A History of Twentieth-Century African Literatures

Lincoln and London :

A HISTORY
OF TWENTIETH-
CENTURY AFRICAN
LITERATURES

Edited by Oyekan Owomoyela

UNIVERSITY OF NEBRASKA PRESS

The paper in this book meets the minimum requirements of
American National Standard for Information Sciences—
Permanence of Paper for Printed Library Materials, ANSI
z39.48–1984.

Library of Congress Cataloging-in-Publication Data
A History of twentieth-century African literatures / edited by
Oyekan Owomoyela.
p.   cm.
Includes bibliographical references and index.
ISBN 0-8032-3552-6 (alk. paper). — ISBN 0-8032-8604-X
(pbk.: alk. paper)
I. Owomoyela, Oyekan.
PL8010.H57   1993
809'8896—dc20   92-37874
                                                     CIP

To the memory of John F. Povey

Contents

Acknowledgments

Sometime in 1984 the editor-in-chief of the University of Nebraska Press asked if I would consider editing a volume on the history of twentieth-century African literatures. I eagerly embraced the opportunity, because I shared his conviction that such a book was both necessary and of potentially great appeal to a sizeable audience. Furthermore, the interest of the press in the subject represented a major advance for African literary studies, and African studies in general—the addition of another top-flight university press to the number making African material available to the serious reader.

The volume makes its appearance now several years behind schedule owing to the difficulties inherent in assembling commissioned original essays according to the timetable I naively established at the start. I have since learned from those with more experience in such ventures that the delays are quite typical. They have nonetheless tested the patience and dedication of those contributors whose chapters came in on schedule.

My greatest gratitude is due, therefore, to my contributors, who have borne with good grace the frustration of long delays in seeing the fruition of their efforts. I hope they will agree that the result has been worth the wait.

Several passages in the following chapters have been translated from other languages. Unless otherwise indicated, the translations have been by the contributing authors. For the rest, I bear the responsibility for whatever flaws the texts contain.

Introduction

In the half millennium that has elapsed since Christopher Columbus's fateful "discovery" of the New World, humankind has experienced profound revolutions directly related to Columbus's voyage and those of the European explorer-adventurers who came after him. Nowhere has the impact of those revolutions been more dramatic than on the African continent, for as a consequence of the voyages Africa quickly became an object of European attention—as either an obstacle or a restocking facility for ships on their way to the spices of the Indian Ocean, as a treasure trove of possessions to be transferred from one European power to another in treaties concluding intra-European wars, as a source of slave labor for the new plantations in the Americas, and as a group of colonies supplying European empires with raw materials, markets for finished goods, and career opportunities for European civil servants.

That original relationship between Europe and Africa has undergone many transformations in the past five centuries. The last of these was decolonization—the formal termination of imposed European rule and the resultant transfer of power to Africans. The colonizers finally acknowledged the inevitability, and even desirability, of that process in the years following World War II, when they began the belated work of cultivating suitable Africans to assume power on the departure of their European rulers. The transformation, observers agree, is still in progress. What is important for our purpose is that, as an integral part of that process, African literatures, essentially a twentieth-century phenomenon, came into being.

In this volume Africa is conceived as a cultural entity, not a geographic entity. Accordingly, the book excludes the countries of North Africa, for while they share some historical experiences (such as colonialism) with the countries below the Sahara, they are in fact Arab in culture, outlook, and lingua franca, and they perceive themselves to be part of the Arab world. The literatures discussed in the following pages, therefore, are those of the sub-Saharan countries, which share a cultural unity. Another result of this cultural conception of Africa is the exclusion of the literature produced by European and other foreign settlers on the continent, past and present. A partial exception is that of the white community of South Africa: the pervasive weight of apartheid on the consciousness of writers, settler or native African, along with its equally pervasive ramifications in the life of the country, necessitates occasional allusions to certain settler writers and their works.

Studies of African literatures implicitly or explicitly argue a continuity with traditional verbal artistry, which, in the absence of a popular writing tradition, was exclusively oral. One can read that intent, for example, in Jonathan Peters's assertion that "the production of fiction in West Africa is virtually as old as communication through the spoken word." Chinweizu, Onwuchekwa Jemie, and Ihechukwu Madubuike similarly see the traditional narrative forms of African societies as "Africa's oral antecedents to the novel" and argue at some length against critics who suggest differences between the two (25–32). But while there can be little doubt that some connection does exist between the traditional forms and the modern, it would be an error to imagine that modern African literatures wholly evolved from, or had an unbroken relationship with, traditional verbal artistry. The modern literatures are quite evidently a legacy of the European irruption on the African scene, and they differ markedly from the traditional forms. It is also futile to suggest that the differences between traditional forms and modern literatures are immaterial, as the proponents of "orature" suggest, or that the distinction that one is oral and the other written is of little significance, as Wellek and Warren argue (21–22), and as Andrzejewski, Piłaszewicz, and Tyloch also do in their book *Literatures in African Languages* (18). Oral performances are by their nature intimately personal and immediate, involving a performer in close physical contact with an audience—performer and audience sharing not only the same spatial and temporal space but also a cultural identity. Literature's audience is characteristically remote, oftentimes separated by vast spatial, temporal, and cultural distances. Fortunately, we need not be concerned with determining the extent of the field covered by the term "literature" (even though a resolution of the question would be desirable, for the manner of its resolution would determine whether or not "orature" was an unnecessary neologism, "written literature" redundant, or "oral literature" an oxymoron).

Another important difference between traditional African oral art and modern African literature involves the identity and social standing of their respective practitioners. Like the Mali *griot,* who according to D. T. Niane "occupie[d] the chair of history" in his village (viii), the traditional oral artist was required to be deeply immersed in the traditional mores and the history of his or her community. This incumbency invested the artist with some formal or informal authority, along with commensurate dignity, even if (as was sometimes the case) he or she eked a living out of mendicancy. The modern writer does not have the sort of worry Niane expresses on behalf of the *griot*—that of being regarded as an object of scorn—since in the postcolonial context he or she is a member of the elite class. But although the modern writer would claim the same legitimacy the traditional artist enjoys, as witness Wole Soyinka's lament that the course of affairs on the continent is set by politicians and not artists (18), that claim has little basis or justification, given the circumstances of writers' constitution as a westernized elite class. African writers bear the traces of their origination as a class in colonialists' desire to hand control to worthy successors they could trust to oversee and preserve the sociopolitical structures colonialism had built. In its present conception, therefore, African literatures inevitably reflect the social and cultural alienation of the writers from their communities, as well as their identity with the Europeans whose languages and cultures they share. In this regard modern African literatures again testify to the great and continuing impact of the colonizing project on the African universe, not least in the persistence of its magisterial role in the definition and self-definition of Africans.

Anyone with a passing acquaintance with discourses concerning African literatures is aware that the mention of the subject automatically suggests writings in European languages. Works in African languages float into consciousness only as an afterthought. Consequently, the arrangement and number of chapters in this book reflect not only this condition but also the relative extent and importance of the literature each linguistic group has produced. For example, literature in English is the subject of five chapters, and French the subject of three, while literature in Portuguese is confined to a single chapter. The paradoxical primacy of European languages in African literatures necessitates another anomaly—the inclusion of a separate chapter on literature in African languages. The chapter, by Robert Cancel, is a useful reminder that another Africa exists besides the one that normally preoccupies the world's attention, and that it also produces noteworthy literatures. The difficulty that confronts any scholar who might be interested in these African-language literatures is considerable, owing, no doubt, to the multiplicity of African languages. A definitive coverage of the subject would demand the collaboration of several scholars who commanded among them all the languages in which significant literature exists. Cancel accomplishes the more modest intention of providing an authoritative discussion of a representative sampling of this body of works.

Russell Hamilton's chapter mentions the reasons that Lusophone African literature was "the first written, the last discovered." Among them one cannot discount the distinction Portuguese colonial policies enjoyed as the most repressive and unenlightened manifestation of a system that is by definition already repressive and unenlightened. Like Belgian colonialism, the Portuguese version concentrated on the exploitation of Africans and their resources, and it failed to follow suit when the French and the British, for different reasons and to different extents, embarked on the westernization of their colonial subjects. Even at the end of the twentieth century the Portuguese enclaves in Africa have not fully divested themselves of their stigma as Portuguese-run prisons for Africans, devoid of much of the romance that attracted European students and tourists to Anglophone and Francophone areas. The interest in Lusophone literature is thus commensurate with that in other aspects of life in the Portuguese spheres.

The story could not be more different with regard to the other two "Europhone" literatures. In all genres the countries that emerged from British colonialism have been the most fecund literary sources, Nigeria being preeminent among them. As far as fiction is concerned, it is customary to cite the publication in 1952 of Amos Tutuola's novel *The Palm-Wine Drinkard* as the beginning of sustained Anglophone literature, although as Peters points out there had been earlier works, especially from the Gold Coast (Ghana). Tutuola was quickly joined in international popularity by his compatriot Chinua Achebe, and it was, not surprisingly, another Nigerian, Wole Soyinka, who became in 1986 the first African, and the first Black writer, to win the Nobel Prize for literature.

Arlene Elder notes the delay in the entry of Anglophone East Africa into the literary arena, and the embarrassed sense of exclusion that people like James Ngugi (Ngũgĩ wa Thiong'o) and Grace Ogot felt when their part of Africa had no representative among the participants in the 1962 African Writers Conference held in Kampala, Uganda. That event became a powerful catalyst for aspiring writers, among whom Ngũgĩ is now one of the most renowned. In South Africa the history of literature has largely repeated that of other parts of Africa, with the difference that it has been more intense and more passionate because of the conditions imposed by apartheid. The all-consuming claim of that system of official racism on the consciousness of African peoples, and consequently its recurrence as a theme in South African writing, are vividly evident in John Povey's chapter.

Servanne Woodward establishes that fiction from Francophone Africa has been quite considerable, both in volume and in quality, and she shows that here too fiction writing commenced much earlier than the 1950s. It began as a trickle in the 1920s, produced by writers well schooled in the French assimilationist system of education, but in the years leading up to and encompassing the anticolonial struggle it was eclipsed by the poetry of the Paris-based African cultural affirmation movement known as Negritude. Edris Makward traces that movement's origins in Paris and its influence in Africa and Madagascar, even among poets who never lived in France. He places emphasis on its initial connection with such European movements as surrealism and existentialism, along with its militant rebuttal of the colonialist misrepresentation of Africanity as the degenerate opposite of westernity, which supposedly embodies the only acceptable paradigm for humanity. The considerable influence of Negritude on the African scene lasted for at least two decades, and both Woodward and Hamilton acknowledge its influence in Francophone fiction and Lusophone poetry. Indeed, even though Anglophone writers such as Ezekiel Mphahlele and Wole Soyinka showed open disdain for the promotion and flaunting of Negritude as a sort of black mystique, Anglophone poetry itself evinced some of the tendencies of the Negritude poets. The "pastoral images of nature and nurture, symbolized often as a woman in tropes that are both maternal and erotic," and the "dance, drums, masks, and other artifacts" that Thomas Knipp identifies as characteristic imagery of modern Anglophone poetry are not much different from the devices popular with Negritude poets. Nonetheless, since the 1960s, when the Negritude movement achieved many of its cultural goals, the work of the Negritude poets has been somewhat eclipsed, as Woodward points out, by the fiction of such Francophone writers as Ousmane Sembène, V. Y. Mudimbe, Ken Bugul, and Aminata Sow Fall.

Despite the general agreement that Africans employed narrative and poetic forms for entertainment, edification, and dissemination of information and ideas in the pre-European past, when discussion turns to drama opinions differ greatly. Some scholars argue that here, too, a long tradition existed among African peoples before the arrival of Europeans. They see the mimetic elements in traditional ritual performance as drama, with some going so far as to assert that modern African drama in fact developed directly from those elements. It is clear from James Amankulor's chapter that he belongs to this school of thought. Others prefer to see rituals, however considerable the mimetic or theatrical instances they include, as phenomena distinct from drama, and point to the clear line of descent of modern African drama from the performances that resident Europeans introduced into their African enclaves for their own amusement. Anglophone Africans have been more concerned with establishing an autonomous origination of drama in Africa than have their Francophone siblings; unlike Amankulor, Alain Ricard states matter-of-factly that drama came to Africa with the Europeans. Whatever the case, the theater has flourished more in Anglophone than in Francophone countries, as the relative proportions of Ricard's and Amankulor's chapters aptly illustrate.

Until very recently one of the most contentious issues among African literary scholars was the near invisibility and inaudibility of women in literary discussions. To some extent their minimal representation for so many years reflected their marginal participation in the creation and analysis of literature. The articulation of colonial policy, as well as African practice, gave men a head start in Western education and consequently enabled them to dominate the early years of literary activity. To some degree, of course, force of habit also contributed to the tendency of the predominantly male literary establishment to ignore or discount women's activities even after these became considerable. The chapter by Carole Boyce Davies and Elaine Savory Fido addresses this issue. It also bears testimony to the extent to which women have breached the male ramparts to make themselves seen and heard as artists and critics, as well as touching upon international feminism and African women's attitudes toward it.

Readers will notice that in several chapters the authors refer to constraints on the production and circulation of literature on the continent, especially to writers' limited access to publishing outlets. As some add, the works that do achieve publication often fail to reach wide audiences because of inadequate mechanisms for distribution. Unimaginative or deliberately unhelpful government policies and severely depressed economic conditions sometimes add to the difficulties. The issue is important enough to warrant its own chapter. Hans Zell, who has for many years been deeply involved in seeking ways to alleviate and solve the problem, provides readers with a vivid account of some of the problems that writers, publishers, and readers face.

I would not wish to leave the impression that the domination of African literary expression by European languages has met with routine approval among African writers and critics. Despite the sometimes strident protests by some of them that Africans have a right to claim those languages as their own (Achebe 74–84; Chinweizu, Jemie, and Madubuike 14), other writers, such as Ngũgĩ, achieved international recognition for their European-language works only to come later to view the embrace of colonial languages as inimical to the furtherance of Africa's cultural interests. This vexing question of language merits a sustained discussion, and it is accordingly addressed in my own chapter.

The essays in this volume emphasize the historical events that have shaped African literatures during the twentieth century. African writers, as readers will find, differ to some degree in their representations and assessments of these key events, but transcending their differences are certain constants: the literatures they produce have in common an undeniable European inspiration and a necessary preoccupation with the vicissitudes that European activities have unleashed all over the continent, activities whose disorienting ramifications persist. These include the abduction of millions of Africans for enslavement in the Americas, the appropriation of African resources and African labor on the continent for the benefit of Europe, the imposition of colonial rule and the attendant disruption of ethnic and national cohesiveness in favor of a mosaic of colonies and later so-called nations, the imposition and underpropping of unworkable postcolonial structures and compliant regimes, and the resultant incoherence of the African world. Also inescapable in the essays, of course, is the sometimes impassioned engagement of the persisting structure of apartheid by the writers of South Africa, whose works have not begun to reflect recent developments in government policy.

This volume joins a growing number of studies on African literatures. It has an advantage over most, however, in its assemblage of eminent scholars who together provide a full coverage of the entire subject with uniform depth and assurance, and in its emphasis on the historical dimension, which contextualizes the various developments in African writing so far. It was conceived to appeal to a wide audience. Readers who seek a better than superficial acquaintance with the entire field of African literary expression, and with the forces that have impinged on it, will find it most rewarding. So will students in courses on African literatures, whether at the undergraduate or the graduate level, as it provides a vivid backdrop for the consideration of individual works. And since few scholars whose specialty is African literatures can be equally versed in all areas of the subject, even they will find in this volume a handy companion. The book is also designed to appeal to students of comparative literature, history, sociology, and cultures. Because our main focus is the historical dimension in the growth of African literatures, we have not gone to great lengths in the critical evaluation of literary works or movements. Yet discussion of significant works and how they reflect their times inevitably implies some critical assessment. For this reason readers in search of critical insight will find much in the volume to interest them.

I began this introduction by pointing out the centrality of European activities in the development of the modern African literary tradition. For so long, the European was such an oppressive fact in African lives that the fiction writer Mongo Beti quoted an old friend and a sage as once predicting that "wherever there was a Negro, there would always be some European colonial to kick his backside" (Beti 2). For most of the years this volume encompasses (by consensus, until the end of 1988) the preoccupation with Europeans evident in African writing would seem to justify the prediction. Moreover, during the heyday of empire the image that the world had of the continent and its peoples was formulated by Europeans, and, as was to be expected, that image was concocted to legitimize colonialism. With the emergence of their own creative writing, Africans began to appropriate from Europeans the right to speak for themselves, to interpret their universe to the world and even to themselves. Achebe, for example, has repeatedly stated that he was inspired to become a writer by such colonial novelists as Joyce Cary, in whose Africans he could not recognize himself, and as a corrective for whose creations he counterposed his own. Thus, through the works of African authors, Africa is being rediscovered by readers around the world, including Africans themselves.

Furthermore, a trend noticeable in recent writing from the continent suggests that the doomsayer in Beti might be wrong after all: the figure of the European, along with direct mention of the European presence, is becoming increasingly peripheral, with the world of Achebe's *Things Fall Apart* yielding to that of Mariama Bâ's *Une si longue lettre*. Works like Ngũgĩ's *Devil on the Cross*, however, serve to remind us that colonialism dies hard, and that old colonialists and their behind-the-scenes manipulation of African affairs have not quite faded away.

Works Cited

Achebe, Chinua. "The African Writer and the English Language." In *Morning Yet on Creation Day*, 74–84. Garden City, N.Y.: Anchor Books, 1976.

Andrzejewski, B. W., S. Piłaszewicz, and W. Tyloch. *Literatures in African Languages: Theoretical Issues and Sample Surveys*. Cambridge: Cambridge University Press, 1985.

Beti, Mongo. *Mission to Kala*. Translated by Peter Green. London: Heinemann, 1964.

Chinweizu, Onwuchekwa Jemie, and Ihechukwu Madubuike. *Toward the Decolonization of African Literature*. Vol. 1, *African Fiction and Poetry and Their Critics*. Washington, D.C.: Howard University Press, 1983.

Niane, D. T. *Sundiata: An Epic of Old Mali*. London: Longman, 1965.

Soyinka, Wole. "The Writer in a Modern African State." In *The Writer in Modern Africa*, edited by Per Wästberg. Uppsala, Sweden: The Scandinavian Institute of African Studies, 1968.

Wellek, René, and Austin Warren. *Theory of Literature*. 3d ed. New York: Harcourt, Brace & World, 1956.

1

English-Language Fiction

from West Africa

JONATHAN A. PETERS

The production of fiction in West Africa is virtually as old as communication through the spoken word. Rich in traditional lore from many ethnic groups, the region has produced folktales that are among the most famous in the world, part of a corpus of what is now usually referred to as *orature* (to distinguish it from literature). West African literature includes the epic tradition kept alive by the *griots*, traditional bards who recounted the history of their clans as well as of heroic figures in their region. In the epic tradition, the exploits of Sunjata, the medieval founder of the Mali empire, is the most celebrated. Although a continuing tradition of oral literature has been passed down over many generations, the written tradition has lagged far behind, because writing arrived only with first Arab and then European influences. Even then, it was not until the twentieth century that an established body of writing began to emerge, first in European languages and then in indigenous ones. While such writing has been in existence for perhaps too short a time for one to talk about a fully established tradition, a number of important phases, landmarks, themes, and trends distinguish its development and form the subject of this essay.

The older oral literatures of West Africa have for the most part been defined from culture to culture, though a handful of studies treat folklore in general and oral traditions in particular as a national or regional phenomenon. Scholars tend to consider the oral tradition separately from the written body of creative literature, even though the latter has been informed to a great degree by the traditional cultures of which the writers are inheritors. One anomaly of the European influence is that some ethnic groups were split by the colonial division of territories between two, often French- and English-speaking, zones. Depending, therefore, on who is doing the collection and analysis, some traditional cultures will be located within either French-speaking or English-speaking Africa, or within a combination of the two, as with Senegambia.[1]

Most studies of African written literatures attempt to define their subjects

9

in regional, national, or linguistic terms. The present discussion, for example, is based on genre, region, and language, the subject being written prose fiction by West Africans originally produced in English. Such a definition is as much a matter of convenience as of established practice. Few critics are fluent in all of the three European languages that dominate the political and literary arenas of West Africa—namely, French, English, and Portuguese— and fewer writers still have a command of more than one of those languages. Most West African countries have retained their linguistic alliances with the former mother country and have continued educational systems introduced from these metropoles. Thus, while the cultural links and similarities among many cultures are strong, there is not the level of cross-fertilization (let alone amalgamation) that would make a comparison of works in these three nascent linguistic traditions very profitable at this time, especially given the variations in accessibility of many works in translation to writers and readers across the region.

Early West African Literatures in English

The development of literatures by West Africans in English, French, and Portuguese is a by-product of colonial domination following the "Scramble for Africa" by European nations. The Berlin Conference on Africa during 1884–85 set in motion the full-scale colonization not just of territories in West Africa but of the entire continent (Flint, "Chartered Companies"), excepting only two countries: Ethiopia, in East Africa, and in West Africa, Liberia—a country that had achieved political independence from the United States in 1847. The establishment of English as the official language in Liberia goes back to the early nineteenth century, when missionaries in the United States set up the American Colonization Society and obtained lands for the settlement of free blacks in West Africa. The other English-speaking countries of West Africa—The Gambia, Sierra Leone, Ghana, Nigeria, and the English-speaking sector of Cameroon—acquired English as a result of British domination. In the case of Cameroon, British influence came as a result of the provision of the armistice following World War I, which placed part of the country under British and part under French control.

The 1890s saw Europeans using expeditions to stake their claim in Africa by wresting control of the territories they had carved out among themselves with virtually no knowledge of natural or ethnic boundaries. That period also marks the flowering of "colonial" novels in English (as well as in French), in which European writers used Africa and Africans as setting and characters. Among the most artistic and the most widely read in and out of Africa from this early period was Joseph Conrad's *Heart of Darkness* (1898), which, while reflecting Conrad's horror at what the Belgians were doing in the Congo, still helped reinforce images of Africa as the "dark continent," cloaking an evil that was almost palpable. Among the most popular were the novels of Sir Henry Rider Haggard set in southern Africa and published between 1885 and 1924 (see Killam, *Africa*). Perhaps the most influential twentieth-century British writer of colonial fiction is Joyce Cary. In response to Cary's four published "African" novels, particularly *Mister Johnson* (1947), which were set in Nigeria, Chinua Achebe, a young man in his midtwenties in the mid-1950s, became determined to write about his people, whom he felt were being caricatured.

Achebe, one of the foremost African writers, depicted in his first novel, *Things Fall Apart* (1958), the clash of cultures attendant on the arrival of European missionaries and colonists. The subjugation of African peoples that they rigorously and sometimes ruthlessly pursued took place in the name of bringing Christianity and civilization to backward peoples. The process of "pacification," as the often brutal expeditions were called, was not always very swift, nor did colonialism in West Africa last as long as is sometimes imagined; indeed, resistance to colonial rule preceded the 1920s, and the achievement of political independence within the national boundaries arbitrarily set up by the Europeans began in earnest with Ghana in 1957 (a generation after Egypt's Independence in 1922), and was soon after followed by territories elsewhere.

The beginning of the twentieth century, as the following excerpt indicates, found the affairs and destinies of African nations largely controlled by Europeans:

> At the dawn of the twentieth century, men of light and leading both in Europe and in America had not yet made up their minds as to what place to assign to the spiritual aspirations of the black man; and the Nations were casting about for an answer to the wail which went up from the heart of the oppressed race for opportunity. And yet it was at best but an impotent cry. For there has never lived a people worth writing about who have not shaped out a destiny for themselves, or carved out their own opportunity. Before this time, however, it had been discovered that the black man was not necessarily the missing link between man and ape. It had even been granted that for intellectual endowments he had nothing to be ashamed of in an open competition with the Aryan or any other type. Here was a being anatomically perfect, adaptive and adaptable to any and every sphere of the struggle for life. Sociologically, he had succeeded in recording upon the pages of contemporary history a conception of family life unknown to Western ideas. Moreover, he was the scion of a spiritual sphere peculiar to himself; for when Western Nations would have exhausted their energy in the vain struggle for the things which satisfy not, it was felt that it would be to these people whom the world would turn for inspiration, seeing that in them only would be found those elements which make for pure altruism, the leaven of all human experience. (Casely-Hayford 1–2)

Thus begins the only work of fiction by Joseph E. Casely-Hayford (1866–1930), the journalist, barrister, and nationalist whom Magnus J. Sampson hails for his public service as "a link between the old order and the new, an 'uncrowned King' of British West Africa" (Ugonna viii). Casely-Hayford, born in the Gold Coast (now Ghana), is better known for his political, sociological, and legal writings, beginning with his first book, *Gold Coast Native Institutions* (1903). His one novel, *Ethiopia Unbound: Studies in Race Emancipation* (1911), reads more like a sociological work than a work of fiction. Yet the ideas he expresses in the opening paragraphs of his novel, with due modification of the propagandist tone in which they are expressed, deal with important concerns about twentieth-century African (or more specifically West African) society and literature.

Casely-Hayford's book is Afrocentric. It looks at African culture from within and endorses its value. It is more anthropological than artistic; many of the chapters are self-contained essays on one issue or another. Although Casely-Hayford uses fictive characters like Kwamankra and the Reverend Silas Whitely, their story is developed spasmodically, only to be abandoned in the novel's final pages. Still, the work expresses the author's views on many issues, not the least being the question of the Black man's claim to greatness along with the white. The novel's title is a tribute to Ethiopia as a land that did not succumb to the yoke of colonialism and thus is a beacon of light, hope, and promise for Africa and her sons. Casely-Hayford shows his interest in African—specifically Ghanaian—culture by referring to traditional customs and by using Fanti names. Interesting episodes paint institutions of the day, Fourah Bay College being a notable one. He also shows some novelistic skills, like the use of allegory in the episode where an African woman confronts the English minister and, after telling a story about an Arab, points out before she passes out and dies that the minister is the Arab in the story. In its conscious use of language, judicious use of Fanti expressions, and concern with malignant colonialism, *Ethiopia Unbound* shares a common spirit with such later works as Achebe's *Things Fall Apart*.

Much of the early twentieth-century writing by West Africans was published in newspapers (Ugonna viii–x)—and Casely-Hayford's first entry to the world of letters was through journalism—but a few authors besides Casely-Hayford produced books as well, such as Edward Wilmot Blyden of Liberia; Samuel Johnson, Dr. Africanus Horton, A. B. C. Merriman-Labor, and Joseph Renner Maxwell of Sierra Leone; John Mensah Sarbah of Ghana; and Henry Carr of Nigeria. Most of their works are either political or socioanthropological. Few are fiction: poetry, influenced by English poetics, is the dominant mode of creative self-expression. Following the appearance of *Ethiopia Unbound* was a lengthy pause in the publication of long fiction by West Africans, at a time when novels on West Africa by British writers proliferated. The second attempt by a West African in English was by another Ghanaian writer, R. E. Obeng, whose *Eighteenpence* (1943) "chronicles the life of Obeng-Akrofi; it also documents the judiciary and legal systems of the Gold Coast (now Ghana) during the colonial days" (Zell, Bundy, and Coulon 135).

Just as English- and French-speaking West Africa as a region has far exceeded other regions in literary production, so within English-speaking West Africa Nigeria has clearly dominated in both creative output and critical commentary. The reason partly relates to size, for the combined population of The Gambia, Ghana, Liberia, Sierra Leone, and the English-speaking sector of Cameroon makes up no more than a fraction of Nigeria's population, estimated at about one hundred million people, close to a third of the population of the entire continent. The country also has, comparatively speaking, a larger number of institutions of higher learning, which provide instruction for students as well as places where academics and artists can interact. It has many printing presses, both private and university-run, and these provide an outlet for reputed writers as well as those who have not secured access to the international press. Moreover, urban and university centers (such as Ibadan in the 1960s) have attracted a concentration of writers and critics who in turn have provided inspiration and role models to aspiring writers. Also, importantly, organizations like the Mbari Club promoted the exchange of views on many issues, and many regional, national, and international conferences have brought writers, critics, and students together. This constant ferment of activity has resulted in Nigerian writers being among the best known and most accomplished on the continent.

Since it is scarcely a generation old, it is probably too early to talk of generations of West African writing in English. I have elected instead to speak of "waves" of West African writing, dictated by developments more in Nigeria than in the other countries. The first wave of writing terminated at 1964, just before the spate of novels that express disillusionment with the outcome of political Independence in 1960; the second constitutes the period from 1965, a period during which the tensions in Nigerian politics climaxed in the military coup in January 1966, to about 1976, when the cycle of war novels subsided; and in the third, from about 1976 to 1988, newer writers began to publish works in which the colonial themes continued during the second phase all but completely disappeared.

The First Wave

AMOS TUTUOLA

It has now become fashionable, if inaccurate, to date the beginnings of West African fiction in English with the publication in 1952 of Amos Tutuola's *The Palm-Wine Drinkard and His Dead Palm-Wine Tapster in the Deads' Town*. Though many of Tutuola's critics predicted that his "miracle" would not be repeated, within fifteen years he went on to publish five other books: *My Life in the Bush of Ghosts* (1954), *Simbi and the Satyr of the Dark Jungle* (1955), *The Brave African Huntress* (1958), *Feather Woman of the Jungle* (1962), and *Ajaiyi and His Inherited Poverty* (1967). After a silence of fourteen years, Tutuola came back with *The Witch Herbalist of the Remote Town* (1981). Still, references to his kind of writing as a cul-de-sac in African literature are not far off the mark. Tutuola created a tradition for himself but not for others to follow, and he proceeded to iron out in his later writings the curious turns of syntax that had endeared him to European readers and alienated him from African ones.

Tutuola's fame as a writer came as the result of a number of accidents, perhaps the most important of which were the rave reviews *The Palm-Wine Drinkard* received from such writers and critics of stature as Dylan Thomas and Kingsley Amis (see Lindfors, "Amos Tutuola"). Ironically, the instant reputation the book received in Britain did not flow quickly across the Mediterranean to colonial Africa. Most of the reading public in Tutuola's own country was unaware of the book's publication, and when Nigerians and other West Africans finally got to read the book they gave it a mixed review.

What was this work of fiction, that it should attract European praise and draw at best a lukewarm reception from the writer's own compatriots? I will let Tutuola summarize the story in the words of his "drinkard," who is addressing his dead tapster:

> I told him that after he had died, I wanted to die with him and follow him to this Deads' Town because of the palm-wine that he was tapping for me and nobody could tap it for me like him, but I could not die. So one day, I called two of my friends and went to the farm, then we began to tap for ourselves, but it did not taste like the wine he was tapping before he died. But when my friends saw that if they came to my house there was no more palm-wine to drink again, then they were leaving me one by one until all of them went away, even if I should see one of them at outside and call him, he would only say that he would come, but I would not see him come. (98)

The drinkard decides to search out his tapster in the Deads' Town and ask him to come back. During the course of his travels he saves a young woman from The Complete Gentleman Reduced to a Skull and marries her. Pointing to his wife, who has accompanied him, he concludes his story as follows:

> And how before reaching here, we met much difficulty in the bush, because there were no roads to this Deads' Town and we were travelling from bush to bush every day and night, even many times, we were travelling from branches to branches of trees for many days before touching ground and it was ten years since I had left my town. Now I was exceedingly glad to meet him here and I should be most grateful if he would follow me back to my town. (99)

It is probably true that not only the Europeans who lavished praise on Tutuola for his "grisly" tale written in "young English," as Dylan Thomas put it (1952), but also the African readers and critics who condemned the work were overreacting to Tutuola's writing. Well-educated West Africans, cognizant of the influence of African languages on the novel's English style, were appalled by what they saw as Tutuola's lapses because they had been so well attuned to writing in the King's English. Indeed, West African educated speech tended to be much more formal, much closer to the written form. Tutuola's writing, a blend of biblical-sounding or Bunyanesque writing with Yoruba idioms rendered directly into English, along with high-flown words that represent Tutuola's attempt to "swank a bit," was seen as utter profanity. Yet it was this very quality of Tutuola's work—a blend of the sacred and the secular with the macabre content of his "ghost novels," as they have been dubbed—that endeared him to his English readers, attuned to a language in which the standard forms and idioms were well worn. To these readers, Tutuola's "accidents" were fresh and new and exciting. His writing sounded original and seemed to portend a new literary trend. Moreover, the adventures in the heart of the forest appealed to Europeans' notions about a mysterious Africa, notions that had held on for centuries and had been made popular in the colonial period through novelists like Haggard, Conrad, and Cary. Revaluations of Tutuola's work since this early period include book-length studies, principal among them Bernth Lindfors's *Critical Perspectives on Amos Tutuola* (1975), which gives a profile of judgments from the earliest reviews through the mid-1970s.

Although Tutuola did not found a tradition of writing in West Africa, he demonstrated that the oral tradition was very much alive and that it was possible for an individual writer to draw on a communal source and use it to create works that bear the writer's individual stamp. He had received little formal education. The factual and the fantastic, the traditional and the technological cohabit in his landscapes without friction, and his settings are invariably the primordial forest peopled more often with creatures who have never been among the "alives." Yet his writing has endured in spite of its odd beginning, though how much longer it will enjoy such a reputation is uncertain. More certain is the significance of the ongoing debate about language, style, and audience in African literature sparked by the reception of Tutuola's works.

Those works have received an uncertain classification. Some see them as basic stories of a hero or heroine, embellished and lengthened by the addition of folktales. Others describe them as romances, for their use of supernatural events and creatures. When critics refer to them as novels, it is often because they see them as picaresques absolved from the necessity of fulfilling the demands of European realist fiction. Still others, rejecting the notion of the novel as a European form, speak of Tutuola's books as novels derived from African oral traditions.

CYPRIAN EKWENSI AND CHINUA ACHEBE

Two years after the publication of Tutuola's *Palm-Wine Drinkard*, Cyprian Ekwensi published his first novel, *People of the City* (1954), which is as urban as Tutuola's work is rural. Preceding it were stories published in magazines as early as 1945 and the novelette *When Love Whispers* (1947), a work whose heroine is something of a prototype for the eponymous protagonist of *Jagua Nana* (1961). *When Love Whispers*, however, belongs less to the realm of so-called serious fiction and more properly to that realm of popular fiction which Ime Ikiddeh has graphically defined as "cooked to the taste of large numbers, finished and served out fast and consumed while it is still hot" (106). And although Ekwensi, with eight full-length novels, a novella, and two collections of stories, not to speak of his thirteen children's books, has been one of the most prolific writers to come out of Africa, his work has not been as enthusiastically received as that of Tutuola, even though his style is much more polished and he writes more often of the sort of individuals who people the rapidly growing towns and cities in Nigeria and other African countries.

In spite of his prolific output, Ekwensi is no more a stylistic trendsetter than Casely-Hayford, Obeng, or Tutuola. For while his writing is considerably more within the scope of the European novel as transposed into West Africa, Ekwensi has not developed a reputation as a skilled craftsman the way Chinua Achebe was to do with his very first book, nor has his art developed much over the years. *People of the City* shows many of his weaknesses and a few of his strengths as a writer. By depicting the seamy side of city life through the story of Amusa Sango, a journalist and bandleader in Lagos, the novel drew protests from many Nigerian readers, just as Tutuola's accounts of jungle life offended many West Africans. Sango's interest in success and the good life leads to triumphs and reverses: triumphs in the praise and promotion that his graphic reports on the coal strike in the "Eastern Greens" bring, as well as his successes as a rake; reverses when he turns his sensational reporting style (hitherto successfully directed at the British) against the "Lebanese Menace" and gets the sack, followed by eviction from his apartment. Ekwensi shows himself capable of telling descriptions and interesting little episodes. But such faults as inconsistencies of plot, episodic and sometimes confusing narration, far-fetched improbabilities, gratuitous sensationalism, melodrama, and lack of a moral code of some sort—in other words, a combination of problems in artistry and vision—have led to its placement more within the category of popular fiction.[2] In an interview published in *African Writers Talking* Ekwensi concedes that he is "a writer who regards himself as a writer for the masses," and he goes on to say, "I don't think of myself as a literary stylist: if my style comes, that is just incidental, but I am more interested in getting at the heart of the truth which the man in the street can recognize than in just spinning words" (Duerden and Pieterse 79). Ekwensi's revelation in the same interview that he spent twelve intense days at the typewriter for the writing of *Jagua Nana* supports critical observations about the weakness of his style.

One important motif that Ekwensi introduced into Nigerian fiction in his pursuit of "the heart of the truth" is the recurring violence in Nigerian politics. In *People of the City* we see it for the most part in colonial violence, but it also occurs in the work of the Ufemfe Society, which lets people in with promises of prosperity but will not let them out, because those who joined its ranks have "literally sold their souls to the devil" (71). The theme of political violence erupts in *Jagua Nana*, considered by most critics to be Ekwensi's best work. This novel first appeared in 1961, shortly after Nigeria had won its political independence in October 1960. Ekwensi ably depicts violence in party politics through links between Jagua, the aging prostitute, and Uncle Taiwo, whose bloated corpse he graphically portrays:

> Rosa told the story of Uncle Taiwo: a terrifying one indeed, and one that taught Jagua that politics was dirtiest to them that played it dirty. Rosa told how she was going to market and she heard that a dead man was lying at the roundabout in the center of the city. She was terrified. It was said to be lying near the market-place, in front of the Hotel Liverpool. . . . The roads were all muddy and pitted; the gutters were full, the farms in the suburbs were overgrown with weeds. Lagos was in a state of chaos that day. It seemed as if the ghost of that corpse had gone abroad among them. The body was lying there twisted and swollen; one knee was drawn up against the chest, the arms were clutching at the breast, rigid like a statue. (139)

Even though the flamboyant Uncle Taiwo was killed not by the opposition represented by Freddie (Jagua's younger lover, whom Taiwo had killed) but by his own party for the loss of the elections, violence goes hand in hand with bribery and corruption. The focus, however, is on the book's heroine, a colorful prostitute whom Ekwensi's portraiture invests with the advertised "grace, space and pace" of the automobile that gave her her nickname. She is so "Jagwaful" that Ekwensi himself becomes captivated with her magnificence and power to the point of exonerating her faults. For while Taiwo receives his just deserts, Jagua, who escaped to Lagos to become a prostitute because her husband did not meet her demands for sex and the good life, ends up with five thousand pounds, which, in an implausible contrivance, her latest lover, Taiwo, had left her before he died. She is able to go to Onitsha to start life as a merchant princess with money that Taiwo had stolen from party coffers.

Despite its faults, *Jagua Nana* succeeds in presenting a slice of Lagos life, albeit the seamy side. Designed for immediate, sensational effect, the novel is memorable for its quick and easy scenes of sex and intrigue, not for a deepened awareness of human conflict and motivation. Jagua Nana has been compared to another picaresque heroine, Defoe's Moll Flanders (Killam, "Cyprian Ekwensi" 86–87), but the similarity has to do with their circumstances as thieves and prostitutes rather than with their motivation and inbred morality (Palmer, "Cyprian Ekwensi" 46–49). All in all, Ekwensi seems to be at his best when dealing with people in the city, whereas those episodes set in the countryside generally lack conviction, vigor, and relevance. When, however, the focus of the action is a rural setting, as in his most artistically successful novel, *Burning Grass* (1962), Ekwensi's prose can take on an evocative charm free of the racy patterns of cheap fiction and imbued with graceful echoes from the oral tradition.

The oral tradition found its most striking and most successful exponent during the transitional period between self-government and independence in the person of Chinua Achebe, whose remarkable first novel, *Things Fall Apart*, quickly established itself as an African classic. The first major work of historical fiction by a West African novelist writing in English, it set to rights the one-sided portrayals of Africa and Africans that had stereotyped the continent and its inhabitants in the colonial writings of not only British writers but also other Europeans, notably the French (see Fanoudh-Siefer). In his essay "The Novelist as Teacher" Achebe views himself as espousing an "adequate revolution" designed "to help my society regain belief in itself and put away the complexes of the years of denigration and self-abasement" (3). Europeans had assumed, in Kipling's phrase, "the white man's burden" as an imposition placed on them from the outside instead of as a deliberate program of worldwide imperialism. That attitude made possible a psychological oppression that in turn had caused "a wound in our soul" (Achebe, "The Black Writer's Burden" 135). Achebe's aim was to teach fellow Africans the truth about the colonial experience so that, unlike the man in the Igbo proverb who did not know where rain began to beat him, African people as a body could know where the colonial "rain" began to beat them and hence the locus in independence where they "dried [their] body" (Achebe, "The Role of the Writer in a New Nation" 163; *Arrow of God* 160).

Things Fall Apart does not express these concerns baldly, but rather with profound evocative power depicts the precolonial Igbo society as a paradigm of traditional African societies, with all their alluring and endearing qualities as well as with their less appealing sides. Unlike other colonial novels, so many of which have a negative and patronizing attitude and a bias against Africans and African institutions, Achebe's novel begins with the African writer looking at his society and conjuring it up for us. By reshaping the borrowed English language he details the life of his central figure, whose "fame spread like a bush-fire in the harmattan," but who in the end, as the point of view shifts to that of the new colonial administration, would be buried like a dog because he tried vainly to prevent the takeover of his patrimony. *Things Fall Apart* does not succeed only or even chiefly because Achebe is attempting a corrective view of African society. The primary reasons for its success include its insight into the culture of the Igbo seen from the point of view of an "inside outsider" (a role he had as an Igbo whose missionary upbringing prevented his participation in traditional rituals), a thorough understanding of narrative organization and style, and a keen observation of and absorption with day-to-day happenings, not through the lenses of the anthropologist, but through the clear sight of one who was involved with and felt at one with his culture while at the same time inculcating Western ideas.

Born Albert Chinualumogu Achebe, the son of Isaiah Okafor Achebe, a catechist with the Church Missionary Society, Achebe was not only barred from traditional Igbo rituals but was also proscribed from eating in the houses of his unconverted fellow Igbos. Achebe developed an involved detachment with his ethnic group that enabled him to see its good and bad sides and to present them honestly in his fiction. Achebe's empathy with the Igbo was one of his greatest assets, enabling him to paint the society in word pictures that have made him the West African novelist—if not simply the African writer—most written about since the definitive beginnings of West African literature in English a generation or so ago. He managed that depiction not only by representing a classic example of racial conflict in an illuminating way but also by selecting episodes and developments that combine to form a composite picture of his society expressed with uncanny exactitude. The debate over language, audience, and style that Tutuola's books sparked expands in the study of Achebe's fiction and takes on additional dimensions dealing with culture, theme, and sensibility.

Achebe's historical depiction did not end with *Things Fall Apart*. He had originally conceived the novel as an extended history that would end in the present, but instead divided the material and brought his first novel to a close with the beginnings of colonial rule. The sequel, *No Longer at Ease* (1960), however, does not pick up where the first novel leaves off, but goes straight to the eve of Independence for Nigeria, in a story about Okonkwo's grandson, Obi Okonkwo. Eventually Achebe completed his history in a sequence of four novels, each set at a crucial moment in history: the first direct contacts and clashes with the Europeans during the 1890s in *Things Fall Apart;* the period when the dual mandate was introduced as British colonial policy in *Arrow of God* (1964), set during the 1920s; the period just before Independence in *No Longer at Ease;* and, in *A Man of the People* (1966), the violent aftermath following Nigeria's Independence in 1960.

A good many readers and critics think that the first novel is unquestionably the best in its evocation of the traditional past; others prefer the more equably balanced *Arrow of God,* where the point of view shifts every chapter or so between Ezeulu and his people on the one hand and Winterbottom and the British colonial administration on the other. The crisis that results from the discrepancy between the arrival of the harvest and Ezeulu's calculation of that arrival precipitates a spate of conversion to Christianity, as the people try to avoid the famine brought on by rotting yams. Their active conversion contrasts with the passivity of the crowd at the end of *Things Fall Apart.* The other two novels do not have the same psychological depth, for Achebe loves the society of yore more than the chaotic present, where alienated people see the government as deserving of no allegiance (*No Longer at Ease*), or where the country is seen as a bounty, with everyone fighting to have his or her share (*A Man of the People*). What is incontestable is that with the publication of his novels West African fiction in English had come into its own.

A number of themes recur throughout Achebe's four-novel cycle. *Things Fall Apart* exhibits the clash of cultures, the destruction of the old value system and authority, and a number of sociocultural themes dealing with religion, custom, taboo, and the supernatural. *No Longer at Ease* best exemplifies the theme of the child of two worlds. The colonial theme receives its most extensive exposition in *Arrow of God,* but Achebe also brings in a wealth of cultural episodes that paint a more complete picture of an Igbo society that has shown tremendous resilience in its recovery from the shock of colonial domination, even though the end of the novel, with Ezeulu gone mad, shows one more blow to traditional ways. The later developments chronicled in *A Man of the People* make it a characteristic novel of the second wave, and accordingly it is discussed later in this essay.

OTHER FIRST-WAVE WRITERS

The novels published by West Africans writing in English during this first wave of writing covered such broad themes as the quest, which typifies Tutuola's books; city life with its glitter, debauchery, and victimization of the unwary; rural life; colonial conflicts; and political violence. The full-length works published in the 1950s, written exclusively by Nigerians, sparked an interest among European writers to find out what the "real" African was like. Accordingly, it was only natural that a book entitled *The African* (1960) should capture the attention of Europeans and Americans who wanted to find out what made the African tick. Its author, the historian William Conton, wrote this interesting but in many parts implausible novel to depict political intrigue in the immediate aftermath of Independence. Conton's book is now important chiefly as a work that introduced first-person narrative into the modern West African realistic novel in English and as the first novel by a Sierra Leonean. Conton wrote no more fiction, nor did the publication of *The African* set off a chain of writings by other would-be writers in Sierra Leone. Another work published outside Nigeria during this phase was *I Was a Savage* (1958) an autobiographical work by Prince Modupeh, a native of Guinea who went to America to study. (The sensational title was changed to an opposing image, that of *A Royal African,* in the 1969 edition.)

In the wake of Chinua Achebe's immediate success as a writer of fiction, a large number of Africans from all over the continent began to write fiction. More and more Nigerian writers began to emerge whose books would number among those introduced into schools as the curricula began to emphasize more African themes and fewer European ones. Among these were Onuora Nzekwu, whose *Wand of Noble Wood* was published by Hutchinson in 1961, followed by *Blade among the Boys* the year after. Probably inspired by Achebe's example, Nzekwu sought to interpret areas of his culture to a predominantly Western audience that was developing an appetite for works by Africans. Nzekwu was, however, ill equipped to convey with the same poise and judiciousness the essence of Igbo society. He may therefore be credited with beginning what has been referred to as the sociological or anthropological novel, a type of work that seeks to explain African traditional customs to aliens to the culture; that credit has also been given to Achebe for his presentation of family and clan life, notably in *Arrow of God*. Critics have pointed to a number of weaknesses in Nzekwu's style, weaknesses that derive not only from his limited schooling but also from his producing his first two novels while also writing sociological essays as editorial assistant for *Nigeria Magazine*, that is, from 1956 until 1962, when he became editor-in-chief (Zell, Bundy, and Coulon 440). Nzekwu simply turned to fiction as an additional outlet for explaining his society to the outside world.

Probably inspired by Achebe's *No Longer at Ease*, where Obi, the child of two worlds, confronts the problem of Clara being an *osu* (an outcast), *Wand of Noble Wood* is the story of Peter Obiesie, who proposes marriage to Nneka, a village schoolteacher, only to find out from his parents (whom he had given limited authority to help him find a wife) that, through her mother, she is under a market woman's curse. The author's idea, derived from tradition but not from Achebe, is to counteract the curse by a ritual of cleansing, but Nneka commits suicide following her discovery in a vision that the rite would be ineffectual. *Blade among the Boys* deals with the problem faced by the hero, whose mother tries to recover him so he can prepare to assume the role of *okpala* (spiritual head of his people) after what she sees as the attempt to "make him a eunuch" by the Catholic seminary that is training him for the priesthood. The more complex plot also sees the hero, Patrick Ikenga, becoming at one point a bribe-taker and, while a seminarian, being seduced by Nkiru, the young woman he was to marry, aided by a love potion. In addition to the sociological cast of both books, in which the author gives running commentaries on customs instead of allowing characters to be the central medium for exhibiting culture, improbabilities of plot and the many breakdowns in the use of language substantially reduce the value of these two novels as examples of successful realistic fiction in English (Taiwo 185–90).

Another Nigerian writer who employs social commentary is Timothy Aluko, who began his literary career with short stories in the 1940s, but whose reputation has come from his novels. Aluko's first novel, *One Man One Wife*, the first full-length work issued by a Nigerian publishing house, was brought out in 1959 by Nigerian Printing and Publishing Company. In the international market, the book was the third of his novels to be published by Heinemann, which brought it out in 1967, behind *One Man One Matchet* (1965) and *Kinsman and Foreman* (1966). As an ethnic historian, Aluko is the Yoruba counterpart of Chinua Achebe, his first five novels serving to depict Yoruba society from the 1920s to the 1960s. The signal conflicts in his works, while often centered on traditional values of the village pitted against modern urban ways, do not focus on race as an issue. *One Man One Wife* deals not only with the theme of polygamy—which is raised when Joshua, a stalwart

Christian, decides to marry a second wife without even consulting his first— but also with such other concerns as the influence of traditional beliefs on urban Yorubas and the conflicts between those who adhere to tradition and those who espouse modern ideas.

One important contribution Aluko makes to the development of West African fiction in English is his use of satire, which pervades his works from the beginning. Unlike Achebe, who reveres ancestral traditions and whose irony or satire is usually directed against those forces antagonistic to traditional mores, Aluko's irreverent satire spares no one. This ability to highlight the comic in both those who are vicious and others who are victims without embracing a moral vision against which the actions of the characters are weighed has led to criticism for his failure to take a moral stand, a charge that Aluko acknowledges (Zell, Bundy, and Coulon 350).

The theme of polygamy is central to another first novel, Obi Egbuna's *Wind versus Polygamy.* According to Egbuna, wind signifies change while polygamy represents "a change of Eves." Like Modupe, the author subsequently changed the sensational title of the 1964 Faber edition, which catered to a European readership, to *Elina,* the name of his heroine, in the second edition, published by Fontana Books in 1980. Like Egbuna's subsequent books, the novel has many weaknesses in conception, design, language, and plausibility, as Oladele Taiwo has pointed out (38–45). The work is another product of a writer who has not developed the technical facility for harnessing creative ideas and whose work is directed at a foreign audience.

This first period of fiction writing by West Africans ends, fittingly enough, with Gabriel Okara's only novel, *The Voice* (1964). While Tutuola's syntactical errors were the result of an imperfect education, Okara's departures from standard English are the conscious choice of a writer seeking to transmit the syntax of Ijaw speech into English. *The Voice* is a poet's novel, a parable about Okolo's search for a nebulous "it." The novel presents a moral world where the search for "it" is a quest for the meaning of life, where people are defined not in terms of their outward appearances but in terms of their "insides," which are either good or bad, and where the protagonist is exiled by his village elders because they fear that his questioning is a threat to their way of life.

The first wave's dozen years of literary activity also saw the organization of conferences on African literature in different regions of the country. Scholars began to be active in producing commentaries on works, and a magazine specifically devoted to the study of African literature, *Black Orpheus,* began publication. Although bibliographical works began to be prepared during this phase and Margaret Amosu brought out her preliminary bibliography, *Creative African Writing in the European Languages,* through the Institute of African Studies at the University of Ibadan in 1964, the bulk of such activities had their fruition later, in publications from 1965 on.

THEMES AND TENDENCIES

In the first wave of West African fiction in English, a limited number of themes emphasized either colonialism and its clash with autochthonous cultures or village life, which was presented, on the one hand, as a whole without outside urban interference or, on the other, as a contrast to city and Western ways. Broadly speaking, fictional works dealt with historical, cultural, social, and religious issues in the past and the present and in urban or rural contexts, which sometimes contrasted and sometimes complemented each other. (In this regard, Tutuola's fiction has been unique insofar as his works center almost entirely on picaresque adventures not within the world of human beings but of the denizens of the forest, who have often never had earthly existence as we know it.) Conflicts ranged from the colonial and the generational through the ethnic, political, and religious to the battle of the sexes, the alienation of the child of two worlds, and the debate on tradition versus modernism. These themes do not disappear in the second wave but, along with new themes, continue the discussion of such subjects as polygamy, supernatural involvements, the importance of offspring, the relationship between the human community and the deities, and the individual's role in the community.

The Second Wave

HOLDOVERS AND NEWCOMERS

The advent of the second wave of fiction writing in English by West Africans may be marked by the Nobel laureate Wole Soyinka's novel *The Interpreters* (1965), which is as much a poet's novel as Gabriel Okara's *The Voice*. Soyinka had already been anthologized as a poet with pieces like "Telephone Conversation" and "Abiku," and Oxford University Press had published *A Dance of the Forests* and *Three Short Plays* in 1963, thus launching his career as Africa's leading playwright. The first part of the novel, with its leaning toward the stream-of-consciousness technique, is an interpretation of the status of the newly independent Nigerian society. The interpreters, a group of young intellectuals, find graft and corruption rampant in their society. Through them Soyinka raps the hypocrisy and pretentiousness in their elders, typified by the bribe-taking Sir Derinola and his half-educated crony Chief Winsala, and by the affected Professor Oguazor, whose railing against "meral terpitude" hides his own culpability in the illegitimate daughter ("the plastic apple of his eye") whom he keeps cloistered from public view.

The second part of the novel takes up the question of what the interpreters are doing with their own lives. Sekoni, the naive, honest engineer, becomes mad and finally dies after his hydroelectric plan is passed over for the proposal of a corrupt contractor. Sagoe, the newspaper columnist whom

Derinola and Winsala try to fleece, to their own discomfiture, is the exponent of the philosophy of Voidancy, an exposition on bowel movements, which he deifies in the expression "To shit is human, to voidate divine"; though more capable of adjustment than Sekoni, he finds that his attempt to expose the engineer's treatment merely plays into Derinola's hands, his piece being used in a "swap of silence" (95). Egbo, another of the interpreters, is caught in a double bind: he has "a choice of drowning" between being a village chief ("the warlord of the creeks") and working as a senior officer at the foreign office ("the dull grey filing cabinet faces of the foreign office" [12]). Kola, the painter, helps to provide continuity in the novel through his painting of the Yoruba pantheon, using his friends as models. The narrative, which focuses on the interpreters' views in part 1, here concentrates on the actions of Lazarus, a beach preacher, and his acolyte, the newly baptized Noah, who is killed when he jumps to his death in order to escape from the African-American homosexual Joe Golder. All in all, the novel provides concrete evidence that the euphoria that Soyinka had warned against at impending Independence in *A Dance of the Forests* has evaporated and that morality and fair play are being set aside.

Following close on the heels of *The Interpreters* was Chinua Achebe's *A Man of the People*. Achebe's only first-person novel, it etches out an unflattering portrait of Nigerian independence through the eyes of an "interpreter," a university graduate who comes into conflict with his former mentor, Chief the Honourable M. A. Nanga (a schoolteacher turned politician), over a young woman and the extension of this rivalry into village and national politics. The alienation Achebe had expressed in *No Longer at Ease* as a distancing from the government and politics, seen as "they" in relation to "us," now becomes a viciously exploitative cynicism that considers the nation as a cake of which everyone is entitled to a piece. The pidgin expression "you chop, meself I chop, palaver finish" (you eat your own share, I eat mine, so we have nothing to quarrel over) epitomizes the contrast between this state of affairs and the well-ordered society of *Things Fall Apart*. This breakdown, coupled with the novel's climax in a military coup prompted by the violence of the national election, prefigures the successive military coups that have plagued Nigeria in the last twenty years or so, and the untamable corruption that has bedeviled Nigerian and other African public and private sectors since Independence.

Although *The Interpreters* and *A Man of the People* gave notice that a mood of pessimism and disillusionment was beginning to set in, that mood was by no means dominant in this early period of the second wave. In 1965, the year Soyinka's novel came out, a work of shorter fiction was published by the Sierra Leonean surgeon Davidson Nicol, writing under the name Abioseh Nicol. *The Truly Married Woman and Other Stories* subsumes "The Leopard Hunt" and "The Devil at Yolahun Bridge," which were also published that same year under the title *Two African Tales*. The stories demonstrate Nicol's fine handling of wit and irony, and they furnish insights into customs and beliefs of Freetown's Creole society, including the engagement ceremony in the title story, as well as the belief in spirits ("The Devil at Yolahun Bridge"), in divination and charms ("As the Night, the Day" and "The Leopard Hunt"), and in the ability of the dead to use kinetic powers ("Love's Own Tears") or to appear in bodily form to the living ("Life is Sweet at Kumansenu"). A typical setting in the stories is the transitional period between self-government and independence, when colonial administrators were on guard against conduct that might promote tension and nationalist fervor. Nicol's competent handling of point of view and tone, of narrative design and dialogue, is nowhere more evident than in one of the two stories that draw on his years in England as a student: "The Leopard Hunt," a finely executed tale that shows a well-developed sensibility.

Nicol far surpasses the two Sierra Leonean writers of fiction who are better known in part because they wrote full-length novels. Yulisa Amadu Maddy's *No Past, No Present, No Future* (1973) examines the lives of three young men, "brothers three," two of whom are from the hinterland, while the third is a Creole from the capital. Maddy plays on ethnic divisions, echoing the prejudice of those Creoles who see themselves as elite in comparison to "provincials." By amassing money through theft at the railway station where they all go to work after their Catholic schooling, they fulfill their ambition to go to London to study. Although Maddy is aware of their faults and, for example, makes Joe Bengoh condemn Santigi Bombolai for being something of a "black Nazi" in taking out his frustrations with European whites on their women, he does not overtly point to their ruthlessness, their lack of a moral core, and their passion for self-gratification as the reasons for their failure. He seems to side with Joe Bengoh in his silent reproach of Ade John, the Creole member of the trio. Eustace Palmer, in his review of Maddy's novel, observes that Maddy "construes [Ade] as another example of Creole tyranny" (164–65) when Ade demands his turn with the girl (also of provincial extraction) whom Joe has just wantonly seduced. Gripping scenes make this morbid novel a better-realized work than Conton's book; yet Maddy's anger and bitterness toward Creoles and whites is hardly disguised. By making his three protagonists as vicious as they are, Maddy makes us feel sympathy by default for their victims.

R. Sarif Easmon, like Nicol a surgeon, is better known for his plays than for his fiction. His novel *The Burnt-Out Marriage* (1967), like some of Nicol's stories, draws on supernatural themes. Its protagonist, Chief Briwa, goes through a death ordeal by fire, the outcome of sorcery earlier in his life, to gain power and prestige. Gondomboh had predicted at the time that the sterile Briwa would die by fire when one of his wives became pregnant, and it is the half-Creole wife Makallay who becomes the agent of fulfillment when she falls helplessly in love with another man and succumbs to him. There have been charges and an effective rebuttal of those charges that Easmon looks down on his African characters and exhibits Creole superiority over non-Creoles, a carry-over from Great Britain's settlement of freed slaves in the Freetown colony in the late eighteenth and nineteenth centuries.

The only published novel by a Gambian writer thus far is by the poet Lenrie Peters. *The Second Round* (1965), whose setting is Freetown, also looks at the Creole society to which Dr. Kawa (and Peters himself) returns after his medical training in England. Like Casely-Hayford's novel, Peters's semiautobiographical work captures something of the ethos of Freetown society, this time in the 1950s to 1960s; it is prefaced by a poem on Freetown, at the foot of the "Lion Mountains" of Sierra Leone, at the heart of which stands the silk cotton tree, "her every root and hope." Though "Free as a summer cloud / and inordinately proud," the city is also "old and worn / uncoordinated" (vii–ix) and caught up in a stagnation that "was the reflection of the British genius for making their colonial peoples march no nearer than a century behind them, so that when frock coats and bowlers were being frowned on and discarded at Westminster, they had become the height of fashion in the tropical heat" (15). Happiness from the enthusiastic welcome home of Dr. Kawa soon fades as Kawa tries to cope not only with an affair whose compass from beginning to end is improbable, but also with the goings-on in the household of his next-door neighbor, Mr. Marshall, who eventually goes mad because, like the turtle the two of them hunt, Marshall is too much in love with his blatantly unfaithful wife and too much restricted by the dictates of the Catholic church to file for divorce. The death in their home from nose cancer of Marshall's nephew, after the nephew's long-drawn-out affair with Marshall's wife, and his wife's death at the hand of their eight-year-old daughter, Sonia, strain the reader's credulity but point to a tragic vision. Peters's characters, whether they speak flawless English or a frequently less than authentic Krio, present us with a number of pithy reflections on religion, morality, politics, and society. Peters also uses symbolism, not just in the turtle love of Mr. Marshall, but also in Sori's carved turtle shell, which depicts the kind of love and friendship Kawa has found elusive thus far in his "second round."

The love theme is treated with much greater effectiveness in *The Concubine* (1966), by the Nigerian novelist Elechi Amadi. Apart from Tutuola, who belongs in a class by himself, Amadi is perhaps the best-known novelist of the supernatural in English-speaking West Africa. *The Concubine* is the finely wrought story of Ihuoma, the wife of a sea god who has permitted her incarnation as a mortal but remains jealous of her. The initially inscrutable Ihuoma grows in human warmth as she grows older, but the men she attracts to her become afflicted with tragedy. Her first husband, Emenike, dies after a fight with Madume, and Madume is blinded by a spitting cobra when he pays court to Ihuoma later on. Finally, Ekwueme, who had for long nursed a love for Ihuoma, is vanquished by his father when he makes a bid to marry the beautiful widow, forcing him to marry Ahurole, an immature woman whom

Ekwueme's parents had chosen for him. When Ekwueme turns mad after ingesting a love potion from Ahurole, it is Ihuoma who nurses him back to health. With every obstacle now cleared from their path, the couple plans to marry, but a respected diviner reveals that marriage to Ihuoma will always be fatal for her husband: she can only be a concubine. Another diviner's attempt to counteract the charm of the sea god yields clear evidence that the gods cannot be vanquished. The diviner may be able to offset the taboo if he can get Ekwueme to the middle of the sea for a midnight ritual. But fate and the gods deal a cruel irony: Ihuoma's son launches a poison arrow to kill a lizard necessary for the sacrifice, and Ekwueme is slain.

Amadi's subsequent novels, *The Great Ponds* (1969) and *The Slave* (1978), treat varying aspects of village society and of conflict within it and between villages, but neither has the same evocative power or enduring charm as *The Concubine*. The practice of consigning families to the service of a god, one of the themes in Achebe's *No Longer at Ease*, is also to be found in *The Slave*, in which the hero, Olumati, returns to his duties as an *osu* in the service of Amadiora, the god of thunder, after his unsuccessful attempt at integrating himself into his village society. Paying tribute to the gods through sacrifice is a theme of *The Great Ponds*, which concerns the conflict between the villages of Chiolu and Aliakoro for ownership of the great ponds; the wrath of the gods comes to the villages in the form of a disease that spares no one, and the people also lose the use of one of the ponds as a result of a suicide.

The Cameroonian writer Mbella Sonne Dipoko's *A Few Nights and Days* (1966) also deals with male-female relationships that end in tragedy. The focus of the novel's conflict is not ethnicity, as in novels by Easmon, Maddy, and to some extent, Peters (even though a Creole element survives in Cameroonian society), but race. The central character plans to wed a French woman who has fallen prey to him and to take her back to Cameroon. Tragedy intervenes, for the prospective wife commits suicide when a reluctantly prospective father-in-law connives in her fiancé's departure from France without her knowledge. In *Because of Women* (1969), Dipoko is alternatively a hedonist, as his hero, Ngosi, indulges in gratuitous acts of sexual intercourse, and a moralist, as he disposes of him with a fever as if to say that he has received his just deserts. Dipoko's talents do not match those of the most accomplished of his French-speaking compatriots like Mongo Beti, Ferdinand Oyono, and Francis Bebey, but he ranks above the few other fellow English-speaking Cameroonians, such as L. T. Asong, Ba'Bila Mutai, and Kenjo Jumbam, who are part of the third wave of writers.

NEW THEMES OF DISILLUSIONMENT

During the first wave of West African fiction in English, every published work had some significance on account of the small corpus of literature being produced. In the second wave, the reverse was true. A large number of new writers entered the scene; their audience and their talents were more diversified, and their styles reflected that variety. In addition, the popular market literature of Onitsha and the popular literature of Ghana provided dozens of chapbooks, which could not be confused with "serious" literature.[3] Optimism over the end of colonialism soon faded, as economic independence lagged far behind political independence. Many Africans soon saw that their newly installed government officials were too preoccupied with feathering their nests to show concern for the poor and disadvantaged. Corruption was rampant, and with it came violence and military coups. From the early euphoria of liberation one moves to the dismal landscapes of West African second-wave fiction, which focuses on disillusionment at the outcome of Independence. For the first time, women writers began publishing works of fiction, thus adding new dimensions and perspectives. Finally, the Nigerian civil war produced a spate of works whose themes and settings were inspired by the war and its aftermath.

The most successful writer of this second phase was not a Nigerian but a Ghanaian, Ayi Kwei Armah, whose scathing denunciation of corruption focused on the themes of corruption and hypocrisy that Soyinka's interpreters had pointed to, without, however, suggesting ways to relieve society of apathy, cynicism, moral degeneracy, and inertia. After having examined the status quo of corruption, graft, and materialism in Ghanaian society in his first novel, *The Beautyful Ones Are Not Yet Born* (1968), Armah proceeded to trace its parallels in revolutionary and capitalist structures within and outside Africa in *Fragments* (1970) and *Why Are We So Blest?* (1972). He traced its African origins in *Two Thousand Seasons* (1973) and laid a foundation for its cure in *The Healers* (1978).

Each of Armah's five novels is an independent work of the imagination that takes a critical look at society. Each novel, nonetheless, also forms part of a comprehensive study reinforcing concepts, themes, and meanings in both earlier and later works as Armah delivers a penetrating analysis of ethnic, African, and world history. Even when the focus of a novel is contemporary society, as in the first three novels, the past acts as an important backdrop against which the actions and conflicts are played out and as a shaping force in their outcomes. The five novels together portray a revalorized history of Ghana and of Africa. Armah is not a cultural historian but a novelist, and his study is not chronological in the sense that subsequent novels offer historical portraits consecutively. Armah's opinions on history contrast with those of Achebe. For Armah, the disintegration of African society began, not with colonialism, but in the distant past, following the encounter with the Arabs. Both writers perceive the same moral decay in contemporary society: Achebe's *A Man of the People* deals with corruption and ends with violence and a military coup; Armah's *The Beautyful Ones Are Not Yet Born* dwells on the choice between poverty and wealth through corruption, with the failure of Kwame Nkrumah's messianism and the 1966 military coup in the background. But while Achebe looks to the past, Armah looks to the future for salvation, because, as the inscription says on the new and smaller bus at the end of the first novel, "The Beautyful Ones Are Not Yet Born."

Images of desolation and despair permeate the first three of Armah's novels. Throughout *The Beautyful Ones Are Not Yet Born* are images of excrement and filth, of rotting wood and rotten people. Even the image of the gleam is not an encouraging one, for it "invariably evokes the sulphur brilliance of artificial light in tropical darkness" as Robert Fraser has observed (21), a white thing enticing people to give up their honesty and morality to obtain wealth and status through corruption. These images are part of a complex symbolism that has as a central motif the archetypal image of the journey, a journey in which the honest people are walkers and the dishonest ones are drivers bent on getting as much speed as they can.

Perhaps because its protagonist, called simply "the man," is so alone and so undifferentiated, Armah's first novel has relatively less autobiographical content than do his next two. In *Fragments* the "been-to" Baako returns from his studies abroad to a rabidly materialistic society, represented by the ostentatious Brempong and his sister, and by Baako's own mother, who had been hoping that he would complete the house she had begun building. Baako is repulsed by this acquisitiveness, which shows itself in the traditional "outdooring" for his sister's child. The event is celebrated on the fifth day after birth, fully three days ahead of the customary eighth day, because it is payday and people will therefore give more generously. What is more, the infant, wrapped up in many folds of *kente* cloth and left unattended while relatives try to squeeze the last cedi from those attending, expires. The grandmother, Nana, asks, "What new power has made them forget that a child too soon exposed is bound to die?" She later opines, "The baby was a sacrifice they killed, to satisfy perhaps a new god they have found much like the one that began the same long destruction of our people" (284).

Baako's own disintegration takes place because he has become willy-nilly a child of two worlds who is now ill at ease in the old/new dispensation of his society. Not even the New World psychiatrist, Juana, who is a kindred spirit, can prevent his falling into the abyss. Sexual intercourse with her is no more fulfilling than Modin Dofu's with either Aimée or Mrs. Jefferson in *Why Are We So Blest?* As an artist, Baako had planned on replacing fiction writing with television scriptwriting, but no one is interested in his scripts, which require attention and reflection. Rather, they prefer inoffensive pabulum that requires no thought or, worse yet, scenarios designed to glorify the everyday events in the life of the country's rulers. Baako's resignation parallels both Dofu's rejection of a scholarship at Harvard University because the officials wanted him to believe that he was an exception to the rule of the African's backwardness and infantilism, on the one hand, and on the other, Dofu's prematurely leaving Harvard without earning his degree. Armah had earned a bachelor's degree from Harvard and a master's degree from Columbia

University before returning home to the same disillusioning experiences of Baako and Modin, who repairs to the fictitious Congheria and works there as a translator. Similarly, Armah had worked in 1963 as a translator in Algeria, a country that, following its successful war of liberation from French domination, had become a refuge for revolutionaries and revolutionary movements. The malaise that besets characters like Maanan, Baako, and now Modin, who loses his identity and his manhood while successfully bringing out Aimee's femininity and her identity, Armah imputes to the historical forces "which began the same long destruction of our people," a slavery that continues in the actions both of the corrupt minister in *The Beautyful Ones* and of the giver and recipient of college scholarships in *Why Are We So Blest?*

In these novels Armah is both castigator and conscience; he uses parody and satire as scourges against the pretentious and arrogant who, using such ploys as high-sounding compound names, ostentatious display of wealth, and cultism, place themselves in a class above everyone else. A writer with a social vision, he advocates a socialist revolution of ideas and of polity, a revolution that would change the view of upward mobility expressed in *The Beautyful Ones Are Not Yet Born.* We learn there that there is "only one way. There would always be only one way for the young to reach the gleam. Cutting corners, eating the fruits of fraud" (112). At age twenty-nine when this work was published, Armah was an angry young man who had left home for America believing in the promise of the future held out to Ghanaians by Nkrumah, only to find himself, after the revolution was betrayed, an iconoclast not only castigating the leadership of the moment but also reaching back into the past to find the seeds of the disease from which his society suffers. This iconoclasm can sometimes go too far, as critics like Wole Soyinka, Gerald Moore, and Robert Fraser have observed. Oyekan Owomoyela writes that *Fragments* "suffers, like many of the new African novels of alienation, from an untempered emotional partisanship." Ironically, it is this very partisanship that serves as the basis of the fourth novel, *Two Thousand Seasons*, without, however, making "discernment difficult and art impossible" (Owomoyela 110).

Two Thousand Seasons provides an important instance of an African novelist meshing the European realistic novel with the narrative art of the traditional African *griot.* Here, however, the narrator is not a single bard who has inherited the knowledge of the history from his forebears but a composite character, a collective "we," that has witnessed both the originating events and the subsequent historical developments. Armah posits an explanation for Africa's centuries of denigration in a moral vision of communal guilt and venality, drawing, in part, on the prophetic literature that is found in many religions and that, in secular literature, goes back to the Middle Kingdom of ancient Egypt. The novel's basic thesis is that Blacks as a people lost a path that Armah calls "the way of reciprocity" (25), and it is clear even from the prologue that this loss is responsible for the travail suffered by Blacks over a period of one thousand years, the "two thousand seasons" of the novel's title. "Receiving, giving, giving, receiving, all that lives is twin. Who would cast the spell of death, let him separate the two. Whatever cannot give, whatever is ignorant even of receiving, knowing only taking, that thing is past its own mere death. It is a carrier of death. Woe the giver on the road to such a taker, for then the victim has found victorious death" (xiii).

Blacks, Armah argues, gave without receiving to two waves of white predators, as the prophetess Anoa foretold. The first came over the desert sands, precipitating the devastation of Black Africans, and the second came over water, sending millions of Blacks to be slaves in lands across the seas. By casting the story into a *griot* framework, Armah is able to cover a vast period similar to that of Yambo Ouologuem in *Le devoir de violence* (1968; *Bound to Violence*, 1971). But the book is not simply a catalogue of woes. In the chapter entitled "The Dance of Love," Armah depicts a successful mutiny of slaves that recalls that of the Black slave dealer Momutu in Ousmane Sembène's story "Le voltaïque" (1962; *Tribal Scars*). The mutiny is significant in that the slaves are able to return to their homeland. Still, as Armah shows, the prophetic necessity of doom cannot be avoided. Not even the teaching of Isanusi, who anticipates Densu of *The Healers*, can save the people from their destiny. Nonetheless, through the collective consciousness of his narrator Armah predicts that "the reign of the destroyers cannot reach beyond these two thousand seasons" (318), for exploitative kings like King Komanche and white predators alike will be destroyed, paving the way for the healing that is the focus of Armah's last novel, *The Healers*.

The Healers covers a much shorter span of history than does *Two Thousand Seasons*, and its tone is much more in keeping with therapeutic impulses than the alternately accusatory and condemnatory voice in the earlier work. *The Healers* is rooted in Ghanaian history of the late nineteenth century, when the British fought and eventually defeated the Ashanti in a war that showed the prowess and skill of Black Africans in war. Armah skillfully but unobtrusively weaves Ashanti history into his novel, revealing that the reason for the kingdom's defeat derived from internal disunity, rivalry, greed, and the psychosocial sickness that recurs in all of Armah's works. In spite of the defeat, Armah intimates that in the work of the great healer Densu, who rehabilitates both Araba Jesiwa and General Asamoa Nkwanta, the period of the Black African's suffering under the curse of the prophecy of slavery and destitution is drawing to a close.

The same year, 1968, that Armah published his first novel, his compatriot Joseph Abruquah published his second, *The Torrent*, which, like his first, *The Catechist* (1965), dwells on the theme of education as a key to prosperity. By that same year Christina Ama Ata Aidoo, another compatriot, had already been hailed as a promising writer with her first play, *The Dilemma of a Ghost* (1965), drawing on a theme of the adjustment of a son lately returned from a stay in the United States, a theme Armah was later to use in the story of

Baako, the hero of *Fragments*. Although her first major work of fiction, *Our Sister Killjoy*, was copyrighted in 1966, it was not published until 1977; consequently, the honor of being the first published woman novelist in English-speaking West Africa goes to the Nigerian novelist Flora Nwapa for her novel *Efuru* (1966). A third woman novelist of note is the Nigerian Buchi Emecheta, who has written several novels set in London (the scene of her married life and of her experience as a single parent of five children) and in Nigeria, to which she later returned. These three writers provided the female voice in an arena that was previously the exclusive preserve of male writers. Together they view from a feminine—and sometimes a feminist—perspective society in English-speaking West Africa.

The heroines in Nwapa's novels tend to be idealized characters, while their male counterparts are often weak-willed or lackluster. In her first novel, *Efuru*, the title heroine grapples with a recurring problem in the writings of male authors, that of an individual whose life is by heredity or custom dedicated to the service of a god (Chinua Achebe's *No Longer at Ease* and Elechi Amadi's *The Concubine* are examples), a problem that is here complicated by the heroine's womanhood. Efuru is blessed with wealth and beauty, but because she is pledged to the goddess of the lake, getting married or having children will prove calamitous, a predicament that echoes the theme of the Ijaw myth "The Woman Who Tried to Change Her Fate," in which Ogboinba finds that her choice of power and prestige as a healer carries with it barrenness.[4] The young, beautiful, and assertive Efuru is unable to succeed as a wife in two marriages and loses her only child when her husband abandons her for another woman. But even though she is assertive and breaks with both husbands when she feels herself victimized by them, Efuru does not develop a strong social consciousness: her problem with Adizua is that he abandoned her, for she accepts polygamy as an institution and was ready to propose that he take the woman he had abandoned her for as his second wife.

Nwapa's second novel, *Idu* (1969), pursues the exploration of the feminine viewpoint, but neither this nor the first novel produces a compelling examination of the African woman's role in society, for Nwapa declines to deal with the moral and philosophical issues that obviously present themselves (Emenyonu 1975). The heroine, Idu, neither affirms the life of the baby she is carrying for her dead husband nor establishes the independence that a progressive woman might be expected to show; instead, she commits suicide in order to join her husband. A recent novel, *One Is Enough* (1981) is about marriage, but the heroine does not take the decisive stand that the title might lead us to expect. The decision not to marry a second time is not one she makes deliberately, but one that comes when the priest she was about to marry has a sudden change of heart as a result of narrowly escaping an accidental death. As its title suggests, Nwapa's collection *This Is Lagos and Other Stories* (1971) dwells on young women's problems in modern, urban

Nigerian society, particularly problems relating to pregnancy, domination by men, and the quest for formal education.

Buchi Emecheta's early novels are autobiographical and sociological studies of women in their involvement with men. Her first novel, *In the Ditch* (1971)—its title drawn from the column she practically forced the editor of *The New Statesman* to allow her to write after a series of evasions—tells the story of Adah, who, like so many other women, Black and white, is forced to live in subsidized housing in London (Zell, Bundy, and Coulon 384–85). Its sequel, *Second-Class Citizen* (1974), continues the story of Adah's life in London. For her third novel, *The Bride Price* (1976), Emecheta takes up a theme treated by writers like Achebe (*No Longer at Ease*) and other Igbo writers. It is the story of the outcast who is rejected by the family of a loved one. Although it is the man who is an outcast, it is the woman who, defying her relatives and marrying her lover, suffers a tragic end: Akunna dies giving birth to her child. *The Bride Price* is the first of three successive novels set in the Nigeria of the past; all three focus on the experiences of female characters within a male-dominated society. The second novel of the series, *The Slave Girl* (1977), deals with a young girl's virtual slavery, and the third, *The Joys of Motherhood* (1979), presents the questionable joys that the heroine, Nnu Ego, experiences in two marriages, the first of which produces no children. The ironic title of this, Emecheta's fifth novel, belies what Eustace Palmer refers to as "the singlemindedness with which she has presented the female point of view" ("Feminine Point of View," 51). Emecheta's use of the limited omniscient point of view, such that much of what goes on is presented from the point of view of the heroine, helps reinforce this singlemindedness of vision (see especially Palmer 44–47). Apart from her adult fiction, Emecheta has also written books for children, the first two of which, *Titch the Cat* (1978) and *Nowhere to Play* (1980), reflect experiences of her children that parallel her own life as an underprivileged, second-class citizen.

Christina Ama Ata Aidoo has written poetry, short stories, and a novel, as well as plays. Her novel, *Our Sister Killjoy; or, Reflections from a Black-Eyed Squint* (1968), echoes her ethnic culture in its fluid blend of poetry and prose. The mixture of styles enables Aidoo to blend the intensely subjective with the less fiercely subjective and with the objective in her narrative of Sissie's experiences, beginning on the eve of her departure for Europe. Sissie's observations of the people she encounters justifies the appellation Aidoo gives her of "a black-eyed squint." These encounters cover a wide spectrum, including male-female, lesbian, and Black-white relationships. In addition, Aidoo uses the opportunity to descant on social and political issues beyond the situations in which Sissie finds herself. Aidoo not only invests her heroine with a consciousness of oppression and of racial and sexual inequality but also takes the liberty as the author to display her own notions about colonialism and other matters. Preoccupation with colonial and neocolonial attitudes is a hallmark of Aidoo's social vision, a concern she also deals with in the opening and closing stories of her collection *No Sweetness Here* (1971), whose title is borrowed from Armah. Aidoo shows a pessimism about Black Africans under a cloud (perhaps even a shroud) of colonial domination past and present. She posits the situation of women within a much broader historical pattern of oppression than either Emecheta or Nwapa.

Kofi Awoonor, Aidoo's Ghanaian compatriot, had distinguished himself as a poet before writing his lone novel, *This Earth My Brother* (1971), whose central character, Amamu, follows a trajectory (much like Baako's in *Fragments*) from his wanderings abroad to his eventual suicide. Here is a capsule of what Awoonor and the book are about from Lewis Nkosi's *Tasks and Masks:*

> As befits a modernist novel, *This Earth My Brother* is a melting pot of varied ingredients: of actual history, personal memories, anecdotes, a mixture of autobiography and invention, linked together by a style which is a constant blending of different genres and literary techniques, an adroit wedding of European and African narrative procedures. The novel uses what must be acknowledged as a fresh device in the handling of African experience. That is to say, we are given a simple narrative in the third person but every chapter has an alternative one consisting of a more undifferentiated, freer flow of images and memory in the Joycean manner of the stream-of-consciousness; each alternate chapter therefore acts as a commentary on the first and *vice-versa.* (63)

Awoonor uses the recurring image of the mermaid or "mammy wata," combining the mythic with the realistic and projecting African history through an individuated consciousness—the central character, who moves through a course of identification and integration through a successful career and self-alienation to chaos and madness, culminating in suicide.

Nigeria's war novels—that is, novels that focus on events during the Nigeria-Biafra War, its aftermath, and its effect on people's lives, or that use the war as a backdrop to unfolding events in the lives of characters—supply ample reminders that internal dissensions, which Armah stressed in his drawing on Ashanti history, are not a thing of the past in African polity. Occasioned by the secession of the eastern region of Nigeria under Colonel Chukwuemeka Ojukwu in the wake of the killing of Igbos in northern Nigeria in 1966, the failure of attempts at a rapprochement, and the decision by the military government under General Yakubu Gowon to prevent the breakup of the Nigerian Federation, the war lasted from 1967 to 1970. The actions of both Western nations and rival Eastern bloc countries in the support of one or the other side, as well as the grim realities of starvation, carnage, and destruction, intensified the war's devastating effects on the Nigerian people's lives and on their psychological well-being. Writers have continued to base works on the war long after its conclusion, leading one critic to refer to "a still lingering 'war consciousness' " (Amuta 83).

Olalere Oladitan has tentatively classified the varied treatment Nigerian writers have given the war. His categories include pioneering forecasts, notably Achebe's novel *A Man of the People;* novels involved "with witnesses to and record of events" (11) of the violent war years, as represented by John Munonye's *A Wreath for the Maidens* (1973) and Chukwuemeka Ike's *Sunset at Dawn* (1976); nonfiction personal accounts such as Elechi Amadi's *Sunset in Biafra* (1973) and Wole Soyinka's prison notes, *The Man Died* (1972); examinations of the "roles of ideology and violence in a revolutionary transformation of society" (14), such as Soyinka's symbolic novel *Season of Anomy* (1973); works dealing with the aftermath of the war, along with the worship of money and materialism, which Samuel Ifejika evokes in the title of his novel *The New Religion* (1973); and satires or parodies of the Nigerian situation, as in Kole Omotoso's two novels, *The Edifice* (1971) and *The Combat* (1972). In addition, purely historical accounts include N. U. Akpan's *The Struggle for Secession* (1971) and R. B. Alade's *The Broken Bridge: Reflections and Experiences of a Medical Doctor During the Nigerian Civil War.*[5]

This sampling of war writings from Nigeria is far from complete, as Oladitan makes clear. Also worthy of note are Chinua Achebe's *Girls at War and Other Stories* (1972), which includes three stories about the war, among them the title story; Isidore Okpewho's *The Last Duty* (1972); Eddie Iroh's *Forty-Eight Guns for the General* (1976) (the "guns" are the white mercenaries hired by the "general" of the Biafran army); Kalu Uka's sensitive examination of the devastating effects of the war on his title hero in *Colonel Ben Brim* (1972); Chukwuemeka Ike's *Toads of War* (1979), the second novel of a projected trilogy; and two novels by Cyprian Ekwensi, *Survive the Peace* (1976) and *Divided We Stand* (1980), the latter reputedly written during the war (Zell, Bundy, and Coulon 149). With the publication of Flora Nwapa's *Never Again*, which is largely fictionalized history from a feminist viewpoint (Amuta 90), and of Buchi Emecheta's *Destination Biafra* (1981), Nigeria's two principal women novelists also added to the number of war-related fictional works.

Soyinka's *Season of Anomy* and Kole Omotoso's *The Combat* stand out for their use of symbolism and allegory. Soyinka had delivered a good deal of personal invective in his angry prison notes, *The Man Died* (1972), and his play *Madmen and Specialists* (1971) depicts a virtual wasteland in stark, dark contours. For *Season of Anomy* (1974) he drew on the myth of Orpheus, which Jean-Paul Sartre had used to characterize the poetry of Negritude in his 1948 essay "Orphée noir." Soyinka's quip that African writers should live their Negritude like the tiger its tigritude, not declaim it, helped to make him a controversial figure. When, however, he experienced a similar psychological privation, which forced him to turn inward, Soyinka had recourse to the same mythic image of the Black artist and his existential situation in a Black nation. Soyinka reworks the myth such that the songs of Ofeyi (Orpheus) become revolutionary songs designed to undermine Nigerian power brokers' "superstructure of robbery, indignities and murder, ending the new phase of slavery" (27). The plaintive song of Negritude becomes a revolutionary weapon, and Soyinka's alter-ego Ofeyi is not beyond using violence to end violence (like Daodu of *Kongi's Harvest* [1967]). He searches for Iriyise, comatose but not dead, and is exposed to madmen in the bowels of Temoko. Soyinka's blend of the realistic with the mythic is well realized, but although much of his anger has been tempered and Iriyise is rescued from the dungeons, the ending conveys the sense neither of a great purgation nor of triumph, but of the quiet stirring of a new and perhaps hopeful dawn.

Soyinka's work is as moderately paced—even in its scenes depicting violence—as Omotoso's *The Combat* is hurried in its course. The allegory in the latter novel is far more direct: a conflict between two friends, Ojo (a federated Nigeria) and Chuku (Biafra), who claim fatherhood of a ten-year-old son, Isaac (Nigeria as an independent nation), born in 1960, the year of Nigeria's birth as a nation. The mother of the child is a prostitute whose father and mother are also interested in dominating Isaac, who, like his biblical counterpart, is an offering for slaughter. She is unsure of which of the contestants is the father and, after having become "fat and sloppy [so that she moves] like one mountain going up another" (23) she no longer has any use for the contestants, only one of whom, Ojo, is interested in her anyway. The central crisis in the novel comes when Chuku runs over Isaac with his taxicab and, rather than go back to apologize, agrees to single combat with Ojo. The plausible narrative realism breaks down as the novel switches back and forth unnervingly between the past and the present. What would have been a serious examination of the conflict between Biafra and the federal forces becomes a mere burlesque as ponderous issues are reduced to trifling matters. The credibility of incidents is also called into question as both combatants go to the same church to prepare for the combat and enlist the aid of the West (Ojo as Nigeria) and the Soviet bloc (Chuku on behalf of Biafra) in their fight.[6] All the same, Omotoso's vision is tragic, for Isaac dies from the hapless crushing under Chuku's taxi and is abandoned to his mother, Moni, transformed as Dee Madam, while everyone, including foreign envoys, go to watch the combat for which the rival blocs of East and West have prepared the adversaries.

The Third Wave

The characteristic features of the third wave of West African fiction in English are somewhat difficult to define, because the issues at stake in the socioeconomic, cultural, and political spheres are far less clearcut than were those of colonialism, the conflict between traditional and modern ways, and the initial disenchantment with new leaders. The problems that now face not just West Africa but the entire continent and indeed the Third World as a whole are far more complex and require far more elaborate solutions than what starry-eyed idealists (whether politicians, bureaucrats, artists, or the average individual) had contemplated.

Still, a number of characteristics present themselves. The writers of the third wave are younger people in the main, writing (by and large) for an African as opposed to a Euro-American audience, and attempting to reach a far wider audience in their countries than the prominent writers of the 1950s and 1960s. Their vision is, on the whole, more down to earth and therefore far less grandiose than that of many of their predecessors. They either oppose the elitism of their precursors with a grassroots orientation and an interest in the fate of the common man or are too preoccupied with the problems of the downtrodden to install themselves on a visionary level. Apart from the few historical novels that appear from time to time, they are concerned less with colonialism than with the remnants of colonialism evident in the neocolonialist attitudes held by many of those in the chambers and corridors of power. This new populist approach is different from that of chapbook literature. Chapbook literature (which is outside the scope of the present examination) has an overwhelming interest in entertainment, while the new wave of writings seeks not only to entertain but to edify and instruct, as well as to forge a common cause with ordinary people.

Buchi Emecheta, although she began writing during the second phase, perhaps more properly belongs to this new phase because of her support of the common woman, whom she portrays as a victim in a male-dominated society. Her early novels draw on her fresh experiences with colonial and male domination, and while subsequent novels go back to the past, she returns to the present in a novel like *Double Yoke* (1983), whose title refers to the "yokes" of the old ways and the new. In *Double Yoke*, Miss Bulewao is a successful writer and university lecturer (obviously a surrogate for Emecheta) who interacts with Ete Kamba, a male-chauvinist student of hers and the hero of the novel. For all the comeback that Miss Bulewao makes to Ete Kamba's remarks, it is still difficult to dismiss the comment he makes about male-female relationships: "Madam, you seem to be forgetting that I am a man. I can do what I like. A man can raise his own bastard, women are not allowed to do that" (162).

Femi Osofisan has tentatively put forward three categories of writing in Nigerian literature in the aftermath of the civil war; these supply a number of handholds useful for grappling with the fiction of the region as a whole. The first is the "war literature," which straddles the second and third waves. The second category is "popular literature," and the third "socialist literature," or what, to avoid misunderstanding, he terms "the alternative tradition" (170–71). The popular literature presented here is more sophisticated than the pamphlet literature of the Onitsha Market variety, which Emmanuel Obiechina has discussed in detail in his *An African Popular Literature* (1973), or for that matter the popular literature that, beginning in Ghana in the 1940s with J. B. Blay's *Be Content with Your Lot*, grew steadily in the 1950s and 1960s (Ikkideh). The flourishing of this new brand of popular literature resulted from greater access by authors to a publishing outlet. It was Faber and Faber's opening of its doors to an unlikely writer such as Amos Tutuola that launched him into a prominent place in the development of African literature; in similar fashion, Heinemann's African Writers Series, Longman's Drumbeats, Oxford University Press's publication of plays in its Three Crowns imprint, and acceptance by other British publishers as well as American ones like Doubleday–Anchor Books in the early days, and by Africana Publishing Corporation and Three Continents Press in the 1970s and 1980s, all provided creative outlets for African writers as well as for critics of their writings. The pamphlet literatures of Nigeria and Ghana were spawned by the establishment of local printing presses to cater to the purely entertainment needs of the masses. The third wave's popular literature did not obliterate that already existing popular literature but represented another tier between market literature and the sophisticated literature that pays homage to exacting aesthetics, form, and style. Its readers, no less than its writers, have been better educated, and the published product is the preserve not exclusively of second-rate printing presses but also of state-of-the-art local and international publishing houses. Among these newer publishers are Onibonoje Press, Ethiope Publishing House, Fourth Dimension, Nwamife, and Flora Nwapa's new publishing company, Tana Press, which brought out her most recent books. In addition, some international publishers established subdivisions that catered to writers in this intermediate group, as Osofisan observes of Macmillan (170).

Among the Nigerians who fall within the category of popular writers is Obi Egbuna, who continued his early work with the following works of fiction published by either a British or Nigerian publisher: *Daughters of the Sun and Other Stories* (1970), *Emperor of the Sea and Other Stories* (1974), *The Minister's Daughter* (1975), *Diary of a Homeless Prodigal* (1978), *The Rape of Lysistrata and Black Candle for Christmas* (1980), and *The Madness of Didi* (1980). Other popular writers include Sulu Ugwu, Anezi Okoro, Victor Thorpe, and Mohamed Sule. Agu Ogali, described as "one of the most prolific and successful of the Onitsha chapbook writers" (Zell, Bundy, and Coulon 161), also produced such works in this intermediate category as *Coal City* (1978) and *The Julu Priest* (1978). Among the women writers are Helen Ovbiagele, who authored *Evbu, My Love* (1983), and Adaora Lilly Ulasi, whose novels *Many Things You No Understand* (1970), *Many Things Begin for Change* (1971), *Who Is Jonah?* (1978), and *The Man from Sagamu* (1978) are set in the colonial past and make conscious use of pidgin, not always with satisfactory results. Flora Nwapa's recent books, *One Is Enough* in particular, fall more nearly within this category. One recurring feature in this popular fiction is the fast-paced detective thriller (which has its counterpart in the Hollywood character of recent Nigerian films), a form that finds a prototype in Ekwensi's short thriller *Yaba Roundabout Murder* (1962). Kalu Okpi's two books, *The Smugglers* (1978) and *On the Road* (1980), exemplify this cops-and-robbers fare, of which one of the more explicitly titled works is Fidel Onyekwelu's *The Sawabas: Black Africa's Mafia* (1979).

In Ghana, Amu Djoleto, whose earlier novel *The Strange Man* (1967) appeared a decade previously, published his second novel, *Money Galore*

(1975), which spikes corruption and the corrupted represented by its hero, Kafu, a businessman and politician. Other writers include J. S. Kwarteng (*My Sword Is My Life*, 1973); E. Y. Egblewogbe (*Victims of Greed*, 1975); Selby Ashong-Katai (*Confessions of a Bastard*, 1976); Afari Assan (*Christmas in the City*, 1978); Nii Ofoli (*The Messenger of Death*, 1979); I. S. Ephson (*Tragedy of False Friends*, 1969); and A. M. Oppong-Affi (*The Prophet of Doom*, 1980). Also of note are the short stories of Kofi Aidoo (*Saworbeng: A Collection of Short Stories*, 1977) and the science fiction of J. O. Eshun (*Adventures of the Kapapa*, 1976). With the exception of Ephson's book, which is from the University of Ghana Bookshop, and Assan's, which was put out by Macmillan, all these other writers were published by Ghana Publishing Company, and this fact indicates the important function played by local publishers in providing access to writers who are unable to secure as an outlet those publishing houses, mostly European and North American, that have a wide network of distribution for their books.

The third category of the third wave, Osofisan's "socialist literature" or "alternative tradition," has fewer adherents than the other two and is also much less distinctive. Osofisan identifies his own novel, *Kolera Kolej* (1975), which chronologically belongs within the second wave, as falling within this tradition, along with the novels of Kole Omotoso, but acknowledges that the new socialist literature regrettably smacks very often of popular literature in its willingness to sacrifice art for immediacy and accessibility to the average reader. He discusses Omotoso's novels as examples of both the aims and shortcomings of the subgenre. Omotoso's *The Edifice* looks at problems confronting the contemporary individual, in this instance a young Nigerian who falls in love with an English girl, marries her, and brings her back to Nigeria, only for the dream to fail and for the wife, abandoned for another white woman and for a woman from her husband's village, to give up her shattered dream. The theme itself is not a new one, for it is found in as early a work in French-speaking West Africa as Ousmane Sembène's *O pays mon beau peuple!* (1957; O my country, my good people!) and again in a recent novel by another Senegalese writer, Mariama Bâ's *Un chant écarlate* (1981; Scarlet Song), as well as in Wole Soyinka's *The Interpreters*, where it is, however, not a central theme. But if the aim of this new kind of socialist writing is to be easily within the capabilities of the masses, then *The Edifice*'s haphazard shifts in narrative progression are difficult to explain, as they serve to make the structure complex while providing little, if anything, in aesthetic appeal. Omotoso's novel has received very favorable literary judgments, and he is himself aware that one should not have to compromise art to educate and entertain the masses.

CHARACTERISTICS AND PREOCCUPATIONS

The socialist view is not new in the evolution of African fiction. It has been overwhelmingly evident in the work of Ousmane Sembène, who did not compromise his art to suit the taste of a less educated or uneducated populace but sought another outlet, that of filmmaking, in order to reach the masses. A social vision was present in the work of Ngũgĩ wa Thiong'o from the first, although his endorsement of socialist principles and the patent influence of Marxism on his work come across most strongly in works like *Petals of Blood* (1977), written after his celebrated novel *A Grain of Wheat* (1967). The move toward endorsing socialist principles came late for Soyinka, whose *Season of Anomy* proclaims such an outlook, but he reverts to the hierarchical in his play *Death and the King's Horseman* (1975). Moreover, in the course of the second wave of writing, Ayi Kwei Armah overtly endorsed Marxism in his works without sacrificing art or complexity, though a stripe of partisanship marks (some would say mars) his works.

A few works stand outside these categories. Among them are Ben Okri's *Flowers and Shadows* (1980) and *The Landscapes Within* (1981), the second of which has been discussed as a novel of personal development; Isidore Okpewho's *The Victims* (1970); Wole Soyinka's *Aké;* and Yaw Boateng's *The Return* (1977).

In *The Return*, the action takes place in the first third of the nineteenth century. The story of the lust for revenge of a younger brother on an older brother he had revered until he felt betrayed by him, this short novel is as Afrocentric in its own way as are *Two Thousand Seasons* and *Ethiopia Unbound*. It does not attempt to set the story of Asante within a vast panorama of myth and history but to flesh out and clothe the bare bones of the actual historical personages and incidents for which, as for many political changes, "history did not give the full reasons" (116). Through the story of Seku and Jakpa, and of the young woman, Asamoa, with whom Jakpa falls in love, Boateng is able to conjure an authentic world infected with the pernicious disease of slavery, which Olaudah Equiano had first described from the African perspective in his autobiography, *Equiano's Travels* (1789), and, in the gripping account by the castrated Imam in the seventh chapter, to give a purview of the tragic bind in which Africans found themselves. Although Boateng does not pursue them, the parallels with contemporary society are all too evident, notably in the view among African Marxists and others that most of the current problems in Africa and in the Third World have to do with methods of capitalist countries that amount to a new form of slavery.

Criticism

This essay would not be complete if I made no reference to the new approaches to criticism that have emerged, since constructive criticism helps engender a budding literature, and indeed, the role of creative writer and critic are complementary and mutually reinforcing. The early reviews and short critiques in chiefly British and American periodicals by pioneering critics such as Janheinz Jahn, Eldred Jones, and Ulli Beier soon gave way to full-fledged periodicals on African literature and society like *Black Orpheus,*

Transition, *African Literature Today,* *Research in African Literatures,* and *Okike;* to full-length studies of individual writers like Achebe, Soyinka, and Armah; and to collections of critical essays by individual writers or in edited volumes. The early preoccupations with theme and language yielded some of their ground to new critical approaches beginning in the late 1960s, including structuralist, deconstructive, semiotic, and Marxist interpretations. The old debate about language took on a new guise as a result of nationalist fervor deriving from frustration over the continuing influence of the former colonial powers on politics, from pride at political independence, and, in the case of the Igbos, from Igbo nationalism arising out of the failure of the first Nigerian republic and their alienation from the much more populous and dominant northerners. The cultivation of literatures written in indigenous languages was part of the new nationalism, so that there emerged not only the notion of a national literature but of an ethnic one, a notable example being the nurturing of an Igbo literature, which was not so much literature written in Igbo but by Igbo writers and purporting to express an Igbo worldview. Similarly, in Cameroon a new nationalism developed, expressed for the most part among French-speaking writers.

The new controversy began in the 1970s with criticism of Soyinka's poetry by Chinweizu and Soyinka's reply that such criticism prescribed the suicide of poetry. The debate has continued into the 1980s with the publication of *Toward the Decolonization of African Literature* (1980), whose authors—Chinweizu, Onwuchekwa Jemie, and Ihechukwu Madubuike—criticize both Eurocentric critics who are patronizing toward African literature or see it as an extension of European literature, on the one hand, and on the other, creative writers, especially bourgeois ones (among them Wole Soyinka), whom these critics find irrelevant to African society and especially to the welfare of the masses. They label themselves *bolekaja* ("Come down, let's fight!") critics, "outraged touts for the passenger lorries of African literature . . . administering a timely and healthy dose of much needed public ridicule to the reams of pompous nonsense which has been floating out of the stale, sterile, stifling covens of academia and smothering the sprouting vitality of Africa's literary landscape" (xii). Soyinka took up the gauntlet this "troika," as he calls them, threw down, calling their approach "neo-Tarzanist" and evidence of the emergence of a "leftocracy" in African literary criticism ("The Critic and Society"). The tone of these three critics is frankly polemical, and their aim of "decolonizing" African literature is a good one, as such critics as Jonathan Ngaté have acknowledged, while pointing up the book's partisanship. Indeed, a good deal of early criticism and some subsequent judgments by both Western and African critics have revealed a Western bias. But the selection by Chinweizu, Jemie, and Madhubuike of whom to praise and whom to criticize is sometimes suspect, especially since they discountenance the discussion of drama, in which Wole Soyinka has excelled. The critics are, however, as careful in their choice of subtitle—*African Poetry and Fiction and Their Critics*—as they are in their avoidance of the Caucasian press. Moreover, they praise Léopold Senghor, the unabashed Francophile whom Soyinka has criticized, while subjecting Soyinka's poetry to "a corrective tussle."

Whatever may be the outcome of these debates, one thing is clear. Both creative writers and critics are committed to a literature centered on Africa and Africans, one that serves a useful purpose. And if disagreements have arisen about the value of art and aesthetics in relation to didactic purpose and accessibility to the average individual, they may be taken as healthy signs of a literary family grown large over a generation and possessing within it gems of literature that have won national and international recognition. Rapidly changing facets of African politics, society, and culture have been tellingly mirrored in works of prose fiction, a genre that thrives in the region and in the rest of the continent. And although the quality of writing has been uneven, one may assert with confidence that already there have appeared several works by gifted writers that will endure.

Notes

1. See Berenger-Feraud, Burton, Christaller, Cronise and Ward, Harris, Koelle, Landeroin and Tilho, Lippert, Prietze, Robinson, Roger, Schön, and Schlenker as examples of folklore collections.

2. Bernth Lindfors dismisses Ekwensi's work as based on the worst possible models in his 1969 article "Cyprian Ekwensi: An African Popular Novelist," provoking a rejoinder from Ernest Emenyonu in *African Literature Today* 5. More balanced judgments include Douglas Killam, "Cyprian Ekwensi" (1971), and another piece, also titled "Cyprian Ekwensi," by Eustace Palmer (1979).

3. For studies of Onitsha chapbooks, consult, inter alia, Obiechina (1973), Lindfors (1967), and Collins (1968).

4. This myth is included in Ulli Beier, ed., *The Origin of Life and Death: African Creation Myths;* it was transformed into the play *Woyengi* by Obotunde Ijimere (a pseudonym for Ulli Beier and Duro Ladipo) and published in *The Imprisonment of Obatala and Other Plays.*

5. The following are suggested by Oladitan as important historical contributions to documentation on the war in note 2 of his essay "The Nigerian Civil War and the Evolution of Nigerian Literature" (93): Madiebo, *The Nigerian Revolution and the Biafran War* (1980); Forsyth, *The Biafra Story* (1979); and Obasanjo, *My Command* (1980).

6. For a short, comprehensive assessment of Omotoso's art, see Femi Osofisan's article, written in 1980, "The Alternative Tradition: A Survey of Nigerian Literature in English since the Civil War" (1986), in particular pp. 176–80.

Bibliography

Abruquah, Joseph. *The Catechist*. London: Allen & Unwin, 1965.
———. *The Torrent*. London: Longman, 1968.

Achebe, Chinua. *Things Fall Apart*. London: Heinemann, 1959 [1958].

———. *No Longer at Ease*. London: Heinemann, 1960.

———. *Arrow of God*. London: Heinemann, 1964.

———. *A Man of the People*. London: Heinemann, 1966.

———. "The Role of the Writer in a New Nation." *Nigeria Magazine* 81 (June 1964): 157–60.

———. "The Black Writer's Burden." *Présence Africaine* 31, no. 59 (1966): 135–40.

———. "The Novelist as Teacher." In *African Writers on African Writing*, edited by G. D. Killam, 3–17. Evanston, Ill.: Northwestern University Press, 1973.

Aidoo, Christina Ama Ata. *The Dilemma of a Ghost*. London: Longman, 1965.

———. *Our Sister Killjoy; or, Reflections from a Black-Eyed Squint*. New York: Nok, 1968; London: Longman, 1981.

———. *No Sweetness Here: A Collection of Short Stories*. London: Longman, 1979 [1971].

Aidoo, Kofi. *Saworbeng: A Collection of Short Stories*. Tema: Ghana Publishing Corp., 1977.

Amadi, Elechi. *The Concubine*. London: Heinemann, 1966.

———. *The Great Ponds*. London: Heinemann, 1969.

———. *The Slave*. London: Heinemann, 1978.

Amuta, Chidi. "The Nigerian Civil War and the Evolution of Nigerian Literature." In *Contemporary African Literature*, edited by Hal Wylie et al. Washington, D.C.: Three Continents Press and African Literature Association, 1983.

Armah, Ayi Kwei. *The Beautyful Ones Are Not Yet Born*. Boston: Houghton Mifflin, 1968; London: Heinemann, 1969.

———. *Fragments*. Boston: Houghton Mifflin, 1970; London: Heinemann, 1974.

———. *Why Are We So Blest?* New York: Doubleday, 1972; London: Heinemann, 1974; Nairobi: East African Publishing House, 1974.

———. *Two Thousand Seasons*. Nairobi: East African Publishing House, 1973; London: Heinemann, 1979.

———. *The Healers*. Nairobi: East African Publishing House, 1978; London: Heinemann, 1979.

Ashong-Katai, Selby, *Confessions of a Bastard*. Tema: Ghana Publishing Corp., 1976.

Assan, Afari. *Christmas in the City*. London: Macmillan, 1978.

Awoonor, Kofi. *This Earth, My Brother . . .* New York: Doubleday, 1971; London: Heinemann, 1972.

Bâ, Mariama. *Un chant écarlate* [Scarlet Song]. Dakar: Nouvelles Editions Africaines, 1981.

———. trans. Scarlet Song. London: Longman, 1985.

Bascom, William. "Folklore Research in Africa." *Journal of American Folklore* 77, no. 303 (January–March 1964): 12–31.

Beier, Ulli, ed. *The Origin of Life and Death: African Creation Myths*. London: Heinemann, 1966.

Berenger-Feraud, L.-J.-B. *Peuplades de la Sénégambie* [The tribes of Senegambia]. Paris: E. Leroux, 1879.

Boateng, Yaw. *The Return*. London: Heinemann, 1977.

Burton, R. F. *Wit and Wisdom from West Africa; or, A Book of Proverbial Philosophy, Idioms, Enigmas and Laconisms*. New York: Negro University Press, 1969 [1865].

Cary, Joyce. *An American Visitor*. London: Michael Joseph, 1936.
————. *The African Witch*. London: Michael Joseph, 1951.
————. *Aissa Saved*. London: Michael Joseph, 1952.
————. *Mister Johnson*. London: Michael Joseph, 1959.
Casely-Hayford, Joseph E. *Ethiopia Unbound: Studies in Race Emancipation* [1911].
Chinweizu, Onwuchekwa Jemie, and Ihechukwu Madubuikwe. *Toward the Decolonization of African Literature*. Vol. 1, *African Fiction and Poetry and Their Critics*. Enugu, Nigeria: Fourth Dimension, 1980; Washington, D.C.: Howard University Press, 1983.
Christaller, J. G. *Three Thousand Six Hundred Ghanaian Proverbs (From the Asante and Fante Language)*. Studies in African Literature, vol. 2. Translated by Kofi Ron Lange. Lewiston, N.Y.: Edwin Mellen Press, 1990. First published as *A Collection of Three Thousand and Six Hundred Tshi Proverbs in Use among the Negroes of the Gold Coast Speaking the Asante and Fante Language*. Basel: Basel German Evangelical Missionary Society, 1879.
Collins, H. R. *The New English of the Onitsha Chapbooks*. Athens, Ohio: Ohio University Center for International Studies, 1968.
Conrad, Joseph. *Heart of Darkness*. London: Macmillan, 1898.
Conton, William. *The African*. London: Heinemann, 1960.
Cronise, Florence M., and Henry W. Ward. *Cunnie Rabbit, Mr. Spider and the Other Beef: West African Folk Tales*. London: S. Sonenschein; New York: Dutton, 1903; Arlington Heights, Ill.: Metro Books, 1969.
Dipoko, Mbella Sonne. *A Few Nights and Days*. London: Heinemann, 1966.
————. *Because of Women*. London: Heinemann, 1969.
Djoleto, Amu. *The Strange Man*. London: Heinemann, 1967.
————. *Money Galore*. London: Heinemann, 1975.
Duerden, Dennis, and Cosmo Pieterse, eds. *African Writers Talking*. New York: Africana Publishing Corp., 1972.
Easmon, R. Sarif. *The Burnt-Out Marriage*. London: Nelson, 1967.
Egblewogbe, E. Y. *Victims of Greed*. Tema: Ghana Publishing Corp., 1975.
Egbuna, Obi. *Daughters of the Sun and Other Stories*. London: Oxford University Press, 1970.
————. *Emperor of the Sea and Other Stories*. Glasgow: Fontana/Collins, 1974.
————. *Diary of a Homeless Prodigal*. Enugu, Nigeria: Fourth Dimension, 1978.
————. *The Minister's Daughter*. Glasgow: Fontana/Collins, 1975.
————. *The Rape of Lysistrata and Black Candle for Christmas*. Enugu, Nigeria: Fourth Dimension, 1980.
Ekwensi, Cyprian. *When Love Whispers*. Yaba, Nigeria: Chuks, 1947.
————. *People of the City*. London: Heinemann, 1954.
————. *Jagua Nana*. London: Hutchinson, 1961.
————. *Burning Grass*. London: Heinemann, 1962.
————. *Yaba Roundabout Murder*. Lagos: Tortoise Series, 1962.
————. *Divided We Stand*. Enugu, Nigeria: Fourth Dimension, 1980.
Emecheta, Buchi. *In the Ditch*. London: Barrie & Jenkins, 1972; Allison & Busby, 1979.
————. *Second Class Citizen*. London: Allison & Busby, 1974.
————. *The Bride Price*. London: Allison & Busby, 1976.
————. *The Slave Girl*. London: Allison & Busby, 1977.

————. *Titch the Cat*. London: Allison & Busby, 1978.

————. *The Moonlight Bride*. Oxford: Oxford University Press, 1980.

————. *Nowhere to Play*. London: Allison & Busby, 1980.

————. *Destination Biafra*. London: Allison & Busby, 1981.

————. *The Wrestling Match*. New York: George Braziller, 1981.

————. *Double Yoke*. New York: George Braziller, 1983.

Emenyonu, Ernest. "African Literature: What Does It Take to Be Its Critic?" *African Literature Today* 5 (1971): 1–11.

————. "Who Does Flora Nwapa Write For?" *African Literature Today* 7 (1975): 28–34.

Ephson, I. S. *Tragedy of False Friends*. Legon: University of Ghana Bookshop, 1979.

Equiano, Olaudah. *Equiano's Travels: His Autobiography*. Abridged ed. of *The Interesting Narrative of the Life of Olaudah Equisno or Gustavus Vassa the African* (1789). Edited by Paul Edward. London: Heinemann, 1966.

Eshun, J. O. *Adventures of the Kapapa*. Tema: Ghana Publishing Corp., 1976.

Fanoudh-Siefer, Leon. *Le mythe du nègre et de l'Afrique noire dans la littérature française de 1800 à 2e guerre mondiale*. Paris: C. Kliucksieck, 1968.

Finnegan, Ruth. *Oral Literature in Africa*. Oxford: Clarendon Press, 1970.

Flint, J. E. "Chartered Companies and the Scramble for Africa." In *Africa in the Nineteenth and Twentieth Centuries*, edited by Joseph C. Anene and Godfrey Brown, 110–32. Ibadan, Nigeria: Ibadan University Press, 1966; N.Y.: Humanities Press, 1966, 1972.

Forsyth, Frederick. *The Biafra Story*. Baltimore: Penguin Books, 1979.

Fraser, Robert. *The Novels of Ayi Kwei Armah: A Study in Polemical Fiction*. London: Heinemann, 1980.

Harris, Herman G. *Hausa Stories and Riddles and a Concise Hausa Dictionary*. Weston-Super-Mare, England: Mendip Press, 1908.

Horton, James Africanus. *West African Countries and Peoples*. Edinburgh: Edinburgh University Press, 1868.

Ijimere, Obotunde [Ulli Beier and Duro Ladipo]. *Woyengi*. In *The Imprisonment of Obatala and Other Plays*. London: Heinemann, 1966.

Ikiddeh, Ime. "The Character of Popular Fiction in Ghana." In *Perspectives on African Literature*, edited by Christopher Heywood, 106–16. New York: Africana, 1971.

Johnson, Samuel. *History of the Yorubas from the Earliest Times to the Beginning of the British Protectorate*. Lagos: CMS, 1921.

Killam, G. D. *Africa in English Fiction, 1874–1939*. Ibadan, Nigeria: Ibadan University Press, 1968.

————. "Cyprian Ekwensi." In *Introduction to Nigerian Literature*, edited by Bruce King, 77–96. Lagos: University of Lagos Press and Evans Brothers, 1971.

Koelle, S. W. *African Native Literature; or, Proverbs, Tales, Fables, and Historical Fragments in the Kanuri or Bornu Language*. London: Church Missionary House, 1854; Freeport, N.Y.: Books for Libraries Press, 1970.

Kwarteng, D. K. *My Sword Is My Life*. Tema: Ghana Publishing Corp., 1972.

Landeroin, M., and J. Tilho. *Grammaire et contes haoussas* [Hausa grammar and tales]. Paris: Imprimerie Nationale, 1909.

Laye, Camara. *L'enfant noir*. Paris: Plon, 1953. *The Dark Child*. New York: Farrar, Straus & Giroux, 1955.

Lindfors, Bernth. "Heroes and Hero-Worship in Nigerian Chapbooks," *Journal of Popular Culture* 1, no. 1 (1967): 1–22.

———. "Cyprian Ekwensi: An African Popular Novelist," *African Literature Today* 3 (1969): 2–14.

———. *Critical Perspectives on Amos Tutuola*. Washington, D.C.: Three Continents Press, 1978.

———. "Amos Tutuola's Search for a Publisher." In *Toward Defining the African Aesthetic*, edited by Lemuel A. Johnson et al., 95–104. Washington, D.C.: African Literature Association and Three Continents Press, 1982.

Lippert, J. "Haussa-Märchen" [Hausa tales]. *Mitteilungen des Seminars fur Orientalische Sprachen* 8, no. 3 (1905): 223–50.

Madiebo, Alexander. *The Nigerian Revolution and the Biafran War*. Enugu, Nigeria: Fourth Dimension, 1980.

Maxwell, Joseph Renner. *The Negro Question; or, Hints for the Physical Improvement of the Negro Race, with Special Reference to West Africa*. London: T. F. Unwin, 1892.

Merriman-Labor. *An Epitome of a Series of Lectures on The Negro Race*. Manchester, England: J. Heywood, 1900.

Modupeh, Prince. *I Was a Savage*. London: Museum Press, 1958. Reissued as *A Royal African*. New York: Praeger, 1969.

Ngaté, Jonathan. "And after the 'Bolekaja' Critics?" In *African Literature Studies: The Present State*, edited by Stephen H. Arnold. Washington, D.C.: Three Continents Press, 1985.

Ngũgĩ wa Thiong'o. *Petals of Blood*. London: Heinemann, 1977.

Nicol, Abioseh. *The Truly Married Woman and Other Stories*. London: Oxford University Press, 1965.

———. *Two African Tales*. London: Cambridge University Press, 1965.

Nkosi, Lewis. *Tasks and Masks: Themes and Styles of African Literature*. London: Longman, 1981.

Nwapa, Flora. *Efuru*. London: Heinemann, 1966.

———. *Idu*. London: Heinemann, 1969.

———. *This Is Lagos and Other Stories*. Enugu, Nigeria: Nwamife, 1971.

Nzekwu, Onuora. *Wand of Noble Wood*. London: Hutchinson, 1961.

———. *Blade among the Boys*. London: Hutchinson, 1962.

Obasanjo, Olusegun. *My Command*. Ibadan, Nigeria: Heinemann, 1980.

Obeng, R. E. *Eighteenpence*. Ilfracombe, England: Stockwell, 1943.

Obiechina, E. N. *An African Popular Literature: A Study of Onitsha Market Pamphlets*. Cambridge: Cambridge University Press, 1973.

Ofoli, Nii Yewoh. *The Messenger of Death*. Tema: Ghana Publishing Corp., 1979.

Ogali, Agu. *Coal City and The Juju Priest*. Enugu, Nigeria: Fourth Dimension, 1978.

Okara, Gabriel. *The Voice*. London: Andre Deutsch, 1964.

Okpi, Kalu. *The Smugglers*. London: Macmillan, 1978.

———. *On the Road*. London: Macmillan, 1980.

Oladitan, Olalere. "The Nigerian Crisis in the Nigerian Novel." In *New West African Literature*, edited by Kolawole Ogungbesan, 10–20. London: Heinemann, 1979.

Onyekwelu, Fidel. *The Sawabas: Black Africa's Mafia*. New York: Vantage Press, 1979.

Oppong-Affi, A. M., *The Prophet of Doom*. Tema: Ghana Publishing Corp., 1980.

Osofisan, Femi. *Kolera Kolej* [Cholera college]. Ibadan, Nigeria: New Horn Press, 1975.

———. "The Alternative Tradition: A Survey of Nigerian Literature in English since the Civil War." *Présence Africaine* 139, no. 3 (1986): 162–84.

Ouologuem, Yambo. *Le devoir de violence*. Paris: Editions du Seuil, 1968. *Bound to Violence*. Translated by Ralph Manheim. New York: Harcourt Brace Jovanovich, 1971.

Ovbiagele, Helen. *Evbu My Love*. London: Macmillan, 1983.

Owomoyela, Oyekan. *African Literatures: An Introduction*. Waltham, Mass.: Crossroads Press, 1979.

Palmer, Eustace. Review of *No Past, No Present, No Future*, by Yulisa Amadu Maddy. *African Literature Today* 7 (1975): 164–65.

———. "Cyprian Ekwensi." *The Growth of the African Novel*. London: Heinemann, 1979.

———. "The Feminine Point of View: Buchi Emecheta's *The Joys of Motherhood*." In *African Literatures Today, 13: Recent Trends in the Novel*. Edited by Eustace Palmer, 38–55. London: Heinemann, 1983.

Peters, Lenrie. *The Second Round*. London: Heinemann, 1965.

Prietze, R[udolf]. *Haussa Sprechwörter und Haussa Lieder*. Kirchhain: Buchdruckerei von M. Schmersow, 1904.

Robinson, Charles H. *Specimens of Hausa Literature*. Cambridge: Cambridge University Press, 1896.

Roger, J[ean]-F[rançois]. *Fables sénégalaises recueillies dans l'Ouolof* [Senegalese fables collected from the Wolof]. Paris: F. Didot, 1828.

Sampson, Magnus J. *Gold Coast Men of Affairs*. London: Dawsons, 1937.

Sarbah, John Mensah. *Fanti Customary Laws: A Brief Introduction to the Principles of the Native Laws and Customs of the Fanti and Akan Districts of the Gold Coast, with a Report of Some Cases Thereon Decided in the Law Courts*. London: W. Clowes and Sons, 1897; 2d ed., 1904.

Sartre, Jean-Paul. "Orphée noir" [Black Orpheus]. In *Anthologie de la nouvelle poésie nègre et malgache de langue française* [Anthology of the new Negro and Malagasy poetry in the French language], edited by Léopold Senghor. Paris: PUF, 1948.

Schlenker, C. F. *A Collection of Temne Traditions, Fables and Proverbs, with an English Translation; also, Some Specimens of the Author's Own Temne Compositions and Translation*. London: Church Missionary Society, 1861; Nendeln, Liechtenstein: Kraus Reprint, 1970.

Schön, James Frederick. *Magana Hausa: Native Literature; or, Proverbs, Tales, Fables and Historical Fragments in the Hausa Language; To Which Is Added a Translation in English*. London: Society for Promoting Christian Knowledge, 1885–86. Nendeln, Liechtenstein: Kraus Reprint, 1970.

Sembène, Ousmane. *O pays mon beau peuple!* [O my country, my good people!] Paris: Amiot-Dumont, 1957.

———. *Voltaiques* [*Tribal Scars and Other Stories*]. Paris: Présence Africaine, 1962.

Soyinka, Wole. *The Interpreters*. London: Deutsch, 1965.

———. *Kongi's Harvest*. Oxford: Oxford University Press, 1967.

———. *Madmen and Specialists*. London: Methuen, 1971.

———. *The Man Died*. London: Rex Collins, 1972.

———. *Death and the King's Horseman*. London: Methuen; New York: Norton, 1975.

———. *Ake: The Years of Childhood*. London: Rex Collins, 1981.

———. "The Critic and Society: Barthes, Leftocracy and Other Mythologies." In *Black Literature and Literary Theory*, edited by Henry L. Gates, 27–57. London: Methuen, 1984.

Spitzer, Leo. "The Sierra Leone Creoles, 1870–1900." In *Africa and the West*, edited by Philip D. Curtin, 99–138. Madison: University of Wisconsin Press, 1972.

Taiwo, Oladele. *Culture and the Nigerian Novel*. New York: St. Martin's Press, 1976.

Thomas, Dylan. "Blythe Spirits." *The Observer*, 6 July 1952, p. 7. Reprinted in Lindfors, Bernth, *Critical Perspectives on Amos Tutuola*, 7–8. Washington, D.C.: Three Continents Press, 1978.

Tutuola, Amos. *The Palm-Wine Drinkard and His Dead Palm-Wine Tapster in the Deads' Town*. New York: Grove Press, 1953.

———. *My Life in the Bush of Ghosts*. London: Faber, 1954.

———. *Ajaiyi and His Inherited Poverty*. London: Faber, 1967.

Ugonna, F. N. Nabuenyi. "Introduction." In J. E. Casely-Hayford, *Ethiopia Unbound*, viii–x. 2d ed. London: Cass, 1969.

Ulasi, Adaora. *Many Thing You No Understand*. London: Michael Joseph, 1970; Glasgow: Fontana/Collins, 1973.

———. *Many Thing Begin for Change*. London: Michael Joseph, 1971; Glasgow: Fontana/Collins, 1975.

———. *The Man from Sagamu*. Glasgow: Fontana/Collins, 1978.

———. *Who Is Jonah?* Ibadan, Nigeria: Onibonoje Press, 1978.

Zell, Hans, Carol Bundy, and Virginia Coulon, eds. *A New Reader's Guide to African Literature*. London: Heinemann, 1983.

2 English-Language Fiction from East Africa

ARLENE A. ELDER

Uncertain Beginnings

"Twenty years ago East Africa was considered a literary desert." This observation, with which Bernth Lindfors begins *Mazungumzo,* his 1976 collection of interviews with East African writers, publishers, and critics, reflects a generally held opinion, especially when literary production in that area of the continent is contrasted with the achievements of West Africa, where Amos Tutuola, Chinua Achebe, Wole Soyinka, and others were already established writers. The Ugandan writer Taban lo Liyong made this deficiency public in 1965 when he raised the controversial question that forms the title of his article "Can We Correct Literary Barrenness in East Africa?" in *East African Journal,* thereby sparking a vigorous debate in the pages of *Transition* (Knight 901). Most of Lindfors's questions to his interviewees, however, were intended to explain why, by the mid-1970s, East Africa had experienced such a growth of artistic vitality that numerous foreign and indigenous publishing houses were thriving there, and the Kenyan writer Ngũgĩ wa Thiong'o had achieved both a local and an international stature comparable to that of Achebe and Soyinka. More than a decade after *Mazungumzo,* one can identify three major influences that have led to this flowering of creativity and publishing and contributed to the shape it has taken. The major determinants of East African writing in English appear to be colonial and postcolonial education; the establishment of local and foreign publishing houses; and pre- and post-Independence politics in East Africa.

If "African literature is a child of education" (Bakari and Mazrui 868), its village forebearer, traditional orature, did not have as much influence on its English-language progeny as its alma maters, the university colleges established by the British. Because of the relative lateness of East African colonization, however, this educational phenomenon occurred in the region long after it had in other areas of the continent: "Though there was a British Resident in Zanzibar, it was not until the end of the nineteenth century that the British attempted to open up the bulk of East Africa, at a time when vast

49

portions of West Africa were already an integral part of the British or French empires" (Bakari and Mazrui 866).

The first graduates of the colonial mission schools were trained to be bureaucratic functionaries and therefore received a vocational rather than an academic education. The earliest East Africans with university degrees received them in America and Britain and produced autobiographical and anthropological works in English, as they were encouraged to do by their Western patrons. The first publication of this type is by the Ugandan Ham Mukasa, secretary to Sir Apolo Kagwa, the Ugandan official representative at the coronation of King Edward VII in 1902. *Uganda's Katikiro in England* concerns that visit to London. It first appeared in 1904 and was translated from Luganda by Taban lo Liyong in 1975 as *Sir Apolo Kagwa Discovers Britain* (Lindfors 49). Twenty years were to pass before the Gikuyu teacher Parmenas Githendu Mockerie, who studied at both the Fabian Summer School in Surrey and the Quaker Fircroft College for Working Men in Birmingham, England, followed Mukasa's literary lead (Mockerie, *An African Speaks* 19; see also Mockerie, "Story"). Mockerie's autobiographical *An African Speaks for His People* (1934), published by Leonard and Virginia Woolf, with a foreword by Sir Julian Huxley, foreshadows Jomo Kenyatta's *Facing Mount Kenya* (1938) in its revelation of Gikuyu society and commentary on the insensitivity of European rule. The next early work, *Story of an African Chief* (1935), republished in London the next year as *Africa Answers Back*, was written by Akiki K. Nyabongo (b. 1907), a prince from Uganda who attended Yale and Harvard and, as a Rhodes scholar at Oxford University, obtained his B.Litt. in 1939 and his Ph.D. in 1940. This autobiographical work, too, has a dual purpose. Nyabongo presents a detailed description of life among the Buganda aristocracy, while implicitly criticizing the highhanded cultural elitism of European missionaries and government functionaries.

Of course, the most politically significant figure of this early group is Jomo Kenyatta (1891–1979), the charismatic Gikuyu political prisoner during the Kenyan Emergency period of the 1950s and president of the nation from the Independence in 1963 until his death. However significant and controversial his later political success, his first prominence came in 1938 with the publication of his anthropological treatise on the Gikuyu, *Facing Mount Kenya*. Kenyatta had been hired part-time at University College, London, as an informant in Gikuyu phonetics and, about the same time, joined the classes taught at the London School of Economics by the functionalist anthropologist Bronisław Malinowski, who subsequently wrote the preface to Kenyatta's work.[1]

Like its predecessors, although considerably more systematic and complete, Kenyatta's study was intended to valorize African traditional life and challenge the racist and elitist assumptions of the Europeans. Tanganyika, too, produced early English works, but ones with completely different motives than those from Uganda and Kenya. Their author, Martin Kayamba (1891–1940), after a visit to Europe in 1931, eventually became the highest African civil servant in the territory, the chief clerk to the provincial commissioner in Tanga (Arnold 950). His two books, *An African in Europe* and *African Problems*, both published posthumously in London in 1948 by the United Society for Christian Literature and commonly considered to have been ghostwritten by whites, present an honorific and appreciative attitude toward British civilization and colonialism. Stephen Arnold notes: "Carefully guided, Kayamba saw through rose-coloured glasses a Britain populated by gods. . . . On returning home, the pious Martin, so inspired by his colonial saviours, changed his name to Kayambason in order to cloak his Bantu name in European garb. He has since become the target of many scornful jokes and is a common symbol in Tanzanian literary culture" (950).

The Influence of Makerere University

It was not until the 1960s that East Africa began to develop literature in English that was imaginative rather than solely historical, anthropological, or political. The single most significant educational force behind this development was Uganda's Makerere University College in Kampala, which had been established in 1939 to provide higher education for all of British East Africa: Uganda, Kenya, Tanganyika, and Zanzibar.[2]

Makerere University attracted an interterritorial group of students— Ngũgĩ wa Thiong'o from Kenya, for example, and Ugandan Asians like Peter Nazareth, as well as Europeans—and after its affiliation with the University of London in 1953, it drew its staff from universities in Europe and America. The "destiny of Makerere as the most significant educational institution in East Africa became closely tied to the destiny of creative writing in this part of the continent" (Bakari and Mazrui 868).

Despite the important role the institution eventually was to play in the promotion of creative literature, its colonial bias, that is, its Great Tradition of canonized British texts, and its rigid insistence upon "correct" British usage, actually mitigated against the early development of an authentic East African voice in English: "It is precisely because of this almost sanctified approach to English that East Africa failed to produce its own Tutuola. The limited usage of the other registers of English led to absurd inflexibility in the creation of near-life characters and even the semi-educated protagonists in Ngũgĩ's novels speak formal, grammatical English. Makerere writers were not favoured with West Africa's luck in having an English based creole and pidgin on whose resources they could draw" (Bakari and Mazrui 874).

Nevertheless, as one of the university's most influential British lecturers, David Cook, is reported to have observed, many of the students in the English Department were there reading English literature with an eye to writing themselves; "language was a tool, not an end in itself" (Bakari and

Mazrui 875). Of those students Mohamed Bakari and Ali Mazrui write: "It was the generation of the fifties in the twentieth century which was to lead the way towards establishing a legacy of literature in the English language, and Makerere College in Uganda was to become the most eminent centre of literary activity. . . . It was there that the first examples of literature in English drawing on the East African experience were created" (868).

Besides the rigorous English-language training and the heady association with members of various African communities and other national and racial groups that the Makerere experience provided, it also offered, through its student journal, *Penpoint* (1958), the opportunity for budding writers to see their works in print. As Bakari and Mazrui point out, the main difference between this journal and its counterparts as West African universities was its multiracial character (875). David Cook's ground-breaking anthology of East African poetry, *Origin East Africa* (1965), is heavily dependent on *Penpoint* for its selections. Student journals were also launched at the universities founded in 1961: from the former College at Dar es Salaam, Tanganyika, came *Darlight* (1966), superseded by *Umma* (1970), and from Nairobi, Kenya, came *Nexus* (1967) and, later, *Busara* (1968). Indeed, as the intellectual and creative center of East Africa shifted in the 1960s from Kampala to Nairobi, it was *Busara* that became the most influential of the student publications. *Penpoint* was superseded in 1971 by *Dhana*, which reflected Makerere's much more Ugandan student population by that date (Heron 923). All of these student journals were extremely important in encouraging and offering outlets for many of the writers later to shape the East African literary scene; Peter Nazareth, Ngũgĩ, and Barnabas Katigula are just a few examples.

Of great significance as well, and reflective of the intellectual activity at the universities, were the two conferences on African literature that serve to frame the decade of the 1960s, the African Writers Conference held in Kampala in 1962 and the East African Writers Conference in Nairobi in 1971. Speaking of the first meeting, Bakari and Mazrui conclude: "This gathering was probably the most important single event that acted as a catalyst for emergent East African authors. . . . The Conference can truly be said to have opened to East Africa new horizons of literary activity and 1962 became the turning point in serious literature in English" (876, 877). Writers, critics, and publishers from throughout English-speaking Africa, the Caribbean, and the United States attended, and the quantity and quality of their publications, contrasted with the dearth of works from East Africa, led to a profound sense of inadequacy and resolve on the part of the young writers at Makerere. Grace Ogot of Kenya remembers the occasion as "a time of heart searching and self-examination." She recalls a "feeling of literary barrenness in East Africa arising from the helplessness of East African writers at this conference. . . . Through sheer embarrassment Ngugi and I took the challenge without any delay. And so did other East African writers who attended the conference" (Lindfors 124). Ngũgĩ praised the meeting in the Nairobi *Sunday Nation* of 1 July 1962 (Bakari and Mazrui 876) and later wrote in *Transition:* "What may be born here and grow as a result is yet too early to predict. I have no doubt that writers from East Africa will rise. The few that I met at Kampala were very enthusiastic and eager to push ahead" (Knight 887).

Push ahead they did, and by 1971 the conference in Nairobi could be focused on East African writing, particularly on its future direction, "the existence or establishment of a distinct East African voice, the nature of the writer's audience and the choice of language" (Knight 902). Two collections of theory and criticism resulted: *Black Aesthetics* (1971), edited by Pio Zirimu and Andrew Gurr, and *Writers in East Africa* (1974), edited by Andrew Gurr and Angus Calder.

Literary Nationalism in the Academy

The difference in tone of the 1962 and 1971 meetings signals a significant movement from the young Makerereans' painful sense of silence to their conscious shaping of their African voices, from their acute awareness of a missing literary identity to their conscious definition of themselves as East African writers. In a historical sense, too, the change in the locales of those two important conferences, from Kampala to Nairobi, represents the shift by the beginning of the 1970s of intellectual and artistic influence from politically chaotic Uganda to Kenya.

Additional evidence of the growing anticolonial self-confidence of this group of writers and critics and its inevitable influence on those following them through the university system is the event that Tanzanian critic Grant Kamenju rightly terms "the 'revolution' that took place during our Annual Interdepartmental Subject Conference in Nairobi in 1969 when, at the initiative of the African members of staff from the three sister Departments of Makerere, Nairobi and Dar es Salaam, it was decided to abolish the three *English* Departments and to set up instead Departments of *Literature*" (Lindfors 38). In "On the Abolition of the English Department," the appendix to his earliest collection of essays, *Homecoming* (1972), Ngũgĩ, one of the architects of this change, comments on the catalyst for it, the proposal presented by his Department to the Arts Faculty Board at the University of Nairobi in September 1968, which raised the "main question: If there is need for a 'study of the historic continuity of a single culture,' why can't this be African? Why can't African literature be at the centre so that we can view other cultures in relationship to it?" (146). The "revolution" led to the end of "the reign of Shakespeare" (Arnold 953) in East African universities, especially at Nairobi, where Ngũgĩ, lo Liyong, and the Ugandan poet Okot p'Bitek were lecturers. Acutely aware of the shaping influence of formal education on young minds, Ngũgĩ also called for a conference of secondary school teachers of literature in Kenya in September 1974 to overhaul their syllabi along the lines of that at the university. In addition to these institutional changes, according to the Kenyan critic Chris Wanjala, the very presence of Ngũgĩ, lo Liyong, and p'Bitek in Nairobi's newly restructured Literature Department "indirectly boosted creativity not only at the campus but in the whole country" (98).

Ngũgĩ's concern with formal education's role in culture formation was well placed, for primary and secondary schools mushroomed in East Africa after colonialism, with obvious and direct consequences for both the writers and those they wished to reach. As p'Bitek observed in 1976, "Written literature depends on a reading audience and that can only be produced in schools. . . . People will begin to express themselves in English through such forms as the novel, the stage play, the poem when there are enough people to read what they write. The place has to ripen educationally first" (Lindfors 139).

Publishing Opportunities

The increase in the literate population after Independence in the three countries led directly to the growth of East African publishing, which meant, of course, that more writers found their way into print than ever before.

Much of the output of the publishers went directly into the classrooms. John Nottingham, formerly with the East African Literature Bureau and later the founder of Transafrica, asserts, "The school market has been the reason why we have had any publishing houses at all, whether they were indigenous firms or branches of British companies. The only exception is the East African Literature Bureau, which has a vast Government subsidy" (Lindfors 115). Nottingham attests to the stimulating effect of the competition among these firms to supply materials for the needs of primary and secondary schools, especially, at first, collections of folktales: "Sometimes it was just a matter of trying to publish the first collection from a particular area or a particular tribe. One was trying to get the first book of folktales from Kisii, from Taita or from Turkana" (Lindfors 116).

The East African Literature Bureau had been founded by the British shortly after World War II to stimulate writing in African languages; its Nairobi and Kampala branches began publishing imaginative work in English in 1970 under their "Student Book-Writing Scheme." This company was dissolved in the late 1970s and replaced by the Kenya Literature Bureau (Knight 888). Another local firm, the East African Publishing House (1965), existed side by side with branches of foreign publishers such as Longman, Heinemann, Macmillan Books for Africa, Oxford University Press, and Cambridge University Press. The influence of the decisions of these firms regarding the needs and desires of their target markets, and of their editorial philosophies in general in stimulating or stifling creative writing in East Africa, can hardly be exaggerated.

As Grace Ogot notes, before Independence there was not such a wealth of publishing outlets; moreover, it was difficult to get manuscripts accepted abroad (Lindfors 124). The popular Kenyan writer David Maillu, for a while a successful publisher himself, attributes that difficulty to a colonial attitude on the part of foreign publishers:

> At that time it was assumed that only English people wrote. The African was hardly given any chance. Those who wanted to be published had to be published outside East Africa in a place like London, and English people had their own way of assessing African writers. I mean, you couldn't publish anything because they thought it was not right for Africans to publish anything. To be published by them, you had to write in a certain way, in a certain style, and depict the African in the image that they liked. And this, of course, discouraged many people from writing. . . . When I sent my manuscripts to England, they were always returned by British publishers who did not want to publish them. (Lindfors 64, 65)

Reflecting a basically anthropological desire to record traditional orature and customs, "literature which could later on be kept in libraries for future research" (Lindfors 125), the East African Literature Bureau was prepared to publish both original work and collections of traditional poetry, tales, and so forth, in both English and the indigenous tongues, but nothing of an imaginative nature in English. The bureau also demonstrated a fairly rigid notion of appropriate subject matter and treatment. Grace Ogot reports that she took

> some of my short stories to the Manager, including the one which was later published in *Black Orpheus*. They really couldn't understand how a Christian woman could write such stories involved with sacrifices, traditional medicines and all, instead of writing about Salvation and Christianity. Thus, quite a few potential writers received no encouragement from colonial publishers who were perhaps afraid of turning out radical writers critical of the colonial regime. . . .
>
> Many people writing today simply did not have an outlet for creative writing. If you wrote a story, you kept it to yourself. I think that the lack of publishers with a correct approach to African literature was a major setback for East African writers. (Lindfors 124)

With Independence in the early 1960s, however, when local people took over the East African Literature Bureau, this colonially inspired, conservative attitude lost force. One indication of the publishers' vigorous new efforts to encourage local imaginative writing was the inauguration of literary contests, such as the "School-Book Writing Scheme," sponsored by various firms, and for which Ngũgĩ wrote *The River Between* (1964) (Lindfors 76). In the 1970s the publishers contributed to the Jomo Kenyatta Prize, which Taban lo Liyong credits with inspiring not only activity among the writers but also a competitive impulse among the publishers themselves: "Soon all of them were trying very, very hard to produce books which could be entered for that competition" (Lindfors 53). A somewhat different viewpoint is expressed by the Kenyan Meja Mwangi, himself the winner of the 1973 Kenyatta Prize for *Kill Me Quick*. Mwangi agrees that the competitions and prize have had some effect but, owing to their scarcity, doubts that people are often motivated to write for such awards. He goes further: "If writing paid, I think we would have a lot more and better writers in East Africa. We have a lot of talented young people at the university, some of whom, I know, would like to do more writing, but they can't because they have to work for a living. So literary development here tends to progress slowly" (Lindfors 77). In the same interview he notes that both the growth of literacy in the region and the "shock of recognition" within the literate public that African writers are worth reading has had a tremendous effect on the publishing houses, thereby encouraging creative production.

Journals

To appeal to this new market, a number of journals providing additional outlets and a regular opportunity for writers to reach the public have been launched by the publishing houses themselves. Before Independence, according to Grace Ogot, aside from the college journals, there were only a few church- and foreign-owned magazines, "but these did not really encourage local participation in their columns" (Lindfors 124). The notable exception to this dearth of journals was *Transition*, founded in 1960 by the Ugandan Asian Rajat Neogy and edited in Kampala until 1969. As suggested earlier, some of the most significant and heated debates about African culture were expressed in its pages, and most of the well-known figures of contemporary East African writing appeared there on occasion. By 1971 *Transition* had moved to Accra, Ghana, but other East African publications had been launched. In 1967 Oxford University Press introduced *Zuka*, "a journal of East African creative writing"; *Ghala*, a regularly published literary issue of the *East African Journal*, was begun the next year by the East African Publishing House (Knight 888). The popular magazines *Drum* and *Viva*, along with the ever-popular humor magazine *Joe*, further extended outlets for writers. As Grace Ogot remarks, the presence of such magazines "is very encouraging for younger writers as well as older writers who are engaged in poetry and short story writing, and don't often have enough collected for a book" (Lindfors 128).

Popular Literature

Increasing literacy in East Africa, obviously a boon to publishers, led in the early 1970s to the immense commercial success of a controversial new popular literature focusing on love stories and urban problems such as unemployment, prostitution, and corruption among politicians and businessmen.

Charles Mangua's crime thriller *Son of Woman* (1971), winner of the literary prize offered by the East African Publishing House, is generally credited with initiating the trend. His subsequent *A Tail in the Mouth* (1972), actually written first, with its emphasis on a genial urban antihero, a former home guard turned Freedom Fighter, assured his prominence (Lindfors 117).

The greatest forces shaping popular literature were the reading tastes and urban experiences of eighteen- to thirty-year-old high school graduates, or "school leavers." According to the editor of *The Weekly Review*, Hilary Ng'weno, whose own crime thriller *The Men from Pretoria* (1976) is a skillful narrative dramatizing undercover links between Kenya and South Africa, the "older generation, including university graduates . . . don't read much. They spend most of their time either making money or drinking" (Lindfors 105). *The Men from Pretoria* began as a screenplay, but was rewritten when Ng'weno could not secure the funds for its filming. As a book, it was intended for an audience similar to that which frequented the popular imported films, what Ng'weno describes as "the average young person who has left school and is seeking two or three hours of light entertainment without having to worry too much about the deeper processes of thought. I believe this is the major reading public in East Africa today" (Lindfors 103, 104).

As his comment suggests, the content and style of the imported films of the 1950s and 1960s cannot be discounted as another important factor shaping the taste of potential readers and, therefore, the selections of publishers. Ng'weno observes, "to a certain extent, this explains the popularity of the so-called popular literature that deals with crime, sex and violence" (Lindfors 104). He notes especially the popularity of American films featuring Black actors triumphing over predictable racist antagonists; films shot in recognizable locales, such as *Shaft in Africa* and *The Wilby Conspiracy*, "most of it . . . shot in Kenya, [so] people could recognize their own friends on the screen"; and kung fu films, providing an exciting, escapist experience (Lindfors 104). In a curious instance of a reversal of the usual literary influence, Meja Mwangi's novel about poaching in contemporary Kenya, *The Bushtrackers*, published as a Drumbeat book by Longman in 1979, is based on a screenplay and bears a dedication "to the four men who died in a tragic aircrash during the shooting of the film which inspired this novel."

Despite the aforementioned Africanization of the primary and secondary school syllabi, the general reader had, during and after colonialism, been heavily exposed to British and American popular literature by authors like Agatha Christie and James Hadley Chase and dashing, amoral heroes like James Bond. Reading material was valued by young readers, as Mwangi comments, mainly as entertainment: "Most of them are more likely to pick up a book by Maillu than one by Ngũgĩ" (Lindfors 78). Lo Liyong agrees, "in Nairobi almost everybody reads crime stories. . . . They don't read the classics, just the popular writing" (Lindfors 56).

"Escapist" would be the kindest of the judgments offered about East

African popular writing by some of its critics. Mwangi, for instance, himself a prolific and popular author of books set both in post-Independence Kenya (*Kill Me Quick* [1973], *Going down River Road* [1976], *The Cockroach Dance* [1979], *The Bushtrackers*) and in the pre-Independence Emergency period (*Carcase for Hounds* [1974], *Taste of Death* [1975]), complains about the effect of what he considers the popular books' overly dramatic, sensational quality: "They become completely distorted. Young people reading them may get the wrong impression of life in the city" (Lindfors 79). According to Ng'weno, this "misconception of life in the city" is precisely the germ that creates the worst of the genre, for he feels the writers themselves are uncomfortable with their urban experience and latch onto the most superficial aspects of it to criticize and exploit: "you are dealing with the first generation of writers, most of them born and brought up in rural areas, who came to the city for the first time when they were admitted to the university. They feel very, very uneasy with the urban situation because they don't understand it at all" (Lindfors 100). Okot p'Bitek sees the trend toward popular writing as both "healthy and unhealthy" (Lindfors 144), regretting most what strikes him as its "light-hearted" nature that precludes any serious discussion of social ills. Mwangi agrees: "Some of these popular works have no message at all. They are simply words, words, words" (Lindfors 79). Chris Wanjala's dismay extends beyond the books to questions about the public they serve: "A society which cherishes the sick fantasies of the American thriller and the sex wasteland of Charles Mangua is decidedly sick" (48).

Whatever their judgment of his art, David Maillu, whose name became synonymous with East African popular writing, is mentioned by every commentator on it. Maillu describes himself as both a serious researcher and a moralist committed to positive social change. He studied for four or five years, he says, the psychology of the general East African reader and of the storyteller "to find out what they liked talking about and hearing" (Lindfors 65). Armed with this information, he founded Comb Books, many of whose volumes are sized small enough to carry around comfortably in a coat or skirt pocket. Comb published Maillu's own works as well as those of others. He considers himself a Christian writer dealing realistically with common experiences and vividly demonstrating the sad consequences of corruption: "I write about what's happening—about corruption, sex or anything. It has not been my interest to dwell on the beautiful or to set my stories in the nicer parts of town. . . . I rather like to believe I am an educator as well as an entertainer and that my books have a moral purpose. Perhaps this is why so many people read them" (Lindfors 68, 69). Indeed, the results of a questionnaire published with the first volume of his three-volume poem *The kommon man* (1975–76) declared Maillu the most popular writer in East and Central Africa (Lindfors 69).

An objective look at many of his fictional works reveals an ambivalence in them reflective of Maillu's yoking together his moralistic intent with his interest in sensational style and subject matter. *No!* (1976), a tale of the downfall and suicide of a corrupt civil servant, rather incoherently alternates between graphic scenes of sex and violence and interludes indicating Washington Ndava's growing awareness of his wasted life, a character development unconvincingly intended to demonstrate that suffering can bring new depths of feeling and understanding. Moreover, Ndava's injuries are so numerous and extreme that they become unintentionally comic, as is the end of the novel, where his chauffeur is feeling up Washington's widow on their way to his funeral. It is difficult to reconcile Maillu's believable statement of his moralistic intentions with the actual horrifying and titillating effect of his works. In contrast to Wanjala's contention that it is Maillu's didacticism that "undermines his artistic means" (Lindfors 152), perhaps a more valid criticism might be that his books do not hold together for the literary critic, as either popular entertainment or cautionary tales, precisely because Maillu lacks the skill to bring together seamlessly two such divergent impulses. It is true, however, that his brief epistolary novels *Dear daughter* (1976) and *Dear Monika* (1976) and a collection of rural tales, *Kisalu and His Fruit Garden* (1972), are more unified. *Dear Monika*, as a matter of fact, is quite effective, almost a primer for replying to abusive husbands.

The body of writing that immediately comes to mind as a sister of writing such as Maillu's or Mangua's is the well-known Onitsha Market literature from Nigeria. The critic Henry Chakava, director of Heinemann East Africa, however, points to a significant difference between the two: "Most of the people who write these novels here have had some education and adopt a more enlightened and sophisticated approach than do the Onitsha writers, who produced some fiction of extremely low quality. As a consequence, East African popular literature may have a much wider audience, too" (Lindfors 11).

A similar realization of the potential popularity of this kind of work occurred to others, and most of the publishers in East Africa initiated subject series geared to what they foresaw as a growing and lucrative market. Oxford University Press began its New Fiction from Africa series in 1972 with *Murder in Majengo* by Marjorie Oludhe Macgoye, a British writer married to a Luo doctor and living in Nairobi. In 1973, the year when Maillu created Comb, Foundation Books started its African Leisure Library with a collection of articles entitled *Bless the Wicked* by the editor of *Drum* magazine, P. G. Malimoto. Transafrica launched its Afroromance series with *Love and Learn* (1974) by "Mary Kise" (Knight 911). John Nottingham later revealed that, despite the different authors listed on the Afroromance publications, all of them actually were produced by a single male writer, "a talented Ugandan[,] and then marketed under various pseudonyms" (Lindfors 120). Nottingham obviously veered from this practice at least once, for he also issued the well-known writer Grace Ogot's collection of short stories *The Other Woman* (1976) as part of this group. As the first title of a different series, New

Writing, Transafrica published *The Day the Music Died and Other Stories* (1978) by Ciugu Mwagiru (Lindfors 116). East African Publishing House brought out J. C. Onyango-Abuje's eerie *Fire and Vengeance* in 1975 as a Heartbeat Book, the same year that Heinemann launched its Spear series with four titles. They produced a further four in 1976, one of which was Mwangi Gicheru's topical *The Ivory Merchant*. Its Longman Crime Series published Ng'weno's *The Men from Pretoria* the same year.

Retrenchment

The boom, however, did not last. All the publishers in the late 1970s cut back their lists or completely collapsed. Reasons for the decline include the comparatively high cost of books for a populace striving to pay for physical necessities; the lack of a book-buying habit in East Africa, as noted by Nottingham (Lindfors 122); and the colonially inspired prejudices of a reading public that still held African writers in less esteem than foreign ones. Moreover, Tanzania's banning of some of the most popular of these writers eliminated one-third of the region to which they could naturally expect to appeal for local support.

Slick urban fiction, it turns out, developed in both Kenya and Uganda in the early 1970s; if anything, Uganda's contribution, according to the critic George Heron, reflected "an even greater interest in sexual themes than its Kenyan counterpart" (924). English-language readers in Tanzania preferred British and American writers such as Ian Fleming and Harold Robbins to the home-grown variety (Bakari and Mazrui 959), although the misleadingly titled *Veneer of Love* (1975) by Osija Mwambungu was a commercial success. In a very real sense, popular literature in Tanzania is exclusively in Swahili, since, because of government philosophy and directives, that language has become almost universal. As Grant Kamenju observes, fewer people in Kenya read the English-language authors than those in Tanzania reading the works produced in Swahili (Lindfors 42–43).

Because of Tanzania's developing sense of its socialist identity and desire, therefore, to purge itself of all Western cultural influences judged detrimental to its progress, popular fiction of the Maillu and Mangua type was banned by President Julius Nyerere's government. It was not only their explicit sexuality, then, that led to their disfavor; they were also judged counterprogressive. Chris Wanjala explains, "Tanzania has put its emphasis on rural development. Urbanization has been played down because they want to try to enhance rural culture. Novels that deal with the urban situation adulterate that emphasis" (Lindfors 159).

As one might expect, David Maillu received the full blast of official Tanzanian disapproval. Comb Books as a group were not banned, but all advertised as written by Maillu definitely were. The writer's response seems remarkably philosophical:

Each country has its ideology, and maybe my books are not compatible with Tanzania's ideology. . . . In the long run, I am sure the books go back and are read there, but I have nothing against Tanzania simply because a few individuals there, thinking on behalf of other people, regard these books as bad. I am not in a position to know whether my books are bad or not, but I would assume that if they were bad, they would have made me bad. (Lindfors 67, 68)

Kamenju admits that despite the book banning, foreign movies continue to contribute to the kind of cultural imperialism that the government, especially since the Arusha Declaration of 1967, with its emphasis on self-reliance, is trying to eliminate (Lindfors 44).

Tanzania and Swahili

In addition to discouraging certain kinds of literature, the Tanzanian government, through its emphasis on Swahili as the official language of the country, and because of its austerity programs and shortages, has greatly limited the amount of English-language writing produced by its citizens. Because of the multiplicity of ethnic groups within its borders (including Zanzibar, since 1964), the Independence government found itself faced with over 120 oral and literate traditions and decided in 1966 on one language, Swahili, in an attempt to unify communication within the country and promote nationalism (Arnold 946). Vigorous efforts were made in both the private and public sectors to guarantee the success of the linguistic experiment; therefore, at the very time when English-language writing was emerging in Uganda and Kenya, it was receiving much less encouragement in Tanzania.[3]

The first Tanzanian novel in English, Peter Palangyo's introspective study of personal and social conflict *Dying in the Sun*, did not appear until 1968. In contrast, the first Swahili novel, an apologia for British rather than German rule, *Uhuru wa Watumwa*, by James Juma Mbotela, had been published in 1934. Mbotela's choice of language reflects the established tradition of literature in non-European languages on which modern Tanzanian policy could build.

Nevertheless, a number of Tanzanian novels in English appeared in the 1970s. Following *Dying in the Sun* came Gabriel Ruhumbika's *Village in Uhuru* (1969) and, in 1974, Barnabas Katigula's *Groping in the Dark*, published in Kenya and notable for its progressive view of women. Ismael R. Mbise's *Blood on Our Land*, also published in 1974, is set among the Meru of Tanganyika during the onslaught of colonialism and contains an introduction by the author raising important issues of genre and style. The last English novel to have been printed in Tanzania was *The Wicked Walk* (1977) by W. E. Mkufya, which, with its focus on urban life, prostitution, incest, and the loss of innocence, could be classified with the disparaged popular literature of Tanzania's neighbors.[4]

According to Steven Arnold, most examples of Tanzanian short fiction in English have been written as school texts to teach grammar, syntax, and morality; "another type, which became nearly extinct in the seventies, was the pulp pamphlet story for youths," for example, F. Kawegere's *Inspector Rajabu Investigates, and Other Stories* (1968) and Akberali Manji's *The Valley of the Dead and Other Stories* (1972) (954). Additionally, one must note the short stories by numerous authors published in *Darlight* and *Umma,* including those by Martha V. Mlangala, who, under her married name, Martha Mvungi, subsequently produced a collection in English of Hehe and Bena folktales, *Three Solid Stones* (1975), and a Swahili novel, *Hana Hatia.* Her progress is typical, says Arnold, for "only expatriate writers (e.g. Asare, Pierce) have ever written more than one novel in English. Almost without exception those who have proven themselves in English . . . later switched to Swahili" (959).

While this linguistic movement might have occurred naturally, given the Swahili cultural tradition of Tanzania, its pace was accelerated by the government's nationalizing the major means of production in the country in 1966, thus cutting off the advertising base of many of the journals that published English material. Moreover, when a severe paper shortage occurred from 1971 to 1974, priority for scarce supplies was given to government documents, school texts, and literature in Swahili: "By 1975 it had become much easier to get published in Swahili than in English and few writers will probably ever turn back. English has lost its prestige" (Arnold 959).

An issue related to that of language choice is one debated hotly in most of the recently independent African countries, namely, the relationship of the artist to his or her society. Grant Kamenju explains that the Tanzanians are aiming toward a less elitist role for the artist than that influenced by colonial attitudes and a return to a more traditional conception of the origin and purpose of art: "We want literature that is worthwhile, that is really grounded in the society itself. This is the direction in which we would like to see it develop, and this is where we hope to play our part, assisting in the establishment of a grass-roots literary tradition. Such a tradition will have to emerge in a language of the people, an African language, and in Tanzania this language is Kiswahili" (Lindfors 44). Taban lo Liyong complains, however, that the writing that aims toward this nationalistic goal is uncritical and simplistically celebratory of Ujumaa, African socialism. In contrast, he judges the writing from his own country as "arriving at the moment of self-criticism and search," an important point in history he attributes to the scourge of Idi Amin, who taught Ugandan writers that they, at least, "can no longer sing songs in praise of Africans because they know that devils come in various colors, guises, religions, standards of education, and so on. . . . So we have been liberated from an uncritical love of Africa and of Africans. I think that is beginning to come out" (Lindfors 59–60).

Hard Times in Uganda

Certainly, if the Tanzanian writers' experience the pressure of political philosophy on artistic choices, the Ugandan situation demonstrates the consequences of political chaos and oppression on the very survival of artists. The upheaval in Uganda could not have been predicted with any certainty, since Makerere University, as already mentioned, served as such a center of academic stability during the colonial period, and, as George Heron notes, the Ganda heartland kept its traditional political system largely intact (923). In other peripheral geographic areas, however, customary authority was weakened during the nineteenth century by large-scale slave raiding, cattle thieving, and ivory trading. Consequently, after Independence, both the incoming *kabaka* of Buganda and Milton Obote, prime minister of Uganda, inherited a fragmented country, ripe for political conflict. Obote's arrest of the *kabaka* in 1964 and the subsequent 1971 coup by Idi Amin attests to that instability. The coup was bloodless, but it soon spawned arrests and massacres of Amin's opponents both military and civilian. The ensuing flight of many educators from the country severely gutted the educational system.

One of the first casualties of Obote's regime was *Transition*. Its editorial staff was decimated by detentions and the threat of long prison terms for sedition; its outspoken editor, Rajat Neogy, was stripped of his Ugandan citizenship and forced to emigrate (Benson 210). Among the writers who fled to neighboring Kenya was the celebrated poet Okot p'Bitek. Okot, already the author of *Lak Tar* (1953), a novel in his native Acholi, had been working in Gulu, in northern Uganda, but in 1966, when his influential poem *Song of Lawino* was published, he had moved to Kampala to direct the Ugandan Cultural Centre. By the end of 1967, however, he was dismissed and went into exile in Kenya, taking up a position at what was then still the English Department at the University of Nairobi. Another exile was Peter Nazareth, for a while a civil servant in the Ministry of Finance, whose political novel *In a Brown Mantle* (1972) provides insight into Ugandan life under Obote, particularly the peripheral position of the Asians shortly before Amin was to exile them. Also to leave was the Lango writer Okello Oculi, author of the long narrative poem *Orphan* (1968), which he describes as a "village opera," and the novel *Prostitute* (1968), frequently classified as popular literature. Henry Kimbugwe, a Ganda writer who goes under the pseudonym of Eneriko Seruma, author of *The Experience* (1970) and a collection of tales, *The Heart Seller* (1971), joined the East African Publishing House in Nairobi. His work reflects the racial and class interests of many African writers of the time. *The Experience* was one "of the first East African novels to use rapid and violent action and a variety of sexual experiences to comment on racial relationships" (Heron 939); the title story of *The Heart Seller* ironically depicts what the recently discovered technique of heart transplants might mean economically to an impoverished African. The controversial Taban lo

Liyong joined Okot p'Bitek at the University of Nairobi. In contrast to the Tanzanian writers in particular, lo Liyong, who was trained in America, demonstrates idiosyncratic and Western attitudes toward art and the autonomy of the artist. His two collections of short stories, *Fixions* (1969) and *The Uniformed Man* (1971), testify to his desire for formal experimentation rather than political or moral didacticism, although some of the stories, "Fixions," for example, ironically treat political topics. A writer who also eventually migrated to Kenya is Barbara Kimenye, who worked in the *kabaka*'s government and produced two genially humorous, but not idealizing, collections of stories about village life, *Kalasanda* (1965) and *Kalasanda Revisited* (1966). These two works, notably, are the "first pieces of [native] Ugandan creative writing to reach book form" (Heron 924). That they and almost all the works written subsequently in the country were published in Kenya attests to the unstable climate in Uganda, which fostered neither money-making publishing ventures nor artistic creativity.

Yet, as Heron points out, "It is conspicuous that Ugandan writers in exile failed, or more probably, refrained, to comment through art on their country's tragedy, which the eviction of Amin Dada did little to alleviate" (947). Moreover, lo Liyong notes that in contrast to the Tanzanians, the Ugandan writers have maintained individual voices and outlooks, rather than a "corporate view" (Lindfors 59). Unlike Ngũgĩ, lo Liyong judges the political influence of the writer to be severely limited and, shortly before Tanzania moved troops into Uganda in the late 1970s to oust Amin, asked, "If even the commanders in the army can't overthrow him, what can you do with a pen?" (Lindfors 61).

One writer who knew precisely what to do with a pen, that is, to poke outrageous fun at the violent leader in the form of the traditional cautionary animal tale, was the author of *Field Marshall Abdulla Salim Fisi; or, How the Hyena Got His!* Writing under the pen name Alumidi Osinya, this author published his extremely funny and effective satire through Joe Publications, an imprint of Transafrica Press, in Nairobi in 1976. The book is a roman à clef, presenting in transparent animal guise many of the major actors on the political stage during the Amin (Fisi) regime. Another author employing a subtle traditional form to make political observations is John Nagenda, whose magical, allegorical *The Seasons of Thomas Tebo* was published in 1986, the year Nagenda returned to Uganda after the overthrow of Amin by the National Resistance Army. A much more straightforward account is *Return to the Shadows* (1969), the account of a post-Independence African country in the throes of a coup, by the Ugandan Robert Serumaga.

Kenya and the Durable Emergency

While the succeeding political upheavals in Uganda served to fragment the society and effectively silence its artists within the country, a comparable pre-Independence situation within Kenya, the British oppression leading to the formation of the Land and Freedom Fighters (designated Mau Mau by the colonialists) and the subsequent Emergency, not only unified many of the African citizens against the British but also provided a compelling subject for a considerable body of literature. The first response to the rebellion of the 1950s and its aftermath came in the form of autobiographical works "which were halfway between the earlier didactic and polemical writings" of aspiring Gikuyu political spokesmen "and genuine fictional narrative" (Bakari and Mazrui 871). These writings include the Gikuyu writer M. P. Joshua Mwangi Kariuki's post-Independence memoir *Mau Mau Detainee* (1963), which provides valuable information about conditions in the various concentration camps established to contain the guerrilla fighters and their sympathizers; *Freedom and After* (1963) by the popular Luo politician Tom Mboya; the more anthropological and personal *A Child of Two Worlds* (1964) by another Gikuyu writer, Mugo Gatheru; and D. Barnett and K. Njamais's *Mau Mau from Within* (1966), which describes the Land and Freedom army as a mass underground movement. That the Emergency period was not the only phase of Kenya's modern history when sudden violence was the order of the day is substantiated by the fate of both Mboya and Kariuki, victims of assassination, Mboya in 1969, Kariuki in 1975.[5]

Fiction writers, too, many of whom were children or adolescents during the Emergency, have been drawn irresistibly to the 1950s period in Kenyan history. Ngũgĩ's novels *Weep Not, Child* and *A Grain of Wheat* (1967) and the stories collected in the section "Fighters and Martyrs" in *Secret Lives* (1975) show the result of the struggle upon ordinary Gikuyu villagers. *A Grain of Wheat*, his most complex interpretation of that extremely difficult period, places moving yet ironic emphasis on betrayal, the need for confession, and psychological as well as physical suffering. Later, in 1976, Ngũgĩ was to team up with his colleague at the University of Nairobi Micere Mugo to write the vivid play *The Trial of Dedan Kimathi*, about one of the heroes of the struggle. It opened that year amid a swirl of controversy at Nairobi's National Theatre, with Micere cast as the Woman.

Meja Mwangi, also a Gikuyu, reveals that *Weep Not, Child* was the only novel he had read on the subject of the Freedom Fighters before he began writing about it himself: "It encouraged me because it was closer to me than anything I had read before. The books I had read earlier were written by Europeans and were alien to me" (Lindfors 75). His own treatments of the guerrilla rebellion, *Taste of Death* and *Carcase for Hounds*, concentrate on the experience in the forest itself. Mwangi is particularly successful at depicting differences among the individuals caught up in the struggle, their insecurities, conflicts, and fear, despite his overall appreciation of the fighters' courageous determination to restore Kenya to its original inhabitants:

> "This is our land," Kariuki said. "The white man is just a foreigner and will have to go back to his country some time."
> ". . . What are we fighting for if we know he will go one day? Why don't we

go back to our villages and wait until he goes back to his accursed country, and then take back our land?"

"You fool, can't you see?" Karuiki swung on Mbogo. "Our land is productive. We have to force him to go."

"Is this the way to force him?" Mbogo sneered. "When you are being wiped out in scores? Do you think he will go now?" He shook his head. "I call this suicide." (146)

In contrast, the semi-autobiographical *Daughter of Mumbi*, by Charity Waciuma (according to John Nottingham, a pseudonym for his sister-in-law [Lindfors 113]), centers on the changed life in the villages during the Emergency period. She writes of "Gitati," the communal work instituted in the so-called White Highlands by the colonizers: "This work was supposed by law to be done for twenty-four days a year by all men on various public works, like roads, schools or dispensaries. But during the Emergency it was done by men, women and children six days a week, every week, and increasingly it was confined to improving the farms of Chiefs, headmen and other 'Loyalists' " (113).

Forced off the white-owned estates, more than a hundred thousand Africans, transformed into squatters on their own land, migrated during this period to the native reserves in the Rift Valley, a mass movement causing untold disruption to already beleaguered families. To help provide a context for the experiences of her young female protagonist, Waciuma concentrates particularly on the situation of the children:

When they moved from the farms, children were separated from their parents and many have never been traced to this day. In many cases they were herded into camps like cattle, men in one place, women in another and children in yet another. After "screening" they were sent back to their district or division. Many small children did not know where they came from and were left, often at railway stations. They spent months wandering about the countryside. (117)

Waciuma is successful in suggesting the sense of tension and isolation that made all Central Province "a prison" (129).

The unequal struggle during the Emergency of the poorly armed Freedom Fighters against the might of the British forces—and often against the members of their own community they took to be traitors and accomplices—is the compelling subject of many Kenyan novels and forms important sections in others. Godwin Wachira's *Ordeal in the Forest* (1968) provides details about how leadership developed among the forest fighters and explains the significance of their frequent oath taking. Like Charity Waciuma, Leonard Kibera and his brother, Samuel Kahiga, in their collection of short stories *Potent Ash* (1968), sensitively reveal the ambivalence toward the dangerous guerillas because of the suffering heaped by the Emergency on ordinary people in the villages. *The Land Is Ours* (1970), by John Karoki Njoroge, tells

the tale of the conflicted Chief Elijah, "torn between the loyalty to indigenous nationalism on the one hand and alien imperialism on the other"
(Foreword). Through the self-serving meanderings of its picaresque hero,
Charles Mangua's *A Tail in the Mouth* also indicates that a desire for survival
was foremost in the minds of most people during the Emergency; thus they
feared the guerrillas and the British alike. Three works actually centered on
other topics—Mwangi Ruheni's comic *The Future Leaders* (1973), Kenneth
Watene's *Sunset on the Manyatta* (1974), and Grace Ogot's *The Graduate*
(1980)—also contain characters affected by the uprising. Similarly, in *A
Curse from God* (1970) Stephen N. Ngubiah briefly depicts a British police
sweep against suspected Mau Mau activists in Nairobi. It is hardly surprising
that even Ngũgĩ's later novels, set in post-Independence Kenya, *Petals of
Blood* (1977) and *Devil on the Cross* (1982), feature important characters
shaped by their experiences during the Emergency.

Despite these numerous attempts to depict this crucial stage in modern
Kenyan history and to account for both the idealism and the heroism of the
Freedom Fighters as well as the fear and ambivalence caused by their dangerous tactics and the bloody response of the British, Meja Mwangi, for one,
opines "that so far not enough has been written about this crucial stage of our
development. Unless it is written now, it will fade from our memory, so it is
very necessary that it be recorded today by the generation that lived through
it. . . . I just keep on tackling certain issues that have not been tackled so far.
In fact, I think I may write a couple more books about the Mau Mau"
(Lindfors 74, 75).

Tradition in Literature

Another important aspect of East African history, specifically, its traditional
culture, has not only been recorded in anthropological or autobiographical works like Nyambongo's, Mockerie's, Kenyatta's, and Gatheru's, mentioned earlier, but it has also led to numerous collections of indigenous
orature and cultural studies. Okot p'Bitek's *Horn of My Love* (1974) and
Africa's Cultural Revolution (1973) are important examples. Traditional culture also provides subject and background for a large body of the fiction
produced in the modern period and appears in snatches in even a work like
Gicheru's *The Ivory Merchant*, concerned with contemporary poaching in
Kenya. Many of these depictions of customary blessings, proverbs, stories,
rituals, ceremonies, and dances are intended primarily to convey the sense
of the lives of the indigenous people, thus providing characterization and
background for the protagonists. Many other examples, however, are used
contrastively to illuminate the differences between African ways and those of
the colonizers.

Various critics of East African literature mention its depiction of the past
as one of its major subjects. Bakari and Mazrui speak of "the conflict

between the African past and the African present, often betraying a deep
nostalgia, an idealization of what once was, or might have been. Related to
this is the clash between tradition and modernity [and] the antimony between the indigenous and the foreign" (878). Elizabeth Knight, too, men-
tioning the "disillusionment that came after the euphoria of independence"
sees one of the resulting trends in Kenyan literature as "an intensification of
the depicting of the traditionalistic orientations of the preceding decade,
contrasting, implicitly or explicitly, the fragmentation of modern Kenyan
society with the cohesion of earlier tribal life" (905). Since their understanding of what traditional life provided to create a positive inheritance of East
African identity is crucial, obviously, even to the author's presentation of
contemporary life, a detailed inclusion here of some of their depictions of
customary life and oral art seems useful.

Traditional songs, for example, enliven the texts of most of these works.
Ngũgĩ's five novels offer songs sometimes intended primarily to reveal Gikuyu legend and myth and to inform readers about his community's traditional culture—the praise of Gikuyu and Mumbi in *A Grain of Wheat* (202)
or the pleas for the gift of oratory in *Devil on the Cross* (9), for example. Some
songs, like those celebrating the Freedom Fighters in *A Grain of Wheat* (26),
those commenting on neocolonial political corruption in *Petals of Bloods* and
Devil on the Cross, and those vowing to overthrow neoimperialism (*Devil* 47),
reflect recent and current political realities. Ngũgĩ's traditional songs also
celebrate circumcision (*Petals* 207), acknowledge the frequent difficulty of
distinguishing good from evil (*Devil* 25), and lyrically express love (*Devil*
241). In *To Become a Man,* the Masai writer Henry ole Kulet offers three
songs celebrating the custom of cattle raiding practiced by the morans (72,
98, 101–2); S. N. Ngubiah's *A Curse from God* presents a song of mockery
against charcoal burners (40); Osija Mwambungu demonstrates how contemporary events like a well-publicized court decision are almost immediately turned into popular songs (*Veneer* 36); Ismael Mbise's *Blood on Our
Land* ends with three women's coded songs to their men, lamenting the exploitation of the white settlers in Tanzania. Most of these verses are presented
in English, but Ngũgĩ does not translate the Congolese popular tune played
at the Devil's feast in *Devil on the Cross* (93), and Mwambungu offers both the
original and a translation of a drinking chant of the Wanyakyusa (*Veneer* 33).

The original educational and social function of the traditional song, then,
not just its content, is presented to suggest subtly the changes wrought by
colonialism. Frequently, that change is demonstrated by the inclusion of
Christian hymns, as in Mwambungu (*Veneer* 81), and by references to Western popular music. In *Devil on the Cross*, Ngũgĩ satirizes missionary hypocrisy with a chant, "The Beatitudes of the Rich and the Imperialists":

> Blessed is he who bites and sooths
> Because he will never be found out.

Blessed is the man who burns down another man's house
And in the morning joins him in grief,
For he shall be called merciful.
(209)

The weakening of traditional culture by colonialism is touched upon by Mwambungu in his depiction of young Africans who feed coins into juke-boxes, playing and replaying American songs like the Everly Brothers' "Devoted to You" (*Veneer* 4).[6]

In contrast to this imported art, traditional songs and dances are shown as both liberating and unifying forces for cultural cohesion. Dances celebrating the activities of certain times of the year, the harvest, for instance, or important religious and social occasions, involve the entire village as participants of one sort or another. Henry ole Kulet pictures women in a Masai village gathering to honor the returning morans after their successful cattle raid:

> Then the women started to sing, their voices rising gradually, until at last, at the peak of the song, they were heaving their chests forward and backwards, throwing up and down their beautiful, multi-coloured jewelry. The jewelry shone beautifully in the moonlight. The song praised the brave men who brought Pukoret to where she belonged. (*To Become a Man* 101)

Osija Mwambungu described an age-old game among the Wanyakyusa, as choreographed as a dance, in which young people select each other for the evening on the basis of beauty of both body and character. Mwambungu goes to some pains to explain:

> Beauty among our people at the time, embraced values which are normally not associated with outside appearance only. A beautiful person to us, in a serious sense of the word, was someone who had a clean body with a smooth skin and an attractive general appearance. He or she was also not a liar, thief, proud, rude, jealous, lazy, disrespectful (usually to older people), dirty, selfish, snobbish, merciless or unkind. He or she had to be a person who was both clean in body and soul. (*Veneer* 27)

Traditionally, the game of selection ended with everyone briefly going into hiding with his or her "beautiful one," a short interval "intended for isolating the unselected ugly children" (29). The narrator and his friend discover, however, that the Christian youth were using this period of isolation for sexual purposes:

> "Boy! It is a complete misunderstanding of our culture," [Roses] moaned.
> Roses had discovered that the big Christian boys and girls were undressing in the dark and were making love! In the pagan game this never happened. . . .
> It is a wonder that when on Independence day we discovered that the Christian missionaries had wrecked our entire philosophy of life in the name of progress without replacing it with anything comprehensible we decided to revive our culture at break-neck speed? (29)

Nowhere in these novels is the societal value of traditional song and dance so often and clearly expressed as in their depictions of the rites and celebrations of male circumcision. Ngũgĩ spends a great deal of time depicting this ritual in both *The River Between* and *Petals of Blood*. Ole Kulet's description of a Masai celebration in *To Become a Man* is arguably the most vivid, detailed, and realistic in all these works, with its dual focus on the protagonist's internal and external experiences.

In general, it is the psychological and social significance of this ordeal, which all the young people are expected to undergo to become adult members of the community, that is emphasized in the fiction, not just the painful details of the operation itself. While among the Wanyakyusa according to Mwambungu, only the Muslims in their midst practiced either male or female circumcision, fictional accounts of the other peoples of East Africa attest to the ritual's central importance in their societies. Leshao's uncle's jibe, "I would like to see an old uncircumcised man, or is he an old boy?" (Kulet, *To Become a Man* 63), signifies the general attitude toward the ritual as a marker of adulthood. Among the Meru in Tanzania, for instance, as Mbise shows, circumcision was essential for complete manhood, and without going through it, a "maseka, an uninitiated boy," could not participate in some official traditional ceremonies and could not dance with or court any of the girls (*Blood on Our Land* 28).

Much of the conflict of Ngũgĩ's *The River Between* stems from the colonial missionaries' attempts to ban female circumcision. As far as male circumcision is concerned, the greatest threat, at least among the Masai, seems to be the preference among the educated boys for having the operation performed in a hospital, a striking evidence of the influence of the West. In *To Become a Man*, Leshao's simple statement that he is considering such an act almost causes a rift between him and his elders. The older members of the clan view the hospital, even more than the school, as evidence of the danger to their way of life:

> Elders are not usually alarmed by anything. But his news undid them.
>
> "Surely it is a new danger. When we first sent our sons to school, we thought they would get lost and we would never see them again. The white men were unable to lure them away. They are still Maasai. But this new threat is dangerous. We have all heard that it is not mere talk. Pushuka's son has been circumcised in that place. He has never come home again. . . ."
>
> "Not only has he not come home," another old man put in. "I understand he no longer wants to speak our language. He puts on long white robes and a red cap!"
>
> "So the plague is spreading?" (Kulet, *To Become a Man* 66)

Even when lamenting the incursion of the Europeans, the African characters in these stories express themselves in traditional modes. Proverbs abound, for in all the areas depicted, the general feeling is that "the witty made frequent use of proverbs" (Ngubiah 131). From the Gikuyu we hear, for example, that "a lamb takes after its mother" (Ngũgĩ, *Weep Not* 54) and "the wood which is in the drying platform above the fire laughs at the one in the fire" (Ngubiah 185); the Masai warn, however, " 'the pots alternate on the fire'; He who has today might not have tomorrow" (Kulet, *To Become a Man* 10); Barnabas Katigula, writing of Tanzania, cautions, "A single hand does not slaughter a cow. You need other people" (*Groping in the Dark* 29). Under neocolonialism, however, the people's wisdom is shown to have become perverted for selfish ends. One of Ngũgĩ's white-worshiping thieves in *Devil on the Cross* confesses, "I have two mistresses, for you know the saying that he who keeps something in reserve never goes hungry, and when an European gets old, he likes to eat veal" (99).

As condensations of wisdom, aphorisms can be seen as "stories" in small. They reflect the didacticism of much orature and indicate the accepted teaching-learning relationship among members of the community. East African novels also present numerous examples of lengthier tales that, through their content and the dynamics of their performance, demonstrate this educative interaction.

Emphasized by the novelists are the emotional and psychological benefits of instructing and being instructed. Both the teller and the listener feel closer to each other and to the community as a whole through the experience. The act of retelling the traditional myths and listening to them, instructing others in legendary knowledge or clan wisdom and partaking of this instruction, is shown to be itself a ritual of unity.

In Ngũgĩ's *Weep Not, Child*, Nganga, an elder, is praised because he "could tell a story. This was considered a good thing for a man" (23). Ngotho, too, the hero's father, while generally austere—"The children could not joke in their father's presence" (26)—draws his children close to him as he recounts the well-known legend of Gikuyu and Mumbi. Other legends and myths Waiyaki and his brothers hear are those of Demi na Mathathi, two generations of Gikuyu giants who communed with the ancestors and cut down the forests to prepare the land for cultivation (10). "Storytelling was a common entertainment in their family" (250). "And when there was no moonlight at night it was the time for story telling" in Mwambungu's *Veneer of Love*:

> All the stories would have been handed down to us by parents, relatives and friends. One of the reasons for visiting your uncles, aunts, cousins and a host of other relatives was to ensure that when it came to story telling you had enriched your knowledge of them after having listened to their stories. A person who knew how to tell nice and new stories was greatly admired. We would sit round a fire with our parents or relatives in the evening and take turns to tell stories while waiting for supper to be ready. (36)

Mwambungu reveals that in his society one was allowed to tell only new stories; clever orators, who could modify a familiar story into something novel, were thus greatly valued.

Clearly, such tales are not intended for enjoyment alone. In addition to strengthening the children's sense of identity and teaching tribal history, many of them inculcate virtues considered essential for survival: "The tribal stories told Waiyaki by his mother had strengthened [his] belief in the virtue of toil and perseverance" (Ngũgĩ, *River* 55). Abdulla, the unlikely hero of Ngũgĩ's *Petals of Blood*, reveals his growing sense of harmony with others and his developing self-esteem by becoming the teller of customary animal stories:

> Abdulla expecially seemed to have gained new strength and new life. His transformation from a sour-faced cripple with endless curses at Joseph to somebody who laughed and told stories, a process which had started with his first contact with Wanja, was now complete. People seemed to accept him to their hearts. This could be seen in the children. They surrounded him and he told them stories. (116–17)

Based upon a traditional Gikuyu poetic form, the song of the *gĩkaandĩ* player, Ngũgĩ's *Devil on the Cross* combines mythic and realistic elements throughout. The Devil appears one Sunday on a golf course in the town of Ilmorog in Iciciri District to tempt Ngũgĩ's heroine, Jacinta Warĩĩnga. By the end of Jacinta's story, with her striking Gikuyu dress, her traditional songs, and, most importantly, her killing of the Rich Old Man from Ngorika, representative of neocolonial vice, Jacinta assumes the characteristics of a tribal saviour. Ngũgĩ uses the tradition of myth, legend, and storytelling to recall the need for heroism to combat dangers to the people.

Mbise's *Blood on Our Land* demonstrates the educative function of storytelling and the loving relationship between the performer/teacher and his audience/students. Kilutaluta begins his lessons for children and adults after evening meals:

> All the children of all the neighbouring houses came for evening talks. At times the initiated came for talks with Kilutaluta. But these talks were hardly comprehensible to the little ones because the conversation started with proverbs and was highly metaphorical. This conversation started after the children's normal classes with the old man. The grown-ups came just before the children left for their beds. (5)

> Kilutaluta often started his teachings by teasing the kids; especially so when he had noticed any of the children sitting carelessly. All the same the children enjoyed Kilutaluta's teasing enormously:
> "You remember, my sons, last time I posed a question before you. Just before I tell you a story I would like to know whether you still remember the question, and of course, the answer. Yes Tareto, what was the question?" Tareto coughed a little and answered.
> "The question was why we should always sit around you at this time . . ."
> "Or around any other elder, don't forget," he reminded them.
> "Or around any other elder," they all repeated smiling.
> "And what was the answer?"
> "Duty. Our real duty," a gallant chorus answered him.

"And it should always remain." He blessed them.
Kilutaluta introduced a new topic. (19)

Charity Waciuma's children's book *Mweru, the Ostrich Girl* (1966) is in its entirety a legend, containing a richness of proverbs, riddles, and stories of ogres, giants, sorcerers, and personified animals and birds. Contemporary East Africans' desire for a positive children's literature to counter the westernizing effect of neocolonial culture has led to the publication of quite a number of children's books. Waciuma has also produced *The Golden Feather* (1966), *Merry-Making* (1972), and *Who's Calling* (1973). Understandably, women writers have been in the forefront in answering this need, but Ngũgĩ, too, has written *Njamba Nene and the Flying Bus* and *Njamba Nene's Pistol*, translated from the Gikuyu by Wangui wa Goro, and other male writers have also been active in this field.[7]

A much more ambivalent attitude than their universal honoring of storytelling is expressed in these writers' presentations of the image and role of the medicine man or witch doctor. Frequently the depiction takes the form of a conflict between Western and traditional medicine. In Waciuma's *Daughter of Mumbi*, for example, a delegation of native doctors comes to the narrator's father, a Western-type doctor, to ask that he stop saying his medicine is better than theirs (26). Grace Ogot's Professor in *The Other Woman* also butts heads with such tradition when he plans to perform a heart transplant operation at the medical school at the University of Nairobi. Not only are the common people suspicious of the transplant procedure itself, but the family of the donor will not touch his body until an artificial heart is sewn into it, for burying "the body without its vital organs is viewed as mutilating the body, as sorcery . . . an abominable act" (237). The full implications of nontraditional acts like heart transplants are reflected upon by Professor Miyare's wife:

> Her husband . . . had cheated the ancestors by giving the donor's heart a new life and by subverting its journey to the land of the dead. Alice Musa would have a dead man's heart ticking away in her bosom, and her own heart would be buried untraditionally at nightfall away from the glaring eyes of the sun, because this was a sacrilegeous act. And the spirit would hover in the oblivion till Alice Musa's body returns to dust to dwell at the bowels of the earth waiting for the days of resurrection. Would the professor's father consult a medicine man to cleanse his son from such an unheard of act which bordered on witchcraft? (239–40)

Indeed, although Miyare believes he is doing God's work by saving lives through science, and the heart-transplant team "felt very close to God during the tedious and delicate operation" (225), his acceptance of Western secularism is made clear when, as he prepares for his second heart transplant, on his laboratory wall hang three wooden placards, proclaiming: "GOD AND MAN, SCIENCE IS GOD and GOD IS DEAD" (246). The title story of Eneriko

Seruma's *The Heart Seller* concerns a contemporary ne'er-do-well, an educated African who offers his heart eagerly to anyone who would pay him a
million dollars and allow him ten years in which to spend it; the religious
implications of such an act never arise.

Jane Bakaluba's heroine, Naiga, reflects a similar, practical attitude toward
native doctors. She admits they perform a useful service to society, but what
she finds unforgivable are the high fees they charge, and the sometimes
humiliating, sometimes impossible acts they demand that their patients
perform for a successful treatment (*Honeymoon for Three* 47).

Many of the writers, however, go into a great deal of interesting detail
about conventions of dealing with native doctors or present them favorably
as not only trustworthy but also representative of the old life shattered by
colonialism. "Customarily a witchdoctor should always be passed on the left
hand side for it is on his right that he carries the sacred objects of his craft"
reports Waciuma (*Daughter of Mumbi* 30). Her narrator's father, despite his
own disbelief, successfully employs a native doctor against thieves who steal
his maize, knowing that they are believers. Such faith is passing with time,
however, as Waithaka, the renowned medicine man in Samuel Kagiri's *Leave
Us Alone* (1975), laments:

> Everybody in the land knows that I, and my ancestors before me, have had the
> power to heal the sick, foresee what is to come, and shield our people from ca-
> tastrophe. . . . On innumerable occasions we have saved our people from suf-
> fering by averting famine, floods, epidemics, and disasters in war. . . . From
> now on . . . things will not be the same. You, my children, will never in your
> life hear the voices that I have spoken. You will not see the sights I have seen.
> (54)

He expresses this change as a retreat of the gods from human affairs:

> The things that have been will cease to be. For the High God and the Spirits of
> our Ancestors will no longer speak. They will no longer understand the
> language in which I have spoken to them. They will no longer meddle in the
> affairs of men. They have withdrawn and gone far, far away from the Holy
> Mountain. They will never return. (55)

While both Meja Mwangi (*Kill Me Quick* 128–29) and Hazel Mugot
(*Black Night of Quiloa* 54–55) also deal briefly with this topic, the most
extensive portrait is that of the old medicine man in Rebeka Njau's *Ripples in
the Pool* (1975), whose lyrical language is intended to remind his young
apprentice of the traditional wisdom of living close to nature and accepting
whatever personal fortune the gods send. By the end of his tale, however, he
realizes that he can no longer communicate with the villagers, who have
become westernized, and so can no longer heal them: "To you the mystery is
dead. / The dew on the leaves is just water to feed the plant" (87). A similar
realization occasions a nostalgic idealization of traditional life in the opening
pages of Samuel Kagiri's *Leave Us Alone* (1975).

The most negative aspect of traditional culture with which East African fiction writers deal is the issue of tribalism. Despite his nostalgic memory of past days, Samuel Kagiri's narrator recalls, "I had seen strangers being badly treated back home during the days of my boyhood. The people of Kagaita, for all the kindness which they showed to each other and to people from the immediate surroundings of the Ridge, did not like strangers" (720). Reflecting on the precolonial battles over cattle, Waciuma recalls, "There used to be fighting always between Masai and Kikuyu and sometimes with the Kamba" (*Daughter of Mumbi* 923). These battles, occasioned by cattle raiding, determine much of the narrative of Kulet's *To Become a Man* and Lydiah Nguya's *The First Seed* (1975). The extremely violent and complex story the grandmother in Bernard Chahilu's *The Herdsman's Daughter* (1974) tells the young girls gathered in her hut begins with a clan murder (178–90), and even Austin Bukenya's satiric look at undergraduate life at the University of Dar es Salaam, *The People's Bachelor* (1972), mentions tribalism continuing among students there.

The Inalienable Land

Even as tribalism is condemned in these works, the communities' commitment to maintaining their homelands is shown to be one of East Africa's most important forces for cultural cohesiveness. The powerful concept of a community existing throughout history in one secure geographic locale is emphasized, particularly in works written about Kenya; the Tanzanian concern is to show the value of the concept of community that traditional life on the land fostered. Before colonialism most of the Kenyan population lived in dispersed rural settlements; villages and towns existed only along the coast. Land was held in traditional, communal ownership.

The homeland of the Gikuyu, the area to be taken over as the "White Highlands," was precisely such a fertile mountain area, and it provided the indigenous people with both physical sustenance and emotional and spiritual security. In his books, Ngũgĩ returns again and again to his people's myths and legends linking them to the land. The legend of God, Murungu, giving the first man and woman, Gikuyu and Mumbi, ownership of the land for their descendants for all eternity is presented in both *Weep Not, Child* and *The River Between*.

In the latter novel, Waiyaki is led by his father to the Sacred Grove, where Gikuyu and Mumbi were brought after their creation on Kerinyaga, "the mountain of He-who-shines-in-holiness" (17). Chege blesses their journey in the traditional way, by spitting on his breast, and instructs his son along the route in the medicinal properties of certain barks and herbs. When they reach the Sacred Grove, he tells Waiyaki:

> "All this is our land." . . .
> "He stood them on that mountain. He showed them all the land."
> . . . His father's voice had a magic spell.

"From that mountain he brought them here"
". . . it was before Agu; in the beginning of things. Murungu brought the man and woman here and again showed them the whole vastness of the land. He gave the country to them and their children and the children of the children, tene na tene, world without end. Do you see?" (17–18)

The integral link between the land and the people's physical and religious well-being is stated explicitly: "These ancient hills and ridges were the heart and soul of the land. They kept the tribes' magic and rituals pure and intact. Their people rejoiced together, giving one another the blood and warmth of their laughter" (3). In *Petals of Blood* Ngũgĩ acknowledges the responsibility of defending this valuable possession: "Gird your loins and always remember everything good and beautiful comes from the soil" (89).

The significance of the land is expressed less mystically in the novels about Tanzania. Their focus is on the mutual use of the land and the people's acceptance of responsibility for it as indicative of the precolonial value of communality. Mbise's portrait of the rural community of Engare Nanyuki, it is true, evokes a precolonial paradise:

Engare Nanyuki looked across Waato river and the green plains rose gradually to the Meru mountain. . . . Along each side of the river were the Meru people who had inherited their land from Lamireny, their great ancestor. Houses, like harmony and love, were scattered all over the green plains. . . . The plains were rich with crops: maize, beans, wheat and millet. There was no hunger. (*Blood on Our Land* 2)

A principal reason for this harmony and love, Mbise suggests, is the communal attitude of the Meru people. People, cattle, and herds of other animals wander over the plains with no concern for boundaries marking private property: "Land was a common property inherited from a common ancestor for a common people under a common chief and rule. Every individual was obliged to utilise it for a common basic purpose" (2). He speaks of the role even children played during the sowing season, keeping birds and domestic poultry out of the fields. Mwambungu, too, writing about the Wanyakyusa of Tanzania, shows the custom of individual farmers seeking assistance from their neighbors to cultivate a large area of land. The number of helpers depends on the number of pots of Kimpumu, a local beer, and the amount of food the farmer's wife can prepare (*Veneer* 32). In a similar setting, Barnabas Katigula, in *Groping in the Dark* (1974), gives a picture of a communal boar hunt to rid the village of the animals that had become a serious menace to their crops: "This was to be a joint activity for the entire village, a collective duty, and nobody except women, children and very old men, could stay away without getting into serious trouble" (17).

Largely because of this sense of an inviolate space and an immutable way of life among these people, the coming of the colonizers is pictured as tantamount to the end of the world. Nothing, for instance, in the Gikuyu's legends or beliefs prepared them for the devastation of being exiled from their lands. On the contrary, the legends reinforced the idea of the continuation of the traditional way of life on the traditional homelands:

"The white man cannot speak the language of the hills."
"And knows not the ways of the land." . . .
"Who from the outside can make his way into the hills?" (Ngũgĩ, *River* 8)

Despite the Africans' confidence in the land's promise of eternal security, the colonizers penetrated deep into East Africa, appropriating the land and uprooting the traditions as they went, until, after listening again to his father tell the legend of Gikuyu and Mumbi, "Njoroge could not help exclaiming, 'Where did the land go?' " (Ngũgĩ, *Weep Not* 28).

While Ngũgĩ, both in his essays and in novels such as *Petals of Blood* and *Devil on the Cross,* strives to answer Njoroge's question with a political analysis of imperialism, most of the other East African fiction writers concentrate more on trying to convey the postcolonial experience itself. The fragmentation, rootlessness, and ultimate sense of despair in independent East Africa is the subject of scores of these novels.

Mwangi's *Kill Me Quick,* for example, is a powerful, naturalistic look at the fate of the relatively privileged school leavers, unable to find work in Nairobi, cut off from their expectant relatives in their villages, and destined only for a life of crime and violence. His other two novels set in an urban environment, *Going down River Road* and *The Cockroach Dance,* examine the same sense of the exploitation of ordinary people in independent Kenya; the latter ends with a sense of hope in political action. Also hopeful at the end is Kenneth Watene's *Sunset on the Manyatta,* which follows a young Masai from the schooling that is to alienate him emotionally from his people, through his hopeless search for employment in the city, to Germany, where he undergoes both training in engineering and immersion in various kinds of racism, and home again with his newfound sense of identity and determination to work for the real liberation of his country. The plight of an individual caught between the traditional and modern worlds is also presented in J. N. Mwaura's study of a Gikuyu father-son conflict, *Sky Is the Limit* (1974); Grace Ogot's depiction of a female M.P. torn between family and political responsibility, *The Graduate;* the Ugandan novelist Bahadur Tejani's examination of interracial love in a racist society, *Day after Tomorrow* (1971); Alfred M. M'Imanyara's *Agony on a Hide* (1973), with its picture of urban violence; and the conflict between urban and rural life in Lydiah Nguya's *The First Seed.*

Women's Writing

Another important subject, fiction by and about East African women, must be mentioned briefly, although the subject of women's writing commands a separate chapter in this volume. It is indicative of the resolve created by the

African Writers Conference at Makerere University in 1962, noted earlier, that the first novel published by the East African Publishing House was a study of traditional-modern conflict, *The Promised Land* (1966) by Grace Ogot. *The Promised Land* was the first imaginative work in English by a Luo writer, and its author the first female novelist in East Africa (Knight 893). Her novel *The Graduate* offers several studies of contemporary African women, and her collections of short pieces, *Land without Thunder* (1968) and *The Other Woman* (1976), contain stories like "The Old White Witch," reflective of her own experiences as a nurse, and the shocking "Pay Day" and "The Middle Door," concerning dangers to women in urban environments. Barbara Kimenye, as mentioned previously, produced the first book-length pieces of Ugandan fiction in English with her 1965 and 1966 tales of Kimenye village. Subsequent East African female fiction writers include Hazel Mugot, whose lyrical *Black Night of Quiloa* (1971) tells of a painful Black/white love relationship; Miriam Khamadi Were, with her disparaging look at polygamy in *The Eighth Wife* (1972) and revelations of the conservative rejection of female education in *Your Heart Is My Altar* (1980); Jane Jagers Bakaluba from Uganda, who contrasts traditional and westernized women in *Honeymoon for Three* (1975); Majorie Oludhe Macgoye, whose *Coming to Birth* (1986) is a sensitive examination of marriage in a political pressure cooker; and Rebeka Njau, whose *Ripples in the Pool* presents one of the most bizarre images of a modern woman in all of these books. Worthy of mention, too, are several novels by East African male writers concerned with issues of polygamy, traditional versus modern notions of the role of women, and the positive and negative aspects of bride price: Samuel Kagiri's *Leave Us Alone*, Bernard P. Chahilu's *The Herdsman's Daughter*, Barnabas Katigula's *Groping in the Dark*, Samuel Kahiga's *The Girl from Abroad* (1974), and Mwangi Ruheni's *The Minister's Daughter* (1975).

Conclusion

"East African writing in English . . . began in 1964 or so with Ngũgĩ's *Weep Not, Child*" (Lindfors 150), asserted Chris Wanjala in 1976, testifying to the great influence of his colleague at the University of Nairobi on the shape of creative literature in English in the region. It seems appropriate, then, to end this brief survey with some observations on what the movement of Ngũgĩ's career might signify for creative writing in East Africa. As indicated by earlier mention of his spearheading the Africanization of the Literature Department at the university and of the school syllabi in Kenya, Ngũgĩ's sense of his own African identity and commitment to espousing anticolonialism and antineocolonialism developed early and has grown steadily in his public utterances, his critical writing, and his creative work. Well-known by now is the story of his detention for almost a year in Kamiti Maximum Security Prison after the opening of the play *Ngaahika ndeenda* (1977; *I Will*

Marry When I Want), written with Ngũgĩ wa Mĩriĩ and the villagers of Limuru, and produced at the community-built Kamiriithu Education and Cultural Center, later razed to the ground by the Kenyan government (see Ngũgĩ, *Detained*). It is ironic that, while earlier English-language works by Ngũgĩ—*The Trial of Dedan Kimathi* and *Petals of Blood*, for instance—have caused controversy and grumbling among those who considered themselves and their class criticized in them, it was when Ngũgĩ turned away from English to Gikuyu to reach his own people, and away from a Western-oriented conception of writing and publishing to traditional, communal involvement in the production of art, that the might of official wrath attempted to silence him.

Dismissed without stated charges from his university position, the writer has been living in exile. Ngũgĩ himself translated *Ngaahika ndeenda* into English, as well as the novel he wrote in prison, *Caithani mutharaba-ini* (*Devil on the Cross*). He has indicated, however, that these translations and the collection of essays *Barrel of a Pen* (1983) will be the last of his writings in English. His musical *Maitu njugira* (Mother Sing for Me), about colonial Kenya, was suppressed by the Kenyan government, and a 1987 political novel, *Matigari*, written in Gikuyu and subsequently translated into English (1987), was banned in Kenya. In effect, then, Ngũgĩ has been silenced in his own country as surely as those artists who fled political oppression in Uganda.

Okot p'Bitek's comment in 1976 seems eerily prophetic of this situation: "Writers in East Africa are becoming timid because they know the hawk is flying overhead. They know there is detention and imprisonment awaiting us, and I think this is discouraging people from commenting on certain political matters that are going on in all East African countries. There is self-imposed censorship because people are afraid to speak out, although occasionally, in their lighthearted way, they do manage to say something" (Lindfors 144). Significantly, the most committed writing in the region at present is not in English at all, but is originating in Tanzania in Swahili.

Notes

1. According to Bakari and Mazrui, Professor Malinowski, already an established anthropologist and a celebrity in his field when Kenyatta made his acquaintance, was an advocate of functionalism (see Malinowski). "Put simply, functionalism was interested in establishing the systematic uniqueness of each culture by emphasizing the specific functions of its institutions and focusing on the differences between cultures rather than their similarities. The functionalist approach to anthropology demanded that the researcher learn the language of the community he was studying as a key towards a full understanding of the social dynamics of the society and its customs. . . . Kenyatta as a native speaker of Kikuyu fascinated Malinowski as a describer of a society which he understood and was qualified to give seminars on" (Bakari and Mazrui 870).

2. While the countries of Somalia, Djibuti, and Ethiopia are commonly considered regions of East Africa as well, this essay covers only the three former British colonies of Uganda, Kenya, and Tanzania (Tanganyika/Zanzibar).

3. According to *The Encyclopedia of Third World Countries*, Tanzania "is the least homogeneous nation in the world with 7% homogeneity (on an ascending scale in which North and South Korea ranked 135th with 100% homogeneity). Africans, who form 99% of the population, are divided into over 130 groups, each with its own physical and social characteristics and languages" (1904).

4. In his study of Tanzanian writing, Steven Arnold mentions several novels written by expatriates, "fully inspired by participatory residence in Tanzania: *The People's Bachelor* (1972) by Austin Bukenya from Uganda; *Bamanga* (1974) and *Leopard in a Cage* (1976) by Bediako Asare from Ghana. Two Kenyans might also be included: Grace Ogot's *The Promised Land* (1966) is set in Tanganyika, and Henry R. ole Kulet has published *Is It Possible* and *To Become a Man* (1972), two tales about the Masai who are as Tanzanian as they are Kenyan" (958).

5. The emotional title story in Grace Ogot's *The Island of Tears* (1980) presents the reaction of the Luo people in Mboya's home district on the day of his funeral.

6. These youths are akin to those in Seruma's *The Heart Seller*, who adopt flashy Western dress and spend their hard-earned shillings on comics and movies, especially Westerns with heroes like Davy Crockett and Jim Bowie, whom they consciously imitate.

7. Other East African books for children and adolescent readers include Miriam Were, *The Boy in Between* (1970) and *The High School Gent* (1972); Asenath Odaga, *Jande's Ambition* (1966), *The Secret of Monkey Rock* (1966), *The Hare's Blanket* (1967), *The Diamond Ring* (1967), *Sweets and Sugar Cane* (1969), and *The Villager's Son* (1971); Marjorie Oludhe-Macgoye, *Growing Up at Lina School* (1971); Pamela Kola, *East African How? Stories* (1966), *East African Why? Stories* (1966), and *East African When? Stories* (1968); John Nagenda, *Mukasa* (1973); and Mwangi Ruheni, *In Search of Their Parents* (n.d.).

Bibliography

Arnold, Stephen. "Tanzania." In *European-Language Writing in Sub-Saharan Africa*, edited by Albert S. Gerard. Budapest: Akademiai Kiado, 1986.

Asalache, Khadambi. *A Calabash of Life*. London: Longman, 1967.

Bakaluba, Jane Jagers. *Honeymoon for Three*. Nairobi: East African Publishing House, 1975.

Bakari, Mohamed, and Ali A. Mazrui. "The Early Phase." In *European-Language Writing in Sub-Saharan Africa*, edited by Albert S. Gerard. Budapest: Akademiai Kiado, 1986.

√   Benson, Peter. *"Black Orpheus," "Transition," and Modern Cultural Awakening in Africa*. Berkeley and Los Angeles: University of California Press, 1986.

Bodker, Cecil. *The Leopard*. Nairobi: East African Publishing House, 1972.

Bukenya, Austin. *The People's Bachelor*. Nairobi: East African Publishing House, 1972.

Chahilu, Bernard P. *The Herdsman's Daughter*. Nairobi: East African Publishing House, 1974.

Gicheru, Mwangi. *The Ivory Merchant.* Nairobi: Spear Books, 1976.

Githae, Charles Kahihu. *A Worm in the Head.* Nairobi: Spear Books, 1987.

Heron, George. "Uganda." In *European-Language Writing in Sub-Saharan Africa,* edited by Albert S. Gerard. Budapest: Akademiai Kiado, 1986.

Kaggia, Bildad. *Roots of Freedom, 1921–1963.* Nairobi: East African Publishing House, 1975.

Kagiri, Samuel. *Leave Us Alone.* Nairobi: East African Publishing House, 1975.

Kahama, C. George, T. L. Maliyamkono, and Stuart Wells. *The Challenge for Tanzania's Economy.* London: Heinemann, 1986.

Kahiga, Samuel. *Flight to Juba.* Nairobi: Longman, 1979.

———. *The Girl from Abroad.* London: Heinemann, 1974.

———. *Potent Ash* (with Leonard Kibera). Nairobi: East African Publishing House, 1968.

———. *When the Stars Are Scattered.* Nairobi: Longman, 1979.

Karnara, Jonathan. *The Coming of Power and Other Stories.* Nairobi: Oxford University Press, 1986.

Karoki, John. *The Land Is Ours.* Nairobi: East African Literature Bureau, 1970.

Karugire, Samwiri Rubaraza. *A Political History of Uganda.* Nairobi: Heinemann, 1980.

Katigula, Barnabas. *Groping in the Dark.* Kampala: East African Literature Bureau, 1974.

Kibera, Leonard. *Voices in the Dark.* Nairobi: East African Publishing House, 1970.

Killick, Tony, ed. *Papers on the Kenyan Economy.* Nairobi: Heinemann, 1981.

Kim, K. S., R. B. Mabele, and E. R. Schultheis, eds. *Papers on the Political Economy of Tanzania.* Nairobi: Heinemann, 1978.

Kimenye, Barbara. *Kalasanda.* London: Oxford University Press, 1965.

———. *Kalasanda Revisited.* London: Oxford University Press, 1966.

Knight, Elizabeth. "Kenya." In *European-Language Writing in Sub-Saharan Africa,* edited by Albert S. Gerard. Budapest: Akademiai Kiado, 1986.

Kulet, Henry R. ole. *The Hunter.* Nairobi: Longman Kenya, 1985.

———. *Is It Possible?* Nairobi: Longman Kenya, 1971.

———. *To Become a Man.* Nairobi: Longman Kenya, 1972.

Kurian, George. "Kenya," "Tanzania," "Uganda." *Encyclopedia of the Third World,* 1032–55, 1900–1921, 2036–51. 3rd ed. New York: Facts on File, 1987.

Lindfors, Bernth, ed. *Mazungumzo: Interviews with East African Writers, Publishers, Editors, and Scholars.* Athens, Ohio: Ohio University Center for International Studies, Africa Program, 1980.

Livingston, I., and H. W. Ord. *Economics for Eastern Africa.* Nairobi: Heinemann, 1968.

Liyong, Taban lo. *Fixions and Other Stories.* London: Heinemann, 1969.

———. *Meditations in Limbo.* Nairobi: Equatorial, 1970.

———. *Meditations of Taban lo Liyong.* London: Collins, 1978.

———. *Thirteen Offensives against Our Enemies.* Nairobi: East African Literature Bureau, 1973.

———. *The Uniformed Man.* Nairobi: East African Literature Bureau, 1971.

Lubega, Bonnie. *The Outcasts.* Nairobi: Heinemann, 1971.

Macgoye, Margorie Oludhe. *Coming to Birth.* London: Heinemann, 1986.

———. *The Present Moment.* Nairobi: Heinemann, 1987.

Maillu, David G. *The Ayah*. Nairobi: Heinemann, 1986.

——. *Dear daughter*. Nairobi: Comb Books, 1976.

——. *Dear Monika*. Nairobi: Comb Books, 1976.

——. *Kadosa*. Machakos: David Maillu, 1975.

——. *Kisalu and His Fruit Garden*. Nairobi: East African Publishing House, 1972.

——. *No!* Nairobi: Comb Books, 1976.

——. *Troubles*. Nairobi: Comb Books, 1974.

——. *Unfit for Human Consumption*. Nairobi: Comb Books, 1973.

Malinowski, Bronisław. "The Language of Magic and Gardening." In *Coral Gardens and Their Magic*. London: Allen & Unwin, 1935.

Mangua, Charles. *Son of Woman*. Nairobi: East African Publishing House, 1971.

——. *A Tail in the Mouth*. Nairobi: East African Publishing House, 1972.

Mbise, Ismael R. *Blood on Our Land*. Dar es Salaam: Tanzania Publishing House, 1974.

M'Imanyara, Alfred M. *Agony on a Hide*. Nairobi: East African Publishing House, 1973.

Mkfuya, W. E. *The Wicked Walk*. Dar es Salaam: Tanzania Publishing House, 1977.

Mockerie, Parmenas Githendu. *An African Speaks for His People*. London: Hogarth Press, 1934.

——. "The Story of Permenas [*sic*] Mockerie of the Kikuyu Tribe, Written by Himself." In *Ten Africans*, edited by Margery Perham. London: Faber, 1936.

Mugo, Hazel. *Black Night of Quiloa*. Nairobi: East African Publishing House, 1971.

Mutiso, G.-C. M. *Socio-political Thought in African Literature: Weusi?* London: Macmillan, 1974.

Mvungi, Martha. *Three Solid Stones*. London: Heinemann, 1975.

Mwambungu, Osija. *Veneer of Love*. Kampala: East African Literature Bureau, 1975.

Mwangi, Meja. *Bread of Sorrow*. Nairobi: Longman Kenya, 1987.

——. *The Bushtrackers*. Nairobi: Longman Drumbeat, 1979.

——. *Carcase for Hounds*. London: Heinemann, 1974.

——. *The Cockroach Dance*. Nairobi: Longman, 1979.

——. *Going down River Road*. London: Heinemann, 1976.

——. *Kill Me Quick*. London: Heinemann, 1973.

——. *Taste of Death*. Nairobi: East African Publishing House, 1975.

Mwaura, J. N. *The Seasons of Thomas Tebo*. London: Heinemann, 1986.

——. *Sky Is the Limit*. Nairobi: East African Literature Bureau, 1974.

Nakibimbiri, Omunjakko. *The Sobbing Sounds*. Kampala: Longman Uganda, 1975.

Nazareth, Peter. *In a Brown Mantle*. Nairobi: East African Literature Bureau, 1972.

——. *The Third World Writer: His Social Responsibility*. Nairobi: Kenya Literature Bureau, 1978.

Ngubiah, S. N. *A Curse from God*. Nairobi: East African Literature Bureau, 1970.

Ngũgĩ wa Thiong'o [James Ngugi]. *Detained: A Writer's Prison Diary*. London: Heinemann, 1981.

——. *Devil on the Cross*. London: Heinemann, 1982.

——. *A Grain of Wheat*. London: Heinemann, 1967.

——. *Homecoming: Essays on African and Caribbean Literature, Culture and Politics*. London: Heinemann, 1972.

——. *I Will Marry When I Want (Ngahika Ndeenda)*. London: Heinemann, 1982.

——. *Matigari*. London: Heinemann, 1987.

———. *Moving the Centre*. Portsmouth, New Hampshire: Heinemann, 1993.

———. *Petals of Blood*. London: Heinemann, 1977.

———. *The River Between*. London: Heinemann, 1965.

———. *Secret Lives*. London: Heinemann, 1976.

———. *The Trial of Dedan Kimathi* (with Micere Githae Mugo). London: Heinemann, 1976.

———. *Weep Not, Child*. London: Heinemann, 1964.

———. *Writers in Politics*. London: Heinemann, 1981.

Nguya, Lydiah Mumbi. *The First Seed*. Kampala: East African Literature Bureau, 1975.

Ng'weno, Hilary. *The Men from Pretoria*. Nairobi: Longman Kenya, 1975.

Njau, Rebeka. *Ripples in the Pool*. Nairobi: Transafrica, 1975; Heinemann, 1978.

Nyabongo, H. H. Prince Akiki K. *The Story of an African Chief*. New York: Scribner, 1935. Republished as *Africa Answers Back*. London: Routledge, 1936.

Oculi, Okello. *Orphan*. Nairobi: East African Publishing House, 1968.

———. *Prostitute*. Nairobi: East African Publishing House, 1968.

Ogot, Grace. *The Graduate*. Nairobi: Uzima Press, 1980.

———. *The Island of Tears*. Nairobi: Uzima Press, 1980.

———. *Land without Thunder*. Nairobi: East African Publishing House, 1968.

———. *The Other Woman*. Nairobi: Transafrica, 1976.

———. *The Promised Land*. Nairobi: East African Publishing House, 1966.

Okello, John. *Revolution in Zanzibar*. Nairobi: East African Publishing House, 1967.

Onyango-Abuje, J. C. *Fire and Vengeance*. Nairobi: East African Publishing House, 1975.

Osinya, Alumidi [pseud.]. *Field Marshall Abdulla Salim Fisi; or, How the Hyena Got His!* Nairobi: Joe, Transafrica, 1976.

Palangyo, Peter K. *Dying in the Sun*. London: Heinemann, 1968.

Ruheni, Mwangi. *The Future Leaders*. London: Heinemann, 1973.

———. *The Minister's Daughter*. Nairobi: Heinemann, 1975.

———. *What a Husband!* Nairobi: Longman, 1973.

———. *What a Life!* Nairobi: Longman, 1972.

Ruhumbika, Gabriel. *Village in Uhuru*. London: Longman, 1969.

Seruma, Eneriko [Henry Kimbugwe]. *The Experience*. Nairobi: East African Publishing House, 1970.

———. *The Heart Seller*. Nairobi: East African Publishing House, 1971.

Serumaga, Robert. *Return to the Shadows*. London: Heinemann, 1969.

Shivji, Issa G. *Law, State and the Working Class in Tanzania, c. 1920–1964*. London: Currey, 1986.

Tejani, Bahadur. *Day after Tomorrow*. Nairobi: East African Literature Bureau, 1971.

Tumusiime-Rushedge. *The Bull's Horn*. Nairobi: Oxford University Press, 1972.

Wachira, Godwin. *Ordeal in the Forest*. Nairobi: East African Publishing House, 1968.

Waciuma, Charity [pseud.]. *Daughter of Mumbi*. Nairobi: East African Publishing House, 1969.

———. *Mweru the Ostrich Girl*. Nairobi: East African Publishing House, 1966.

Wanjala, Chris. *The Season of Harvest: Some Notes on East African Literature*. Nairobi: Kenya Literature Bureau, 1978.

Watene, Kenneth. *Sunset on the Manyatta*. Nairobi: East African Publishing House, 1974.

Wegesa, Benjamin S. *Captured by Raiders*. Nairobi: East African Publishing House, 1969.

Were, Miriam K. *The Boy in Between*. Nairobi: Oxford University Press, 1969.

———. *The Eighth Wife*. Nairobi: East African Publishing House, 1972.

———. *The High School Gent*. Nairobi: Oxford University Press, 1972.

———. *Your Heart Is My Altar*. Nairobi: East African Publishing House, 1980.

3 English-Language Fiction

from South Africa

JOHN F. POVEY

The history of South African literature contains several strands, beginning with the English and Afrikaans settler traditions, which should be recognized for their influence on more recent work. Alongside those strands, an extensive and significant African literature, originally oral, has developed as well, including works both in several of the indigenous languages and, more recently, in an English aimed at the growing educated urban readership.

The Early Works

The earliest South African written literature was connected with British colonization and is comparable with similar literature that emerged from other so-called Old Dominions. As in Canada and Australia, nineteenth-century British immigrants to South Africa, beginning with the 1820 settlers, began to force an identifiable and original voice in response to their new environment. At first they merely appended a description of the newly encountered topography to their residual but deep-seated British cultural inheritance. Later, decades of geographic separation necessitated the expression of a local viewpoint, from which emerged a recognizable national ethos and attendant literature.

In South Africa, Dutch settlements predated British colonization by more than one and a half centuries. While fervently retaining their individuality as a separate people, these Afrikaaners failed to develop even a minor literature, partly because of their migrant lifestyle and more certainly because of their religious beliefs, which proclaimed the Bible as virtually the sole acceptable reading matter. Only in the last forty years has there been Afrikaans writing vigorous and independent enough to achieve international consequence.

Publication in South African languages—especially Sotho and Zulu—is unexpectedly extensive, for elsewhere on the continent, where oral forms predominate, printing (other than biblical translation) generally began with the adoption of a European language. One innovative novel in Sotho,

Thomas Mofolo's *Chaka* (1925), has received justifiable critical acclaim as a historical tragedy. Unlike most of these African-language books, *Chaka* transcends the restrictions imposed by the missionary-controlled presses, whose authors, to be published, needed to adopt the requisite moral and educational tone.

Literature in African languages is treated in depth elsewhere in this volume (chapters 10 and 12). The emphasis of this chapter is on English-language writing from South Africa of the last forty years. To see this writing in perspective, it is necessary first to have some awareness of the historical British tradition, which provides antecedents and influences all contemporary writing in South Africa, even that recently produced by Africans.

The first British South African work of major caliber was Olive Schreiner's *Story of an African Farm* (1883). In her introduction to a recent paperback reprint, Doris Lessing describes how central this work was to the awakening of her own national cultural awareness. The novel powerfully conveys the awesome violence that the South African veld inflicts on its white farmers. Ironically, it ignores African inhabitants, seeming to find them merely one aspect of the landscape. This attitude allows Schreiner to make South Africa itself the central aspect of her tale. Her descriptions are visibly those of the resident, not the immigrant, and a good deal of subsequent writing—the work of Pauline Smith, for example—draws on her perceptions.

A New Uniqueness

At this early stage, there was little difference between the emerging patterns of South African writing and Australian writing, but already by the 1920s the uniqueness of the South African situation was becoming evident. Writers began to reflect on the central problem that continues to suffuse all subsequent writing: the issue of race. Sarah Gertrude Millin's popular *God's Step Children* (1924) was original for addressing the problem of the "colored" people of the country, if in a somewhat sentimental and patronizing tone. A more sophisticated and penetrating early statement was made in William Plomer's *Turbott Wolfe* (1925), which was found to be most prescient and relevant when it was republished in 1965. Plomer's merciless condemnation of white arrogance, his sympathy for Africans, and his understanding depiction of miscegenation caused an outcry, and Plomer became one of the first writers driven to exile by antagonistic racist public reaction.

In spite of such relatively early criticism of the racial situation, it was not until after World War II, fought with an idealism that found colonialism intolerable, that South Africa, resistant to the winds of change, became recognized as a reactionary bastion of racism and was universally condemned by world opinion. The book that best expressed this new mood of moral concern was the impassioned novel by Alan Paton, *Cry, the Beloved Country* (1948). Perhaps nowadays one may find its tone too sentimental, its compassion too paternalistic, its solution too naively optimistic. Many also find Paton's sonorous biblical style excessively rhetorical, particularly when it seeks to emulate in English the cadences of Zulu speech. It is interesting to learn Mbulelo Mzamane's opinion of a version translated into Zulu by Cyril Sibusiso Nyembezi: it "exceeds the original since it doesn't have to strain for an appropriate register for African characters, something that makes the dialogue in the English version so stilted" (Mzamane, *Mzala* x).

Paton himself has written elsewhere with more penetrating urgency. The far harsher *Too Late the Phalerope* (1953) avoids the earlier novel's condescension of tone and excess of style. But the theme of *Cry, the Beloved Country* remains worthy. One should not too casually dismiss Paton's plea for Christian understanding and compassion, nor scorn the earnest sympathy in which he delineates the quandary of the liberal conscience affronted by his society. Only more recent events have made it seem a less than adequate response. The influence achieved by its fame has made it not a negligible book. It may prove, like *Uncle Tom's Cabin*, a book that exerts a profound impact out of all proportion to its historical accuracy or its literary quality, a novel, for all its visible limitations, capable of moving a mass audience to active concern. Even now it may be the only South African work known to other than a specialized readership.

That Paton's optimistic mood of idealized racial reconciliation was not solely confined to white writers is proved by the plot of Peter Abrahams's *Mine Boy* (1946), the first "nonwhite" novel to reach an international audience. Though written from the other side of the color bar, it takes a similar philosophical stance in suggesting that racial problems are as much moral as political issues, and that personal goodwill can heal a divided society. The plot has become familiar and has been characterized by Nadine Gordimer as the "countryman-comes-to-town" story (*Black Interpreters* 29). Xuma, an innocent and honorable African, comes to Johannesburg to work in the mines. Though honest and hardworking to the point of nobility, he experiences the hardships that the system imposes on those who live in the segregated slums. He also encounters decent and dedicated people of all races who challenge the regime by refusing to follow racist codes of behavior. The conclusion, where the white miner abandons his own group to support the Black strikers, may seem too much like Paton's expectations, optimistic and sentimental, but at the time it had some legitimate plausibility.

The change of attitude that the years of continuing oppression have caused can be seen in the contrast in a later Abrahams book, written while in exile, entitled *A Night of Their Own* (1965). It is little more than a crude adventure story interrupted with political harangues. Its plot replaces the solution to racism through Christian tolerance with more belligerent events—for example, a mysterious submarine landing an armed guerrilla on the coast—that bring sabotage to the country. Abrahams's implicit assertion provides that violence, not tolerance, is now the inevitable means of change.

Paton's attitudes are carried forward in the novels of other white writers who share the historical inheritance but retain little of his sublime optimism. Dan Jacobson and Jack Cope exhibit an increasing pessimism and anxiety as the long dream of justice and understanding proves an inadequate response to the racial intolerance and the penal political circumstance they see about them. Their several novels present different situations, but they all dwell upon the impossibility of achieving any personal or political equality given the mode of life they are forced to live. Their despair generates a cynicism that undermines even potential means to achieve their long-sought ends.

Jacobson's *Evidence of Love* (1960) describes a London group, dedicated as the Free African Society, that can achieve nothing, being a base for incompetent white fatuity and Black manipulations. Its members are "free thinking Jews and devout Anglicans in the usual admixture among the whites, and earnest students and untrustworthy politicians in the usual admixture among the blacks" (Jacobsen 172). The novel tells of a colored man and a white woman who find that they can discover a nonracial humanity in exile but feel morally obligated to return to South Africa and to inevitable persecution and jail. They come back "because we are South Africans." That is a stigma of birth that exile cannot cure. Their return is a useless but heroic gesture-making, better than absence; it is "evidence of love" for country as much as each other. Their solution is pointless and romantic and yet tragically profound.

The title of Jack Cope's *The Dawn Came Twice* (1969) is ironic, because in this novel no illumination comes, unless death be considered an enlightenment. In its place is constant moral conflict, of a young white man torn between his inbred sense of moderation and the obligation to become a terrorist to advance the cause in which he believes, and of the woman who tries to abandon her rich and privileged upbringing to join the freedom struggle. They desire to find a basis for personal tenderness, yet they pursue violence. That may be a necessity, but it destroys the decency and hope that are their declared ends in a country "where there is no place for justice or love or hope," not ultimately for those who may wish to serve those ends. The final dismissal of these two white ideals is made in this exchange:

> "Well, I want people to accept freedom. I want them to accept good as a motive in life."
> "That sounds fine but it's all shit." (Cope 70)

Contrasting Attitudes

WHITE VOICES

The problem for the South African novel, if the conclusion of Cope's novel is accepted as reasonable, is that the moral qualities that mark human experience elsewhere are in this country rendered worthless and impossible and therefore can sustain neither the society nor its literature. A violent pessimism rules, one that justifies a writing based on anger and revolt. Since the 1960s, when the expression of a liberal optimistic sensibility became blighted by political extremism, the development of white and Black writing demonstrably diverged. The discrepancy is not simply one of different beliefs. Honorably enough, there is no South African equivalent of those Soviet authors who gained reputation and rewards for reverently following the party line. No defenders of this regime exist outside of parliament, no national bard sings to commend apartheid.

All South African writers of consequence and conscience condemn the absurd and malevolent policies under which they live. But recognizable variations mark their attitudes and approaches. The white writers' indignation and shame derives from an intellectual rather than a visceral assessment. They have to recognize that their privileged existence plays its part in the maintenance of apartheid, and they cannot abdicate the elitist status their skin color awards. Not only are Black persons more closely tied to the suffering and brutality of daily events, but they remain permanently committed by their race, whereas white support of political activism can be withdrawn at will. No matter how dedicated to social reform honest, concerned whites may be, they remain to some degree outsiders in the struggle, whether they present a sympathetic or antagonistic face toward the essential reformation.

Authorial expectations and assumptions, consequent upon this inevitable distinction, are clearly observed in the contrasting tones and styles of writers of the different races. White writers, determined to scarify an intolerable regime, brilliantly employ a range of subtle devices that allow them to explore with fearsome sarcasm the metaphysical absurdity of the system and the inconceivable crimes it generates. Black writers speak more directly, preferring to oblique reference an exact and pungent description of the atrocities that make up the daily circumstances of their lives. This distinction is more than technical, since it touches on a very arguable issue in conveying reality: what is the function of artistic construct and what is the appropriate formal stance of a writer in times of political oppression? Blacks sometimes express scorn at formal technique, dismissing skillful devices as artificial, even frivolous in a situation that to them requires only vehement condemnation. White writers consider that literary technique in itself is part of the means by which they forge their moral stance and guide readers to a deeper comprehension of the situation.

Undoubtedly, the finest white South African writer is Nadine Gordimer, whose brilliant short stories and powerful novels surgically expose the bizarre attitudes and behavior that become manners of survival in so repugnant a system. With exquisite penetration she exposes the raw vulgarity of racial prejudice. With even more acute wit she strips away the pretensions and posturings that mark the self-satisfied liberals, finding them more self-deluding than self-aware. She perceives their assertions of sympathetic comprehension acting only as a mask, which often slips to expose the unconsidered racism of their instinctive and inherited responses.

In her earlier works, no matter how incisively she writes, there appears to be almost an element of satire. This may not be entirely a literary contrivance. Local behavior, merely scrupulously observed and accurately reported, often seems to merit the accusation of being as much ludicrous as wicked. But as South African conditions became more bleak she jettisoned this characteristic tone, and her later novels, *The Conservationist* (1974), *Burgher's Daughter* (1979), and *July's People* (1981), have taken on a far darker texture, as if confronting the imminence of Armageddon. In *July's People* a wealthy Johannesburg family, living in the immediate future, fears the increasingly reactionary urban violence. They seek safety in the village of their longtime servant, July. Here they are shocked to encounter the daily privations that have been July's lifelong norm. Gradually they fall under the dominance of the African way of life. The ending brings the landing of an unidentified helicopter. One does not learn whether it brings conquering guerillas to round up white escapees or victorious government troops to reinstate white authority. Such is the emotional power of the book that neither ending brings comfort nor the resolution of the moral conflict propounded. The family has lost any sense of the legitimacy of their elitist status, but the future can provide no encouraging alternative, whichever way the temporary military and political impasse is resolved.

Recently, J. M. Coetzee, a writer of extraordinary and disturbing power, has extended Gordimer's increasingly apocalyptic vision into the presentation of a surreal nightmare of violence. *Waiting for the Barbarians* (1980) has received the most attention. It has a disturbing mixture of tone, in which atrocious cruelties are described with horrendous realism and then carried beyond realism into hallucinatory dreams akin to madness. The novel, like Conrad's *Heart of Darkness*, makes clear that the boundless horrors inflicted derive not from Africa but from the vile recesses of the human heart, justified by debased principles. As Nadine Gordimer correctly observes, Coetzee writes "with an imagination that soars like a lark and sees from up there like an eagle" ("Idea" 3). She could also be describing the effect of her own masterly works.

The stylistic switch from intolerable reality into symbolic statement constitutes one of the means by which whites seek to engineer some literary mode that will prove capable of expressing the moral horrors among which they live. They require this more complex intellectual and psychological interpretation to comprehend their world and achieve some measure of sanity. African writers assume that the very description of the realities that they regularly encounter provides the kind of moral judgment that whites reach after much more convoluted analysis.

By about 1970, the increasing degeneration of the political situation finally brought forth condemnation from several Afrikaaner writers who for the first time exhibited an urgent, liberal conscience not commonly associated with their kind. To the dismay of the bigoted orthodox Afrikaaner, condemnation of the regime began to be heard, not from the hated British, whose national loyalties had always been suspect, but from renegades who employed the revered Afrikaans language previously used only to sanctify religious identity and racial purity. The all-powerful censorship board was appalled to discover the disturbing necessity of banning works written in Afrikaans, an unthinkable extension of the harsh authority they had so widely exerted to render English-language literature free of dangerous taint.

The most influential and provocative Afrikaan writers banded together to form the "sixties" or "sestiger" group. It included André Brink, Etienne Leroux, Jan Rabie, and Breyten Breytenbach, whose *Confessions of an Albino Terrorist* (1985) describes his own imprisonment under the Terrorist Act. André Brink is the member of this group who has achieved the greatest international recognition, partly because he translates his own work into English, a language that appeals to other than a parochial local readership. In his judgment, the cruelty of the present system does not derive from recent legislation but has its origins in the broader context of Afrikaaner nationalism and its assertion of the eternal and irresistible superiority of the "volk."

Refusing to take shelter behind Paton's generalized compassion or Gordimer's protective irony, Brink insists in his indicatively titled *Looking on Darkness* (1974) that "nothing in this novel has been invented." For his plots he draws on past history rather than present experience, but that history becomes a kind of metaphor for the more immediate disaster. His unforgiving and apparently true story describes a crescendo of white savagery culminating in a shameless execution. Brink recognizes that savagery as his own inheritance. His theme condemns his people through a truthful reexamination of the history that had been propagated to justify their destiny.

BLACK VOICES

Parallel to these developments in white writing grew a vigorous Black writing that expressed the African perception of events and inevitably gave challenge to the regime under which they were forced to live. An early influential work was Ezekiel Mphahlele's *Down Second Avenue* (1959). Like much African writing—for example, Peter Abrahams's *Tell Freedom* (1954), Bloke Modisane's *Blame Me on History* (1963), and Alfred Hutchison's *Road to Ghana* (1960)—Mphahlele's book is autobiographical. It draws on the young boy's experience as he was brought up by a kindly aunt in the Black section of Pretoria. Despite hardships and oppression, the book displays a tolerant and affectionate tone, recognizing that even in the harshest conditions for children there are always times of happiness, and that to deny this is political posturing. It is this evenhanded tone that gives Mphahlele's writing a strength and honesty that escapes those who vehemently stress only the intolerable elements of experience. His is the writing of a humanist rather than a polemicist.

Mphahlele began his writing career as a journalist for the legendary *Drum*. The magazine continues to exist, but is now a slick commercial production, far from the bright, inventive periodical initially aimed at a new audience: the Black urban population. Socially committed and yet lively and popular, *Drum* boasted columnists who can be considered primarily responsible for the development of a new South African writing: Henry Nxumalo, Can Themba, Todd Matshikaza, Nat Nkasa, Bloke Modisane. They exploited the new market with investigative journalism and descriptions of life seen from the African point of view.

A *Drum* "Hall of Fame" included in the anthology *Reconstruction*, edited by Mothobi Mutloatse, reprints some of the more renowned articles, among them, Henry Nxumalo's "The Story of Bethel," a shocking exposé of the exploitation of prison labor on the farms, and Can Themba's "Dinokana: The Target," which describes the women's revolt against carrying the abhorred passbooks. Todd Matshikaza's lively description is recalled in his "We Invented 'Majuba' Jazz." These are typical examples of the material that sustained this widely read magazine, topical, cheerful, familiar, but closely identifying with the concerns of a growing literate proletariat. A characteristic example, blending wry humor and bitter anger, comes from the professional hand of Mphahlele, writing an editorial column under the pseudonym of Bandi Mvovo. He describes one of those situations incomprehensible to the outsider and yet commonplace in South Africa, where prejudice leads inevitably to the most absurd contrivances. A white lady is explaining to her tea-time guest that she cannot allow her servant to use her toilet because "natives are so dirty." When the maid brings in the tea, the guest questions the convolutions of the racial situation: "If she is so filthy that she can't use your toilet—how do you drink her tea? I don't think I'll wait for it, thank you" (Mutloatse, *Reconstruction* 179).

The Short Story

THE FIRST GENERATION OF WRITERS

Perhaps it is because of the importance of *Drum*'s influence that a review of the last thirty years of Black South African writing shows clearly that the most popular genre is the short story. Some argue that this preference derives from the pressure of external threats, which prevented people from committing themselves to elongated composition. That theory does little justice to other writers who in far worse circumstances have created extended masterpieces. Rather, the short story fits the present intention of Black South African writing. Its anecdotal form allows authors to draw directly from their experiences and present the social environment to a wider world. It also bridges the gap between true autobiography and quasifictional events. Mbulelo Mzamane, with deliberate overmodesty, suggests that in his case "the short story is a genre most suited to my prosaic mind, without making the kinds of demands (in terms of self-discipline, concentration and sustained effort) which the novel form makes on the writer" (*Mzala* viii). More important than this objection to the hardship of expansion is the recognition that reality and art blend most readily in the short story, which—consider even the tales of Somerset Maugham—always contains an element of reportage and factual incident. In a reversal of the usual authorial denials, Mzamane prefaces his collection with the determination "to make it categorically clear, that all the 'characters' in these stories are actually based on people I know . . . I claim absolutely nothing for myself" (*Mzala* xii).

Ezekiel Mphahlele in the mid-1950s developed a natural and personal style that combined the immediacy of *Drum* with the formal literary style found in international short stories. With this technical combination he wrote a series of stories that explored the subjects and form that were later to become common, and anticipated the many vigorous writers who were later to draw on his initial efforts.

Mphahlele's characters carry out a day-to-day existence in the midst of violence, both mental and physical, and in spite of strife and various forms of official persecution. When employed as servants, his people are forced to interact not only with snobbish racists but also with vigorously involved activists, whites like the title character in "Mrs. Plum," who "loved dogs and Africans and said that everyone must follow the law even if it hurt" (*The Unbroken Song* 216). Her affectation of tolerance does not survive the rumor that Africans may murder her vicious dogs, nor the discovery that her daughter wishes to marry one of the Africans she so generously and nobly invited to the house. She asks her servant, "Tell me, Karabo, what do you people think of this kind of thing between a white woman and a black man? It cannot be right is it?" Believing that "what I think about it is my business," the maid's mental response is pragmatic rather than political. "I said to myself, I say these white women, why do not they love their own men and leave us to love ours!" (236–37).

In spite of racial strains, a strange intimacy develops. After the servant is dismissed, Mrs. Plum feels compelled to drive to her village and beg her to return, even accepting her insistent demands for higher wages and longer holidays. Clearly the relationship has become not that of mistress and servant, nor even that of racial equals, but a kind of inescapable and intense symbiosis. This intimate connection suggests a significant and often-ignored element in the complex interrelationships that dominate the South African situation. The inevitability of the mutuality makes for circumstances very different from the white-Black divisions of Kenya, where a transient elite profit from a period of residence while reserving their most specific allegiance for elsewhere. Most whites and Blacks in South Africa recognize the unavoidable continuance of close association.

The Johannesburg scene seemed to dominate publications until Richard Rive, himself a distinguished writer, edited a timely and important anthology of short stories, *Quartet* (1963), which presented to a wide audience four new Cape Town writers: Rive himself, James Matthews, Alex La Guma, and Alf Wannenburgh. Rive's own much-anthologized contribution includes "The Bench," which describes a weary African's refusal to move off a "whites only" seat when commanded by railway officials. By his skill Rive takes a common enough, even minor, incident and extends its consequences beyond reportage into political evidence.

James Matthews draws his stories directly from experience, often to the degree that they become virtual anecdote or journalism. But they exert a powerful effect for just that reason. They have a precise sense of context and a striking immediacy in their record of the hard days when the misery of poverty spills out into active grievance. His most famous tale, "The Park," also provides the title of his collected stories. Denied access to amenities provided for white children, the young protagonist gazes wrathfully through the railings that both actually and metaphorically enforce the racial separation. His resentment explodes into a cosmic anger caused by his deprivation, directed not at the whites who cause his misery but at the environment it forces on him. "Rage boiled up inside him. Rage against the house with streaked walls and smashed panes, filled by too many people; against the overflowing garbage pails outside the doors, the alleys and streets; and against a law he could not understand . . ." (Matthews 206). Only at the end is causation hinted at, and even then it seems unbelievable that the consequences should be so grim. The boy's rage exposes his impotence and he bursts into tears, only to suffer the unsympathetic jeers of his friends who prefer a small victory over him to sharing his bitter alienation. "Cry baby!" they shout, and in self-defense the boy is forced to deny his entirely legitimate reaction. "Who say I cry? Something in my eye and I rub it." In this way matters of conscience remain private, their public admission impossible.

In "The Party" Matthews satirizes the pretenses of white liberals by describing an attempt to socialize between races. The party is hosted so that white intellectuals can meet Black artists and implicitly patronize them in both senses of the word. The gesture allows them a warm glow of generosity as evidence of their particular sympathy and understanding. Matthews views the event more harshly, condemning both the hostess and Ron, the African intermediary, for putting Africans' talents "on display like virgins to be sold to those like her and Ron was their pimp" (Matthews 128). When the protagonist mischievously pretends he neither writes nor sculpts but works as an office messenger, he is immediately denounced and evicted. Who would want to waste the gesture of goodwill on an untalented common worker? By such satires Matthews describes the impossibility of links across the race barrier under present circumstances. The two different worlds cannot impinge on any level of equality.

"The Party" is one of the rare stories that cross the color line. Nadine Gordimer has also attempted this double vision. Many hold the opinion that an author's own color determines the accuracy of character portrayal, claiming that both sides tend to be less accurate, less aware when they depict the other race. This shortcoming would be understandable in so divided a society, though the imagination of great writers can compound all worlds. It is indicative that within Matthews's story a white admirer, intending to expose only her respectful admiration on encountering the African author, is made to remark, "I always thought that those stories were not written by white writers. They were too authentic, too close to the subject . . . you know what I mean" (Matthews 182).

There is a general truth in her observation: used as a means of characterizing the foolish speaker, at the same time, taken in itself, it makes a critical statement concerning African short story writing and the broader issue of the relationship between literary quality and authenticity. It is not necessarily unqualified praise to observe that as artists some Africans do get "too close to their subject." Equally, it is hard to see how, given their present lives, detachment can be seen as a practical alternative for South African writers.

Like Matthews, La Guma draws on his experience in the "colored" section of Cape Town, the legendary District Six. But he is sometimes more skillful than Matthews in deriving profounder moral judgments from the events he describes. His plots demonstrate his instinctive recognition of an acute danger that confronts the African writer. When good and evil are so clearly ranged within the society, it is easy to make characters equally extreme, to make suffering Africans represent all the virtues and whites unmitigated evil. There are understandable personal reasons for such an attitude, but it does not allow the subtle examination of the complexities that motivate human actions, which is central to major literature.

La Guma impressively avoids such a simplistic dichotomy in his novella *A Walk in the Night* (1962). This work describes the brutal circumstances of slum living: the arrogance of the bosses, the sadism of corrupt policemen, and the dehumanizing quality of poverty-induced despair. Yet La Guma makes his plot prove a far deeper and in some ways a more painful truth than the obvious injustice of oppression: that the human capacity for violence when stirred by misery can take directions that serve no purpose or reveal only iconoclastic ferocity.

La Guma's protagonist, Michael Adonis, commits a murder, not to assert any heroic cause of racial justice, but in a moment of uncalculated drunken resentment. His anger explodes, not against the cruel police, but against someone who, if technically white, is in every way more broken and impoverished by the system than Michael is. As his victim protests when attacked for the elitist rank of his color, "Here I am in shit street and does my white help?" As if this irony were not sufficient, in La Guma's conclusion the police shoot and arrest for Adonis's crime a completely innocent character, who in turn seems not the least surprised by such injustice, having suffered during his entire youth equivalent cruelties from his own father.

The tone of such a conclusion, where not a hint of poetic justice is represented or expected, does not permit any easy political attitudinizing about the system, yet obviously La Guma is urgently aware of the underlying causes. His condemnation is the more profound because it exposes the ideology of a system that prevents all normal standards of morality from operating. La Guma's sequence of harsh and ultimately irrational injustices is no more absurd and improbable than those continuing, persistent injustices that are the very substance of his society. La Guma says nothing more than that in a depraved world mad things happen.

THE SECOND GENERATION OF WRITERS

With their individual skills, the first generation of Black short story writers established accepted models, which accelerated the development of a contemporary Black South African literature. Newer writers such as Mbulelo Mzamane had the historical advantage of being able to draw on the works of those pioneers. Mzamane realized that censorship robbed him of access to several proscribed authors, but the early works of R. R. R. Dhlomo and Ezekiel Mphahlele were available to build upon. Similarly, La Guma, Rive, and Matthews "all captured my imagination in a way no other group of writers had done before . . . the literature that had the greatest impact on me stylistically and theatrically, was what I read in *Classic*" (Mzamane, *Mzala* ix).

Classic (inaugurated in 1963) was a vital transitional publication, which is still existent in a much modified form. More self-consciously literary than *Drum,* it provided an early and vital outlet for the publication of contemporary writing by South Africans of all races—a desirable policy of integration rarely maintained subsequently on either side of the color bar. By making African writers adapt to the expectations of more formal publication and by imposing literary standards more openly, *Classic* directed individual experiments into channels that were to become more clearly part of the overall development of a significant modern South African literature.

Typical of this next generation of short story writers is Mothobi Mutloatse. In *Mama Ndiyalila: Stories* (1982) he makes the familiar denunciation of racist restrictions, but more original is his protagonist observer, Mada Yeke, a schoolgirl who witnesses and rejects her father's habitual and docile acceptance of the existing regime. His assumption that one can best seek survival within the limited opportunities that regime permits provokes the girl into outright criticism that would be unforgivable in the traditional family. As a representative of a more aware and educated generation, she condemns as delusion her parents' belief that if only they display surface cooperation their lives will be made easy and they will achieve some acceptable measure of success. Her words presage the motivation of the present township violence and give evidence of the generational change and heightened expectations that occasion it. Rhetorically she proclaims her dissatisfaction: "How long have we appealed to them to do their duty as parents and make their voices known? It would seem as if our parents are refusing to defend the right of their own flesh and blood" (Mutloatse, *Mama* 12). Her vigorous spirit soon moves other young people to join her vehement attack. They have none of the fears of their parents. As Mada Yeke wryly remarks, "Havenotians are not easily intimidated."

Mzamane's story collection *Mzala* (1983) is a remarkable example of the adoption of a tradition. He takes the familiar theme of the country boy coming to Jo'burg and extends it into a very up-to-date mode. There is none of the earlier naïveté and admiring innocence in his story "Jim." Mzal'u Jola from his first arrival in the city becomes a slick operator, adapting his wits to the agreeable process of hoodwinking all the people he encounters. He is a jaunty, amoral creature living happily by his own measures of achievement, which go considerably beyond any satisfaction with drab survival. Such a bold, extravagant character, displayed at the same time as both amusing and dangerous, is a development of authorial sophistication within the context of the common township environment. The author's tone is satiric, balancing dismay and admiration at such provocative posturing.

A curiosity of Mzamane's writing is his contrast between a highly realistic setting and an occasional use of very formalized language. Not for him the regular use of township argot that marks the dialogue embraced by many similar writers as an evidence of realistic legitimacy. He describes a lecherous relative as follows: "Devouring like some omnivorous beast, ready to co-habit with any woman who crosses his path, his behavior has been as unjust to his victims as it has been degrading to my family" (Mzamane, *Mzala* 14).

Yet Mzamane's striking and perceptive tales, simultaneously bitter and comic, fix the experience of the Black urban areas. "The Soweto Bride" is a sarcastic description of an African bringing home his conceited Black American wife, who is appalled by local custom. The story is a masterpiece of accurate reportage and deliberate irony. "To me the 'back to Africa call' would always remain a black American myth" (Mzamane, *Mzala* 141). In what seems little more than a casual aside, Mzamane tosses the relationship between Africans and African Americans a deadly dismissive shaft.

Njabulo Ndebele's collection *Fools* (1983), the winner of a Noma Award for Publishing in Africa, introduces a new element into the continuing development of the short story form. Like earlier authors, Ndebele draws upon the township experience, but because the writer has returned to South Africa with a master's degree from Cambridge and an American doctorate, he inevitably sees things somewhat more dispassionately and with a more literary control of circumstances. He deals with another stratum of township society: not the deprived unemployed, but those to be judged as successful, the upwardly mobile bourgeoisie. His characters are eagerly seeking more than survival; they strive for visible achievement within a system that allows a modest advantage to those who neither challenge the restricted opportunities it provides nor fret at the human inhibitions it imposes.

Ndebele's stories tell of the evolving Black middle class, whose acquired, secondhand values contrast with the vigorous defiance of the streets. In "The Music of the Violin," parents who have a daughter "started in ballet recently" and wish their son, Vukani, to learn to play Mozart on the violin, have less in common with the average Black than with whites inspired by similar expectations. For their cultural dedication Vukani suffers constant mockery from the street gangs, but his desperate appeals for release from his musical obligation achieves nothing. At one level he is assaulted with the common parental argument that what is, is. "A violin you have and a violin you will play" (Ndebele 141). At another level their determination exposes the clearest evidence of their profound conviction that it is only by those values certified by white arts, by ballet dancing and violin playing, that their social distinction will be made credible.

It consequently follows that only by repudiating indigenous values and Black attitudes will the family be able to free itself from their inherent sense that it is degrading to be associated with vulgar urban workers. Success is measured by a changed allegiance, by developing lifestyles that seem superior to the slum existence of neighbors. Their attitude, which relates achievement to snobbery, is common enough in many parts of the world. The difference in South Africa is that it requires a double rejection, one impossible, the other regrettable, of pigmentation and of tradition.

A bitter irony is suggested by the author but entirely unrecognized by the father, who asserts, "How difficult it is to bring a child up in Soweto" (Ndebele 150). So far there would be a total agreement, but he continues, "To give him a culture. African people just turn away from advancement." Many questionable layers of conviction are expressed in those lines. Why do Africans have to be "given" a culture when they have inherited a distinguished one? African advancement is not measured in the expectation of political change, since to some degree the parents benefit from the existing discrimination. Advancement is to be measured only against the yardstick of white expectation and white cultural values.

The platitudes advanced by the father are not so different from the unctuous phrases of government spokesmen. The father attacks a teacher who is not sufficiently uplifting the Black nation because "that fellow was just not teaching gardening and that is dead against government policy" (Ndebele 127). He complains about the racist system only when his own search for white values is challenged. He grieves against the "Boers," not so much because they apply oppressive legislation, but because they unsympathetically deny him his opportunity to escape from the blackness that both parties feel is a measure of inferiority. Boers tell Blacks that "Western civilization is spoiling us and so we have to cultivate the indigenous way of life" (Ndebele 143). The family fights such a threat, advertising their commitment to Western civilization by violin lessons and more openly by extravagant purchases of china. The mother gloats, "How many households in the whole of Johannesburg, white and black, can boast of such a set?" (Ndebele 145). It is a practice too depressing to be laughable.

Again and again Ndebele's title—*Fools*—echoes in the mind as his characters expose their self-delusion and their folly. There is the school principal who solemnly and without sarcasm after the assassination of Hendrik Verwoerd, a primary architect of apartheid, gives "an inspired eulogy" for "a man whose strength of mind and character stood before the world as a shining example of leadership" (Ndebele 126). Then there is the absurd reaction of an interviewer who proclaims, "Ordinary people have no problems. They don't make a nuisance of themselves . . . but you have to display your education" (Ndebele 270). Such an attitude is breathtaking in its ability to turn facts on their heads. The equation that education makes Blacks a nuisance is profoundly believed by the reactionaries in this society, not all of whom are white. Such blindness in the face of racism is extraordinary, but this principal has his eyes opened in a way that might be anticipated: he is given an unprovoked beating by a Boer thug. Only then, with the lacerations on his body, does he recognize the truth that he is confronting a people "whose sole gift to the world has been the perfection of hate . . . they will forever destroy, consuming us and themselves in a great fire" (Ndebele 276). It is a likely but despairing conclusion.

The Novel

Overall, the quality of Black South African novels has been less consistent, although there have been several impressive individual examples. An important early work, Richard Rive's *Emergency* (1964), takes as its factual basis the happenings that followed the massacre at Sharpeville in 1960 and the state of emergency declared by the government in an attempt to control subsequent unrest. By showing the effect of events on a series of fictional characters, Rive develops a structure that was to be commonly followed: an imaginative recreation of a historical situation. It is an extended example of the technique of the short story writers and exposes again the South African necessity to come to grips with actual experience within the context of creating fiction.

Understandably, jail is a common experience, since it is likely that the most sensitive and articulate people will attract the immediate attention of the government. An early example was La Guma's haunting and claustrophobic novel *The Stone Country* (1967). Moses Dlamanini has published "reminiscences" of a maximum-security prison, *Robben Island, Hell-Hole* (1983). D. M. Zwelonke's *Robben Island* (1973) painfully exposes the atrocities of this prison, where criminals and political activists serve together. This body of work has counterparts in a regrettably similar vein from several countries. The experience of the political prison is so familiar that its description has almost become a twentieth-century genre in itself. Wole Soyinka's denunciation in *The Man Died* (1972) of the indignities he suffered in a Nigerian jail is a powerful example from elsewhere in Africa, and one remembers that part of his indignation derives from his resentment that his incarceration was not happening in South Africa, where it should reasonably be expected, but in his own independent Nigeria.

Zwelonke's novel raises, in a most acute form, the problem for the South African writer of how to turn realistic narrative into art. Reality is so desperate that it may seem diminished by the fabrication of fiction. Zwelonke insists, "I had decided to bar my mouth from telling the story of the place. But I am going to write about it." He then argues the complexity of discriminating between factual truth and artistic truth. "For various reasons I have written it as a work of fiction. Fiction, but projecting a hard and bitter truth; fiction mirroring nonfiction, true incidents and episodes. The characters are all fictional, including in a sense myself" (Zwelonke 3). The last wry dismissal exposes the problem for the author/activist.

Zwelonke's assertion that he will attempt some aesthetic distancing through fictionalizing his subject has additionally to be set against the clear recognition that the events in the life of his fictional hero, Bekimpi, most precisely parallel the tragedy of Steve Biko's actual jail torture and murder. For that reason, it is not so much the construction of the novel that carries the deepest conviction as the undoubted realism of its incidents. The information Zwelonke records seems quite probable. Prisoners become aware of a fiery anti–South African speech in the United Nations only when they are immediately and additionally abused. Equally convincing, because it replicates Nazi history, is the observation that wardens tolerate crooks in a relatively friendly manner—they were familiar game. They hated and feared political prisoners because they perceived them as threatening to the entire social and prison system, and therefore to the self-confidence of the guards, by constituting "a new subject: self-disciplined, cool, not begging, not crouching, not expecting favours but always complaining his rights within the regulations" (Zwelonke 68).

In the brutal ending, Bekimpi is hanged upside down until he suffocates. The novel expresses an eternal verity of human nature when the regular army colonel, trained to some standards of martial gallantry, condemns the Special Branch inspector, saying, "This is your work." But he takes no action. Such Pontius Pilate evasions have a long history. Horror at excesses of brutality do not produce justice in South Africa any more than they have elsewhere. In this case, the power of color allegiance overrides a more general sense of human decency.

Two important novels have been written, indicatively, by distinguished poets: Sipho Sepamla's *A Ride on the Whirlwind* (1983) and Mongane Serote's *To Every Birth Its Blood* (1981). Sepamla's title sounds prescient, given subsequent South African events. His plot is a kind of political thriller, with the protagonist, Mzi, returning from revolutionary training abroad to advance the violent revolution. The novel emphasizes two major confrontations of political philosophy. Suspicion rather than collaboration arises between two generations of activists: the younger, represented by Mzi and Mandela, and the established resistance group, which finds these upstart student revolutionaries and their motives dubious, when their experience has been so limited. The second touches on the antagonism toward those Blacks who serve the white regime. Mzi is commanded to assassinate a Black policeman who has collaborated too enthusiastically with the regime and thus is seen as a "legalized terrorist."

After the successful bombing of the police station, the authorities angrily respond with all their power. As the Security Police colonel observes, "The death of Sergeant Ntloko is to be regretted, gentlemen . . . but we must all appreciate the damage done to the police station" (Sepamla 51). When one of the group is finally arrested, he is tortured not by the white police but by Batata, an African, who like all efficient torturers enjoys his role. Gleefully and absurdly he shouts amid the blows, "I am practising for power." With cynicism the guard supports him with the challenge: "Batata is a black man, he's just showed you what is meant by black power" (181).

This incident provides the new recognition that the color divisions accepted by earlier authors, that Blacks are good and whites are bad, are too simple to be applied with conviction. That admission goes far to explain the violence in the South African townships in the 1980s and 1990s, which seems directed less against whites than against Africans who sustain the regime by accepting positions of personal authority within the structure and who enjoy the power it permits them. Later historical developments, as so often, are anticipated by a writer's imaginative formulation.

Serote begins his novel, as most must, with his experience of ghetto township life: a world of "tins, broken bottles, bricks, dirty water running freely on the street . . . a dead cat or dog lying somewhere in the donga." It is a world where police "came on horseback, in fast cars, in huge trucks, and shot for real; they came in Saracens and with machine guns" (Serote 30). It is a world where Blacks battle police authority and whites yearn for exile because, by departure, "[t]hey would leave behind them all the bloody problems. Servants, nasty neighbors. Guilt of being white. Shit, the lot" (200).

Both sides, differently motivated, whether sympathetic or antagonist, confront the appalling recognition that violence is inescapable: "There was no way any other thing could be done with the present way of life, with this South Africa, with the South African way of life; there was nothing else that could be done to save it" (Serote 232). With an impassioned rhetoric approaching poetry, Serote mounts his indictment: "The country had gone mad. By 'country' I mean the government and those who protected it, those who lubricated it with money, wealth, oppression, violence and their lives. They had no choice but to go mad. We had no choice but to stop the madness, to achieve this" (344). The novel's conclusion juxtaposes the new headlines of "Daring Terror Attack" against a pregnant woman about to give birth who is commanded by her attendant to "push push push." These words, echoing in the hero's mind as he walks away, become a suggestive metaphor. In the last lines of the book the author has moved from toleration into challenging action. "Push push push" will painfully bring to birth the new society. The agony of parturition will be the same for a race as for a single mother.

To Sing or to Rage?

Straddling the corpus of writing from the early days of *Drum* to the present and emphasizing its continuity is Ezekiel Mphahlele, now choosing to write as Es'kia Mphahlele. He has become the senior spokesman of South African literature. His collection *The Unbroken Song* (1981) brings together the majority of his stories, most of them first printed in important but ephemeral publications. His title comes from a suggestive quotation from Vinoba Bhave: "Though action rages without, the heart can be tuned to produce unbroken music." This expression seems to apply at several levels to the consistent humanism of Mphahlele's own work: to the continuity of African literary self-expression and, more philosophically, to the vital question of the relationship between external event and creativity, which provides such a consistent division in the approach of the contemporary writer in South Africa.

It is Mphahlele who has best and most consistently attempted to explore the difficulties that this dilemma presents. Literature continues, as he beautifully expresses it, when "our players refuse to hang up their harps, because they daren't forget this lovely bleeding land, lest their tongues cleave to the roof of the mouth" (Mphahlele, *The Unbroken Song* viii). His idealism causes him to deplore above all the separation that racism imposes: "We keep on talking across the wall, singing our different songs, beating our different drums." Mphahlele, better than other writers and critics, perceives and articulates this dilemma, trying to balance the vicious input of experience against the means of its literary expression. He recognizes that the unbalanced impetus that the South African experience brings to local writing can be dynamic but can equally be destructive. He reports a dialogue that occurred some years ago as friends tried to dissuade him from the immediate necessity of exile:

> You've got all the material you want here, and the spur is always there. That's the trouble: it's a paralyzing spur; you must keep moving, writing at white heat everything full of vitriol hardly a moment to think of human beings as human beings and not as victims of political circumstance. . . . I'm sick of protest creative writing and our South African situation has become a terrible cliché as literary material. (Mphahlele, *Down Second Avenue* 199)

This dichotomy between the political and the aesthetic has dictated an attitude to South African authors, though few openly admit it for fear they might be deemed insufficiently committed to the cause of liberation. But for the true writer the dilemma is a real one. It affects all the writing produced under existing circumstances. Every creative writer believes in the necessity to devote his or her creativity to an examination of race relations in the country. This direction leads to propaganda rather than literature, but the necessity to continue to proclaim the injustice of apartheid and to demand a remedy must preoccupy a writer, though it need not in itself preclude a deeper and more general human statement.

South Africa is unique. As Nadine Gordimer observes in a tone almost of puzzlement, "It is an extraordinarily interesting society you never come to an end of discovering its strangeness. There's never a point where all that can be said has been said." There is a professional dispassion about this comment. The immediate fate of African writing is more likely to follow the outline suggested by D. M. Zwelonke in the introductory statement to *Robben Island*. It affirms the motivating belief of the Black South African writer, for in its lines the literary figure and the political activist have finally merged:

> My concept of fighting is not limited only to action on the battlefield. Fighting means making no surrender to irrationality, not abdicating from one's convictions even when chained to a tree at the point of a gun. (Zwelonke 2)

If all South African writers refuse to "surrender to irrationality," they will not only produce a significant literature but also make a vital contribution to the resolution of the divisions within their unhappy land.

Bibliography

Brink, André, and J. M. Coetzee, eds. *A Land Apart: A South African Reader.* London: Faber, 1986.

Brown, Godfrey N. *Apartheid: A Teacher's Guide.* Paris: UNESCO, 1981.

Cope, Jack. *The Dawn Came Twice.* London: Heinemann, 1977.

Daymond, J. M., J. U. Jacobs, and Margaret Lenta, eds. *Momentum on Recent South African Writing.* Pietermaritzburg: University of Natal Press, 1984.

Gordimer, Nadine. *The Black Interpreters: Notes on African Writing.* Johannesburg: SPRO-CAS/RAVAN, 1973.

―――. "The Idea of Gardening." *New York Review of Books,* 2 February 1984, pp. 3, 6.

Gray, Stephen. *Southern African Literatures: An Introduction.* New York: Barnes & Noble, 1979.

Heywood, Christopher. *Aspects of South African Literature.* London: Heinemann, 1976.

Jacobson, Dan. *Evidence of Love.* London: Weindenfeld & Nicholson, 1960.

Kunene, Daniel P. "Ideas under Arrest." *Research in African Literatures* 12, no. 4 (1988): 421–39.

La Guma, Alex, ed. *Apartheid: A Collection of Writings on South African Racism by South Africans.* New York: International Publishers, 1971.

Lapping, Brian. *Apartheid: A History.* London: Grafton, 1986.

Lonsdale, John. *South Africa in Question?* Cambridge: African Studies Centre, University of Cambridge; Portsmouth, N.H.: Heinemann, 1988.

Matthews, James. *The Park and Other Stories.* Athlone, South Africa: BLAC, 1974.

Motsoko, Pheko. *Apartheid: The Story of a Dispossessed People.* London: Marram Books, 1984.

Mphahlele, Es'kia [Ezekiel]. *Down Second Avenue.* Garden City, N.Y.: Doubleday, 1971.

―――. *The Unbroken Song.* Johannesburg: Ravan Press, 1981.

―――. *Voices in the Whirlwind.* New York: Hill & Wang, 1972.

Mutloatse, Mothobi. *Mama Ndiyalila.* Johannesburg: Ravan Press, 1982.

―――, ed. *Reconstruction: 90 Years of Black Historical Literature.* Johannesburg: Ravan, 1981.

Mzamane, Mbulelo. *Hungry Flames and Other Black South African Short Stories.* Harlow, Essex: Longman, 1986.

―――. *Mzala.* Johannesburg: Ravan Press, 1980.

Ndebele, Njabulo. *Fools and Other Stories.* Johannesburg: Ravan Press, 1983.

Ndlovu, Duma, ed. *Woza Africa: An Anthology of South African Plays.* New York: George Braziller, 1986.

Nkosi, Lewis. *Tasks and Masks.* Harlow, Essex: Longman, 1981.

Omer-Cooper, J. D. *A History of South Africa.* London: Heinemann, 1987.

Parker, Kenneth. *The South African Novel: Essays in Criticism and Society.* London: Macmillan, 1978.

Sepamla, Sipho Sidney. *A Ride on the Whirlwind.* Johannesburg: Ad. Danker, 1981.

Serote, Mongane. *To Every Birth Its Blood.* London: Heinemann, 1981.

Shava, Piniel Viriri. *A People's Voice: Black South African Writing in the Twentieth Century.* London: Zed, 1989.

Wauthier, Claude. *The Language and Thought of Modern Africa.* New York: Praeger, 1964.

Writers from South Africa: Fourteen Writers On Culture, Politics, and Literary Theory and Activity in South Africa Today. TriQuarterly Series on Criticism and Culture 2. Evanston, Ill.: TriQuarterly Books, 1989.

Zwelonke, D. M. *Robben Island.* London: Heinemann, 1973.

English-Language Poetry

THOMAS KNIPP

The composition and publication of Anglophone poetry in Black Africa has a long but disjointed history. In one form or another, poetry has been and is being written in English in all areas of the continent and has been composed for well over one hundred years. Because of these factors of time and space, it is useful to think of this poetry as having several interrelated regional "histories" and to consider its development in terms of generations. South African poetry, however, has developed under such different circumstances as to require its own unique historical approach, taken up in the last section of this essay.

The Pioneers

In the nineteenth century anglophone poetry was composed in places as widely separated as Sierra Leone and the Cape Colony. Most of this verse was religious. Hymns, hymn adaptations, and verse expressions of religious sentiment and moral instruction were encouraged by Christian missions and published by small mission presses and in ephemeral mission journals. Much of this material has been lost. What survives reveals an unsophisticated piety expressed in a prosody modeled on that of the Protestant hymnals. As the twentieth century progressed, these religious verses were augmented by expressions of racial pride and assertions of continental destiny. The piety, the pride, and the prosody are all illustrated in the following quatrain by a Ghanaian resident of Sierra Leone, Gladys Casely-Hayford (1904–50):

> Rejoice and shout with laughter
> Throw all your burdens down
> If God has been so gracious
> As to make you black or brown.
>
> (Nwoga 6)

Gladys May Casely-Hayford, daughter of Joseph E. Casely-Hayford, is one of a number of heterogeneous West African poets of the 1940s and early 1950s who have been called the "pioneer poets." They bring to a culmination the racial and religious themes of the earlier poetry and are a last expression of Protestant and Edwardian prosody. Because of the increase of both mission- and government-sponsored schools in the middle third of the twentieth century and increased access to university and professional training and the consequent formation of fairly extensive "elites," the generation of late pioneer poets is fairly numerous. Prominent in its numbers along with Casely-Hayford are Michael Dei-Anang of Ghana, Dennis Osadebay of Nigeria, Crispin George of Sierra Leone, and Roland Dempster of Liberia. Perhaps the most significant of them is the Ghanaian R. E. G. Armattoe.

Armattoe (1913–53) is more of a transitional figure than the other pioneers, closer in spirit to the ironists of the succeeding generation. In his two collections *Between the Forest and the Sea* (1950) and *Deep Down in the Black Man's Mind* (1954) he deals with the two dominant themes of modern Anglophone poetry: the meaning and uses of the African past and the nature and meaning of the modern African's life and experience. Often he does this in unworkable stanzas and rime schemes, but sometimes he is effective in simple unrhymed lines.

> I am not sure of anything here
> No known values hold, nothing certain
> Save uncertainty, nothing expected
> Save the unexpected.
>
> (Dathorne 155–56)

He takes the great themes of anglophone African poetry farther than any of his contemporaries, but he stops well short of his successors.

In *African Literature in the Twentieth Century* (1974), O. R. Dathorne said of the pioneer poets, "Their influence cannot be disregarded" (172). This is really not the case. They have proved to be not pioneers at all but rather the last inheritors of a dying tradition. The important poets of the following generations have learned not from them but from encounters—at Ibadan, Legon, and elsewhere—with the major English and American poets of the Euromodernist tradition and from their determined return to the forms and figures of African oral poetry.

West Africa

The break—the important alteration in tone and technique—between the poetry of the pioneers and that of the "moderns" who follow them coincides with a generational shift. Most of the pioneers were born between 1910 and 1920 and published their work in the 1940s and early 1950s. With the exception of Gabriel Okara, the poets of the first modern generation were born between 1926 and 1936. The major poets of this generation are Lenrie Peters of The Gambia, Kwesi Brew and Kofi Awoonor of Ghana, and Gabriel

Okara, Wole Soyinka, John Pepper Clark Bekederemo, and Christopher Okigbo of Nigeria. Of course, significant poetry was written by other members of this generation, including Ayitey Komey and Frank Kobina Parkes of Ghana and Michael Echeruo, Chinua Achebe, and Emmanuel Obiechina of Nigeria.

Sharing a particular moment in time, these poets share similar educational and political experiences as well. Educated in developing African institutions such as the University of Ibadan and the University of Ghana, they encountered the Anglo-American expression of the Euromodernist poetic tradition. They read Hopkins and Yeats, Eliot and Pound. Their early poetry, which began to appear in the late 1950s, is often imitative of those masters. The presence of Eliot is strongly felt in Okigbo's earliest lines, and some of Pepper Clark's early poems are inscapes in sprung rhythm in the manner of Hopkins. But one thing they learned from the Euromodernists is the efficacy, indeed, the primacy, of the individual voice. These poets learned, they did not imitate. As a result they developed individual, highly distinctive voices and styles. They arrived at their individuality through complex processes: by selecting and adapting Euromodernist techniques, by developing unique personae as responses to their experiences as men and as Africans, by interacting with—coming to terms with—Negritude, and above all, by working their way back to their own indigenous oral poetry.

However distinctive their voices, tropes, and techniques, they are nevertheless united thematically. They all write about the same things, the same two great, deep themes: the meaning of African history and the significance of their own experiences as modern Africans. These themes can best be explained as two intersecting myths. The first is a paradigm of African history, and the second might be called the psychological myth of the cyclical journey.

The historical paradigm is the conjugation of a long historical process consisting originally of five "tenses":

1. A rich traditional past that is both pastoral and romantic and is made up of both villages and empires

2. A ruthless European conquest against heroic resistance

3. A period of oppression and exploitation in which Black character was purified through suffering

4. A determined struggle for liberation culminating in triumphant independence

5. A returning glory to independent Africa.

This vision of the African past is, in effect, a kind of countermyth, a repudiation of the European myth of the dark continent to which Europeans were bringers of light. It provides African poets with a tropology and with a set of moral assumptions on the basis of which African experience can be interpreted.

The psychological myth casts the experience of the westernized African into the pattern of a cyclical journey. Born into the tradition of hearth and village, the African is pulled away in the disorienting world of the West. Through schools and universities and often extended periods of time spent in Western countries, he is transformed into a modern African. But in the process he finds himself rejected by the West while, at the same time, he learns to see—and then see through—its racism, imperialism, and material- ism. The cycle of this journey is completed as the altered African returns to an altered Africa, often to help in the attempt to build a meaningful future out of a usable past.

Much of the imagery of the modern Anglophone poets is derived from the historical myth. Africa is depicted in pastoral images of nature and nurture, symbolized often as a woman in tropes that are both maternal and erotic. The traditional past, figured by dance, drums, masks, and other artifacts, is both sustaining and creative. The Europeans who violate it are presented as birds of prey or other predators. The psychological myth often determines the character of the persona and its relation to historic Africa. Awoonor writes from Stoneybrook, New York, as an exile; Okigbo presents himself to Idoto as a prodigal; Okara wanders as the lonely African between the piano and the drum.

These myths are seen in their purest form in Léopold Senghor and David Diop, the Francophone poets of Negritude. Writing later, after a different set of political experiences, the Anglophone poets bear a complex, ambivalent relationship to the two myths and the images derived from them. They completed their education during the struggle for political freedom and matured as artists during the first decade of independence, when, amid coups, wars, and scandals, glory simply failed to return to Africa. This first generation of modern Anglophone poets developed strategies for coping with the dysfunction between myth and experience. The bereft personae men- tioned above, suspended between the past and the future, are one example. Most importantly, the Anglophone poets develop strategies of irony that enable them to take this dysfunction to the brink of tragedy without quite abandoning hope in Africa's future. Thus, on the basis of their most distin- guishing common trait, they can be thought of as the ironic generation.

All seven major poets have produced a substantial body of work, and each is represented by at least one collection. Collections are the result of design and arrangement; they are wholes greater than the sums of their parts. It is in their collections that one can see the common themes of these poets and hear their unique voices. It is in the collections that one can see the members of the ironic generation bring together in personal, individual ways the rich traditions of Anglo-American and vernacular poetry. The result is what Gerald Moore and Ulli Beier call "a fresh exploration of language" (22).

THE NON-NIGERIAN IRONIST POETS

Lenrie Peters. The Gambian poet Lenrie Peters has produced four collections of poetry: *Poems* (1964), *Satellites* (1967), *Katchikali* (1971), and *Selected Poetry* (1981). This last collection contains selections from his previous volumes and fifty-four new poems. In all these he is something of a literary maverick and very much his own man, though he writes within the mythopoeic matrix. That is, he writes with an awareness of the personal consequences of the cyclical journey, and he focuses frequently on the dysfunction between the promise of the African past and the experience of the present. In fact, the center of his poetry is an African present of grief, violence, oppression, loneliness, and death.

In *Satellites* Peters calls this Africa "a house without a shadow / lived in by new skeletons" (31). This dead land is the result of a "bartered birthright" (44). And he views it from the perspective of one devastated by westernization:

> We have come home
> From bloodless wars
> With sunken hearts
> Our boots full of pride
> From the true massacre of the soul.
>
> (31)

Peters believes that what happened to the individual and the race is the result of a rupture, not a transformation. In a quatrain of remarkable insight he suggests that the rupture has occurred because change has been so sudden that a healing mythopoeic process has not had time to work.

> Too strange the sudden change
> Of the times we buried when we left
> The times before we had properly arranged
> The memories that we kept.
>
> (39)

In the new poems of *Selected Poems* the primary focus is the present, depicted in the lives of individuals, in the clash of cultures, and in the exploitation of neocolonialism. Peters is compelled to make the simple, sad assertion: "It has been dismal / since the new freedoms came" (91). Juxtaposed against this view of the present is an intense nostalgia expressed in pastoral images of traditional Africa. He speaks longingly of "messages from wood fires and the warm / pungency of cooking" (113), messages he receives in the "shanty town sinks" of modern urban Africa. One of the best of these nostalgic poems begins with what seems to be the poet's claim to both of these worlds, but it ends with the sad failure of separation. Speaking of men roasting nuts and girls dancing by firelight, he says:

> They know where sorrow ends,
> and I, the broken bridge
> across the estuary,
> across worlds, cannot reach them
>
> (129)

Nostalgia is the mood that enables Peters to explore the suffering of contemporary Africa and the disconnection between the present and the past.

Kwesi Brew. In two collections, *The Shadows of Laughter* (1968) and *African Panorama* (1981), the Ghanaian poet Kwesi Brew writes longingly of the past and hopefully of the future, but he does so while maintaining a personal sense of a present made up of uncertainty and fear. In the earlier collection Brew focuses on the process by which Africa was forced to encounter change and the process that took the poet persona from the secure center of tradition to the painful realization that he had been "crippled by a god / I do not know" (53). In the title poem, this alienation and discontinuity are presented in lines as moving as any in West African verse.

> We fear the look in the eyes of our old men
> Where they sit in the corners
> Of their crumbling huts
> Casting tremulous looks
> At the loud crashing waves.
>
> (1)

Section 3 of *The Shadows of Laughter* begins and ends with poems that incorporate either implicitly or explicitly the entire historical myth. "The Lonely Traveller," the often-anthologized first poem of the section, begins with the Senghor-like oxymoron "sweet enemy" and develops through a series of characteristically African images—the spear, the shield, the drum, the green hills of the African savannah. Here the past is a source of strength. Then the image shifts from the martial to the musical. "Our hands that slept on the drums / Have found their cunning" (33). The result of this quickening of the present by the invocation of the past is the promise of the future:

> Now far on the horizon
> The red suns set
> The tired suns set
> To turn old nights into new dawns
> And people the skies with black stars.
>
> (33)

This is pure Negritude, not only the imagery and the myth but also the hopeful attitude. But neither here nor in the second volume is Brew able to maintain the optimism. He is subdued by the broken dream of the present.

Brew's second volume shows his creative staying power. Its greatest strength is his ability to construct images that are sharp and detailed and mythopoeically resonant. Even the titles illustrate this ability: "Our Hillside Home," "Drum Song," "Consulting a Fetish," "Dancers." The persona folds the historical myth within his own psychological journey by writing of the past and the future from the vantage point of the disordered present. It is there that the ironies gather to make the poet aware of his own contradictory role as a modern African poet—African and Western, son and stranger:

> We are the old dancers of a new dance
> an old dance revived by new men,
> strangers who are no strangers to our songs.

(55)

Kofi Awoonor. Kofi Awoonor, Ghana's most important poet, has produced five overlapping volumes of poetry: *Rediscovery* (1964), *Night of My Blood* (1971), *Ride Me, Memory* (1973), *The House by the Sea* (1978), and *Until the Morning After* (1987). In all of them he develops his own richly textured version of the historical myth in which a sustaining tradition is celebrated as

> The trappings of the past, tender and tenuous
> woven with the fiber of sisal and
> washed in the blood of the goat in the fetish hut.

For Awoonor this is the old, which must become the basis for the new. "Sew the old days for us, our fathers / That we can wear them under our new garment" (*Night of My Blood* 29).

Awoonor is resolutely a poet of hope. Encouraging his African readers (and, indeed, all of us) with the concept of ongoing revolution—the need for continued struggle in the present against the forces of oppression—he promises a triumphant future based on the values and strengths of the past. "The Wayfarer Comes Home," the final poem in *The House by the Sea*, is one of the best mythopoeic poems in all West African poetry. In it Awoonor offers this affirmation:

> . . . the dance has begun
> the drummers all in place
> this dreary half life is over
> our dream will be born at noon.

(77)

But this rich past and bright future are viewed from within the broken dream of a present in which the exploitive white West and its Black bourgeois henchmen bring suffering and sorrow to Africa. The house by the sea in his fourth collection is in fact a cell in Fort Ussher prison in Accra, from which he complains, "I never had known that my people / wore such sad faces" (41).

In each of the collections Awoonor infuses the historical myth with two highly personal components: first, the record of his own cyclical journey to the West and back, and second, his sense of the special role of the artist in building the African future out of the past. He makes many references to his own journey and subsequent disillusionment.

> If only I had known
> I would have stayed at home
> to clear the bush.
>
> (*Night of My Blood* 49)

Beyond this, *Ride Me, Memory* and *The House by the Sea* are structured around the journey. In the former Awoonor writes from America about his disillusioning experiences there and about an Africa to which he returns in memory. The latter collection begins with American recollections of Africa and concludes with poems, many of them painfully ironic, of his return to a troubled land. Still, he returns to Africa to carry out the task of the artist as a man of action, that is, to weave Africa's future out of the raffia of its past.

> . . . I plait my hope
>   into poems
> The sounds I make here
> part of the landscape
>   of my new homeland
>
> (62)

These themes are restated in the few new poems included in *Until the Morning After*, in which his tough, idealistic hope is expressed as a promise to continue the poet's militant task "until the morning after freedom" (206).

THE NIGERIAN IRONIST POETS

The largest number of significant poets of the ironic generation come from Nigeria, most of them connected at one time or another with either the University of Ibadan or the University of Lagos. They share with their fellow West Africans a preoccupation with the two dominant mythic themes, the historical experience of the continent and the psychological experience of the individual African. All of their work, however, was deeply affected by the Nigerian civil war. For all Nigerians the war was the most devastating experience of the 1960s. For the Nigerian poets it became the primary symbol of the failed present and their third great theme.

Gabriel Okara. Gabriel Okara has produced a smaller body of poetry than any other major poet of the ironic generation. His one collection, *The Fisherman's Invocation*, was published in 1978. Nevertheless, he had been publishing verse since the 1950s and has composed poems before, during, and after the civil war. He has written a half dozen of the finest lyrics to come out of West Africa, all of which are contained in the collection.

In most of his prewar poetry Okara deals with the two mythic themes, the African past and the African's journey. To depict the latter he projects an alienated persona, longing for death: "And O of this dark halo / Were the tired head free" (21). He makes this alienated voice specifically African, the product of the cyclical journey. In contrast to Awoonor's and Okigbo's prodigal, his is the voice of the lonely African. In "One Night at Victoria Beach" the poet observes the ritual of the Aladuras, a syncretistic religious sect, taking place on a stretch of beach symbolically situated between a traditional fishing village and a string of "modern" highlife bars. He longs to join them, to connect, but instead,

> . . . standing dead on dead sands
> I felt my knees touch living sands
> but the rushing winds killed the budding words.
>
> (29)

Cut off in midjourney from both traditional Africa and the West, he finds himself, in his most famous poem, "Piano and Drums,"

> lost in the labyrinth
> —wandering in the mystic
> rhythm of jungle drums and the concerto.
>
> (20)

From the perspective of the lonely African, Okara explores the historical relationship of the two worlds, tradition and the West. In "The Snowflakes Sail Gently Down" he presents this relationship in surreal but very African pastoral imagery.

> I dreamed of birds, black
> birds flying in my inside, nesting
> and hatching on oil palms bearing suns
> for fruits and with roots denting the
> uprooters, spades. And I dreamed the
> uprooters, tired and limp, leaning on my roots—
> their abandoned roots
> and the oil palms gave each of them a sun.

He then points out that Africa's tragedy is that the uprooters frowned and rejected the suns which "reached not / the brightness of gold" (30).

In the war poems Okara struggles with the central irony in the historical myth, the failure of independence to ameliorate and enrich the lives of Africans. The suns are gone; instead the poet sees "sad smoke curling skywards" (37), "bodies stacked in the morgue," and "children playing at diving jets" (31). The postwar poems suggest that a great spiritual fatigue has been added to the poet's sense of alienation. He speaks of "tired songs" and complains: "I am tried, tired. / My trembly feet drag" (56). Since then Okara has fallen silent in his loneliness.

J. P. Clark (Bekederemo). J. P. Clark Bekederemo has published five volumes of poetry: *Poems* (1962). *A Reed in the Tide* (1965), *Casualties* (1970), *A
Decade of Tongues* (1979), and *State of the Union* (1985). *A Reed in the Tide*
incorporates and rearranges the poems from the first collection. *A Decade of
Tongues* incorporates poems from the first three collections with very little
new material. *State of the Union* comprises new, highly political poems
composed between 1975 and 1980.

Pepper Clark is very much a man of his time and place and, in his early
verse, very much a poet of the two great mythic themes. He weaves those
themes together in the long early poem "Ivbie," in which he speaks of
traditional Africa's "treasures so many and beautiful" (*Poems* 45). And he
attempts to speak for those "that cry out of a violated past" but fails because,
as a result of the westernization to which he has been subjected, he finds that
he is only the Niger's "bastard child" (*Poems* 51).

A Reed in the Tide is designed to reflect the first half of the cyclical journey.
The poems are arranged to reflect the persona's movement from childhood to
adulthood and from the banks of the Niger to Times Square. All through this
journey the imagery of the individual poems is derived from the historical
myth. In the best poems Africa is symbolized by images of women: maternal
images of a grandmother's protective hug and a mother securing her home
against the rain and erotic images of dancers and bathers both emanating
from and integrated with nature. In "Agbor Dancer" he says of the dancing
girl:

> In trance she treads the intricate
> Pattern rippling crest after crest
> To meet the green clouds of the forest.
>
> (7)

Africa contrasts with the West, to which he journeys only to find that
"spirits / sink with sirens" (34) and "all [is] sterile and faceless" (35).

Casualties and *State of the Union* are poetic reflections on the civil war and
life in postwar Nigeria. Both reflect contemporary Nigeria as a betrayal of the
past—a bitterly ironic conclusion to the historical process and to the promise
of independence. *Casualties,* a controversial book, is a poetic record of the
war and the poet's involvement in it. It concludes with the following lines:

> A song was begun one night,
> The song should have begun
> A festival of three hundred tribes,
> Instead it lit for cantor
> And chorus a funeral pile.
>
> (40)

Burning on that pile was a nation—its myths, its men, its past, and its culture. Along with several miscellaneous poems, *State of the Union* consists of

twenty-five poetic comments on life in postwar Nigeria. The first line of the first poem reads "Here nothing works" (3). The last poem begins "It never was a union" (30). Everything in between is a variation or a particularization of the vision of contemporary Nigeria implicit in those two statements.

Wole Soyinka. Wole Soyinka, best known as a dramatist, is also a significant poet. His four main poetry publications are *Idanre and Other Poems* (1967), *A Shuttle in the Crypt* (1972), *Ogun Abibiman* (1976), and *Mandela's Earth and Other Poems* (1988). All these works reflect Soyinka's awareness of the mythopoeic power of art and the social significance of myth. In *Myth, Literature, and the African World,* a collection of essays and lectures, Soyinka speaks of "one of the social functions of literature: the visionary reconstruction of the past for purposes of social direction" (196). His poetic works are, or contain, visionary reconstructions of the past, present, and future.

Soyinka has always insisted on the appropriateness of Yoruba mythology and metaphysics as instruments for the interpretation of modern life. He finds this appropriateness especially in the irony with which the Yoruba mind contemplates the relation of violence to creativity, war to peace, and life to death. In *Idanre and Other Poems* these ironies are reflected in a number of fine lyrics and especially in the title poem, "Idanre," in which they are all personalized in Ogun, the Yoruba god of creation and war, life and death, "the shield of orphans who is also the orphan-maker." As a cautionary tale, "Idanre" contains the same wry warning that is found in Soyinka's play *A Dance of the Forests.* The poem tells of Ogun's "reluctant kingship," assumed only at the insistence of the people, and of his battle slaughter—how, after leading his people to victory, he turned and slaughtered them:

> . . . their cry
> For partial succor brought a total hand
> That smothered life in crimson plains
> With too much answering.
>
> (78)

On the brink of civil war, Soyinka reminds his people that the blood of mankind is on the hands of men for having made Ogun king.

The second collection, *A Shuttle in the Crypt,* comprises poems written in prison during the civil war. It constitutes a harrowing personal record of the consequences of having made Ogun king. The central experience in the collection is the poet's coming to terms with the hanging of five prisoners, and the image that haunts the volume is the image of the dead dangling men. "Their hands are closed on emptiness" (43). It ends on a personal note close to despair. In the last poem the poet suggests to the shade of Christopher Okigbo that it might be better to be killed than to survive—to die like Christ than to endure like Prometheus.

This is the point where the tragic ironist must fall silent or turn to new visions. In his next published major poem, *Ogun Abibiman*, Soyinka turns to the concept of ongoing revolution by recasting Ogun as a "revolutionary archetype" who "appears to be a definitive symbol of Africa's immediate destiny" (jacket note). In the poem Ogun meets Shaka, and of that meeting of north and south, myth and history, Abibiman, the triumphant black nation, is born. The future stands clear on the horizon, and "the clans are massed from hill to hill / Where Ogun stood" (22).

Mandela's Earth is more ironic and less militant than *Ogun Abibiman*. It focuses on the South Africa of Soweto and the Mandelas and on the New York of befouled subways and "packaged" news. Its prevailing tone is controlled rage—rage at Africa's failure to rise to the challenge of Mandela's courage and vision and at the rest of the world's indifference to it, as symbolized by a New York television anchorman's "Mind calloused to universal loss" (43).

Christopher Okigbo. In 1967, at the age of thirty-five, Christopher Okigbo was killed while serving in the Biafran army. He left behind a group of "organically related" poems that were published together in 1971 under the title *Labyrinths*, arguably the most important single volume of poetry to emerge from Anglophone Africa. Certainly it is the most difficult and complex. The early sections are very much in the Euromodernist tradition of Eliot; the later sections are increasingly enriched by the incorporation of elements from traditional oral literature. Okigbo said the poems constitute "a fable of man's perennial quest for fulfillment" (xiv). That quest is depicted in the African context of the cyclical journey. "Heavensgate," the first section of *Labyrinths*, begins with the persona, having returned bereft from his journey, invoking the spirit of an African river and river goddess—the African muse:

> Before you, mother Idoto,
> > naked I stand
> before your watery presence
> > a prodigal.
>
> (3)

Having invoked the muse, the poet depicts a series of departures and returns by a lonely, abandoned African who is himself "sole witness to my homecoming" (53).

Through this cycle of cyclical journeys key images emerge from the historical myth. Traditional Africa and Africanness are personified as Idoto and the lioness and also depicted in images of river and grove. In contrast, the Africa to which the persona returns is violated and abandoned. Okigbo compresses the whole history of colonialism into a quatrain:

> A fleet of eagles
> > over the oilbean shadows

> Holds the square
> > under curse with their breath.
>
> (31)

But the prodigal African also bears a burden of guilt because he has abandoned his traditions. "Our gods lie unsung . . . Behind the shrinehouse" (34).

The cruelest irony on which the collection insists is that the prodigal returns not to a living tradition but to this violated and abandoned land about to self-destruct. The last section of the volume, "Path of Thunder," is subtitled "Poems Prophesying War." Here, as in Soyinka's *A Shuttle in the Crypt* and Clark's *Casualties,* the Nigerian civil war constitutes the failure of myth. Independence brings not glory but self-destruction.

> The smell of blood already floats in the lavender mist
> > of the afternoon.
> The death sentence lies in ambush along the corridors
> > of power.
> And a fearful great thing already tugs at the cables of
> > the open air.
>
> (66)

The result is, seemingly, the death of myth and of hope:

> The glimpse of a dream lies smouldering in a cave
> together with the mortally wounded birds.

And the Ibo poet's only consolation is the Yoruba ontology of cyclical change, the "going and coming that goes on forever" (72).

OTHER IRONIST POETS

To these major voices of the ironic generation it is possible to add the voices of other talented West African poets. Included among these are A. W. Kayper Mensah of Ghana and Michael Echeruo of Nigeria. An important early collection is *Songs from the Wilderness* by Frank Kobina Parkes. Parkes, who complains in one poem that "the hour of hope is long, long lost" (9), is among the earliest to lament the failed dream of independence. The Cameroonian Mbella Dipoko records the disillusionment and alienation of the cyclical journey in *Black and White in Love* (1972). Several members of the generation better known in genres other than verse have published important collections. Chinua Achebe published *Beware, Soul Brother* in 1971. In 1973 he added seven new poems to the collection, then retitled *Christmas in Biafra.* Along with searing images of war's cruelty, Achebe's collections communicate the fear that the modern African may "become / a dancer disinherited in mid-dance" (47). In *Locusts* (1976) the scholar and critic Emmanuel Obiechina expresses the same fear in a parallel image: "Musician, you lost your song. / Your tune is a dry echo" (32).

THE DISILLUSIONED GENERATION

A second generation of Anglophone West African poets has established itself in the late 1970s and 1980s. Like their predecessors, these poets, who were born in the 1940s, come from different countries and draw on different indigenous traditions as well as different aspects of the Euromodernist tradition. The result is a poetry of great range and diversity, yet united by theme and mood. Having experienced their own cyclical journey and acquired a strong sense of disillusionment, the younger poets continue variations on the theme of African history, in which the present is seen as a betrayal of the past and of the political leaders and intellectuals of the previous generations.

Although this disillusionment is more pronounced in some poets' work than in others, the mood and subject are pervasive. Themes of disillusionment can be found in Ghanaians as different as Atukwei Okai (*Lorgorigi Logarithms and Other Poems*, 1974) and Kobina Eyi Acquah (*The Man Who Died*, 1984) and in Nigerians like Ken Saro-Wiwa (*Songs in a Time of War*, 1985), Tanure Ojaide (*The Blood of Peace*, 1991), and Niyi Osundare. Osundare's *The Eye of the Earth* (1986) is an effective fusion of nostalgic pastoralism and revolutionary vision. Together with his earlier collections, it establishes him as a poet of major importance. But perhaps the three most significant poets of the generation are Syl Cheney-Coker of Sierra Leone (*The Graveyard Also Has Teeth*, 1980), Odia Ofeimun of Nigeria (*The Poet Lied*, 1980), and Kofi Anyidoho of Ghana (*A Harvest of Our Dreams*, 1984, and *Earthchild*, 1985).

Syl Cheney-Coker. At his best, Syl Cheney-Coker is a strong, angry poet. He is also conscious of influences, among which he includes the social vision of radical Latin American poets like Pablo Neruda and the surrealist techniques of Tchicaya U Tam'si. These influences suggest a closer affinity to Francophone African poets than we find in other West African Anglophones—an affinity seen in the surreal imagery and in the declamatory rhetoric and invective of which he is fond. More important, however, is the moral dimension of Cheney-Coker's work, expressed over and over again in judgmental terms—rages against past and present betrayals of the cause of Africa and the cause of man. There is little variety of mood in his poetry, which is shrill with anger and sorrow. What redeems it is its confessional intensity.

The confessional quality is presented in terms of the myth of the cyclical journey. The title of Cheney-Coker's slim early collection, later incorporated into *The Graveyard Also Has Teeth* (1980), is *Concerto for an Exile*. His exile is similar to Awoonor's, but he adds his own Krio dimension to it. His alienation is not just geographical or cultural but genetic, carried in his "tainted" Creole ancestry, which he calls "the plantation blood in my veins / my foul genealogy" (7). The only way he can end his exile is to "return" to Africa as a poetic man of action, a poet of revolution. "I write the brushfire that spreads," he promises (61). This revolutionary poetry emanates from the historical myth. Cheney-Coker depicts a Sierra Leone of rich tradition violated by the Creole taint. His most focused rage, however, is directed at that tradition's betrayal by the contemporary black bourgeoisie:

> my poetry assumes its murderous intensity
> because while remaining quiet I have observed the
>   politicians
> parcelling out pieces of my country.

(65)

Odia Ofeimun. Odia Ofeimun has been West Africa's angry young man. He is also the poet as a man of action, translating his anger into poetic indictments and promises of revolutionary triumph. He insists on the political significance of the poet's craft. "At the moment Í can't think of putting anything down on paper unless I want to influence some situation" (Osofisan et al., 9). Poetry's social utility is the basis of Ofeimun's evaluation of the poets of the ironic generation. He praises Achebe, Okigbo, and Soyinka for their conduct and their vision of the African past and future while he excoriates Clark for his ambivalence during the civil war and his failure to provide vision.

The Poet Lied is a collection of forty-one poems in four sections: "The New Brooms," "Where Bullets Have Spoken," "Resolve," and "The Neophytes." These titles reflect a thematic organization. The first section deals with post–civil war life and leadership, the second with the war and its consequences. His disillusionment and sense of betrayal can be seen in the following lines:

> the magic promises of yesterday
> lie cold like mounds of dead cattle
> along caravans that lead nowhere.

(4)

Three persistent themes run through all four sections: the exploitive corruption of the elite, the sordidness of contemporary Nigerian life, and the role of the poet in African society. In sections 3 and 4 he carries out the poet's role by projecting a bright future that might result from his own generation's revolutionary action. He alternates between hopelessness and hope. In one place he confesses the need "to scream / on paper" (36). But he concludes by offering hope for the future if the integrity of the myth and the future of the continent are in the hands of the resolute of his generation, who are determined "that the locust shall never again visit our farmsteads" (42).

Kofi Anyidoho. Kofi Anyidoho, perhaps the best poet of the disillusioned generation, is the author of three collections: *Elegy for the Revolution* (1978),

A Harvest of Our Dreams (1984), and *Earthchild* (1985). The best of what this good poet has done can be found in *A Harvest of Our Dreams,* a collection filled with echoes. His use of Ewe forms suggests Awoonor. The controlling images of seedtime and harvest remind one of Soyinka's *Idanre,* while other images—heaven's gate, the sun bird—suggest Okigbo. But he is not a deliberately derivative poet. He speaks in his own voice, but where the ironic generation learned from their encounter with Euromodernism, Anyidoho and his contemporaries have learned by reading the ironists.

A Harvest of Our Dreams is divided into six sections, some of which contain very personal poems, others of which contain the poet's reflections on America. But the two most important sections are the first and the last, "Seedtime" and "Elegy for the Revolution," the latter a reprinting of the first collection. The poems in the other sections exist in a parenthesis of mood controlled by these two sections.

The title of the first section seems hopeful in its own pastoral way, but it is ironic rather than hopeful. The irony derives from the vantage point from which the persona contemplates the hopes of seedtime—the failed harvest, the ruined present. Everywhere are images of despair—references to "discarded myths," "sickness of soul," "famished dreams," "exiled gods." In every poem in the section are lines that speak of the poet's sorrow and the country's desolation: "Our hive went up in flames"; "Harvests go ungathered in our time" (6).

"Elegy for the Revolution" suggests the mood and tone of the collections of nearly all the poets of the post-Independence generation. The dedication of the section is "to the memory of / The revolution that went astray" (57). In it the dreams are "unhatched," "corpses lying strangled" in "smouldering wastelands." The collection ends with pastoral images made tragically ironic: images of the calabash, the gourd, the iron pot, in all of which "there was a void." Faced with this void, the poet is forced into grotesque art. "Mine is the dance of the hunchback," he says (83), and then a generation's cri de coeur: "My mind fails / my heart dies" (85).

East Africa

Anglophone poetry in East Africa reflects the same mythic patterns and the same generational development as poetry in West Africa, but its flowering came later and has been less abundant. This slower, thinner growth has been discussed extensively by East African critics and scholars. There is no agreement about the causes of this rate of "development," but the character of the indigenous cultures, the smaller populations in East Africa, the vitality of Swahili literature, and the characteristics of colonial rule all play a part. Two important stimulants to Anglophone literary growth in East Africa have been Makerere University, where undergraduate literary activity has been encouraged since the 1950s, and the East African Publishing House in

Nairobi, which, in the 1960s, published much important East African literature, including Okot p'Bitek's masterpiece *Song of Lawino* (1966) and the first important anthology of East African verse, *Drumbeat* (1967). A number of good, potentially important ironic-generation poets appeared in *Drumbeat*, including John Mbiti, the transplanted David Rubadiri, and Taban lo Liyong.

THE IRONIC GENERATION

Okot p'Bitek. The most important East African poet in English is the late Okot p'Bitek of Uganda, author of three remarkable volumes: *Song of Lawino, Song of Ocol* (1970), and *Song of a Prisoner* (1971). The first two are extended dramatic monologues, the third a series of monologues. They all deal with the relationship of the past to the present in Africa and with the dilemma of the modern African, but the mood in which they treat those fundamental issues deepens and darkens from volume to volume, progressing from the comic through a kind of self-reflexive satire to rage. Each volume contains startlingly effective images and short, clear, rapidly moving lines that owe much to Acholi oral verse and to p'Bitek's habit of composing first in Acholi.

Song of Lawino is possibly the most successful comic work in modern African literature. It is the lament of Lawino, the naive, abandoned traditional wife of Ocol, a westernized Acholi. Lawino tells her husband, "The ways of your ancestors / Are good" (29), and warns him, "Let no one / Uproot the pumpkin" (63). Her indictment of Ocol for abandoning these ways and treating them contemptuously is simple and powerful:

> Like beggars
> You take up white men's adornments
> Like slaves or war captives
> You take up white men's ways.
>
> (47–48)

Later she cries, "You behave like / A dog of the white man" (204). Along the way (there are thirteen sections and 216 pages), Lawino satirizes Western food, fashion, religion, education, and politics. Her lament ends poignantly as she comes to embody the tradition she defends.

> Let me dance before you
> My love,
> Let me show you
> The wealth in your house.
>
> (216)

Okot's two succeeding volumes are increasingly ironic acknowledgments of the African dilemma. In *Song of Ocol* the persona defends change and westernization with despairing intensity and indicts tradition with a passion

that suggests self-hatred. *Song of a Prisoner* takes the modern African deeper
into his self-dividing dilemma by making him a prisoner of his own independence. Functioning as synecdoche for all Africans, the prisoner calls himself

> A broken branch of a tree
> Torn down by the whirlwind
> of UHURU.
>
> (120)

Taban lo Liyong. Taban lo Liyong is one of the most versatile and flamboyant
men of letters in East Africa. He has written criticism, including some
negative comments on Okot p'Bitek, and four volumes of poetry: *Eating
Chiefs* (1970), *Frantz Fanon's Uneven Ribs* (1971), *Another Nigger Dead*
(1972), and *Ballads of Underdevelopment* (1976). The first is a recasting into
blank verse of a number of Luo oral poems, a sustained example of his own
injunction to "treat . . . tribal literature as raw material" (x).

The next two titles suggest a connection with the predominant myths of
modern Black African poetry, but the voice that runs through them is heavily
Americanized. They are written, for the most part, in Whitmanesque free
verse. In the first, a Whitmanesque "I" predominates, often functioning as
a cosmic ego speaking for and to his generation. The allusions, too, are
American—an invocation to Whitman, a poem about Stokely Carmichael,
satiric wordplay around the negative stereotypes of Uncle Tom and Aunt
Jemima. The attacks on racism are more generic and less specifically African
than in other Anglophone poets.

Though often flip, sarcastic, and Americanized, lo Liyong nevertheless
projects the image of the alienated African and presents the tragic message of
Africa's failed present: "We have at last nationalized POVERTY" (*Another
Nigger Dead* 9). In *Ballads of Underdevelopment* he contrasts Black and white
and plays Africa against Europe. He never stops being a mainstream African
poet, but he does seem to subside finally in the shadows of a more universal,
more existential angst.

> The world goes where it goes
>   The captainless ship
> the beast without a rudder
> Our mother divine
> Born in woes and woos.
>
> (*Ballads* 51)

THE DISILLUSIONED GENERATION

The East African poets born in the 1940s and 1950s share the themes and
moods of their contemporaries in West Africa. The similarity, apparent in the
early work that appeared in university publications in Kampala and Nairobi
and in Cook and Rubadiri's anthology *Poems from East Africa* (1971), be-

comes very clear in the collections that begin to appear after 1970, as the younger poets achieve maturity and accumulate substantial bodies of work. Among the more interesting volumes are two from Uganda and three from Kenya: *Orphan* (1968) by Okello Oculi, *Words of My Groaning* (1976) by p'Bitek's son-in-law Cliff p'Chong, Jared Angira's *Silent Voices* (1972) and *Cascades* (1979), and Gerald Kithinji's *Whispers at Dawn* (1976).

Orphan is a sequence of statements about, by, and especially to an orphan (the symbolic modern African) by a series of shifting personae. The orphan's absent mother, the symbol of traditional Africa, is the great unifying force and focus of the book. The orphan learns that he can reunite with his mother and reclaim his past only by struggling to build the future. If he struggles "through the thorns on strange pathways," he is told, he will be able to "Enshrine the spirit of your Mother / In the new homestead" (100–101).

Cliff p'Chong's small volume is a collection of painful, angry images of life in newly independent Africa—rampaging elephants, leaky houses, drunkenness, degraded sexuality. In "Lament for Alumya the Voter" p'Chong projects these images into the future with a devastating sense of hopelessness.

> My children
> Will die
> Slaves
> Of Joblessness
> And their children
> Will be tethered
> To the pole
> Of poverty.
>
> (52)

Jared Angira's *Silent Voices* is a varied, almost random collection. Lacking design or development, it is held together by image motifs that owe a debt to Christopher Okigbo, to whom two of the poems are dedicated—images of collapsing mud walls and children wailing in hunger. It is also held together by a unifying voice, a kind of persona that stands and speaks bereft in the center of Africa's shattered present. The voice speaks over and over again of dysfunction, disconnection, and despair:

> Disconnected circuit
> The stones that roll down
> Thunder that tears humanity.
>
> (54)

Kithinji is not as good a poet as Angira—not as complex or as resonant—but he reflects all the characteristic themes and modes of Angira and the others. He has the same enemies—the West, with its materialism and its ideologies, and the exploitative Black bourgeoisie—and the same hero-victim, the suffering African, and even the same pastoral images of trees and huts and fields. Occasionally he is able to gather all the angst of modern Africa into one image, as in his reference to "kinsmen / dancing on a volcano" (70).

Central and Southern Africa

Serious modern Anglophone poetry also developed later in Central and Southern Africa than in West Africa. There are a number of reasons for this slower growth in Malawi, Zambia, and Zimbabwe: their isolation, the oppressive colonial administrations, and the repressive and disruptive effects of industries, especially mining, under European control. One consequence was the later development of Western education, especially at the university level. As a result, writers contemporaneous with the ironic generation were dispersed, forced to seek education and careers elsewhere in Africa. David Rubadiri (b. 1930) of Malawi, the author of prose fiction and several fine poems, was educated at Makerere University in Uganda and later returned there to teach. Although a Malawian, he became part of the literary community that produced Okot p'Bitek, Ngũgĩ wa Thiong'o, and Taban lo Liyong. Dennis Brutus was born in Zimbabwe (at that time Rhodesia) in 1924 but educated in South Africa. His subsequent career as a poet and as a leader in exile of the literary opposition to apartheid has placed him firmly in the South African literary orbit. Thus modern Anglophone poetry did not really develop in the region until the 1970s and 1980s, but in those decades an important body of work emerged, especially in Malawi and Zimbabwe.

MALAWI

One significant development in the 1980s in Malawi was the evolution of an indigenous publishing industry capable of printing collections and anthologies by Malawian poets, such as *Raw Pieces* by Edison Mpina (1986) and Steve Chimombo's *Napolo Poems* (1987). Nevertheless, the most important collections have been produced outside the country: Jack Mapanje's *Of Chameleons and Gods* (1981), Felix Mnthali's *When Sunset Comes to Sepitwa* (1982), and *O Earth, Wait for Me* (1984) by Frank Chipasula.

The sociopolitical situation out of which these collections emerge is contemporary Malawi, that is, Malawi in the first decades of its independence. These have not been happy years. Politically Malawi has developed into an authoritarian one-party state in the firm grip of a dictatorial ruler who, in his determination not to tolerate discussion, much less dissent, has not hesitated to use detention and even torture. The country has suffered from an economic stagnation marked by agricultural deterioration and very limited development in mining and manufacture. The population has steadily drifted toward urban and semiurban areas, with a consequent spread of slum neighborhoods. In other words, Malawi has shared the fate of its neighbors and much of the rest of Black Africa.

The special feature of Malawi's malaise is its relationship to the Republic of South Africa. It was for a long time the only Black state to have diplomatic relations with the republic. The reason for this connection is that Malawi's largest export and greatest single source of hard currency is manpower contracted to work in the South African mines. Thus, although separated from South Africa by hundreds of miles, it is, like Swaziland and Lesotho, a client state. This is arguably the most odious form of neocolonialism. It results in an exploitive symbiosis in which the elite (the Black bourgeoisie) become, willy-nilly, collaborators in apartheid. It is this ongoing tragedy over which Malawian poets brood and to which their verse responds.

In *Of Chameleons and Gods* Jack Mapanje's response takes the form of an attempt "to find a voice or voices as a way of preserving some sanity" (introduction). The "voice" he seems to settle on is a very personal one. The design of the search for this voice—and thus the design of the collection—is that of the cyclical journey. The book is arranged in four sections, in the first of which Mapanje focuses on rooted Malawian subjects ranging from Chiuta, the traditional god of creation, to John Chilembwe, an early liberation hero. These are his reference points for condemning the tawdriness and repression of contemporary Malawian life. The second section, "Sketched from London," shows that this furthermost point in the cyclical journey is no viable alternative to the tragedy at home. Section 3, "Re-entering Chingwa's Hole," portrays the completion of the cyclical journey—the return to oppression and torture on the one hand and to shrines and the buried heart of Africa on the other. In the fourth section, "Assembling Another Voice," the returned African finds his new voice and a new vision of Africa.

Running through all the sections are an evocation of the strength of the past and a harsh indictment of the Malawi of the 1970s and of those responsible for its tragedy. "The Palm Trees of Chigawe," for instance, is an elegiac piece of nature imagery in which trees that once produced fruit and milk and served as "banners for night fishermen" are "now stunted" and "stand still beheaded" (24). Elsewhere the poet returns from England to a diminished present in which rivers "without their hippos and crocs / merely trickle gratingly down" (42). "The gods have deserted," Mapanje says, "these noble shrines" (43). But he discovers that the past lives in him in memory:

> I remember . . .
> . . . watching the endless blue waters of
> The vast lake curl, break, lap-lapping at my
> Feet as little fishes nibbled my toes. Then
> A loin-cloth fisherman, emerging from the men
> Bent mending their broken nets under the shade
> Of the lone beachtree, jumped into a canoe
> Fettered to a nearby colony of reed and grass
> He sculled away lazily perhaps to check the night's
> Fishtraps.
>
> (54)

This pastoral past becomes the moral and psychological base from which the poet indicts the present, symbolized vividly by the detention of Mapanje's friend Felix Mnthali. Included in the indictment of the present are those who cause its suffering—the "hounds in puddles," he calls them (49)—the Black bourgeoisie and their white neocolonial collaborators. He asks:

> The canoe has capsized, the carvers are drowned . . .
>   . . . should we fell
> More poles to roll another canoe to the beach?
> Is it worth assembling another voice?
>
> (69)

Of Chameleons and Gods is his answer, given in the name of the violated past and the sufferers of the present. And the answer is yes.

Like Mapanje's collection, Felix Mnthali's *When Sunset Comes to Sapitwa* is primarily a product of the 1970s. In it the substructure of historical myth, though muted, is nonetheless evident, with an emphasis on the broken dream of the present. In the first section an invoked voice or muse instructs the poet write for those

> who suffer the void
> of a prison without walls
> and groan at the tread
> of idols without a face.
>
> (3)

The most important poem he writes to and for this suffering audience is the culminating poem of the first section, "December seventh, 'seventy-six." The title refers to the date on which Mnthali was released from detention. The poem depicts the forces that imprison him, the factors that lead to his release, and the physical and psychological alterations consequent upon confinement and release. We learn that he is arbitrarily locked away "in this walled wilderness" with "some of the best brains in the land" and that his release is the result of the arbitrary attention of the world press to "ideas whose time had come." Against this background of malign and indifferent forces, the persona moves from confinement to freedom. Before his release he stands on the brink of emotional collapse and depression: "It's the walls within me / that are beginning to cave in." Then, as his name is read from the release rolls, his response is a multilayered irony of self-parody. Verbally he embraces his liberators, who are also his captors, with one of the most hated nouns of colonial subservience: "B W A A A N A A A" (23). The final irony is that, released from prison, he finds not joy but another kind of sadness.

This is the dominant poem in the collection. In it the broken dream of the present is symbolized by the poet's own detention. Fuguelike, the theme is restated in the third section, "Until the next encounter with our diminished selves," in a series of mutually reinforcing images: the mean lives of the poor, the contrast between the poor and the bourgeoisie, the contrast between the diminished present and the heroic past. The section concludes with a picture of what Mnthali calls "the looters' / contemptuous largesse":

> Crumbs of bread
> and mildewed chips
> from the white man's table
> will keep us on our feet
> until the next encounter
> with our diminished selves.
>
> (45–46)

In Frank Chipasula's *O Earth, Wait for Me* the prevailing mood is one of lamentation rising occasionally to exhortation. A close reading reveals a pattern of two interwoven thematic threads holding the collection together. One thread is overtly political and comprises poems and images of oppression and exploitation. The other theme is aesthetic—an inquiry into the nature of art (song) and the function of the artist in contemporary Malawi.

The dominant political image of the collection is the victim, who appears in a variety of manifestations. Diminished descendants of those who fought for independence, modern Malawians are a people who merely "smile sickly from postcards." They are excluded from the high-rise buildings they themselves had built only to have "come-back-tomorrows" flung in their faces. The most powerful image of victimization is found in the poem "A Hanging." The hanged man's writhing body dangles and swings for Malawi:

> His body sang until it could not
> stand its own song . . .
> All his blood stood up and sang
> twisting toward his throat.
>
> (14)

The role of the poet and the nature of the poem under conditions like those in Malawi constitute the most persistent theme in the collection. The titles scattered throughout make this theme clear: "A Singer's Dilemma," "The Blind Marimba Player," "Bangwe Player," "The Witch Doctor's Song." In the second of these the blind musician is a symbol of the African artist who creates "melody . . . resurrecting the spirits / of our ancestors." It is on the basis of this vital and authentic past that he builds his creative protest and points the way:

> But I, attentive, watched him strum the sweet past
> Touch the present momentarily, letting the threads of
>   rhythm
> Grope for truth and proceed violently almost bringing
>   down heaven

To challenge us to fill in the dark gaping blanks . . .
Where the future should be.

(20–22)

The whole myth of African history is here, past, present, and future. Activism and militancy are of the very nature of African poetry for Chipasula. For the African poet a poem should be a weapon. Armed with his song, he must play his part. Accepting that role himself, Chipasula says in "Everything to Declare," "I will start the world afresh" (59). But if Chipasula is a poet of the future rooted in the past, he is nevertheless overwhelmed by the present. In "A Singer's Dilemma," the final poem of the collection, he wonders if the poet can make poetry out of Africa's reality.

Is this the right material for my poetry . . . ?
Today I must wait for the wind to blow more gently
. . . but death's omnipresent stench creeps into my peace . . .
Give me a metaphor that is not scared of shrapnel wounds.

(82–83)

Napolo Poems by Steve Chimombo is perhaps the most interesting of the collections published within Malawi. In it the poet weaves a collection out of a great seismic upheaval in Malawi in 1946 and the concept of Napolo, "the mythical, subterranean serpent residing under mountains and associated with landslides, earthquakes, and floods" (vii). These two motifs—the earthquake and the mythological monster—enable Chimombo to operate on many levels, through strategies of indirection made necessary by the political climate in which he composes and publishes. In the introduction he insists on "different levels" and speaks of "the reception of the phenomenon on the physical, psychological, social, religious, and political planes" (vii). That is, he uses the historical and mythological to comment on the contemporary and political. Like many of his contemporaries, he pokes "fingers into the myth-infested crevices" (49) on behalf of his countrymen. He too is the poet as a man of action.

ZIMBABWE

Like Malawi, Zimbabwe produced little significant poetry in the 1950s, 1960s, and early 1970s, but experienced something of a poetic renaissance in the late 1970s and 1980s. The results of this late and modest outpouring include a number of significant locally published collections: F. E. Muronda's *Echoes of My Mind; Counterpoint*, a joint production of the poems of Hopewell Seyaseya and Albert Chimedza (1984); and Chenjerai Hove's *Red Hills of Home* (1985). These poets are stylistically very dissimilar. Seyaseya's rather stately free verse bears no resemblance to Hove's two- and three-foot lines. But they all write from the same perspective, and they see and say very similar things. They are poets of the "broken dream," poets who stress the anguish of contemporary life. But they do not see the viable past as a point of reference and departure. There are very few allusions to traditional gods and heroes and a notable absence of the pastoral. In this they are more like the poets of South Africa, especially the poets of the Sharpeville generation, than like the poets of West and East Africa. The reason is not that they are imitative but that they developed as artists in circumstances analogous to those found in the Republic of South Africa. Less urbanized and "detribalized" than the township poets of South Africa, they nevertheless matured as members of a Black proletariat struggling against white settler domination.

Seyaseya's is a voice of sorrow and controlled rage speaking from the center of the broken dream of the present, "the rubble of a failed coup." He speaks of "my people's wounds / The bleeding of the land," and wonders, "Is this the gods' twisted sense of humour?" (9). He connects the suffering of his country with that of neighboring lands. He looks to Mozambique, where Samora Machel has begun "the journey without end" (21) and to South Africa where, on Robben Island, "the spears are whetted . . . on the hard road to Azania" (13). His poems alternate between hope and despair. At one point, contemplating the present, Seyaseya cries,

> I hang
> on the edge
> of insanity.
>
> (22)

But he also finds consolation in the promise of the future: "When our time comes, we shall join hands" (22). And this future, he promises, will be the result of revolution:

> Tomorrow they will come from the east blowing like the wind
> To right a wrong done
> To destroy the chains of slavery.
>
> (12)

Seyaseya's poetry is controlled; it focuses the reader's attention steadily on the people's painful present and promised future. Albert Chimedza's voice and focus are notably different. His work is self-indulgent and out of control, an unstructured, undisciplined hallucination marked by the gratuitous use of shocking language—"Slow goes this fucking train" (35)—and outrageous characterization: "I screw my brother's wife / I am the slithering snake in the grass." This latter quote begins a self-depiction by a Black bourgeois exploiter that is not without power; still, the overall effect of the verse is exhibitionist, like a sudden burst of beat poetry in the Zimbabwe of the 1980s. Still, Chimedza is a symptom—an occasionally moving one—of the suffering of the modern African artist. He is, as he says, both "the dreamer / of sunsets" and "cold and hungry and away from home" (35).

Chenjerai Hove is one of the more finished and complex poets of Zimbabwe, and his work in English and Shona has been widely anthologized. He is best seen in his collection of English-language poems *Red Hills of Home*, which is dominated by the poet's sense of the suffering of contemporary Africa. The focus and tone are set in the prologue, in which he quotes Neruda: "Come and see / the blood in the streets." The images of that suffering are scattered everywhere in the collection. For him African history is "the interrupted tale / of hunger and strife" (43).

More than any other Zimbabwean poet, he depicts this present suffering as an aberration—a departure from the African essence and the African past. He does this by weaving two large motifs through the collection. The first is the disruption of the flow of the seasons: "There was no explanation / of the season's withdrawal" (56). The second, linked to the first, is of the scattering of the migratory birds. In one poem the bird asks, "Why did I migrate?" and laments:

> . . . I shall never sing
> the seasons' flow again
> Till my people rescue me
> With yesterday's echoes.
>
> (42)

And the poet, in turn, stands as synecdoche for the modern African struggling to reconcile tradition and change:

> Maybe I will carry my coat
> my new coat
> on my torn shoulders.
>
> (9)

Like the West African poets, Hove gives unity and focus to the collection by means of this symbology. He is able to create, out of personal experience and interior landscapes that parallel the African landscapes, images that reflect the experience of a whole generation of Africans. Those images link poet and reader to the experience of the mass of Africans struggling in the poverty of the village:

> If you stay in comfort too long
> you will not know
> the weight of the water pot
> on the bald head of the village woman.
>
> (3)

South Africa

The history of Black Anglophone poetry in South Africa is long and complex. Like poetry in West Africa, it can be traced through a series of pioneer generations back into the nineteenth century. For well over a hundred years, pious and patriotic verse appeared in mission journals and emanated from mission presses. Most of this early verse is of limited thematic or aesthetic interest. By the middle of the twentieth century, however, two concerns dominate the works of the last of the "pioneer" generations: nostalgia and politics, the longing to reclaim a lost past and the determination to oppose white oppression. B. W. Vilakazi, for instance, a poet who composed in Zulu and translated his own work into English, brought the two themes together by depicting the plight of the migrant mine worker. Perhaps the best-known work of this generation, however, is *Valley of a Thousand Hills* (1941), by Herbert I. E. Dhlomo, brother of novelist R. R. R. Dhlomo. This long poem—over a thousand lines—demonstrates the thematic concerns and prosodic limitations of the tradition.

The analysis of more recent Black poetry—that written after the coming to power of the Nationalist party in 1948 and the consequent hardening of political and poetic lines around the issue of apartheid—is complicated by four factors: (1) the development of a parallel poetic tradition in African languages like Zulu and Xhosa; (2) the urban, essentially proletarian experience of "coloured" writers with no real ties to indigenous African cultures; (3) the interaction of Black and "coloured" writers with an extensive indigenous white literature; and (4) the disruptive effect of the forced exile of a generation of militant poets. This extensive body of work can best be appreciated by considering Black and "coloured" poets together (as they now consider themselves) and by grouping them into two generations—the Sharpeville generation and the Soweto generation.

The Sharpeville generation includes Dennis Brutus, Arthur Nortje, Cosmo Pieterse, Keorapetse Kgogsitsile, and Mazisi Kunene. These poets range in age from Dennis Brutus (b. 1926) to Arthur Nortje (1942–70). Two things hold them together and mark them as a group: (1) their lives and art were shaped by the increasing racial oppression of the Nationalist government through the 1950s and given focus by the tragedy of Sharpeville in 1960; (2) by the end of the 1960s they were all forced into exile by that oppression.

Brutus has made an important distinction among the militants between protest poets and resistance poets. Protest poetry might be thought of as a Black expression of liberalism—a poetry of personal response to oppression based on assumptions of justice, rights, and human dignity. Resistance poetry is provocative, defiant, confrontational—a call to action. To the extent that poets have target audiences, the former attempts to awaken the liberal sensibility of an international community of poetry readers, while the latter calls the oppressed themselves to action. The two best poets of the Sharpeville generation, Brutus and Nortje, are protest poets.

Nortje was an enormously talented poet who took his own life in 1970. His most important collection, *Dead Roots*, was published posthumously in

1973. It offers many images of oppression, humiliation, and detention—the appalling but numbing facts of life under apartheid. Yet his best poems are not about life in South Africa but rather about exile and its consequences: isolation, alienation, and self-hatred. In fact, chronologically arranged in *Dead Roots,* the poems constitute an autobiographical descent into hell. There is no evidence that the self-absorbed, Camus-like Nortje would not have followed the same descent had he not been victimized by his country's racist policies, but he was indisputably a victim. And as a victim he left a record of loneliness ("The heart is a stone in water," 98), dissipation ("I have felt my loins go numb at the blue burn of alcohol," 112), and self-disgust ("The poisoned spring has bubbled through my veins," 133).

The best-known and most prolific poet of the Sharpeville generation is Dennis Brutus. He is the author of four major collections and several smaller ones. The larger collections are *Sirens, Knuckles and Boots* (1963). *Letters to Martha* (1968), *A Simple Lust* (1973), and *Stubborn Hope* (1978). All these collections demonstrate Brutus's passionate love for his country. That love has made his actions militant, but it has made his voice ironic and controlled. He has been forced to develop poetic strategies that enable him to communicate his love of the land itself and his hatred of the day-to-day experience of that land. When he sings to his country like a troubadour to his lady, and even when he writes of his experiences on Robben Island and uses prison as a metaphor for South Africa, Brutus maintains a rhetorical distance and detachment.

In the later poems written in exile—he left South Africa in 1966—he is able to claim with justice after many years of labor, "I am a rebel and freedom is my cause" (*Stubborn Hope* 95). But even in exile and wearing the mantle of prophesy, his voice is quiet, controlled, understated:

> Behind the dark hills
> the spears of dawn advance
> . . . .
> the fieldflowers, drenched and bowed,
> lift with the coming light:
> the long night lumbers grudgingly
> into the past.
>
> (*Stubborn Hope* 95)

On either side, as it were, of these two protest poets of the Sharpeville generation are Mazisi Kunene and Keorapetse Kgogsitsile. Like Brutus, Nortje, and Pieterse, Kunene has lived in exile for many years, but unlike them, he is a Zulu, not a "coloured" writer. He writes in the Zulu language and in Zulu forms, translating his work later into English. The first of his major collections, *Zulu Poems,* was translated and published in 1970; the most recent, *The Ancestors and the Sacred Mountain,* in 1982. Kunene's work may raise the question of the place of translations in the study of English-language literatures, but his best pieces are very effective in English. They bring together two themes of Black South African poetry: the fate of traditional culture and the fate of Black South Africans confronting technology, industry, and apartheid. On the one hand, he writes poems with titles like "The Rise of the Angry Generation" and "Police Raid," while on the other hand he promises a future based on the traditional past:

> My child takes the poem that is old
> And learns from it our legends
> To see life with the eyes of the Forefathers.
>
> (*Ancestors* 17)

If Kunene is a traditionalist and a protest poet, Kgogsitsile, who has been in exile since 1961, is a resistance poet pointing the way to the Soweto generation. The title of his major work, *My Name Is Afrika* (1971), makes this clear. It is a collection shot through with images of fire and expressions of defiant rage.

> It is the rhythm of unchained spirit
> will put fire in our hands
> to blaze our way
> to clarity to power
> to the rebirth of real men
>
> (85)

Oswald Mtshali is a more truly transitional figure than Kgogsitsile for two important reasons: he lived, wrote, and published in South Africa in the grim years between Sharpeville and Soweto, and his transformation from a protest poet to a resistance poet parallels and reflects the growing militancy of Black South Africans. His first collection, *Sounds of a Cowhide Drum*, was published in Johannesburg in 1971. It is a protest collection, the possibility of censorship and even imprisonment imposing on the poet strategies of obliqueness, allusiveness, symbolism, and irony. But in his second collection, *Fireflames* (1981), the subtle, even sly tonalities give way to direct, confrontational verse. "I'm a burning chimney" is subtitled "A Militant's Cry." It begins with the poet acknowledging that he stands "on the debris of . . . the Black man's life," but it ends with the promise:

> We will ascend to take up our rightful places,
> we will sing a song in unison,
> "At last victory is ours
> the whole household now belongs to us."
>
> (*Fireflames* 37)

Militancy is one of the tones of the Soweto generation, poets who matured and emerged in print in the 1970s. That generation, most of whom continue to live and publish in South Africa, includes the older short story writer

James Matthews, who in the 1970s turned to popular verse as a way of reaching the masses. His poems in *Cry Rage* (1972) convey both a warning and a prophesy—almost a prediction of the Soweto uprising in 1976, the tragedy waiting to happen. The best-known poet to emerge in the early 1970s is Mongane Wally Serote, who overcame detention in the Transvaal and exile in Botswana to publish four volumes in that decade. In spite of the Zulu titles of his first two collections, *Yakhal'inkomo* (1972) and *Tsetlo* (1974), and the occasional poem he has composed in Zulu, Serote is a location or township poet. His diction is hip—deliberately shocking in a streetwise way, as in the famous "What's in This Black 'Shit'" (*Yakhal'inkomo* 9). But he is also capable of distilling the fire imagery that is so characteristic of the Soweto poets into simple, moving language:

> White people are white people,
> They are burning the world.
> Black people are black people,
> They are the fuel.
>
> (*Yakhal'inkomo* 50)

Two other important poets of the Soweto generation are Mafika Pascal Gwala and Sipho Sepamla. Like Serote's, their style owes more to the American poets of the civil rights movement—Imamu Amiri Baraka, Etheridge Knight, Haki Madhubuti—than to their exiled predecessors of the Sharpeville generation. It is hip, jazzy, bluesy, a poetry made out of the incidents and the language of the streets of Soweto and the other Black townships. Sepamla is, perhaps, the most prolific of the poets who found their voices in the 1970s. He has published both before and after Soweto. In the earlier collections like *Hurry Up to It* (1975) and *The Blues Is You in Me* (1976), he sings the blues: "the blues is the shadow of a cop / dancing the Immorality Act jitterbug" (*Blues* 70). After Soweto, however, the blues and the anger he kept at an ironic distance with a cool, even comic tone are transformed into simpler, more immediate images of horror and expressions of hope. In *The Soweto I Love* (1977), he describes the results of the uprising this way:

> bullets
>   pierced the backs of kids killed and
>   killed and killed.
>
> (12)

Still, in the face of that atrocity, he dares to hope that those who remain in the township

> will carry on with the job
> of building anew
> a body of being
> from the ashes of the ground.
>
> (24)

The themes of South African poetry are, of course, more varied than these excerpts imply. Nevertheless, the dominant themes parallel those found in the poetry of independent Black Africa—they parallel and yet they differ. In spite of the living literary traditions in indigenous languages, the English-language poets are not greatly concerned with roots and the recovery of a lost heritage. But they are deeply concerned with the immediate effects of fascist, racist oppression. This is inevitable. They have not lived *uhuru* ("freedom")—even *uhuru* betrayed. Their art, like their lives, is determined—contained—within the events that have labeled the generations: Sharpeville and Soweto.

Bibliography

Achebe, Chinua. *Christmas in Biafra and Other Poems*. New York: Doubleday, 1973.

Acquah, Kobena Eyi. *The Man Who Died*. Accra: Asempa, 1984.

Angira, Jared. *Cascades*. London: Longman, 1979.

———. *Silent Voices*. London: Heinemann, 1972.

Anyidoho, Kofi. *Earthchild*. Accra: Woeli, 1985.

———. *A Harvest of Our Dreams*. London: Heinemann, 1984.

Armattoe, R. E. G. *Between the Forest and the Sea*. Londonderry: privately printed, 1950.

———. *Deep Down in the Black Man's Mind*. Ilfracombe: Stockwell, 1954.

Awoonor, Kofi. *The House by the Sea*. Greenfield Center, N.Y.: Greenfield Review Press, 1978.

———. *Night of My Blood*. Garden City, N.Y.: Doubleday, 1971.

———. *Rediscovery*. Ibadan, Nigeria: Mbari Press, 1964.

———. *Ride Me, Memory*. Greenfield Center, N.Y.: Greenfield Review Press, 1973.

———. *Until the Morning After*. Greenfield Center, N.Y.: Greenfield Review Press, 1987.

Brew, Kwesi. *African Panorama*. Greenfield Center, N.Y.: Greenfield Review Press, 1981.

———. *The Shadows of Laughter*. London: Longman, 1968.

Brutus, Dennis. *Letters to Martha*. London: Heinemann, 1968.

———. *A Simple Lust*. London: Heinemann, 1973.

———. *Sirens, Knuckles and Boots*. Ibadan, Nigeria: Mbari Press, 1963.

———. *A Stubborn Hope*. Washington, D.C.: Three Continents, 1978.

Cheney-Coker, Syl. *The Blood in the Desert's Eyes: Poems*. Oxford: Heinemann, 1991.

———. *The Graveyard Also Has Teeth*. London: Heinemann, 1980.

Chimombo, Steve. *Napolo Poems*. Zomba, Malawi: Manchichi, 1987.

Chinweizu, Onwuchekwa Jemie, and Ihechukwu Mandubuike. *Toward the Decolonization of African Literature*. Vol. 1, *African Fiction and Poetry and Their Critics*. Washington, D.C.: Howard University Press, 1983.

Chipasula, Frank. *Nightwatcher, Nightsong*. Johannesburg: Ravan Press, 1986.

———. *O Earth, Wait for Me*. Johannesburg: Ravan Press, 1984.

———. *Whispers in the Wings*. Oxford: Heinemann, 1991.

Clark [Bekederemo], J. P. *Casualties*. New York: Africana, 1970.

———. *A Decade of Tongues: Selected Poems, 1958–1968*. London: Longman, 1981.

———. *Poems*. Ibadan, Nigeria: Mbari Press, 1962.

———. *A Reed in the Tide*. London: Longman, 1965.

———. *State of the Union*. London: Longman, 1985.

Cook, David, and David Rubadiri, eds. *Poems from East Africa*. London: Heinemann, 1971.

Dathorne, O. R. *African Literature in the Twentieth Century*. Minneapolis: University of Minnesota Press, 1974.

Dhlomo, H. I. E. *Valley of a Thousand Hills*. Durban, Natal: Knox, 1962.

Dipoko, Mbella Sonne. *Black and White in Love*. London: Heinemann, 1972.

Hove, Chenjerai. *Red Hills of Home*. Harare: Mambo Press, 1985.

Kgogsitsile, Keorapetse. *My Name is Afrika*. New York: Doubleday, 1971.

Kithinji, Gerald. *Whispers at Dawn*. Nairobi: East African Literature Bureau, 1976.

Kunene, Mazisi. *The Ancestors and the Sacred Mountain*. London: Heinemann, 1982.

———. *Zulu Poems*. London: Deutsch, 1970.

Liyong, Taban lo. *Another Nigger Dead*. London: Heinemann, 1972.

———. *Ballads of Underdevelopment*. Nairobi: East African Literature Bureau, 1976.

———. *Eating Chiefs*. London: Heinemann, 1970.

———. *Frantz Fanon's Uneven Ribs*. London: Heinemann, 1971.

Mapanje, Jack. *Of Chameleons and Gods*. London: Heinemann, 1981.

Matthews, James. *Cry Rage*. Johannesburg: Spro-Cas, 1972.

Mnthali, Felix. *When Sunset Comes to Sapitwa*. London: Longman, 1982.

Moore, Gerald, and Ulli Beier. *Modern Poetry from Africa*. Baltimore: Penguin Books, 1963.

Mpina, Edison. *Raw Pieces*. Blantyre, Malawi: Hetherwick, 1986.

Mtshali, Oswald. *Fireflames*. Pietermaritzburg, South Africa: Shuter & Shooter, 1980.

———. *Sounds of a Cowhide Drum*. New York: Third Press, 1972.

Muronda, F. E. *Echoes of My Mind*. Harare: College Press, n.d.

Nortje, Arthur. *Dead Roots*. London: Heinemann, 1973.

Nwoga, Donatus. *West African Verse*. London: Longman, 1967.

Obiechina, Emmanuel. *Locusts*. Greenfield Center, N.Y.: Greenfield Review Press, 1976.

Oculi, Okello. *Orphan*. Nairobi: East African Publishing House, 1968.

Ofeimun, Odia. *The Poet Lied*. London: Longman, 1980.

Ojaide, Tanure. *The Blood of Peace and Other Poems*. Oxford: Heinemann, 1991.

———. *Children of Iroko and Other Poems*. Greenfield Center, N.Y.: Greenfield Review Press, 1973.

Okai, Atukwei. *Lorgorigi Logarithms and Other Poems*. Accra: Ghana Publishing Corp., 1974.

Okara, Gabriel. *The Fisherman's Invocation*. London: Heinemann, 1978.

Okigbo, Christopher. *Labyrinths*. New York: Africana, 1971.

Osofisun, Femi, San Aseir, and Kole Omotoso. "Interview: Odia Ofeimun." *Opon Ifa* 2, no. 1 (1976): 7–9, 12–18, 21–22, 24, 27–29.

Osundare, Niyi. *The Eye of the Earth*. Ibadan, Nigeria: Heinemann, 1986.

Parkes, Frank Kobina. *Songs from the Wilderness*. London: University of London Press, 1965.

p'Bitek, Okot. *Song of a Prisoner*. New York: Third Press, 1971.

———. *Song of Lawino*. Nairobi: East African Publishing House, 1966.

———. *Song of Ocol*. Nairobi: East African Publishing House, 1970.

p'Chong, Cliff. *Words of My Groaning*. Kampala: Uganda Literature Bureau, 1976.

Peters, Lenrie. *Katchikali*. London: Heinemann, 1971.

———. *Poems*. Ibadan, Nigeria: Mbari Press, 1964.

———. *Satellites*. London: Heinemann, 1967.

———. *Selected Poetry*. London: Heinemann, 1981.

Saro-Wiwa, Ken. *Song in a Time of War*. Port Harcourt, Nigeria: Saros, 1985.

Sepamla, Sipho. *The Blues Is You in Me*. Johannesburg: Donker, 1976.

———. *Hurry Up to It*. Johannesburg: Donker, 1976.

———. *The Soweto I Love*. London: Collins, 1977.

Serote, Mongane Wally. *Tsetlo*. Johannesburg: Donker, 1974.

———. *Yakhal'inkomo*. Johannesburg: Renoster, 1972.

Soyinka, Wole. *Idanre and Other Poems*. London: Methuen, 1967.

———. *Mandela's Earth and Other Poems*. London: Deutsch, 1989.

———. *Myth, Literature, and the African World*. London: Cambridge University Press, 1976.

———. *Ogun Abibiman*. London: Collins, 1976.

———. *A Shuttle in the Crypt*. New York: Hill & Wang, 1972.

5 English-Language Drama and Theater

J. NDUKAKU AMANKULOR

Drama and theater—that is to say, dramatic literature and the art of theatrical presentation—have the same unity that goes for bread and butter as food. As bread and butter is food so is drama and theater performance art. Describing the two terms as a singular notion or activity does not imply that there is no discrimination to be made, but rather that both terms perform together, and hardly could the one be talked about without the other being implied. They may be taken together to refer to the technique of telling a story directly to an audience or spectators, through actors who impersonate the characters in the story, thereby giving the impression that the events are taking place there and then.

The forms in which the story may be preserved and disseminated are various in modern times; they include printed literature, film, and videotape. Because stage performances, unless captured in one of the latter two media, are ephemeral, the playscript remains the most reliable method of preserving the dramatic material independent of a specific performance. The convenience of storing and retrieving the play in its literary form, and the fact that it can be read and appreciated cerebrally without a formal staging, have tended to invest the written play with a life of its own, to the extent that cultures lacking their own scripts or story maps preserved in writing are thought of as not having drama. African societies are categorized as such; hence drama is said not to be indigenous to the continent. The controversy over this issue is now itself part of the history of drama in Africa.

I have drawn attention elsewhere to the complex structure of indigenous African religious and social practices, including festivals, in which, I believe, we can locate several art forms, including drama, dance, music, poetry, and storytelling, either in their distinct forms or in performance combinations (Amankulor, "Concept and Practice"). If we realize that sculpture, which Wole Soyinka (*Art, Dialogue and Outrage* 192) aptly calls "a sister art" to drama, was denied a place in African culture by missionary-colonizer pioneers until European artists themselves redressed the erroneous assessment, we should be able similarly to correct the judgment by the same Europeans that drama in Africa is nothing but ritual ceremony.

The process of reassessment has indeed already begun. With the work of such concerned theater artists as Antonin Artaud, Peter Brook, and Jerzy Grotowski, the theater world is making an objective journey into non-Western theater cultures and considering a theory of drama in which the techniques transcend the merely material and which regards a journey into the spirit as the ultimate function and essence of performance.

The distinction between drama and theater, as well as their interdependence, must be kept in mind throughout any discussion of drama and theater in contemporary English-speaking African society. In such discussions the tendency too often is to go straight to the published plays because they represent the modern tradition and are easily retrievable and accessible. Such an approach gives a misleading impression of contemporary African theater, which I consider to include both the indigenous and Western traditions of the art. I therefore attempt to discuss both forms in their historical perspectives in the following pages. Moreover, many of the contemporary African playwrights are products of two cultures, indigenous African and Western, so that the English-language plays cannot be fully understood without recourse to their traditional cultural backgrounds. Also, if we locate the contemporary African theater only in the historical period beginning in the 1960s, when the majority of English-speaking African states achieved independence, we risk ignoring earlier play and theatrical traditions, including not only that theater which was part of the colonial encounter but also the evolution of popular traditions such as the concert party and operatic performances, sometimes in English and sometimes in African languages, which are still part of the contemporary scene.

Indigenous African Theater in the Contemporary Setting

The strength of indigenous African theater before the coming of the Europeans and Arabs resided in cultural associations and community institutions. These associations, which were community-based, were often distinguished in their varying functions by the age, sex, and sometimes occupation of the members. In addition to the political, social, and artistic obligations they fulfilled for their people, which included the initiation of new members, the associations formed performance groups for drama, music, and dance, as well as sculpting, decorative, and other artistic groups.

Since public performance is the usual medium adopted by the arts in indigenous African as in other societies, it was not difficult to find one kind or another going on throughout the year's cycle. Drama, dance, poetry, story-telling, music, and the creation of sculpture lent themselves readily to performances, which naturally exploited contemporary religious and social realities. That these performances drew large crowds indicates that they were fully supported by the community; it is therefore not difficult to see why the Islamic and Christian organizations tried hard to stamp them out. The Muslims banned the use of the principal form of character representation, the mask, while the Christians raided ancestral shrines and forbade African converts to participate in their cultural association's activities, or even play their musical instruments. The attacks on the Yoruba *Egúngún*, the Igbo *Mmonwu*, the Mende *Poro*, the Chewa *Nyau*, or the Luo *Isinyago* and *M'dimu* were aimed at the peoples' indigenous religious and political ethos, as dramatized in these performances. To attack the cultural associations and pronounce their practices evil or barbaric was the best way to stamp out the art forms and politics engendered by them. Nevertheless, the reappearance of the banned performances and their incorporation of characters and themes involving the colonizers themselves in performances such as in the *ikoro* of the Ngwa in Igboland, the *egúngún* of the Yoruba, or the *gule wa mkulu* of the Chewa, shows the resilience of indigenous dramatic art and its ability to cope with the changing political and historical climate. Indigenous artists remained faithful to the tradition of their art, through which they interpreted political, religious, and social developments.

Before Africa's contact with Europe's colonialism, Africans were already accustomed to treating political and religious matters in their drama. Performances reached the highest state of artistic inclusiveness and excellence during festivals at which certain central myths and rituals were reenacted by the people as a whole, and which also provided opportunities for the treatment of purely social issues through the use of masked characters, puppets, and other techniques. The use of masks for character representation had the effect of liberating the actor from psychological inhibitions and imbuing him at the same time with the sacred essence that, by convention, enabled him to be unique and to project a role that nobody would dare challenge or contest. The masked actor thus embodied the holy actor, spirit essence, ancestor, or supernatural essence the dramatic role transformed him into.

In the contact with the colonial administration the mask was a symbol of both mystical and political authority, hence the reluctance of masked performers to submit to colonial law enforcement. According to Isaac O. Delano, when a Yoruba *egúngún* was arrested for committing a criminal offense during a performance, he claimed he was "a native of another planet, and therefore outside this world's police authority" (164–65). In spite of strong protests the *egúngún* was tried in court and sentenced to two weeks' imprisonment with hard labor. This incident best illustrates the easy confusion of the artistic, religious, and political functions of the masked performer. Nor has the situation changed in post-Independence African states, where performances by cultural associations still constitute a claim to power and display a willingness to court danger by defying civil law. In Nigeria, where a rich diversity of performances is sponsored by cultural associations, masked performers have often been known to clash with the police. In the cosmopolitan city of Lagos, *Èyò* performances hold sway, and efforts by the police to control their activities have often ended in social disorder. The same can be said of the *Egúngún* in Ibadan, the *Mmonwu* in Enugu, the *Ekpe* in Calabar, or the *Bori* in Kaduna. John Nunley reports the same situation about the Ode-lay masking society in Freetown, Sierra Leone, which courts confrontation with police and government in its street performance as an integral aspect of its aesthetic and spiritual success (102). Ode-lay groups, whose names—such as Firestone, Rainbow, Bloody Mary, and Joyce Wata— suggest a certain physical toughness and supernatural association, have remained part of the reality of the urban environment, and they delight in choosing strategic locations in the streets for their performances.

In the true sense of artistic development and awareness, indigenous the-atrical performances mirrored the historical realities of the colonial period and therefore contributed to helping rural Africans develop what David Kerr describes as "cross-cultural competitive organizational skills . . . an essential element of the consciousness-raising that preceded the formal struggle for independence" ("Unmasking the Spirits" 116). British colonialism came down heavily on indigenous African culture, especially the performing arts. The reaction of the indigenous theater to colonial efforts to gag it was similar in many African countries. The Igbo in Nigeria created new plays featuring British colonial officers—administrators, police, missionaries—and their families as characters to replace the banned traditional characters. The new plays were satiric comedies imitating the manners and foibles of the Euro-pean in a very broad sense, but also more incisively where historical circum-stances provided materials on such characters. The colonial district commis-sioner, popularly known as "Nwa D.C." (*nwa* being an Igbo term for "child," which the elders used in this context to draw attention to the young administrative officers who were made to rule over and command their elders, contrary to the Igbo system of authority), has become a stock charac-ter in contemporary indigenous theater. He can be seen in a variety of performances strolling along with his aides and muttering instructions to them. The policeman is another stock character, frequently sheepish in his execution of authority. Colonial Europeans, men, women, and children, feature in the *Ijele, Uzoiyi, Odo, Omabe*, and *Ikoro* performances, to mention only a few in Igboland.

In *Ikoro* the repertoire of European characters includes the King and Queen of England, the Governor General in Lagos, the Residents and District Commissioners in the provinces and districts, and the law enforce-ment officers (Amankulor, "Concept and Practice"). The performance takes the form of an official visit by the king and queen of England to their subjects at Ngwa in Igboland and the ceremonies and protocols performed to receive them, including the presentation of the welcome address and the response to it. In spite of the obvious satire of the performance, the *ikoro* drum, the original symbol of the performance before colonial intervention, still occupies the center of the arena stage, surrounded by a chorus of dancers. Other social dramas, such as the negotiation for medicines hawked by an itinerant Hausa trader, take place on the outskirts of the ring formed by the dancers. Also, the Aba Ugwu festival of Okpatu Udi in Igboland features a district commissioner of the 1930s, a Mr. Chadwick, who was notorious for sending men on forced labor for weeks without considering the effect their absence would have on their families. Elsewhere in Africa, the Nyau cult leaders in Malawi reacted to colonial interference in their *Gule wa Mkulu* (big dance) "by incorporating stereotypes of colonial political and religious figures into the satire of the anthropomorphic masking traditions" (Kerr, "Unmasking the Spirits" 116, quoting Schofeleers and Linden 1972), and in the Bamana puppet plays in Mali the characters include colonial as well as modern-day police (Arnoldi 66).

The contradictions of colonial contact that led to the incorporation of European characters into indigenous African plays have become a regular, albeit anachronistic, feature of the performances. Their place within the total structure of the performance, however, shows that although they form a constellation of history, they are only peripheral to the people's lives and worldview. Thus, in the variety of festival and other performances where they are featured, the colonial figures yield the center of the performance space to the enactment of the original myths or stories at the basis of the performance.

The foregoing is only a brief overview of indigenous theatrical performances in Africa. The scholarly debate on the question of indigenous theater and drama in Africa has been conducted by such scholars as Ruth Finnegan, M. J. C. Echeruo, Oyekan Owomoyela, Alain Ricard, Oyin Ogunba, J. Ndukaku Amankulor, Ossie Enekwe, and S. O. Obuh, to name but a few. In my view, indigenous theater and drama are alive and well in contemporary African culture, conflicting theories of the drama notwithstanding.

The Colonial Legacy

There was no lack of enthusiasm by the British to build theaters, especially in the cosmopolitan cities where the seats of government were located. As early as 1800 Sir George Yonge had built the African Theatre in Cape Town, South Africa. Although it was forced to close in 1839 because of the puritanical campaigns against it by the Methodist church, which accused it of "sinful practices," the African Theatre's premiere production, Shakespeare's *Henry IV*, showed its strong cultural orientation. Similar theaters, sometimes all-purpose town halls, were built in Lagos, Accra, Lusaka, and Nairobi, to mention only a few capitals, and thrown open for cultural uses by Europeans and sometimes by elite Africans whose aesthetic taste mimicked that of the whites. Lagos still has its Glover Memorial Hall, and Nairobi its Donovan Maule Theatre and the Kenya National Theatre, which Ngūgī wa Thiong'o (*Decolonising the Mind* 41) decried because they were still European-dominated. The Glover Memorial Hall opened in Lagos in 1899 and catered to the interest of Europeans, as well as of Black elite clubs formed by returnee ex-slaves such as those who formed "The Academy" in 1866, the Philharmonic Society, the Lagos Glee Singers, and Brazilian Dramatic Company. The preoccupation with European culture was so undisguised in these colonial theater establishments that any play with an African cultural theme presented in them was considered greatly favored. Thus in 1904 when D. A. Oloyede's premier Nigerian drama, *King Elejigbo and Princess Abeje of Kotangora*, was performed at the Glover Memorial Hall, the event made history because it was the first play written by a Nigerian (and the first church-sponsored drama group) to be presented there (Ogunbiyi 19).

Colonial theaters were designed as institutions to showcase European culture and civilization, a function that church organizations and educational institutions were later to help promote and perpetuate. The establishment of the European form of theater in complete indifference to traditional forms, which Robert Serumaga and Janet Johnson lament, was aided by the formal study and practice of the European tradition in the schools and among church groups. According to Serumaga and Johnson, the theater of Europe "did not even superimpose itself onto the traditions, but rather led an isolated existence related only to the needs of the few who fell within its ambit" (52–53). I have offered cultural and political reasons why this could have happened. Moreover, Serumaga is aware that the major aim of colonialism was not to promote indigenous culture and give the Africans a sense of pride in themselves and in their institutions, but, to the contrary, to "civilize" Africa, which means bringing up its people in the image and likeness of the colonizers.

In South Africa the formation of the Bantu Dramatic Society in 1933 led to the production of English plays, the first being Oliver Goldsmith's *She Stoops to Conquer*. The founder of the society, Herbert I. E. Dhlomo, was in 1935 to write the first published African play in English. *The Girl Who Killed to Save* explores an aspect of a traditional story, which he gives a Christian moral twist by attacking traditional dependence on mystical and magical powers as worthless. Dhlomo's heroine, Nongqause, leads her people to famine and dependence by her announcement that the ancestors of the Ama Xhosa have told her that the invading white people will be defeated if the Ama Xhosa slaughter their cattle and leave their soil uncultivated. They follow her advice and suffer famine and hardship, later to be restored to prosperity through the efforts of the same invaders in the persons of the commissioner, his wife, his brother-in-law, and a missionary.

Elsewhere in Africa the British system of education, which encouraged the use of indigenous languages at the early stages, led to the production of plays in those languages first. The church-sponsored schools frequently organized social, educational, and religious celebrations and activities where plays in African languages were performed, interspersed with music, dance, and recitations, most of which drew their creative origins from indigenous art forms. Biblical stories were dramatized and presented in programs containing dramatized local tales, selected local dances, and songs. In West Africa this medley of theatrical presentation, often known as concerts, offered inspiration for further dramatic creativity, which blossomed into the Yoruba operas in Nigeria and the concert party groups in Ghana. The organizers of the church and school concerts frequently kept the performances indoors— in the assembly or social halls, which may or may not have raised stage areas, but which in terms of spatial and conventional standards constituted direct borrowings from the presentation techniques of Europe. Many church and government school assembly halls were therefore furnished with raised-platform stages, house curtains, and backdrops, which became standard equipment for all kinds of performances, no matter how inappropriate the halls were for the materials being presented in them. Thus with school concerts and plays the proscenium stage became the model for all performances and occasions. It became a legacy that the universities would later adopt, and as such the spatial point of reference for African playwrights and producers. Popular European playwrights such as Shakespeare, Molière, George Bernard Shaw, and Henrik Ibsen were featured in the school productions by literature students, who constituted the backbone of the dramatic societies and participated in the productions, because doing so they had the opportunity to memorize the lines of the relevant plays on which they were to be tested in their literature examinations. The performances were duly reported in the local papers as well as in the teachers' educational journals, such as the *Native Teacher's Journal* in South Africa and the *Nigerian Teacher* in Nigeria.

Achimota College, in Ghana, also became involved in dramatic activities from the early 1920s. Here students produced their own plays in indigenous African languages. By 1933, after a two-year assistance by the staff to help the students produce English plays, there came a decision by the students "never to put on a vernacular play again" (Williams 63). In a reverse situation in the same country, the Accra Dramatic Society (founded by Africans in 1929) was discouraged by their mentor and British educator, J. M. Winterbottom, from producing Ibsen, Shaw, and Galsworthy, because "they were concerned with situations the majority of which have not yet arisen in West Africa" ("Experimental Drama" 113). In any case, the dramatic fare in Ghana, as in Nigeria, was largely foreign. Even on the eve of independence, in the 1950s, the University College Ibadan dramatic presentations featured such performances as *Arms and the Man* by the Student Dramatic Society (1958), *H.M.S. Pinafore* by the Ibadan Operatic Society (1958), and the *Mostellaria* in Latin and the *Cyclops* in Greek by the Classics Society (1957 and 1961 respectively). Dramatic activity that encouraged indigenous playwrights started in earnest in both countries with the founding of the Arts Theatre Group in 1958 at the University College Ibadan and of the Ghana Experimental Players by Efua Sutherland in Ghana.

School plays did not become a popular tradition despite their medley performance convention, and neither did the African elite club performances. They lacked grass-roots supports. With the eruption of World War I cultural development diminished in importance as attention was diverted to helping the British in their war effort, and there was less interest in theatrical development. In West Africa, it took the efforts of people like Hubert Ogunde in Nigeria and Ishmael Johnson in the Gold Coast (Ghana), working within the syncretistic tradition of the Western church-oriented morality musical plays and the indigenous aesthetic conventions, to build a popular tradition of African theater outside the walls of the secondary schools, colleges, and universities. Hubert Ogunde was influenced in his operatic performance convention by the theatricalized church services of the breakaway African churches in Nigeria, especially the Aladura sect, which made use of African and European music and musical instruments along with dance, song, and mimes in their worship. As an organist and composer of native airs, Ogunde became involved in dramatic presentations for his church. The moral religious emphasis is evident in his first two plays, *The Garden of Eden and the Throne of God* (1944) and *Worse Than Crime* (1946), which respectively deal with Adam and Eve's rebellion against God, and the evils of the slave trade.

The success of those two plays encouraged him to resign from the police force to become a professional theater artiste, and with his total savings of only nine pounds he founded his first theater company, the African Music Research Party. Acknowledging the reality of his indigenous Yoruba culture and its influence on him as a product of "the ritual ceremony, the ritual priest and communal life" (Ogunbiyi 10), Ogunde strove to reflect his society by focusing on its social, political, and moral concerns. He contributed actively through theater to the fight against colonialism with such plays as *Strike and Hunger* (1945)—for which the colonial police arrested, tried, and fined him at Jos in 1947 on the charge of inciting the workers to rebel—and *Bread and Bullet* (1950), which treats the Enugu coal miners' strike of 1949 and the massacre of eighteen miners by the police. With other Yoruba artistes, especially Kola Ogunmola and Duro Ladipo, Ogunde created a distinct theatrical tradition in contemporary Nigerian theater, the Yoruba operatic theater. It is believed that there are about one hundred Yoruba traveling theater groups today in the Association of Nigerian Theatre Practitioners.

Like Ogunde in Nigeria, Ishmael Johnson pioneered a popular tradition of theater, the concert party, in the former Gold Coast, now Ghana. Kwabena N. Bame writes that the history of this new form of dramatic entertainment, which drew upon indigenous as well as foreign influences, may be traced to a certain Teacher Yalley, headmaster of a Sekondi elementary school who began giving "concerts" and acting in his school's Empire Day celebrations back in 1918 (Bame 8). Yalley's performances were a medley of "jokes, singing and dancing," in which he disguised himself with fancy clothes, wigs, false mustaches, and minstrel makeup. His audiences were the elite of society, and it took Ishmael ("Bob") Johnson, himself a pupil of Yalley in the Sekondi school, to bring the "concert" to the masses by playing to popular audiences in the towns. Influenced by the Yalley tradition, church morality and musical plays, Charlie Chaplin's characteristic walk in the silent movies, Black American vaudeville, and the *Anansesem* (Spider folktales) storytelling conventions of the Akan peoples, Johnson created in 1930 a concert trio known as The Two Bobs, including himself and his two school friends J. "Bob" Ansah and C. B. Hutton. Johnson and Ansah played the "Bobs" (male roles) and Hutton played the female character, in which she was later to be popularly featured as "the Carolina Girl." According to E. J. Collins, these shows were publicized "by a masked bell-ringer wearing a billboard" (52).

The performance structure consisted of one half hour made up of an "Opening Chorus," an "In" and a "Duet," and the "Scene" or the play proper. The opening chorus was sung and danced by the three actors, the "in" comprised ragtime sung by one of the Bobs, and the duet, which closed the thirty-minute introduction, featured the two Bobs in a joking session. The scene (or play) lasted one hour. The language of presentation was English (occasionally translated into Akan and Pidgin English), which was also the language of the highlife lyrics. In effect the performance catered to a wide variety of audiences, including those who had received some Western education, people whose education was picked up in the city streets, and people who knew no English.

Between 1935, when Johnson left The Two Bobs to join another concert party, The Axim Trio, and 1960, twenty-eight guitar bands with concert parties had been registered, and about the same number had become members of the Musicians Union of Ghana (MUSIGA), formed on 24 June 1978. The MUSIGA—whose constitution included, among other aims, the protection of the creative and performing rights of the musicians and the encouragement of talent and research into indigenous music and culture—is a tribute to the creative seed sown by Ishmael Johnson and his friends in the popularization of the performing arts. Like Ogunde, they brought the practice of theater within the reality of a profession capable of earning them a living while also entertaining and educating their audiences. Presentations such as "The Jealous Rival" and "The Ungrateful Husband" were not just invitations for the audience to "come and laugh" (Bame 103–90) but also pleas to them to reflect on the moral, social, and cultural implications of the actions of the people they laughed at.

On the eve of the 1960s, when the majority of African countries were granted independence by the British and the French, some African playwrights had started to demonstrate sufficient mastery or competence in the dramatic form to declare their independence from the earlier religious, educational, and cultural tutelage of the churches, the schools, and the British Broadcasting Corporation. Plays from West Africa, like Kobina Senyi's *The Blinkards* and J. B. Danquah's *The Third Woman* (both from the Gold Coast), were already exploiting the themes of social responsibility and the cultural image of the African in the light of his acquired European civilization. In general the plays urged the ideal of a balance between traditional African and European cultures so that the African might still identify with the masses in the rural villages as well as the elite in the urban environment.

In Nigeria, the same concern with the conflict between indigenous and European cultures marked Wole Soyinka's early plays, *The Swamp Dwellers* and *The Lion and the Jewel*, written between 1957 and 1958. Igwezu, the protagonist of *The Swamp Dwellers*, finds no comfort in the swamps, where his parents live, nor in the city, where his twin brother now lives. In the swamp his crops are washed off by the floods in spite of the mandatory sacrifices he makes to the Serpent god through his priest, Kadiye, and in the city his own wife is seduced by his twin brother—an abominable offense in traditional society. Igwezu is no longer at ease in either environment. In *The Lion and the Jewel* Lakunle's mindless application of Western strategies to indigenous situations results in failure. Traditional culture, symbolized in the character of Baroka, the Lion of Ilujinle, proves to possess greater stability and common sense. Sidi, who stands in the middle of the two cultures, prefers to seek a union with Baroka rather than Lakunle. Baroka's mesmerizing address to her, urging that "the old must flow into the new," suggests the playwright's solution to the conflict, a realization that one culture cannot now exist independent of the other: Africa and the West, the old and the young.

Unlike the healthy conflict and optimism of the West African plays on the eve of independence, the plays written by Africans at the same time in South Africa were rather less robust and more pessimistic. Dhlomo's *Dingane* (1959), like his earlier play, reveals a fixed pessimism from which there appears to be no relief except for the moral religious recourse to forgiveness. The play takes its title from the name of one of Shaka's brothers, who planned and executed his death. Dingane is hated fiercely by Shaka's sister, who, however, by the end of the play decides to forgive him, saying, "I must cease to hate." In other words, the entire heroic tone of the Shaka story, based on revenge tragedy, sobers into a morality tale of forgiveness. Tjaart Coetzee's *Kwa-Namakunde* is another pessimistic portrayal of an African kingdom after its conquest by the Europeans. Anthony Graham-White attributes the pervading pessimism in South African plays to the political reality the Africans there faced, which was different from that in West Africa (81).

The British Broadcasting Corporation, an active partner in the cultural formation of Africa in the European tradition, played a significant role in the development of contemporary African theater of English expression. The BBC African Service program featured a monthly series, "African Theatre," designed to encourage dramatic creativity among African writers and to further the cultural development of the theater through the medium of radio. Shirley Cordeaux writes that the first production in the new series was an adaptation of a part of the Wakefield Cycle of medieval English mystery plays by a South African author, Tjaart Coetzee, writing under the pseudonym Chawanda Kutse (147). *The Creation* was aired on 21 March 1962. But why adapt from the Wakefield Cycle? Cordeaux explains, "The reasoning went as follows: These Mystery plays were the beginning of theatre in England. Adapt them to an African setting, and update the language to be comprehensible to a present-day audience, and this will make an acceptable introduction to radio drama for an African audience" (148).

This reasoning, I daresay, has had an overwhelming effect in the development of contemporary African drama, which has largely followed the structure and form of the English tradition of literary dialogue while adapting the local materials to fit into this form. Chawanda Kutse's *The Creation* obviously explored a Christian religious theme that perhaps was considered safe for the African audience. Two more radio plays by the same author, *The Crucifixion* and *The Resurrection*, broadcast in the next two months, completed this Christian trilogy and fulfilled, as it were, the messianic introduction of the African radio audience to the aesthetics of modern theater.

The BBC "African Theatre" audience was very narrow indeed. Although people from different walks of life could listen to and enjoy the broadcasts and satisfy a variety of their aesthetic interests, the plays were beamed especially at the educated African class "able to speak and think comfortably in English . . . people who have undergone some course in higher education" (Cordeaux 150). While Cordeaux makes excuses for the BBC African Service for not wishing "to set itself up as an arbiter of African radio drama," yet the organization through the "African Theatre" series "acted as a radio nursery for African writing talent . . . a nursery for African actors and actresses." The influence of the BBC on the educated African elites in English-speaking Africa is an important factor in the formation of a new taste in dramatic art. That this influence has remained a tradition among many in contemporary society probably explains why the struggle between the integration of indigenous and western dramatic tastes and concepts remains unrealized.

Participation in the "African Theatre" series attracted the cream of Africa's creative writers in English. Apart from the sense of achievement and publicity they received from having their works broadcast worldwide, they were also paid a modest stipend into the bargain. It is therefore not surprising that almost all the well-known and the not-so-well-known English-speaking African playwrights participated in the African Theatre Competition organized between 1962 and 1969, and their works were broadcast whole or in part. Wole Soyinka's *The Detainee* was broadcast on 5 September 1965, six months after his *Camwood on the Leaves* was aired. Later (in 1966 and 1969, respectively), his *Lion and the Jewel* and *The Swamp Dwellers* were broadcast. Other names that have become famous in contemporary African theater and that appeared in the program include those of Ngũgĩ wa Thiong'o, formerly James Ngugi, and Kuldip Sondhi (Kenya); Ama Ata Aidoo and Joe de Graft (Ghana); John Pepper Clark [Bekederemo], Femi Euba, and Obi Egbuna (Nigeria); Pat Maddy (Sierra Leone); Guillaume Oyono-Mbia (Cameroon); and Chewanda Kutse and Bloke Modisane (South Africa), among many others. Judging from the level and quality of participation the BBC African Service "African Theatre" series attracted in the decade immediately following Independence in the 1960s, one may assert that contemporary African theater in English would never have been the same without it.

Independence and After

The attainment of political independence in the 1960s by the majority of the Anglophone and Francophone African countries was a boost to contemporary African literature. Although the groundwork had been laid through a variety of cultural, religious, and educational institutions, the arrival of political freedom triggered the need for freedom in other fields of national endeavor, including literature and the arts. The Kampala Conference on African Literature in 1964 and the Congress for Cultural Freedom meetings in Senegal and Sierra Leone in 1963 were concerned with the definition of African literature and the need for its study in the universities. They were clear recognitions by Africans that the time had come for them to be conscious of the national and cultural relevance of that literature which they could call their own.

That many Anglophone African countries, except perhaps Kenya and Zimbabwe, may be said to have attained their independence without much bitterness and bloodshed meant that the need to examine the historical, political, and cultural imperatives of African identity was not considered pressing in the era before political independence. As a result, the treatment of the conflict with colonial authority was not as strident in the drama and theater of independent English-speaking African states as was the case in South Africa. The conception of the relevance of African literature, especially drama, was that it had to examine a variety of contemporary social, political, and religious issues. Although the phenomenon of the contemporary African personality as one delicately balanced between indigenous culture and western civilization has already been explored in pre-Independence writing, there was an intensification of its probing by post-Independence playwrights and an expansion of its application to include economic and political implications. The sheer outpouring of creative energy was a symbolic declaration of independence by the playwrights, even though they continued to rely largely on European dramatic form and production conventions.

From playwrights commanding a high degree of national and international visibility, like Wole Soyinka, Ngũgĩ wa Thiong'o, and others, to the more local, like the Onitsha Market playwrights, came plays that tackled the problems of society, social relationships, and national independence with varying degrees of success, and that appealed to different social classes. Soyinka's plays, for example, could be visually appealing to popular audiences, and also had the intellectual sophistication that made them an intellectual challenge for university audiences. Hubert Ogunde and other Yoruba traveling theater practitioners, on the other hand, reached the masses more easily, and the Onitsha Market plays found ready audiences among high school students, who often produced them to entertain fellow students.

Themes

The themes of the plays written from the late 1950s through the 1980s range over a wide spectrum of issues, which include social relationships and institutional changes affecting marriage and family life, ethnic taboos, prejudices, chauvinism, and social responsibility. Political themes, including corruption among the ruling classes, are also explored by the playwrights. Even religion, especially the conflict among the new religions and their corruptive influences, finds its way into the plays. In thematic terms, it is fair to say that African playwrights writing in English, like their French-language counterparts, have displayed considerable concern for the problems of their society even though their styles of treating the issues naturally vary according to the influences affecting them and the degree of their social commitment to those issues.

The theme of conflict between African and European traditions is pervasive in the early plays of Wole Soyinka. This concern continues in his plays of the 1960s (including *The Trials of Brother Jero* [1960], *Camwood on the Leaves* [1960], *Childe Internationale* [1987], *The Strong Breed* [1963], *Kongi's Harvest* [1965], and *The Road* [1965]), and in the post–civil war plays (including *Madmen and Specialists* [1971], *The Bacchae of Euripides* [1973], *Opera Wonyosi* [1981], and *Death and the King's Horseman* [1975]). His interest in cultural nationalism, for which he reinvents the myth of Ogun, may be seen in many different guises in his plays. In *Brother Jero* the conflict between Jero and Old Prophet dramatizes the corruptions that have permeated the field of religion as a result of the selfish quest for material gains. In *Camwood* the conflict is between Isola, the rebellious son of a Christian pastor who has made the daughter of the Olumorins pregnant, and his father, whom he kills in an attempt to shoot a boa that threatens to exterminate a tortoise and her young ones. *Childe Internationale* is a light-hearted treatment of cultural conflict. In it Titi, the daughter of a local politician and student at an international school, returns home to practice her newfound European freedom, actively encouraged by her "been-to" mother. Indigenous culture prevails here, as in *The Lion and the Jewel*.

In *The Strong Breed* and *Kongi's Harvest*, Soyinka explores two kinds of conflict, the one cultural and metaphysical and the other cultural and political. The ritual ceremony of the scapegoat in the former play is one of those cultural practices that may offer society a psychological renewal but that, in the light of contemporary civilization, needs to be abolished. In the latter play the cultural celebration of the New Yam Festival by Oba Danlola is usurped by Kongi, president of the Republic of Isma. This usurpation of ritual authority by a political leader creates a conflict in which both cultural and political stability are threatened. In *The Road* cultural symbols are exploited for the personal and selfish benefit of the Professor, whose death becomes a victory for Say Tokyo Kid and the other layabouts whom he had continuously exploited. The conflict (with regard to moral responsibility) is played out in *Death and the King's Horseman*, in which Elesin Oba's delay to perform the ritual suicide demanded of him causes his British-educated son and medical student, Olunde, to commit suicide in his place. Although Olunde's death brings shame to his father and prompts him to kill himself rather belatedly, it is questionable whether his personal sacrifice represents a triumph for the younger generation in any meaningful or progressive sense. Biodun Jeyifo has criticized Soyinka's resolution of the conflict as a typical African "bourgeois" historical tragedy characterized by conformism (106–7).

With regard to political themes, Soyinka is at his best with the satiric portrayal of corrupt and power-hungry political figures. *Kongi's Harvest*, *Opera Wonyosi*, and *A Play of Giants* are full-length plays dealing directly with politics and power. In *Kongi's Harvest* a life-giving institution, the New Yam Festival that constitutes the permanent backdrop of the play, is travestied by Kongi, who turns it into a sterile, life-threatening celebration. The travesty in turn breeds plotters like Daodu and Segi, who plan to assassinate Kongi in order to restore the communality and spirituality of the traditional celebration. The failure of the assassination plot creates a confusing denouement that leaves Kongi still in control and likely to become even more ruthless in the consolidation of his political power.

Extreme degrees of such callous ruthlessness characterize the actions of the African leaders portrayed in *A Play of Giants*, published in 1984. Idi Amin, the deposed Ugandan tyrant (Kamini in the play), is the central butt of this deadly satire. With such other political tyrants as Macias Nguema of Equatorial Guinea, Jean Bedel Bokassa, the self-styled emperor of the Central African Empire, and Mobutu Sese Seko of Zaire, respectively disguised in the play as Benfacio Gunema, Emperor Basco, and Barra Toboum, he poses for a sculptor attended by Gudrum, a hypocritical and fawning Scandinavian journalist. Soyinka chronicles the sadistic and blood-chilling repressive measures adopted by these leaders, the "giants" of Africa, in keeping themselves in power with the active connivance of the imperialist forces, East and West, and the support of local functionaries, including intellectuals, economists and image-makers. Kamini, a symbol of evil in all its ramifications, unleashes a desperate assault on the United Nations (symbol of superpower politics) when news reaches him that he has been overthrown with arms supplied by the superpowers to his country of Bugara. Although *A Play of Giants* is set in New York rather than Africa, its symbolic denouement is unmistakably positive for the oppressed in Africa, who are the ultimate victims of the ineptitude of the African political process created and exploited by imperialist forces. The play endorses the stand that when true freedom comes in Africa with the entry of patriotic and well-informed leaders, the monsters forced on the people as leaders will, like Frankenstein's, turn against the very powers that created or nurtured them. Thus the giants in the play are political midgets in fact, whose leadership is both an imposition and an insult to the natural potential of the African.

Soyinka's countrymen who have won international recognition as playwrights include John Pepper Clark, Ola Rotimi, Obi Egbuna, and Femi Osofisan. While J. P. Clark's *Song of a Goat* (1964) established him as a playwright, his *Ozidi* (1966) testified to his indebtedness to traditional folk material and Ijo performance tradition. Other plays such as *The Raft* and *The Masquerade* (both 1964) equally exploit the folktale models for contemporary social and political meaning. Ola Rotimi is well known for his successful adaptation of Sophocles's *Oedipus Rex* into an African play with a Yoruba background, titled *The Gods Are Not to Blame* (1971). *Kurunmi* (1971) deals with the nineteenth-century Yoruba wars, and *Ovonramwen Nogbaisi* (1974) tells the story of an Oba of Benin who was forced to surrender to British soldiers in the last decade of the nineteenth century. Both plays are fatalistic tragedies in the classical Greek mode, and Rotimi has been criticized for adopting a tragic form that does not serve the needs of contemporary Nigerian society in any positive way. *If . . .* (1983), subtitled *The Tragedy of the Ruled*, purveys a concept of the hero and of collective action consistent with those of the other plays. In it the collective action of renters against a corrupt landlord and politician fails, and the young boy who represents the future continuation of the struggle is killed during the police action to evict the renters. Rotimi's plays, though culturally interesting and dramatically moving, fail to suggest a positive basis for a new social order.

The younger generation of Nigerian playwrights have, since the civil war, been critical of their predecessors for not providing a guiding social vision for contemporary society. They have therefore written plays to fill this artistic ideological vacuum. The outstanding playwright of this generation is Femi Osofisan. Others are Tunde Fatunde, Egiab Irobi, and Segun Oyekunle, whose plays demonstrate the same urgency and social awareness that suffuse contemporary Black South African drama. Among the female playwrights, Zulu Sofola's depiction of the traditional role of women is contrasted with her younger counterpart, Tess Onwueme's, who challenges the traditional gender assumptions in her plays.

In Ghana, Efua Sutherland, Ama Ata Aidoo, and J. C. de Graft have played major roles in the establishment of contemporary drama and theater. Efua Sutherland especially has worked consistently since the days of Kwame Nkrumah in the early 1960s toward the founding of a national theater and dramatic culture in Ghana. Her most important plays, *Edufa, Foriwa,* and *The Marriage of Anansewa,* show her development within the European dramatic tradition as well as her determination to create a new dramatic aesthetic that would define for her what a truly African theater should be. She founded an open-air theater called the Ghana Drama Studio in Accra, and the Kodzidan (Story House) in Ekumfi-Atiwa.

Edufa (1967) is the story of a man of that name who seeks to escape death by manipulating his wife, Ampoma, to succumb to a death the oracles predicted for him. Although the similarities between this play and *Alcestis* by Euripides have been remarked, Sutherland nevertheless exploits traditional beliefs in divination and the interplay of traditional and European ceremonies in the attempt to portray a rich and successful modern Edufa held in high esteem by his people. In *Foriwa* (1967) Sutherland uses her protagonists, Foriwa, the beautiful and enlightened daughter of the queen mother of Kyerefaso, and Labaran, a graduate from the north of Ghana who lives a simple and unostentatious life, to bring enlightenment to the town of Kyerefaso, which has been abandoned to ignorance and backwardness by its elders' refusal to learn new ways. The theme of the play is obviously national, namely, the promotion of a new national spirit in Ghana that would encourage inter-ethnic cooperation and openness to new ideas. This is the significance of the queen mother's promise to use the festival of the town as a symbol of positive renewal, because "Kyerefaso needs the new life . . . and men to make it true." *The Marriage of Anansewa* (1975) is Sutherland's most valuable contribution to Ghanaian drama and theater. In it she transmutes the traditional Akan Spider tales *(Anansesem)* into a new dramatic structure, which she calls *Anansegoro.* In the play the storyteller occupies his traditional prominent position as the wise commentator and narrator, uniting the audience with the actors onstage and preventing false emotions from passing for facts by debunking the actions of pretenders such as Ananse and his aides.

Ama Ata Aidoo has produced literary works in drama, fiction, and poetry. She is not as strongly attached to practical theater as Sutherland, but her two plays, *The Dilemma of a Ghost* (1965) and *Anowa* (1970), are strong contributions to the Ghanaian theater of the mid-1960s and early 1970s. Both plays deal with the role of positive communication and mutual confidence, or the lack of them, in the relationship between men and women. In *The Dilemma* Ato Yawson, a Ghanaian, marries Eulalie Rush, an African American, in the United States, promising her a life full of pleasure and free from extended family intervention in his native Ghana. The conflict between the couple arises from Ato's romantic promise, which the realities of an African marriage will not support. It takes Ato's mother, Esikom, to educate Eulalie and save the marriage. In *Anowa* the marriage of Kofi and Anowa heads for a disastrous tragedy because of the failure of Kofi, though a wealthy and handsome businessman, to communicate positively with his wife, especially about his impotence, which appears to have resulted from a curse placed on him by the ghosts of the slaves he keeps to promote his business. Unable to stand the shame they have brought on each other and on themselves, Kofi and Anowa commit suicide, leaving behind their alienated families and townspeople to pass judgment on them.

Like Aidoo's, J. C. de Graft's plays *Sons and Daughters* (1964) and *Through a Film Darkly* (1970) had a tremendous impact on African theater in English in the 1960s and 1970s. They have been produced by drama groups in universities and urban areas throughout the continent. *Sons and Daughters*, which deals with the choice of suitable professions for the youngest son and daughter of a self-made African whose two oldest sons are a doctor and accountant respectively, was topical in the early days of independence. It remains so today. The desire of the father to have his youngest son and daughter become an engineer and a lawyer respectively, against their wishes of becoming an artist and a dancer, amounts to a critique of the value of education in contemporary African society. *Through a Film Darkly* explores the tragedy inherent in the sort of lack of honest communication we have observed in Ama Ata Aidoo's two plays. John breaks his promise to marry Rebecca when he falls in love with an English girl, but eventually he breaks up with the latter also. When he returns home, he marries Sewah. Rebecca learns the truth of John's insincerity, confronts him with his deception, and finally kills herself. Unable to accommodate his deceit of Rebecca and his humiliation at the hands of his English girl, who in fact used him only as an anthropological specimen, John commits suicide. The dilemma for the emergent educated African who must play a role in divergent contemporary cultures is clearly evident in John's fate. De Graft's last play, *Muntu* (1977), is a philosophical portrayal of the history of Africa from its mythic origins, through the scramble for Africa and the slave trade, to the struggle for independence. The inability of Muntu's children to remain united, aggravated by pressure from external forces, leads to political turmoil and rapid changes of governments, civilian and military, with dictatorial tendencies. Commissioned by the All Africa Council of Churches, *Muntu* projects a religious yet deterministic image of man, who must always continue to struggle in life and death, "Because at the heart of Creation / There seems to lie a will counter-purposed" (89).

Other major Ghanaian playwrights include Kwesi Kay, whose plays have been broadcast on radio, and Kofi Awoonor, whose one-act plays include *Ancestral Power* and *Lament* (both 1972). Kwesi Kay's *Laughter and Hubbub in the House* (1972) and *Maama* (1968), Darlene Clems's radio plays *The Prisoner, the Judge, and the Jailor* and *Scholarship Woman* (both 1973) have also been published. Asiedu Yirenkyi's collection of five plays, titled *Kivulu and Other Plays* (1980), deals with a variety of domestic problems, sometimes set against the background of traditional ritual or urban environment.

Post-Independence plays in other parts of English-speaking West Africa, including Sierra Leone and The Gambia, have been influenced by similar social, cultural, and political pressures observable in the plays from Nigeria and Ghana. Sarif Easmon put Sierra Leone on the map of African drama and theater with his two plays, *Dear Parent and Ogre* and *The New Patriots* (both 1965), both of which are peopled by characters who control the wealth, influence, and top positions in society, flaunt their decadence shamelessly, and drown their corruption in champagne, fine talk, and the superior mannerisms of cozy affluence. *Dear Parent and Ogre* shows how dirty politics gets among people of this class even in negotiating a marriage. *The New Patriots* reveals in a rather melodramatic way the corrupt record of a minister of state and his associates who scramble to grab their country's money. "These are the NEW PATRIOTS," Easmon says.

Yulisa (Pat) Amadu Maddy's handling of the social and political problems of society is more effective than Easmon's. Maddy has published many plays since the 1960s, and he is still quite active, especially in his commitment to bringing a theater of conscience to the people. His plays, published in 1971, include *Obasai, Yon-Kon, Life Everlasting, Gbana-Bendu*, and *Alla Gbah*. They expose the hypocrisy of those who are supposed to have the public trust, especially men who are supposedly called to God's service. *Alla Gbah* is the social tragedy of Joko Campbell, a young man conceived and raised in deceit and hypocrisy, the offspring of a local pastor and a widow. He learns the truth of his parentage and exposes their hypocrisy in his death cell as he awaits hanging for the murder of his lover. In his later plays, Maddy embraces the role of the theater activist, turning to the problems of the poor masses of his country and raising the battle cry for social reforms.

In The Gambia Ramatoulie Kinteh's full-length play *Rebellion* (1968) joins those celebrating African independence in the 1960s. Here, the daughter of a village chief who has hitherto been protected from the world travels abroad and returns home as a doctor to a new kind of life in the public service. Another playwright, Gabriel J. Roberts, has written for radio, his works including *The Trial of Busumbala* (1973).

In East and Central Africa the situation has changed radically since Martin Banham wrote in 1976: "East Africa has not, perhaps, produced any playwrights in recent years of the quality and substance of the leading playwrights from Nigeria and Ghana" (81). However, as Banham also correctly observes, dramatic activity grew in this part of Africa in the 1960s, especially in the universities, unlike in Nigeria and Ghana, where the development of popular drama and theater took place outside the universities.

Kenya became independent in 1963, but it was not until five years later that its National Theatre came under the direction of an African, Seth Adagala. The year following Independence witnessed the founding of a new theater group, the Chemchemi Theatre Company, by the then-exiled South African writer Ezekiel (Es'kia) Mphahlele. The company performed in both English and Swahili. The National Theatre, in spite of national independence, remained dominated by foreign interests and aesthetics. However, a great deal of creative revolt with strong nationalistic flavor did take place in the 1960s and 1970s, when Kenyan playwrights, directors, and actors began displaying their vibrant dramatic creativity in a variety of communication media, including radio, television, and theater. High school students wrote and produced plays in Swahili, and the University of Nairobi expanded its drama and theater program to include experimental theater. With this explosion in dramatic and theatrical activity emerged prominent names like Francis Imbuga, Kenneth Watene, Kibwana Micere Mugo, Seth Adagala, Tirus Gathwe, Waigwa Wachiira, and David Mulwa, who are involved in writing and directing for the contemporary Kenyan theater.

Kenya's leading novelist, Ngũgĩ wa Thiong'o, wrote the first full-length play by an East African, *The Black Hermit*, in 1968. He followed with a collection of three short plays published under the title *This Time Tomorrow* (1970) comprising the title play, *The Rebels*, and *The Wound in the Heart. The Black Hermit* is the story of an educated man who causes the suicide of his village wife in his attempt to condemn and distance himself from the tribal bigotry that hampers national consciousness and unity. In a short preface to the play Ngũgĩ condemns tribalism, "the biggest problem besetting the new East African countries," and urges national cooperation to stamp out the cancerous effects of "tribalism, racialism and religious factions." Ngũgĩ's social realism permeates his creative works. The insensitivity of the rich to the sufferings of the poor is the subject of *This Time Tomorrow*, in which slums erected by the poor are bulldozed by the city government in order to boost income from tourism. The crowd, representing the masses of the people, is totally alienated from the system and bemoans the fact that *uhuru* "has brought us nothing."

Francis Imbuga and Kenneth Watene are two other contributors to the nationalistic spirit of contemporary Kenyan theater. Imbuga's *The Fourth Trial* and *Kisses of Fate* (both 1972) are based on the theme of the clash of values between educated young people and their old parents or relations. *Kisses of Fate* furthers the theme of sociocultural responsibility by exposing an incestuous relationship between a brother and his sister. Both have been separated for a long time, and the riotous encounter of a promiscuous student life provides the occasion for the incest. Kenneth Watene's earliest play is *My Son for My Freedom* (1973), the title piece in a volume that also includes *The Haunting Past* and *The Broken Pot*. These plays, like Ngũgĩ's, are committed to educating the people on the need for social responsibility, reconciliation between the past and the present, and commitment to a true nation-building program. While *The Broken Pot* underscores the dignity of manual work and the dangers in overrating one's position in society, *The Haunting Past* cautions against the total rejection of traditional values in preference for an alien one. The theme is similar to that of *Sarzan*, adapted by Lamine Diakhate from a story by Birago Diop during the colonial period (Graham-White 82). Watene's plays, *My Son for My Freedom* and *Dedan Kimathi* (1974) come closer to Ngūgī's revolutionary plays of the 1970s and 1980s.

On the eve of Independence in 1962, the appointment of the director of Uganda's National Theatre was terminated. He was charged with trying to indigenize that country's theater productions. Events, however, moved rapidly thereafter. Ngūgī's *The Black Hermit* was performed by the Dramatic Society at Makerere University in that year, and in the next the university started a Free Travelling Theatre, while the National Theatre founded a drama school. The result is that since Independence Uganda's theater and drama activities have been Africanized, and today the country's prominent playwrights and creative producers like John Ruganda and Mukotani Rugyendo work within or outside the country and contribute to contemporary African theater.

Robert Serumaga (now deceased) founded a professional theater company, Theatre Limited, in 1968, and the company presented his play *The Elephants* at the National Theatre the following year. It has participated in several international theater festivals in Manila, Belgrade, and elsewhere. His plays are concerned with form as an essential ingredient for an authentic African theater aesthetic. He freely uses music, dance, and song to strengthen or replace verbal dialogue, as his play *Renga Moi* illustrates (*Renga Moi* is unpublished but was staged in London in 1975). *The Elephants* offers a huge dramatic irony when the symbolism of the title is applied to what it signifies, the protagonists. They may be huge on the outside, apparently strong and self-confident, yet in reality they are dependent and insecure, "no better than just big mice." A situation in which people will exploit others to boost their own feeling of self-importance best defines the social relationship in the play. Serumaga's Theatre Limited productions reveal the contradictions of an artist of his stature who aspires to make African theater a viable commercial venture. After the financial disasters that followed the company's production of Athol Fugard's *Blood Knot* and Wole Soyinka's *The Road*, Theatre Limited was forced to present Molière's *School for Wives* in order to attract a wider international patronage at the box office. In Africa as elsewhere, financial dependency has been the bane of many an effort to establish professional theater companies. At the present level of economic activity, the prospects for success are even bleaker.

John Ruganda, a graduate of Makerere University and a Ugandan citizen, currently directs and practices theater at the University of Nairobi in Kenya.

His plays to date include *The Burdens* (1972), *Black Mamba: Covenant with Death* (1973), *The Floods* (1988), *Music without Tears* (1982), and *The Glutton* (unpublished). *The Floods* deals with the issue of naked power. Apparently based on the murderous regime of Uganda's Idi Amin, and by extension other military regimes in Africa in which the innocent victims suffer brutally at the hands of culpable psychopaths, the play penetrates the depths of human feeling by exposing horrible murders by the gory agents of death, two of whom are the head of the secret police and a pseudointellectual. The play is structured as the flow and ebb of three successive floods, whose flows spawn crimes, the gory results being revealed after the ebbs. Ruganda has become a master of psychological realism, which he employs to great success. *The Burdens,* which brought him to theatrical prominence, deals with the inability of an erstwhile politician, Wamala, to live with the reality of his failure in politics. Instead he clings to unrealistic dreams. His wife, Tinka, finally shatters his make-believe world and kills him to relieve the family of the burden he has inflicted on it. *Black Mamba* is a satiric treatment of the sexual adventures of an expatriate, Professor Coarx, with the wife of his houseboy, Namuddu, whenever the professor's ill-natured wife is away. *Covenant with Death* explores the ravages of a curse that destroys mind and body as well as fertility and life in a couple, Mutama and her white-man city friend; it is based largely on a folkloric background. On the whole Ruganda explores a wide range of contemporary conflicts, including poverty, prostitution, class conflict, land seizure, and power control.

Tanzania's contribution to contemporary African drama and theater comes from playwrights such as Ebrahim Hussein; Mukotani Rugyendo (a Ugandan national and editor in the Tanzanian Publishing House), and Bob Leshoai, a South African playwright who became the first African to head the Department of Theatre Arts at the University College, Tanzania, the only such department among East African universities. It is also important to note that President Julius Nyerere himself has an abiding interest in dramatic art, as is evident in his translation of some of Shakespeare's works into Swahili. Moreover, his political ideology as an African committed to the building of African socialism was bound to affect dramatic and theatrical expression as an instrument in the service of national consciousness and aspiration.

The conviction that theater should be a medium of mass communication unhindered by language constraints has led such playwrights as Ebrahim Hussein, Farouk Topan, and Penina Muhando to write in Swahili in order to make the plays accessible to a wider Tanzanian public. This approach to a national theater unencumbered by the distraction of an alien language recalls Ngũgĩ's. Some of the Swahili plays have been translated into English, though, either by the playwrights themselves or by others. Ebrahim Hussein's *Kinjeketile* (1970) is one of the finest African plays, embracing the unity of ideology and art and employing theater as a consciousness-raising medium. The same is true of Mukotani Rugyendo's plays such as *The Barbed*

Wire, The Contest, and *And the Storm Gathers* (all 1977), plays that advance the argument for a socialist African state. In *The Barbed Wire* Rugyendo presents the conflict between a small peasant community and a rich farmer who tries to acquire their communal land to make himself an even bigger and richer farmer. In *The Contest* the playwright demonstrates how a modern African play can speak to popular audiences and still remain relevant in terms of its approach to social issues.

In Central Africa, as in East and West Africa, the development of modern African drama and theater has been nurtured through the schools, the radio, and the universities, which, apart from fostering dramatic activities on the campuses, have sponsored traveling theater groups and companies. Although the writing and publishing of plays did not flourish here in the 1960s as in other parts of Africa, Malawi and Zambia today boast a vibrant theater culture, especially in those experiments that bring theater to the local audiences. Andrew Horn, James Gibbs, Michael Etherton, Fay Chung, and David Kerr are among the expatriates who have helped to develop a tradition of African theater in the universities in Zambia and Malawi through theater workshops and traveling troupes. But their work could not have succeeded without the enthusiastic and creatively robust contributions of indigenous artists like Kabwe (Godfrey) Kasoma, Masauto Phiri, Stephen Chifunyise, Fwanyanga Mulikita, and Andrea Masiye in Zambia; and James Ngombe, Joe Mosiwa, Innocent Banda, Chris Kamlongera, and other playwrights published in *Nine Malawian Plays* (1976), as well as Steve Chimombo, Peter Chiwona, and Father Joseph Chakanza in Malawi.

Kabwe Kasoma's plays include *The Long Arms of the Law* (unpublished), *The Fools Marry* (1976), *Katongo Chala* (n.d.), and the *Black Mamba* trilogy (1970). Like his counterparts in Tanzania, Kasoma models his plays on the Zambian national philosophy of humanism and the leadership of Dr. Kenneth Kaunda, whose political career is the focus of the *Black Mamba* trilogy. Masautso Phiri has published a play titled *Nightfall* (n.d.) dealing with Ngoni history. Another play of his, *Kuta* (unpublished), is a dance-drama. *Soweto: Flowers Will Grow,* the product of an extensive research and theater experiment by Phiri and other collaborating artists, symbolizes the radical contribution of a frontline African state to the cultural dimension of the struggle against apartheid. The epic proportion of Mulikita's *Shaka Zulu* (1967) and the title of Masiye's play *The Lands of Kazembe* (1973) indicate the concern of Zambian playwrights for the political realities of Southern Africa. Stephen Chifunyise, a Zimbabwean national, is perhaps better known for his contributions to the Zambian theater through radio, television, and the stage. His plays, such as *Shimakamba's Dog, The District Governor Goes to a Village,* and *I Resign* (all unpublished), address the issues confronting the poor in an independent African state, educating party cadres in the process (Etherton 326–34). Back home in Zimbabwe, Chifunyise has resumed the crusade for a humane society that caters to the interests of all. *Medicine for*

Love and Other Plays (1984) ranges over issues such as domestic jealousies (*Medicine for Love*), rape (*Women of Courage*), and society's reluctance to reintegrate those of its members who have acquired the stigma of imprisonment (*When Ben Came Back*).

Nine Malawian Plays comprises pieces that resulted from creative writing courses in the Department of English, University of Malawi, and that were subsequently broadcast on radio or performed at drama festivals. Chris Kamlongera's *The Love Potion* won a BBC runner-up prize, while Innocent Banda's *Lord Have Mercy* has been broadcast on Malawi Broadcasting Corporation. The plays are as diverse as their authors, in the sense that they do not seem to be as socially committed and cohesive as those by Tanzanian and Zambian playwrights, for example. But this is to be expected, judging from the relative conservatism of the Malawian writers and the conservative political ideology of their government. Spencer Chunga and Hodges Kalikwembe satirize the dangers of a little learning in *That Man Is Evil*, while Joe Mosiwa adapts a local folk material in *Who Will Marry Our Daughter?*, using a narrator-chorus technique. The play presents a fight between modernity and tradition, which ends in a compromise resolution that accommodates both. Steve Chimombo's *The Rain Maker* (1975) integrates the ancient M'bona legends with extant M'bona cult masking tradition, following the advice by Fr. Matthew Schoffeleers that Nyau cult and its protodramatic characteristics should be used as the basis for a modern Malawian theater (Roscoe 271). *Opera Extravaganza* (1976), as the name suggests, represents another direction in the search for identity in Malawian theater. Its slight plot, comprising issues such as courtship, marriage, and peacemaking, is augmented by extraordinary dancing, drumming, and singing.

Ethiopia, the oldest self-ruling African country, has not produced great drama and theater that can match those of the newly independent African states. Tsegaye Gabre-Medhin is the country's best-known playwright. His *Oda Oak Oracle* (1965) is a legend of Black peoples and their relationships with their gods as well as a tale of their hope, love, fears, and sacrifices. Another play, *Collision of Your Altars* (1970), is based on the fall of Emperor Kaleb's Axumite kingdom in sixth-century Ethiopia, which was considered the third greatest power in the world. It foreshadows the overthrow of Emperor Haile Selassie of Ethiopia by radical forces in 1974. Menghistu Lemma, another Ethiopian playwright, has published *The Marriage of Unequals* (1970). It dramatizes the story of a Western educated elite who returns home and settles among the rural population, builds a school for them, and marries his maid. His aunt, a social snob, wants him to assume his proper place among the country's elite and to choose a wife among them. The popular orientation of his protagonist notwithstanding, the playwright does not succeed in making his play into a radical social statement of any significance.

Contemporary Radical and Experimental African Drama and Theater

In the foregoing pages, in which we have taken a rather sweeping view of the contemporary drama and theater scene in English-speaking African countries, we have observed in a number of countries a style of dramaturgy that does not merely describe the contemporary situation but appears to interpret sociopolitical phenomena in such a way as to educate the reader or spectator on the desirability of mass enlightenment and commitment to the issues raised.

The task of tackling those issues has been the major burden of African drama and theater since the 1970s. In the independent African countries, where the powerful ruling military, political, or religious classes appear to have generated more poverty and social strife than existed during colonial times, the playwrights engage in historical or social analyses of the situation to arrive at an enlightened interpretation. In those parts of Africa where Africans are still politically dominated, the need for such social education becomes even more urgent. Thus we have so far not discussed the contemporary South African dramatic and theatrical scene, because the plays of that country are of the radical political type. Also in this section, we shall examine the phenomenon of experimentation as a crucial factor in the development of modern African drama and theater. Experimentation flourished in the 1970s and 1980s and promises to significantly affect the African theater in the twenty-first century.

Ngũgĩ wa Thiong'o has become one of the most important writers to emerge on the contemporary African scene. Among his most revolutionary contributions to African theater are *The Trial of Dedan Kimathi* (1976), which he coauthored with Micere Mugo, and *I Will Marry When I Want* (1982), an English translation from the Gikuyu of the play *Ngaahika ndeenda*, the result of his experiments on African theater with Ngũgĩ wa Mĩriĩ at the Kamiriithu Community Education and Cultural Center, inaugurated in 1977. *The Trial of Dedan Kimathi* is an interpretation of history. It examines the intensity and commitment of ordinary Kenyan citizens in the social mobilization led by Dedan Kimathi twenty years earlier, during the struggle for independence from the British. The play also clearly analyzes the self-interest of the Kenyan bourgeoisie, and their consequent role aborting this grass roots–inspired revolution.

I Will Marry When I Want, according to the author, "depicts the proletarization of the peasantry in a neo-colonial society" (44). It is in many ways the follow-up of the events in *The Trial of Dedan Kimathi*, especially after Kimathi's execution. It thus deals with a Kenyan society that is independent only in name, and that is materially and socially controlled and exploited by the erstwhile colonial forces. Focused on the land question, the play shows how a multinational firm owned by Japanese and European businessmen enters into an alliance with their African counterparts to deprive the Kiguunda family of their one-and-a-half acres of land, which they depend on for subsistence. As a continuation of the Kimathi-led Kenya Land and Freedom Army revolution, the play examines how the struggle for independence in Kenya, for which thousands of its citizens died, has now been hijacked by neocolonial forces extending from America to Japan. In the process of researching the play at Kamiriithu, a town that historically was involved in the Kimathi struggle, Ngũgĩ wa Thiong'o and his creative associates had to contend with the problem of the language, the history, the social and working conditions of the people, and the artistic elements of the indigenous African theater, such as song, dance, mime, and ceremony, in their quest for an authentic African drama and theater. In 1981 they devised another production, *Maitu njugira (Mother Sing for Me)*, which extended their search for a socialist-oriented society, using more than eighty songs from eight ethnic nationalities in Kenya to celebrate and to bemoan the joys and sorrows of the Kenyan people's struggles. Ngũgĩ's commitment to the struggle for real freedom has even prompted him to abandon the English language and to write in Gikuyu and Swahili in order to reach the vast majority of ordinary Kenyans. The English versions of his future works will therefore come only as translations. Still, he uses his essays and critical commentaries on culture and other sociopolitical issues to communicate to a wider English-speaking world.

Ngũgĩ's commitment to the use of drama and theater as a potent instrument for mass education through a clearer interpretation of history is shared by his countryman Kenneth Watene. Watene chose the Kimathi-led revolution as his subject in *My Son for My Freedom* and *Dedan Kimathi*. In the former, he uses the struggle to reveal the contradictions and fratricidal conflicts members of the same family may experience as a result of divided loyalties. The fact that Mwaura has taken the oath of solidarity with the struggle while his brother-in-law, Gacem, wavers angers Mwaura to the point of total hatred. In *Dedan Kimathi* (1974) the playwright brings the hero down to earth by exposing the suspicious and autocratic dispositions that prompt him to kill Nyati, his best friend and ritual leader of the Mau Mau.

In Nigeria, Femi Osofisan leads the group of new playwrights advocating radical social change. Unlike their older predecessors Soyinka, Clark, and Rotimi, these playwrights are unequivocal in their sympathies with the working masses, and even when they use myth as their backdrop for dramatic action it is manipulated in such a way that the message comes out clearly in favor of radical change. From the early social farce *Who's Afraid of Tai Solarin* (1978), in which Osofisan takes a roll call of corrupt Nigerian citizenry, to the more mature political plays such as *Once upon Four Robbers* (1980), *Moróuntódùn* (1982), and *The Chattering and the Song* (1977), he has demonstrated a commitment to social justice and political change. *The Chattering and the Song* is ideologically situated to reflect the struggle of the farmers—the neglected masses of the population—to be free. Their freedom will not materialize until such a time as "everyone's a farmer." In *Moróun-tódùn* the playwright demystifies an ancient Yoruba myth by transforming Moremi, the mythical heroine whose self-sacrifice saved Ile-Ife from its erstwhile marauders, into a sympathizer and advocate for the peasants after sharing their material condition. The class war continues in *Once upon Four Robbers*. A group of armed robbers forms a syndicate under the spiritual leadership of Asafa, a *babaláwo* (seer). As it turns out, the syndicate becomes an instrument for fighting the overprivileged military class. Their principle of robbing public places only but never the poor or private homes demonstrates their sympathy with the underprivileged in society, and the subversive ideological import of the play.

Ebrahim Hussein's *Kinjeketile* (1970) is set in the colonial period and explores the Maji Maji revolt against the Germans in 1904. Hussein selects only such historical details as contribute to and clarify his point of view. Kabwe Kasoma's *Black Mamba* trilogy is based on Kenneth Kaunda's *Zambia Shall Be Free* and therefore represents the same sort of artistic extension of a political program or historical reality as is observable in the plays of Ngũgĩ and Hussein. Kasoma means the trilogy not only to portray Kaunda as a political leader but also to propagate his views among the people of Zambia. His creative work is also part of the experiment to take theater to the people rather than wait for them to come to the theater; this strategy facilitates reaching wider urban and rural communities with plays designed to be stageable anywhere. Moreover, Kasoma believes in improvisations, especially in the use of appropriate linguistic registers to drive home the points of his plays. The three *Black Mamba* plays may be roughly divided into the three crucial stages in Kaunda's struggle for Zambian nationhood: (1) colonial domination and the inability of even the most qualified Africans to secure suitable jobs in the colonial administration; (2) the political struggle by Africans for independence, including the arrest of the Black Mambas: Nkumbula, Kaunda, Kapwepwe, Kalulu, and Kamanga; and (3) the emergence of an independent Zambian nation.

Stephen Chifunyise's plays are squarely set in this new Zambian nation. They portray the undermining of its independence by neocolonialist forces and the fate of the poor in the rural areas. *I Resign* exposes the machination of Mr. Leeds, the white managing director of a British company based in Zambia, to further mechanize the company's production assembly with "a British machine," thereby depriving 115 Zambian workers of their jobs and livelihood. Although Leeds wins the support of some Zambian collaborators, the stalwart stand of Mr. Banda, the Zambian general manager, on behalf of the Zambian workers wins the day. In another play, *The District Governor Goes to a Village*, Chifunyise exposes the corruption among public servants, in this case in the guise of a regional secretary who misrepresents the governor's message to the villagers.

Soweto: Flowers Will Grow (1979) represents another effort at using theater to aid the struggle for political emancipation and freedom in contemporary South Africa. It emerged out of an experimental workshop by Masautso Phiri and members of his Tikwiza Theatre between 1976 and 1979. It comprises fragments of songs, poetry, music, testimonies, and history by prominent indigenous South African authors such as Dennis Brutus, A. N. C. Khumalo, Mazisi Kunene, Oswald Mbuyiseni Mtshali, and Tandie Rankoe. *Soweto* is a collage of the foregoing as well as other extracts from Aimé Césaire, Parnell Munatamba, Donald Wood's *Biko,* and the creative input of the artistic collaborators. In this technique history and creativity mix to produce a play that raises strong political emotions in three movements respectively captioned "Soweto: A Dirge to the Youth of Soweto," "Soweto Revisited," and "Soweto Remembered." The play was presented at the Lagos Black Arts Festival, and in the frontline states of Zambia and Botswana. Among the themes it exploits are the exposure of the double roles religious influences play in the struggle, and an examination of the origin of the oppressive policies in South Africa. The events are selected to create an awareness among those fighting apartheid.

Inside South Africa Black drama and theater have been prominent and successful on the cultural front of the war against apartheid. Playwrights of the early 1960s like Lewis Nkosi (whose play is among those described by Anthony Graham-White as "bitterly anti-European" [87]) can fit into Phiri's category of "postermen," or moderates, only if their plays are compared with those by their more militant countrymen of the 1970s and after. Both Nkosi and Athol Fugard wrote plays that preached racial integration and tolerance. In Nkosi's *Rhythm of Violence* (1964) an interracial plot by a club of young people determined to change society is frustrated by the intrusion of their personal affairs, which hinders any united effort and causes them to fail in their mission.

Younger Black playwrights have tended to eschew the intrusion of such personal problems by devoting their energies to raising the consciousness of their fellow Africans in the light of the historical and cultural contradictions inherent in apartheid. Steve Biko and other leaders of the Black Consciousness Movement encouraged the formation of grass-roots theater organizations in the African townships. The result has been the reinvention of old techniques essentially drawn from the traditional African performance conventions such as storytelling, music, song and dance, multiple role playing, open-space utilization, and the active involvement of the audience during performance to suit the demands of an urgent guerrilla-like urban theater.

There has existed, from the 1970s, what the International Defence Aid Fund calls "a new wave of cultural energy" resulting from the conscious education of the participants to recognize and promote the identity and dignity of the Black person even in the face of the oppression inherent in all forms of apartheid legislation. Among the theater groups formed for this purpose were TECON (Theatre Council of Natal, 1969), PET (People's Experimental Theatre, 1973); and MDALI (Music, Drama, Arts, and Literature Institute, 1972). Other groups are The Serpent Players (1963) and Workshop '71 (1971). The vigorous political orientation of these theater groups quickly attracted the attention of the government, which has wasted no time in declaring them "prejudicial to the safety of the state," and has therefore proceeded to arrest, interrogate, detain, and imprison their members and ban the organizations. Furthermore, the government, seeing in what it considered the permissive conditioning of the young one of the methods of international communism, reinvigorated its censorship regulations with the new Publications Act of 1974. The result was that the three Black theater groups, TECON, PET, and MDALI, formed under the auspices of the Black Consciousness movement, were forced to disband following constant banning orders and harassment of their members. Gibson Kente, Khayalethu Mqayisa, John Kani, and Winston Ntshona are among several Black South African theater activists who have been arrested and detained by the police at one time or another.

Contemporary Black South African plays reflect the material existence of Black people under the apartheid government. Theater is considered an effective method of portraying that existence. This is what John Kani and Winston Ntshona meant when in an interview they declared, "We believe that art is life and conversely, life is art" (5). It is also the concern of contemporary Black South African plays. Black theater artists are turning away from such white-masterminded "blacksploitation" musicals as *King Kong* and *Ipi Tombi* and creating their own powerful plays, like *Sizwe Bansi Is Dead, u Nosilimela, Shanti, Too Late, Survival, Woza Albert, Gangsters, Born in the RSA, Asinamali!, Bopha!*, and many others. The plays, which are mostly created under experimental or workshop conditions, collectively signify the intensification of the political struggle on the cultural front through grass-roots mobilization and consciousness raising among the urban masses. As experimental plays, they are unencumbered by Western production conventions, and this quality gives the artists the freedom to experiment with techniques with which the audience is already familiar in traditional performances.

The play *u Nosilimela* (1981, *South African People's Plays*), by Credo V. Mutwa, is taken from an epic. In it the playwright exploits a variety of traditions indigenous to African people such as narrative, satirical, ritualistic, and realistic sequences, all rolled into one performance. In doing so, Mutwa touches on the history, tales, allegory, and the future aspirations of his people. The heroine of the play, u Nosilimela, goes through a difficult process to attain self-knowledge and greater awareness of the conditions surrounding her; she emerges as a conscious inheritor of a proud African civilization. The play thus tells the audience members to cease being mindless imitators of foreign cultures and civilizations and understand the values of their own.

The majority of contemporary Black South African plays are not based on myths and legends but on contemporary history. *Sizwe Bansi Is Dead* (1974), by Athol Fugard, John Kani, and Winston Ntshona, attacks the evils of such apartheid legislations as the Group Areas Act and the Pass Law. The protagonist, Sizwe Bansi, is forced to inherit a dead African's name and passbook so that he may legally stay and work in New Brighton. Mthuli Shezi's *Shanti* (1981) addresses, in addition to the issues raised in *Sizwe Bansi*, the question of color classification and the effects of the Immorality Act and the Terrorism Act. Because Thabo, an African student, is in love with an Indian girl, he is accused of theft, while the girl's family is charged with running an illegal drinking place. Thabo is imprisoned, but he escapes and joins General Mobu's guerrilla fighters across the border in Mozambique. In Gibson Kente's *Too Late* (1981) a young boy, Saduva, is imprisoned for defending his handicapped cousin against the menace of a scheming, illiterate, and rude Black policeman, Pelepele. In prison the innocent lad is further brutalized by other prisoners, and he comes out an embittered, violent, and angry young man. *Survival* (1981), by Workshop '71, like *Shanti*, is one of the most radical plays from contemporary South Africa. It is a call for the oppressed people of the society to join hands, "to go forward" and change the system. According to Themba, one of the five narrators on the oppressions of apartheid:

> THEMBA: A people survive by grimly holding on. But at the same time they achieve what their oppressors cannot help envying them for. The strength lies with the people, who carry with them in their lives the justification for the struggle—the victory that is . . .
>
> ALL [*together*]: SURVIVAL! (170)

Woza Albert, a collaboration by Percy Mtwa, Mbongeni Ngema, and Barney Simon; *Gangsters*, by Maishe Maponya; *Born in the RSA*, another collaboration by Barney Simon and the cast of the Market Theatre; *Asinamali!*, by Mbongeni Ngema; and *Bopha!*, by Percy Mtwa, together represent a continuum of the historical and material realities of apartheid as well as its contradictions for Black people. As Imamu Amiri Baraka writes in his preface to the anthology *Woza Afrika* (1986), the plays constitute a "poignant and purposeful self-evaluation" and "reveal the joy of bearing witness" (Ndlovu xv). *Woza Albert* reviews the scenes of evil and oppression in contemporary South African society and speculates on what would happen if Jesus Christ were to return to that country in the 1980s. *Gangsters* tackles the issues raised in the death of Steve Biko, by revealing details of his murder and the police role in covering it up. *Born in the RSA* is a complex story reflecting the attitudes of Blacks and whites in a racially segregated South Africa. *Asinamali!* is the story of five persons imprisoned for their role in rent-boycott protests led by Msizi Dube in Lamontville against substandard government housing.

Bopha! examines the effects of apartheid on a Black family in which the father is a police sergeant and the son of a young student activist of the Sowetoan generation. Initially divided by their conflicting emotions about their employment as policemen in a repressive regime, employment that both demeaned them and set them against their own people, the Njadini family finally finds harmony by abandoning the false security of the police force and embracing their people's cause.

The vibrancy and vitality of contemporary Black South African theater is the result of an ideological commitment to promote the image and views of Black people in their struggle against apartheid. The creative vigor that has flourished in the 1970s and 1980s corresponds with the heightening of awareness of the role art must play in the fight for freedom and a distinct identity. This cultural struggle is not confined to South Africa but can be observed as well in other parts of the continent where the legacy of European theater conventions is being challenged, modified, or replaced with new forms of performance expression. Such replacements have not been based on mere cultural chauvinism. On the contrary, they are the benefits of research into indigenous African performance traditions in the effort to take theater down from the ivory towers to the grassroots of Africa's population.

Playwrights like Efua Sutherland of Ghana have succeeded in converting the traditional African folktale convention into a contemporary dramatic form. Some may see her dramaturgy as being influenced by Brecht's epic theater techniques; nonetheless, Sutherland is simply using an indigenous African performance format that may have been lost to those Africans who seek cultural and artistic validation from without the continent. Sutherland has continued to experiment with storytelling and other dramatic forms rooted in indigenous Ghanaian traditions.

The search for indigenous performance forms and techniques and the effort to reach the rural masses of Africa with contemporary performances are typical of the Zambian National Theatre Arts Association and Chikwakwa Theatre, the Kenyan Kamiriithu project, grass-roots theater experiments in Uganda and Tanzania, the Botswana Popular Theatre Movement, and the experiments taking place in many Nigerian universities—in Benin, Ife, Nsukka, and Zaria, where the theater is either being indigenized or serving as an instrument for raising consciousness. The Zaria experiments, or Popular Theatre Workshops, have succeeded in increasing the concerned awareness of a number of Hausa communities around the university by getting the people to participate in performance projects designed to help them identify and articulate their local problems with a view to finding appropriate solutions to them.

Conclusion

Western theatrical practices were undoubtedly part of the complex of cultural imports Europeans brought with them to Africa. Through government-

and church-sponsored formal education in the colonial era, Africans were taught western dramatic and theatrical aesthetics, following which they quickly learned to write plays in the European tradition. The British Broadcasting Corporation and other local radio and later television establishments contributed largely in the successful tutelage of English-speaking African playwrights. Meanwhile, the traditional forms of dramatic expression were either ignored or only grudgingly accepted. However, the independence of several African countries meant less interference in cultural matters by outsiders, and African playwrights and performers began looking inward for artistic resources, from which they have devised new contemporary plays and performance modes that define their culture and personality in a more authentic and relevant way. The concern of playwrights has also shifted from the colonial theme of the clash of cultures (African and European) to the sociopolitical concerns of post-Independence Africa, especially the justification of that independence and the raising of the masses' consciousness. In this regard, indigenous African performance conventions and techniques are being harnessed to foster a livelier, people-oriented African theater.

The future of the continent's drama and theater is very bright indeed, so bright that the ongoing experiments and workshops, which are sometimes integral with real-life history and political struggles, as in South Africa, must produce models that will further define the direction of contemporary African drama and theater. Wole Soyinka and the older playwrights whose works were accepted in the 1960s without question have, since the early 1970s, been the butts of critical attacks by radical critics who do not now see the relevance of their mythopoeic dramas to the sociopolitical contradictions of contemporary society. The result is that African drama and theater in the 1970s and 1980s increasingly adopted a Marxist approach to social criticism, a response to the large-scale corruption among government officials and the widening of the economic gap between the rich and the poor. It is to the credit of contemporary African dramatists that they are able to address Africa's post-Independence social, political, and economic problems, and that they do so through techniques of mass appeal and recourse to indigenous performance traditions. It is only a matter of time before the gap between indigenous African and European dramatic conventions is completely bridged.

Bibliography

Aidoo, [Christina] Ama Ata. *Anowa*. London: Longman, 1970.
————. *The Dilemma of a Ghost*. London: Longman, 1965.
Amankulor, J. Ndukaku. "The Concept and Practice of Traditional African Festival Theatre." Ph.D. diss., University of California, Los Angeles, 1977.
————. "The Traditional Black African Theatre: Problems of Critical Evaluation." *Ufahamu* 6, no. 2 (1976): 27–61.
Arnoldi, Mary Jo. "Playing the Puppets: Innovation and Rivalry in the Bamana Youth Theatre of Mali." *Drama Review* 33, no. 2 (1988): 65–82.

Awoonor, Kofi. *Ancestral Power and Lament: Short African Plays*. Edited by Cosmo Pieterse. London: Heinemann, 1972.

Bame, Kwabena N. *Come to Laugh: African Traditional Theatre in Ghana*. New York: Lilian Barber Press, 1985.

Banham, Martin, with Clive Wake. *African Theatre Today*. London: Pitman, 1976.

Chifunyise, Stephen. *Medicine for Love and Other Plays*. Gweru, Zimbabwe: Mambo Press, 1984.

Clark, J. P. *Ozidi*. London: Oxford University Press, 1966.

———. *Three Plays* [*Song of a Goat, The Masquerade*, and *The Raft*]. London: Oxford University Press, 1964.

Clem, Darlene. *The Prisoner, the Judge and the Jailer: Nine African Plays for Radio*. Edited by Gwyneth Henderson and Cosmo Pieterse. London: Heinemann, 1973.

Collins, E. J. "Comic Opera in Ghana." *African Arts* 9, no. 2 (1976): 50–57.

Cordeaux, Shirley. "The B.B.C. African Service's Involvement in African Theatre." *Research in African Literatures* 1, no. 2 (1970): 147–55.

de Graft, J. C. *Muntu*. Nairobi: Heinemann, 1977.

———. *Sons and Daughters*. London: Oxford University Press, 1964.

———. *Through a Film Darkly*. London: Oxford University Press, 1970.

Delano, Isaac O. *The Soul of Nigeria*. London: Laurie, 1937.

Dhlomo, H. I. E. "The Nature and Variety of Tribal Drama." *Bantu Studies* 13 (1939): 33–48.

Easmon, Sarif. *Dear Parent and Ogre*. London: Oxford University Press, 1965.

———. *The New Patriots*. London: Longman, 1965.

Echeruo, M. J. C. "The Dramatic Limits of Igbo Ritual." *Research in African Literatures* 4, no. 1 (1973): 21–31.

Enekwe, Ossie O. "Modern Nigerian Theatre: What Tradition?" *Nsukka Studies in African Literature* 1, no. 1 (1978): 26–43.

———. "Myth, Ritual and Drama in Igboland." In *Drama and Theatre Nigeria*, edited by Yemi Ogunbiyi. Lagos: Nigeria Magazine, 1981.

Etherton, Michael. *The Development of African Drama*. London: Hutchinson University Library for Africa, 1982.

"Experimental Drama in the Gold Coast." *Overseas Education* 5 (1934).

Finnegan, Ruth. *Oral Literature in Africa*. Oxford: Clarendon Press, 1970.

Fugard, Athol, with John Kani and Winston Ntshona. *Statements: Three Plays* [*Sizwe Bansi Is Dead, The Island*, and *Statements after an Arrest under the Immorality Act*]. London: Oxford University Press, 1974.

Gabre-Medhin, Tsegaye. *Collision of Your Altars*. Unpublished MS, SRLF, 1970(?).

———. *Oda Oak Oracle*. London: Oxford University Press, 1965.

Gibbs, James. *Wole Soyinka*. New York: Grove Press, 1986.

———, ed. *Nine Malawian Plays*. Limbe, Malawi: Popular Publications, 1976.

Graham-White, Anthony. *The Drama of Black Africa*. New York: Samuel French, 1974.

Gugelberger, Georg M., ed. *Marxism and African Literature*. Trenton, N.J.: Africa World Press, 1986.

Horton, Robin. *The Gods As Guests: An Aspect of Kalabari Religious Life*. Lagos: Nigeria Magazine, 1960.

Hussein, Ebrahim. *Kinjeketile*. Dar es Salaam: Oxford University Press, 1970.

Imbuga, Francis. *The Fourth Trial: Two Plays* [with *Kisses of Fate*]. Nairobi: East African Literature Bureau, 1972.

International Defence and Aid Fund. *Black Theatre in South Africa.* Fact Paper on Southern Africa 2. London: International Defence and Aid Fund, 1976.

Jeyifo, Biodun. "Tragedy, History and Ideology: Soyinka's *Death and the King's Horseman* and Ebrahim Hussein's *Kinjeketile.*" In *Marxism and African Literature*, edited by Georg M. Gugelberger, 94–109. Trenton, N.J.: Africa World Press, 1986.

Julien, Eileen. "Introduction." In *African Literature and Its Social and Political Dimensions*, edited by Eileen Julien, Mildred Mortimer, and Curtis Schade, 1–3. Washington, D.C.: Three Continents Press, 1986.

Kani, John, and Winston Ntshona. "Art Is Life and Life Is Art." Interview with Ufahamu and the African Activists Association, University of California, Los Angeles. *Ufahamu* 6, no. 2 (1976): 5–26.

Kasoma, Kabwe. *Black Mamba Two.* Vol. 2 of *African Plays for Playing*, edited by Michael Etherton. London: Heinemann, 1975.

———. *The Fools Marry.* Lusaka, Zambia: Neezam, 1976.

Kavanagh, Robert Mshengu. *Theatre and Cultural Struggle in South Africa.* London: Zed Books, 1985.

———, ed. *South African People's Plays: Ons Phola Hi* [plays by Gibson Kente and others]. London: Heinemann, 1981.

Kay, Kwesi. *Laughter and Hubbub in the House: Five African Plays.* Edited by Cosmo Pieterse. London: Heinemann, 1972.

———. *Maama: Ten One-Act Plays.* Edited by Cosmo Pieterse. London: Heinemann, 1968.

Kerr, David. "Theatre and Social Issues in Malawi: Performers, Audiences, Aesthetics." *New Theatre Quarterly* 4, no. 14 (1988): 173–80.

———. "Unmasking the Spirits: Theatre in Malawi." *Drama Review* 31, no. 2 (1987): 115–25.

Kinteh, Ramatoulie. *Rebellion.* New York: Philosophical Library, 1968.

Lemma, Menghistu. *The Marriage of Unequals.* London: Macmillan, 1970.

Maddy, Pat Amadu. *Obasai and Other Plays.* London: Heinemann, 1971.

Masiye, Andreya. *The Lands of Kazembe.* Lusaka, Zambia: NECSAM (National Education Co. of Zambia), 1973.

Mulikita, Fwanyanga. *Shaka Zulu.* Lusaka: Longman of Zambia, 1967.

Ndlovu, Duma, ed. *Woza Afrika: An Anthology of South African Plays.* New York: George Braziller, 1986.

Ngũgĩ wa Thiong'o. *The Black Hermit.* Nairobi: Heinemann, 1968.

———. *Decolonising the Mind: The Politics of Language in African Literature.* London: Currey, 1986.

———. *Moving with the Face of the Devil: Art and Politics in Urban West Africa.* Champaign: University of Illinois Press, 1987.

———. *This Time Tomorrow.* Nairobi: East African Literature Bureau, 1970.

Ngũgĩ wa Thiong'o and Micene Mugo. *The Trial of Dedan Kimathi.* London: Heinemann, 1977.

Ngũgĩ wa Thiong'o and Ngũgĩ wa Mĩriĩ. *I Will Marry When I Want* [*Ngaahika ndeenda*]. London: Heinemann, 1982.

Nunley, John. "Purity and Pollution in Freetown Masked Performance." *Drama Review* 32, no. 2 (1988): 102–22.

Obuh, Sylvanus O. "The Theatrical Use of Masks in Southern Igbo Areas of Nigeria." Ph.D. diss., New York University, 1984.

Ogunba, Oyin. "Ritual Drama of the Ijebu People: A Study of Indigenous Festivals." Ph.D. thesis, University of Ibadan, Nigeria, 1967.

———. "Traditional African Festival Drama." In *Theatre in Africa*, edited by O. Ogunba and A. Irele, 3–26. Ibadan, Nigeria: University of Ibadan Press, 1978.

Ogunbiyi, Yemi. *Drama and Theatre in Nigeria: A Critical Source Book.* Lagos: Nigeria Magazine, 1981.

Osofisan, Femi. *The Chattering and the Song.* Ibadan, Nigeria: Ibadan University Press, 1977.

———. *Moróuntódùn.* Ikeja: Longman Nigeria, 1982.

———. *Once upon Four Robbers.* Ibadan, Nigeria: Bio Educational Publishers, 1980.

———. *Who's Afraid of Tai Solarin?* Ibadan, Nigeria: Scholars Press, 1978.

Owomoyela, Oyekan. "Give Me Drama Or . . .: The Argument on the Existence of Drama in Traditional Africa." *African Studies Review* 28, no. 4 (1986): 29–45.

Phiri, Masautso. *Soweto: Flowers Will Grow.* Lusaka, Zambia: National Educational Co. of Zambia, 1979.

Roberts, Gabriel J. *The Trial of Busumbala: Nine African Plays for Radio.* Edited by Gwyneth Henderson and Cosmo Pieterse. London: Heinemann, 1973.

Ricard, Alain. "Theatre Research: Questions about Methodology." *Research in African Literatures* 16, no. 1 (1985): 38–52.

Roscoe, Adrian. *Uhuru's Fire: African Literature East to South.* Cambridge: Cambridge University Press, 1977.

Rotimi, Ola. *The Gods Are Not to Blame.* London: Oxford University Press, 1971.

———. *Kurunmi.* Ibadan, Nigeria: Oxford University Press, 1971.

———. *Ovoramwen Nogbaisi.* Ibadan, Nigeria: Oxford University Press, 1974.

Ruganda, John. *Black Mamba: Covenant with Death.* Nairobi: East Africa Publishing House, 1973.

———. *The Burdens.* Nairobi: Oxford University Press, 1972.

———. *The Floods.* Nairobi: East African Publishing House, 1980.

———. *Music without Tears.* Nairobi: Bookwise, 1982.

Rugyendo, Mukotani. *The Barbed Wire and Other Plays* [*The Barbed Wire, The Contest,* and *And The Storm Gathers*]. London: Heinemann, 1977.

Schofeleers, Matthew, and Ian Linden. "The Resistance of Nyau Societies to the Roman Catholic Missions in Colonial Malawi." In *The Historical Study of African Religion*, edited by T. O. Ranger and I. N. Kimbambo, 252–73. London: Heinemann, 1972.

Serumaga, Robert. *The Elephants.* Nairobi: Oxford University Press, 1971.

———. *Majangwa.* Nairobi: East African Publishing House, 1974.

Serumaga, Robert, and Janet Johnson. "Uganda's Experimental Theatre." *African Arts* 3, no. 3 (1970): 52–55.

Soyinka, Wole. *Art, Dialogue and Outrage: Essays on Literature and Culture.* Ibadan, Nigeria: New Horn Press, 1988.

———. *Before the Blackout.* Ibadan, Nigeria: Orisun, 1971.

———. *Collected Plays*, vol. 1 [*A Dance of the Forests, The Swamp Dwellers, The*

Strong Breed, The Road, and *The Bacchae of Euripides*]. London: Oxford University Press, 1973.

——. *Collected Plays,* vol. 2. [*The Lion and the Jewel, Kongi's Harvest, The Trials of Brother Jero, Jero's Metamorphosis,* and *Madmen and Specialists*]. London: Oxford University Press, 1974.

——. *A Play of Giants.* London: Methuen, 1984.

——. *Six Plays.* [*The Trials of Brother Jero, Jero's Metamorphosis, Camwood on the Leaves, Death and the King's Horseman, Madmen and Specialists,* and *Opera Wonyosi*]. London: Methuen, 1984.

Sutherland, Efua. *Edufa.* London: Longman, 1967.

——. *Foriwa.* Accra: State Publishing Corporation, 1967.

——. *The Marriage of Anansewa.* London: Longman, 1975.

Vandenbroucke, Russell. "Chiaroscuro: A Portrait of the South African Theatre." *Theatre Quarterly* 7, no. 28 (1977–78): 46–54.

——. "Introduction: African Theatre." *Yale/Theatre* 8, no. 1 (1976): 6–10.

Watene, Kenneth. *My Son for My Freedom and Other Plays* [*The Haunting Past* and *The Broken Pot*]. Nairobi: East African Publishing House, 1973.

——. *Dedan Kimathi.* Nairobi: Transafrica, 1974.

Williams, C. Kingsley. *Achimota: The Early Years.* Accra: Longmans, Green, 1962.

Yirenkyi, Asiedu. *Kivulu and Other Plays.* London: Heinemann, 1980.

French-Language Fiction

SERVANNE WOODWARD

The Beginnings

African voices were initially heard in French around the end of the eighteenth century, in the form of translations of oral fables in travelogues. Abbé Henri Grégoire (1750–1831), a philanthropist who championed the cause of slaves and of women during the French revolution, published *De la littérature des Nègres* (1808; On Negro literature), thus becoming one of the few to signal to French-speaking audiences the existence of African authors such as Olaudah Equiano and Phillis Wheatley in the Anglophone tradition. Mohamadou Kane observes that the Francophone African novel, when it finally emerged, had no other choice than to follow the lead of French colonial novels (106). Both were considered to be "African" literature and touched the same European public. Kane cites Roland Lebel's *Histoire de la littérature coloniale en France* (1931; History of colonial literature in France) as an indication of French colonial interest in ethnographic information, which French and African colonial novels sought to satisfy. Such works provided the public and the authorities valuable knowledge that could be exploited by administrative and political agents (M. Kane 109).

Philippe van Tieghem traces the "exotic" themes in French literature, as well as in those of England, Spain, and Italy, in *Les influences étrangères sur la littérature francaise (1550–1880)* (1961). Prosper Mérimée ("Carmen") and George Sand (*Indiana*) in the nineteenth century were followed by Loti in the twentieth. Greenwich Village and the Harlem Renaissance served as catalysts for Negritude. Josephine Baker, dancing in a banana skirt, became the star of Paris in the 1920s, while sculptors and painters such as Picasso, Derain, and Matisse adopted new forms suggested by museum collections and souvenirs brought back from Africa. But the French public was probably not ready to purchase works by African authors before the 1920s.

Albert S. Gérard points out that if French-language publications appeared later than English ones, the blame lies with French publishers (*European-Language* 145). His other suggestion—that French is a difficult language to master—is unconvincing. Senegal had been in contact with the French, based at the Fort of Saint-Louis and on the coast, since 1639. In 1854 Louis-Léon-César Faidherbe became the first governor of Senegal. Saint-Louis,

173

Gorée, and later Rufisque and Dakar were the four communes whose citizens were given French nationality. A few decades later, those citizens were fighting to retain their full privileges. Thus the first African Francophone authors were interested in becoming part of the fabric of French society.

Ahmadou Mapaté Diagne, a Senegalese schoolteacher, authored the first piece of imaginative writing published in French by a Black African: *Les trois volontés de Malic* (1920; The three wishes of Malic). Diagne's book is often discounted because it belongs in the genre of juvenile literature, and, according to European aesthetic categories and values, children and the literature devoted to them are at the lowest end of its scale. Diagne chose the same means of entry into writing as that adopted over a century earlier by such French women as Mme Leprince de Beaumont, Mme d'Epinay, and Mme Campan.

In 1921, however, *Batoulala* by René Maran, a French Guyanese, received the prestigious Goncourt Prize. Maran, a French citizen and a métis born in Martinique, became one of the most prolific Negro authors. Léopold Sédar Senghor nevertheless regards him as the father of the African novel (Chevrier, *Littérature nègre*, 32). *Batouala* does not differ substantially from colonial literature, but its strongly anticolonialist preface, which earned him the prize, also created a scandal because it exposed to the French public the crude abuses of colonizers. The French right counterattacked, and the author lost his job and career with the colonial administration.

After World War I the redistribution of certain African colonies as mandates to the victorious allies brought Africa to the forefront of European politics. Sylvester Williams convened the first pan-African conference in London in 1900. In 1919 William Edward Burghardt Du Bois convened what is commonly referred to as the first Pan-African Congress in Paris. This was followed by another gathering in 1921 which convened in London and continued in Brussels and then Paris. Du Bois's *The Souls of Black Folk* (1903) and his role in the creation of the National Association for the Advancement of Colored People in 1909 were aimed at the celebration of the African heritage and the reconstruction of the image of Blacks in white European consciousness. The diverse fashions of Black exoticism in vogue, combined with political events, created a favorable moment for a Pan-African movement that eventually embraced the mulatto *élite* and the diaspora as well as continental Africans.

More African novels in French were published in the next several years: *Le réprouvé* (1925; The outcast), in a Senegalese periodical edited by the author, Massyla Diop; *Force-bonté* (1926; Benevolent force) by Bakary Diallo; *L'esclave* (1929; The slave) by Félix Couchoro; *Doguicimi* (1938) by Paul Hazoumé; *Karim* (1935) and *Mirages de Paris* (1937; Mirages of Paris) by Ousmane Socé; and in the late 1940s, works by Abdoulaye Sadji. While the novelists started rooting their identity in Africa, it would take many more years for them to reorient their attitudes toward France. Albert Memmi's

The Colonizer and the Colonized and Frantz Fanon's *Black Skin, White Masks* analyzed the sort of mental alienation that informs these early novels.

Incipient Anticolonialism

Although the tone in these works is procolonial, it might be intriguing to analyze the ways in which protest subsists even in such alienated expression. For example, the paean to France in *Force-bonté*, though enthusiastic, is at times unconvincing (Riesz 17, 19). Diallo praises the French as essentially strong and benevolent at the most unlikely moments, when they have demonstrated brutality and weaknesses. Praise may indeed be an indirect reproach against the state of affairs, the projection of an ideal world of fiction rather than realistic representation. Although Paul Hazoumé of Dahomey (now Benin) did not address the issues of colonialism directly in his historical novel *Doguicimi*, his affirmation of African culture and history "firmly rejected the notion that Africa lay in darkness before the European arrived," according to Priscilla P. Clark (122). In these early novels, therefore, whether through irony or by direction representation, the authors confront the French reader with the logical necessity of becoming reformist or anticolonialist.

The writers identified with the transition to a more militant literature are Ousmane Socé and Abdoulaye Sadji. Both were politicians, and both were involved with *Bingo,* a journal founded by Socé, who was later to become a part of the Negritude movement. With Massyla Diop, the elder brother of the poet Birago Diop and a witness of cultural conflict, they are the original enunciators of the themes that would later be fully developed by Ousmane Sembène of Senegal. These early novelists had a considerable thematic or psychological effect on the careers of later writers; Camara Laye credits Ahmadou Diagne with his inspiration to become a writer, and Mohamadou Kane acknowledges Félix Couchoro as the first author to treat the problem of cultural identity (111). Their influence continues to be felt even today.

The history of African publications in French has inevitably been determined to some extent by political events and the material conditions available for the creation and publication of books. Thus, of the early writers previously mentioned, only Diop and Sadji published in Dakar, while Couchoro worked in Togo; the others had their works published in France. Couchoro's public consisted of the bourgeois readers of local journals that promoted literary works. Togo now produces detective stories aimed at the same public. Adrien Huannou, identifying Couchoro as the founder of Benin's literature (15), reminds us that these journals predate *L'esclave* by twenty-four years (31).

The nature of the colonial presence was also important in the development of early African literature. Upper Volta and Niger were poorer regions of lesser interest to the French, and were therefore late in developing a literature. French Equatorial Africa (AEF) did not contribute to early writing either, probably because it was colonized late. Likewise, Cameroon, a German colony before it was mandated to France, was not as intimately integrated into the French academic system as were Senegal and the other West African colonies. Joseph Owono was the first Francophone novelist from this territory, and his *Tante Bella* (1959; Aunt Bella) is, interestingly, not an anticolonial work but a denunciation of the traditional abuse of women and an expression of hopes for some equity with the advent of colonization. Tante Bella cannot be vindicated by her young nephew, who narrates her story. A social change is intensely desired and called for, but neither colonization nor independence fulfilled the expectation of the people, according to African novelists.

Madagascar, with a strong poetic tradition (the *hain-teny*) that predated European contacts, produced mainly poets. The first Madagascan novel (published in Paris) was *La soeur inconnue* (1932; The unknown sister) by Edouard Bezoro; it may have been the transcription of a play and is comparable to *Force-bonté*. It is also oddly detached from ideological revolt, especially when one considers that 1932 also witnessed the creation of the journal *Légitime défense* (Self-defense), and that in 1934 *L'étudiant noir* (The Black student) articulated the tenets of Negritude. With the decline of the Pan-African and Negritude movements, Madagascar is now mostly absent from African anthologies.

The first novel purported to be published by an African author from the Belgian sphere is *L'éléphant qui marche sur des oeufs* (1931; The elephant that walks on eggs). Mukala Kadima-Nzuji believes, however, that the book was a hoax perpetrated by its Belgian authors, Gaston-Denys Périer and J. M. Jadot ("Belgian Territories" 160). He blames the long delay in literary creativity in the Congo on Belgium's colonial policy, the practical effect of which was that no schooling system existed comparable to those in the territories under French control. Education was left in the hands of missionaries, and consequently, the first generation of French-language authors in Belgian Africa were people whose education was preparatory to entering the priesthood. Modern authors from this area are still heavily involved in the disciplines of theology and philosophy. They include Alexis Kagame (from Rwanda), Antoine-Roger Bolamba, Paul Lomami-Tshibamba, and Joseph Saverio Naigiziki (all from Zaire). Lomami-Tshibamba is one of the occasional novelists among the crop; his *Ngando* won the Literature Prize at the Colonial Fair in Brussels in 1948. The launching of *La voix du congolais* (The voice of the Congolese) in January 1945 in Léopoldville (now Kinshasa) and the inauguration of the Union Africaine des Arts et des Lettres in December 1946 in Elisabethville (now Lubumbashi), with its magazine *Jeune Afrique* (Young Africa), translated into more published opportunities for these early authors, even more than were available to writers in the French territories. As Robert Pageard notes, however, it is a telling fact that the first university in the Belgian Congo, the Université Lovanium, founded in 1954, had produced no more than six graduates by the time of independence in 1960 (29).

Negritude and Francophonie

In the aftermath of World War II, the cultural crisis that prompted Gen. Charles de Gaulle to promote *francophonie* (probably aimed more at European countries than at the African territories) tied in with the efforts at self-definition undertaken by the proponents of Negritude. Lylian Kesteloot is convinced that Léopold "Senghor . . . made use of it [*francophonie*] to accord legitimacy to African literature" ("Senghor" 52). In the Hegelian tradition of artistic theory then prevailing, Western art was felt to be in decline, as if it were becoming moribund at the end of its life cycle. In that perspective, Africa stood to offer renewed vitality to European art, and France and Belgium would be beneficiaries in a true relation of exchange with their former colonies.

Negritude's major literary achievement was in poetry. The movement had intimate ties with the surrealists, whose principles were embraced by the originators of Negritude: Senghor, from Senegal, and Aimé Césaire, from Martinique. In French aesthetics, poetry is held to be the highest form of art, and thus poetry best served the wish of Francophone African artists in the 1930s to achieve recognition. The choice of the genre was particularly fortuitous for those artists, since the French had had few poets to boast of since the beginning of the century. Jacques Chevrier also suggests other reasons in favor of poetry as the genre of choice for the time; most important was its ability to skirt the censorship enforced by the Vichy government, as demonstrated by Césaire's explosive but cryptic *Tropiques* (1941–45; Tropics) (66).

While poetry enjoys a greater prestige than does prose, the latter genre has certainly not been neglected. It has in fact been employed extensively for historical and folkloric subjects. Clark suggests that such subjects enabled prose writers to achieve the same sort of escape from present realities that the Negritude writers found by other means:

> One problem is that if the writer wished to deal with contemporary life (as the poets did not), he was all but forced to deal with changes wrought by the colonial presence. The negritude poets, encouraged in their aestheticism by surrealism, escaped from the colonial reality into a mystical Africa which obviated any necessity of a realistic presentation. The early African writer of prose fiction had no such solution. His model was the nineteenth-century (European) novel firmly anchored in the study of contemporary society. (129)

It is futile to criticize Negritude for its benign and tolerant attitude toward France and Belgium, and for its escape into symbolism (see Makward, "Negritude"). The major contemporary literary figures in Europe—Ionesco, Beckett, Artaud, Genet, and those involved in the Eastern European formalist school of criticism—all participated in a revolt that was muted at best. Indeed, they were publishable only because of their symbolic and abstract style, which bypassed censorship. Jean-Paul Sartre was exceptionally allowed to express himself clearly (in classical French) and without constraint. President de Gaulle likened him to Voltaire ("On n'embastille pas Voltaire"—One does not imprison Voltaire) and turned down demands for his imprisonment when, in May 1968, the leftist philosopher addressed Renault workers of Billancourt in an inflammatory manner. It is not by sheer chance that Sartre's "Orphée noir" (Black Orpheus) prefaces Senghor's first anthology of Negro poetry.

Commentators harshly criticize the colonized mentality evident in the novels preceding World War II. They also point to their formal awkwardness (Chinweizu, Jemie, and Madubuike 3). The authors stand accused of being either too slavish in emulating their French models, such as the colonial novels of Pierre Loti, or sociological models provided by naturalism and Marxism. Otherwise, they are at fault because they do not respect the Western model and intervene too frequently in their text.

Speaking of *Force-bonté*, Frederic Michelman represents the awkwardness as indicative of tensions with African oral traditions: "The perfectly linear narrative is broken from time to time by philosophical reflections inspired by event and usually dealing with what the author conceives as the basic oneness of the universe and all its creatures, despite its astonishing diversity" ("Beginnings" 11–12). Clark is of a similar opinion: "The absence of an African vision in the early West African novel is compounded by the lack of a personal voice. The tone is generally didactic and highly moralistic, perhaps another legacy of the folk tales whose function is precisely to teach" (130).

Adèle King extends the criticism to the authors of Senghor's generation, three of whom appear in her *Trois écrivains noirs* (1947; Three Black writers): Jean Malonga of the Congo, Sadji, and Alexandre Biyidi. With the exception of Bernard Binlin Dadié of the Ivory Coast, a graduate of colonial Senegal's Ecole William-Ponty (see chapter 8), King has little regard for the first generation of post–World War II novelists. She finds them overdetermined by colonial culture, whether they abide by it or oppose it. While Malonga's themes are anticolonialist, *Le fils du fétiche* (1955; The son of the fetish) by David Anamou of Togo betrays a strong missionary influence. King dismisses Ibrahim Issa's *Les grandes eaux noires* (1959; The great black waters) as a novel of "confused ideology," wavering between anticolonial, Islamic, and French values. On the other hand, Dorothy S. Blair, who sympathizes with Issa's Muslim perspective, commends him for producing a "pioneering study of an era and subject otherwise untouched by African Literature" (*African Literature in French* 78). With regard to Nazi Boni, a teacher, journalist, and politician from Upper Volta (also a graduate of William-Ponty), King raises other questions:

Boni's style and sense of structure are not those of a novelist. The typical folk tales included in *Crépuscule* [*des temps anciens*, 1962; The twilight of old times] comes closest to narrative art. The richness of the ethnological detail is perhaps impossible to blend with the story. Rather than judge it as a failed novel, however, one should see *Crépuscule* as a successful presentation of the validity of a traditional society, without reference to another cultural tradition. The poetic story of Térhé and Hakanni, whose tragedy parallels the decline of the tribe, also has epic dignity. (497)

Since Présence Africaine reprinted Boni's work in 1976, King has revised her opinion of him, acknowledging his affirmation of traditional values.

The Question of Africanity

Beyond the problem of identity, these novels raise the question of a coherent aesthetic for the development of a new African genre. In *Essais d'histoire littéraire africaine* (Essays on African literary history), Gérard suggests that the novel is a genre born out of Western civilization at a specific moment in the development of the bourgeoisie, and that its premises are incompatible with African cultures (206). Claire L. Dehon is ready to recognize that Cameroonian authors have transformed the aesthetics of the novel. They redefined the genre: "It often resembles a long short story; the events tend toward generalization and follow each other often without true separation. The characters appear not to think and not to know internal deliberations" (6; my translation).

It is legitimate to ask whether the Francophone African novel in the golden age of the 1950s and 1960s is less "African" because the form is not African, even if the authors openly contested the colonial ideology. Chinweizu and his collaborators in *Toward the Decolonization of African Literature* would answer in the affirmative, but such a view would be too negative and confining, and ultimately alienating as well, since it would define Africanity in terms of race, color, geography, residence, nationality, adopting approved "purist" models, and rejecting modes of expression that are not "African." A comic dialogue by Werewere Liking, from her novel *Elle sera de jaspe et de corail* (1983; She will be of jasper and coral), pokes fun at the desire to construct "African art" in a way that precludes for the artists all the available possibilities: her ironic dialogue forbids theater, painting, poetry, and novels as non-African genres (55–61). Her book is a "song-novel," freely borrowing from traditional and Western forms.

Jonathan Ngaté chooses an image from Valentin Yves Mudimbe's *L'autre face du royaume* (1973; The other side of the kingdom), the metaphor of the elevator, to illustrate the stance of the African author of the first generation, trapped in an unlikely asylum of mobile ambiguity. Ngaté recasts the infernal couple depicted by Memmi in *The Colonizer and the Colonized* as the hypocritical reader, the double, and the brother of the Francophone African writer (40). Ngaté refers here to René Girard's theories—articulated by Tobin Siebers in *The Mirror of Medusa*—whereby the colonizer and the colonized find themselves in a sort of sibling rivalry for the seduction of their French-speaking public. At stake also is the shared anxiety as to legitimate authorial ancestry, the African author suddenly claiming French letters. Gérard suggested that Corneille, Alexandre Dumas, Victor Hugo, the surrealists, and Gorky are so many literary fathers to Francophone African literature (*Essais d'histoire* 215–16). For Ngaté this pioneering literature, produced by Camara Laye (Upper Guinea), Alexandre Biyidi (alias Erza Boto and Mongo Beti), Ferdinand Oyono (Cameroon), and Cheikh Hamidou Kane (Senegal) is "a literature of trace and influence, be it Bloomian in its anxieties, Derridean in its deconstructive possibilities, or negritudist in its unacknowledged illustration of the celebrated 'double-consciousness' of Du Bois's *The Souls of Black Folk* (1903)" (40). Kane's *L'aventure ambiguë* (1961; *Ambiguous Adventure*, 1963), which was awarded Le Grand Prix Littéraire d'Afrique Noire d'Expression Française in 1962, is an autobiographical manifestation of the ambiguous African identity.

The Uses of French

The adoption of French for creative expression has been the subject of some debate. Many authors and critics consider it simply to be an expedient "tool." While asserting his belief that African national literatures should be written only in African languages, the Togolese writer Victor Weka Yawo Aladji, author of *La voix de l'ombre* (1985; The voice from the shadow), nevertheless adopts French as an "instrument" (Herzberger-Fofana 112–13). Likewise, Ide Oumarou of Niger, author of *Gros plan* (1977; Close-up) and *Le représentant* (1984; The representative) uses French as "un outil de travail" (a work tool) that offers him access to a broader international audience than he would have otherwise (Herzberger-Fofana 38). Whatever misgivings he might have about the expediency of his linguistic choice, they are eased by his ability to rationalize French as a "weapon" (39) as well as a tool, a role that a more immediate African language would be inadequate to play.

Gaoussou Diawara of Mali also compares his writing to the weaponry befitting a warrior: "I am a poet, but also a prose novel author. At some point I abandon the light arm, the machine gun, of poetry to use the tanks that are the novels, the short stories" (Herzberger-Fofana 20; my translation). Statements such as these may be typically male, and may indicate an intriguing relationship between the writer and the language he uses.

Makouta-M'Boukou's impatience with Mudimbe (225–26, 314–18) derives from the latter's use of language. Mudimbe typically resorts to several languages (Greek, Latin, Italian) in his novels, which are consequently out of reach for most African readers. But inasmuch as books are so exorbitantly priced as to be beyond the means of the generality of the people, and inasmuch as the isolating habit of reading is not one that they have cultivated, M'Boukou's criticism may be pointless (cf. Mbwil a Mpaang, in Herzberger-Fofana 119). On the other hand, that criticism raises such important questions (since the 1950s) as the public envisaged by the writer, the actual readership of literatures (from popular and local to world class), and the politics of the authors.

Language and Audience

One of the most innovative approaches to the language issue has come from Sembène. Having studied cinema with Mark Donskoï in the late 1950s, he has also made several highly successful movies based on his novels; his interest in the cinema derives from his determination to find a genre through which he could better address his African public. In *L'Harmattan* (1963) he addresses the problem of using a foreign language to create a national literature. Sembène believes, like Memmi, that the use of French rather than African languages must be a temporary expedient (*L'Harmattan* 68). It would appear that Mudimbe and Sembène write for different audiences. But if language use alienates the majority of Africans from Mudimbe's writing, Blair has commented that Sembène's syndicalism also isolates him from the public, in comparison with other authors from the 1950s who, continuing the "tradition of *Karim* and *L'Enfant Noir*," were more representative of the bulk of African Francophone writing (245). What Dehon says about Cameroonian writers is generally applicable over the field: most authors opt for a "craftsmanship" and style that would make them accessible to the people, as opposed to an "art" of writing that would allow the African authors to reach international and Western spheres and elitist readership. Typically, authors who opt for the latter apply considerable work to their linguistic medium, which may include several Western languages as well as traces of African proverbs and syntax. Makouta-M'Boukou places himself in a paradoxical bind by requiring that the text be toned down and "clearly" written for the people, when such transparency derives from classical French—the most conservative style issued from a French colonial and monarchic system of expression. Mpang, who sympathizes with the most sophisticated writers—as most intellectuals probably will—decries what he calls "myths of readability and opacity" (Herzberger-Fofana 119).

The Moderns and African Identity

It is customary to date the modern Francophone African novel from the time of the appearance of Camara Laye's *L'enfant noir* (1953; *The Dark Child*, 1954). Robert Pageard notes that before its publication Parisian publishing houses shied away from African authors (28). Mongo Beti criticized *L'enfant noir* when it came out because its idyllic, autobiographic theme was not obviously anticolonialist. To the contrary, Laye was interested in affirming the world of his youth, untouched by Europeans, before Africa was defined as the negative of Europe, in the era of autonomy. He was defended by Senghor in *Liberté I: Négritude et humanisme* (1964; Liberty I: Negritude and humanism); but in contrast to *L'enfant*, which was an affirmation of African identity, when Laye's *Dramouss* appeared in 1966 (translated as *A Dream of Africa*, 1968) it turned out to be a bitter attack against the tyrannical regime of his country (M. Kane 115).

Dadié's *Climbié* (1956), reminiscent of *L'enfant noir*, is also autobiographical to some extent, as are his travel books, *Un nègre à Paris* (1959; A Negro in Paris), *Patron de New York* (1964; Boss of New York), and *La ville où nul ne meurt: Rome* (1968; The city where no one dies: Rome). The travels are in fact a process of arriving at self-identity. Tracing the theme of cultural identity in the Francophone African novel, Mohamadou Kane (1986) spoke of the enduring influence of Negritude; he named Oyono and his compatriot Beti as the forefathers of modern African identity. Both use more humor in their depiction of social chaos than do their West African counterparts. Beti's *Mission terminée* (1957; *Mission to Kala*, 1958) exemplifies a trend in this Cameroonian type of humor analyzed by Roger Berger in "Comedy in Mongo Beti's *Mission to Kala*." Humor has long been integrated in the African identity by Negritude as emotional. Lylian Kesteloot sees in the theme of "African personality" a continuation of Negritude ("Senghor" 51–57) as Senghor originally defined it in the preface of *Liberté I*.

The second generation of Negritude novelists, born in the 1920s, steered away from cultural identity toward a more aggressive political assertion. Their stance, which was strongly anticolonial, received a strong impetus from Césaire's *Discours sur le colonialisme* (1950; Discourse on colonialism, revised in 1955, 1958). Independence, achieved in Senegal in 1960, significantly interrupted the development of this theme, Ousmane Sembène being one of the few major authors to consistently pursue it in the early 1960s. Unlike the other Senegalese authors, Sembène had no higher education. Instead, his preparation was as a docker in Marseille, in which career his trade union affiliation converted him to Marxism. His first novel, *Le docker noir* (1956; *The Black Docker*, 1987), was followed shortly by *O pays mon beau peuple!* (1957; O my country, my good people!), and in 1960 by his masterpiece, a prose epic titled *Les bouts de bois de Dieu* (*God's Bits of Wood*, 1962). Later came *Voltaïques* in 1962; *L'Harmattan*, a collection of short stories, in 1963; *Vehi Ciosane* and *Le mandat* (*The Money-Order*, 1972) in 1966; *Xala* in 1974, all published by Présence Africaine; and *Le dernier de l'empire* in 1981 (*The Last of the Empire*, 1983). His most important innovation, for our present purposes, is that he creates full-fledged female characters who cannot be stereotyped as African, French, or even as some abstract muse. They are individuals, produced by certain historical conditions and taken in a given context, but they also have their own aspirations. This achievement is noticeable in his novel *Fatou Ndiaye Diop,* with reference to which he says, "The idea behind the book is that without the liberation of women, if women do not escape conformism, Africa will not be free" (Novicki and Topouzis 67). Tante Bella will have to free herself, since neither colonization nor independence helped her much.

Zairian authors of the late 1960s continued to dwell on the themes that characterized the second generation of Negritude writers of some twenty years earlier. The new preoccupation with anticolonialism, as seen in Timothée Malembe's *Le mystère de l'enfant disparu* (1962; The mystery of the lost child) is reminiscent of *L'enfant noir.* National literature, it seems, is destined to repeat a prescribed pattern at each emergence.

The Senegalese writer Ken Bugul for her part combines the "been-to" with the anticolonialist themes in her 1982 novel *Le baobab fou* (The crazy baobab). A mother separates from her child after her husband leaves. The baby girl is next to a baobab pit, which grows into a tree of sympathetic psyche; in France, the girl becomes crazy along with the baobab, which dies upon her return to Africa. The female hero may now grow new roots. The novel is made of a series of new beginnings, with the new hopes they entail. To a degree, it is symbolic of each new emancipation. The first female African authors adopted the same strategy (of anticolonialism) against domination that all quests for emancipation require.

Another development, which Pierrette Herzberger-Fofana applauds, is the recent growth of a children's literature, in particular from the pens of writers like Ken Bugul, Aminata Sow Fall, and Abdou Anta Kâ (12). Another author of juvenilia is Nafissatou Diallo of Senegal, whose *Awa, la petite marchande* (Awa, the petty trader) came out in 1981. Diallo became the first woman to break into the ranks of African Francophone novels in 1975, with a fictional autobiography, *De Tilène au plateau: Une enfance dakaroise* (1975; From Tilène to the plateau: A Dakar childhood). Susan Stringer considers that her accomplishments helped women in a way comparable with what Camara Laye did for African men (165–66). Diallo's work is also reminiscent of Diagne's *Les trois volontés de Malic,* which was Laye's inspiration as well.

Gabriel Ilunga-Kabalu's *Journal d'un revenant* (1968; Journal of a ghost) is another "been-to" account of a young man who confronts the unknown and deculturation in a European country, according to the Orphic theme. In this sense, it is not original, but it affirms the necessity to repeat a familiar African experience, and it inaugurated what has become known a "Zairian concretism" in the early 1970s: "The rehabilitation of the African tradition and the questioning of contemporary society" (Kadima-Nzuji 553). It could be described as a conflation of Negritude and the post-Independence nationalism. The most prominent exponent of concretism is Mudimbe, who achieved an international reputation through his novels: *Entre les eaux* (1973; Between the waters), *Le bel immonde* (1976; *Before the Birth of the Moon,* 1989); and

L'écart (1979; The gap). *L'écart* might be indicative of a breach that corners the main character into madness. Characteristic of Mudimbe's style is the juxtaposition, in a most sophisticated fashion, of social structures and thoughts from Africa and Europe.

For these writers, literature serves a self-constitutive function. It adopts the earlier strategies of Negritude for an inward glance toward the essential self, anchored in childhood or ancestry; it also determines the author's perception of his or her relationship to Europe. As long as the politico-economic world situation remains as it is, the tendency will probably persist.

Drought in the Late 1960s

The career of the Malian writer Seydou Badian Kouyaté is typical of the profiles of the authors who became active in the 1950s. His first published work, *Sous l'orage* (Beneath the storm), appeared in 1957, but after the ensuing *La mort de Chaka* (1961; The death of Shaka) he stopped writing, when he became a government minister (1960–66). He resumed writing, though, when he was imprisoned after a military coup in 1968. *Le sang des masques* (Blood of the masks) was published in 1976, and *Noces sacrées* (Sacred nuptials) in 1977. A similar hiatus occurred in the creative career of Aké Loba; ten years of silence were to elapse after *Kocoumbo, l'étudiant noir* (1960; Kocoumbo, the Black student) before he was heard of again with *Les fils de Kouretchka* (1970; The sons of Kouretchka) and *Les dépossédés* (1973; The dispossessed). The former attracted hardly any notice, while the latter simply rehashed outdated anticolonialist themes. Similarly, Beti's *Remember Ruben* and *Perpétue* (1974) came after fully sixteen years of midcareer silence (Blair 282).

John D. Erickson has indicated that in the late 1960s and 1970s no new authors seemed to be emerging from Francophone Africa (254). The production of fiction did indeed drop in the years immediately preceding and following Independence. But Herzberger-Fofana points out that Zaire and Togo emerged on the literary scene in 1960 with novelists who were more interested in existential themes than in anticolonialist ones. Blair identifies four works between 1966 and 1968 that she finds "completely original and outstanding" (293). *Sur la terre en passant* (1966; On the earth in passing) by François-Borgia Marie Ewembe of Cameroon, which Blair describes as "economically composed," "most moving," and "rich in social implications and philosophical significance" (295), depicts a man who is terminally ill, and strives to maintain his dignity. Malik Fall's *La plaie* (1967; The wound), influenced by the former but with "greater subtlety of treatment" and "more poetry" (296), shows how an accidental wound shapes the social interaction of a young man who voluntarily reopens his flesh to maintain his social status. Ahmadou Kourouma's *Les soleils des indépendances* (1968; The suns of independences, 1981), characterized by "kaleidoscopic," "exotic" style and "picturesque neologisms" (301), addresses Malinke people independently from the new sovereign national borders. And Yambo Ouologuem's *Le devoir de violence* (1968; *Bound to Violence*, 1971), which received the Prix Renaudot and acclaim from France until it was accused of being plagiarized from André Schwarz-Bart's *Le dernier des justes* (1960; The last of the just [Prix Goncourt 1960]). Ouologuem's work is a sadistic and iconoclastic reconstruction of African history from the thirteenth-century empire of Nakem onward; the combination of plagiarism and sadism is reminiscent of Lautréamont's *Chants de Maldoror*, the bible of the surrealist poets, who in turn strongly influenced the poets of Negritude. It appears as though the authors of the African "new novel" have opted for strategies similar to the surrealists' in waging their literary revolution with a view to transforming society.

Beyond Anticolonialism: The New Realism

Jonathan Ngaté identifies Camara Laye's *Dramouss*, Ouologuem's *Le devoir de violence*, and Kourouma's *Les soleils des indépendances* as signaling the move away from anticolonial subjects. Gérard cites the same authors as evidence of liberation from both anticolonialism and the myth of Negritude. As for Laye, Gérard chooses *Le regard du roi* (1954; *The Radiance of the King*, 1965) rather than *Dramouss* (Gérard, *Essais* 19). *Dramouss* contrasts starkly with *L'enfant noir* in style, having none of the limpid classicism of the earlier novel, a possible indication of the author's emancipation from French academism. *Dramouss* portrays the country as a prison run by a sinister giant. The same type of country appears in Tierno Monénembo's *Les crapauds-brousse* (1979; The bush toads), where the whole country revolves around concentration camps; some will almost manage to cross the border, until they realize external help or escape is beyond reach and the only issue left is to fight, albeit hopelessly. Ouologuem and Kourouma share the credit for breathing new life into the Francophone African novel in the late 1960s. Sunday O. Anozie has described their style, in particular Ouologuem's, as a "new realism" (250). Ouologuem employs narrative devices from old Muslim chronicles, while Kourouma adapts the French language to Malinke idioms and syntax. Makouta-M'Boukou provides a rigorous investigation of Franco-African expression that could serve for further studies (294–324). Amadou Kone, Gérard D. Lezou, and Joseph Mlanhoro, in the introduction to their anthology of literature from the Ivory Coast, remark that Kourouma was the initiator of the most modern novelistic trend, adding that by the late 1960s the novel had become the most important genre (13).

Ngaté writes that these three authors (Laye, Ouologuem, and Kourouma) demonstrate "a noticeable decrease in the obsession with Europe and Europeans: the colonial era has ceased to be the temporal frame in which events are set; strong and pointed criticism has assumed a key function, and an African audience is clearly being cultivated" (58). He also recognizes in their works, along with Makombo Bamboté's *Princesse Mandapu* (1972) and Mudimbe's *Le bel immonde*, the beginning of a new form, which he describes in the words of Henri-Daniel Pageaux:

> In these "new" novels, it is less theme and argument in the usual sense (bad living conditions in Africa, disappointment in the face of dictatorial and corrupt politics) that matter as it is the search for a new novelistic diegesis: the revision of the notion of character, a new way of organizing dialogues, chronology and a questioning of meaning (be it social or textual). . . . Here, the novels selected create a problematic space (Sassine's "sand") where the internal imperfection of the individual and his decentering in relation to the social, political, cultural space, and to a confused and crushing "hic et nunc," never cease to turn themselves into words. (Pageaux 33, translated and quoted by Ngaté 70)

Although Pageaux's comment addressed novels produced between 1979 and 1984, Ngaté notes that Dorothy Blair had made a similar observation in her 1976 *African Literature in French* (70).

In these new novels, experimentation is meant for the informed African reader able to submit to the guidance of a discreet but demanding narrator. A good example is the Ivorian writer Charles Nokan's *Le soleil noir point* (1962; The black sun rises), of which P. Ngandu Nkashama writes: "[It] is not a continuous narrative but a juxtaposition of short vignettes and sketches consisting of dialogues, descriptions, letters, excerpts from diaries, dreams or prose poems. This loose structure evidenced the author's determination to experiment outside the conventions of the traditional French novel" (538). An indication of *Le soleil noir point*'s unconventionality is the apparent confusion about which genre it belongs in, since the *Anthologie de la littérature ivoirienne* (Anthology of Ivorian literature) lists it as a play (Kone, Lezou, and Mlanhoro 306).

While Ngaté and Pageaux speak of a new novel, others see a continuation of surrealism in the telescoping of words and spaces, continents and cultures:

> Some authors, such as Bernard Nanga, Moussa Konaté, Ibrahima Ly in *Spiderwebs*, etc. . . . borrow repeatedly from the realist-naturalist novel of the past, this "ready-made writing" of belles lettres. But more and more, the African novel is distancing itself from this type of epic enunciation in favor of a jarring, violent writing, baroque and polyphonic at times, surrealist at other times, as if for a disjointed world only fragmentary and disarticulated narrative forms are appropriate. (Chevrier, "L'image" 11; my translation)

Chevrier's assessment of it notwithstanding, *Toiles d'araignées* (1982; Spiderwebs) did win the first prize of the Foundation L. S. Senghor in 1985.

Critics and authors are ever alert to any indications of new aesthetics. Blair, proclaiming an African "New Novel," hailed Pierre Makambo Bamboté's *Princesse Mandapu* (1972) as a "loosely connected baroque narrative," and the best or only example of "literature of the absurd" in African Francophone literature (*African Literature* 316), although A. C. Brench had earlier noted that Camara Laye's *Le regard du roi* (1954) shared some kinship with Kafka (*Writing* 120).

Another form of experimentation worthy of note is the attempt to merge genres, as in *Assoka, ou les derniers jours de Koumbi* (1973; Assoka, or, The last days of Koumbi), a historical novel by Amadou Ndiaye, which combines "cinematic techniques with the traditional narrative devices of the *griots*" (Gérard "Nouvelles Editions" 1986: 574). Jacques Chevrier predicted in 1989 that future developments in Francophone African fiction will be in the direction of allegory, parable, and fables. They are supposedly more "African." These forms are also conveniently cryptic and relatively anodyne compared to realist novels, and afford authors greater flexibility in repressive political contexts.

The Harvest of the 1970s

The growth of national literatures in the 1970s was not confined to Zaire and the Ivory Coast, but involved Cameroon and the Congo as well. According to Fernando Lambert, the Centre de Littérature Evangélique (CLE) was responsible for the development with regard to Cameroon and the Congo between 1963 and the mid-1970s (571). Francis Bebey of Cameroon won the Grand Prix Littéraire de l'Afrique Noire in 1968 with his first book, *Les fils d'Agatha Moudio* (1967; Agatha Moudio's Sons, 1972). Henri Lopès of the Congo, author of *Le pleurer-rire* (1982; The tearful laughter), is among the major writers to emerge during this period. One should also mention Sony Lab'ou Tansi, who published four novels with Le Seuil between 1979 and 1985.

The Senegalese writer Aminata Sow Fall's first novel, *Le revenant* (1977; The ghost) is about a young man just out of prison, but in 1979 she published *La grève des battù* (*The Beggars' Strike*, 1981) which redirected literary focus onto the plight of the subproletariat in the megalopolis. *L'appel des arènes* (1982; The call of the arena) is more traditional, as she deals with African identity. Sow Fall has also published *Ex-père de la nation* (1987; Ex-father of the nation), thus becoming one of the most prolific female authors in French from Africa.

Based in Senegal and the Ivory Coast, the publishing house Nouvelles Editions Africaines was flourishing and offering new opportunities for African writers. By publishing local authors, it brought to the local reading public works that featured places, events, and names recognizable to them. Many of these works are autobiographical and suitable for creating self-constitutive mirror narratives. Although these pieces address an African audience with the aim of constructing an Afrocentric identity, they are written in comprehensible—in classical—French.

Variations in Style

A recent new form is what P. S. Diop has described as "psychological novels" written in the first person singular. Mariama Bâ (1929–81) is typical of the authors in this literary current. *Une si longue lettre* (1979; *So Long a Letter*, 1981) is an epistolary novel, which Diop asserts is almost purely autobiographical. A mature traditional marriage falls apart when the combined greed of the in-laws deprives the wife of all her rights. She is compelled to leave her husband, to whom she writes a long letter. Among the novel's distinctions is the fact that it is a rare instance of social criticism by a woman, and that its target is neither the colonial past nor the politically troubling present, but rather the problems of polygamy. Bâ continued to explore the issue in *Un chant écarlate* (1981; A scarlet song), with the added twist of a mixed marriage. What would appear to be the debunking of the combined project of Negritude and *métissage* is further complicated by the authorial identification, which may bind the heroine of *So Long a Letter* with the white woman who is the first Muslim wife of a weak and egocentric husband.

Other novels in the psychological tradition are Mudimbe's *Entre les eaux*, about a man unable to commit himself to any ideal or relationship; Ken Bugul's *Le baobab fou* and *Rilwan, ou la chute des nuages* (1987; Rilwan; or, The fall of the clouds), Abdou Anta Kâ's *Mal* (1975; Evil), and Mbwil a Mpaang Ngal's *Giambattista Vico, ou le viol du discours africain* (1975; Giambattista Vico; or, The rape of African discourse), which questions the aesthetic appropriateness of the novel as a means of expressing African traditions (Diop 88–91).

Ngal, whose other works include *L'errance* (1979, 1985; Wandering), applauds the formal revolution that is shaping new Francophone African novels, the better to respond to their new political contexts (Herzberger-Fofana 117). He agrees with Gérard and Ngaté in his assessment of the new tendencies of the African novel: "One may say that the movement begun by Yambo Ouologuem's *Le devoir de violence* and Ahmadou Kourouma's *Les soleils des indépendances* received added impetus from the arrival on the literary scene of Labou Tansi's *La vie et demie*, Tierno Monénembo's *Les crapauds-brousse*, and Henri Lopès' *Le pleurer-rire*" (Herzberger-Fofana 117; my translation). The three new authors are inspired by Latin American authors (Gabriel Garcia Marquez, Augusto Roa Bastos, Alejo Carpentier) in their criticism of dictatorship and their depiction of social realities (Herzberger-Fofana 118). What is "African" in these works, according to Ngal, is their use of European languages "impregnated" by African languages (118). In his view Henri Lopès's *Le pleurer-rire* and Monénembo's *Les crapauds-brousse* are Afrocentric insofar as their French is transformed by African languages (119): several sentences appear in Arabic, from Koranic expressions to common exclamations. Diouldé, the protagonist of *Les crapauds-brousse* is a "handful of flesh" of mythical dimensions. He is also a tragic character whose political awareness develops too late. He dies secretively, and faceless, having been unable to construct his personality (Ngal 12). Dehon regards *Le nègre de paille* (1982; The straw Negro) by Yodi Karone, *Elle sera de jaspe et de corail* by Werewere Liking, and Bernard Nanga's *La trahison de Marianne* (1984; Marianne's treachery) as exemplifying both the new tendency and the ability of Cameroonian writers to find ingenious solutions to aesthetic problems (282).

Stressing the importance of style, Huannou writes: "Revolutionary writers of Benin will produce valuable aesthetic works when they have understood and accepted the fact that what is essential in literary creativity is not the message but the manner of its delivery, in other words, the style" (272; my translation). Gaoussou Diawara has made much the same point: "The people of Mali cannot read their own languages. A literature that aspires to compete in style and syntax with the great literatures of the world must be of good craftsmanship" (Herzberger-Fofana 16; my translation).

Richness and Uniformity

At the turn of the 1970s, Bernard Mouralis notes, a malaise descended upon compilers of African anthologies and literary history, because the corpus of production had become so extensive that it would be practically impossible for any single person to keep track of what was being written in European languages alone (38). Analytical works about Francophone literature from Togo, Cameroon, and the Congo are wrapped in ambiguity because, he believes, one cannot speak of a national literature by applying the notion of "nation" derived from the results of the political developments in Europe between 1750 and 1850 (see also Mpang, in Herzberger-Fofana 120–21). A national literature, in his view, is articulated in a language accessible to the "people," a term that remains to be defined in terms of culture, since social structures affect literary production and their reception. Developments since the 1970s would suggest that the term covers a wider part of the population in Africa than in Europe. Furthermore, Mouralis recommends the study of the cross-cultural effects of hegemonic or dominant cultures on national literatures (42–44). In any case, he views the concept of national literatures as restrictive compared to the earlier Pan-Africanism, and he questions its pertinence in view of the arbitrary manner in which national boundaries were drawn in Africa (48–49).

Also commenting on the recent flood of Francophone literary works, Diop observes that there are "no less than 2,900 titles and close to 1,800 authors to this day. And each year the number grows" (61; my translation). For Cameroon alone, Dehon counts more than fifty titles between 1954 and 1984 (6). But the harvest has not been uniformly plentiful. Huannou remarks that despite the impressive early showing of Benin the novel no longer flourishes there. *L'esclave*, the first regionalist novel in Africa, and *Doguicimi*, the first historical novel, came from that country, but by 1979 a definite drought had occurred (272). He conjectures that the explanation might be the waning fortune of French in that country, especially since oral genres are flourishing. Another obstacle that authors face is a lack of encouragement from local publishing houses, who often consider them to be unacceptable financial risks. Furthermore, increasing materialism among the youth is not conducive to the emergence of new authors. Ahmadou Ousmane makes similar points about his native Niger, where the publishing houses display little interest in their national authors, among the most prominent of whom are Ide Oumarou and Abdoulaye Mamani (Herzberger-Fofana 42–43). Diawara notes that even where authors enjoy publication by their national publishing outlets, as in Mali, they still cannot hope for international recognition because of inadequate distribution (Herzberger-Fofana 14). There have been some ameliorating developments in Benin, however, such as the founding of an association of writers and literary critics (1980); the institution of festivals, colloquia, and prizes; and the inauguration in 1983 of a radio program devoted to cultural affirmation. Comparable developments have taken place in other Francophone African nations.

The Future of the Francophone African Novel

Memmi predicted that "colonized literature in European languages appears condemned to die young" (*Colonizer* 111). Whether Francophone African literature is a "colonized" literature even today may be debatable. Meanwhile France is embarking on a campaign to revitalize French influence in Europe and the Francophone world. On 26 February 1990 the French ministers of *francophonie* and of education, Alain Decaux and Lionel Jospin, urged French high school professors to commend *francophonie* to their classes on its official celebration day, 20 March. Three Francophone summits took place recently (Paris 1986, Quebec 1987, Dakar 1989) with the same end in view. What effect such efforts will have on the fortunes of literary production in the French-speaking African communities remains to be seen.

Léopold Senghor offers his prediction for the future in responding to two questions addressed to him in 1991 (personal correspondence, 11 April 1991). With regard to prospects for *francophonie* after the establishment of a unified European community he predicts, "La construction européenne sera d'autant plus solide que l'Europe aura conservé, mieux, renforcé, sa coopération économique, mais aussi culturelle avec l'Afrique" (The unification of Europe will be that much stronger, in that it will have retained and, better yet, strengthened its economic and cultural cooperation with Africa). As for Francophone literature, he says, "En ce qui concerne la littérature Francophone en Afrique, celle-ci se développe, année après année. D'autant qu'elle est inscrite dans les programmes des enseignements secondaires, mais surtout supérieurs. Je vous dirai même que mes oeuvres sont beaucoup plus étudiées au Maghreb qu'en Afrique noire" (As far as Francophone literature is concerned, it grows year by year, inasmuch as it is part of the syllabus for secondary education, and especially for higher education. I will even tell you that my works are studied more frequently in North Africa than in sub-Saharan Africa).

Bibliography

Ananou, David. *Le fils du fétiche* [The son of the fetish]. Paris: Nouvelles Editions Latines, 1955.

Anozie, Sunday O. *Sociologie du roman africain: réalisme, structure et détermination dans le roman moderne ouest-africain* [Sociology of the African novel: realism, structure, and determination in the modern West African novel]. Paris: Aubier-Montaigne, 1970.

Bâ, Mariama. *Une si longue lettre*. Dakar: Nouvelles Editions Africaines, 1980. *So Long a Letter*. Translated by Modupé Bodé-Thomas. London: Heinemann, 1981.

———. *Un Chant écarlate* [Scarlet Song]. Translated by Dorothy S. Blair. Essex: Longman, 1986.

Badian [Kouyaté], Seydou. *Sous l'orage* [Beneath the storm]. Paris: Présence Africaine, 1957.

———. *La mort de Chaka* [The death of Shaka]. 1961; Paris: Présence Africaine, 1962.

———. *Le sang des masques* [Blood of the masks]. Paris: Robert Laffont, 1976.

———. *Noces sacrées* [Sacred nuptials]. Paris: Présence Africaine, 1977.

Bamboté, Pierre Makambo. *Princesse Mandapu*. Paris: Présence Africaine, 1972.

Bebey, Francis. *Les fils d'Agatha Moudio*. Yaoundé: CLE, 1967. *Agatha Moudio's Sons*. Translated by Joyce A. Hutchinson. New York: Lawrence Hill, 1973.

Berger, Roger. "Comedy in Mongo Beti's *Mission to Kala.*" In *Selected Papers of the 1989 African Literature Association*, edited by Edris Makward. Washington, D.C.: Three Continents Press, in press.

Beti, Mongo. *Mission terminée*. 1957; Paris: Buchet, Chastel, 1972. *Mission to Kala*. Translated by Peter Green. 1958; New York: Collier Books, 1971.

———. *Remember Ruben*. Paris: UGE, 1974. *Remember Ruben*. Translated by Gerald Moore. London: Heinemann, 1980.

———. *Perpétue et l'habitude du malheur*. Paris: Buchet, Chastel, 1974. *Perpetua and the Habit of Unhappiness*. Translated by John Reed and Clive Wake. London: Heinemann, 1978.

Bezoro, Edouard. *La soeur inconnue* [The unknown sister]. Paris: Figuière, 1932.

Blair, Dorothy S. *African Literature in French*. Cambridge: Cambridge University Press, 1976.

———. *Senegalese Literature in French*. Edited by David O'Connell. Boston: Twayne, 1984.

Boni, Nazi. *Crépuscule des temps anciens* [The twilight of old times]. Paris: Présence Africaine, 1962.

Brench, A. C. *The Novelists' Inheritance in French Africa: Writers from Senegal to Cameroon*. London: Oxford University Press, 1967.

————. *Writing in French from Senegal to Cameroon*. London: Oxford University Press, 1967.

Bugul, Ken [Marietou Mbaye]. *Le baobab fou* [The crazy baobab]. Dakar: Nouvelles Editions Africaines, 1982.

————. *Rilwan, ou la chute des nuages* [Rilwan; or, The fall of the clouds]. Dakar: Nouvelles Editions Africaines, 1987.

Césaire, Aimé. *Tropiques. Revue culturelle*, April 1941–45. Reprint. Paris: Jean-Michel Place, 1978.

Chevrier, Jacques. *Littérature nègre* [Negro literature]. Paris: Armand Colin, 1974.

————. "L'image du pouvoir dans le roman africain contemporain" [The image of poverty in contemporary African literature]. *L'Afrique littéraire* 85 (1989): 3–13.

Chinweizu, Onwuchekwa Jemie, and Ihechukwu Madubuike. *Toward the Decolonization of African Literature*. Vol. 1, *African Fiction and Poetry and Their Critics*. Washington, D.C.: Howard University Press, 1983.

Clark, Priscilla P. "West African Prose Fiction." In *European-Language Writing in Sub-Saharan Africa*, Vol. 1, edited by Albert S. Gérard, 118–29. Budapest: Akadémia Kiado, 1986.

Couchoro, Félix. *L'esclave* [The slave]. Paris: Dépêche Africaine, 1929.

Dadié, Bernard. *Climbié*. Paris: Seghers, 1953.

————. *Un nègre à Paris* [A Negro in Paris]. Paris: Présence Africaine, 1959.

————. *Patron de New York* [Boss of New York]. Paris: Présence Africaine, 1964.

————. *La ville où nul ne meurt: Rome* [The city where no one dies: Rome]. Paris: Présence Africaine, 1968.

Davies, Miranda. *Third World–Second Sex: Women's Struggles and National Liberation: Third World Women Speak Out*. London: Zed Books, 1983.

Dehon, Claire L. *Le roman camerounais d'expression française* [The Cameroonian novel in French]. Birmingham, Ala.: SUMMA, 1989.

Diagne, Ahmadou Mapaté. *Les trois volontés de Malic* [The three wishes of Malic]. Paris: Larose, 1920.

Diallo, Bakary. *Force-bonté* [Benevolent force]. Paris: Rieder, 1926.

Diallo, Nafissatou Niang. *De Tilène au plateau: Une enfance dakaroise* [From Tilène to the plateau: a Dakar childhood]. Dakar: Nouvelles Editions Africaines, 1975.

————. *Awa, la petite marchande* [Awa, the petty trader]. Dakar: Nouvelles Editions Africaines; Paris: EDICEF, 1981.

Diop, Papa Samba. "Au coeur de la littérature négro-africaine d'écriture française: Problèmes littéraires et sociologiques" [At the heart Black African literature in French: Literary and sociological problems]. In *Littératures africaines francophones*, 61–122. Bayreuth African Studies Series 3. Bayreuth: German Research Council and the University of Bayreuth, 1985.

Duclos, Jocelyn-Robert. "Bibliographie du roman africain d'expression française" [Bibliography of the African novel in French]. *Présence francophone* no. 10 (1975): 145–52.

Erickson, John D. *Nommo: African Fiction in French South of the Sahara*. York, S.C.: French Literature Publications, 1979.

Evembe, François-B. M. *Sur la terre en passant* [On the earth in passing]. Paris: Présence Africaine, 1966.

Fall, Malick. *La plaie* [The wound]. Paris: Albin Michel, 1967.

Fanon, Frantz. *Peaux noires, masques blancs*. Paris: Seuil, 1952. *Black Skin, White Masks*. Translated by Charles Lam Markmann. New York: Grove Press, 1967.

Gérard, Albert S. *Essais d'histoire littéraire africaine* [Essays on African literary history]. Quebec: ACCT and Editions Naaman de Sherbrooke, 1984.

———. "The 'Nouvelles Editions Africaines.'" In *European-Language Writing in Sub-Saharan Africa*, Vol. 1, edited by Albert S. Gérard, 574–80. Budapest: Akadémia Kiado, 1986.

———. "The Western Mood." In *European-Language Writing in Sub-Saharan Africa*, Vol. 1, edited by Albert S. Gérard, 342–53. Budapest: Akadémia Kiado, 1986.

Gleason, Judith I. *This Africa: Novels by West Africans in English and French*. Evanston, Ill.: Northwestern University Press, 1965.

Grégoire, Henri Abbé. *De la littérature des Nègres* [On Negro literature]. Paris: Maradan, 1808.

Hazoumé, Paul. *Doguicimi*. Paris: Larose, 1938.

Herzberger-Fofana, Pierrette. *Ecrivains africains et identités culturelles: Entretiens* [African writers and cultural identities: Interviews]. Tübingen: Stauffenburg, 1989.

Huannou, Adrien. *La littérature béninoise de langue française des origines à nos jours* [Beninois literature in French from the beginnings to our times]. Paris: Editions Karthala and ACCT, 1984.

Issa, Ibrahim. *Les grandes eaux noires* [The great black waters]. Paris: Scorpion, 1959.

Jahn, Janheinz, Ulla Schild, and Almut Nordmann. *Who's Who in African Literature: Biographies, Works, Commentaries*. Tübingen: Horst Erdmann, 1972.

Kâ, Abdou Anta. *Mal* [Evil]. Dakar: Nouvelles Editions Africaines, 1975.

Kadima-Nzuji, Mukala. "The Belgian Territories." In *European-Language Writing in Sub-Saharan Africa*, Vol. 1, edited by Albert S. Gérard, 158–68. Budapest: Akadémia Kiado, 1986.

———. "Congo/Zaïre." In *European-Language Writing in Sub-Saharan Africa*, Vol. 1, edited by Albert S. Gérard, 541–57. Budapest: Akadémia Kiado, 1986.

Kane, Cheik Hamidou. *L'aventure ambiguë*. 1961; Paris: Julliard, 1972. *Ambiguous Adventure*. Translated by Katherine Woods. 1963; New York: Collier Books, 1971.

Kane, Mohamadou. "Le thème de l'identité culturelle et ses variations dans le roman africain francophone" [The theme of cultural identity and its variations in Francophone African fiction]. In *Literature and African Identity*, 105–25. Bayreuth African Studies Series 6. Bayreuth: German Research Council and the University of Bayreuth, 1986.

Karone, Yodi. *Le nègre de paille* [The straw Negro]. Paris: Silex, 1982.

Kesteloot, Lylian. *Black Writers in French: A Literary History of Negritude*. Translated by Ellen Conroy Kennedy. Philadelphia: Temple University Press, 1974.

———. "Senghor, Negritude and Francophonie on the Threshold of the Twenty-first Century." Translated by Ellen Conroy Kennedy. *Research in African Literatures* 21, no. 3 (Fall 1990): 51–57.

King, Adèle. "The Growth of the Novel." In *European-Language Writing in Sub-Saharan Africa*, Vol. 1, edited by Albert S. Gérard, 489–500. Budapest: Akadémia Kiado, 1986.

Kone, Amadou, Gérard D. Lezou, and Joseph Mlanhoro. *Anthologie de la littérature ivoirienne* [Anthology of Ivorian literature]. Abidjan: CEDA, 1983.

Kourouma, Ahmadou. *Les soleils des indépendances.* 1968; Paris: Seuil, 1970. *The Suns of Independences.* Translated by Adrian Adams. London: Heinemann, 1981.

Labou Tansi, Sony. *La vie et demie* [The life and a half]. Paris: Seuil, 1979.

———. *L'état honteux* [The shameful state]. Paris: Seuil, 1981.

———. *L'anté-peuple* [The prior people]. Paris: Seuil, 1983.

———. *Les sept solitudes de Lorsa Lopez* [The seven solitudes of Lorsa Lopez]. Paris: Seuil, 1985.

Lambert, Fernando. "Cameroon." In *European-Language Writing in Sub-Saharan Africa,* edited by Albert S. Gérard, 557–73. Budapest: Akadémia Kiado, 1986.

Laye, Camara. *L'enfant noir.* Paris: Plon, 1953. *The Dark Child.* Translated by James Kirkup and Ernest Jones. New York: Farrar, Straus & Giroux, 1954.

———. *Le regard du roi.* Paris: Plon, 1954. *The Radiance of the King.* Translated by James Kirkup. New York: Macmillan, 1971.

———. *Dramouss.* Paris: Plon, 1966. *A Dream of Africa.* Translated by James Kirkup. New York: Collier Books, 1968.

Lebel, Roland. *Histoire de la littérature coloniale en France* [History of colonial literature in France]. Paris: Larose, 1931.

Liking, Werewere. *Elle sera de jaspe et de corail* [She will be of jasper and coral]. Paris: L'Harmattan, 1983.

Loba, Aké. *Kocoumbo, l'étudiant noir* [Kocoumbo, the Black student]. 1960; Paris: Flammarion, 1980.

———. *Les fils de Kouretcha* [The sons of Kouretcha]. Nivelles: Francité, 1970.

———. *Les dépossédés* [The dispossessed]. Bruxelles: Francité, 1973.

Lomami-Tshibamba, Paul. *Ngando.* Bruxelles: G. A. Deny, 1948.

Lopès, Henri. *Le pleurer-rire.* [The tearful laughter]. Paris: Présence Africaine, 1982.

Ly, Ibrahima. *Toiles d'araignée* [Spiderwebs]. Paris: L'Harmattan, 1982.

Makouta–M'Boukou, J. P. *Introduction à l'étude du roman négro-africain de langue française: Problèmes culturels et littéraires* [Introduction to the study of the Black African novel in French: Cultural and Literary problems]. 2d ed. Dakar: NEA; Yaoundé: CLE, 1980.

Makward, Edris. "Negritude and the New African Novel in French." *Ibadan* 22 (1966): 37–45.

Makward, Edris, and Leslie Lacy. *Contemporary African Literature.* New York: Random House, 1972.

Malembe, Timothée. *Le mystère de l'enfant disparu* [The mystery of the lost child]. Léopoldville: Bibliothèque de l'Etoile, 1962.

Malonga, Jean. *Coeur d'Aryenne* [Aryan's heart]. Paris: Présence Africaine, 1954.

Maran, René. *Batouala.* Paris: Albin Michel, 1921.

Mayer, Jean. "Le roman en Afrique noire francophone: Tendances et structures" [The novel in Francophone Black Africa: Tendencies and structures]. *Etudes françaises* 3, no. 2 (1967): 169–95.

Memmi, Albert. *Portrait du colonisé précédé du portrait du colonisateur* [Portrait of the colonized preceded by the portrait of the colonizer]. Corrêa: Buchet, Chastel, 1957. *The Colonizer and the Colonized.* Translated by Howard Greenfeld. New York: Orion Press, 1965.

Michelman, Frederic. "The Beginnings of French-African Fiction." *Research in African Literatures* 2, no. 1 (1971): 5–17.

———. "The West African Novel since 1911." *Yale French Studies* 53 (1976): 29–44.

Monénembo, Tierno. *Les crapauds-brousse* [The bush toads]. Paris: Seuil, 1979.

Mouralis, Bernard. "Le concept de littérature nationale dans l'approche des littératures africaines" [The concept of national literature in the approach to African literatures]. In *Littératures africaines francophones*, 37–60. Bayreuth African Studies Series 3. Bayreuth: German Research Council and the University of Bayreuth, 1985.

Mudimbe, Valentin Yves. *L'autre face du royaume: Une introduction à la critique des langages en folie* [The other side of the kingdom: An introduction to the critique of language in insanity]. Lausanne: L'Age d'Homme, 1973.

———. *Entre les eaux* [Between the waters]. Paris: Présence Africaine, 1973.

———. *Le bel immonde* [Before the Birth of the Moon]. Translated by Marjolijn de Jager. New York: Simon and Schuster, 1989.

———. *L'écart* [The gap]. Paris: Présence Africaine, 1978.

Nanga, Bernard. *La trahison de Marianne* [Marianne's treachery]. Dakar: Nouvelles Editions Africaines, 1984.

Ndiaye, Amadou. *Assoka, ou les derniers jours de Koumbi* [Assoka; or, The last days of Koumbi]. Dakar: Nouvelles Editions Africaines, 1973.

Ngal, M[bwil] a M[paang] [Georges Ngal]. *Giambattista Vico, ou le viol du discours africain* [Giambattista Vico; or, The rape of African discourse]. Lubumbashi, Zaire: Alpha-Oméga, 1975; Paris: Hatier, 1984.

———. *L'errance* [Wandering]. Yaoundé: CLE, 1979; Paris: Hatier, 1985.

Ngaté, Jonathan. *Francophone African Fiction: Reading a Literary Tradition*. Trenton, N.J.: Africa World Press, 1988.

Nkashama, P. Ngandu. "The Golden Years of the Novel." In *European-Language Writing in Sub-Saharan Africa*, Vol. 1, edited by Albert S. Gérard, 512–39. Budapest: Akadémia Kiado, 1986.

Nokan, Charles. *Le soleil noir point* [The black sun rises]. Paris: Présence Africaine, 1962.

Novicki, Margaret A., and Daphne Topouzis. "Interview: Ousmane Sembène: Africa's Premier Cinéaste." *Africa Report* 35, no. 5 (November–December 1990): 66–69.

Nyembwe, Tshikumambila. "From Folktale to Short Story." In *European-Language Writing in Sub-Saharan Africa*, Vol. 1, edited by Albert S. Gérard, 475–88. Budapest: Akadémia Kiado, 1986.

Oumarou, Ide. *Gros plan* [Close-up]. 1977; Dakar: Nouvelles Editions Africaines, 1982.

———. *Le représentant* [The representative]. Paris: Nouvelles Editions Africaines, 1984.

Ouologuem, Yambo. *Le devoir de violence*. Paris: Seuil, 1968. *Bound to Violence*. Translated by Ralph Manheim. New York: Harcourt Brace Jovanovich, 1971.

Owono, Joseph. *Tante Bella* [Aunt Bella]. Yaoundé: Au Messager, 1959.

Pageard, Robert. *Littérature négro-africaine: Le mouvement littéraire contemporain dans l'Afrique noire d'expression française* [Negro-African literature: The contemporary literary movement in Black Africa of French expression]. 2d ed. Paris: Livre Africain, 1966.

Pageaux, Henri-Daniel. "Entre le renouveau et la modernité: Vers de nouveaux modèles?" [Between renewal and modernity: Toward new models?]. *Notre librairie* no. 78 (January–March 1985): 31–35.

Périer, Gaston-Denys, and J. M. Jadot. *L'éléphant qui marche sur des oeufs* [The elephant that walks on eggs]. Brussels: L'Eglantine, 1931.

Riesz, Janòs. "The First African Novels in French: A Problem of Authenticity." In *Toward African Authenticity: Language and Literary Form*, 5–30. Bayreuth African Studies Series 2, edited by Eckhard Breitinger and Reinhard Sander. Bayreuth: German Research Council and the University of Bayreuth, 1985.

Sartre, Jean-Paul. "Orphée noir" [Black Orpheus]. Preface to *Anthologie de la nouvelle poésie nègre et malgache de langue française* [Anthology of the new Negro and Malagasy poetry in the French language], edited by Léopold S. Senghor. Paris: PUF, 1948.

Sassine, Williams. *Le jeune homme de sable* [The young sable man]. Paris: Présence Africaine, 1979.

Schwarz-Bart, André. *Le dernier des justes* [The last of the just]. Paris: Seuil, 1959.

Sembène, Ousmane. *Le docker noir*. Paris: Nouvelles Editions Debresse, 1956. *The Black Docker*. London: Heinemann, 1987.

———. *O pays mon beau peuple!* [O my country, my good people!] Paris: Amiot-Dumont, 1957.

———. *Les bouts de bois de Dieu*. Paris: Livre Contemporain, 1960. *God's Bits of Wood*. Garden City, N.Y.: Doubleday, 1962.

———. *Voltaïques*. Paris: Présence Africaine, 1962.

———. *L'Harmattan* [Harmattan]. Paris: Présence Africaine, 1963.

———. *Vehi Ciosane, suivi Le mandat* [Vehi Ciosane, followed by The money order]. Paris: Présence Africaine, 1966.

———. *Xala*. Paris: Présence Africaine, 1974.

———. *Le dernier de l'empire*. 2 vols. Paris: L'Harmattan, 1981. *The Last of the Empire*. London: Heinemann, 1983.

Senghor, Lamine. *La violation d'un pays* [The violation of a country]. Paris: Bureau d'Editions, de Diffusion et de Publicité du Faubourg Saint-Denis, 1927.

Senghor, Léopold S. *Liberté I: Négritude et humanisme* [Liberty I: Negritude and humanism]. Paris: Seuil, 1964.

Siebers, Tobin. *The Mirror of Medusa*. Berkeley and Los Angeles: University of California Press, 1983.

Socé [Diop], Ousmane. *Karim, roman sénégalais* (Karim, a Senegalese novel). Paris: Nouvelles Editions Latines, 1935.

Sow Fall, Aminata. *Le revenant* [The ghost]. Dakar: Nouvelles Editions Africaines, 1976.

———. *La grève des battù*. Dakar: Nouvelles Editions Africaines, 1979. *The Beggars' Strike; or, The Dregs of Society*. Translated by Dorothy S. Blair. Harlow, Essex: Longman, 1981.

———. *L'appel des arènes* [The call of the arena]. Dakar: Nouvelles Editions Africaines, 1982.

———. *Ex-père de la nation* [Ex-father of the nation]. Paris: L'Harmattan, 1987.

Stringer, Susan. "Nafissatou Diallo: A Pioneer in Black African Writing." In *Continental, Latin-American and Francophone Women Writers*, vol. 2, edited by Ginette Adamson and Eunice Myers. New York: University Press of America, 1990.

Taylor, Richard. "The Question of Ethnic Traditions within a National Literature: The Example of Nigeria." In *Toward African Authenticity: Language and Literary Form*, 31–47. Bayreuth African Studies Series 2, edited by Eckhard Breitinger and Reinhard Sander. Bayreuth: German Research Council and the University of Bayreuth, 1985.

Tieghem, Philippe van. *Les influences étrangères sur la littérature francaise (1550–1880)* Paris: PUF, 1961.

Wake, Clive. "Madagascar." In *European-Language Writing in Sub-Saharan Africa*, edited by Albert S. Gérard, 141–50. Budapest: Akadémia Kiado, 1986.

Weka, Victor Yawo Aladji. *La voix de l'ombre* [The voice from the shadow]. Lomé: Habo, 1985.

7 French-Language Poetry

EDRIS MAKWARD

Beginnings in Paris

In the early 1930s a group of French West Indian students in Paris united their energies and their voices to express their radical opposition to the colonial conformism of their elders. The names of the leaders of this group were Etienne Léro, René Ménil, and Jules Monnerot. The nature of their protest was twofold, political and literary. These young men were all from the mulatto middle class of the French Caribbean island of Martinique. They all had been sent to Paris by their parents to complete and crown the latter's dream of total assimilation to French culture with successful French university degrees, and subsequently to return to their native island to join the dignified civil service and professional classes. These young men, however, decided to resist violently their elders' dream of assimilation. Instead of quietly pursuing their studies, they launched their own organ of protest on 1 June 1932: *Légitime défense* (Legitimate defense).

Ménil and his friends had deliberately borrowed from André Breton's 1926 surrealist manifesto not only the title but also the tone of revolt. They proclaimed that they were "suffocating with this capitalistic, Christian, bourgeois world," that "among the filthy, vile, bourgeois conventions" they abhorred "particularly human hypocrisy, this stinking emanation of Christian rottenness" (Kesteloot, *Les écrivains* 25; my translation). Above all, they wished to reject vehemently what they saw as the "fake personality" of the imitative Black and mulatto middle class of the French West Indies from which they came. Most of these young men were budding poets whose vision was strongly influenced by the surrealists' new and invigorating approaches. Thus, following in the footsteps of Michel Leiris, Ménil predicted the advent of a man "armed with poetic power" who will overturn the social, political and moral life of his country through the power of the word (Kesteloot, *Les écrivains* 50; my translation).

This group of young poets and intellectuals, mainly from Martinique, living and studying in Paris, and known as the *Légitime défense* group, from the name of their single-issue magazine of June 1932, are seen by scholars as the precursors of a more mixed group, also composed of young students, poets, and intellectuals living in Paris in the 1930s but originating not only from French-speaking countries of the Western hemisphere, such as Martinique, Guadeloupe, and French Guyana, but also from continental Black Africa and Madagascar. This group in 1934 assembled around their own journal, *L'étudiant noir* (The Black student), under the emerging leadership of Aimé Césaire from Martinique, Léopold Sedar Senghor from Senegal, and Léon Damas from French Guyana.

In Damas's own words, the first merit of *L'étudiant noir* was to bring together Black students of different horizons and backgrounds, for as he put it, it was "a corporate magazine of combat whose objective was the end of tribalization, of the clannish system then commonly practiced in the Latin Quarter. One was now no longer essentially a Martiniquan, a Guadeloupean, a Guyanese, an African, or a Malagasy student, but just one and the same Black student. Life was no longer to be lived in isolation" (Kesteloot, *Les écrivains* 91; my translation).

The Negritude Poets

It is among the members of this latter group, under the leadership of Senghor, Césaire, and Damas and including Léonard Sainville, Aristide Maugée, Birago Diop, and Ousmane Socé Diop, that the ideology and the movement of Negritude was to emerge and develop, sustained above all initially by the works of poets. The principal concern of these poets was indeed the assertion of their confidence and pride in the originality and beauty of Black and African cultures.

The study of contemporary African literature in French, whether prose or poetry, almost always starts with reference to the ideology and poetry of the Negritude movement. And while some critics would assert the chronological precedence of prose writing and fiction by Africans from the former French Empire over the later appearance of poetry, there is an almost universal consensus with regard to the initial primacy of poetry and the importance of Negritude in the development of contemporary African literature in French. It is undeniable that the influence of these earlier works of prose by Francophone Africans as negligible in comparison to the influence, both literary and political, of the poetry of the Negritude era.

Thus, at the opening of the historic Dakar colloquium "African Literature and the Curriculum," sponsored by the Congress for Cultural Freedom in March 1963, Senghor, then president of Senegal, could exclaim with emotion:

> Unthinking people will no doubt look for something exotic. Because what we are to discuss is, after all, not just any literature written in French, but negro literature, nurtured on the full and vigorous sap of *négritude*. Yes, I have used the word that does not appear in the title of your colloquy. I understand why you did not use it. You had no wish to attract a crowd of tourists, in dark glasses and topees. (Moore 13)

RABÉARIVÉLO AND THE LURE OF FRANCE

While it is possible to extract some earlier poetic activity by French-speaking Africans in such colonial publications as *La revue coloniale* (The colonial review), or in even more obscure local publications, the study of Francophone African poetry must start with the poetry of Senghor and his generation, that is, the poetry of Negritude. There is, however, one remarkable exception: Jean-Joseph Rabéarivélo from Madagascar, who died in 1937 without achieving his cherished dream of visiting the "mother country." Although his troubled life was prematurely ended by suicide at the age of thirty-four, Rabéarivélo left us with a rich legacy of some of the most sophisticated and arresting Francophone poetry, and he unquestionably deserves the conspicuous place that he receives in anthologies and collections of contemporary Francophone literature. Albeit a contemporary of Senghor and his friends, Rabéarivélo wrote his poetry outside the framework of his Black African and Caribbean counterparts, and his work must be studied separately yet simultaneously with the poetry of Negritude.

A true autodidact whose formal schooling was interrupted at the age of eleven and terminated about a year later, Rabéarivélo was an avid reader who devoured the works of his self-appointed masters: Baudelaire, Hugo, Claudel, Valéry, and Gide. Also a compulsive letter writer, he corresponded with Gide and a number of contemporary French poets whose works had some influence on him: Pierre Camo, P. J. Toulet, Ormoy, and others referred to in French literary history as *les poètes fantaisistes* (the whimsical poets). Although he had to work at several menial jobs for a living and was burdened with a large family, Rabéarivélo was a prolific poet. His first poems appeared in *Le journal de Madagascar*, and in 1923 his brilliant essay on Malagasy poetry appeared in the Austrian review *Anthropos;* he was only twenty years old. Soon other volumes of poetry followed: *La coupe de cendres* (1924; The bowl of ashes), *Sylves* (1927; Virgin lands), and *Volumes* (1928). These early poems were clearly influenced by the nineteenth-century French symbolists and Parnassians. Rabéarivélo's later works, *Presque-songes* (1934; Half dreams) and *Vieilles chansons du pays d'Imérina* (Old songs from the land of Imerina), published posthumously in 1939, show a genuine and strong attachment to the people, the traditions, and the literary culture of the Imerina high plateau. His fascination with death, the other world, and the ancestors was apparently intensified by the premature death through illness of one of his daughters, Voahanny. This almost morbid sensitivity, coupled with his vivid awareness of the ambiguity of his cultural condition, has marked some of the most moving poetry of the Francophone world:

> You who left at dawn
> and who thus entered a doubly walled night,
> human words can no longer reach you,
> nor can these floral stalks be a crown for you

having turned into bursting buds around the trees of Imerina
The very morning you departed from us.

A stone door separates us:
A door of wind divides our lives.
Do you sleep on the red earth of your couch
on that red earth where no grass grows
but where blind ants get intoxicated
by the wine of the dark grapes of your eyes?

(*Presque-songes*, in Chevrier 113; my translation)

While Rabéarivélo's correspondence reveals a passionate love and aware-ness of the literary Paris of the 1920s and 1930s, whence he would order recent publications at devastating cost to his modest purse, and while he was aware of the presence in Paris of René Maran, the author of the prestigious Goncourt Prize–winning novel *Batouala* (1921) to whom he even sent a few early poems, he apparently had not heard of Senghor, Césaire, and their friends or of the idea of Negritude.

Rabéarivélo was indeed a predictable product of the French assimilation policy; for him, France, and Paris in particular, was the birthplace of the poets and writers he admired above all others and whom he passionately wished to emulate. But unlike his contemporaries from the French West Indies or from the African continent then living and studying in France, he had not reached the stage of protest and denunciation. In fact, in spite of constant humiliations and indifference, he continued to strive for recognition and acceptance by the French colonial administration through wearying and frustrating efforts to obtain a government position and a place among the Malagasy delegation that was to represent the territory at the historic Paris Exposition Universelle of 1937. The latter would have naturally fulfilled his lifetime dream of visiting his poetic and cultural Eldorado.

The final rejection, which he received on 20 June 1937, was doubtless an immediate cause of his suicide two days later. This final blow was probably only the straw that broke the camel's back, however, for Rabéarivélo had been deeply troubled and frustrated throughout his adult life. His daughter Voahanny's premature death four years earlier, which plunged him into an extensive gloomy meditation, was most certainly one other decisive cause of his suicide.

Nevertheless, this deep introversion, on the one hand, and his apparent total acceptance of the colonial order, on the other, did not prevent him from expressing in many of his poems the ambiguity of his condition between two cultures. This is exemplified in the poem *Flûtistes* (Flute players), which ends with the following lines:

His flute
 is like a reed bending

under the weight of a bird of passage
not a bird captured by a child
and whose feathers rise up,
but a bird separated from its kind
looking at its own shadow, for comfort
on the running water.

Your flute,
and his—
they mourn their origins
in the songs of your troubles.

(*Presque-songes*, in Wake 26)

But even in his expression of loss between two cultures, Rabéarivélo's words ring more like a resignation and the acceptance of a dilemma than the characteristic challenge or the deliberate rejection of a Damas or a Senghor.

Rabéarivélo will continue to occupy an important place in Francophone African and Black poetry, by virtue of the depth and the harmony of his images and the rigorous form of his verse. It is no accident that his work is included in Senghor's historic *Anthologie de la nouvelle poésie nègre et malgache de langue française* (1948; Anthology of the new Black and Malagasy poetry), which is preceded by Jean-Paul Sartre's celebrated preface "Orphée Noir" (Black Orpheus) and which continues to be viewed as the true manifesto of Negritude. Nevertheless, his poetry belongs to a different ideological stance and era in the history of Francophone African and Black poetry.

THE IDEOLOGIES

Like most world literatures, contemporary African and Black literatures, whether in French or in other languages, are generally characterized by specific ideological stances within which individual literary trends as well as individual authors and works can be easily classified. Borrowing from the landmark analyses of Frantz Fanon in *Les damnés de la terre* (1961; *The Wretched of the Earth*, 1963) and Albert Memmi in *L'homme dominé* (1968; The dominated man), we can identify four basic stances in a loosely connected chronological order, starting with the ideology of white superiority, used by colonial rulers to justify their domination of darker races and faithfully internalized by generations of Africans and Europeans alike up to about the advent of World War II.

This first ideological stance is not well represented in the poetic genre in Francophone Africa, but it is abundantly so in the French West Indies and in Haiti through a host of faithful imitators of the nineteenth-century Parnassian and symbolist schools of French poetry. This servile imitation is naturally to be seen as just one confirmation of the unquestioned acceptance of the stance of absolute white superiority by the colonized educated elite.

The prose narratives of the period between the two wars, such as Ousmane

Socé Diop's first novel, *Karim, roman sénégalais* (1935; Karim, a Senegalese novel), all belong to this first stance of unconditional acceptance of the supremacy of Western European civilization. The same is true for some of Birago Diop's early poems, which Damas dismissed as not "Black" enough, as "classical reminiscences," and in which Mohammadou Kane finds "the characteristic themes of the poetry of the early 1800s: the tears, the sighs, death, the flight of time, impossible love, the pangs of passion" (Kane 81; my translation). Even Senghor, known as one of the "founding fathers" of Negritude, does not escape completely, in Jacques Chevrier's words, "from the temptation of imitation of the symbolists and the Parnassians in his early poetic attempts" (Chevrier 27; my translation).

The second ideological stance corresponds to the era of the struggle for independence—roughly the period from immediately before World War II to the early 1960s. This stance is that of a new consciousness, of one's legitimate pride in one's cultural and historical heritage, a stance of protest, of criticism and challenge to the colonial ideology of absolute white and Western superiority. This new consciousness started with Senghor and his friends in Paris in the mid 1930s, but the influence of their ideas did not spread from the banks of the Seine to those of the Senegal, the Niger, or the Congo until the post–World War II years. The two principal landmarks associated not with the birth or the development of Negritude but with its dissemination to the four corners of the Black world, and to Africa in the first place, are undeniably the publication in 1948 of Senghor's *Anthologie* and the simultaneous appearance a few months earlier of the first issue of *Présence africaine* in Paris and in Dakar, in December 1947. This is confirmed by Senghor himself, in a letter to Lylian Kesteloot:

> Naturally, Paris is small . . . at least for the Black intellectuals who always end up meeting in the Latin Quarter or in Saint-Germain-des-Prés. It is in those circumstances that I came into contact with a good number of Black intellectuals of the second generation, during the years of the Occupation. . . . Thus was *Présence africaine* born after the war. (Kesteloot, *Les écrivains* 207; my translation)

Alioune Diop, the late founder of *Présence africaine*, expressed eloquently the raisons d'être of this important review in its first issue:

> We were a number of overseas students in Paris who, in the middle of the sufferings of a Europe that was reexamining her own essence and the authenticity of her values, came together to study our situation and the distinguishing elements that defined us. . . . As it was no longer possible to return entirely to our original traditions or to assimilate ourselves to Europe, we felt that we were now a new race, mentally the result of a cross between several cultures. (A. Diop 7; my translation)

For Diop, in those years following the liberation of France, the principal preoccupation of the Black African intellectual, whether poet, journalist, or historian, could only be "the search for a true understanding and a definition of the African's originality and his insertion into the modern world."

The promoters of Negritude were initially more concerned with the creative and aesthetic expression of their new consciousness than with establishing a comprehensive and coherent statement explicating their position in the world. That explication would come only later. Thus, at the 1963 meeting in Dakar referred to earlier, Senghor felt the need to reiterate a precise definition of Negritude:

> Once more, *négritude* is not racialism; it does not spring from a vulgar and distorted attitude of mind. It is simply the sum of civilised values of the black world; not past values but the values of true culture. It is this spirit of Negro-African civilisation, which is rooted in the land and in the heart of the black man, that is stretching out towards the world of men and things in the desire to understand it, unify it and give expression to it. (Moore 15)

In an earlier statement—and significantly, at an important political gathering, the 1959 congress of the Parti du Rassemblement Africain (PRA)—Senghor the political leader had insisted on the role of Negritude as an instrument of struggle against colonialism and domination: "To stage an efficient revolution, our revolution, we had above all to rid ourselves of our borrowed garments—those of assimilation—and to assert our own existence, that is to say, our Negritude" (Kesteloot, *Les écrivains* 110; my translation).

SENGHOR AND THE POETRY OF RECONCILIATION

It is first in the poetry of Senghor and his friends, and later in that of younger Black African poets, some of whom are true disciples of Negritude, that the themes that characterize this second ideological stance are most eloquently developed. For instance, the persistence of one's culture over the centuries and the sense of a continuity between the dead and the living in the traditions of Black Africa are recurrent themes in many poems of that early era:

> O Dead ones who have always refused to die, who have known
>   how to fight death
> All the way to the banks of the Sine, to the banks of
> the Seine, and in my fragile veins, my indomitable
>   blood
> Protect my dreams as you have protected your sons, the
>   thin-legged migrants.

> (Senghor, "In Memoriam," *Chants d'ombre* [Songs of darkness],
> in *Poèmes* 9–10; my translation)

> Woman, light the clear oil lamp, that the Ancestors
> may chat and the parents as well, with the children in bed.

> (Senghor, "Nuit de Sine" [Night of Sine], *Chants d'ombre*,
> in *Poèmes* 14; my translation)

Those who are dead have never gone away.
They are in the shadows darkening around,
They are in the shadows fading into day,
The dead are not under the ground.
They are in the trees that quiver,
They are in the woods that weep,
They are in the waters of the rivers,
They are in the waters that sleep.
They are in the crows, they are in the homestead.
The dead are never dead.

(B. Diop, "Souffles" [Breaths], in Reed and Wake 20–23)

There is naturally the evocation of a glorious Africa, the Africa of the prestigious empires, of brave warriors and audacious princesses, the Africa of
beauty, wisdom, and splendor characterized also by a closer intimacy of man
with his environment, with nature, as opposed to a dry, lifeless, and decadent
Western world characterized by excessive rationality and materialism, and
by its remoteness from nature and its propensity for the destruction of life. In
an early poem, "Neige sur Paris" (Snow on Paris), Senghor wishes to forget

The white hands that fired the shots that brought the
        empires crumbling
The hands that flogged the slaves, that flogged you.
The white dusty hands that buffeted you, the powdered
        painted hands that buffeted me.
The confident hands that delivered me to solitude,
        to hatred
The white hands that felled the forest of palm trees
        that commanded the heart of Africa.

("Neige sur Paris," *Chants d'ombre*, in *Poèmes* 22; my translation)

Senghor has often been referred to as the poet of reconciliation in comparison
to say, a more aggressive Césaire. Such an assessment, however, does not
preclude the denunciation of colonialism and its abuses in Senghor's poetry,
as in the lines quoted above or in "Ndéssé":

Oh! How heavy is the pious burden of this falsehood.
I am no longer the functionary with authority, no
longer the holy man surrounded by charmed disciples.
Europe has crushed me like the flat warrior under the
monstrous paws of her tanks.
My heart is more bruised than my body on my return from
faraway escapades to the enchanted realm of the
Spirits, in the days of old.

(*Hosties noires* [Black sacrifices], in *Poèmes* 81–82; my translation)

The tone of reconciliation, of pardon, is sounded in many of Senghor's
poems. An example is the beautiful "Prière aux masques" (Prayer to masks):

Let us report present at the rebirth of the World
Like the yeast which white flour needs.
For who would teach rhythm to a dead world of machines and guns?
Who would give the cry of joy to wake the dead and the
        bereaved at dawn?
Say, who would give back the memory of life to the man
        whose hopes are smashed?
They call us men of coffee cotton oil
They call us men of death.
We are the men of dance, whose feet draw new strength
        pounding the hardened earth.

(*Chants d'ombre*, in *Poèmes* 23–24; my translation)

LÉON DAMAS AND AIMÉ CÉSAIRE

Similar themes are echoed in the poetry of Damas and Césaire. In Césaire's celebrated *Cahier d'un retour au pays natal* (1956; *Return to My Native Land*, 1969), heralded in the book's preface, by the French surrealist poet André Breton, as "the greatest lyrical monument of our time" (17), there are many instances where the poet defines and redefines Negritude, what it is and what it is not, always in that high tone characterized by Breton as "that culmination into the concrete, that unceasingly elevated quality of the tone that distinguishes so readily major poets from minor ones" (17). Here is one of the most eloquent examples:

O friendly light
my Négritude is not a stone, its deafness
thrown against the clamor of the day
my Négritude is not a speck of dead water
on the dead eye of earth
my Négritude is neither a tower nor a cathedral

it thrusts into the red flesh of the soil
it thrusts into the warm flesh of the sky
it digs under the opaque dejection of its rightful patience

Eia for the royal Kailcedrat!
Eia for those who invented nothing
for those who have never discovered
for those who have never conquered

but, struck, deliver themselves to the essence of all things,
ignorant of surfaces, but taken by the very movement of things
not caring to conquer, but playing the game of the world

truly the elder sons of the world
porous to all the breath of the world
fraternal space of all the breaths of the world

bed without drain of all the waters in the world
spark of the sacred fire of the world
flesh of the flesh of the world
panting with the very movement of the world.

(Césaire, *Cahier* 114–19, trans. Snyder)

Again, Césaire expresses not only his rejection of hatred and revenge against any race but also his commitment to what Senghor will develop in numerous essays and speeches as "la civilisation de l'universel" (Civilization of the universal):

But so doing, my heart, preserve me from all hatred
do not make me that man of hate for whom
I feel nothing but hate
for cantoned in this unique race
you know, however, that my tyrannical love
is not out of hatred for other races

that I am the toiler of this unique race
what I want
is for the universal hunger
for the universal thirst

I call the race to be finally free
to produce out of its closed intimacy
the succulence of fruit.

(Césaire, Cahier 122–25, trans. Snyder)

It was undoubtedly such passages that were already included in Senghor's anthology that led Sartre to exclaim in his preface "Orphée noir" that "this antiracist racism is the sole road that can lead to the abolition of racial differences" (Senghor, *Anthologie* xiv).

DAVID DIOP: POETRY OF COMBAT

The only continental African poet represented in the Senghor anthology, other than Birago Diop and Senghor himself, was David Mandessi Diop, a much younger man then living in the southwest of France, where he was born of a Senegalese father and a Cameroonian mother. Born in Bordeaux in 1927, Diop was definitely not a member of Senghor's initial Paris Negritude group of the mid-1930s. A sensitive adolescent and avid reader, he was already writing poetry in the ninth grade (*quatrième* in the lycée), and Senghor had had a chance to see some of these initial efforts. By the time Senghor was in the process of compiling the material for his anthology, several of Diop's more mature poems had appeared in the second issue of *Présence africaine*. While choosing to include Diop's poems because of their compelling directness and vigor, Senghor felt the need to point out the young poet's aggressive tone and to state his belief that that tone would no doubt change when Diop came to understand that the "Negritude of a poem lies more in its form . . . than in its theme" (Senghor, *Anthologie* 173). Here is one example of David Diop's vigorous, committed poetry:

> The White killed my father
> My father was proud
> The White raped my mother
> My mother was beautiful
> The White bent my brother under the sun of the roads
> My brother was strong,
> The White turned toward me
> His hands red with black blood
> And said in his Master's voice
> "Boy! A drink, a towel, some water!"
>
> ("Le temps du martyre" [The time of the martyr],
> in *Hammer Blows* 40–41)

Appropriately, Senghor described David Diop's poems as aggressive, direct, and efficient in displaying an acute, uncompromising race consciousness. But in light of Diop's later poems and other activities up to the time of his premature death in a 1960 plane crash off the coast of Senegal, these traits, which Senghor attributed mainly to youth, remained the trademark of this genuine representative of the stance of protest to European supremacy. Significantly, what Senghor describes as the principal characteristic of the Negritude poem, that "emotional warmth that gives life to words and transmutes the word into Logos" (*Liberté I* 24; my translation), is definitely one distinguishing feature of Diop's poetry. This is true of almost every verse of his thin but invaluable volume of poems *Coups de pilon* (1956; *Hammer Blows*, 1973), from the moving poem about the African mother "A ma mère" [To my mother] to the thought-provoking "Nègre clochard" [Nigger tramp], dedicated to Césaire. In sum, Diop's poems can be said to be thematically circumscribed within a framework of uncompromising and sometimes deliberately harsh denunciation of prejudice and exploitation, and an unconditional faith in the Black man's capacity to rise triumphantly into a new and scintillating dawn. And it is within this framework that the secondary themes of love, brotherhood, beauty, tenacious courage, and admiration for one's elder's visionary example of dedication are developed. Here are two additional examples from *Coups de pilon:*

> Your smile that spoke old vanquished miseries
> O mother mine and mother of all
> Of the negro who was blinded and sees the flowers again
> Listen listen to the voice
> This is the cry shot through with violence
> This is the song whose only guide is love.
>
> (*Hammer Blows* 2–3)

From the biting *A un enfant noir* (To a Black child):

> And that justice might be done there were two of them
> Exactly two on the pan of the scales
> Two men on your fifteen years and the glimpsed kingdom.
> They thought of the mad blind man who saw
> Of their women besmirched
> Of their tottering rule
> And your head flew off to hysterical laughter.
>
> In air-conditioned mansions
> Around cool drinks
> An easy conscience relishes its rest.
>
> (*Hammer Blows* 26–27)

The latter excerpt is from one of the most biting denunciations of racism, inspired by the lynching in Mississippi in 1955 of Emmett Till, a Black youngster from Chicago.

It is clear from these excerpts that David Diop, though not a member of Senghor's inner circle of Negritude poets and intellectuals, had read Senghor's works and those of Césaire, and his own poems were indubitably in the same protest vein. The tone of his protest was, however, much more uncompromising and harsh. A poet of pardon and reconciliation he was not.

JACQUES RABÉMANANJARA: THE POETRY OF COMMITMENT

Along with Rabéarivélo, two other Malagasy poets were included in Senghor's anthology: Jacques Rabémananjara, born in 1913, and Flavien Ranaïvo, born in 1914. Of the two, the former was unquestionably the closest to the Paris group of Black poets both ideologically and poetically. A sincere admirer of his elder Rabéarivélo, whom he revered as a mentor, Rabémananjara was allowed the two privileges that had been refused his predecessor: to complete a solid secondary education and join the colonial civil service, and be allowed to visit Paris. His formal education was with the Jesuits at the Tananarive Seminary, and in 1939 he traveled to Paris as a member of the Malagasy delegation to attend the commemoration of the 150th anniversary of the French Revolution. With the outbreak of World War II, he did not return to Madagascar but stayed in Paris to study for a degree in literature. He became an active member of the Black literary and intellectual circles in Paris and a friend of Senghor and Alioune Diop. At the end of the war he was elected deputy of his native island in the French National Assembly in Paris. One of the first Francophone African leaders to state unequivocally his commitment to total and immediate independence, he was arrested, charged, and sentenced to death as one of the instigators of the tragic upheaval of 1947 in Madagascar. After almost ten years in prison in Madagascar and later in Marseilles, he was released on parole in 1956. He then moved to Paris and resumed his literary activities with the Black intelligentsia. With the advent of independence, in 1958, he returned to Madagascar and came to occupy prominent positions in the government up to the time of the military take-over in 1975.

Unlike his compatriots Rabéarivélo and Ranaïvo, Rabémananjara believed staunchly in the poet's duty to participate in the effort to resolve the problems of his nation and not to leave the latter solely in the hands of politicians. With this idea of the function of the poet as a fighter and a liberator for his people, it is not surprising that the principal themes of Rabémananjara's poems and plays center on the lyrical expression of the poet's pride and love for the national past, and his determination in the struggle for freedom and justice.

Rabémananjara is the author of several long poems and collections: *Antsa*, *Lamba*, *Antidote*, *La lyre à sept cordes* (The seven-stringed lyre), and *Aux confins de la nuit* (To the ends of the night). His plays include *Les dieux malgaches* (Malgasy gods), *Les boutriers de l'aurore* (The armors of the dawn), and *Les agapes des dieux Tritiva: une Tragédie* (The love feast of the Tritiva Gods: A tragedy). Despite the horrors of prison and later of poverty and humiliation in France, the tone of his poems, even of those written in prison, is always controlled, almost serene. Jacques Chevrier calls this the "paradox of this poetry of combat that rejects the hatred of France, which remains for Rabémananjara, in spite of the varied experiences resulting from colonization, a spiritual mother and lover" (Chevrier 119; my translation).

Many images in *Antidote* (1961) and *Antsa* (1956) are reminiscent of Senghor's favorite themes: the urge and call of the simple pleasures of dance, of communion with nature, of love, of the kingdom of childhood—"le royaume d'enfance," the innocence of Africa confronted with treacherous Europe, characterized by the harshness of stone and rock and by the cold solitude she brings with her:

> When will I dance covered with roses
> in a frenzy of corollas
> and of paschal chimes!
> Oh when shall we dance,
> on the esplanades of love!

> A sky purer than all the dreams
>   of childhood
>   Oh! the rape of innocence
>   on Easter day
>   in the double clamp
>   of rock and of solitude.

> (*Pâques* [Easter], in Wake 119)

> Lodged in the naked heart of the South,
> I shall dance, Oh! Beloved

I shall dance the flash dance
Of the reptile hunters,
Madagascar!

I shall throw my mythic laughter
On the bold face of the South
I shall throw to the stars my transparent blood!
I shall throw the luster of your nobility
on the thick nucha of the Universe,
Madagascar!

But tonight, the machine gun
Scrapes the kingdom of sleep
Death prowls
Among the lunar songs of the lilies.
The great night of the earth,
Madagascar!

(*Antsa*, in Wake 121)

FLAVIEN RANAÏVO: A BLEND OF CULTURES

Ranaïvo, a contemporary of Rabémananjara who also considered Rabéari-vélo as a master and a mentor, has been accurately referred to as "l'incarna-tion même du métis culturel" (The true incarnation of the cultural hybrid) so dear to Senghor. Born in 1914 in the traditional Merina nobility of Tanana-rive (now Antananarivo), the modern capital city of Madagascar, he had a sheltered childhood and grew up in a relatively affluent and open environ-ment where the hostility and even the ambiguity of a divided or pluralistic world was not apparent to him. This explains partly, in Senghor's view, the harmonious serenity of his "retour aux sources" (Senghor, *Anthologie* 207)—his return to the sources.

Ranaïvo's poetry—*L'ombre et le vent* (1932; Shadow and wind), *Mes chan-sons de toujours* (1955; My songs of forever), and *Retour au bercail* (1962; Return to the fold)—is intimate and deeply rooted, both thematically and in its form and inspiration, in the tradition of the ancient Malagasy *hain-teny*. In an era where the formerly colonized world perceived literature and art in general as always functional and committed, Ranaïvo writes apparently with-out any affectation or regret, in an "art for art's sake" vein. His themes cen-ter on the chaste flutterings of the lover, the pains of separation and distance, and the humorous and often witty confessions of the village sage. Here are two characteristic examples, which were included by Senghor in his anthol-ogy as unpublished items and have since appeared in separate collections:

Epithalamium
Just one word, Sir,
Just a piece of advice, Madam.
I am not one-who-visits-often

like a spoon of feeble volume,
nor am I one-who-talks-all-day-long
like a bad brook across the rubble
I am one-who-speaks-of-love-of-one's-neighbor.
I am not the slight-canoe-that-drifts-on-the-tranquil-water
Nor the pumpkin-that-draws-itself-a-figure-on-its-belly,
And if I cannot make a great deed,
I can always make a small one.

Regrets
Six paths
start from the foot of the traveling tree:
the first one leads to the village-of-oblivion,
the second is a cul-de-sac,
the third is the wrong one,
the fourth saw the beloved one go by,
but did not keep track of her footprints,
the fifth
is for the-one-whom-wisdom-stings,
and the last . . .
I know not if it leads anywhere.

(Senghor, *Anthologie* 216–17)

While Ranaïvo is genuinely enjoyable and pleasant and a true poet indeed, he must be the only African poet of this century who escapes classification in the ideological framework around which this chapter is written. He fits neither with the poets of Negritude, like his contemporary Rabémananjara, nor with the preceding generation of writers whose stance correspond to an unquestioned acceptance of the French assimilation policy.

THE FECUND POSTWAR YEARS

The years following the end of World War II were years in which the influence of Black intellectuals expanded and developed both in Paris and in the overseas territories. A number of factors contributed to this expansion. First, the ranks of colonial students in the metropole, or "mother country," grew from just a few score in the 1930s to thousands after 1946. Second, the French intelligentsia, who after the occupation of their own country by a foreign power had become more sympathetic to the aspirations of their colonized counterparts, were now ready to support the publication of works by Black writers and poets. The latter's presence in the book and print markets became more visible, and consequently their ideas circulated more widely in metropolitan France, at least. Third, even without the encouragement of local colonial authorities, these writings circulated in the overseas territories, where they understandably caught the keen attention of a growing number of younger African men and women who had not had a chance to go abroad for further studies. This did not just happen by chance, for it must be remembered that when the first issue of *Présence africaine* appeared in 1947, the venture was announced officially as appearing simultaneously in Paris and in Dakar, which was then the capital of French West Africa (AOF), a federation comprising eight territories: Mauritania, Senegal, French Sudan (renamed Mali after independence), Guinea, Upper Volta (now Burkina Faso), the Ivory Coast, Niger and Dahomey (now Benin), and the United Nations trusteeship territory of Togo (a former German colony).

This simultaneous official launching was definitely not just a symbolic ceremonial gesture. It was intended to be a significant step toward reeducation and a better circulation of relevant information in Africa itself. And this deliberate move did produce results: some new poets, true disciples who had not left the African continent, began to produce some noteworthy poems. The influence of the two International Conferences of Black Writers and Artists (Paris, 1956, and Rome, 1959) was also an important factor.

BERNARD BINLIN DADIÉ: A HOMEGROWN ORIGINAL

Within the expansion of the Negritude movement to the African continent, the most significant and genuine poet was undoubtedly Bernard Binlin Dadié, from the Ivory Coast, a founding member of *Présence africaine* in Dakar. Dadié is the author of many poems appearing in that and in other periodicals and of two early collections of poems: *Afrique debout* (1950; Rise Africa!) and *La ronde des jours* (1956; The passing of days). While Senghor was correct in warning against sterile imitation or futile repetition at the Dakar Colloquium on Negritude in April 1971, he could not have been thinking of the poems of Dadié, his junior by ten years when he confessed, "When I recognize in the poems that I am sent by young writers reminiscences of Damas, Césaire, or Senghor, I can hardly suppress a yawn" (Chevrier 123, my translation).

Though Dadié is now better known for his prose writings and his plays, he made his initial mark on African literature as a Negritude poet. His themes were then centered on the denunciation of prejudice, the reassertion of racial pride, and the determination to partake in the making of a new Africa. Thus his poem "La vie n'est pas un rêve!" (Life is not a dream), dedicated to "mes frères" (my brothers), ends with:

> Together, let us build the new city.
> You, bent over your books, your distilling vases
> And I, with my spade in hand, in the marshes
> You, draped in broadcloth, in smock
> And I in coarse canvas, my feet in clogs.
> Let us think of Africa wanting for us,
> Let us think of the world to which we owe so much!
> Let us continue the struggle without respite, my brother
> For life is not a dream!

> (Dadié, *Légendes et poèmes* [Legends and poems] 28; my translation)

There is also the poem "Sèche tes pleurs" (Dry your tears):

> Dry your tears, Africa!
> Your children are returning to you
> With hands full of toys
> And the heart filled with love.
> They return to dress you
> With their dreams and their hopes.

(Dadié, *Légendes et poèmes* 245; my translation)

Poems dealing essentially with the theme of pride in one's blackness, such as "Je vous remercie mon dieu" (I thank you, Lord) or "Le noir de mon teint" (The black of my complexion) may be read today as unnecessarily obsessional, but not if one is aware of the early 1950s context in which they were written:

> White is a color for special occasions
> Black the color for every day
> And I have carried the World since the first evening.
>
> I am happy with the shape of my head
> Made to carry the World,
> Content with the shape of my nose
> That must sniff every wind of the World.

(Dadié, *Légendes et poèmes* 239–40; my translation)

Post-Negritude Poetry

In 1966, as part of the activities surrounding the Premier Festival des Arts Nègres in Dakar, Senegal, *Présence africaine* brought out another literary landmark: a five-hundred-page collection of poetry, *Nouvelle somme de poésie du monde noir* (New sum of poetry from the Negro world). While we may notice today, with regret, the volume's lack of poetry in the African languages or in the various creoles of the diaspora, this collection was an unprecedented and important cultural and literary endeavor. It was indeed the most eloquent and effective way of showing the world the flourishing of poetry in Africa and in the rest of the Black world, in the preceding twenty-year period. It brought together some younger but already established poets such as David Diop, Lamine Diakhaté, Edouard Maunick, Cheik A. Ndao, Paulin Joachin, Tchicaya U Tam'Si, and some other greener but promising men and women who were appearing in print for the first time. Among this latter group, one should include Charles Nokan and T. M. Bognini from the Ivory Coast, Annette Mbaye from Senegal, Yambo Ouologuem from Mali, and Henri Lopès from the Congo.

Aimé Césaire's opening statement on the first page of this special issue of *Présence africaine* constitutes a fitting introduction to the discussion of post-Negritude Francophone African poetry:

But why poetry? One might ask.

Do we need to look hard for an answer?

A victim of the colonial traumatism and in search of a new equilibrium, the Black man is still in the process of liberating himself. All the dreams, the yearnings, all the accumulated rancors, all the unspoken hopes that were suppressed for a century by colonialist domination, all this needed to come out, and when it does and expresses itself and spurts out carrying along indistinctly the individual and the collective, the conscious and the unconscious, the present and the future, then what you get is poetry.

Suffice it to say that that essential language, that language of the essential that characterizes poetry is resorted to here, and that poetry plays fully its liberating role.

That the themes have changed, that the media are more varied, that in some instances, the French or the English influence is more perceptible, that in other instances, in contrast, the traditionalist element prevails; that is appropriate.

This evolution and this variety show one thing: that Negritude expands as well as it renews itself. A sign that Negritude continues. (*Nouvelle somme* 3; my translation)

It is easy to agree with almost everything said here. However, to agree with the closing point, that is, that Negritude "expands," that it "renews itself" and "continues," one has to agree on the meaning of the word *Negritude*. If the word implies the unconditional rejection of domination, of exploitation, of prejudice in all its overt or covert forms, if it implies, to paraphrase Fanon, the "interiorization" of the sense of equality and self-worth, and the staunch commitment and effort to rebuild a strong, harmonious and fulfilling homeland for one's people, then one could readily agree with Césaire that Negritude renews itself and continues. One would then see how this progression leads naturally in fact to a third and even a fourth ideological stance, which are both translated poetically in the works of some of the younger poets mentioned above and which will be discussed later in this chapter.

But if the word continues to convey above all what Sartre called that "coming into consciousness" (*prise de conscience*) or that "being-in-the-world" of the Black man, or to convey that exacerbated race consciousness that we have seen in some of Dadié's early poems, and does not evolve to include the reconstruction and the true development of the African nation, then one would have to reject Césaire's closing point, for it then would not account for some of the best poetry included in the *Nouvelle somme* or for most of the more recent poetic contributions of the younger African poets from all over the continent.

And here the sometimes acrid critique of Negritude by the Beninois scholar Stanislas Adotévi comes to mind:

The Black man who is conscious of his race is a good Black man, but if he loses the memory of our fall, if he forgets himself and fades into a mystical trance, if he sees black instead of seeing right, he will lose himself, he will lose the Black man while losing his own sight. In other words, one will not help cure the Black man if one becomes ill or insane. (Adotévi 102; my translation)

For Adotévi and for many African writers and intellectuals of his generation, Fanon's analysis of the colonial condition and his conclusion that race and racism are only accessory to economic subjugation and control in the process of domination remain fundamental. Thus, quoting Fanon's *Peau noire, masques blancs* (1952; *Black Skin, White Masks*, 1967), Adotévi (102) emphasizes the urgency of further action for his generation to move beyond the stage of *prise de conscience*, beyond Negritude, in order to rid Africa of economic domination and inferiority:

> For us the disalienation of the Black man implies an abrupt awareness of the social and economic realities. If there is a complex of inferiority, it has come as a result of a double process:
> −economic first
> −then through internalization or better still through the "epidermization" of this inferiority. (Fanon 28, my trans.)

Consequently, for Adotévi and those of his generation who belong to the third and fourth ideological stances, some of Senghor's pronouncements on the specificity of the Black man's mind are simply unacceptable: for instance, his often quoted "l'emotion est nègre, comme la raison hellene" (emotion is Black as reason is Hellenic), which appeared first in print in 1939 ("Ce que l'homme noir apporte" in *Liberté I* 24).

Apparently, Senghor was aware of these reservations well before Adotévi's time, for in a 1956 article, "L'esthétique négro-africain" (Negro African aesthetics), he protested as follows:

> This is to say that the Black man is devoid of reason, as I have been accused of saying. But his reason is not discursive, it is synthetic. It is not antagonistic, it is sympathetic. It is another mode of learning. . . . *European reason is analytical through utilization, and Black reason intuitive through participation.* (*Liberté I*, 203; Senghor's italics, my translation)

As can be expected, these attempts at further clarification and elaboration did not convince Senghor's detractors.

THE POETS OF THE AGE OF DISILLUSION

The third ideological stance appeared in the 1960s. It is a stance of disillusionment with the new independence and the new African rulers, and it is expressed sometimes with great bitterness. Although a number of poems included in the Francophone section of the *Nouvelle somme* were still in the vein of the second stance—that of protest and denunciation of colonial abuses and prejudice—the new stance was already apparent.

Thus Alpha Sow, from Guinea, probably already disillusioned with Sékou Touré's leadership after the euphoria of his country's symbolically courageous vote in 1958 against membership in de Gaulle's French Community, wrote:

> One sees only Night, the demons on our heels;
> One feels only time, mournings, sobs
> Of a country that wails in the spring of life!
> Where did they go, the indomitable heroes,
> Who used to brave the storm, pull us away from distress,
> Revive our confidence and lead us in battle?
> Under the weight of demons, of lackeys, of accomplices,
> To revive the Voices, their complaints, their revolt,
> To scorn death, march to battle, snatch victory,
> A thousand years! We looked for the ray to draw the furrow!
> Revive the fire, sister;
> The dark night has come;
> We must walk noiselessly.
>
> ("Où sont-ils donc allés?" [Where Then Have They Gone?],
> in *Nouvelle somme* 75; my translation)

The Malian writer Yambo Ouologuem, the author of the controversial novel *Le devoir de violence* (1968; *Bound to Violence*, 1971), a bitter satire of the new order, which seems to have swallowed up the exalting dream of the previous era, writes as follows:

> We eat grapes pasteurized milk gingerbread all imported
> And we eat little
> It's not your fault
> Your name was Bimbircokak
> And all was just fine
> Then you became Victor-Emile-Louis-Henri-Joseph
> Which as far as I can remember
> does not indicate that you are related to Roqueffelère
> (Pardon my ignorance I know nothing about finances and fetishes)
> But as you can see Bimbircokak
> It is your fault that
> From being underdeveloped I have now become undernourished.
>
> ("A mon mari" [To my husband], *Nouvelle somme* 95; my translation)

In the Beninois poet Emile Hologoudou's lines that follow, the ambiguity of the people's victory tempers all exhilaration:

> On the mound of anger,
> they celebrate outrageous triumphs,
> and,
> on their chests,
> their throbbings of bravery burst in fine droplets
> tomorrow,
> at dawn, they will all leave across the desert,
> shoddy goods of vermin and dust

palpitating and hairy joy,
Never mind the lukewarm thousands,
the heroism of some
makes up for the trembling of others,
They trudge along for moons and moons,
and suddenly, in front of them,
nearing the crumbling hour when dawn
lights up its brushfires on the hill,
the promised land appears,
that chilly hallucination of the confines of the valley.

("Légende et mythe" [Legend and myth],
Nouvelle somme 67; my translation)

A NEW GENERATION OF ACTIVISTS

Of the many poets of the *Nouvelle somme*, those who were to become most outstanding in the Francophone literary scene were without any doubt the Congolese poets Tchicaya U Tam'Si and Henri Lopès, the Mauritian poet Edouard Maunick, and the Senegalese poet Cheik Aliou Ndao. Although he was not included in the *Présence africaine* volume, another Congolese poet was soon to join this group with some of the most compelling and engaging poetry of the 1970s: J. B. Tati-Loutard.

It is in the poetry of this latter group that the fourth and most current ideological stance—that of genuine commitment to national, political, economic, and social reconstruction—has its most convincing representatives. The themes and tone of these poets go one important step beyond either a sterile imitation of their immediate predecessors or simply a harsh expression of their disillusionment and their denunciation of the latter.

There is, on the part of this more current group, a genuine attempt to participate in the effort toward true social reform and development. Though some of these poets may have started with works belonging to either the second or the third stances—or even to both stances consecutively—they would subsequently move to the fourth stance of more constructive involvement.

The most prolific and original of these poets is Tchicaya U Tam'Si (the pen name of Gérard Félix Tchicaya), the author of six volumes of poems, the most recent of which, *Arc musical* (Musical bow), came out as long ago as 1970. Tchicaya U Tam'si's first collection was published in 1955, when he was in his early twenties. Born in the Congo in 1931, he went to France as a high school student when his father was elected deputy of his territory in the French National Assembly in Paris, in 1946.

With his six volumes of poetry—*Le mauvais sang* (1955; Bad blood), *Feu de brousse* (1957; Brush fire), *A triche-coeur* (1960; To a tricking heart), *Epitomé* (1962), *Le ventre* (1964; The belly), and *Arc musical* (1970), Tchicaya U Tam'Si established himself as the most prominent Francophone African poet to have emerged after the generation of Senghor. Tchicaya is not a disciple or a convert to Negritude; neither is he a disciple of surrealism, though he no doubt read abundantly the surrealist and the Negritude poets. His poetry is characterized by a personal and acute exploratory inspiration combined with a deeply rooted abhorrence of dogmatism of any kind. His best poetry is strikingly sincere and reveals a keen, sensitive soul striving for an ever-illusory world where true harmonious love and unselfish sacrifice are a reality.

Tchicaya's imagery is often spontaneous and convincing, but his symbolism is not always readily decipherable, even to the most attentive reader. This has led to his reputation as a difficult, almost hermetic poet. Tchicaya himself reacted to that reputation in a 1970 interview during the African Studies Association annual meeting in Montreal by insisting that his poetry should be seen as an intimate and sincere unveiling of his soul to his reader. And he added that, as can be expected in his kind of intimate communications, the flow is not always continuous, and one will naturally encounter here and there obstacles, which are only indications of one's reluctance to strip completely one's soul at once, so to speak; but this should not be taken as the consequence of the poet's desire to be hermetic.

It is in his 1962 volume *Epitomé* that Tchicaya U Tam'Si's poetry becomes most revealing and convincing. This volume was clearly inspired by the mental and physical confusion caused by the poet's brief experience as the editor-in-chief of Patrice Lumumba's Congolese National Movement (MNC) newspaper, *Congo*, in Léopoldville (now Kinshasha) during the traumatizing months that led to the assassination of the charismatic leader and the chaos and misery that followed. Gerald Moore advises that Tchicaya's poetry be read in extended passages for a full appreciation of the intensity and all-consuming passion of his explorations (Tchicaya, *Selected Poems* viii–ix). Here are two eloquent short excerpts from *Epitomé:*

> Already there were showers of flesh
> of younger flesh under your sky
> drenching the year 1908
>
> Then 1959
> Splendid meteorites
> fell on the earth
> at Kin and Kinshasa
> A dove fell
> upon a slaughterhouse
> so fatally
> that she had hallucinations.
>
> (*Selected Poems* 57)

> Am I quite sure that backbone was mine
> Said she, who perpetrated the crime
> And then who was that woman I loved

She had the blue scent of burnt grasses
on the savannah at pitch of noon
at noon when the cicada sings
in the shadow of some murdered shade
a woman with arms blackened by the sun
a woman with empty cradled arms that rocked me
poisoned my soul to love no one but her.

(*Selected Poems* 68)

Another remarkable Francophone poet of the second generation is J. B. Tati-Loutard, born in 1938 in Pointe-Noire, French Equatorial Africa (now in the People's Republic of Congo). While Senegal dominated the Francophone poetry and the literature of the first contemporary generation of African writers, the Congo seems to have played that role for the current generation.

Tati-Loutard, a graduate of the University of Bordeaux, taught at the University of Brazzaville before becoming dean of the faculty of arts there, and then director of higher education and research. He is the author of six volumes of poetry—*Poèmes de la mer* (1968; Poems of the sea), *Les racines congolaises* (1968; Congolese roots), *L'envers du soleil* (1970; The reverse side of the sun), *Les normes du temps* (1974; The standards of the time), *Les feux de la planète* (1977; The fires of the planet), and *Le dialogue des plateaux* (1982; The dialogue of the plateaus)—and the editor of an *Anthologie de la littérature congolaise d'expression française* (1976; Anthology of Congolese literature in French). One feature that Tati-Loutard's poetry shares with Tchicaya's is the absence of dogmatism. It is also characterized by a genuine warm concern and love for Africa. But while Tati-Loutard's theme and tone are often also intensely personal and sincere, Tchicaya's sense of loss, of angry revolt and despair is absent here. Tati-Loutard's poetry, together with the few poems and several important prose works of his countryman Henri Lopès (born 1937), belong definitely in that fourth ideological stance of the poet's determined involvement in the reconstruction of the African nation and continent. Cheik Aliou Ndao, from Senegal, Francis Bebey, from Cameroon, and a number of younger poets are also representatives of this ideological stance.

Thus Tati-Loutard advises in "Retour au Congo" (Return to the Congo):

Follow not the river!
Let the cicada rip the rays of sun
In search of a marrow of shade;
Leave the hummingbird and its piercing song
Among the red bougainvilleas.
Do not fall for the slender plant
That only the wind can hold by its waist;
Return toward the men of the new Africa
Where the factory raises its nostril
Among the high palm trees.

(*Racines congolaises* 37; my translation)

In the same section of *Racines congolaises* is a moving statement on the poet's concern and compassion for those who suffer from poverty and from the inhuman indifference of those who made it to the top in the new economic and social order in Africa:

> This is my concern
> Up there the sun is endlessly exploding
> And the moon is endlessly milking the sun
> And generously offering us its milk
> Month after month day after day.
> Thus goes the world which from the poles
> Has stopped turning round on its cushions of ice.
> But that is the way God suns his world;
> It is an ancient pact I would not mingle in.
> But you my brother who would not stop wearing away
> Your hands and always hard up
> Day after day month after month
> May I say to you without jamming my heart
> Just this one time between two hard days:
> "Your misfortune is a pact with which I do not meddle"?

(*Racines congolaises* 45; my translation)

THE FUTURE

It is appropriate to end this chapter with quotations from two Senegalese poets, Cheik Aliou Ndao and Marouba Fall, and from former Congolese statesman and prime minister Henri Lopès. These quotations from West and Central Africa epitomize the most current trends in Francophone African poetry. They also exemplify what the directions of this poetry are likely to be, namely, a poetry that thematically will still continue to explore some of the areas pioneered by the Negritude predecessors. These themes will naturally include the pride and genuine admiration and respect for one's past and the exaltation of one's heroes from the remote as well as from the recent past. A strong sense of race, but without undue ostentation, will still pervade this poetry; there may still be some references to past abuses and prejudices, but such themes will no longer be a principal concern.

Indeed, this poetry will continue to convey a genuine confidence in the making of a new and strong Africa, but the abuses by the post-Independence rulers and leaders of Africa will also continue to be denounced. More often than before, these themes are likely to be treated in a more personalized and less grandiose tone. Lastly, the mastery of the poetic medium and the confidence and competence of these younger poets will continue to be more and more convincing. There will also be more attempts at borrowing from traditional African verbal art forms.

Ndao, who holds an English degree from the University of Grenoble in France, wrote in English a tribute to Kwame Nkrumah, the architect of

Ghanaian independence and a passionate champion of Pan-Africanism. In another poem whose inspiration stems from pride in one's culture. Ndao describes the beautiful African hairstyle using the traditional braids. This hairstyle is now the fashion all over the continent:

> Braids
>> Simple clusters
>> Of complex lines
>> savannah's forests
>> Ancestral witchcraft
>> Dissipate the overseas era
>> And bring back the dance of naked Breasts.
>
> Braids.

(Ndao, *Mogariennes* 34; my translation)

And from the younger Marouba Fall, born in 1950, a message of determination and commitment to an Africa devoid of corruption and war:

> But I say that Paradise can be invented here
> Let nations be to one another
> What milk is to couscous
> Let each one cultivate its garden
> For the joy and repletion of all.

(Fall, *Cri d'un assoiffé de soleil*
[The cry of one parched by the sun] 30; my translation)

In a 1963 poem Henri Lopès reveals his mixed-blood origin and the painful but real sense of rejection it often implies, despite his undivided loyalty to the continent of his birth:

> The teeth and the hair
> Married
> One day in a smile
> under the arch of the mangrove
> I am the flower of their love
> The child of Ebony and of Ivory
> The color of clay
>
> But child of a premarital love
> Nobody wants me
> In the family council
> Though tomorrow I see
> Fields covered with flowers of clay
> Filling the horizon
> You may at once
> Howl like a dog
>
> I am African.

(Tati-Loutard, *Littérature congolaise* 177; my translation)

Lopès ended an earlier (1961) praise song to a modern African hero, Patrice Lumumba, in words of determination and confidence in the future:

> We will swear to go
> And march in warlike
> Four by four
> To the nonburial
> Of this giant
> For in a whisper his heart still in our hearts beats
> A pointed finger
> In the direction of Katanga
> To the burial we will go
> Of the colonial helmet
> Of the tyrants' helmets
> White black or khaki
> never mind the color.

(Tati-Loutard, *Littérature congolaise* 176; my translation)

Bibliography

Abraham, W. E. *The Mind of Africa*. London: Nicolson, 1962.

Actes du Colloque sur la littérature africaine d'expression française [Proceedings of the colloquium on African literature in French]. Dakar, 26–29 March 1963. *Langues et littératures* [Languages and literatures] 14 (Dakar, 1965).

Adotévi, Stanislas. *Négritude et négrologues* [Negritude and Negro ideologues]. Paris: Union générale d'éditions, 1972.

Andrade, Mario Pinto de, ed. *Antologia da poesia negra de expressão portuguesa* [Anthology of Negro poetry in Portuguese]. Paris: P. J. Oswald, 1958. *La poésie africaine d'expression portugaise*. Paris: P. J. Oswald, 1969.

Anyinefa, Koffi. "Bibliographie de la littérature congolaise" [Bibliography of Congolese literature]. *Research in African Literatures* 20, no. 3 (Fall 1989): 481–507.

Aubert, Jean, ed. *Huit poètes de Madagascar* [Eight poets of Madagascar]. Paris: Centre, 1959.

Aujoulat, L. P. *Aujourd'hui l'Afrique* [Africa today]. Paris: Casterman, 1958.

Balandier, Georges. *L'Afrique ambiguë* [Ambiguous Africa]. Paris: Plon, 1957.

Ballagas, Emilio, ed. *Antologia de la poesia negra hispanoamericana* [Anthology of Hispano-American Negro poetry]. Madrid: Agvilar, 1935; 1964.

Bassir, Olumbe, ed. *An Anthology of West African Verse*. Ibadan, Nigeria: Ibadan University Press, 1957.

Beier, Ulli, and Gerald Moore, eds. *Modern Poetry from Africa*. London: Penguin Books, 1970.

Brachfeld, Georges. *Lumière noire* [Black light]. New York: Macmillan, 1972.

Cendrars, Blaise, ed. *Anthologie nègre: Folklore des peuplades africaines* [Negro anthology: Folklore of African tribes]. Paris: Sirene, 1921. Reprint. Paris: Correa, 1967.

Césaire, Aimé. *Le cahier d'un retour au pays natal*. Bilingual edition with English translation by Emile Snyder. Paris: Présence Africaine, 1956. *Return to My Native Land*. Translated by John Berger and Anna Bostock. Hammondsworth: Penguin Books, 1969.

————. *Lettre à Maurice Thorez*. Paris: Présence Africaine, 1956. *Letter to Maurice Thorez*. Paris: Présence Africaine, 1957.

————. *Discours sur le colonialisme* [Discourse on colonialism]. Paris: Présence Africaine, 1958.

————. *The Collected Poetry*. Translated by Clayton Eshlemen and Annette Smith. Berkeley and Los Angeles: University of California Press, 1983.

Chevrier, Jacques. *Littérature nègre* [Negro literature]. Paris: Armand Colin, 1974.

Collins, Marie. *Black Poets in French*. New York: Scribner, 1972.

Cook, Mercer. *Five French Negro Authors*. Washington, D.C.: Associated, 1943.

Damas, Léon. *Pigments*. Paris: Guy Levy Mano, 1937.

————, ed. *Poètes d'expression française: Afrique noire, Madagascar, Réunion, Guadeloupe, Martinique, Indochine, Guyane* [French-language poets: Black Africa, Madagascar, Reunion, Guadeloupe, Martinique, Indochina, Guyana]. Paris: Seuil, 1947.

Dadié, Bernard Binlin. *Légendes et poèmes*. Paris: Seghers, 1967.

De Schutter-Boucquey. *Négritude et poètes noirs: Mémoire de philologie romane presenté a l'Université libre de Bruxelles* [Negritude and Black poets: Report on novelistic philology at the Free University of Brussels]. 1959.

Diop, Alioune. "Niam n'goura, ou les raisons d'être de *Présence africaine*" [Niam n'goura; or, The reasons for the birth of *Présence africaine*]. *Présence africaine*, November–December 1947.

Diop, Birago. *Leurres et lueurs* [Lures and glimmers]. Paris: Présence Africaine, 1961.

Diop, Cheick Anta. *Nations nègres et culture* [Negro nations and culture]. Paris: Présence Africaine, 1954.

————. *L'Afrique noire précoloniale* [Precolonial Black Africa]. Paris: Présence Africaine, 1960.

Diop, David Mandessi. *Coups de pilon*. Paris: Présence Africaine, 1956. *Hammer Blows and Other Writings*. Translated and edited by Simon Mpondo and Frank Jones. Bloomington: Indiana University Press, 1973.

Eliet, Edouard. *Panorama de la littérature négro-africaine* [Panorama of Black African literature]. Paris: Présence Africaine, 1966.

Fall, Marouba. *Cri d'un assoifé de soleil*. Dakar: Les nouvelles éditions Africaines, 1984.

Fanon, Frantz. *Peaux noires, masques blancs*. Paris: Seuil, 1952. *Black Skin, White Masks*. Translated by Charles Lam Markmann. New York: Grove Press, 1967.

————. *Les damnés de la terre*. Preface by J. P. Sartre. Paris: François Maspéro, 1961. *The Wretched of the Earth*. Translated by Constance Farrington. New York: Grove Press, 1968.

Goodwin, Ken. *Understanding African Poetry: A Study of Ten Poets*. London: Heinemann, 1982.

Grégoire, Abbé Henri. *De la littérature des nègres, ou recherches sur leurs facultés intellectuelles*. Paris: Maradan, 1808. *An Inquiry Concerning the Intellectual and Moral Faculties and Literatures of the Negroes. Followed with an Account of the Life and Works of Fifteen Negroes and Mulattoes Distinguished in Science, Litera-*

ture, and the Arts. Translated by D. B. Warden. College Park, Md.: McGrath Publishing Co., 1967. (First published 1810.)

Grunebaum, Gustave Edmond Von. *French African Literature: Some Cultural Implications*. Paris: Mouton, 1964.

Guibert, Armand. *L. S. Senghor, l'homme et l'oeuvre* [L. S. Senghor, the man and his work]. Paris: Présence Africaine, 1962.

———. *Selected Poems*. Translated by John Reed and Clive Wake. New York: Atheneum, 1969.

Hell, Henri. *Poètes de ce temps* [Poets of the present time]. Number 57. Paris: Fontaine.

Hughes, Langston, ed. *An African Treasury*. New York: Crown, 1960. *Anthologie africaine et malgache*. Translated by Christiane Reynault. Paris: Seghers, 1962.

Jahn, Janheinz. *Muntu: An Outline of Neo-African Culture*. Translated by Majorie Green. London: Faber, 1961.

———. *Manuel de littérature neo-africaine: Du XIV siècle à nos jours, de l'Afrique à l'Amérique* [Manual of neo-African literature: From the fourteenth century to the present, from Africa to America]. Paris: RESMA, 1969.

Jahn, Janheinz, and John Ramsaran. *Approaches to African Literature*. Ibadan, Nigeria: Ibadan University Press, 1959.

Justin, Andrée, ed. *Anthologie africaine des écrivains noirs d'expression française* [African anthology of Black writers of French expression]. Paris: Institut pedagogique africaine, 1962.

Kane, Mohammadou. *Birago Diop, l'homme et l'oeuvre* [Birago Diop, the man and his work]. Paris: Présence Africaine, 1971.

Kesteloot, Lilyan. *Les écrivains noirs de langue française: Naissance d'une littérature*. Brussels: L'université libre de Bruxelles, 1965. *Black Writers in French*. Translated by H. Kennedy. Philadelphia: Temple University Press, 1976.

———, ed. *Anthologie négro-africaine* [Black African anthology]. Paris: Marabout université. 1967.

Lebel, Roland. *L'Afrique occidentale dans la littérature française depuis 1870* [West Africa in French literature since 1870]. Paris: Larose, 1925.

———, ed. *Le livre du pays noir: Anthologie de la littérature africaine* [The book of the Black country: Anthology of African literature]. Preface by M. Delafosse. Paris: Monde moderne, 1928.

Lewis, William H., ed. *French-Speaking Africa: The Search for Identity*. New York: Walker, 1965.

Makward, Edris, and Leslie Lacy. *Contemporary African Literature*. New York: Random House, 1972.

Maquet, Jacques. *Les civilisations noires*. Paris: Marabout université, 1965. *Civilizations of Black Africa*. Revised and translated by Joan Rayfield. New York: Oxford University Press, 1972.

Melone, Thomas. *De la négritude dans la littérature négro-africaine* [On Negritude in Black African literature]. Paris: Présence Africaine, 1962.

Michelman, Frederick. "The Beginnings of French African Fiction." *Research in African Literatures* 2, no. 1 (Spring 1971): 5–17.

Moore, Gerald. *Seven African Writers*. London: Oxford University Press, 1962. Revised and enlarged as *Twelve African Writers*. London: Hutchinson, 1980.

————. *African Literature and the Universities*. Ibadan, Nigeria: Ibadan University Press, 1965.

Mphahlele, Ezekiel. *The African Image*. New York: Praeger, 1974.

Mveng, P. Engelbert. *Dossier culturel pan-africain* [Pan-African cultural dossier]. Paris: Présence Africaine, 1965.

Ndao, Cheik Aliou. *Mogariennes*. Paris: Présence Africaine, 1970.

Ngaté, Jonathan. *Francophone African Fiction: Reading a Literary Tradition*. Trenton, N.J.: Africa World Press, 1988.

Nouvelle somme de poésie du monde noir [New sum of poetry from the Negro world]. Special issue. *Présence africaine* 57 (1966).

Nwoga, Donatus. *West African Verse*. Paris: Présence Africaine, 1970.

Ouologuem, Yambo. *Le devoir de violence*. Paris: Seuil, 1968. *Bound to Violence*. Translated by Ralph Manheim. New York: Harcourt Brace Jovanovich, 1971.

Perham, Margery. *Ten Africans*. London: Faber & Faber, 1936. Reprint. 1963.

Perier, G. D. *Petite histoire des lettres coloniales* [Brief history of colonial letters]. Brussels: Collection nationale, 1944.

Price-Mars, Dr. Jean. *Ainsi parla l'oncle* [Thus spake the uncle]. Paris: Compiegne, 1928.

Reed, John, and Clive Wake. *French African Verse*. London: Heinemann, 1972.

Rutherford, Peggy, ed. *Darkness and Light: An Anthology of African Writing*. London: Faith; Johannesburg: Drum, 1958.

Sainville, Léonard, ed. *Anthologie de la littérature négro-africaine: Romanciers et conteurs* [Anthology of Black African literature: Novelists and storytellers]. Paris: Présence Africaine, 1963.

Senghor, Léopold Sédar. *Liberté I: Négritude et humanisme* [Liberty I: Negritude and humanism]. Paris: Seuil, 1964.

————. *Poèmes*. Paris: Seghers, 1973.

————, ed. *Anthologie de la nouvelle poésie nègre et malgache de langue française* [Anthology of the new negro and Malagasy poetry in the French language]. Preface ("Orphée noir") by J. P. Sartre. Paris: PUF, 1948.

Shelton, Austin J., ed. *The African Assertion: A Critical Anthology of African Literature*. New York: Odyssey, 1968.

Taravant, J. *Essai sur une nouvelle poésie nègre d'expression française* [Essay on a new negro poetry in French]. Report presented to the Ecole Nationale de la FOM. Paris, 1946–48.

Tati-Loutard, J. B. *Les racines congolaises* [Congolese roots]. Paris: Oswald, 1968.

————, ed. *Anthologie de la littérature congolaise d'expression française* [Anthology of Congolese literature in French]. Yaoundé: CLE, 1976.

Tchicaya U Tam'si [Gérard Félix Tchicaya]. *Arc musical; Epitomé*. Honfleur: Oswald, 1970.

————. *Selected Poems*. Translated by Clive Wake. London: Heinemann, 1970.

Thompson, Virginia, and Adolff, Richard. *French West Africa*. New York: Allen & Unwin, 1958.

Wake, Clive, ed. *An Anthology of African and Malagasy Poetry in French*. London: Oxford University Press, 1965.

Wauthier, Claude. *L'Afrique des africains*. Paris: Seuil, 1964. *The Literature and Thought of Modern Africa*. Translated by Shirley Kay. New York: Praeger, 1966.

French-Language Drama

and Theater

ALAIN RICARD

The first book-length study of theater in Africa, Bakary Traore's *Le théâtre négro-africain et ses fonctions sociales* (1958; *Negro-African Theater and Its Social Functions*, 1972) clearly shows the influence of missionaries and of the public school system in French-speaking Africa. Unfortunately, Traore does not draw a strict line between the concepts of theater and drama. Drama is a constant in social life: dances, rituals, and burials all have an element of show and action that is indeed dramatic. But theater is something different: it originates in a desacralized society that is willing to play with its problems, even with its myths. The Bambara *koteba*—sketches acted out by youngsters—is no doubt one of the indigenous African theater forms; so are the Malinke puppets. Both deserve to be included in a history of theater in Africa. The same can be said of other, very different forms that also contain this element of narrative playacting. The Togolese *kantata* in Ewe—religious drama using biblical themes—dates as far back as the 1920s and is still being staged today. In other parts of what was considered French-speaking Africa, in Malagasy, one can cite the *mpilalao*—a kind of musical vaudeville—whose origins are traditional and which also persists today. Strictly speaking, these forms (*koteba, kantata, mpilalao*) do not belong to the history of theater in French, but they have had an influence on writers in French. They flourished throughout the colonial era and are still being maintained.

To write the history of African theater in French is to write the history of texts staged by actors, that is, by people playing a role for fun or for money, but certainly not for ritual reasons. There are very few professional actors in Africa today, yet the existence of a professional society of actors is what would define, for the sociologist, the presence of theater. In the case of theater in French-speaking Africa, let us say that such a corporation exists in embryonic form and that the texts produced during the last two decades have helped shape it.

Actors attempt to create a work of art by presenting a story composed by somebody else. Their craft is a form of art, not a part of daily or ceremonial

227

life. Theater is thus a way of telling stories using people and relying on a fixed scenario, which then allows the actors to improvise. A breakthrough transforms the traditional performances. Language, gestures, and music are suddenly presented in a new synthetic form, or rather should be. Language is now an imported one. What happens then to a medium—theater—that strives for a synthesis of the arts when the relationship between spoken language, music, and dance is no longer embedded within a tradition, and has to be totally re-created? The story and the future of theater as an art form in French-speaking Africa is the record of several such attempts to re-create this relationship.

I concentrate in this study on those texts that can function as works of art, that can communicate a message beyond the boundaries of their original ethnic group, and that can exist independently of those who first composed them. The essay is divided into three parts: (1) a historical overview of the birth and development of theater in Francophone Africa; (2) an analysis of the plays, grouped into three categories; and (3) remarks on the new directions present writers are taking and an attempt to assess what this means for theater as an art form.

Historical Survey: The William-Ponty Formula

It can rightly be said that theater in French on a stage in Africa started at the Ecole William-Ponty, a teachers' training college established in 1930 in Senegal by the French colonial administration. Here, schoolteachers from all over West Africa were trained. Dramatic activity within the school curriculum emphasized stories and dances from the different cultural groups to which the students belonged. As these stories were dramatized, a dialogue in French was added, and an annual theater show presented the results of this interesting pedagogical experiment.

These shows became African theater: at the 1937 Colonial Exposition in Paris the students won critical acclaim. Their dramatic training would have numerous consequences throughout West Africa, since the students came from all the different French territories. They brought to their home countries a concept of theater that has had profound influence, until the 1980s, on dramatic productions in French-speaking Africa. The "Ponty formula"—if we judge by the texts published in the journal *Présence africaine*, such as *Sokame* (1948), a ten-page historical play about a Dahomean queen—consisted of spoken text in French with sung text in an African language. Text was interspersed with songs and dances, which probably attracted most of the audience response, at least during the European tour. The spoken text was, according to L. S. Senghor, "bland and stiff, without style" (*Liberté I* [Liberty I] 66), and could not pretend to the dignity of literature if it were not for the formula that invented this type of didactic folkloristic theater, so widespread until today and so well suited to the students' demands. The

Ponty formula provided an outlet for the students' two basic and suddenly complementary desires: to speak French in a public situation, and to present publicly on a stage their native songs and dances.

In 1938 in the Ivory Coast, Ponty alumni Coffi Gadeau and Amon d'Aby created the Théâtre indigène de Côte d'Ivoire. Bernard Dadié, also a Ponty alumnus from the Ivory Coast, was to become the most famous dramatic writer in French in the late 1960s. And in 1958 another Ponty alumnus, Bakary Traore, published his book on African drama.

Theater was in the hands not only of schoolteachers but also of missionaries. Missionary forms paid more attention to African languages and thus aimed at a better aesthetic synthesis, mediated by indigenous African music. The Togolese *kantata*, with its blend of music, songs, dances, and biblical evocations, is directly descended from that effort. But missionary theater, rarely being in French, does not fall within the scope of this study, even though it had a considerable influence on the concept of dramaturgy that was to preside over the efforts of many an aspiring writer.

Theater in the Ponty vein, acted by students, was to experience a kind of revival (after the school changed emphasis during the overhaul of the colonial educational system in 1948) with the creation by the French colonial government of the Cultural Centers in French West Africa in 1953. These centers subsidized and controlled cultural life within the colonies. Buildings were provided that could be used as libraries and theaters under the aegis of the French colonial administration. The annual drama competition of the Cultural Centers rapidly became a feature of African dramatic life and created the competitive pattern so important even today in African theater.

Not enough attention has been given to the two most original dramatic texts of the end of the colonial era: from Senegal, Senghor's *Chaka* (1956), and from Guinea, Fodeba Keita's *Aube africaine* (1955; African dawn). *Chaka* is a poetic drama, a kind of oratorio, "a dramatic poem for several voices with a drum accompaniment." The text, included in the collection *Ethiopiques*, is dedicated to the "Bantu martyrs of South Africa." It is a meditation on power, a drama of the man of action sacrificing his love to the necessity of armed struggle: "Power is not obtained without sacrifice. Absolute power is obtained by giving the blood of the most cherished being." *Chaka* is a short play with a choir, an interesting experiment in marrying French text and African music. *Aube africaine* is a dance drama, marked by the hope for better days after the end of colonization. Both *Chaka* and *Aube africaine* try to reconcile the spoken text with music and with dance, because as self-conscious artists, Senghor and Keita Fodeba know that theater is an art form that seeks a dynamic synthesis of image, words, and sounds, and not an educational medium, as was the fashion in the Ponty vein. Their example was not followed (was it understood?). Independence saw the flourishing of school drama to an extent that even the most enthusiastic Ponty zealots could not have envisaged.

The Dominant Genres: Village Drama, Urban Drama, and Historical and Political Drama

Jacques Scherer, head of the Institute for Theater Research at the Sorbonne, undertook a survey of African theater in 1965; in six months he read 136 plays and met with many authors. He found that the proclaimed goal of universal primary education and the correlated development of high schools in all countries had given the necessary manpower to theater in French. The output of plays has been large, but their quality has remained low, and no writer stands out, as for instance, Wole Soyinka does in the same period in Nigeria. Works can easily be grouped into three categories: the village drama, the urban drama, and the historical drama.

The paradigm of village drama is the Cameroonian playwright Guillaume Oyono-Mbia's *Trois prétendants, un mari* (1964; *Three Suitors, One Husband,* 1968). The play has been a best-seller (fourteen editions to date) and the all-time favorite of school groups for over two decades, and rightly so. It deals with the cupidity of a father who wants to marry his daughter to a rich suitor in disregard of the girl's preference. In the best Molièresque style the play is written with a touch of lightness, a zest for social criticism. It has all the ingredients to ensure its success among students wishing to separate themselves from so-called backward village practices. Oyono-Mbia's achievement remains unchallenged. Unfortunately, the play uses only the resources of the classical comedy and does not show the theatrical inventiveness of a comparable work by Wole Soyinka: *The Lion and the Jewel* (1963), which addresses the same kind of audience but, for instance, uses dance in a very creative way.

The Congolese playwright Guy Menga also produced a play, *L'oracle* (1969; The oracle), whose topic is the humorous condemnation of village practices, in this case, fetish priests. *L'oracle* is a great favorite of school groups and one of the repertory classics in French-speaking Africa. *L'os* (1973; The bone), by Birago Diop from Senegal, a poet and an accomplished writer of folktales, was first produced in Dakar in 1965. In the vein of the village comedy but with the bite of satire, *L'os* deals with human greed in a situation of extreme need such as prevails in many Sahelian villages.

Just as village life is a great topic for the satirist, so is office life, but the urban dramas' achievements do not measure up to the standards of the village dramas. Corruption in high places, graft, and abuse of women are the topics of many plays, from *La secrétaire particulière* (1970; The private secretary) by the Republic of Benin's Jean Pliya and *Monsieur Thôgô-Gnini* (1970) and *Papa Sidi, maitre escroc* (1975; Papa Sidi, master swindler) by Senegal's Bernard Dadié to *Le club* (1984) by Togo's Senouvo Agbota Zinsou.

Independence also saw the development of historical drama. It had been in the Ponty tradition to present the ways of the old African kingdoms, but no political discussion was included. After Independence, the new states tried to reflect upon their history, and drama was seen by the students and the new elite as a proper vehicle for such soul-searching. A long list of plays using the pageantry of traditional courts were written and presented. Among them we can cite, from Mali, Seydou Badian's *La mort de Chaka* (1961; The death of Shaka) and Djibril Tamsir Niane's *Sikasso, ou la dernière citadelle* (1971; Sikasso; or, The last citadel); from Senegal, Amadou Cissé Dia's *Les derniers jours de Lat Dior* (1965; The last days of Lat Dior) and Cheik Ndao's *L'exil d'Albouri* (1968; The Exile of Albouri); from Benin, Jean Pliya's *Kondo le requin* (1966; Kondo the shark); from Niger, André Salifou's *Tanimoune* (1974); and from the Ivory Coast, Raphaël Atta-Koffi's *Le trone d'or* (1969; The golden throne).

Themes of death and exile are dominant; they can be confronted now that the new nations have been born. These plays have been widely presented in their respective countries of origin as well as in festivals, and they constitute another salient feature of the repertory of school companies. Unfortunately, their artistic achievement does not match the interest of their political content. No balance has been achieved between the spoken and the sung parts, and the result is often weak. Reflection on history should be combined with a reflection on artistic forms, as is the case in Soyinka's *A Dance of the Forests* or *Kongi's Harvest,* where poetry becomes an instrument of power in itself and not a mere illustration of political theories and of historical knowledge.

Some plays try to deal with the political theme in a more ambitious way, attempting an aesthetic as well as political debate of the dominant discourse on history. Such is the Ivorian playwright Charles Nokan's *Les malheurs de Tchako* (1968; The trials of Tchako), which heralds the type of critical outlook that would become the norm in the next decade, although in a rather unaccomplished way.

The best work of the 1960s is probably *Béatrice du Congo* (1969; Beatrice of the Congo), written by the grand old man of African drama, the former Ponty student Bernard Dadié, who, along with Amon d'Aby and Coffi Gadeau, was a former leader of the Cercle culturel et folklorique de la Côte d'Ivoire. Beatrice is the daughter of the King of the Congo. She exhorts her father and her people not to submit to the people of Bitanda (i.e., Portugal), not to abandon their wealth and their culture for a mere mimetism of European ways. Her speeches and her personal commitment make her a kind of African Antigone. She is sentenced to death, her last scream a call for a grant of happiness and joy by the elemental forces of the continent. The play is written with mastery; dialogues are fast paced and the historical setting well constructed. *Béatrice du Congo* was the only African play to be produced at the Avignon Drama Festival (1971), one of the best-known drama festivals in Europe, under the direction of Jean-Marie Serreau, former director of many of Aimé Césaire's plays.

One of the more original plays of the 1960s was *L'Europe inculpée* (1969, 1977; Europe indicted) by the Congolese writer Antoine Letembet-Ambilly, first produced in 1969. Here is the argument of the play as presented by the author:

> This play uses the biblical episode of Noah with his three sons Sem, Cham and Japhet.
>
> In this five-act play, Japhet, father of Europe, upon learning that his daughter Europe is accused in front of judge Humanity, exhorts his father Noah, back on earth, to intervene and stop the trial. (Letembet-Ambilly 5–6)

The schematism of the situation, as well as the coded rhetoric, has an interesting, operatic quality. It belongs to the universe of religious drama, of passion plays, often produced, but in an African language, by missionaries. This is the first example, and still a rare one, of the influence of this type of dramaturgy on theater in French.

This survey of the first period of African theater in French would not be complete if we neglected Guinea and Zaire, where historical developments have been quite different from the other French-speaking countries. In Guinea, the promising debut of Fodeba Keita came to a halt with the dictatorship of Sékou Touré: writers and poets were killed (Keita, himself once a minister, disappeared) or went into exile. Theater was reduced to the competitive singing of praise for the so-called revolution.

A Guinean play presented in Lagos in 1977, *L'aube sanglante* (Bleeding dawn), was an obvious sequel to Keita's *Aube africaine*. Its aesthetic treatment was "based on socialist realism using a fighting vanguard technique opposed to the contemplative theater" (d'Aby, Dadié, and Gadeau, *L'aube sanglante;* my translation). In its ethical proposal, it glorifies "all fighters who fell on the front of the anticolonial struggle." And true to this announcement, the play treats anticolonial struggle in a realistic and prosaic way, using all the techniques of the so-called bourgeois theater it claims to replace. It is supposed to be "a collective creation," which probably expresses the difficulty of finding a self-respecting writer in the nightmarish republic that Guinea had become at that time.

In Zaire, the theatrical movement has deep roots in missionary activities. Many groups existed in the 1950s and put on plays in African languages. There even existed a popular theater in broken French, which was often broadcast over the radio. Plays written by Albert Mongita enjoyed vast popularity. Theater was thus at the same time a popular and an educational medium to an extent unknown in other French-speaking countries.

Plays by Justin Disasi were published in the journal *Présence congolaise* in 1957, while plays by Mongita appeared in *La voix du congolais* in the same year. It is fair to say that this theater, although active and popular, remained poor artistically. The schooling of the authors did not go far, since the intellectual promotion of an African elite was not high on the agenda of Belgian colonization. Still, granting the crudeness of the language and artistic devices, these plays had a strange revealing power, according to the

Zairean scholar P. Ngandu Nkashama, who has written a profound and simulating study of theater in Zaire. It is because of the plays' very marginality "that they signify the relevant manner in which colonial reality was reflected in the frightened and troubled eyes of the elite of the Belgian Congo . . . and of Rwanda Burundi. They [the elite] remained inhibited and panicked at the thought of a theatrical discourse that would investigate deeply and reflect upon their very conditions of existence" (Nkashama 65; my translation).

One could not better express the limitations of colonial drama. In a way, the lack of formal slickness, of that Ponty polish, makes Zairean theater more revealing, more in touch with the essential realities. It has a more direct relationship to truth, and this may be a better road to art.

In the mid-1960s Zairean theater was very active inside the country: students in the big cities such as Kinshasa and Lubumbashi provided a large and receptive audience. Hardly anything was known of the outside world, although eager Zairean students would put on foreign plays. Nkashama has documented some of this activity: names such as D. Bolamba (*Geneviève, martyre d'Idiofa*—Geneviève, martyr of Idiofa) and Valerien Mutombo-Diba (*Le trône à trois*—The throne for three) were well-known among students (Nkashama 68). In 1967 a national theater group was created, and by the early 1970s it counted as many as four hundred people in its company.

New Perspectives

I would like, in this final section, to reflect upon the sociological conditions of theater production and to analyze in this light recent developments and essential trends.

INSTITUTIONS

The creation of national theater companies was for a time a new element in the picture. Senegal built the Théâtre Daniel Sorano in 1965; the Ivory Coast had the Institut national des arts and later the Ecole nationale de théâtre. Zaire, as mentioned above, created a national company in 1967, as did the Congo in 1972 and Togo in 1973.

Today (1985), few countries are without some kind of official support of or involvement in theater: in the Cameroons it was the university theater that, following the Nigerian example, was supposed to stimulate dramatic creativity. Official cultural polices were developed in the early 1970s and varied from a liberal and tolerant attitude, as in Senegal or even in the Congo, to the militant, verbose, and more or less totalitarian postures of Zaire and Guinea. These policies have direct bearing on dramatic writing and production. For instance, how can one speak of theater in what was the Central African Empire? Reality was far beyond anything that could be written, so writers went into silence or exile.

More beneficial to the long-term development of theater has probably
been the gradual development of publishing. In the late 1960s only a few
publishers—P. J. Oswald, who started the *Théâtre africain* series in 1967;
Présence africaine; and CLE—included plays in their catalogues. The French
radio network (ORTF) started its own series (Ricard, "The ORTF"). Then a
new multinational company, Nouvelles Editions Africaines, created by Senegal and the Ivory Coast, built quite a sizable theater list, as did Hatier, which
now publishes the prize-winning radio plays of the Concours Théâtral Inter-
africain, sponsored by the ORTF, now Radio France Internationale (R.F.I.).

The diffusion of drama through the radio is still a significant feature of
cultural life in French-speaking Africa. The aforementioned competition is a
major event, and the grand prize is usually won by writers who are either
confirmed—Jean Pliya from Benin and Guy Menga from the Congo, for instance—or of great promise, like the Congo's Sony Lab'ou Tansi or Togo's
Senouvo Agbota Zinsou.

A permanent hindrance for the development of theater is the lack of
qualified professional actors. Guillaume Oyono-Mbia comments thus:

> It is unnecessary to recall, I believe, that there is still no professional theater
> troupe in the Cameroons. Many African countries are in the same situation.
> Consequently, there is nothing astonishing in the fact that dramatic authors
> are themselves not professionals. . . .
> One of my dearest desires would be, as you might guess, the creation of one
> or several professional theater troupes in the Cameroons and elsewhere in
> Africa. This is so, on the one hand, for the reasons already enumerated above
> and, on the other hand, because authors who merit it should be able to earn
> a living with their work or at least be justly remunerated. (Oyono-Mbia, *Le
> train* 8)

Where professional companies exist (Senegal and the Congo, for instance),
they have become bureaucratized: administration and diplomacy take precedence over responsiveness to innovation and creativity. Where they do not
exist, authors and actors have hopes that soon they will. A rather difficult
balance must be achieved between a strictly administrative approach and an
approach that would encourage only specific productions. If actors are unable to secure a means of livelihood, how can they improve their art? How
can authors experiment and develop their skills? It is worth noting that some
of the most creative groups of the last decade have been only marginally
supported by cultural institutions. Such was the case of the Mwondo Theater
from Lubumbashi, which experiments with dance drama. The same is true
of Rocado Zulu from Brazzaville, which uses (in an independent way) actors
from the national theater group to produce Sony Lab'ou Tansi's plays, and of
Koteba, which borrows the name of the traditional genre from Abidjan and
experiments with dance drama and popular French, trying thus to achieve a
new synthesis of words, gestures, and music.

EXPERIMENTS

The key problem remains one of achieving this new synthesis of words, gestures, and music. Several playwrights have tried to respond to this challenge: Werewere Liking in the Cameroons with the ritual theater, and Porquet Niangouran in the Ivory Coast with *griotique*. One grasps the intent, but unfortunately, few works exist, and the results are difficult to judge.

Other experiments tackle the language problem and in the name of social realism try to reconcile the spoken French on the stage with the language spoken in the streets. One of the most successful such attempts is by the Congolese playwright Sylvain Bemba in *Un foutu monde pour un blanchisseur trop honnête* (1979; A wretched world for a too honest washerman).

The quest for new means of expression, for a new dramatic form, goes along with the desire for a more direct political expression. Such at least is the case with Sony Lab'ou Tansi, especially in *Je soussigné cardiaque* (unpublished; I, the undersigned cardiac), and Chadian M. Naïndouba in *L'étudiant de Soweto* (1981; The Soweto student). The recent interest for the Soweto theme should also be put in perspective, since it has a strong element of parody in Zaire, but also elsewhere, as P. Ngandu Nkashama remarks: "In denouncing apartheid . . . in South Africa, by sublimating the unarmed struggle of students in the face of violence and weapons, in the search for a more just and freer society, the authors are in fact superposing two distinct languages: the general revindication of all African countries and their personal revolt against a society that rejects them" (74; my translation).

This perceptive quote helps us understand the frequent re-creation of the South African political scene in Francophone theater. It forces us to deal with an interpretative sociological criticism that cannot simply describe the contents of the play. The transition is from Shaka as emblem of the political ruler to Soweto as metaphor of political oppression, valid south as well as north of the Limpopo. For many writers caught in small countries that stifle freedom of expression, South Africa offers an easy and efficient way to parody their own situation.

In many countries, what is not possible on a stage is the direct questioning of abusive political power, of what political scientists call the patrimonial character of many African regimes, especially in French-speaking Africano in Togo and Zaire, to name a few. The concept of patrimonialism is of direct relevance to the art of drama, since it is meant to describe the concentration of power in the hands of the head of state, leading to confusion between the private and public domains. The state tends to become the private property of the president, and accordingly, political criticism is taken personally and castigated directly. It is, then, quite understandable that political plays should be written by expatriate writers. Tchicaya U Tam'si, a well-known poet from the Congo, has taken to drama, and his play *Le zoulou* (1977; The

Zulu) was produced in France. Aside from the resources of exile and parody, little room remains for directly political plays.

The last and probably central problem of African theater in French has been, and still is, the lack of theoretical reflection, of confrontation between theory and practice. The conservatory tradition—by which I mean special technical schools of drama such as exist in Senegal, the Ivory Coast, and Zaire—by separating technical training from general university education in the humanities and social sciences, is probably responsible for this state of affairs. The situation is on the way to change. The work of P. Ngandu Nkashama on Zairean theater and of Senouvo Agbota Zinsou on Togolese theater, as well as their own plays, for instance Zinsou's *On joue la comédie* (1984; We are doing comedy), show a new direction, conscious of the necessity to combine social and historical information with an aesthetic awareness. Both writers are particularly concerned with the development of popular forms, either in French or in African languages, and try to adapt their writing to this grass-roots creativity. Neither writer theorizes his work in an ideological sense. Zaire, for instance, is not a place for social criticism. But their example opens new avenues of freedom to dramatic writing.

Conclusion

Our harvest has been meager. No writer of Soyinka's stature has emerged in African theater in French, and too few confirmed poets and novelists have tried their hand at dramatic writing. A strange phenomenon has occurred, though: creativity in representational arts seems to be concentrated in movies. This is where the good actors and the good directors are to be found. No dramatists equal cinematographers like Souleymane Cisse or Sembène Ousmane in the mastery of their art. The question arises, Why are there such good films and such poor plays in French-speaking Africa? One might suggest an answer by taking into account the development of the film industry as well as the history of theater. Filmmaking in French-speaking Africa was introduced at the time of the New Wave movement in France. African filmmakers had the best possible training in the late 1950s and were in the vanguard of film as an art form. On the contrary, theater was taught by schoolmasters who were not real artists. Training in the dramatic arts was continued in second-rate conservatories trying to emulate French institutions. Many African actors worked with Jean-Marie Serreau, one of the best French directors of the 1960s, but Serreau never worked in Africa, and many African actors lived in Paris. In English-speaking Africa, the reverse was true: in Nigeria, for instance, the film industry was started by second-rate Hollywood directors working with brilliant Nigerian actors and it failed, whereas a young Nigerian writer could work for several years with the Royal Court Theater, one of the leading centers of theater in the late 1950s. Theater, like film, is a specific art form, and its development cannot be confined to a mere didactic medium. African film in French was directly in tune with the New Wave. African theater in French was never really in tune with the development of the medium: the Living Theater or the Performance Group never went to Africa, and Peter Brook limited his stay to Nigeria. In the 1970s many repressive regimes came into power, hiding their cultural conservatism under the disguise of authenticity; but this authenticity is only folklore and not the adventurous search for a language that would create a new synthesis of word, music, and gesture, which would be real theater.

The history of African theater in French has so far been the history of an artistic failure. Recent years have shown an awareness of this situation among young writers striving to confer autonomy on theater as an art form and to separate it from the schools. Only by cutting the umbilical cord that links it with the school can theater thrive as an art form.

Bibliography

Anonymous. *L'aube sanglante* [Bleeding dawn]. Conakry, Guinea: Imprimerie Patrice Lumumba, 1977. A play presented by the Republic of Guinea at the Second World Festival of African Arts and Culture, January 1977, Lagos.

————. *Le Théâtre populaire en république de Côte d'Ivoire* [Popular theater in the Ivory Coast]. Abidjan: Cercle culturel et folklorique de Côte d'Ivoire, 1965.

Atta-Koffi, Raphaël. *Le trône d'or* [The golden throne]. Paris: ORTF-DAEC, 1969.

Badian [Kouyaté], Seydou. *La mort de Chaka* [The death of Shaka]. Paris: Présence Africaine, 1962.

Bemba, Sylvain. *Un foutu monde pour un blanchisseur trop honnête* (A wretched world for a too honest washerman). Yaoundé: CLE, 1979.

Bonneau, Richard. *Ecrivains, cinéastes et artistes ivoiriens, aperçu bio-bibliographique* [Writers, filmmakers, and artists of the Ivory Coast: a bio-bibliographical survey]. Abidjan: NEA, 1973.

Chevrier, Jacques. *Littérature nègre* [Black literature]. Paris: Armand Colin, 1984.

Cornevin, Robert. *Le théâtre en Afrique noire et à Madagascar* (Theater in Black Africa and Madagascar) Paris: Le Livre Africain, 1970.

Culture française 3 and 4 (1982) and 1 (1983). Colloquium on theater in countries where French is the national, official, cultural, or popular language, 26 and 27 May 1982.

Dadié, Bernard B. *Assémien Déhylé roi du Sanwi, précédé de Mon pays et son théâtre* [Assémien Déhylé, king of Sanwi, with My country and its theater]. Abidjan: CEDA, 1979.

————. *Béatrice du Congo* [Beatrice of the Congo]. Paris: Présence Africaine, 1970.

————. *Monsieur Thôgô-Gnini*. Paris: Présence Africaine, 1970.

————. *Papa Sidi, maître escroc* [Papa Sidi, master swindler]. Dakar: NEA, 1975.

Dia, Amadou Cissé. *Les derniers jours de Lat Dior; La mort du Damel* [The last days of Lat Dior; The death of Damel]. Paris: Présence Africaine, 1965.

Diop, Birago. *L'os* [The bone]. Dakar: NEA, 1973.

Disasi, Justin. *Arrivé tardive* [Late arrival]. Présence Congolaise, 1957.

Ecole William-Ponty. "Sokame." *Présence africaine* 3 (1948): 627–41.

Huannou, Adrien. *La littérature béninoise de langue française des origines à nos jours* [Beninois literature in French from its origins to the present]. Paris: Karthala/ ACCT, 1984.

Keita, Fodeba. *Aube africaine* [African dawn]. In Frantz Fanon, *Les damnés de la terre* [The Wretched of the Earth], 157–62. Paris: F. Maspero, 1961.

Le théâtre indigène et la culture franco-africaine [Indigenous theater and Franco-African culture]. Special number of *L'education africaine* (Dakar, 1937).

Letembet-Ambilly, Antoine. *L'Europe inculpée* [Europe indicted]. Paris: 1969; Yaoundé: CLE, 1977.

Liking, Werewere. *Une nouvelle terre, suivi de Du sommeil d'injuste* [A new land, with About the sleep of injustice]. Abidjan: Nouvelles Éditions Africaines, 1980.

Menga, Guy. *La marmite de Kola-Mbala* [Kola-Mbala's cooking pot]. Paris: ORTF, 1969.

———. *L'oracle* [The oracle]. Paris: ORTF, 1969.

Mongita, Albert. *La quinzaine: Cabaret Ya Botember* [The fortnight: Cabaret Ya Botember]. *La voix du congolais*, November–December 1957.

Mouralis, Bernard. "L'Ecole William-Ponty et la politique culturelle." In *Le théâtre négro-africain* [Negro-African theater]. Proceedings of the Abidjan Colloquium 1970; 31–36. Paris: Présence Africaine, 1971.

Naïndouba, Maoundoé. *L'étudiant de Soweto* [The Soweto student]. Paris: Hatier, 1981.

Ndao, Cheik Aliou. *L'exil d'Albouri, suivi de La décision* [The Exile of Albouri, with The decision]. Paris: P. J. Oswald, 1967.

Niane, Djibril Tamsir. *Sikasso, ou la dernière citadelle* [Sikasso; or, The last citadel]. Paris: P. J. Oswald, 1971.

Niangoran, Porquet. *Soba, ou la grande Afrique* [Soba; or, The great Africa]. Abidjan: Nouvelles Éditions Africaines, 1978.

Nokan, Charles. *Les malheurs de Tchako* [The trials of Tchako]. Paris: P. J. Oswald, 1968.

Nkashama, P. Ngandu, "Le théâtre et la dramaturgie du masque au Zaïre" [Theater and mask dramaturgy in Zaire]. *Culture française* 8 (1982–83): 58–76.

Nzuji, Mukala Kadima. *La littérature zairoise de langue française* [Zairean literature in French]. Paris: Karthala/ACCT, 1984.

Oyono-Mbia, Guillaume. *Jusqu'á nouvel avis* [Until further notice]. Yaoundé: CLE, 1981.

———. *Le train spécial de son excellence/His Excellency's Special Train*. Bilingual edition. Yaoundé: CLE, 1979.

———. *Trois prétendants, un mari*. Yaoundé: CLE, 1964. *Three Suitors, One Husband*. London: Methuen, 1968. *Three Suitors, One Husband and Until Further Notice*. London: Methuen, 1974.

Pliya, Jean. *Kondo le requin* [Kondo the shark]. Cotonou: Editions du Bénin, 1966; Yaoundé: CLE, 1981.

———. *Le secrétaire particulière* [The private secretary]. Cotonou, Benin: ABM, 1970; Yaoundé: CLE, 1973.

Ricard, Alain. "Francophonie et théâtre en Afrique de l'ouest: Situation et perspectives" [Francophony and theater in West Africa: Situation and perspectives]. *Etudes littéraires* 71, no. 31 (December 1974): 449–76.

————. *L'invention du théâtre* (The invention of the theater). Paris: L'Age d'Homme, 1986.

————. "The ORTF and African Literature." *Research in African Literatures* 4, no. 2 (1974): 189–91.

————, ed. *Le théâtre en Afrique de l'ouest* [Theater in West Africa]. Special issue, *Revue d'histoire du théâtre* 1 (1975).

Salifou, André. *Tanimoune*. Paris: Présence Africaine, 1974.

Scherer, Jacques. "Le théâtre en Afrique noire francophone" [Theater in Francophone Black Africa]. In *Le théâtre moderne*, vol. 2, edited by Jean Jacquot, 103–16. Paris: Editions du Centre national de la recherche scientifique, 1967.

Senghor, Léopold Sédar. *Chaka*. In *Poèmes*. Paris, 1956; Paris: Seuil, 1964.

————. *Liberté I: Négritude et humanisme* [Liberty I: Negritude and humanism]. Paris: Seuil, 1964.

Sokame. *Présence africaine* 4 (1948): 627–41.

Soyinka, Wole. *A Dance of the Forest*. Oxford: Oxford University Press, 1964.

————. *Kongi's Harvest*. Oxford: Oxford University Press, 1964.

————. *The Lion and the Jewel*. Oxford: Oxford University Press, 1963.

Tansi, Sony Lab'ou. *La parenthèse de sang* (Brackets of blood). Paris: Hatier-Paris, 1981.

Tchicaya, U Tam'si [Gérard Félix Tchicaya]. *Le zouluo, suivi de Uwene le fondateur* [The Zulu, followed by Uwene the founder]. Paris: Nubia, 1977.

Traore, Bakary. *Le théâtre négro-africain et ses fonctions sociales*. Paris: Présence Africaine, 1958. *The Black African Theater and Its Social Functions*. Translated by Dapo Adelugba. Ibadan, Nigeria: Ibadan University Press, 1972.

Waters, Harold A. *Black Theater in French: A Guide*. Sherbrooke, Quebec: Naaman, 1978.

Zinsou, S. Agbota. *Le club*. Lomé, Togo: Haho, 1984.

————. "La naissance du théâtre togolais moderne" [The birth of the modern Togolese theater]. *Culture française* 3, no. 4 (1982): 49–57.

————. *On joue la comédie* [We are doing comedy]. Paris: ORTF, 1972; Lomé, Togo: Haho; Haarlem: In de Knipscheer, 1984.

Portuguese-Language

Literature

RUSSELL G. HAMILTON

R. G. Armstrong observed that the "serious business of the mid-twentieth century is carried on in four languages: English, French, German and Russian" (quoted in Roscoe 5). And Chinua Achebe, after a visit to Brazil in the mid-1960s, reported that a "number of the writers I spoke to were concerned about the restrictions imposed on them by their use of the Portuguese language" (18).

The lesser international prestige of Portuguese (despite its nearly 170 million speakers worldwide), compared to English and French, has much to do with the relative obscurity of the writing from Cape Verde, Guinea-Bissau, São Tomé and Príncipe, Angola, and Mozambique. A paucity of translations has also kept this writing largely inaccessible to the non-Portuguese-reading world.[1] But even those who do know the language have had limited access to works from the former Portuguese colonies, which were themselves generally closed to outsiders. Although by now its existence is at least known to most serious students of African literature, writing from Lusophone Africa still gets short shrift in an Anglocentric and Francocentric Africanist universe.

Ironically, Lusophone African writing has been around for a long time. Gerald Moser argues this point in his appropriately titled "African Literature in Portuguese: The First Written, the Last Discovered" (1967). Moser documents the mid-nineteenth-century origins of a Portuguese-language literature written from what can be loosely defined as an African perspective. Although never in large numbers, the Portuguese have had the longest, most sustained European presence in Africa. Centuries-long contact with Portuguese traders, adventurers, slavers, missionaries, and outcasts, including not a few political exiles of a liberal bent, exposed segments of the local African populations to a process of acculturation that led to sporadic social and linguistic creolization, especially in urban centers. During long periods of neglect by the metropole, Africans and Europeans, to varying degrees in

240

all five colonies, were virtually left to their own devices. Often out of expediency Europeans, especially in rural areas, adapted to African ways and spoke local languages just as Africans and *mestiços* (mixed race), principally in the colonial towns and cities, were westernized and spoke Portuguese.

In Angola, Mozambique, and Guinea-Bissau—the colonies with the largest numbers of unassimilated Africans—only a small fraction of the indigenous population learned to speak Portuguese beyond a rudimentary level. Conversely, the unique history of acculturation in all five colonies gave rise to small but significant African and *mestiço* urban elites, many of whose members spoke and wrote Portuguese as their first and, in some cases, only language. In Cape Verde, São Tomé and Príncipe, and Guinea-Bissau, Portuguese-based creoles have served as the first, second, or only language for large segments of the population. In Cape Verde, especially, and to a significant degree in Guinea-Bissau and São Tomé and Príncipe, many of the Portuguese-speaking members of the privileged social strata have also been fluent in the local creole vernacular. The indigenous middle classes in all five colonies gave rise to the intellectual and, in some cases, interracial elites from whose ranks emerged the majority of the writers who produced the earliest acculturated literature of sub-Saharan Africa.

After independence, even as they attempted to validate the nineteenth-century precursors of their respective literatures, most Lusophone African writers and critics would probably concede that the mainly Portuguese-language works truly worthy of being labeled Angolan, Cape Verdean, and so forth, are products of the twentieth century. With the exception of Cape Verde, whose modern literary movement dates from the mid-1930s, a nativistic literature emerged in the late 1940s and early 1950s simultaneously with the crystallization of nationalist sentiments among influential members of the Lusophone African intelligentsia and their Portuguese allies.

African Poetry in Portuguese

Members of the urban intelligentsia, in search of an emotive means of expressing their growing social and political consciousness in the years before independence, seized upon poetry as a more accessible and malleable medium than prose fiction and drama. Whether occasional or "serious," poets could often overcome editorial, economic, and governmental restrictions by surreptitiously distributing their typed or handwritten poems among like-minded intellectuals. Despite government-imposed censorship, writers often found outlets for their poems and occasional stories in a few local newspapers, magazines, and publishing houses run by sympathetic Europeans, and in even fewer African-owned newspapers in cities like Luanda and Lourenço Marques (now Maputo). Some writers even managed to publish their works in Portugal. Starting in the 1950s in Lisbon and Coimbra,

Black, *mestiço*, and white students from the colonies, along with their Portuguese sympathizers, controlled a few editorial outlets for their largely socially conscious poetry and prose.

The Casa dos Estudantes do Império (CEI—House of students from the empire) was founded in Lisbon in 1944 with, ironically, the blessings of António Salazar, the chief architect of Portugal's fascist New State. By the 1950s the CEI had become a hotbed of political and literary activity. This activity led to three anthologies and a number of slim volumes of poetry of cultural revindication and implicit social protest, as well as to the CEI's demise, in 1965, at the hands of PIDE (the Portuguese acronym for the infamous International Police for Defense of the State). In its heyday the CEI's roster of members read like a who's who of Lusophone African nationalist leaders and writers—in several cases, the former and latter being one and the same.

A POETRY OF CULTURAL REVINDICATION

A poetry "of," as opposed to "about" or simply "in," Africa is an emotive form of cultural resistance predicated, to a greater or lesser degree, on a desire for social change. With antecedents dating back to the mid-nineteenth century, a poetry of cultural revindication flourished in the Portuguese colonies before anything comparable emerged elsewhere south of the Sahara.

Cape Verde. Jorge Barbosa (1902–71) published *Arquipélago* (1935; Archipelago), the first of his three books of a poetry of cultural revindication, ten years before Léopold Senghor's *Chants d'ombre* (Songs of darkness). If Senghor's first book of poems harbingered the themes and discourse of the Senegalese poet's most rhapsodic Negritude, Barbosa and other Cape Verdeans had long before fashioned nativistic poems around a unique ethnic ethos.

"Momento" (For just an instant), one of Barbosa's most compelling nativistic and geocentric poems, codifies the archipelago's ambiance of bittersweet melancholy in the expression of a hushed sense of peoplehood:

> who here has not felt
> this, our
> refined melancholy?
> that which unexpectedly suspends
> a laugh just begun
> and leaves a sudden bitterness
> in the midst of our joy
> in our hearts,
> and for no reason at all
> clouds our speech with some sad utterance.
>
> (*Arquipélago* 18; my translation)

Barbosa, along with Manuel Lopes (b. 1907) and Osvaldo Alcântara (the pseudonym of Baltasar Lopes da Silva [1907–89]), form a triad of poets belonging to the *Claridade* generation (so named for the literary journal they and others founded in 1936). Members of this generation hit on the idea of a single ethnic group with a creole language and ethos as the stuff from which Cape Verdean cultural revindication could be fashioned.

Angola. In Luanda in the early 1950s, a nucleus of Black, *mestiço*, and white intellectuals and high school students, members of the Regional Association of Angola's Native Sons (Anangola), rallied around the banner of cultural revindication as they intoned their hortatory poems. "The Young Intellectuals," as they dubbed themselves, founded *Mensagem* (The message), a literary journal, of which only two issues were published, in 1951 and 1952, but which launched the so-called Generation of 1950, with its preponderance of poets, who invoked Africa and vowed to "discover" Angola.[2]

Out of this initial flurry of literary activity emerged Viriato da Cruz (1928–73), a *mestiço* who was *Mensagem*'s prime mover and whose best poetic efforts resulted in ballads composed in an innovative, hybridized Portuguese-Kimbundu language that revindicated the semicreolized city of Luanda and, by extension, a reinvented Angola. Cruz's poem "Sô Santo" (*sô* being a black corruption of the standard Portuguese *senhor*, which, in the poem's title, is equivalent to the English "mister") tells the story of a local Kimbundu entrepreneur and landlord who has fallen on hard times. To the rhythm of the *rebita*, a popular Luandan dance, a chorus of *bessanganas* (Kimbundu for "young women") sings, in creolized Kimbundu:

> Mauari-ngana Santo
> dim-dom
> ual'o banda o calaçala
> dim-dom
> chaluto mu muzumbo
> dim-dom . . .
> [Mister Santo
> *dim-dom*
> down the street he goes
> *dim-dom*
> a cigar stuck in his mouth
> *dim-dom* . . .].
>
> (166; my translation)[3]

At the poem's end the narrator wonders whether Mister Santo offended the gods or whether he is just a symbol of the fate of the race, all of which is coded commentary on the influx, around the end of World War II, of Portuguese settlers that sent many of Luanda's black and *mestiço* residents into a downward socioeconomic spiral, as they lost middle-level jobs to the new arrivals and were forced, paradoxically, to move up to shantytowns (*musseques*) that ringed the European lower city. Thus the members of the Generation of 1950 came of age at a time when Luanda was becoming two cities: a prosperous European one, with skyscrapers and bustling commerce, and a poor African one, with its squalor and cheap source of labor.

Mário António (1934–89), along with other poets of his generation, evoked that real and imagined creole-Kimbundu Luanda that existed before the arrival of waves of settler families. In "Rua da Maianga" (Maianga street), António poetically captured, with sentimentality and irony, a toponymic detail that emblematized the creeping Europeanization of a traditional Luanda neighborhood:

> Maianga Street
> now bears the name of some missionary or other,
> but for us it is still the street of Maianga.
>
> (*Crónica da cidade estranha* 154; my translation)

Other significant poets of the *Mensagem* generation are António Jacinto (1924–91), Alda Lara (1930–62), and Agostinho Neto (1922–79). The latter, about whom I have more to say shortly, is Angola's best-known poet of cultural revindication and social protest. Also significant among the poets of cultural revindication are Aires de Almeida Santos (b. 1922), Samuel de Sousa (b. 1927), Ernesto Lara Filho (1932–75), António Cardoso (b. 1933), Manuel Lima (b. 1935), Arnaldo Santos (b. 1936), Costa Andrade (b. 1936), and Henrique Guerra (b. 1937), all of whom opened the way for and contributed to the next phases of social protest, proindependence, and combative poetry.

Mozambique. The interrelated socioeconomic conditions and cultural and political factors that gave rise to Angola's nationalist literary movement brought about a similar phenomenon on the opposite side of the continent in the Mozambican cities of Beira and, especially, Lourenço Marques. While Angolan intellectuals were coalescing under the banner of such racially integrated organizations as Anangola and the Cultural Society of Angola, comparable groups were forming in Mozambique, but largely along color lines. South Africa's recently officialized apartheid and the color bar in the British-owned Rhodesias directly influenced racial mores in neighboring Mozambique. As a result, much Mozambican poetry of cultural revindication reveals a stronger sense of racial affirmation than Cape Verdean and Angolan writing of the same period.

José Craveirinha (b. 1922), Mozambique's most celebrated modern poet, is a *mestiço* who, years before independence, carried cultural and racial revindication to rhetorical heights unequaled in Lusophone African writing. Craveirinha assaulted an acculturated discourse still allied with a European canon. With affirmation and sardonic posturing, he wrote: "On my thick

lips ferment / the grains of sarcasm that colonized my Mother Africa"
("África" in *Xigubo* 15)

Noémia de Sousa (b. 1927) has the distinction of being the first female poet
of color writing in Portuguese, and perhaps, in any language in all of southern Africa. Eugénio Lisboa, a Euro-Mozambican critic of considerable acu-
men, but with little patience for what he deemed to be artistic ineptitude,
characterized Sousa's poems as prolix and babbling. Ironically, it is these
apparent defects that lend vigor and urgency to her diction. Verbosity and a
stammering search for a liberated mode of expression were the weapons the
mestiça Sousa used, in the 1950s and 1960s, to lay siege to acculturated
language. Her persona's voice is throaty and almost frenetic in "Sangue
Negro" (Black blood):

> Because the strength of your vigor conquers all!
> And nothing more was needed, than the incomparable sorcery
> of your war drums calling out,
> dundundundun-ta-ta-dundundun-ta-ta,
> nothing more than the raw madness
> of your wildest and terribly beautiful rites . . .
> —so that I could tremble
> —so that I could scream
> —so that I could feel, deep, in the blood, your voice, my Mother!
> And overcome, I saw that which joins us . . .
> And so I returned to my millennial origins.
>
> (Ferreira, *No Reino* 92; my translation)

With only a handful of poems and no book to her credit, Noémia de
Sousa's passionate voice faded early, and in the 1950s she went into voluntary exile in Paris (in the 1980s she moved to Lisbon, where she lives today).
Craveirinha remained in Mozambique, where he continued to write (to date
he has published four volumes of poetry) throughout the years of war and
persecution, to which he himself fell victim when he was imprisoned, from
1965 to 1969, as an enemy of the state. Both poets set a standard for a poetic
discourse that defied the very language of its acculturated composition.

Other noteworthy poets who, in the 1950s and 1960s, sought to revindi-
cate a cultural Africanness or protest colonial rule in Mozambique are Orlando Mendes (b. 1916), Virgílio de Lemos (b. 1929), and Sebastião Alba (b.
1940). In line with the unique racial/ethnic composition of literary movements in Lourenço Marques and Beira, it is also worth noting that these
three, along with the majority of the poets publishing in Mozambique during
that period, were Portuguese or Europeans born and raised in the colony.

A Poet from São Tomé and Negritude in Portugal. In 1974 a military coup
overthrew the Portuguese dictatorship, and within a year all of Portugal's
African colonies had been granted independence. Only a few months after

the coup, a curious event took place in Lisbon. Léopold Senghor, by invitation of the Lisbon Academy of Sciences, delivered an address titled "Lusitanianism and Negritude." The celebrated Senegalese poet attributed the deposed Portuguese regime's downfall to its abandonment of Lusitanianism, which, Senghor assured his august audience, is grounded in the ethnic character of a people whose civilization has much in common with that of Black Africa. According to Senghor, the Portuguese possess African *politesse*, civility, and xenophilia, and, like Africans, they are instinctively and congenitally poets. Negritude and Lusitanianism may seem strange bedfellows, but the relationship dates back to well before the 1974 coup.

In "Portugueses e Negritude," a three-part essay that first appeared in 1970 in a Lisbon newspaper, Maria da Graça Freire compares Negritude to the tropicalist ideology of the Portuguese colonies. As proof of a genuinely Portuguese brand of Negritude, Freire quotes from "Canção do Mestiço" (*Mestiço*'s song"), by Francisco José Tenreiro (1921–63):

> When I make love to a white woman
> > I am white . . .
> When I make love to a Black woman
> > I am Black
> > Oh yeah!

> (Freire 62; my translation)

Although the poem perhaps better exemplifies "Mulattitude," Freire's characterization of Tenreiro as a poet of Negritude—the Portuguese way—has some validity.

Tenreiro, born to an African mother and a Portuguese father on the tiny equatorial island of São Tomé, was taken as a child to Lisbon. In Portugal he rose to unprecedented heights as a scholar (he was a professor of geography), a politician (he served in the Portuguese National Assembly), a respected literary critic, and a much-heralded poet. Although held aloft by the right as living proof of Portugal's vaunted racial tolerance, Tenreiro traveled in circles ideologically inimical to the regime. He coedited *Caderno de poesia negra de expressão portuguesa* (1953; A collection of Negro poetry in Portuguese), the first anthology of its kind to be published in the Portuguese sphere. Mário Pinto de Andrade (1928–90), Tenreiro's Angolan coanthologist, has impressive anticolonialist and antifascist credentials. He cofounded, in 1956, the People's Movement for the Liberation of Angola (MPLA), and he has distinguished himself as a literary critic and an articulate, militant essayist who became a close associate of Amílcar Cabral (1924–73), the father of Guinea-Bissau's and Cape Verde's independence.

Death overtook Tenreiro before the appearance of his *Coração em África* (1964; With my heart in Africa), which was issued posthumously as part of a volume of his collected *Obra poética* (1967; Poetic works), and which established him as a formidable Lusophone African poet. And insofar as Negritude was launched in Europe as a cultural formulation of the ideologies of Pan-Africanism and Black consciousness, many of Tenreiro's poems fall into that category (Tenreiro was also influenced by Langston Hughes, Countee Cullen, and other poets of the Harlem Renaissance). In the title poem of Tenreiro's collection, the persona proclaims:

> With my heart in Africa, I tread these foggy city streets
> with Africa in my heart and a bebop rhythm on my lips,
> while all about me they whisper, look,
>   a black man (OK), look, a mulatto (same difference),
>   look, a darky (ridiculous).

(*Coração* 126; my translation)

The quasiofficial acceptance, in Portugal, of Tenreiro's Negritude constituted, in effect, an adaptation of his broader sense of Pan-Africanism to a mitigating justification of a Lusotropicalist ideology out of step with a decolonizing world. In a way, Tenreiro is as much a paradox of Portuguese colonialism as are those Angolans and Mozambicans of European extraction who joined the nationalist movements and wrote literary works of African cultural revindication and social protest.

A POETRY OF PROTEST AND COMBAT

Some Lusophone African intellectuals have declared that their literary movements were born in struggle, while Negritude was conceived in defeat. However exaggerated that contention may be, it is true that in the 1960s, with the outbreak of the wars of independence in Angola, Guinea-Bissau, and Mozambique, cultural revindication and racial affirmation became handmaidens to social protest and combativeness. Mário de Andrade, who lived many years in Paris and who once had praised Negritude as a potent weapon in Africa's struggle for independence, later characterized the Black ideology as having outlived its usefulness. And in 1972 Amílcar Cabral, during a visit to the United States, told a group of African-American students that Negritude had little relevance for his people in their struggle for liberation, because it and Pan-Africanism "were propounded outside of black Africa" (*Return to the Source* 62–63). Indeed, it was chiefly in Portugal, during the years of the wars of liberation in Africa, that a few poets, including Tenreiro and the Angolan Geraldo Bessa Víctor (1917–89), practiced the art and adhered to the precepts of Negritude, Lusitanian style.

Cape Verde and Guinea-Bissau. Cape Verde, as the poet and short story writer Gabriel Mariano (b. 1928) argues in his essay "Negritude e caboverdiani-dade" (1958; Negritude and Cape Verdianism), the Cape Verdeans' collective sense of cultural singularity and ethnic identity precluded the need for any imported racial ideology. And so it is that on the archipelago, some three hundred miles west of Senegal, Cape Verdean intellectuals have long clung to their creole ethos of the biological, linguistic, and cultural mulatto. (Estimates put the islands' population at around 70 percent *mestiço*, 20 percent Black, and 10 percent white.)

Writers of the group known as *Certeza* (Certainty—so named for yet another short-lived but historically significant literary journal, founded in 1944) generally evinced a keener social awareness than their *Claridade* predecessors. In 1952 Amílcar Cabral wrote, however, that although both the *Claridade* and *Certeza* groups had made undeniable contributions to a new Cape Verdean social consciousness, their message had to be transcended in favor of a poetic expression that would reveal "another land within our land" ("Apontamentos" 8).[4] Cabral's own phrase was transcended by the fervent avowal: "We will not go to Pasargadae!"

The reference to Pasargadae, the capital of ancient Persia, comes from a poem by Manuel Bandeira, Brazil's celebrated modernist poet, who, along with other Brazilian writers, profoundly influenced the *Claridade* group. For Bandeira's persona Pasargadae was a Camelot to which he escaped to live out hedonistic fantasies. And following that line, the Cape Verdean poet Osvaldo Alcântara wrote "Itinerário de Pasárgada," in which the persona expresses a "keen longing" for that mythical place.

Militant Cape Verdean writers and intellectuals seized on the Pasargadae metaphor to contest what they saw as the *claridosos'* failure to address the archipelago's chronic socioeconomic problems and political dependency. Thus was born a literary movement based on *anti-evasão*, which is the title of a poem, written around 1962, by Ovídio Martins (b. 1928). With terse and unembellished diction, Martins's persona avows:

> I will scream
> I will shout
> I will kill
>
> I will not go to Pasargadae!
>
> (Burness 117)

Without totally abandoning the ethnocentric notions of creole singularity, these militant poets attempted to locate Cape Verde's destiny in a more African context than had their *Claridade* and *Certeza* predecessors. They also more vehemently protested the chronic economic and social ills that plagued the islands, including the institution of contract labor, which, beginning in the nineteenth century, sent thousands of Cape Verdean peasants to the harsh conditions of the cacao and coffee plantations of São Tomé.

Onésimo Silveira (b. 1935), one of the firebrands of the antievasionist group, chronicled, in poetry and short stories, the abuses of the plantation island, where he himself had lived from 1956 to 1959. Silveira's experiences in São Tomé and, later, Angola undoubtedly led to his insistence on Cape Verde's African roots, in contrast to the *Claridade* claim of the islands as "a mixture of two cultures—but, more European than African" (34; my translation).[5]

The war in Guinea-Bissau, under the leadership of the African Party of the Independence of Guinea[-Bissau] and Cape Verde (PAIGC), led a number of young Cape Verdean intellectuals to identify even more closely with the continent and its destiny. One such intellectual, Felisberto Vieira Lopes (b. 1937), using the provocative creole name of Kaoberdiano Dambará, authored *Noti* (1964; Night), a collection of militant poems written in the creole of Santiago, usually characterized as the most African of the ten inhabited Cape Verde islands.[6]

The patterns of European settlement, with the imposition of Western social institutions and economic structures, which in the other Lusophone colonies gave rise to a small but significant indigenous bourgeoisie, applied to a much lesser degree in the enclave of Portuguese Guinea. Due in part to the virtual absence of a homegrown acculturated elite (the colony's first high school opened in 1949, in contrast to 1917 in Angola and 1860 on the Cape Verde island of Santiago), Guinea-Bissau's modern literary movement began to materialize only after Independence. In a very real sense, cultural revindication, social protest, combativeness, and an exaltation of the word came about almost simultaneously in post-independence Guinea-Bissau poetry.[7]

São Tomé and Príncipe. The Portuguese- and creole-language writing on the two equatorial islands that form the republic of São Tomé and Príncipe is another distinctive phenomenon within the singular history of Lusophone African literature. During colonial times on these plantation islands of largely absentee Portuguese landlords, social and economic conditions made for the emergence of a black and *mestiço* managerial class known as *filhos da terra* (sons and daughters of the land), more or less the equivalent of the Cape Verdean *crioulos*. However, unlike Cape Verde, with its early and unprecedented cultural and literary activities, before independence there was virtually no coordinated literary movement in São Tomé and Príncipe. Many of the *filhos da terra* left their native islands at a tender age to be educated and often to live out their lives in Portugal. Tenreiro, with his nativistic and Negritude poetry, all but initiated modern island literature—in Portugal. Some fifty years before him, Caetano da Costa Alegre (1864–90), a black *filho da terra* also from São Tomé, lived most of his short life and wrote all of his poems, contained in the posthumous volume *Versos* (1916), in Portugal.

Alda Espírito Santo (b. 1926), Maria Manuela Margarido (b. 1926), and Tomás Medeiros (b. 1931) formed the nucleus of an embryonic São Tomé and Príncipe literary movement, similar, in terms of cultural revindication and protest writing, to what occurred in the 1950s and 1960s in Cape Verde, Angola, and Mozambique. Espírito Santo and Medeiros, from São Tomé, and Margarido, from the smaller island of Príncipe, were active in the 1950s in the Lisbon-based House of Students from the Empire (CEI), where they rubbed shoulders with other militant writers from the Lusophone African colonies. But of the three, only Espírito Santo, after completing her education in Portugal, returned to the islands, where she taught school during the final decades of colonial rule and where, after independence, she became a government official.

É' nosso o solo sagrado da terra (1978; The sacred soil of this land is ours), a volume of Espírito Santos's collected poems, bears the subtitle *Poesia de protesto e luta* (Poetry of protest and struggle). Included in the volume is "Onde estão os homens caçados neste vento de loucura" (57; Where are the men hunted in this wind of madness), a poem written in the 1950s to commemorate the police massacre that in 1953 took the lives of nearly one thousand striking São Tomé dock workers. If Espírito Santo had published nothing else, this poem alone would have established her reputation in the constellation of Lusophone African writers.[8]

Margarido and Medeiros also wrote nativistic poems of protest, such as the former's "Vós que ocupais a nossa terra" (You, who occupy our land) and the latter's "Meu canto, Europa" (My song, Europe). It is, however, to Angola and Mozambique that one must turn for the best examples of literary events and works as aesthetico-ideological artifacts of Lusophone Africa's proindependence movements.

Angola. In quantitative and qualitative terms, the poetry of cultural revindication, social protest, and combativeness, produced mainly by Black, white, and *mestiço* members of Angola's urban middle social stratum, stands out in the Portuguese-language writing of mid-twentieth-century Africa.

In the original Portuguese, poems by more than fifty Angolans appear in Manuel Ferreira's anthology *No reino de Caliban 2*. The anthologies, whether those compiled by Ferreira, Mário de Andrade, or, in English translation, Wolfers and Burness, include, among the most socially conscious Angolan poets, Agostinho Neto, António Jacinto, António Cardoso, Arnaldo Santos, Costa Andrade, Deolinda Rodrigues (1939–69?) Jofre Rocha (b. 1941), Jorge Macedo (b. 1941), and Manuel Rui (b. 1941), to mention but a few.

Between the late 1940s and the early 1960s, Agostinho Neto, who in 1975 became Angola's first president, wrote several poems in which the public and private voices merge in expressions of nationalist resolve and anticipatory patriotism. In October of 1960, while a political prisoner in a Lisbon jail, Neto wrote "Havemos de voltar" (We shall return), an anthem in which the persona promises that

> to marimbas and finger pianos,
> to our carnival,
> we shall return,
> to the beautiful Angolan homeland,
> our land, our mother, we shall return.
>
> (132; my translation)[9]

"Havemos de voltar," along with others of Neto's poems, was spirited out of Lisbon's Aljube prison to Milan, Belgrade, and Dar es Salaam. Ironically, speakers of Italian, Serbo-Croatian, and English had access to Neto's poem in translation before it was available, in the original Portuguese, to most Angolans. Fourteen years later, after the coup, "Havemos de voltar" found its way back to Portugal and then "returned" triumphantly to its intended constituency in newly independent Angola.

Neto's collected poems—like those of any number of poets who had lived in exile, spent time in political prison, or remained in Angola, where throughout years of repression they wrote surreptitiously—went from clan-destineness to legitimacy. Almost overnight underground poems became the core of a national literature. During the first years of independence, poets and writers in general, riding the crest of a wave of patriotism and socialist revolution, produced circumstantial art, replete with political slogans.

Some fifteen years after independence, public poetry—some of it quite good, some painfully bad—continued to be important as Angolans attempted to set the historical markers and establish the terms of the literature of their new nation and of a nationality still in formation. With political independence, overtly combative, anticolonialist poems lost their immediacy and were turned into historical artifacts. Tensions between the public and private voices that date back to the 1950s resulted, by the late 1970s, in a group of Angolan poets who, as I attempt to demonstrate in a later section, increasingly appreciated the subtleties and exalted the power of the word.

Mozambique. The word as political message and social instrument received special expression among practitioners of poetry who lived in or gravitated toward those areas of northern Mozambique that had fallen, by the late 1960s, to the forces of the Mozambican Liberation Front (FRELIMO). Because it was, for all intents and purposes, Mozambique's only nationalist movement, and because it was early able to consolidate its power among substantial numbers of peasants, FRELIMO succeeded in institutionalizing a relatively small but significant body of political and combative poetry. This poetry, written in Portuguese, served didactic purposes, including that of mnemonic aid and pedagogical tool in alphabetizing the members of several ethno-linguistic groups brought together under the flag of a single, embryonic nationality. After serving their often didactic purpose in the liberated zones of northern Mozambique and, in the exterior, a morale-boosting end among anticolonialist exiles and their sympathizers, more than eighty such poems were issued by FRELIMO's Department of Ideology in two volumes under the title *Poesia de combate* (1971 and 1977; Poems of combat).

Several of the poets included in the volumes are anonymous. Among the best known of those whose names do appear are José Craveirinha, Marcelino dos Santos (b. 1929), Rui Nogar (b. 1932–93), Armando Guebuza (b. 1935), Fernando Ganhão (b. 1937), Jorge Rebelo (b. 1940), and Sérgio Vieira (b.

1941). Circumstantial poems like Rebelo's "Carta de um combatente" (Letter from a combatant) and Rui Nogar's "Na zona do inimigo" (In the enemy zone) set the tone for the two volumes. But it is Marcelino dos Santos who qualifies as the foremost practitioner of what might be called the "communique poem."

Pamphletary verse, like Marcelino dos Santos's "Para uma moral" (To teach a moral truth), is testimony to and a codification of collectivized experiences as prime requisites for a sense of nationality among diverse ethnic groups and social classes. These militant, revolutionary poems by a relatively small group of educated individuals are testimonials to the transition from colony to nation-state.

An episode that illustrates the holistic socioaesthetic function of "good" public poetry took place in Mozambique shortly after independence. The newly installed FRELIMO government published *Eu, o povo: Poemas da revolução* (1975; I, the people: Poems of the revolution) in an unprecedented printing of thirty thousand copies. According to a story circulating in Maputo and Beira at the time, the collection's twenty-seven poems were discovered among the belongings of one Mutimati Barnabé João, a FRELIMO soldier killed in action. In reality, the poet/freedom fighter is a heteronym of António Quadros (b. 1931), a Portuguese poet who lived in Mozambique from 1964 until the early 1980s and who played a prominent role in the literary and the other cultural activities dominated, during the latter years of colonial rule, by a small cadre of politically liberal Europeans.

Rather than a hoax, the episode is, in effect, revolutionary theater. On the level of verbal gesture, the poet combined his private and public voices so that message and form coincide in such a way that the former does not—as is frequently the case with overtly political poetry—overwhelm the latter. The poet as witness to momentous events in the lived collective experience dignifies such terrifying occurrences, turned banal in war, as the death of one stranger by the hand of another: "And I regret that only now, by the hand of death, / Has he come to the same side of Life" (João 14; my translation)

Quadros/Mutimati is typical of a number of serious poets in all of the former colonies who, although they practiced an art form that was often transitory by virtue of its historical-political immediacy, also exalted the word. By the end of the 1970s, this exaltation of the word became a standard for those who wrote poetry with a sense of craft.

POETRY AS EXALTATION OF THE WORD

Angola. In celebration of Angola's independence, Manuel Rui wrote, in his "Poesia necessária" (Essential poetry), "Of new words a country is also made / in this country so made of poems" (*11 Poems em novembro* 20; my translation).[10] Indeed, an inordinate number of former freedom fighters and other nationalists were writers who began their literary careers simultaneously with the awakening of their political consciousness. Rui, who himself has served as a high government official, is one of a cohort of Angolan poets who have sought to express changing social realities and produce a new Angolan poetry. Along with Rui, chief among these poets is Arlindo Barbeitos (b. 1941), whose *Angola, Angolé, Angolema* (1976; Angola, hail Angola, Angola the word), contributed to a new poetic diction in the fledgling country. In the volume's preface Barbeitos states his intention of avoiding "the conventional paths of African poetry of Portuguese expression," by which he means to throw off the mantle of cultural dependency inherent in that outmoded appellation and to eschew the clichés of cultural revindication, protest, and combativeness. Barbeitos further states that "poetry is a fictionalized symmetry between words and things, expression and reality" (2), as evidenced by these lines from one of his titleless poems:

> In the forest
> of your eyes
> only night is seen
>
> In the night
> of the leopard
> only eyes are seen
>
> In the dawn
> of the night
> only your eyes are seen
> and
> in your leopard eyes
> only the forest is seen.
>
> (45; my translation)[11]

Barbeitos and other poets of his generation discovered what "primitives," like the Kwanyama of southeastern Angola, had long known, and what many of the acculturated had forsaken in their revolutionary zeal to fashion art out of abstractions: poetry—whether intimist or popular—as a fictive compromise between expressions and reality, often suggests as much as it states, which is, of course, the essence of the symmetry between words and things.

Similarly, Ruy Duarte de Carvalho (b. 1941), an Angolan of Portuguese extraction, has combined concretist phrasing with the tonality of ancient African chants to produce poems, collected in three slim volumes, that are visual, audial, and kinetic codifications of the culture and social practices of southern Angola's nomadic peoples. As do Rui and Barbeitos, Carvalho offers some thoughts on the nature of Angolan cultural expression in a new age: "The question of culture [in Angola] is, in the final analysis, a question of lore. Today we can identify, in an abstract way, of course, three types of lore: traditional lore, the lore that comes from the colonial experience, and revolutionary lore whose emergence and dissemination characterize the present" ("Angola" 48; my translation). "Revolutionary," in this sense, transcends the message-laden, rhetorical glosses of political upheaval; rather, it has to do with the formal and thematic restructuring of culture within an open-ended temporal and circumscribed spatial context.

The open-endedness is also social in nature, and an undeniable factor in the uniqueness of Lusophone Africa's acculturated literature is the imposing presence of somatically European individuals among engagé writers of Angola and Mozambique, to cite the two former Portuguese colonies that most often capture the attention of the outside world. In the parlance of the Western media, these two nations of southern Africa—a region that more often than not makes headlines in Europe and America because of racial strife—have "Black-run" governments. Yet in Angola and Mozambique racial labeling, on any official level, is nothing short of heresy. Idealistically, this lack of racial categorizing constitutes a progressive exercise in democracy; pragmatically, official color blindness is a component of the effort to create a single nationality without regard to ethnic group or race (tribalism and distinctions based on color being two negative legacies of colonial rule). Moreover, pragmatism also dictates that these new societies use all their human resources, whether the individual be African, European, East Indian, or of mixed ancestry.[12] Idealism and pragmatism notwithstanding, even the most open-minded outsider, whether from Europe, America, or other African countries, may experience at least mild surprise upon verifying that several of Angola's most prominent contemporary writers, such as the poets Carvalho, Barbeitos, Costa Andrade, and David Mestre (b. 1948), are phenotypically European.

In Angola and Mozambique some writers of European ancestry have displayed an overcompensatory Africanness and revolutionary zeal. But poets such as Carvalho, Barbeitos, and Mestre have not so much overcompensated as they have attempted to combine those distinctive historical and cultural experiences. In some of the best of Lusophone African poetry, by members of the three social-racial groups, these combinations have surpassed categorizations with imaginative exaltations of the word.

Cape Verde. After independence the imperative of the reintegration of a historical time and geographical space occupied the attention of poets in all five of the emerging nations of Portuguese-writing Africa. In Cape Verde, this poetic reintegration of time and space has special implications for the other former colonies.

Beginning with the rise of Cape Verdean nationalism and culminating with independence, a creole ethos, combined with an intensified sense of an African time and space, has lent an especially epic tenor to poets' exaltation of the word. Arlindo Barbeitos coined the term *angolema* to invoke and codify a nation "so made of poems." For similar purposes, the Cape Verdean poet Corsino Fortes (b. 1933) gave the title *Pão e fonema* (1974; Bread and phoneme) to his collection of poems. A symbol of human sustenance joins with the force of pure utterance to exalt the word, which, in Fortes's poetry, frequently reaches epic levels. *Pão e fonema* contains three cantos, and the poetic voice, as if inspired by a creole muse, takes on heroic proportions in the volume's twenty-two poems, which can be read as a single narrative. Fortes's bilingual (Portuguese-creole) phantasmagoria and his epic flights of surrealism are an exaltation of the word that metaphorically reveals Cape Verde in its cosmic dimensions.

No less exuberantly, João Varela (b. 1937), under the creole pseudonym of Timóteo Tio Tiofe, wrote the long poem *O primeiro livro de Notcha* (1975; Notcha's first book—Notcha being the creole sobriquet of Varela's grandfather). With no false modesty, Varela confides in his preface that "I suppose I have written a poem that my generation expects or expected of me" (8; my translation). Apparently, the same creole muse who inspired Fortes also compelled Varela to recount the deeds of a historic people. But Varela had deferred his Cape Verdeanness during a long interlude in Europe, where, under the name of João Vário, he wrote metaphysical verse. The narrator of *O primeiro livro de Notcha* returns as a prodigal to reclaim his and his people's birthright in the epic poem his generation expected of him. The result is a verbal and imagistic pastiche that surpasses Fortes's poetry in surrealistic phantasmagoria. What most distinguishes Varela's poem is its discursive, soaring regeneration of the Cape Verdean people in their historic time, African space, and proverbial wanderlust. The persona waxes prophetic in his regenerative diction and spiritual re-Africanization of Cape Verde:

> Because they shall say: there is a man of this century,
> a man of Africa, under his mango tree
> and under his papaw, a man
> yearning for audience and history . . ."
>
> (13; my translation)

Fortes's and Varela's lofty verse reflects a trend toward exultant rhetoric in contemporary Cape Verdean poetry. One of the best contemporary practitioners of this kind of verbal exuberance is Oswaldo Osório (b. 1937). Osório, along with Arménio Vieira (b. 1941) and the latter's more contemplative exaltation of the word, forms the core of an important generation of Cape Verdean poets. While many Cape Verdean writers were living abroad—some in voluntary exile—Osório and Vieira remained on the islands, where they bore witness to the events that accompanied social and political change and wrote poems from these experiences, before and after Independence, that helped lend continuity to a literary thread that had become tenuous in the late 1960s and early 1970s. During that period Osório wrote the patriotic poems contained in his exuberantly, if somewhat pretentiously, titled *Caboverdeamadamente, construção, meu amor* (1975; Cape Verde–lovingly, building a nation, my love) and the spiritually epiclike poems of *O cântico do habitante* (1977; The inhabitant's hymn). For his part, in a volume bearing the decidedly unpretentious title of *Poemas* (1981; Poems), Vieira brought together some sixty poems—several of them prize winners—written between 1971 and 1979. Although Vieira's persona speaks most often with a private voice, both he and Osório figure significantly among those Cape Verdeans who would regenerate a national poetry by exalting the word.

Guinea-Bissau. In this tiny West African country, wedged between Senegal and the Republic of Guinea, the traditional orature of several ethnolinguistic groups had begun, during the long guerrilla war, to influence writing in Portuguese and the Portuguese-based creole. The poems published in *Mantenhas para quem luta!* (1977; Hail to those who struggle!) and *Antologia dos jovens poetas* (1978; Anthology of the young poets) hold interest as overdue aesthetico-ideological artifacts, even though the revindication, anticolonialist protest, and combativeness come somewhat after the fact. As might be expected, many of these poems are cliché-ridden anthems. There are, however, a few among these mainly beginning poets who succeed in turning that rare phrase or capturing that ineffable moment that gives even overtly political art a feeling and integrity that surpass its explicit message. One such poet is Helder Proença (b. 1956), several of whose poems appear in both anthologies. But it is perhaps with five poems published in 1979 in the Lisbon-based journal *África* that Proença realizes his true potential. "Pérola cintelante" (The sparkling pearl) and "Reconstrução, se! . . ." (Reconstruction, if! . . .) display a verbal complexity that mediates between the intimist soliloquy and the collective voice.

The 1980 coup that toppled the government of Luís Cabral also dealt something of a blow to the incipient processes of a national cultural integration in Guinea-Bissau. A casualty of what some called ethnic-inspired political conflict was Mário de Andrade, who, although an Angolan, had served in Luís Cabral's government as Guinea-Bissau's minister of culture.[13] Andrade was a mentor to the young poets who, in the cities of Bissau and Bolama, were beginning to organize around national cultural integration. The setback was, however, temporary. By the mid-1980s, and with the impetus of the two modest anthologies of the late 1970s and the leadership of writers and intellectuals like Proença, the young poets began working anew toward the attainment of a national literary expression.

Mozambique. At the end of 1971 and the beginning of 1972, in the colonial capital of Lourenço Marques, Rui Knopfli (b. 1933) and J. P. Grabato Dias (another pseudonym of António Quadros, of Mutimati João fame) coordinated the three issues of *Caliban,* an unassuming but disarmingly important poetry journal, which, as its title suggests, had much to do with language as empowerment. Several years later, in the People's Republic of Mozambique, the abiding influence of Craveirinha and the *Caliban* legacy were points of departure for a new Mozambican poetic expression.

One of the first important heirs to a legacy established during the waning years of colonialism is Luís Carlos Patraquim (b. 1953), author of *Monção* (1980; Monsoon), a volume that ushered in a period of innovative poetry in Mozambique. Patraquim's "Metamorfose," a poem dedicated to Cravei-rinha, begins: "when fear pulled light to the city / I was a little boy," a line inspired by the latter's "Lustro à cidade" (When light comes to the city), originally published in the first issue of *Caliban*. Craveirinha used grotesque totemic symbols and opulent surrealistic imagery to convey, however cryp-tically, a message of cultural resistance and social protest:

> Old hyena
> eyes streaked with blood
> suck the anguish from my kidneys
> and with teeth of carniverous loathing
> gnaw on the unbreakable marrow of my dreams.
>
> (*Caliban* 1:22; my translation)

Patraquim's likewise oneiric and sensuous poetry has a tropical exuber-ance that metaphorically overcomes fear and tests the waters of experimen-tation. Through this sense of aesthetic and thematic freedom defied the prescriptive language of structured, revolutionary poetic discourse—still prevalent in Mozambique of the late 1970s—and resulted in sometimes esoteric symbology, Patraquim's use of dream imagery is a statement of cultural liberation. In "Adágio" Patraquim constructs an ecology of tropical sensuality:

> I open wide the afternoon curtains
> to have you fully
> within the poem
>
> and dressed in your *capulana* you walk by my window
> and your body is like the dunes
> planted to pines
> murmuring near
> the waves' fury
> falling softly
> on my gesture.
>
> (*Monção* 38; my translation)

The literal meaning of the Italian word *adagio* is "at ease," a state that describes the aesthetic and ideological posture of a group of serious poets in Lusophone Africa in the penultimate decade of the twentieth century.

African Prose Fiction in Portuguese

In spite of the material and political difficulties of publishing prose works in colonial Lusophone Africa, members of the acculturated elites knew that short stories and novels were indispensable components of any corpus of works that presumed to constitute a national literature. The novel, like the epic poem before it, is a cultural icon and linguistic marker of a people, especially one seeking to rewrite history and consolidate itself into a nationality. Even before nationalism had crystallized in Lusophone Africa, those acculturated intellectuals who had begun to define history from their and not the former colonialists' perspective, responded to the storytelling urge and the desire to relate individual and shared experiences. Not only did socially conscious writers of prose fiction face economic and material barriers, but they also had to contend with concerns stemming in part from the existence, starting in the late nineteenth century, of the *novela colonial*. Cultivated by Portuguese expeditionaries, missionaries, adventurers, and settlers, this subgenre of ethnographic tales and novels bears such titles as *Princesa negra: O presço da civilização em África* (1932; Black princess: The price of civilization in Africa), by Luiz Figueira. These novels were exotic portrayals of the ways and customs of peoples depicted as existing on the margins of civilization.

By the mid-1950s those Black, *mestiço*, and white writers committed to a revindication of African culture and belief systems found prose narrative ideal for adapting oral traditions to acculturated literary expression. And therein lay the danger, for no matter how noble and politically well-informed their intentions, those acculturated writers who simulated orature or fashioned stories in Portuguese about precolonial or semiassimilated societies ran the distinct risk of appearing patronizing or condescendingly folkloric.

ETHNOGRAPHY AND SOCIAL REALISM

The ethnographic narrative and the literary text that simulate oral expression can attain artistic integrity only when their language is adequate to social and cultural referents. Whether consciously or intuitively, engagé writers knew that the Portuguese words and syntax they used had to capture and transmit at least the essence of the worldview embedded in indigenous languages and cultural values.

There are some important precursors of those who sought that "right" language. In Angola, António de Assis Júnior (1878–1960), one of a handful of assimilated Africans who fired the first salvos for self-determination in the Portuguese colonies, published *O segredo da morta* (1934; The dead woman's secret). Subtitled *Romance de costumes angolenses* (Romance of Angolan customs), this novel is a curious blend of the narrative style of Victor Hugo, a plot reminiscent of an Anatole France work, a positivistic faith in a civilizing process, and a republican political outlook. But true to his subtitle, Assis Júnior also filled his romance with Kimbundu proverbs and depictions of the ways and customs of those with whom he simultaneously identified and characterized as the "others."

Early writers, like Assis Júnior and Fausto Duarte (1903–55), a Cape

Verdean *mestiço* who lived in Guinea-Bissau and wrote several novels about the Mandinkas and other local ethnic groups, gave a more sympathetic twist to the conventional *novela colonial*. Fernando Castro Soromenho (1910–68), born in Mozambique to Portuguese parents and raised in Angola, qualifies, according to some historians, as the father of the modern Angolan novel. Although he began his writing career within the tradition of the colonial novel, in his second phase Soromenho wrote *Terra morta* (1949; Dead earth) and the posthumous *A chaga* (1970; The bleeding sore) to dramatize the clash of cultures and the exploitation inherent in colonial social structures. Soromenho's combining of neorealism and ethnography set a standard for the social realism and cultural revindication that inform much of the prose fiction produced in the 1950s and 1960s by engagé writers from Angola and Mozambique.

In assessing the overall uniqueness of Lusophone African writing, we must take into account that for decades most writers from the former Portuguese colonies had limited contact with the literary currents in the rest of Africa. (A handful of these writers, especially those who lived or traveled in Europe, did have some knowledge of other African literatures as well as the poetry of the Anglophone, Francophone, and Hispanophone diasporas of the Americas.) On the other hand, intellectuals in the Lusophone colonies had long and sustained contact with literary currents and access to works from Portugal and Brazil. By the mid-twentieth century, in the eyes of many members of the indigenous elites of Cape Verde, Angola, and Mozambique, Brazil was a model. Moreover, numbers of these intellectuals embraced the Lusotropicalist ideology that romanticized Brazil as a new world in the tropics where European, African, and Amerindian peoples, values, languages, and customs had blended harmoniously.

On a less romanticized, if still somewhat idealized, plane, Brazilian modernism and Northeast regionalism gave birth to a sociological novel of cultural revindication, which influenced Portuguese neorealism and, together with the latter, engaged the imagination of a number of Lusophone African writers. The Brazilian cultural and literary movements and Portugal's neorealism contributed to the early emergence of a relatively small but significant body of social realist short stories and novels in Cape Verde, Angola, and Mozambique.

Cape Verde. Chronologically, Cape Verdeans, because of the early consolidation of their intellectual elite, were the first Lusophone Africans to produce a number of characteristic short stories and novels. Imbued with a sense of their islands' creole originality, the *Claridade* intellectuals saw Cape Verde as a sort of mini-Brazil. Some even claimed that their tiny archipelago had surpassed the South American giant as an example of biological and cultural homogeneity in the tropics.

One of the fiercest proponents of Cape Verde's creole preeminence in the so-called Portuguese space was Baltasar Lopes da Silva, whose poetry appeared under the pseudonym Osvaldo Alcântara. As early as 1937, in the pages of *Claridade*, Lopes da Silva published excerpts from his novel *Chiquinho* (1947), which, in opposition to the *novela colonial*, he subtitled a *romance caboverdeano*.

Lopes da Silva sets the tone for his tropical bildungsroman with an epigram in the creole of his native windward islands: "The slave body departs / the unshackled heart remains" (my translation). Wanting to stay and having to leave (and vice versa) is an intertextual theme and structural motif in Cape Verdean social realist fiction. Chiquinho's decision to set sail for New Bedford, Massachusetts, as his father had done years before, completes the novel's socially homologous structure. Moreover, in Cape Verdean literature a centrifugal force (i.e., wanderlust and the economic imperative to emigrate) juxtaposes with a centripetal force (i.e., a sentimental attachment to the land).

Manuel Lopes, Baltasar Lopes da Silva's *Claridade* colleague, wrote two novels around the dyadic theme-motif of departing/staying. Much of the appeal of Manuel Lopes's *Chuva braba* (1956; Torrential rain) and *Flagelados do vento leste* (1959; Victims of the east wind) lies in the author's nativism, similar to that which characterizes many nineteenth- and twentieth-century New World novels, like those of the Brazilian northeast. In these "frontier" narratives the forces of nature (in Manuel Lopes's novels, the devastating Harmattan blowing off the Sahara and the resulting drought) take on the grandeur of prosopopoeia.

For Manual Lopes and others of his generation, Cape Verde was a harsh land where those who survived had to persevere in the face of adversity. The Social Darwinism that informs Manuel Lopes's prose fiction, as well as his poetry, led later, more militant Cape Verdeans alternately to praise and criticize the pioneering writer's works. They praised *Chuva braba* because the protagonist, after the rains come, resolves to stay on the ancestral land rather than emigrate to Brazil. But they criticized Lopes and other *Claridade* intellectuals for evading the issue of colonial rule as the ultimate source of the islands' endemic social and economic ills. Manuel Lopes, Baltasar Lopes da Silva, and the majority of writers of their generation did stop short of challenging the political order, but their social realist works, as reformulations of acculturated fictive discourse, constituted meaningful texts of cultural resistance.

António Aurélio Gonçalves (1902–84), a third major writer of the *Claridade* group, anticipated the concerns of the antievasionists when he characterized the principal determinants of Cape Verdean literature as "the conviction that there was a Cape Verdean regionalist originality, the necessity of calling attention to and protesting against an economic crisis caused by drought, the abandonment of the port of São Vicente, and the hardships brought about by the closing off of emigration to North America" (xxix; my translation). Gonçalves's five novellas portray Cape Verdeans enmeshed in situations caused by the archipelago's chronic problems. All of Gonçalves's principal characters are strong-willed women, such as Nita, the protagonist of *Noite de vento* (1970; A windy night), who defy the rules that govern conventional male-female relationships in a social environment in which temporary unions are a function of the economic crisis and the long-standing male emigration. In Gonçalves's stories women are the focal point of rebellion against the system; implicitly they are metaphors of protest.

Social protest intensified in the short stories of members of the next generation, particularly those associated with *Certeza*. Henrique Teixeira de Sousa (b. 1918), with his "Dragão e eu" (1945; Dragon and I) and Gabriel Mariano, with "O rapaz doente" (1957; The sick boy), were more explicit in their neorealist portrayals of Cape Verde's social ills.

Over the years, what the *claridosos* routinely referred to as "regionalist" singularity—in other words, Cape Verde as a unique region in the Portuguese space—evolved into an ethos that nurtured later nationalist and Pan-Africanist sentiments. Prose writers, during the last two decades of colonial rule, sought with their sociological short stories and novels to provide the historical substance of that ethos, just as poets like Corsino Fortes resorted to heroic verse to celebrate Cape Verdeans as a historic people. Teixeira de Sousa subordinated the lyrical-nostalgic quality of the ethos to sociological documentation in several short stories. And with *Ilhéu de contenda* (1978; Isle of contention), Teixeira de Sousa expanded his short docudramas into a monumental historical romance.

Since its beginnings in the 1940s much Cape Verdean fiction, including Teixeira de Sousa's novels, retain a somewhat outmoded neorealism. But there is also something unconventional about many of these works, from the tropical Gothic romances of Manuel Lopes to Luís Romano's (b. 1922) *Famintos* (1961; The famished), a decidedly non-novel novel, despite its stylistic and thematic similarity to some late nineteenth-century Brazilian fiction.[14] Historically, the belief, on the part of Cape Verdean writers of diverse political persuasions, in their culture's singularity—whether regional within the Portuguese sphere or as a sui generis extension of Africa—has contributed to that unconventionality as represented in novels and short stories.

Because of historical factors that allowed for the early formulation of the terms of a unique ethos, Cape Verde, with fewer than 200,000 inhabitants, gave rise—in advance of the fact—to a "national" literature. Cape Verde's creole literary preeminence notwithstanding, it is, however, the larger milieu of Angola that has produced some of the most compelling examples of ethnographic and neorealist writing in a conflictive colonial sphere of social action.

Angola. Oscar Ribas (b. 1909), a Luanda *mestiço*, although blind since the age of twenty-one, carefully documented Angolan (principally Kimbundu) lore in such fictionalized ethnographic works as *Uanga: Romance folclórico angolano* (1951; Enchantment: an Angolan folkloric novel). Among members of the Generation of 1950, the Guerra brothers, Henrique (b. 1937) and Mário (b. 1939, also known as Benúdia), cultivated stories of cultural revindication based on indigenous Angolan societies. In the same vein of fictionalized ethnography, Henrique Abranches (b. 1932) produced *A konkhava de Feti* (1981; Feti's Hatchet), the novelistic recreation of a legend of southern Angolan peoples.[15]

Another writer worthy of note is Manuel Pacavira (b. 1939), whose *Nzinga Mbandi* (1975) chronicles the exploits of the legendary Angolan queen, who in the early seventeenth century led an alliance of tribal groups in resisting Portuguese domination. Pacavira's work qualifies as the first historical romance to be produced in Angola.

As did poets, fiction writers among the Young Intellectuals achieved some of their best successes when they set their works in the city of Luanda. In his *Crónica da cidade estranha* (1964; Chronicle of this uncommon city) and *Farra no fim de semana* (1965; Weekend spree), Mário António adopted the chronicle, which had developed as a literary subgenre in Brazil, to depict the outwardly subdued but socially charged day-to-day existence of Luanda's *mestiço* middle class. Much of the success of António's chronicles stems from the author's skill in converting the ambivalence of the relatively privileged mulatto, perched precariously on a social ledge in the "uncommon" colonial city, into something more than the conventional neorealist statement on the half caste caught between two worlds. In his chronicles, the "true" mulatto—meaning the legitimate child of stable *mestiço* parents, as opposed to the often illegitimate *mestiço* offspring of a Black mother and a white father—acts out his or her angst in the alienating space of colonial Luanda.

The chronicle, as a literary codification of quotidian events, suited the ends of Angolan intellectuals seeking to define the temporal and spatial dimensions of a colonial reality that itself seemed a fiction. *Farra no fim de semana* gives a different psychological twist to the conventional dichotomy of the city and the countryside when a group of urban mulattoes gathers at a seaside home, on the outskirts of town, for an all-night party that banishes them to a kind of twilight zone between the hubbub of the modern, Europeanized city and a mystified primitive world, which inspires one of the revelers to pose the rhetorical question: "Don't you find their songs very beautiful, carefree, really the image of a people who still place great value on the joy of living?" (49; my translation).

In a similar way of qualifying trivializations that lie between illusion and reality, Arnaldo Santos (b. 1936) wrote *Quinaxixe* (1965) (the name of an old neighborhood of Luanda) and *Tempo de munhungo* (1968; Vertigo time), two collections of chronicles that capture the essence of the absurd in the social and cultural contradictions inherent in the daily life of a city at odds with itself. The chronicle-story "Bessanganas de mentira" (Make-believe African maidens) revolves around a social gathering of "true" mulattoes, during which two women bedecked in colorful Kimbundu robes pose for photographs. At the height of the posturing a bemused guest observes that "we exoticize our own race" (*Munhungo* 57).

António's chronicles depict psychologically charged encounters among the middle-class colonized who blankly contemplate their ambivalent places in a city divided by its Africanness and that European-defined tropicalism that earned colonial Luanda its reputation as the Rio de Janeiro of Africa. The characters of Santos's chronicles indulge in philosophical ruminations that adduce reflectiveness to the social realist narrative. Both writers' works convey a sense of waiting for something to happen, and this fictive air of expectation helped establish a thematic framework for the contemplative prose fiction that would emerge in Angola after independence.

Other significant short narratives, written after Independence and set in Luanda, are Jofre Rocha's (pseudonym of Roberto de Almeida, b. 1941) *Estórias do Musseque* (1977; Musseque tales) Jorge Macedo's (b. 1941) *Gente de meu bairro* (1977; People from my neighborhood) and Boaventura Cardoso's (b. 1944) *Dizanga dia muenho* (1977; The lagoon of life) and *O fogo da fala* (1980; The fire of words). All of these works constitute reworkings of acculturated language and validations of cultural values engendered in a changing urban milieu.

Mozambique. João Dias (1926–49) was born into a middle-class African family in Lourenço Marques. His legacy to an emerging acculturated literature is *Godido* (1952), a posthumously published collection of short stories. If Dias's autobiographical and journalistic stories presaged the beginning of a genuine Mozambican prose fiction, then *Nós matamos o cão tinhoso* (1964; *We Killed Mangy Dog and Other Mozambique Stories*, 1969), by Luís Bernardo Honwana (b. 1942), was that beginning.

The English translation of Honwana's book has the distinction of being the first Lusophone African work to be included in Heinemann's African Writers Series. The stories' principal appeal stems from the author's narrative timing and rhythm, his often humorous use of irony, and his ability to combine the styles of neorealism and the oral expression of his own Ronga origins.

Although there were several other works of note, such as Orlando Mendes's racial novel *Portagem* (1965), until Independence *Nós matamos a cão tinhoso* was the prose work quintessentially *of* Mozambique. With the collection's title story, as well as with "Papa, Snake & I" and "Dina," Honwana established the epistemological contours of a Mozambican prose fiction.

THE VERBAL STRATEGIES OF FOUR ANGOLAN WRITERS

José Luandino Vieira. Born José Vieira Matéus da Graça, in 1935, in rural Portugal, and raised from about the age of one in Luanda, José Luandino

Vieira qualifies as a true phenomenon in the realm of Lusophone African letters. The son of a shoemaker, Luandino (the name by which he is most commonly known) grew up in and around Luanda's working-class neighborhoods and shanty towns with playmates from the three racial-social groups, in a world dominated by African foods, music, and verbal cadences. *A cidade e a infância* (1957; Childhood and the city), Luandino's first collection of stories, written when he was in his late teens, bears the dedication: "For you, childhood companions."

In 1959, accused of being an MPLA sympathizer, Luandino spent a month in a Luanda jail; in 1961 he was arrested again for distributing subversive pamphlets. By the time *Luuanda* (1964; *Luuanda: Short Stories of Angola*, 1980), his first major work of fiction, appeared in print, Luandino had begun serving nearly eleven years as a political prisoner. And it was in prison, mainly in the infamous concentration camp at Tarrafal, that Luandino wrote at least four of his eight books of stories and one of his two novels.

Although he wrote all of his published works before independence, Luandino has had the greatest influence on the Angolan prose fiction of the 1970s and 1980s. He is a language innovator and the creator of a subgenre he calls the *estória*, a term he prefers over the conventional *conto* (short story). According to the author, *estória* is the closest Portuguese equivalent of *musoso*, a Kimbundu word meaning "fable" or "moral narrative." Moreover, Fernão Lopes, the fifteenth-century chronicler to the Portuguese kings, used *estória* to signify "narrative." And João Guimarães Rosa, who revolutionized contemporary Brazilian narrative, defined *estória* as a short, popular epic. The word's Kimbundu, Portuguese, and Brazilian interconnectedness has suited Luandino's attempts to formulate a hybridized, uniquely Angolan literary form and language. Many writers, from Cape Verde to Mozambique, have since adopted *estória* as a generic term.

Luandino, whose own sobriquet combines a Kimbundu root word with a Portuguese suffix, experimented with language in such ways that lexical items, syntax, and the cadences of *musseque* speech—which many Portuguese settlers and even some members of the indigenous middle class pejoratively labeled *pretoguês* (literally, "blackieguese")—suggested a creolized Kimbundu and lent legitimacy to an even more creolized Portuguese. His purpose has been to dignify the stigmatized black vernacular by elevating it to the level of a literary language, not just in dialogue, but also in the narrative voice of a kind of urban and suburban *griot*. Luandino went beyond most of his predecessors and many of his contemporaries who Africanized acculturated writing in an ostensively European language by sprinkling their narratives with indigenous words and phrases. Luandino has bent Portuguese syntax to simulate Kimbundu word order and has used whole sentences in Kimbundu without providing Portuguese translations. Tamara Bender, the American translator of *Luuanda*, writes that "Vieira refused to provide a glossary for his book because, as he explained, he wrote his *estórias* for the very people whose language he used, adding that ignorance of *musseque* speech was the problem of the Portuguese colonizer, not his" (vii).[16]

For all his populism, Luandino has also been sensitive to the risks of being labeled a déclassé and exoticizer. In all his mature works Luandino's concern with finding the right mode of expression has resulted in metalanguage and metatexts. In a revised, second edition of *Luuanda* he modified the verbal and situational formulas conventionally associated with oral expression to suggest, rather than explicitly state.

After independence, a number of Angolan intellectuals, struggling with how their literature could better serve the revolution, began to question those works that eluded the masses. Other intellectuals of a cultural nationalist bent, also committed to a restoration of Angola's indigenous languages in their purest form, took issue with linguistic hybridization. Thus, starting with its title, Luandino's *Macandumba* (1978) caused a stir among Angola's relatively tiny but growing and avid readership. The Kimbundu word *macandumba*, freely translated, means "big happenings," and is a combination of *maka* (literally, "conversation," and, by colloquial extension, "heated discussion") and *ndumba* (literally, "a great quantity" or "a lot"). In colonial times newsboys from the *musseques* hawked their papers in the European lower city with cries of *macandumba* (i.e., the equivalent of "read all about it!"), and the term entered into the vocabulary of even those colonists who generally disdained "native dialects."

After independence some purists, decrying lexical and semantic bastardization, pointed out that Kimbundu orthography called for *k*, a letter that does not figure in the Portuguese alphabet. Luandino has argued that the *c* and the word's semantic shift resulted from *macandumba*'s status as a loan word used in colonial Luanda by Africans and Europeans alike. The term *maka*, on the other hand, popularized in post-independence Angolan usage, retains its original Kimbundu meaning and spelling.

Luandino coined numerous hybridized words that forsake neither the purity of Kimbundu nor that of Portuguese. And Luandino's *estórias* have set a standard for those Angolan writers of prose fiction searching for new discourses for new realities.

Uanhenga Xitu. Uanhenga Xitu was born in 1924 in the village of Calomboloca in the heart of Kimbunduland. The name Agostinho Mendes de Carvalho is, according to the writer himself, the pseudonym Xitu uses in his public life as party member, the former governor of the province of Luanda, and Angola's ambassador to East Germany.

If Luandino, true to his hybrid name, has cultivated "creole" texts, Uanhenga Xitu and Mendes de Carvalho exist in a dyadic relationship from which derive discourses formed on the tensions that occur first at those points where Kimbundu, a semicreolized Kimbundu, standard Portuguese, and Black Portuguese converge and then separate to confront each other at short range. Thus the verbal uniqueness of *Manana* (1974), Xitu's first novel, and "'Mestre' Tamoda" (1974; "Professor" Tamoda) derives from the conscious and unconscious use of sociolinguistic juxtapositions and unorthodox verbal strategies that challenge the conventions of acculturated discourse.

Xitu came to the city with his Kimbundu identity and his official Portuguese name. In Luanda he worked as a nurse and joined the nationalist movement; in 1959 he was sentenced to ten years in the Tarrafal concentration camp. During his confinement he began to write fiction with the help of fellow prisoners, including Luandino. And like Luandino, he sought to neutralize that which was imposed and impose that which was disdained by the colonial system.

Luandino used untranslated Kimbundu epigraphs to parody Portuguese writers' penchant for untranslated English and French inscriptions. Xitu went beyond parody of a Western literary convention by introducing *Manana* with a barrage of nine dedications to those who, like himself, do not speak "the Portuguese you learn in school," and to those who, attempting to do so, appear ridiculous. As the implied author of Xitu's works flaunts his less-than-standard Portuguese, he simultaneously ridicules the pompous, malapropism-laden speech of those Africans who outdo themselves in using the king's Portuguese. Tamoda, the self-styled professor, is the embodiment of and, ultimately, the quintessential tragicomic, semiassimilated African.

At one extreme, Xitu's works display a pure, almost reverently treated Kimbundu. And despite his implied author's professed disdain for the Portuguese one learns in school, at the opposite extreme he flaunts a scrupulously written, erudite Portuguese in footnotes and glossaries, presumably provided by Mendes de Carvalho to explain the Kimbundu words and phrases used by Xitu and his characters. Thus Xitu's works somewhat ambivalently sort out the components that make up the linguistically variegated and socially amorphous world of the city that encroaches on the indigenous languages, belief systems, and customs of traditional rural society.

Pepetela. Artur Carlos Maurício Pestana dos Santos (b. 1941) is, like Luandino, a highly touted Angolan writer of Portuguese descent. Unlike Luandino, Pestana dos Santos—whose nom de plume and de guerre, Pepetela, means "eyelash" in Umbundu—was born in Angola, in the city of Benguela, a kind of smaller replica of creole Luanda. After a few years of studying in Portugal and exile in Algeria, Pepetela returned to Angola in the late 1960s as an MPLA combatant.

Since 1969 Pepetela has published two plays, three novels, and two novellas, including the enormously successful *As aventuras de Ngunga* (1976; Ngunga's adventures). Written in 1972, this short, didactic novella about a small boy caught up in the war was originally distributed, in five hundred typed copies, on the MPLA's eastern front. With the arrival of independence Ngunga became a national symbol, and three successive editions of the book, with a total printing of seventy-four thousand copies, sold out in Angola. Not only did the book's success serve as added evidence of literature's and writers' prestige in revolutionary Angola, it afforded Pepetela the opportunity to publish, after Independence, a reputedly controversial novel he had completed in 1971.

Some citizens of the fledgling one-party state predicted that the authorities would prohibit the novel's publication. In the security-conscious climate of a country with a tenuous hold on its polity and whose sovereignty has been threatened from within and from the outside, ideological zeal and proscriptive measures, if not outright censorship, came as no great surprise. Much to the surprise of many, however, not only was the manuscript published, but the novel won the government-sponsored Angolan National Prize for Literature. The book in question, *Mayombe* (1980; English translation, 1984), is a monumental novel in which Pepetela takes a hard, analytical look at the Angolan nationalist war.

Set in the Mayombe rain forest of Cabinda, that tiny enclave separated from the rest of Angola by Zaire, the novel is a study in solitude and introspection during the virtual impasse that occurred in the tenth year of the protracted war. Pepetela broke with the linear narration and patriotic message of conventional war novels by using quasiallegorical characters who speak discursively and synchronically, often in stream of consciousness, as they contemplate their individual roles in an endless armed struggle and as part of a nonexistent nationality). In arriving dialectically at the core of this nation(ality), threatened by tribalism, regionalism, class and racial divisions, and individual ambitions pitted against the will of an abstract collective, Pepetela fashioned a bold verbal universe.

Following the pioneering lead of Luandino's *Nós, os do Makulusu* (1975; We, the folks from Makulusu), Pepetela wrote *Yaka* (1984), a novel whose title refers to a mysterious statue and whose story revolves around the settler experience in Angola. In Luandino's quasiautobiographical novel, a second-generation white Angolan repeats, refrainlike throughout the narrative, variations on the wistful statement: "We were almost bilingual." This state of almost bilingualism stands as a metaphor for the biculturation that hangs precariously on the ambivalent settler experience.

On one narrative level *Yaka* is the saga of an old settler family, and the novel's emotional and ideological message is one of a difficult, albeit inevitable, Angolanization of settlers over five generations. On another level the novel is a mythic transfiguration, as represented by the enigmatic statue. Together with Luandino's experimentalist fiction and Uanhenga Xitu's liberties with acculturated discourse, *Yaka*, along with those other of Pepetela's works with an African mythic base, represents a high point in the verbal strategies used by Angolan writers in their search for new discourses.

Manuel Rui. A *mestiço* from the south central city of Huambo (formerly Nova Lisboa), Manuel Rui started his own revolution in Angolan poetry and prose fiction. Rui earned a law degree at Coimbra, published two books of poetry in Portugal, and in 1974, when he went home to Angola, his ironically titled *Regresso adiado* (Postponed return) was published in Lisbon. This collection of short stories established Rui as one of Angola's foremost fiction writers. Rui entered into a course of history that swept him to notoriety: he participated in the transitional government that ruled Angola briefly after the Portuguese military coup of 1974, and he presided as judge at the trial of a multinational group of captured mercenaries. He also achieved literary fame as a witness to the momentous events, including the bloody civil war, that marked the troubled eve and hope-filled dawn of Angola's independence.

Rui's most original writing grew out of the vital day-to-day experiences in that short span roughly between 1974 and 1979, the period covered in *Sim camarada!* (1977; *Yes, comrade*, 1992) and *Quem me dera ser onda* (1982; Oh, that I were a wave in the sea). The five *estórias* that make up *Sim camarada!*, from "O conselho" (The council) to "Cinco dias depois da independência" (Five days after independence), cover the period from the installation of the transitional government to the establishment of the People's Republic of Angola. The stories are largely circumstantial and directed to those who also witnessed the dramas played out in the national microcosm of Luanda when these episodes were becoming part of a collective, lived history. The volume's final three *estórias* recount incidents from the civil war, or what MPLA adherents call their "second war of liberation," much of it waged in and around Luanda, in neighborhoods like Vila Alice and on city streets like the once fashionable Avenue of Brazil.

Manuel Rui's *estórias* convert the urban geography into a theater for the historic events that unfolded in Luanda. These testimonial vignettes derive their uniqueness from the ways in which colloquial speech and attitudes toward language work on an emotional and ideological plane. Ironically, the role of Portuguese, as the language of national unity, heightens in a tension-breaking, burlesque scene in the story "O último bordel" (The last brothel). A frightened Angolan prostitute, in a burst of patriotic defiance and linguistic chauvinism, refuses to go to bed with a Zairean soldier (sent to Angola to bolster the forces of the National Front of the Liberation of Angola [FNLA]) because she does not sleep with any man who speaks French.

Manuel Rui, like no other Angolan writer, has capitalized on the language usage that characterized a sometimes overreaching attempt to forge a vernacular of national unification during the first, heady years of independence. Thus the story "Cinco dias depois da independência" represents the apotheosis of Rui's ability to encode urban slang, political and military acronyms, and new forms of social address.

As a chronicler Rui blends humor with intense involvement and cool detachment that at once celebrate the power and expose the banality of patriotic rhetoric. With *Quem me dera ser onda*, Rui tests the waters of social, if not overtly political, satire. This short novel focuses attention on the institutions, social attitudes, and language generated just before and after independence. As the latter approached, the civil conflict drove thousands of rural people into Luanda in search of refuge. Villagers unaccustomed to city dwelling moved into the apartment buildings abandoned by middle- and upper-class Europeans who fled Angola in droves. Stories circulated in Luanda about livestock transported in elevators and fish laid out to dry on the roof tiles of once-fashionable apartment buildings. In Rui's novella, a family turns a section of an apartment veranda into a fattening pen for a pig. When the couple's young sons take pity on the doomed animal and concoct a scheme to save it from its fate, the story becomes a clever satire of social mores as well as an artful commentary on the unsolidified institutions that accompany the new social order.

More so than occurred with Pepetela's *Mayombe*, speculation ran high that the authorities would prohibit the book's publication. Once again proving the skeptics wrong, *Quem me dera ser onda* was published in Luanda and awarded the grand prize in the first Comrade President Literary Contest (established in memory of Agostinho Neto).

Manuel Rui remains firmly in the vanguard of Angolan writers. He has joined with Luandino, Xitu, and Pepetela in significantly altering and enhancing the dialect of acculturated literary discourse (see Butler, "Colonial Resistance and Contemporary Angolan Narrative").

Lusophone African Drama

In their African colonies the Portuguese authorities controlled theater and film as tightly as they did the news media and certain other forms of information and entertainment accessible to broad segments of the indigenous population. Despite this repression and the self-censorship prudently practiced by members of the acculturated elites, there were a few sporadic breakthroughs in the area of live theater. Manuel Ferreira attributes the scarcity of theater to a corresponding paucity in Portugal and Brazil (*Literaturas* 70).

A historically important breakthrough came in 1971, when Norberto Barroca, a young Portuguese director recently arrived from Lisbon, staged in Lourenço Marques *Os noivos, ou conferência dramática sobre o lobolo* (The newlyweds; or, Dramatic consultation on the bride price), by Lindo Lhongo (b. circa 1940). This drama, by an African educated in Protestant mission schools, is based on the theme of "tribal life in transition," with all that such transformations implied in social, economic, and cultural terms. It played to packed audiences of mainly Europeans, in a downtown theater, and mainly Africans, in an Indian-owned movie house in the suburb of Xipamanine. If the play itself, with its social message and use of traditional musical and dramatic dance expression, was a major cultural breakthrough, that it was allowed to be staged at all was of historical and political significance. (Some speculate that although the war continued in the northern zones, the Portuguese, believing they were winning, could afford to be cosmetically tolerant of African cultural expression.)

In Luanda, during this same period of relative liberalization in the colonies, Domingos Van-Dúnem (b. 1925), who in the late 1940s had founded the short-lived theater group Teatro Gesto (Gesture theater), wrote and staged *Auto de natal* (1972; Christmas play). Van-Dúnem's bilingual (Kimbundu and Portuguese) musical drama of religious and cultural syncretism played to racially mixed and socially heterogeneous audiences.

Although Lhongo's and Van-Dúnem's plays have artistic appeal and historical significance, neither signaled the start, during colonial times, of a socially conscious theater in Mozambique and Angola. The authorities apparently had second thoughts about their permissiveness, and for the duration of colonial rule any popular, socially conscious theater was confined to the liberated zones. Indeed, makeshift folk and agitprop productions were common in the *maquis* bordering Angola's eastern war zone, in the FRELIMO strongholds of northern Mozambique, and in the PAIGC-controlled areas of Guinea-Bissau.

Starting in 1974, a more sophisticated agitprop, social realist theater, with Brechtean influences and heavily laced with regional music and dance, accompanied the return of nationalist revolutionaries to the cities of all five former colonies. In Luanda, during the tumultuous days before the installation of the MPLA as the government of Angola, intellectual revolutionaries organized worker-student theater groups. By 1977 there were three such groups in Luanda: Xilenga Theater, National Theater School, and Ngongo Theater. Plays with such epic titles as *História de Angola* (The history of Angola) were brought to the proscenium stage. These ambitious productions captured the patriotic fervor of the times, and if they occasionally reached heights of exciting musical and folk spectacle, they were also mainly transitory and often banal attempts at bridging the gap between the drama-poor colonial period and the early years of independence, with its need for collective, emotive expression.

In 1978 Pepetela staged his *A corda* (The rope), a patriotic play that makes up for its tendentious message with its appealing allegory. Similarly, Henrique Guerra, under the influence of Bertolt Brecht by way of the Spanish dramatist Alfonso Sastre, wrote *O círculo de giz de bombó* (1979; The Manioc chalk circle).

When independence came to Mozambique, in villages, towns, and especially in the cities of Nampula, Beira, and the newly named capital of Maputo, a spate of social nationalist dramatic presentations, performed by students and workers, accompanied the nation-building imperative. In May of 1978 Belo Marques, a Portuguese-born journalist and dramatist, initiated in Maputo a highly successful series of radio plays with the broadcast of an African fable presented in the simulated sound environment of oral expression, complete with audience response. Some of these experimental radio dramas were adaptations of literary works, including stories from Honwana's *We Killed Mangy Dog*.

In São Tomé and Príncipe, Guinea-Bissau, and most notably, Cape Verde, theater based on folk forms and with social and political themes helped fill a cultural void during the first years of independence. In 1977 Kwame Kondé (the pseudonym of Francisco Fragoso, b. 1940) founded Korda Kaoberdi (creole for "Awaken, Cape Verde"), a theater group organized as a "Scenical Nucleus of Workers and Students." Kondé collaborated with Kaoberdiano Dambará, the poet and playwright, in producing original folk musicals and social dramas.

Korda Kaoberdi's limited success—measured in part by sparse attendance at its performances—can be laid to a number of factors. Not the least of these factors is a political tendentiousness, which, even though mitigated by music and dance, largely failed to engage the imagination of enough of the people for whom the spectacles were intended. Similar factors, including amateurism and a tendency toward the superficially folkloric, likewise accounted for the limited successes that theatrical experimentations met with in Angola during the late 1970s.

In spite of the false starts and shortcomings, enthusiasm, improvisation, and the combining of folk and classical elements contributed to a theatrical infrastructure. By the early 1980s, in all five Lusophone countries, playwrights with a sense of craft were beginning to build on that base.

Lusophone African Literature in the 1980s

Despite war, drought, and famine in Angola and Mozambique and varying degrees of socioeconomic woes in all five Lusophone countries, writers continued to write and publish during the 1980s. By 1987 all five countries had associations of artists, writers, or both. In Luanda the Union of Angolan Writers, to cite the outstanding example of productivity, had published by 1989 more than 250 titles, amounting to more than two million copies.

Our temporal proximity to recent literary and editorial events in Lusophone Africa precludes the kind of sifting and filtering that normally allows for the identification of literary canons. But in the Lusophone African countries, where for only a decade and a half relatively few writers have been engaged in defining the terms of their national literatures, nearly every work—pre- or post-independence—commands the attention of the literary critic and historian.

Because of the historical period and the manner in which many Third World countries came into being, there has been an inevitable acceleration and truncating of the normally long-term and slow processes that resulted in the formation of the nation-states and nationalities of the West. In the fifteen short years since the achievement of political independence, the national unification that has been taking place in Lusophone African countries—

despite the problems of ethnic diversity and regional rivalries, and in part because of these very difficulties—has given special importance to the cultural and literary events and works of the 1980s. Thus a concluding attempt at sifting and filtering, so as to highlight some of what might at least tentatively be considered the major events, writers, and works of the 1980s, will ideally put the phenomenon of twentieth-century Lusophone African literature into sharper focus.

In the 1980s, along with the founding of writers' organizations in four of the emerging nations (The Union of Angolan Writers was founded in December 1975, about a month after the declaration of independence), young and beginning writers formed into brigades and launched several literary journals. A group of aspiring Cape Verdean writers, led by José Luís Hopffer Almada (b. circa 1958), formed the Pro-Culture Movement, which in 1987 published the first issue of *Fragmentos*, a magazine of Cape Verdean letters, arts, and culture.

Hopffer Almada, himself a promising poet, also edited the anthology *Mirabilis* (forthcoming), containing the works of about sixty young poets. The established poets Corsino Fortes, with his *Arvore e Tambor* (1986; Tree and drum), and Oswaldo Osório, with *Clar(a)idade assombrada* (1987; the Portuguese title is a play on words that can be read as "Overshadowed clarity"—an allusion to the famous journal *Claridade*—or "Bright age overshadowed"), have contributed to the refinement of the epic discourse and rewriting of history that began to emerge in the immediate post-Independence period. A preoccupation among Cape Verdean intellectuals with redefining the archipelago's place in history and its national identity led Henrique Teixeira de Sousa to write *Xaguate* (The hotel Xaguate, 1987), his second historical novel. In *Xaguate* a note to the reader explains that the text contains expressions in the islands' creole, which Teixeira de Sousa, holding on to a rather outmoded notion, assures us is a dialect of Portuguese.

Manuel Veiga (b. circa 1955), a linguist from Santiago, more than likely disagrees with Sousa's characterization of Cape Verdean *crioulo* as a regional dialect of Portuguese. *Oju d'agu* (1987; The wellspring), Veiga's first attempt at fiction, may well be the most hotly debated Cape Verdean novel ever published. Written in creole, this landmark novel may also be one of the least-read Cape Verdean works of the decade, for the simple reason that even many of those who normally read creole with no difficulty find the language of the text nearly unreadable due to the effort required to decipher the spelling of individual words. Veiga, applying his considerable linguistic knowledge, and wanting to establish the vernacular's phonological and morphological distinctiveness from Portuguese, adapted the international phonetic alphabet to a standardization of creole orthography. The linguistic parameters of Cape Verdean literature are as much a preoccupation of Veiga's creolist and cultural nationalist novel as is a symbolic, literary rewriting of the island's history.

Literary texts in Portuguese and creole have been produced by Cape

Verdeans living abroad, particularly in the large communities of the United States and Portugal. For one, Orlanda Amarilis (b. 1924), who published her first volume of stories at the age of fifty, has emerged as one of the most powerful writers of the Cape Verdean diasporas. The stories collected in her three volumes—*Caís do Sodré té Salamansa* (1974; From the docks of Sodré to the port of Salamansa), *Ilhéu dos pássaros* (1983; Bird island), and *A casa dos mastros* (1989; The house of the masts)—build an imaginative bridge between Lisbon and the islands.

Since the archipelago's independence, in cities like Boston and Providence a growing group of mainly young Cape Verdeans, many U.S.-born, have begun to write poetry and prose in creole, Portuguese, and English. Some of these writers founded, in Boston, Atlantis Publishers, which since the late 1970s has issued such works as *Descarado* (The shameless man), a creole-language play by Donaldo Macedo (b. 1950), and *Across the Atlantic: An Anthology of Cape Verdean Literature* (1988), containing poems and stories in English translation.

In Guinea-Bissau, despite such setbacks as the 1980 coup and the departure of Mário de Andrade, there have been some literary bright spots. A notable one is Helder Proença's *Não posso adiar a palavra* (1986; I can no longer postpone the word), a most appropriate title, given the lull in Guinea-Bissau writing, for this collection of poems. Proença's work, as well as that of a handful of others, and the founding, in 1986, of the Union of Artists and Writers of Guinea-Bissau helped bring that tiny nation into line, on the level of literary and cultural activities, with the newly formed confederation known as PALOP—the Portuguese acronym for the somewhat awkward designation African Countries Whose Official Language Is Portuguese.

In São Tomé and Príncipe, on 30 September 1986, even as the tiny, two-island republic struggled with a myriad of economic and political problems, the Association of Writers and Artists, with some fifty members, came into being. A year before the association's founding, Albertino Bragança (b. circa 1960) published *Rosa do Riboque* (1985; Rose from Riboque). This "modest but significant work," as the preface accurately terms the volume of short stories, is important because it constitutes the first such effort since Independence. Bragança was a genuine revelation, and the association was a major breakthrough in the institutionalization of São Tomé and Príncipe art and literature.

Frederico Gustavo dos Anjos (b. 1957), who, ironically, refused to become a member of the association (he believed its founding to be premature), was in the 1980s one of the islands' most productive writers. His *A descoberta das descobertas, ou as descobertas da descoberta* (1984; Discovery of the discoveries; or, Discoveries of the discovery) is a small anthology of only forty pages containing ten short selections by six island poets. Except for Alda Espírito Santo, who began her career as a poet in the late 1940s, all of the contributors (Conceição Lima, Carlos Vaz de Almeida, Armindo Aguiar, Armindo Vaz, and dos Anjos himself) came of age after independence. Dos Anjos followed his anthology with three equally modest volumes of his own poetry, one short story, and an essay. The twenty-page critical essay, included in *As descobertas da descoberta, ou a dimensão de uma mensagem poética* (1985; The discoveries of the discovery; or, The dimension of a poetic message) summarizes the literary history of São Tomé and Príncipe. What is fascinating is the very existence of an evolving literary expression and criticism in a nation of fewer than 100,000 inhabitants.

In Angola in the 1980s, the prevailing climate of discussion and debate gave added impetus to an evolving literary criticism. One of the principal post-Independence critics is the poet David Mestre, whose *Nem tudo é poesia* (1987; Not everything is poetry) brings together six essays on individual writers—including Agostinho Neto, António Jacinto, and Aires de Almeida Santos—with two articles on the history and nature of Angolan literary criticism.

Other Angolans, especially those who, in 1985, launched *Archote* (Torchlight), the official journal of a group of aspiring writers who call themselves the "Young Flame of Angolan Literature," began to devote themselves to serious criticism and commentary. One of the most assiduous of these commentators is E. Bonavena (b. circa 1950), who has been a regular contributor of editorials and a section, called "Documentos," to *Archote*. In the same category of research and close analysis is Luís Kandjimbo (b. circa 1955), whose *Apuros de vigília* (1987; Anguishes of vigilance) revealed him to be a well-read scholar, versed in theory and familiar with several literatures.

Ruy Duarte de Carvalho, with *Ondula, savana branca* (1982; Roll on, white savanna) and *Hábito da terra* (1988; Habit of the land), and David Mestre, with *Nas barbas do bando* (1985; In the face of the mob), continued to be two of Angola's most productive poets in the 1980s. They, along with other seasoned poets, transmitted their feel for language to several promising poets, including E. Bonavena, Rui Augusto (b. circa 1950), and José Luís Mendonça (b. 1955). Of particular interest and importance are Paula Tavares (b. 1952) and Ana de Santana (b. 1960), two female poets in what has been a male domain. Tavares's *Ritos de passagem* (1985; Rites of passage) and Santana's *Sabores, odores e sonho* (1985; Tastes, scents, and dream) demonstrate that, as poets, they have given original dimension to the discourse of tropical sensualism that characterizes some of the best contemporary poetry of Angola and Mozambique.

Pepetela, one of four Angolan writers with a readership among the entire Portuguese-speaking world and beyond, published *O cão e os caluandas* (The dog and the Luandans, 1985), a futuristic and satirical fable set in post-Independence Angola. Uanhenga Xitu's *Os discursos do "Mestre" Tamoda* (1985; "Professor" Tamoda's speeches), capitalized on the popularity of his first Tamoda book. And Arnaldo Santos, after a long silence, published *O cesto de Katandu* (1986; Katandu's Basket), a collection of five chronicle stories, all but one of which were written in 1982.

A conjura (1989; The conspiracy), a historical novel and first published work of Jose Eduardo Agualusa (b. 1962?), won the Sonangol Prize for the Revelation of the Year. Manuel dos Santos Lima, who wrote the preface for *A conjura*, produced, with his own *Os anões e os mendigos* (1984; Dwarfs and beggars), what he himself has called a political fable about African reality. Lima, who has lived abroad since the 1960s, has retained his membership in the Union of Angolan Writers, but has felt generally disaffected from the social and political directions of his native land—hence his novel contesting the post-Independence state of affairs in sub-Saharan Africa in general and Angola in particular.[17]

With regard to theater, with all its potentially socially contentious possibilities, Domingos Van-Dúnem, with *O panfleto* (1988; The pamphlet), and Jose Mena Abrantes, with *Ana, Zé e os escravos* (1988; Ana, Joe, and the slaves), are two experienced playwrights who, although not in an overtly contentious way, use their art for social commentary.

In Mozambique, the 1980s witnessed a resurgence in literary activity and productivity. Under the aegis of the Association of Mozambican Writers, established in 1981, young writers organized the João Dias Brigade. They launched *Charrua* (The plow), which along with the news magazine *Tempo* (Time) and the literary supplement of the newspaper *Domingo* (Sunday), became as important an outlet for individual poems, stories, and essays as the association's several Mozambican Authors series were for books by experienced as well as beginning writers.

In the capital city of Maputo—one of the urban islands of relative normality in a country beset by a brutal insurgency—the writers of the brigade have held, starting in 1982, a monthly open-air "happening" known as a *msaho* (a Cicope or Chope word meaning, literally, song), and consisting of singing, dancing, theater, and poetry readings.

The first of the *msahos* held in Maputo's Tunduro Park honored and celebrated José Craveirinha, who has become a living legend in Mozamique. *Maria* (1988), a volume of homage to Craveirinha's wife, who met with a tragic death, contains poems that inspired Rui Knopfli to write, in the volume's preface, that "I consider Jose Craveirinha to be—by far—the greatest African poet of Portuguese expression" (*Maria* 10). And Craveirinha's persona, in "O genero" (The genre), the final poem in the collection, acknowledges his role in the convoluted, acculturated world of intimist and public poetic discourse:

> I take increasing pride
> in the undeserved honor of belonging
> to the majority in which I am confined.
>
> A bothered and pathetic citizen
> I rigorously recopy
> the genre: Ze Craveirinha.
>
> (62; my translation)

Craveirinha, as an institution unto himself, became a major force in the reshaping of contemporary Mozambican poetry. Luís Patraquim followed his aforementioned *Monção* with *A inadiável viagem* (1985; The urgent voyage), the best poems of which also display the unmistakable influence of Craveirinha's diction, phrasing, and images.

Prominent among a new generation of Mozambican poets is Hélder Muteia (b. 1960), whose first poem was published in 1979 and whose first book, *Verdades dos mitos* (1988; The truths of myths), contains some of the most imaginative African poetry in Portuguese to appear since Independence. Armando Artur (b. 1962), who published his first poem in 1982, also produced a book, *Espelho dos dias* (1988; Mirror of the days), that contains poetry that—as does much of the most compelling of contemporary Lusophone African poetry—seeks to take the measure of relationships between the past and the present and the private and public voices.

In their attempt to balance the two voices, many recent Mozambican poets—beginning with Patraquim, but harking back to some of Craveirinha's surrealistic and erotic poetry—use tropicalist, sensual imagery and symbology. The Indian Ocean, most notably in the verse of Patraquim and Eduardo White (b. circa 1960)—whose *Amar sobre o Índico* (1987; To love over the Indian ocean) established him as another significant poet—became a kind of nature icon in the literary expression of an evolving Mozambican ethos.

In the 1980s the words "calamities" and "emergency" took on special meaning as RENAMO, also known as the MNR (the Mozambique Resistance Movement), continued to terrorize the rural populace. As a response to the calamities, there emerged a kind of emergency literature, like Eduardo White's *Homoine* (1988), eight short poems to honor the victims of the MNR's massacre of dozens of men, women, and children in the village of Homoine, about two hundred miles north of Maputo.

Lina Magaia (b. 1946) produced the first emergency stories, published first in several issues of the magazine *Tempo* and then in a volume titled *Dumba nengue* (1987; *Run for Your Life!*, 1989). The title is a Xitsonga expression meaning "trust in your feet,"[18] and the book, whose Portuguese subtitle translates as Tragic stories about banditry (the RENAMO guerrillas are commonly referred to as *bandidos*), sold out its first printing of ten thousand copies.

The 1980s ended the virtual impasse in Mozambican prose fiction that followed the seemingly intimidating success of Honwana's *We Killed Mangy Dog*. A growing group of Mozambican fiction writers began to manifest a concern—shared with their Angolan and Cape Verdean counterparts—for the retelling and remythification of history. Albino Magaia (b. 1947)—a poet, the editor of *Tempo*, and the brother of Lina Magaia—published *Malungate* (1987), a narrative that rewrites a portion of the history of the final decades of colonial rule.

In 1986 Mia Couto (b. 1955), a white Mozambican from the city of Beira, published *Vozes anoitecidas* (Voices turned to night). This book of *estórias* (Couto's use of this designation pays homage to Luandino's influence) revolutionized Mozambican fiction writing by establishing a new literary discourse from the perspective of those who dwell in the cultural interstices between two societies.

Along with Mia Couto, another revelation in Mozambican narrative of the 1980s is Ungulani Ba Ka Khosa (the Tsonga name of Francisco Esau Cossa), born in 1957 in the province of Sofala. Khosa's *Ualalapi* (1987) contains phantasmagoric stories that, in a manner similar to Mia Couto's *estórias*, reintegrate the past and present and fashion a new literary language to transmit Mozambique's transitional social history. Drawing on the oral traditions of the Sena and Changane peoples, and influenced by such writers as Luandino and the Colombian novelist Gabriel García Márquez, Khosa's first book demystifies and remythifies Mozambique's historical time and space.

Mia Couto and Ba Ka Khosa are among the Young Turks who have challenged and even influenced the "consecrated" writers—meaning those who came of age before Independence, under the banners of cultural revindication and social protest. One of the younger "consecrated" writers is Raul Calane da Silva (b. 1945), who, as a founding member of the Association of Mozambican Writers, joined with the João Dias Brigade in organizing the monthly *msahos*. Silva, who began his literary career as a poet, turned to prose in 1987 with *Xicandarinha na lenha do mundo* (Teapot on the wood fire of the world), a collection of *estórias* whose uniqueness derives from the author's ability to transform the time-honored neorealist story into surrealistic social vignettes.

The resurgence of the Mozambican short story and novel has also given new life to theater. In the decade of the 1980s Maputo's historic Avenida Theater has been the stage for several experimental plays, mainly adaptations of short stories, including those by Mia Couto, and other Young Turks.

Finally, individually and as a whole, these five literatures in Portuguese have already fulfilled their promise as the first acculturated writing from modern Africa. From its precursors in the late nineteenth and early twentieth centuries, through its origins in the 1930s, and up to the present, Lusophone writing is a unique social and aesthetico-ideological phenomenon.

Notes

1. Gerald Moore and Ulli Beier characterized the poetry from the then Portuguese colonies as "little more than a cry of sheer agony and loss" (23–24). In a revised 1984 edition the anthologists included a few more poets and selections from the former Portuguese colonies, and they expanded on their original, reductionist characteriza-

tion of that poetry. Michael Wolfers's and Don Burness's anthologies, among others, have made greater numbers of the poems by more Lusophone African writers available to English-speaking audiences.

2. According to Mário de Andrade, he and Viriato da Cruz used "Vamos Descobrir Angola" (literally, "Let's Discover Angola") in letters they exchanged while the former was living in Paris and the latter in Luanda, but the phrase was not the war cry of the Generation of 1950, as many literary critics and historians consistently and erroneously have claimed.

3. *Muari-ngana* is the Kimbundu equivalent of "mister," *calaçala* is a Kimbun-duized version of *calçada*, Portuguese for "sidewalk," and *chaluto* is a corruption of *charuto*, meaning "cigar."

4. In the 1940s Cabral himself wrote a number of poems, most of which were discovered only after his death. See O. Osório, *Emergência*.

5. This is indeed a departure from the usual creole ethnocentrism. The poem is, in effect, a celebration of a "black being in the world."

6. *Noti* was issued by the Central Committee of the PAIGC. The 1980 coup resulted in the splitting of the binational PAIGC into separate parties, the PAIG and the PAICV.

7. In a 1979 issue the Lisbon journal *África* carried ten previously unpublished poems by Vasco Cabral (b. 1926). The Guinea-born Cabral had lived in Portugal from early childhood through college and beyond. With independence he became a high official in the newly formed government of Guinea-Bissau. Some students of Luso-phone African literature, on the basis of these ten poems of revindication and protest written in Portugal, see Vasco Cabral as an important precursor of modern Guinea-Bissau literature.

8. The poem has been translated into English, French, Russian, and Swedish, among other languages, and ranks as one of the most anthologized of Lusophone African poems. It appeared, for example, in Moore and Beier's *Modern Poetry from Africa* and, in French, in Mário Andrade's *La poésie africaine d'expression portugaise*.

9. M. Wolfer's English translation of the poem as "We Must Return" is included in his *Poems from Angola* (19–20). Burness's version, also titled "We Must Return," appears in his anthology (37).

10. Angola's independence became official on 11 November 1975.

11. Burness has an English version of this poem, "In the Forest of Your Eyes," in his anthology (73).

12. At this historical juncture it is, however, doubtful that a European, East Indian, or a *mestiço*, for that matter, could rise to head of state in these countries, where, as a legacy of colonialism, ethnic, if not racial, politics do play a role. See Hamilton 1985.

13. After the 1980 coup, Andrade relocated to Paris. He died in London in 1990.

14. Romano has lived much of his adult life in Brazil; before that he lived in Senegal and Morocco. It seems plausible that Romano's sometimes flamboyant Cape Verdeanness, in both his poetry and prose, is in part an aesthetic and ideological overcompensation for having lived most of his adult life away from his native land.

15. The Portuguese-born Abranches emigrated at the age of fifteen to Angola, where, as a young man, he became an MPLA militant. He began writing his monu-mental ethnographic novel in 1961 while confined in a Luanda prison. Along with being a novelist and short story writer, Abranches is also a poet, literary critic, historian, painter, cartoonist, anthropologist, and museum curator.

16. For the Brazilian edition Luandino reversed his policy by providing two glossaries, one of typical Luandan terms, the other of Kimbundu words and phrases.

17. Lima, although his novel is a thinly veiled criticism of the regime, is nonetheless not a persona non grata in Angola. One of the few cases in independent Angola, and certainly the most notorious, of the apparent political persecution of a writer occurred when Costa Andrade was imprisoned for nearly a year, in 1979–80, because of allegedly offensive allusions to government officials in his play *No velho ninguém toca* (1980; Nobody touches the old man).

18. The term apparently became popularized in Maputo, where makeshift black markets sprang up on many city streets. As the story goes, when the police approached, the cry *dumba nengue* would go up, and the illegal vendors would gather their wares and literally "trust in their feet."

Bibliography

Abranches, Henrique. *A konkhava de Feti* [Feti's hatchet]. Lisbon: Edições 70, União dos Escritores Angolanos, 1981.

Abrantes, José Mena. *Ana, Zé e os escravos* [Ana, Joe, and the slaves]. Porto, Portugal: Edições ASA for the União dos Escritores Angolanos, 1988.

Achebe, Chinua. "English and the African Writer." *Transition* 4, no. 18 (1965): 27–30.

Agualusa, José Eduardo. *A conjura* [The conspiracy]. Lisbon: Caminho, 1989.

Alegre, Caetano da Costa. *Versos* [Poetry]. 3d ed. Lisbon: Ferin, 1951.

Amarilis, Orlanda. *Cais de Sodré té Salamansa* [From the docks of Sodré to the port of Salamansa]. Coimbra, Portugal: Centelha, 1974.

———. *Ilhéu dos pássaros* [Bird island]. Lisbon: Plátano, 1982.

———. *A casa dos mastros* [The house of the masts]. Linda-a-Velha, Portugal: Africa—Literatura, Arte e Cultura, 1989.

Andrade, Fernando Costa. *No velho ninguem toca: Poema dramático com Jika* [Nobody touches the old man: A dramatic poem featuring Jika]. Lisbon: Sá da Costa, 1979.

Andrade, Mário Pinto de, ed. *La poésie africaine d'expression portugaise* [African poetry in Portuguese]. Honfleur, France: Pierre Jean Oswald, 1969.

Anjos, Frederico Gustavo dos, ed. *A descoberta das descobertas, ou as descobertas da descoberta* [Discovery of the discoveries; or, Discoveries of the discovery]. São Tomé: Direcção de Cultura, 1984.

———. *As descobertas da descoberta, ou a dimensão de uma mensagem poética* [The discoveries of the discovery; or, The dimension of a poetic message]. São Tomé: Empresa de Artes Gráficas, 1985.

Antologia da ficção cabo-verdiana contemporânea [Anthology of contemporary Cape Verdean fiction]. Praia, Cape Verde: Achamentos de Cabo Verde, 1960.

Antologia dos jovens poetas: Momentos primeiros da construção [Anthology of the young poets: The first moments of nation building]. Bissau, Guinea-Bissau: Conselho Nacional de Cultura, 1978.

António [Fernandes de Oliveira], Mário. *Crónica da cidade estranha* [Chronicle of this uncommon city]. Lisbon: Agência-Geral do Ultramar, 1964.

Artur, Armando. *Espelho dos dias* [Mirror of the days]. Maputo, Mozambique: Associação dos Escritores Moçambicanos, Colecção Início, 1986.

Assis Júnior, António de. *O segredo da morta: Romance de costumes angolenses* [The dead woman's secret: Romance of Angolan customs]. 2d. ed. Lisbon: Edições 70, União dos Escritores Angolanos, 1979.

Barbeitos, Arlindo. *Angola angolé angolema* [Angola, hail Angola, Angola the word]. Lisbon: Sá da Costa, 1967.

Barbosa, Jorge. *Arquipélago* [Archipelago]. Mindelo, Cape Verde: Claridade, 1935.

———. *Caderno de um ilhéu* [Notebook of an island]. Lisbon: Agência-Geral do Ultramar, 1956.

Bragança, Albertino. *Rosa do Riboque e outros contos* [Rose from Riboque and other stories]. São Tomé: Cadernos Gravana Nova, 1985.

Burness, Donald, trans. *A Horse of White Clouds: Poems from Lusophone Africa*. Athens: Ohio University Press, 1989.

Butler, Phyllis Reisman. "Colonial Resistance and Contemporary Angolan Narrative: *A Vida Verdadeira de Domingos Xavier* and *Vidas Novas*." *Modern Fiction Studies* 35, no. 1 (Spring 1989): 47–54.

Cabral, Amílcar. "Apontamentos sobre poesia caboverdiana" [Notes on Cape Verdean poetry]. *Cabo Verde: Boletim de propaganda e informação* no. 28 (1952): 5–8.

———. *Return to the Source*. New York: Monthly Review Press, 1973.

Cardoso, Boaventura. *Dizanga dia muenhu* [The lagoon of life]. Lisbon: Edições 70, União dos Escritores Angolanos, 1977.

———. *O fogo da fala* [The fire of words]. Lisbon: Edições 70, União dos Escritores Angolanos, 1980.

Carvalho, Ruy Duarte de. "Angola, conscience politique et culture populaire" [Angola, political conscience and popular culture]. *Afrique-Asie* 124 (1976): 48–50.

———. *Ondula savana branca: Expressão africana: Versões, derivações, reconversões.* [Roll on, white savanna: African expression: Versions, derivations, reconversions]. Lisbon: Sá da Costa, 1982.

———. *Hábito da terra* [Habit of the land]. Porto, Portugal: Edições ASA, União dos Escritores Angolanos, 1988.

Couto, Mia. *Vozes anoitecidas* Lisbon: Caminho, 1987. *Voices Made Night*. Translated by David Bradshaw. Oxford: Heinemann, 1990.

Craveirinha, José. *Xigubo*. 2d. ed. Lisbon: Edições 70, 1980.

———. *Maria*. Linda-a-Velha, Portugal: Africa—Literatura, Arte e Cultura, 1988.

da Cruz, Viriato. *No reino de Caliban: Antologia panorâmica da poesia africana de expressão portuguesa* [The kingdom of Caliban: Comprehensive encyclopedia of African poetry of Portuguese expression], edited by Manuel Ferreira. Vol. 2. Lisbon: Seara Nova, 1976.

Dambará, Kaoberdiano [Felisberto Vieira Lopes]. *Noti* [Night]. Bissau, Guinea-Bissau: Comité Central do PAIGC, 1964.

Dias, João. *Godido e outros contos* [Godido and other stories]. Lisbon: Casa dos Estudantes do Império, 1952.

Ellen, Maria M., ed. *Across the Atlantic: An Anthology of Cape Verdean Literature*. North Dartmouth, Massachusetts: Center for the Portuguese-Speaking World, 1988.

Espírito Santo, Alda. *É nosso o solo sagrado da terra* [The sacred soil of this land is ours]. Lisbon: Ulmeiro, 1978.

Ferreira, Manuel, ed. *Literaturas africanas de expressão portuguesa* [The kingdom of Caliban: Comprehensive encyclopedia of African poetry of Portuguese expression]. 2 vols. Lisbon: Instituto de Cultura Portuguesa, 1977.

————, ed. *No reino de Caliban: Antologia panorâmica da poesia africana de expressão portuguesa*. Vols. 1 and 2. Lisbon: Seara Nova, 1975, 1976. Vol. 3. Lisbon: Plátano, 1985.

Figueira, Luiz. *Princesa negra: O preço da civilização em África* [Black princess: The price of civilization in Africa]. Coimbra, Portugal: Coimbra Editora, 1932.

Fortes, Corsino. *Pão e fonema* [Bread and phoneme]. Mindelo, Cape Verde: Privately printed, 1974.

————. *Arvore e tambor* [Tree and drum]. Praia, Cape Verde: Instituto Caboverdiano do Livro and Publicações Dom Quixote, 1986.

Freire, Maria da Graça. *Portugueses e negritude* [The Portuguese and Negritude]. Lisbon: Agência-Geral do Ultramar, 1971.

Gonçalves, António Aurélio. "Problemas da literatura romanesca em Cabo Verde" [Problems of romantic literature in Cape Verde]. In *Antologia da ficção Cabo-Verdiana Contemporânea* [Anthology of contemporary Cape-Verdian fiction]. Praia: Archamenti de Cabo Verde, 1960.

Guerra, Henrique. *Círculo de giz de bombó* [The bombo chalk circle]. Luanda, Angola: UEA, Cadernos Lavra, 1979.

Hamilton, Russell. "Class, Race, and Authorship in Angola." In *Marxism and African Literature*, edited by Georg M. Gugelberger, 136–49. London: James Currey, 1985.

————. "Language and Literature in Portuguese-Writing Africa." *Portuguese Studies* 1 (1985–86): 196–207. Reprint. *Callaloo* 14, no. 2 (1991): 313–23.

————. "Lusofonia, Africa, and Matters of Languages and Letters." *Callaloo* 14, no. 2 (1991): 324–35. Rev. ed. *Hispania* 74, no. 3 (September 1991): 610–17.

Honwana, Luís Bernardo. *Nós matamos o cão tinhoso*. São Paulo, Brazil: Atica, 1980. *We Killed Mangy Dog and Other Mozambique Stories*. Translated by Dorothy Guedes. London: Heinemann, 1969.

João, Mutimati Barnabé [António Quadros]. *Eu, o povo: Poemas da revolução* [I, the people: Poems of the revolution]. Maputo, Mozambique: FRELIMO, 1975.

Kandjimbo, Luís. *Apuros de vigília* [Anguishes of vigilance]. Lisbon: Sá da Costa, União dos Escritores Angolanos, 1988.

Khosa, Ungulani Ba Ka [Francisco Esau Cossa]. *Ualalapi*. Maputo, Mozambique: Associação dos Escritores Moçambicanos, Colecção Início, 1987.

Lhongo. Lindo. "Os noivos, ou conferência sobre o lobolo" [The newlyweds; or, Dramatic consultation on the bride price]. *Caliban* 3, no. 4 (1972): 105–6.

Lima, Manuel dos Santos. *Os anões e os mendigos* [Dwarfs and beggars]. Porto, Portugal: Edições Afrontamento, 1984.

Lisboa, Eugénio. "Nota nuito sumária: a propósito da poesia em Moçambique" [A very summary note: About poetry in Mozambique]. Introduction to Rui Knopfli, *Mangas verdes com sal* [Green mangoes with salt]. Lorenço Marques (Muputo): Publicações Europa-América, 1969.

Lopes, Manuel. *Chuva braba* [Torrential rain]. 1956. 2d. ed. Lisbon: Edições 70, 1982.

Lopes da Silva, Baltasar. *Chiquinho*. 2d. ed. Lisbon: Prelo, 1961.

————. *Os flagelados do vento leste* [Victims of the east wind]. 1959. São Paulo, Brazil: Atica, 1979.

Magaia, Albino. *Malungate*. Maputo, Mozambique: Associação dos Escritores Moçanbicanos, Colecção Karingana, 1987.

Magaia, Lina. *Dumba nengue: Histórias trágicas do banditismo*. Maputo, Mozambique: Colecção Karingana, 1987. *Run for Your Life! Peasant Tales of Tragedy in Mozambique*. Translated by Michael Wolfers. Trenton, N.J.: Africa World Press, 1988.

Macedo, Donaldo. *Descarado* [The shameless man]. Boston: Atlantis Publicações, 1979.

Macedo, Jorge. *Gente de meu bairro* [People from my neighborhood]. Lisbon: Edições 70, União dos Escritores Angolanos, 1977.

Mantenhas para quem luta!: A nova poesia da Guiné-Bissau [Hail to those who struggle!: The new poetry of Guinea-Bissau]. Bissau, Guinea-Bissau: Conselho Nacional de Cultura, 1977.

Mariano, Gabriel. "Negritude e caboverdianidade" [Negritude and Capeverdianism]. *Cabo Verde: Boletim de propaganda e informação* no. 104 (1958): 7–8.

Mendes, Orlando. *Portagem* [Toll]. Beira, Mozambique: Notícias da Beira, 1965.

Mestre, David. *Nas barbas do bando* [In the face of the mob]. Lisbon: Ulmeiro, União dos Escritores Angolanos, 1985.

————. *Nem tudo é poesia* [Not everything is poetry]. Lisbon: Edições 70, União dos Escritores Angolanos, 1987.

✓ Moore, Gerald, and Ulli Beier, eds. *Modern African Poetry*. 3d. ed. Baltimore: Penguin Books, 1984.

Moser, Gerald M. "African Literature in Portuguese: The First Written, the Last Discovered." *African Forum* 2, no. 4 (Spring 1967): 78–96.

————. *Essays in Portuguese African Literature*. Pennsylvania State University Studies in Romance Literatures, no. 26. University Park, Pa.: Pennsylvania State University Press, 1969.

Muteia, Hélder. *Verdade dos mitos* [The truths of myths]. Maputo, Mozambique: Associação dos Escritores Moçambicanos, Colecção Timbila, 1988.

Neto, Agostinho. *Sagrada esperança*. 2d. ed. Lisbon: Sá da Costa, União dos Escritores Angolanos, 1979. *Sacred Hope*. Translated by Marga Holness. Dar es Salaam: Tanzania Publishing House, 1974.

Osório, Oswaldo. *Caboverdiamadamente, construção, meu amor* (Cape Verde–lovingly, building a nation, my love). Lisbon: Publicações Nova Aurora, 1975.

————. *O cântico do habitante* [The inhabitant's hymn]. Lisbon: Terceiro Mundo, 1977.

————. *Emergência da poesia em Amílcar Cabral: 30 poems* [The emergence of Amílcar Cabral's poetry]. Praia, Cape Verde: Dragoeiro, 1985.

————. *Clar(a)idade assombrada* [Overshadowed clarity]. Praia, Cape Verde: Instituto Caboverdiano do Livro, 1987.

Pacavira, Manuel. *Nzinga Mbandi*. 2d. ed. Lisbon: Edições 70, União dos Escritores Angolanos, 1979.

Patraquim, Luís Carlos. *Monção* [Monsoon]. Maputo, Mozambique: Instituto Nacional do Livro e do Disco, 1980.

————. *A indiável viagem* [The urgent voyage]. Maputo, Mozambique: Associação dos Escritores Moçambicanos, Colecção Timbila, 1985.

Pepetela [Artur Carlos Maurício Pestana dos Santos]. *As aventuras de Ngunga* [Ngunga's adventures]. 3d. ed. Lisbon: Edições 70, União dos Escritores Angolanos, 1978.

———. *A corda* [The rope]. Luanda, Angola: UEA, Cadernos Lavra, 1978.

———. *Mayombe.* Lisbon: Edições 70, União dos Escritores Angolanos, 1980. *Mayombe.* Translated by Michael Wolfers. London: Heinemann, 1984.

———. *Yaka.* São Paulo, Brazil: Atica, 1984.

———. *O cão e os caluandas* [The dog and the Luandans]. Lisbon: Publicações Dom Quixote, 1985.

Poesia de combate [Poems of combat]. 2 vols. Maputo, Mozambique: FRELIMO, Departamento do Trabalho Ideológico, 1971, 1977.

Proença, Hélder. *Não posso adiar a palavra* [I can no longer postpone the word]. Lisbon: Inquérito, 1982.

Reisman [Butler], Phyllis. "José Luandino Vieira and the 'New' Angolan Fiction." *Luso-Brazilian Review* 24 (Summer 1987): 70–78.

———. "Manuel Rui's *Sim camarada:* Interpolation and the Transformation of Narrative Discourse." *Callaloo* 14, no. 2 (1991): 307–12.

Ribas, Oscar. *Uanga: Romance folclórico angolano* [Enchantment: An Angolan folkloric novel]. 2d. ed. Luanda, Angola: Privately printed, 1969.

Rocha, Jofre [Roberto de Almeida]. *Estórias do Musseque* [Musseque tales]. Lisbon: Edições 70, União dos Escritores Angolanos, 1976.

Romano, Luís. *Famintos* [The famished]. Rio de Janeiro, Brazil: Leitura, 1961.

Roscoe, Adrian A. *Mother Is Gold: A Study in West African Literature.* Cambridge: Cambridge University Press, 1971.

Rui, Manuel. *11 Poemas em novembro* [11 poems in November], vol. 1, 2d. ed. Luanda, Angola: UEA, Cadernos Lavra, 1977.

———. *Regresso adiado* [Postponed return]. 2d. ed. Lisbon: Edições 70, União dos Escritores Angolanos, 1977.

———. *Sim camarada.* Lisbon: Edições 70, União dos Escritores Angolanos, 1977. *Yes, Comrade!* Translated by Ronald W. Sousa. Minneapolis: University of Minnesota Press, forthcoming.

———. *Quem me dera ser onda* [Oh, that I were a wave in the sea]. Lisbon: Edições 70, 1982.

Santana, Ana de. *Sabores, odores e sonhos* [Tastes, scents, and dreams]. Luanda, Angola: União dos Escritores Angolanos, 1985.

Santos, Arnaldo. *Quinaxixe.* Lisbon: Casa dos Estudantes do Império, 1965.

———. *Tempo de munhungo* [Vertigo time]. Luanda: Nós, 1968.

———. *O cesto de Katandu e outros contos* [Katandu's basket and other stories]. Lisbon: Edições 70, 1986.

Senghor, Léopold S. *Lusitanidade e negritude* [Lusitanianism and Negritude]. Instituto de Altos Estudos, Nova Série. Lisbon: Academia das Ciências de Lisboa, 1975.

Silva, [Raul] Calane da. *Xicandarinha na lenha do mundo* [Teapot on the wood fire of the world]. Maputo, Mozambique: Associação dos Escritores Moçambicanos, Colecção Karingana, 1987.

Silveira, Onésimo. *Hora grande* [A long hour]. Nova Lisboa (Huambo), Angola: Colecção Bailundo, 1962.

Soromenho, Fernando Castro. *Terra morta* [Dead earth]. 2d. ed. Lisbon: Edições 70, União dos Escritores Angolanos, 1978.

——. *A chaga* [The bleeding sore]. 2d. ed. Lisbon: Edições 70, União dos Escritores Angolanos, 1979.

Tavares, Paula. *Ritos de passagem* [Rites of passage]. Luanda, Angola: União dos Escritores Angolanos, Cadernos Lavra, 1985.

Tenreiro, Francisco José. *Obra poética* [Poetic works]. Lisbon: Memórias da Junta de Informações do Ultramar, 1967.

——. *Coração em África* [With my heart in Africa]. Linda-a-Velha, Portugal: Africa—Literatura, Arte e Cultura, 1982.

Tenreiro, Francisco José, and Mário Pinto de Andrade, eds. *Caderno de poesia negra de expressão portuguesa* [A collection of Negro poetry in Portuguese]. Lisbon: Privately printed, 1953.

Teixeira de Sousa, Henrique. "Dragão e eu" [Dragon and I]. In *Antologia da ficção cabo-verdiana contemporânea*, 257–76. Praia, Cape Verde: Achamentos de Cabo Verde, 1960.

——. *Ilhéu de contenda* [Isle of contention]. Lisbon: O Século, 1978.

——. *Xaguate* [The hotel Xaguate]. Lisbon: Publicações Europa-América, 1987.

Tiofe, Timóteo Tio [João Varela]. *O primeiro livro de Notcha* [Notcha's first book]. Mindello, Cape Verde: Publicações Gráficas, 1975.

Van-Dúnem, Domingos. *Auto de natal* [Christmas play]. Luanda, Angola: Privately printed, 1972.

——. *O panfleto* [The pamphlet]. Porto, Portugal: ASA, União dos Escritores Angolanos, 1988.

Vieira, Arménio. *Poemas* [Poems] (1971–79). Lisbon: Africa Editora, 1981.

Vieira, José Luandino. *A cidade e a infância* [Childhood and the city]. 2d. ed. Lisbon: Edições 70, União dos Escritores Angolanos, 1977.

——. *Luuanda*. 8th. ed. Lisbon: Edições 70, 1981. *Luuanda: Short Stories of Angola*. Translated by Tamara Bender. London: Heinemann, 1980.

——. *A vida verdadeira de Domingos Xavier*. 7th ed. São Paulo, Brazil: Atica, 1979. *The Real Life of Domingos Xavier*. Translated by Michael Wolfers. London: Heinemann, 1978.

——. *Nós, os do Makulusu* [We, the folks from Makulusu]. 4th. ed. Lisbon: Edições 70, 1985.

——. *Macandumba*. Lisbon: Edições 70, União dos Escritores Angolanos, 1978.

White, Eduardo. *Amar sobre o Índico* [To love over the Indian ocean]. Maputo, Mozambique: Associação dos Escritores Moçambicanos, Colecção Início, 1986.

——. *Homoine*. Maputo, Mozambique: Associação dos Escritores Moçambicanos, 1988.

Wolfers, Michael, trans. *Poems from Angola*. London: Heinemann, 1981.

Xitu, Uanhenga. *Manana*. 2d. ed. Lisbon: Edições 70, União dos Escritores Angolanos, 1978.

——. *"Mestre" Tamoda e outros contos* ["Professor" Tamoda and other stories]. 2d. ed. Lisbon: Edições 70, União dos Escritores Angolanos, 1977.

——. *Os discursos do "Mestre" Tamoda* ["Professor" Tamoda's Speeches]. Lisbon: Ulisseia, Instituto Nacional Angolano do Livro e do Disco, União dos Escritores Angolanos, [1985]. *The World of "Mestre" Tamoda*. Translated by Annella McDermott. London: Readers International, 1988.

10 African-Language Literatures:

Perspectives on Culture and Identity

ROBERT CANCEL

> Thus one of the most humiliating experiences was to be caught
> speaking Gikuyu in the vicinity of the school. The culprit was given
> corporal punishment—three to five strokes of the cane on bare
> buttocks—or was made to carry a metal plate around the neck with
> inscriptions such as I AM STUPID or I AM A DONKEY. Sometimes the
> culprits were fined money they could hardly afford.—(Ngũgĩ wa
> Thiong'o, *Decolonising the Mind* 11)

During the 1980s two extensive studies appeared that explore the history and
content of literatures written in African languages from most regions of the
continent. Albert Gérard's *African Language Literatures* (1981) is a broad
survey of the corpus, from the oldest to the most contemporary literatures in
African languages. One of the author's main points is that for the amount of
writing and the length of time some of it has existed, there is a woeful lack
of scholarship about these literatures. Similarly, he points to the unevenness
of our knowledge regarding these traditions. On the one hand, aspects of
Swahili, Amharic, Xhosa, and Zulu literatures have been studied by European and African scholars in some degree of depth. On the other hand, our
knowledge about writing in Gikuyu, Ewe, Shona, and Bemba, for example,
suffers from great lacunae in both criticism and explication. Three Polish
scholars, B. W. Andrzejewski, S. Piłaszewicz, and W. Tyloch, in their study
Literatures in African Languages: Theoretical Issues and Sample Surveys (1985),
acknowledge the impossibility of a thorough survey of all African-language
writing and concentrate instead on a sizeable sample of literatures from
various parts of the continent. They also include the consideration of "oral
literature" from each of the traditions studied, thus emphasizing the continuity between oral art forms and the written genres of particular African
languages.

This essay proposes to find a path between these seminal studies to focus
on certain issues as they are exemplified in several African literary traditions.
Perhaps the best way to suggest, at least in a modest way, the richness of

285

artistry and the cultural and political significance of literatures in the vernacular languages of African people is to begin with a brief historical overview of writing in Africa, then to examine a few case studies, and finally, to consider the sociocultural implications of African-language literatures.[1]

Early Writing Traditions

The hieroglyphics of the ancient Egyptians was one of the continent's oldest forms of writing. There was also the writing, in an epigraphic script, of Ge'ez in Ethiopia which dates back to at least the fourth century B.C.E.. Amharic followed Ge'ez as another language that has for centuries been written in Africa.[2] But perhaps contemporary writing in African languages can more readily be traced back to the advent of Arabic writing in several regions of the continent. The West African trading empires that grew at the southern margins of the Sahara desert included numerous scholars, scribes, and holy men who used Arabic as their literary or at least record-keeping language. The great founder of the Malian Empire, Sunjata (thirteenth century), encouraged writing and its related arts at court, as did his successors. These states can be dated from the end of the first millennium on. Though Arabic has largely remained a language of religion in most of sub-Saharan Africa, it provided the valuable service of stimulating the so-called Ajami writing traditions (Gérard, *African Language Literatures* 47–170). Simply put, these were cases of African peoples using Arabic script as a medium to reproduce their own languages. This happened among the Fula people of Cameroon, Guinea, and Senegal; among the Hausa, in Nigeria and Niger; and among the Wolof in Senegal and Gambia. The art form most commonly appropriated for these efforts was Arabic religious and secular poetry, which had strict rules of prosody and rhyme—though these written poems were often sung for audiences and were tied to an oral tradition. Chronicles and histories also appeared in these languages, written in Arabic script.

Several other regions of Africa used Arabic script to reproduce the local languages. Ajami writing in Madagascar, for instance, dates back at least as far as the thirteenth century, and it was not until the nineteenth century that Latin script was officially sponsored by the government. Swahili was another African language that was not only written in Arabic script but whose very formation was heavily influenced by the Oriental, and later Muslim, culture that grew and flourished on Africa's east coast from around the first century C.E. As in other cases, the most popular genre was poetry, eventually written in the local language but following the formal, and often moral and didactic, tenets of Islam and Arab culture.

As time went on and colonial powers from Europe made themselves felt in such matters, most indigenous languages turned to Latin script. An unusually old example of European influence is the case of the Kongo kingdom, which had trade ties with the West since the fifteenth century, and whose court regularly sent selected members to Portugal for higher education. On returning, they employed Portuguese as an official language of written communication between functionaries. Ironically, Kongo itself was written down and used in literary endeavors only after the Berlin Conference of 1884–85, when Protestant missionaries developed and disseminated a system in which to publish and read the language (Gérard, *African Language Literatures* 286–93). A further irony, one of many produced by conditions and consequences of the slave trade, was that English became the first literate language of the leaders of the modern states of Sierra Leone and Liberia. As former slaves, taken mostly from West Africa and repatriated by the British and Americans, the people who became the elites and rulers of these countries, by the late eighteenth and early nineteenth centuries, had been trained to read, write, and communicate—first with their masters then among each other—in English. While many of the intellectuals of these groups, or their descendants, kept English as their medium of scholarship, a number of them took on the task of evangelizing local and neighboring peoples. For this vital work they took to heart the methods of their European Protestant teachers. That is, they settled areas, learned the local languages (if they did not already know them), created an orthography, and went about translating the Bible into those languages. Furthermore, the English-speaking elites, of Sierra Leone in particular, were responsible for the creation of a new language that drew on elements of English (mostly vocabulary) and the indigenous languages (syntax, pronunciation, and elements of tone): Krio. It was also in Sierra Leone and Liberia that several ethnic groups, as a means of rejecting European languages and script, developed their own local orthographies for writing their languages, the best known of these being the Vai script.[3]

Missionaries and the Emergence of Yoruba Literature

By far the most common pattern of reducing African languages to European script was the one established in the British colonies.[4] For reasons of religion and, I suspect, control, early missionaries, especially Protestants, would from the earliest contact set out to learn and write down local languages. They recognized the importance of allowing people to pick up this new knowledge in their own languages, in their own patterns of thought and philosophy. The missions therefore developed an early generation of "educated" converts whose facility with European languages would allow them to fill the crucial civil service and labor ranks needed to run the colonies. Many in this educated class used those metropolitan languages as a means of personal advancement and status. Others went beyond producing translations of Biblical works or—that most ubiquitous of translated texts—John Bunyan's *Pilgrim's Progress,* and began writing creatively in their own languages for readers of their ethnic-linguistic groups. The type of writing they produced and the information conveyed in this writing is of central interest to this discussion. We can examine these dimensions by considering a few linguistic regions where writing in local languages took place before and especially during the twentieth century.

In what would eventually become the nation of Nigeria, the Yoruba people made up a sizeable group when missionaries arrived to begin the work of evangelization. It is relevant to consider the development of their written literature because it is a fairly long-standing one and because the Yoruba remain one of the larger ethnic and linguistic groups in Africa. Perhaps the most remarkable of the early missionaries was Samuel Ajai Crowther (1807?–91). Taken as a slave, then freed and repatriated to Sierra Leone, this Yoruba graduated from Fourah Bay College in 1827 and, after his ordination as a Church Missionary Society (CMS) minister, returned to Nigeria as a missionary. Some of his earliest accomplishments were the production of a Yoruba dictionary and five school primers. In 1900 Crowther's full Bible translation was published, and this was followed in 1911 by the issuing of his translation of *The Pilgrim's Progress*. While he produced these important works, Bishop Crowther formalized a Latin script orthography for Yoruba, in the process developing a written form of "standard" Yoruba based mainly on the Oyo dialect, though three of the nine major dialects also contributed to this form. As was the case for numerous African languages entering the medium of written traditions, poetry was an early popular genre of expression. Oral poetry, so prevalent in Africa, was an important part of traditional art and expression for the Yoruba and was the source for early writers such as J. Sobowale Sowande (1858–1936), who is credited with writing the first published "original" Yoruba poems. This means that, as opposed to the early hymn-writers who used Western models for their efforts or merely reproduced the words of oral Yoruba poetry, Sowande began with the formal model of traditional poetry—specifically, the chants employed in the Abeokuta festivals of Orò, the ancestor of the Earth Spirit—and infused them with Christian themes and personal experiences and observations.[5] The first two collections of his poems were published in 1905 and 1906, respectively.

Literacy was embraced as a means to success in colonial Africa—success being defined as employment and eventual financial security. The Yoruba people took to the preservation and promotion of their language in the form of cultural societies and Yoruba-language newspapers and periodicals. The first novelette written in Yoruba found its initial forum in such a newspaper, *Akéde èkó* (Lagos herald), where it was serialized before its 1929 publication. The plot detailed a cautionary tale, narrated by a "fallen woman" who had debased herself through prostitution, adultery, and abortion and is afflicted at the end with an incurable illness. The irresistible title of this work, by Isaac Babalola Thomas (1888–1963) is *Sègilolá, eléyinjú egé* (Segilola, woman of ensnaring eyeballs).

It was not until 1938 that the first full-fledged novel in Yoruba was published, and this turned out to be a signal occasion for the future of Yoruba literature. A church primary school headmaster named Daniel Olorunfemi Fagunwa produced a vivid, fantastic story called *Ògbójú ode nínú igbó irúnmalè* (1938; *The Forest of a Thousand Daemons*, 1968). In a narrative that draws on Yoruba cosmology and oral traditions, as well as Greek, Latin, and Middle Eastern mythologies, Fagunwa weaves an episodic quest tale that depicts fantastic creatures and adventures in the mysterious bush combined with observations on many elements of traditional Yoruba life: "the virtue of courage and perseverance; rivalry between co-wives in polygamous families; various vices such as wickedness, cruelty, treachery, theft, greed and ingratitude; the laws of retribution; parents' problems in choosing a husband for their beautiful daughter; belief about spirits and witches" (Babalola in Andrzejewski, Piłaszewicz, and Tyloch 167). Fagunwa's book became very popular; in fact, it set the pattern for three more successful novels.[6]

For virtually the remainder of his life, Fagunwa was known as *the* Yoruba prose stylist. He published collections of traditional Yoruba tales and reports on his eighteen-month visit to England. Fagunwa's last novel departed from the familiar pattern by depicting a much more realistic, yet no less didactic and moralistic, situation: *Adììtú-Olódùmarè* (1961; [Biography of a man named] God's mystery knot). By writing about fantastic events and traditional values, Fagunwa partly combined the two streams of early African writers who had, or at least felt, the responsibility to preserve, to preach, or both. He drew from and therefore approximated the oral tradition while also setting up lessons in ethical and moral values for younger readers to absorb. Much of his writing was destined, often intended, for primary and secondary school readership, and the didactic bent was part and parcel of the literary effort.

In 1947 Adekanni Oyedele published a fictional autobiography, *Ayé rèè!* (Thus goes the world!), set before the arrival of whites in the Yoruba area. It differed notably from Fagunwa in its "realistic" depiction of characters and events. Adeboye Babalola points out that this novel's "overriding theme" was the notion of predestination and fate.

Another well-known novelist is Chief Isaac Oluwole Delano (b. 1904), an officer in the Yoruba cultural society Egbé Omo Odùduwà (Association of the children of Oduduwa). His first novel, *Aiyé d'aiyé òyìnbó* (1955; The world has become a white man's world), is set in the Yoruba area before the coming of Europeans and, cast as a fictional autobiography, covers that period up to the current era. Babalola says that the "author brilliantly adopts a narrative style fashioned on the characteristic mode of Yoruba elders' delivery of their recollections. Consequently the novel is rich in Yoruba proverbs and idioms and the prose has a delightful measured tread" (Andrzejewski, Piłaszewicz, and Tyloch 169). Chief Delano eventually devoted his full attention to writing, producing a Yoruba monolingual dictionary and another historical novel.

Yoruba dramatists produced, in addition to contemporary types of plays, a new genre termed "folk opera." As a departure from the syncretic dramas performed in earlier colonial contexts, a transitional sort of play set out to dramatize scenes from the Bible but ended up as free interpretations, at times rather ribald and accompanied by Yoruba music (Babalola and Gérard 255). These dramas, when combined with traditional Yoruba dramatic festival forms (masks, ritual celebrations, acting out of historical and mythical events), eventually evolved into the folk opera. The pioneer in the genre was Herbert Ogunde, who in the 1940s "began to secularize this syncretic medium" (Babalola and Gérard 255). Drama, music, song, and historical and mythical sources were combined with topical and satirical commentary to constitute a vital and popular art form. Many actor/writer/producers succeeded Ogunde, but it was not until 1969 that Duro Ladipo's popular *Oba kò so* (The king did not hang), first performed in 1963, reached print to become the first published version of the genre.

Contemporary Yoruba writers are numerous, thus it is important to identify at least two more. Adebayo Faleti, an acknowledged master of language, is a dramatist, poet, and novelist. His lengthy novel *Omo olókùn esin* (1970; Son of the keeper of horses) is called by Babalola "a feast for the reader." It has a historical, pre-nineteenth-century setting, and the author employs three separate narrators to tell different parts of the complex tale. Faleti depicts the various tactics employed by slaves both to free themselves and to depose the slaver rulers of the Otu kingdom. Several collections of poems, a novelette, and two plays, one of which is a densely evocative historical epic, have placed Faleti among the best-known and most highly regarded Yoruba writers.

Afolabi Olabimtan is also a playwright, poet, and novelist. His play *Oláòré afòtèjoyè* (1970; [Chief] Olaore, king by treachery) is allegorical, alluding to the downfall of a good king due to an error of judgment. The allusions to contemporary politics of the 1960s are quite clear, as is the play on the name of the good king, Obalowo.[7] Olabimtan's poems have been praised for their evocative qualities as well as their adherence to traditional Yoruba poetic patterns. Says Babalola of the second collection, *Ewì orísìírísìí* (Poems of various types), which deliberately showcases several styles of oral poetic genres, "The compositions are remarkably successful; those which are divination poems have provided scholars with an insight into the process of the growth of the Ifa literary corpus in the oral traditions" (Andrzejewski, Piłaszewicz, and Tyloch 174). Finally, Olabimtan has written two novels, both noted for their realism and unflinching portrayals of urban and rural life, with their various problems and consequences.

Adeboye Babalola, on whose scholarship this section is based, points to a situation that no longer strictly applies to Yoruba writing and its readership, though his statement holds true for the current status of African-language writing in a majority of countries:

The contemporary creative writer in Yoruba has a relatively small audience among the adults because of the still high percentage of adult illiteracy and the continuing indifference of many educated Yoruba citizens to their mother tongue. It appears the further development of Yoruba literature will depend on the determination of talented writers to continue to produce Yoruba literary works in obedience to the dictates of their genius and not merely to meet the demands of the market existing in the primary and secondary schools. (Andrzejewski, Piłaszewicz, and Tyloch 175–76)

Perhaps the greatest influence colonial rule had on Africa was a linguistic, and therefore cultural, one. Frantz Fanon suggested that to adopt a new language was to "take on a world," and the process that moved Africans towards the adoption of a foreign language is still, I think, not properly understood. Ngũgĩ wa Thiong'o, for instance, notes the early growth of a "messenger class" in colonial times and how these purveyors of translation "for a price," as depicted in some of Achebe's novels, used the European language as a tool for personal gain (Ngũgĩ, *Decolonising the Mind* 63, 67). Before going into this question in more depth, it is worthwhile noting the growth of written African literatures in other sections of the continent.

The Southern African Experience

In southern Africa, the Xhosa people were among the first and largest indigenous groups to begin writing creatively in their own language. As early as the 1820s a mission station of the Church of Scotland was established in the vicinity of Tyume, among the Ngqika people of the Xhosa group. When a small press was introduced in 1823, the Ngqika dialect was launched as the future "standard" form of Xhosa literature, in much the same way that the Oyo dialect became the model for written Yoruba. In 1825 the Tyume mission was rechristened Lovedale and, after a shift to a new site following the 1834–35 frontier war, became the center of Xhosa publishing activity. As with the Yoruba, Xhosa was first reduced to writing by the missionaries, then converts were to take up the tasks of translating—at times retranslating— some of the important religious or literary works brought from Europe, such as the Bible and *The Pilgrim's Progress*. Vernacular poetry and prose were screened by officials of the mission press, and the works that were selected were distributed among the growing numbers of literate Xhosa people. One of the most influential early writers was Tiyo Soga (1825–71). Gérard may have been referring to Soga, as much as to any number of early African writers, when he said,

> That is where modern African literature may truly be said to have begun: with Christian hymns composed by Africans, with recording of oral lore (especially in the form of traditional stories), with the earliest attempts at oral prose composition imitating the kind of stories that the pupils had read at school, either in English or in vernacular versions. (*African Language Literatures* 180–81)

Tiyo Soga's earliest contributions were indeed church hymns. He also translated sections of the Xhosa Bible and a large portion of Bunyan's classic—the translation being completed years later (published in 1926) by his son, John H. Soga. The elder Soga was, like Crowther for the Yoruba, one of the earliest codifiers of written Xhosa literature.

The advent of the twentieth century in what was to become the Republic of South Africa was a sobering time for Xhosa and other Bantu-language writers. These early convert/teacher/intellectuals were to find that their prose was most often confined to newspapers when they wrote in protest of oppressive conditions.[8] By the middle to late 1800s the relatively liberal mission encouragement of Black writing and advancement had turned much more conservative. Elements of racial determinism in European scholarship and colonial policies combined readily with the discovery of precious metals and gems in the Orange Free State to institutionalize the subservient position of Black Africans, especially the Black writer, in South Africa (see Gérard, *Four African Language Literatures*, 174–98 and Scheub in Andrzejewski, Piłaszewicz, and Tyloch 542–50). The gifted and committed Christians among the Xhosa and other peoples were hard pressed to find a sympathetic ear for their growing discontent. Censorship or repression of manuscripts and eventually even newspaper writing—for many of the liberal Xhosa-language newspapers were white owned and controlled—were to force writers to shift their emphasis from blatant protest to subtler or even mundane themes.[9] Two major outlets became feasible for the Christian intellectuals: political activity and agitation, and pedagogical pursuits. As the former alternative resulted in more frustrations and official censure, the latter choice became the more common for activists.

In southern Africa, as in many other parts of colonized Africa, Christian mission activity often encouraged converts to renounce their precolonial practices and beliefs and to embrace an essentially Western ethos. Daniel Kunene, who refers to this process as "deculturation," claims that many southern African writers were channeled into themes that made for an exercise in "self-devaluation." The main character of a Nyanja-language novel from Zambia illustrates Kunene's argument effectively when he warns his son that a traditional festive dance is "dirty and evil, and those people dance naked, with only small patches of cloth around their loins—very shameful indeed. . . . Most of their songs are obscene. It fills one with shame to watch those dancers. And what is good in them anyway?" (Kunene, "African Vernacular Writing" 648). Indeed, that was the attitude fostered by many mission-run educational systems. On the other hand, even from early times the traditional life was often a draw to the Xhosa writer. For some it was merely the convenient target of editorial moralizing, ending with the lauding of the coming of new Christian ways. Yet there was also the recognition of positive elements of Xhosa culture, and those elements would eventually be paired with the good things of rural life in thematic contrast to the evils and perils of the city.

Samuel Edward Krune Mqhayi (1875–1945) is considered to be "the father of Xhosa poetry." He was said to be equally skilled in the traditional art of the *imbongi* (the oral bard) and written poetry. His earliest themes lauded Christianity, but he later turned to lamenting the rising and inevitable conflict between Black and white South Africans. The two themes alternate in Mqhayi's work. His utopian novel *U-Don Jadu* (1929; Don Jadu) hypothesizes a South Africa where all races would live peaceably and profitably. In 1925 Mqhayi addressed to Britain's Prince of Wales an at times ironic praise poem, in the traditional form, that contains the following allusions:

> Ah, Britain! Great Britain!
> Great Britain of the endless sunshine!
> . . . .
> You gave us Truth: denied us Truth
> You gave us ubuntu: denied us ubuntu
> You gave us light: we live in darkness
> Benighted at noon-day, we grope in the dark.

> (Cited in Jordan 114)

Harold Scheub says of James J. R. Jolobe (1902–76) that "he is the greatest of the Xhosa literary poets, an experimenter, an eloquent manipulator of imagery" (Andrzejewski, Piłaszewicz, and Tyloch 558). Like Mqhayi, Jolobe was an ordained minister with a solid education. The winner of various literary prizes in his lifetime, Jolobe wrote the earliest collection of essays by a Xhosa writer, *Amavo* (1940; Personal impressions). Though he experimented with various forms of poetry and rhyme, his poem "The Ingqawule," considered the finest in Xhosa literature, approximates the traditional oral form. The poem depicts a crucial event in Xhosa history, whereby the lethal threat of hostile settler armies is responded to by an extreme milennarian solution. A prophetess is inspired by a vision to advise the people to kill all their cattle and destroy their crops as a mass sacrifice to the spirits, thereby ensuring deliverance from this grave and impending danger.

> . . . all the livestock
> And the harvest of the earth were to be sacrificed.
> Even the corn reserves would be destroyed.
> The promise was a new abundance:
> Great herds of cattle, a surfeit of maize;
> Old women would be revitalized,
> They would acquire the freshness of youth.
> The long hills, the low lands,
> From the Mbashe to the Nxuba, would be ruled by Xhosa
> And the foreigners would be swallowed by the sea.

> (Scheub in Andrzejewski, Piłaszewicz, and Tyloch 566)

Jolobe was also a thoughtful educator and man of letters who not only wrote, in addition to his poetry, a novel and a play, but translated numerous works from English and Afrikaans into Xhosa as well. He also wrote about Xhosa literature.

The novel in Xhosa was inaugurated by Henry Masila Ndawo in 1909 with *uHambo lukaGqoboka* (Journey of a convert), an allegorical novel influenced in great part by *The Pilgrim's Progress*. Again, a common theme is reiterated as Xhosa tradition is tied in with Christian mores. Speaking about another Xhosa novel, *u Nomalizo, okanye izinto zalomhlaba ngamajingiqiwu* (1918; Nomalizo, or the things of this life are sheer vanity), by Enoch S. Guma, Scheub echoes the observations of Kunene when he says, "the characters in the novels of this period in Xhosa literary history are not subtle psychological studies. They are frequently caricatures, their functions and actions being far more significant than their characters" (Andrzejewski, Piłaszewicz, and Tyloch 575). Kunene, examining fiction in southern Africa, laments that "full, rounded characters are apt to be rare." He goes on to suggest that the problem is a narrow and relentless didacticism, saying of a Xhosa novel that "the writer's worst offense as an artist is his apparent determination to give us the sermon for its own sake, in a work that nevertheless purports to be art" (Kunene, "Problems" 91).

All scholars of Xhosa literature agree that the 1940 novel by A. C. Jordan, *Ingqumbo yeminyanya* (The wrath of the ancestors), was a breakthrough work. Its success is in part due to Jordan's skillful and imaginative use of the language. Moreover, the novel combines the conflicts of old and new, Xhosa culture and the West, tradition versus Christianity, into one unifying work. Scheub says that "with Jordan, the Xhosa novel becomes a purely literary form" (Andrzejewski, Piłaszewicz, and Tyloch 581), owing to both formal and thematic attributes. Formally, Jordan is able to combine tenets of the oral narrative tradition with those of the Western literary forms adapted by the early Xhosa writers. Thematically, he goes beyond the "right and wrong" polarization of traditional and contemporary mores and, rather than argue about whether or not change will come, insists that it has already arrived and been accepted. His point is that people must decide what kind of change is to be embraced and how it is to happen. Significantly, the only character in the book who is able to weather the devastating events is among the most flexible of the novel's protagonists. The many themes and questions raised by Jordan and those who preceded him were to be further explored by the generation of writers who followed.

INFLUENCES OF THE ORAL TRADITION

Two elements raised so far deserve closer examination. The first is the debt to the oral tradition, and here again Scheub (Andrzejewski, Piłaszewicz, and Tyloch) is the strongest proponent of the idea that formative elements in Xhosa fiction stem from the tenets of the so-called *ntsomi* tradition. He argues that the basic oral narrative movements, most often from a known place to an unknown or dangerous one, are preserved in much Xhosa prose. Further, the rapid action and often minimal characterization are traits of the oral tradition. Most of all, symmetrical patterning is a means of structuring both fiction and oral narrative. For example, in the "good girl/bad girl" pattern, found in oral traditions throughout the continent as well as in Xhosa written fiction, a virtuous or obedient character is consistently compared with one who acts in the opposite manner, the good person in the end winning out over the bad one. Hence, there was a built-in attraction to the familiar patterning and allegorizing in a work like *The Pilgrim's Progress*. Kunene notes the same kind of pattern in a subcategory of his "transgenerational story progression": the "pampered child" versus the "harshly-treated step-child" ("Problems").[10]

The Government and African Languages

A second problem raised by the examination of Xhosa fiction is the question of African languages and their use by African governments. In the case of Xhosa, censorship and repression were common concerns from before the turn of the century. The example of the Sotho writer Thomas Mofolo is a famous case in point. Mofolo's first novel, *Moeti oa bochabela* (1907; Traveler to the east), was eagerly published by a mission press because it was written in the Bunyanesque allegorical format, praising the great bounties of the Christian West and condemning the excesses and savagery of traditional Sotho life. Mofolo's second novel, *Pitseng* (1910), was also published expeditiously because its theme again reaffirmed the values of Christianity and a solid Western-type education. When the author offered his classic work *Chaka* for publication in 1910, there was a delay of fifteen years before the novel saw print. Though the book was a rather unflattering portrait of the great Zulu king, it did not contain a clear Christian message. In fact, it used as one of its central literary devices the decidedly non-Christian practices of divination and "magic." Furthermore, whether the portrait was unflattering or not, the mission press was probably not prepared to publish an account of such a powerful African conqueror for a readership whose past it sought to erase or denigrate. Colonial government presses preferred works for the primary or secondary school child. Ideally, these works were simplistically wrought, providing a bit of "moral" guidance while the student learned to read and appreciate the connections between his own writers and the translations of the "great" books from Europe. Kunene, when talking about the process of "self-devaluation," gives several causes for the problem, and among them are both conscious and unconscious constraints that led to moralizing and unimaginative syncretisms ("African Vernacular Writing"). On the other hand, there always existed the possibility for writers to appropriate the imported literary elements and use them for their own, often nationalistic, purposes.[11]

Somali Literature

Though the area that was to become the independent nation of Somalia had for centuries embraced Islam and therefore had a long history of scholars and poets who wrote in Arabic, the Somali language has been written for only a relatively short period of time. At first Somali poets and record keepers used the Arabic script to write the language. Over time several scripts were developed, and these reflected the complex colonial history of Somalia; because each of these scripts carried some kind of sociopolitical baggage, it was not until 1972 that the nation finally adopted an official orthography.[12]

The Somali-speaking people have for centuries possessed a popular and highly valued oral poetry, traditionally sung and composed by bards at all levels of Somali society. Despite its association with oral Arabic poetry and later with written Arabic poetry, Somali poetry, even when written with Arabic characters, managed to maintain its distinctive identity, in part because the Arabic language in Somalia did not have the intrinsic artistic or political prestige that accrued to it in, say, East Africa.

The origins of modern Somali literature can arguably be traced to the man who is still acknowledged as the nation's greatest poet: Sayyid Maxamed Cabdulle Xasan (1856–1921). Referred to as the Mad Mullah by the British, his longtime political enemies, Maxamed can rightfully be called the first great Somali nationalist. He led a group known as the dervishes on a protracted campaign of resistance to English imperial efforts. He was also a master of oral Somali and Arabic poetry. An example of why he is held in such high esteem as both poet and nationalist is provided by B. W. Andrzejewski. In his poem "Xuseenow caqligu kaa ma baxo idam Ilaahaye" (O Xuseen, God willing may good sense never leave you), Maxamed righteously criticizes

> The men who of their free choice carry out menial tasks
>   for the infidels
> Those who, though uncoerced, go on errands for them as if
>   they were bound to them by the loving bonds of kinship
> And who became like the offspring of the Christians and made
>   a life-protecting pact with the Europeans.

(Andrzejewski, Piłaszewicz, and Tyloch 348–49)

Despite arguments about how Maxamed, a consummate politician, really felt about the majority of Somalis who were not of his own lineage (Laitin), he is unquestionably venerated today for both his art and political struggles.

It is important to note this link between the poet and the politician in Somalia for, as David Laitin emphasizes, the spoken word has more than purely aesthetic power in that society:

> The extensive and conscious cultivation of the art of speaking is one of the most striking features of Somali culture. . . . Quotations from poems and

alliterative proverbs, characterized by their pithiness and condensed imagery, adorn the prose style of sermons and speeches at assemblies, arbitration tribunals and political meetings. . . . And so poets in Somalia have political power in their own society far beyond their colleagues in other cultures. (37)

Given the importance of verbal forms of art and wisdom on the continent of Africa, this claim requires a contextual tempering and qualification. But it must also be acknowledged that Somalia is in the almost unique situation of having essentially one culture and language in one nation—recognizing the great diversity of families and clans, as well as a small minority whose first language is not necessarily Somali—and it may therefore be quite true that the language and its literature exert an exceptionally powerful influence on contemporary culture and politics.

Somali writing of this century has mainly consisted of poetry, a good deal of it constituting the written record of orally composed works. Said S. Samatar has written an extensive study of Somali oral poetry and prose, and his work on the oral prose of rural Somalia is exceptionally helpful in understanding the forms of Somali oratory and the roots of the nation's written literature. Written prose has been sporadic, at least until recently. A short story by Axmed Cartan Xaarge "Qawdhan iyo Qoran" (Qawdhan and Qoran), which reached print in 1967, depicts the tragic situation of two lovers forced apart by the woman's arranged marriage. Apart from this story, Andrzejewski notes only a published but unproduced play, some poetry appearing in journals, and some literary essays. After 1969 activity picked up, with plays and historical novels representing a trend whereby written prose was moving away from oral influences. Yet above all, poetry still dominates the Somali literary scene, and the most prevalent medium of dissemination, aside from live recitation, is nationwide radio broadcasts. John Johnson, B. W. Andrzejewski, and David Laitin all emphasize the great power and passion of this art form; whether the content is mainly nationalistic or harks back to older times, the poems are appreciated, argued over, and interpreted by many Somalis:

> Most Somali poets now rely on writing in the composition of their works, but their poems reach the public mainly in oral form at private or public recitals, through the radio and more recently through tapes, which circulate throughout the country. Those poets who have achieved fame in the New Era have done so through such oral channels and not through their published works. (Andrzejewski, in Andrzejewski, Piłaszewicz, and Tyloch 375)[13]

The emphasis on nation-building by the Somali government has put a premium on literacy, and most Somali writers are today urged to develop new texts for primary and secondary school students, as well as technical manuals for farmers and medical workers. There are, to be sure, a considerable number of unpublished manuscripts of Somali prose fiction, poetry, and drama, but the concerns and priorities of the government printers make it unlikely that these works will see print for some time. For Somalia, the greatest literary battle had been won when the government finally chose a controversial Latin script to represent the language—a choice based, among other concerns, on the facility of typesetting and publishing the language for workers, teachers, and students. Somalia was not, in practice, differing much from the policies implemented by British colonial educational mandates. The essence of the literacy policy differs substantially, however, from its colonial predecessors. The educational materials are geared toward furthering true nationalist goals for an independent nation, forming them in the language *and* culture of the entire polity.

Literature in Swahili

Farther south along the East African coast, including the southern part of Somalia, Swahili has for centuries been spoken as a first language. It is important, when discussing Swahili literature, to distinguish between the language and the people. The language was first the sole property of the people who lived in areas of the coastlines of what are now modern Kenya and Tanzania. It is their form of the language that is still referred to as classical Swahili. As the language spread in this century to people of non-Swahili descent, the most popular form of the language came to be called standard Swahili. Over the years, the Arab and Indian settlers who helped to establish commerce between this region of Africa, the African peninsula, and the Indian subcontinent mixed with the indigenous African population to form the people who are, rather generically, known as the Swahili. This contact with the Arab and Asian worlds can be dated back to the first century C.E. Arabic was the spoken and written language of these early traders who came to stay. Literature, in the form of historical records and poetry, was exclusively written in Arabic. As the Swahili language developed, it became the chosen medium of daily speech, but Arabic remained the language of literature and religious rite.

The oldest known literary manuscript in Swahili, written in Arabic script, is the seventeenth-century poem "Hamziya." As in numerous African literatures whose written forms were associated with either Christianity or Islam, a good deal of Swahili writing was hagiographic. Heroes of stories or poems were often either Muslim saints or allies of famous religious historical figures. In fact, one of the great epic poems of the Swahili people is about the "pagan" king Fumo Liyongo (1160–1204?), though in most literary accounts of his life he is somehow associated with the Muslim heroes who fought against the non-Muslim Bantu-speaking peoples (Ohly, in Andrzejewski, Piłaszewicz, and Tyloch 462).

Most early writing in Swahili was carried out by scholars, poets, and clerics who were devout Muslims and who had little empathy for the lives or cultures of the nonbelievers in the interior. That situation would change with the coming of colonial rule and the use and eventual official adoption of Swahili as a lingua franca in the Tanganyika (later Tanzania), Uganda, and Kenya colonies. Though the Swahili language had been spread by the interior trade routes of the East Coast slave trade and other forms of long-range commerce, the use of the language to facilitate colonial efforts was to lead to a much wider network of speakers and writers.[14]

Gérard and others look to 1925 as a marker for the birth of "modern Swahili literature" (see Gérard, *African Language Literatures* 134 and Hellier). At that time an education conference moved to adopt a single vernacular language for schools in British East Africa. Simply put, this meant that non-Muslims and non-Swahili were to begin reading and eventually writing creatively in that language. The early writers of this new era, as in many parts of Africa, wrote for juvenile audiences, in publications that became school "readers" or primers. During this early period, the most popular Swahili writer by far was a customs official from Tanga named Shaaban Robert (1909–62). Shaaban was a poet, novelist, and essayist. Though his parents were Yao, from Malawi, Shaaban's writing, personality, and ethos were quintessentially Swahili. A master of the language, Shaaban Robert extolled the virtues of his culture, a culture that, he emphasizes, is African and not Arab or Western. He, like many Swahili and Arabic poets, was an inveterate moralizer, going so far in his didacticism as to include glossaries at the end of his works so that non-Swahili Swahili-language readers could delve into the nuances of the language (Harries, "Tale," "Swahili Literature"). Along these lines, he was an advocate of culture and language as important adjuncts to the colonial types of education:

> Perhaps better literature than that from my own wretched pen already exists in East Africa, but the disadvantages of the foreign language in which it is written are not negligible. Africans are forced to get knowledge from it with much difficulty, like children fed from the bottle instead of from their mother's breast. My writing will be in the one important language of East Africa. (Cited in Gérard, *African Language Literatures* 138)

By 1951 Shaaban was a full-time writer and chair of the Swahili Language Committee and a member of the East African Language Bureau.[15] He was, in other words, in a position to promote the language he called the most important in East Africa. Though at times the moral elements of his poems and prose recalled the mostly conservative elements of the Muslim roots of the literature, Shaaban is today revered as a patriot who strove to create a truly national literature. He remains immensely popular.

But my desire here is not so much to focus on Shaaban Robert, or even the many talented poets and prose stylists of the pre-Independence era—before, say, 1960—as it is to see Swahili in both its national and nationalist contexts. Though a major national language at the time of Tanzania's Independence (1961), it did not immediately become that nation's official language. Similarly, Swahili in Uganda was treated as simply one of several national languages, as it was, despite its greater historical and immediate constituency, in Kenya. In all three East African nations, then, Swahili was a language of varied importance, yet it was English, the language of the former colonial rulers, that became the official language. It was not until after the famous Arusha Declaration (1967) of Tanzania's president, Julius Nyerere, that the choice was made to use Swahili as the nation's official language. That decision meant that education, commerce, science, parliamentary debate, newspapers, and the electronic media were to use that one language as the principle means of communication.

One outcome of this new focus was the establishment of the Society for Swahili Composition and Poetry (Chana cha Usanifu wa Kiswahili na Ushairi Tanzania, or UKUTA), which was mandated to promote Swahili writing that would both aid in the literacy education of the populace and provide inspiration for the understanding and conceptualizing of national goals. An immediate outcome of UKUTA's effort was a flood of poetry, referred to as *ngonjera*, that stressed patriotism and the various collective projects instituted by the government. Poems about the Arusha Declaration, Tanzania's struggle against imperialism, and the glories of the Ujamaa village projects were the order of the day. One is reminded of the cynical description of Soviet socialist realism in writing and film as a case of "boy-meets-tractor" romantic plotting. Not surprisingly, Western, and not a few African, literary critics were not impressed by such heavy-handed efforts, suggesting that the social content of the poetry was overwhelming any aesthetic or artistic considerations (Harries, "Swahili Literature," and Gérard, *African Language Literatures* 147–48).

As in other regions of Africa, prose was often relegated to the role of a recorder, a tool to reproduce and preserve oral narrative traditions and historical events. One of Shaaban Robert's many contributions to Swahili literature was his role as a bridge between the older generation of Muslim poets and the newer post-Independence writers. In that role he introduced the novel to the language, or at least a prose form that was as close to the European idea of "novel" as Swahili had up to that time come. In 1960 Muhammad Said Abdullah took the Swahili novel further by writing the first full-length detective story, which nonetheless was still set in the classical Swahili/Arabic mode of moralizing literature. Faraji Katalambulla moved further away from Shaaban Robert by writing an urban police thriller in standard Swahili, *Simu ya kifo* (1965; Phone call to death). By the late 1960s writers in Tanzania and Kenya were producing novels in growing number. In many ways, these newer themes and directions were presaged by the so-called Tales from Tanga in the mid-1960s. During this period in the Tanga area of Tanzania, young journalists and writers published stories in magazines and newspapers that ran serially and became very popular. They were often violent and explicitly sexual—a combination that any bookseller would confirm as a sure-fire formula—depictions of contemporary urban and rural lifestyles (Harries, "Tale"). The language of these narratives was also a contemporary form of Swahili as it is spoken by urban dwellers. It is filled with slang and borrowings that are often the provenance of non-first-speakers. The stories are comparable, at least in tone, with the Onitsha literature of Nigeria, wherein urban realism and the depiction of the plight of the innocent in such settings was a real and vibrant focus. Ironically, the political goals of the Tanzanian government proved to be the liberating force that would allow nondoctrinaire new writers, some influenced by the Tanga example, to see publication.

Various styles and themes were to grow out of that post-Arusha era. Perhaps the most liberating effect was the sense that Swahili was to be used as an official language and that the growth of the language was open to new ideas and vocabulary. The government formed scholarly bodies to renovate and shape the language to suit a modern world of science and technology. New vocabulary had to be found for things that had never needed description before. In the field of literature this has had similar ramifications. For instance, the Swahili detective novel soon became one of the most popular contemporary genres. In both Kenya and Tanzania, newspapers, magazines, and books carried the works of writers like Eddie Ganzel, who successfully borrowed from such pulp stylists as Mickey Spillane and Ian Fleming. The detective writers had to coin new phrases to describe the blue smoke that was alternately curling up either from the hero's nostrils as he coolly smoked a cigarette or from his gun after he coolly dispatched his enemies.

In the valuable introduction to her current bibliography of Swahili literature, Elena Zubkova Bertoncini provides information on themes and trends. She points out that the audience for "popular" writing is growing so quickly that it is an almost causal element in the concurrent rapid growth of literacy in Tanzania. The growing audience of readers has spurred a parallel boom in publishing houses. She notes that reader preferences have shifted from "tale and romance" to the "realistic novel and short story"—*realistic*, in the context of Swahili literature, being a relative term. Bertoncini observes that the detective genre is so popular that "serious" Swahili writers have attempted to use it as a means for getting across socially relevant themes to the masses. Finally, she refers to the sizeable percentage of thrillers listed in her bibliography, almost one third of the titles, many of which are carbon copies of U.S. and foreign spy and detective films (527–28). While these thrillers lack the moralizing and didacticism of traditional Swahili writing, Bertoncini suggests that a lot of this social prescriptiveness is being carried out in contemporary Swahili written drama. The reason for this, she theorizes, may be that "theatre is near to the oral tradition which is basically didactic" (528).

Popular literature is not the only product of Swahili authors. Tanzanian and Kenyan writers have produced some extremely interesting and successful works, pleasing to both the average reader and the more demanding literary critic. Among these writers, the Tanzanian Euphrase Kezilahabi is the most praised for his innovative and linguistically evocative efforts. His novels include the highly regarded *Rosa mistika* (1971), which exposes a serious problem of the abuse and harassment of schoolgirls by their teachers, and *Dunia uwanja wa fujo* (1975; The world—a field of chaos), a complex story that moves its protagonist from life in a rural area to a small town, where he experiences all the concomitant corruptions, then to a form of salvation on the land as he works hard to amass a large farm, and finally, ironically, to a tragic end when the state collectivizes and socializes all large landholdings.

Ebrahim Hussein is Tanzania's best-known playwright, and his works *Mashetani* (1971; Devils), *Wakati ukuta* (1971; Time is a wall), and especially *Kinjeketile* (1969) are critically lauded. Another Tanzanian, Penina Muhando, has also gained fame for her dramas. She differs from Hussein in her approach to both audience and plotting, but some scholars feel she is reaching the masses more effectively than any other playwright.[16] Her works include *Tambueni haki zetu* (1973; Recognize our rights), *Heshima yangu* (1974; My dignity), and *Pambo* (1975), as well as several unpublished plays. Across the border from Tanzania, one of Kenya's best young novelists is Katama G. C. Mkangi, whose novel *Ukiwa* (1975; Desolation) is a depiction of a tragic love story wherein a young Mombasa couple are separated when the girl goes off to study in Nairobi, forgetting her lover and, more importantly, her background and cultural ties.

In Tanzania the proliferation of works published in Swahili, initially encouraged by government decree, is accelerating as the reading audience similarly grows. In Kenya the growth is less obvious, perhaps owing in large part to the still-nebulous status of Swahili as a semiofficial language. Theorists such as Ngũgĩ wa Thiong'o go so far as to suggest that Swahili and other Kenyan languages have not only lacked active promotion from the government but have in some cases been repressed, especially when they threaten to raise the general level of consciousness of a "national culture." Whatever the actual situation, it is not unfair to say that the popularity of Swahili writing is nonetheless growing and appealing to many readers across ethnic and national boundaries. That growth alone is a positive sign, since the lively evolution of Swahili literature is assured as its audience and pool of potential writers and critics grows. Despite the many economic and political problems facing Tanzania internally and externally, its language policy has irreversibly led the nation towards the fulfillment of the linguistic integration of a national culture.

Bemba Literature

The final African-language literature to be examined here is Bemba writing from Zambia. Historically, the Bemba people were among the most powerful groups in what is today the nation of Zambia. They live in the northern part of the country, and Bemba is spoken over a wide area. Again, it is important to separate the people and the language, since Bemba is the best known of a cluster of languages in northern Zambia and has, since the days of colonial rule, been promoted in literature, school texts, and radio broadcasting. Though linguists might argue over the current definition of the languages in the Bemba family—that is, whether some of the languages are actually dialects—it is safe to assume that because of its status as a national language Bemba is today the dominant member of that family. Like Yoruba in Nigeria and Xhosa, in southern Africa, Bemba was the language of the earliest group in Zambia to be evangelized, and consequently it was used in early translations and education, thus becoming the standard model for literary language. In the case of the Bemba people it is also significant that they were the dominant military state in their region of Zambia at least two centuries before the coming of colonial rule.[17]

As was a general trend in the British colonies, an African Literature Committee was established in 1937 for what was then Northern Rhodesia. Writing in local languages was encouraged by the offering of annual prizes for the best works. This committee also sought teaching texts for schools, which were to be produced by local writers. By 1948 the committee combined with one in Nyasaland to form the Northern Rhodesia and Nyasaland Publications Bureau. One of the first publications of the bureau was a Nyanja-language novelette by Ned B. Linje, *Nthano ya Tione* (1947; The story of Tione). In a short time, as in other parts of the continent, European and South African publishers saw the potential for a sizeable market and began publishing works in local languages, especially, at first, in Nyanja, a language spoken in Malawi and Zambia. It was not long, however, before the largest language group in Zambia, Bemba, found outlets for publication in the literary market. Though Gérard (*African Language Literatures*) and Kunene ("Analysis") locate the origin of modern Bemba writing in the publication in 1960 of Stephen A. Mpashi's novel *Cekesoni aingila busoja* (Jackson becomes a soldier), the novel actually was first published in 1948. Mpashi had therefore been an active writer and chronicler for some years and had a loyal readership among the literate Bemba-speakers and schoolchildren. Two of Mpashi's earlier works were also popular: *Uwakwensho bushiku* (1951 [1955]; He who hurried you through the night) and *Uwauma nafyala* (1955; He who beats his mother-in-law).[18]

Scholars tend to praise the above three works for their structure, themes, and language—the latter quality being as important as the other two among Bemba readers. A look at some of Mpashi's other publications suggests his important role as a chronicler of Bemba culture, mores, and history: *Umucinshi* (1952; Traditional manners, [lit. Respect or Homage); *Icibemba cesu na mano yaciko* (1955; Our Bemba language and its wisdom), a collection of proverbs and their explication; and *Ubusuma bubili* (1955; [Two kinds of] goodness[es]), detailing desirable qualities in women. Mpashi's role as a cultural preserver and, at times, validator recalls the seminal functions of many early writers in African languages. Where numerous elements of language and culture may have originally been fluid or relatively localized, the African-language writer became the conduit and editor-arranger for much of this information, and after a while the published works themselves became not only codifiers but sources of linguistic and cultural validation.[19] And of course Mpashi was not alone, even within Bemba literature. Many writers followed his example in one genre or another, whether it was in producing didactic school readers, chronicling oral traditions, or writing history or fictional narrative.

At least among the writers of the 1950s and early 1960s, there was often a tie to either an educational or a religious organization. Didacticism and some sort of religious or moral message was, as in other similar literatures, the order of the day. Several of Mpashi's books were published or sponsored by the Catholic church, the most obvious instance being his historical work *Abapatili bafika ku babemba* (1956; The Catholic priests arrive among the Bemba). A similar work by M. K. Chifwaila, *Ululumbi lwa mulanda kuka-kaata* (1956; The fame of the stubborn poor person), details some of the difficult times brought to the Bemba by the slave trade and the concurrent wars with the Ngoni people. The "solution" to those hard times was found in the coming of missionaries and the institution of a new and benevolent colonial administration.

Aside from Mpashi's writings on culture, many writers put together collections of traditional tales. For instance, Paul M. B. Mushindo, a renowned Bemba minister, wrote *Imilumbe ne nshimi: Shintu bashimika ku lubemba* (1957; Stories [with and without songs]: The ones they tell in the Bemba area). M. K. Chifwaila also wrote *Amalibu ya kuilombela* (1958; Self-inflicted misfortunes), a book of traditional tales, mostly of the *imilumbe* type, that is, stories without songs that usually have explanations appended to the end. The title of the collection is also the title of one of the stories and is, itself, a common saying used to warn others about greed or meddling in things best left alone. An offshoot of this type of writing can be seen in J. M. Bwalya's *Umupushi na bambi* (1970; The beggar and others), a collection of stories based in part on oral narratives but admittedly reworked into something more akin to literary short stories.

These titles suggest both continuity and diversity. Mpashi was clearly a role model of sorts for other Bemba writers. A perceptive dissertation by Dr. Kalunga Lutato, "The Influences of Oral Narrative Traditions on the Novels of Stephen A. Mpashi," examines "traditional Bemba aesthetics." Lutato's information is drawn in part from Mpashi's own *Ifyo balemba amabuku* (1962; How they write books), a kind of how-to manual for prospective Bemba authors, and in part from Lutato's knowledge of traditional life and art of the people he grew up with. One of the more interesting outcomes of his discussion is its reminder of the powerful role played by "explanation" or didacticism in traditional thinking about art. This is not to say that the colonial-era presses encouraged any other type of writing for what eventually would be used for school readers; they most often selected this very kind of sermonizing over other themes or forms. Still, the confluence of the didactic oral tale—there were of course other kinds of oral tale—and the colonial-missionary criteria for publications is obviously responsible for the overall frequency of didactic writing in earlier versions of African-language literatures.

Mpashi himself advises writers of the value of didacticism:

> In fiction, one should bear one thing in mind, and this is that, although the book is fiction, it should have something to teach the readers. . . . It would not be aesthetically pleasing to write a book from which, when one is done with the reading, one does not retain a worthwhile message at all because, then, the writer will have failed. Written fiction is similar to oral narrative performances. You perform a narrative, the audience apprehends a worthwhile message. (Cited in Lutato 32)

One is tempted to see in Mpashi's words a slightly subversive piece of advice that has more to do with getting published in the colonial-era press than with a real Bemba aesthetic description. In any event, various studies of oral traditions indicate that the so-called didactic elements in those traditions are much more fluid than earlier researchers had supposed. (See, for instance, Okpewho and Cosentino.) In fact, what writing initially does is to reduce many of the elements of fluidity into a frozen set of truisms and pieces of lore and law. Although Bemba sources themselves may point to the importance of a story's message or moral, such a comment is based on the overall effect of a live performance, not just its obvious homiletic qualities. Lutato accordingly notes elements of the Bemba aesthetic, *ubusuma*, which also relate to form and "effect." It is only when all salient aspects are skillfully worked that a tale or, today, a piece of literature may be considered a successful work of art.

The Writer's Language

African authors have been reassessing their own roles vis-à-vis the languages in which they write. One of the earliest to do so was Ousmane Sembène, who, tired of "enriching the French language," chose to make films that would reach his desired audience in Senegalese languages—specifically Wolof and Diolla. In reality, literacy that is functionally greater than being able to read and write one's name is still decades away from a truly representative proportion of African people. The Kenyan writer Ngũgĩ wa Thiong'o discovered, through personal experience, that his many critical essays and speeches in English did not bring down government censure onto his head. However, his involvement with the production and writing of a Gikuyu-language play that had a theme critical of current conditions directly resulted in his imprisonment and the loss of his position as chair of the Department of Literature at the University of Nairobi. Gérard says of this incident:

> As long as Ngũgĩ, or Kibera or the many others who were critical of the corruption and exploitation characteristic of the Kenyatta regime voiced their objections in English novels and plays which can only be understood by a small number of highly educated people, most of whom belong to the privileged class anyway, there was obviously no need to ban them, for as Fibi Muene aptly put it, "if a play is in English or Kiswahili, it leaves out the majority of the people in this country." Conditions become vastly different when a gifted writer manages to phrase his message in the language really spoken by men, so that the majority of the people can grasp what he has to say. (*African Language Literatures* 314)

Conclusion

In most cases, African-language writing was initially sponsored by outside religious or political interests. There was a need at those periods for merging local languages and conceptual frames with the information and concerns being spread by the newer institutions. In almost every case, literature growing out of such conditions began by imitation: Arabic poetic forms, church hymns, allegorical tales inspired by *The Pilgrim's Progress*, hagiographic works, or the recording of texts of traditional narratives and poetry. Over time, themes of immediate relevance inevitably crept into these literatures. Depending on the sociopolitical situation of the languages and governments where these literatures were evolving, experimentation was either encouraged or censured. While Babalola does not suggest a strong degree of colonial or independent government censorship of Yoruba writing, he does lament that the promotion of the language was for some time not all it should have been. In South Africa, and among other colonial-era literatures, Xhosa writing was subject to official control. Before 1990 the most common forms of Black South African literary activity seem to have been urban street theater and poetry published quickly on mimeograph or photocopy machines, or even recited at gatherings and not written down at all. The format of the art work reflects both the immediacy and volatility of the situation as well as the obvious risks taken when "seditious" ideas are committed to paper or print.

A survey made by the Zambian government's Institute for African Studies in 1973 unearthed a revealing statistic. Of the many Zambians polled on their preference of language for broadcasts from Radio Zambia, a large majority stated that if they could not listen to their own language they preferred to hear programming in other Zambian languages, even those they did not understand, rather than in English (Mytton 27–39). Shaaban Robert's comparison of foreign and native languages to bottle feeding and breast feeding may be the ultimate statement on the relevance of African-language literatures and their role in shaping the future of the continent.

Notes

1. I am greatly indebted to several scholars who are working in the field of African-language writing for their help and advice in the preparation of this chapter. David Laitin, at the University of Chicago, provided information on Somali literature; Richard Lepine, at Northwestern University, commented on an earlier draft of the material on Swahili writing; John Chileshe of the University of Zambia, in 1986–87 a visiting Fulbright scholar at the University of Wisconsin, added suggestions and corrections of the entire chapter and on the Bemba material in particular; and Oyekan Owomoyela provided an overall critique of the article as well as specific comments on the Yoruba-language section.

2. In addition to the numerous studies of Ethiopian-language literature, Albert Gérard's *Four African Language Literatures* offers a fairly comprehensive examination, with a broad-ranging bibliography of earlier scholarship as well. See also Gérard, *African Literatures*, and Andrzejewski, Piłaszewicz, and Tyloch.

3. Again, Gérard, *African Language Literatures*, has a valuable bibliography of work on Sierra Leonean and Liberian language writing. Some of the more illuminating studies include Jones, Dalby, and Goody, Cole, and Scribner. Simon Battestini, at Georgetown University, is currently preparing a book-length study of indigenous African writing, including systems that are not specifically syllabic scripts as well as plastic arts used as symbolic systems of communications.

4. Gérard (*African Language Literatures* 173–86) discusses the differences in, say, French and British colonial policies concerning the uses of indigenous languages for education and literary purposes. While I think there was in actuality a more complicated situation (for instance, Ngũgĩ [*Decolonising the Mind*] sees no essential differences in these policies), an exploration of this history is slightly out of the realm of the current examination. Gérard's bibliography for his discussion is an informative one for anyone wanting to explore the question in greater detail.

5. Besides sections on Yoruba writing in Gérard, *African Language Literatures*, and Andrzejewski, Piłaszewicz, and Tyloch, see also Babalola and Gérard; Babalola; and Olatunji.

6. Fagunwa's three successive fiction works are *Igbó Olódùmarè* (1949; The jungle of the almighty), *Ìrèké-oníbùdó* (1949; The camp-commandant's sugarcane), and *Irinkerindo ninu igbo elegbeje* (1954: Wanderings in the forest of innumerable wonders). See also Bamgbose.

7. The king's name is a thinly veiled approximation of that of the Nigerian politician Chief Obafemi Awolowo.

8. A. C. Jordan cites an example where the Xhosa newspaper *Isigidimi* publishes such a protest. The protest, using direct allusive and allegorical references to Tiyo Soga's translation of Bunyan's classic, treats the issue of voting and the dilemma of having such poor candidates to choose from. Jordan's study, cut short by his untimely death, remains one of the more lucid and revealing works on an African-language literature written by a native speaker of that language.

9. See Jordan (100–102) for an example of how literate Xhosa wrote letters to protest a certain newspaper's editorial policies.

10. Scheub makes the same point in a much broader survey ("Review"), claiming that the roots of the novel were indigenous to Africa and owed only a small debt to the coming of Europe.

11. See for instance, the discussion below of Shaaban Robert's reputation as a

nationalist. Also, Ngũgĩ (*Decolonising the Mind*) provides several examples of Gikuyu nationalists writing protest literature during the time of the so-called Mau Mau struggle.

12. David Laitin documents the history of Somali writing and the many political ramifications inherent in the search for an official orthography.

13. Andrzejewski has an extensive bibliography at the end of his article; see in particular Johnson.

14. For a powerful and thought-provoking study of how one colonial power used the Swahili language for its own purposes, see Fabian, and also Whiteley.

15. Shaaban, often seen as the father of modern Swahili writing, held a position in the Language Bureau that paralleled the job performed by Stephen Mpashi as head of the Zambia Publications Bureau after Independence. Mpashi too is the acknowledged father of another African-language literature, Bemba.

16. An extensive discussion in English of Muhando's work may be found in Jesse L. Mollel and Stephen Arnold's "An Introduction to the Drama of Penina Muhando and the Theme of *Wapotovu na kuwarudi* (Deviants and rehabilitation)." See also Mugo.

17. See Roberts for a detailed exposition of Bemba history and their expansion in the northern part of what is now independent Zambia.

18. The translations of Bemba titles are my literal renderings. Both Lutato and Chileshe translate some of the same titles in a more poetic or allusive way. For instance, to suggest the actual proverbial reference that *Uwauma nafyala* makes, Chileshe uses a title taken from a familiar English proverb: "As well be hanged for a sheep as for a lamb." See Chileshe and Lutato.

19. Though Mpashi is seen as someone who wrote down and thereby preserved the "true" Bemba language and body of traditions, he often used borrowed English terms in his urban novels. See Lehmann, Kashoki, and Chileshe. See also Maxwell for his account of how once-fluid cosmological beliefs and ritual practices became formalized and narrowed into a more monotheistic framework when writing was introduced to Bemba society through missionary and colonial intervention.

Works Cited

Andrzejewski, B. W., S. Piłaszewicz, and W. Tyloch, eds. *Literatures in African Languages: Theoretical Issues and Sample Surveys.* Cambridge: Cambridge University Press, 1985.

Babalola, Adeboye. "A Survey of Modern Literature in the Yoruba, Efik, and Hausa Languages." In *Introduction to Nigerian Literature*, edited by Bruce King. New York: Africana, 1972.

Babalola, Adeboye, and A. Gérard. "A Brief Survey of Creative Writing in Yoruba." *Review of National Literatures* 14, no. 2 (1971): 188–205.

Bamgbose, Ayo. *The Novels of D. O. Fagunwa.* Benin City: Ethiope Press, 1974.

Bertoncini, Elena Zubkova. "An Annotated Bibliography of Swahili Fiction and Drama Published between 1975 and 1984." *Research in African Literatures* 17, nos. 1–2 (1971): 525–62.

Chileshe, John. "Literacy, Literature and Ideological Formation: The Zambian Case." Doctoral thesis, University of Sussex, 1983.

Cosentino, Donald. *Defiant Maids and Stubborn Farmers: Tradition and Invention in Mende Story Performance*. Cambridge: Cambridge University Press, 1982.

Dalby, David. "A Survey of the Indigenous Scripts of Liberia and Sierra Leone: Vai, Loma, Kpelle and Bassa." *African Language Studies* 7 (1981): 3–5.

———, ed. *Language and History in Africa*. New York: Africana, 1970.

Fabian, Johannes. *Language and Colonial Power: The Appropriation of Swahili in the former Belgian Congo, 1880–1938*. Cambridge: Cambridge University Press, 1986.

Fagunwa, D. O. *Ògbójú ode níní igbó irúnmalè*. London: Nelson, 1950. *Forest of a Thousand Daemons: A Hunter's Saga*. Translated by Wole Soyinka. London: Nelson, 1968.

Gérard, Albert. *Four African Literatures: Xhosa, Sotho, Zulu, Amharic*. Berkeley and Los Angeles: University of California Press, 1971.

———. *African Language Literatures: An Introduction to the Literary History of Sub-saharan Africa*. Washington, D.C.: Three Continents Press, 1981.

Goody, Jack, M. Cole, and S. Scribner. "Writing and Formal Operations: A Case Study among the Vai." *Africa* 46, no. 3 (1971): 289–304.

Harries, Lyndon. "Tale from Tanga: A Literary Beginning." *East African Journal* 3, no. 2 (1966): 4–6.

———. "Swahili Literature in the National Context." *Review of National Literatures* 2, no. 2 (1971): 45–50.

Hellier, A. B. "Swahili Prose Literature." *Bantu Studies* 14, no. 1 (1940): 247–57.

Johnson, John W. *Heellooy Heelleellooy: The Development of the Genre of the Heello in Modern Somali Poetry*. Bloomington: Indiana University Press, 1974.

Jones, Eldred D. "The Potentialities of Krio as a Literary Language." *Sierra Leone Studies* 9 (1957): 40–48.

Jordan, A. C. *Towards an African Literature: The Emergence of Literary Form in Xhosa*. Berkeley and Los Angeles: University of California Press, 1973.

Kashoki, Mubanga E. "Town Bemba: A Sketch of Its Main Characteristics." *African Social Research* 13 (1972): 161–86.

Kunene, Daniel P. "African Vernacular Writing: An Essay in Self-Devaluation." *African Social Research* 9 (1970): 639–59.

———. "Problems in Creative Writing: The Example of Southern Africa." *Review of National Literatures* 2, no. 2 (1971): 81–103.

———. "An Analysis of Stephen Mpashi's *Uwauma nafyala*." In *Neo-African Literature and Culture: Essays in Memory of Janheinz Jahn*, edited by Bernth Lindfors and Ulla Schild. Wiesbaden: B. Heymann, 1976.

Laitin, David. *Politics, Language, and Thought: The Somali Experience*. Chicago: University of Chicago Press, 1977.

Lehman, Dorothea. *Loanwords in S. A. Mpashi's Bemba Story "Uwakwensho bushiku."* University of Zambia, Institute for Social Research Bulletin, no. 4 (Lusaka, 1969).

Lutato, Kalunga S. "The Influence of Oral Narrative Tradition on the Novels of Stephen A. Mpashi." Ph.D. diss., University of Wisconsin, 1980.

Maxwell, Kevin B. *Bemba Myth and Ritual*. New York: Peter Lang, 1985.

Mollel, Jesse L., and Stephen Arnold. "An Introduction to the Drama of Penina Muhando and the Theme of *Wapotovu na kuwarudi* (Deviants and rehabilitation)." *Greenfield Review* 8, nos. 1–2 (1980): 188–202.

Mpashi, Stephen Andrea. *Cekesoni aingila ubusoja* [Jackson becomes a soldier]. Cape Town: Oxford University Press, 1950.

———. *Uwakwensho bushiku* [He who hurried you through the night]. Cape Town: Oxford University Press, 1951; 1955.

———. *Uwauma nafyala* [He who beats his mother-in-law]. Lusaka: Publication Bureau, 1955.

Mugo, Micere G. "Gerishon Ngugi, Peninah [*sic*] Muhando and Ebrahim Hussein: Plays in Swahili." *African Literature Today* 8 (1976): 137–41.

Mytton, Graham. *Listening, Looking and Learning: Report on a National Media Survey in Zambia, 1970–73*. Lusaka, Zambia: Institute for African Studies, 1974.

Ngũgĩ wa Thiong'o. *Writers in Politics*. London: Heinemann Educational Books, 1981.

———. *Decolonising the Mind*. London: Heinemann Educational Books, 1986.

Okpewho, Isidore. *Myth in Africa*. Cambridge: Cambridge University Press, 1983.

Olatunji, Olatunde. "Religion in Literature: The Christianity of J. S. Sowande (Sobo Arobiodu)." *Orita* 7 (Ibadan, 1974): 3–21.

———. *Adebayo Faleti: A Study of His Poems, 1954–1964*. Ibadan, Nigeria: Heinemann Educational Books, 1982.

———. *Features of Yoruba Oral Poetry*. Ibadan, Nigeria: Ibadan University Press, 1984.

Roberts, Andrew. *A History of the Bemba*. Madison: University of Wisconsin Press, 1973.

Samatar, Said S. *Oral Poetry and Somali Nationalism: The Case of Sayyid Mahammad 'Abdille Hasan*. Cambridge: Cambridge University Press, 1982.

Scheub, Harold. "A Review of African Oral Traditions and Literature." *African Studies Review* 28, nos. 2–3 (1985): 1–72.

Whiteley, Wilfred. *Swahili: The Rise of a National Language*. London: Methuen, 1969.

11

African Women Writers:

Toward a Literary History

C A R O L E   B O Y C E   D A V I E S   A N D

E L A I N E   S A V O R Y   F I D O

African Women Writers and the African Literary Canon

African women writers[1] engage in several different discourses, which give voice to their many realities. They are conscious of neocolonialism and are interested in fighting through their work for a greater genuine independence for Africa. They are critical of the exploitation of women. African women explore what is useful and what is dangerous to them as women in traditional cultures. At the same time, they examine which influences from the West (or from countries such as the former Soviet Union and Japan) are positive or negative in their environment. They write of realities in ways male African writers do not. They also pay particular attention to the insider-outsider dichotomy, because they are often aware of participating in their societies but not always being part of the contemporary political decision-making structures. Because of these varied challenges, African women writers bring specific perspectives to the evaluation of their societies. They become not just artists but also pathfinders for new relations between men, women, and children.

The study of the work of African women writers is an engaging experience, not only for of all of the above reasons, but also because there now exists a rich opportunity for critics in the field of African literature to reevaluate, in the light of the special contributions of women writers, all earlier critical canons, which heretofore have been the work of male critics evaluating male writers. The relative scarcity of women writers in the African literary canon may be partly explained by the opposition of colonial education, family, and gender policies to women's engaging in pursuits apart from domestic ones. After colonial education established the literary arts in general, a few women, through migration, or family privilege, or exceptional brilliance and determination, or strong support from others, were able to publish their writing. When women did begin to write in Western languages, however, more commonly during the late colonial period, their work was not recognized like that of male African writers of the same generation (with the exception of Nadine Gordimer, who has a large audience outside Africa).

O. R. Dathorne includes a few references to women writers in his *African Literature* (1976), but most other works do not. Course syllabi, textbooks, and anthologies of African literature have been dominated by male writers. The situation is changing gradually now, but an acceptance of different conceptions of what African writing is and how it should be approached is needed to comprehend some of the experiments that women writers are making. The tendency of literary critics in each generation to establish certain expectations, based on the career patterns of the dominant group of writers (i.e., male writers) with which they deal, requires that we alter these assumptions for women writers, whose career patterns are different.

Some of the domestic pressures on women writers easily explain gaps in writing. Women may stop writing because their male relatives feel they are being immoral or disloyal by telling too much about issues considered private. Husbands have been known to threaten to take actions such as leaving the marriage or establishing other relationships if their wives do not stop writing. Buchi Emecheta writes about her husband's destruction of her manuscript in her autobiographical *Second-Class Citizen* (1975). Also, women writers must often, if free from marital pressures, function as mothers and breadwinners in a world where career levels are based on work expectations of men who are fully supported in domestic arrangements by their womenfolk. Relatives of African women writers may feel that traditional hospitality must be extended at all times to them, because they assume that the woman writer's life is primarily centered in domestic functions. Domestic tasks remain for most women a tremendous user of time. Much depends on the ability of the women to pursue self-set goals rather than be endlessly at the service of their families.[2]

Beyond the personal, women still have relatively less access to publishers than do men. Many African women writers speak of manuscripts that are ignored for years by male editors and reviewers. Criticism of African women writers must therefore be responsive to the politics of their individual lives.[3] A critic must engage not only with the hermeneutic concerns but with all the peripheral issues that relate to the politics of writing and publishing as well.

African Women and Oral Literature

The question of whether constraints on the development of female talents with language have always existed is an area for much-needed research.[4] Women told tales or sang songs to children in the family compound, and excellent women narrators were appreciated by the family and community. Several African societies have female oral artists who travel beyond the confines of their villages, but the common misconception is that the "professional" oral performer or *griot* is male. Ruth Finnegan makes the distinction that some genres are the specific preserve of men, others of women, but that there is variation in specialization throughout the continent:

> Certain kinds of poetry are typically delivered or sung by women (particularly dirges, lullabies, making verses or songs to accompany women's ceremonies or work), and each culture is likely to have certain genres considered especially suitable for women. However, references to men seem to occur even more often, and, with a few striking exceptions, men rather than women tend to be the bearers of the poetic tradition. (98)

Finnegan suggests that gender conventions and specializations vary from culture to culture, but that by and large, "serious tales" like myths and oral history tend to be the preserve of men (375–76). The image of the *griot* is always male.

Traditional scholarship on oral literature has also tended to focus on male oral artists. At a 1977 University of Ibadan conference on African oral poetry, the bulk of the papers showed an overriding assumption that oral artists are male. Only one paper, that of G. G. Darah on Urhobo dance songs, made references to women's participation in communal culture. This imbalance suggests that major research is necessary to uncover the extent of women's creativity in orature. One breakthrough in this respect is Harold Scheub's collection *African Oral Narratives, Proverbs, Riddles, Poetry, and Song,* which has a large concentration of female contributors. Scheub suggests this female emphasis also in his preface, where he quotes the Xhosa performer Nongenile Masithathu Zenani on the art of composing: "and our grandmothers said that oral narrative had been created years before by their grandmothers" (vii).

A number of recent studies have begun to establish concern for the orature of women in different parts of Africa. Enoch T. Mvula, in "Tumbuka Pounding Songs in the Management of Familial Conflicts," reveals how women use poetic license and a number of other "veiling devices" to comment publicly on issues that affect them and that propriety dictates they should keep private. Mvula concludes that "by singing about their familial problems, the women construct and reconstruct their personal histories, as well as reflect on the values and attitudes of the society" (113). Beverly Mack's work on Hausa women's oral lore demonstrates "how traditional women, using traditional literary art forms, advocate women's independence through the pursuit of both new and customary professions" (15–16). The study also shows how Hausa women's songs emphasize the role of choice in women's lives and speak of women's need for solidarity. Thomas Hale's *Scribe, Griot, and Novelist: Narrative Interpreters of the Songhay Empire* (1990) has some work on *griottes,* or female keepers of the Songhay-Zarma oral tradition.

Much of the work available on women's oral literature is still in doctoral dissertations or is unavailable in the West. A doctoral dissertation by Pauline Nalova Lyonga, "Umahiri: A Feminist Approach to African Literature" (1985), demonstrates a thematic continuity between African women's oral lore and written literature. May Balisidya's "Language Planning and Oral Creativity" (1988) is another important work. Some studies have been done in East Africa by Penina Muhando and published in Swahili. Micere Mugo's work in Zimbabwe on oral literature and her article on "Orature Aesthetics" (1987) have as well to be noted. One recognized extended study of Yoruba women's orature is Karin Barber's *I Could Speak until Tomorrow: Oriki, Women, and the Past in a Yoruba Town* (1991).

According to Mamadou Diawara in "Women, Servitude and History: The Oral Historical Traditions of Women of Servile Conditions in the Kingdom of Jaara (Mali) from the Fifteenth to the Mid-Nineteenth Century" (in Barber and Farias), the literature concerning African women as a source for the history of their society is meager in the extreme. Diawara contends that this paucity has not been significantly improved, the rise in women's studies notwithstanding, because African studies continues to be "profoundly marked by the male point of view," with the result that women frequently are not cited when they supply information or are not interviewed at all. Studies such as Diawara's, however, reveal that in many cultures, women are the experts in oral traditions and are central in the transmission of group ideology, values, history, and literature. Further, there is often a female mode in the transmission of narrative that Western or male researchers would never find out. Joan Russell, for example, in "Women's Narration: Performance and the Marking of a Verbal Aspect," looks at ways in which women present their narratives.

The above survey points only in the very barest of ways to the substantial work in women's oral literatures still unknown or undone. In the West, one can know these stories only in translation or transmission to print. Martha Mvungi, for example, has a story, "Mwipenza the Killer," which she heard from her mother, published in Charlotte Bruner's *Unwinding Threads* (1983), an anthology that has been instrumental in bringing many women's work to the reading public. As a teacher, for example, Mvungi has collected and recorded oral narratives from older people and has published *Three Solid Stones* (1975), comprising twelve folk narratives from Tanzania. Writers such as Penina Muhanda Mlama (1991) have worked oral narratives into dramatic presentations. Moreover, a number of oral personal-experience narratives or life stories have been collected and are being transmitted in print form, with all the implications of oral-written literary conversions applicable. This reveals the whole area of orature and writing as a rich one for literary examination. It allows us, as well, given the contemporary work on speech act and discourse theory, to move from a specifically reductive construction of "women's writing" to women's oral and written discourses.

Obviously, oral art is especially nourished by a strong cultural and spiritual environment that can relate to the past. It requires also a sense of community and time to experience it. Urban and oppressed conditions alienate women from traditional orature as much as they interfere with other kinds of creativity. As one South African woman says in the anthology *Lip:*

> I get up every day at 4:30, and I only get home about 6:15 P.M. By then my daughter has already made the fire. But I do the cooking. After supper we wash ourselves and go to bed. I read the paper when I go to bed—not novels and things. I usually have a headache and I am too tired. (Brown, Hofmeyr, and Rosenberg 95)

But as the following pages demonstrate, that creativity flourishes nevertheless and is expressed through accessible media.

African Women Writers: Shaping Forces

GENERATIONAL AND CLASS DIFFERENCES

As in the case of other writers in the continent, African women writers have to be seen partly in terms of the changing concerns of and changing societal pressures on different generations. One early woman writer who offered critiques of the colonial situation was Adelaide Casely-Hayford (1868–1959). Of Fanti and British parentage, Casely-Hayford was born in Sierra Leone, educated in England and Germany, and married to the well-known lawyer Joseph Casely-Hayford. The combination of her privileged social status, mixed race, and international travel gave her special perspectives on her society. Her story "Mista Courifer" (1961; reprinted in Bruner 8–16) concentrates on the problem of the collision between African and Western elements of culture in a person's life, a theme that was to become familiar in later African writing. The story's central character rejects his father's desire that he project a British exterior and instead favors African dress. He also, importantly, rejects expectations of wifely subservience. His unusual encouragement of a woman's autonomy is matched by his friendly and affectionate relations with his sister. The story, while exploring aspects of mediation between African and European customs, is definitely written with a woman's consciousness.

Mabel Dove Danquah (b. 1910 in the Gold Coast [now Ghana]) presents polygamy from an amusing though distinctly critical female point of view in "Anticipation" (1947; reprinted in Bruner 3–7). The story shows a chief remarrying a wife (and paying a second bride price) because his having so many other wives has confused him and caused him to forget about having married her before. Danquah's vision here is opposed to that part of her tradition that is male and exploitative.

The earliest writings of a people in the process of self-identification are often autobiographical in form. By such means people write themselves into history, as in the narratives of enslaved Africans, which began the African-

American literary tradition. Adelaide Casely-Hayford's "Reminiscences" (in Dathorne and Feuser 131–38), taken from material she used for her *Memoirs*, compiled at the age of ninety-one, relate how as a young schoolteacher Casely-Hayford began to develop views on the role and behavior of women in modern African societies—for example, that African women should wear traditional dress and not copy European fashions.[5] Like Casely-Hayford, Noni Jabavu (b. 1919), the daughter of Professor D. D. T. Jabavu and granddaughter of the journalist, teacher, and editor John Tengo Jabavu, looked back on her life in the earlier part of the century in *The Ochre People* (1963), which gives us a strong impression of her attachment to her family, describing her patriarchal father, who holds court while female servants bustle about.

In neither fiction nor memoir did these writers discuss women's fruition as such. Nonetheless, their very existence as women writers, necessarily focused on what they saw as major issues of their day (cultural change, inequality, African identity), signals the beginning of a tradition of writing in European languages that continues today.

During the period 1900–1950 a number of women writers, working mainly in African languages, emerged. As early as 1913 or 1914, Lillith Kakaza (circa 1885–1950) wrote and published a short novelette and a long piece of fiction in Xhosa. Victoria Swaartbooi also wrote Xhosa fiction in the 1930s. Violet Dube published a volume of Zulu short stories in 1935 and a novel in 1936. The life histories of these women suggest that they were part of intellectual writing communities.[6]

Poetry by African women was rarely included in early African poetry anthologies. Langston Hughes was an exceptional editor in this respect, including several women in *Poems from Black Africa* (1963).[7] Martin Banham's early anthology of Nigerian student verse (1959) includes one poem by a woman, Minja Kariba, whose subsequent poetry has been anthologized in various volumes (see Bankier and Lashgari). In the 1960s a few other woman poets, such as Noemia de Souza, Maria Manuela Margerido, and Efua Sutherland, began to be recognized.

Similarly, the 1960s saw the emergence of fiction writers such as Grace Ogot (b. Kenya, 1930). A number of the women writing in Kenya seem like Ogot (b. Kenya, 1930). A number of the women writing in Kenya seem, like woman Rebeka Njau (b. 1932) has had a distinguished career as headmistress of the Nairobi Girls School from 1964. Flora Nwapa (b. Nigeria, 1931) is another of this generation, which is chronologically the same as the generation of Soyinka, Achebe, Ngũgĩ, and others.

The writing of women of this generation, which was educated in colonial schools and came to maturity at about the time of Independence and early post-Independence in their various countries, has received much less attention than that of men. Although Sutherland's *Edufa* (1967) and Ogot's *The Promised Land* (1966) and *Land without Thunder* (1968) were clearly important, their work never received proper critical attention in comparison to the attention give to male writers of comparable achievement. Although the publication in 1962 and 1963, respectively, of Noni Jabavu's *Drawn in Color: African Contrasts* and *The Ochre People: Scenes from a South African Life*, when their author was then in her midforties and previously unpublished, might be taken to signal the beginning of a more receptive literary climate for women's work than had existed before, recognition of Jabavu's work did not come until the 1980s.

Only since the 1970s has the writing of African women really come into its own and found acceptance. Writers such as Ama Ata Aidoo, Buchi Emecheta, Bessie Head, Lauretta Ngcobo, Mariama Bâ, Miriam Tlali, Nafissatou Diallo, and Aminata Sow Fall have received attention lately partly because of the awareness raised by the women's movement, which has also been an important stimulus in getting the writing done. Mariama Bâ (b. Senegal, 1929) did not emerge until after her strong involvement with the feminist movement there. Her first novel, *Une si longue lettre* (1980; *So Long a Letter*, 1981), appeared after she was fifty. Each year, new voices are added (too slowly, it still seems), but they arrive to critical encouragement from a growing body of women critics, many of whom write themselves. Tsitsi Dangarembga, the author of *Nervous Conditions* (1988), began her publishing career in her twenties. African-language writing by women is also continuing to develop. Penina Muhando (or Penina Mlama) is a Tanzanian dramatist whose work in Swahili, Tanzania's national language, has become well known inside her own country and enjoys a growing reputation outside (see Balisidya 15–19). Her keynote speech at the 1990 African Literature Association annual conference identified many issues related to audience, orality, literacy, and writing in Africa.

The conditions that encourage writing by African women are complex and various. In some cases, as with Ama Ata Aidoo, a family with respect for education and the written word stimulates a daughter's achievements. Publication often depends on catching a publisher's notice. Faith in the power of literature is also important. Buchi Emecheta, with an experience of urban poverty in Britain, believed strongly in education and in the power of the written word to help her change her condition, and that belief enabled her to study successfully and to write, whereas other women in her situation might have been silenced by their difficulties.

Emecheta's story brings us to the question of class contexts in women's writing. Although some significant women writers in Africa are centrally concerned with peasant or working-class women, Micere Mugo has challenged many middle-class women writers for too often portraying these women as victims who lack the enduring, fighting spirit she finds in the true peasant women of Africa. From this kind of debate comes stimulation, freshness, new directions: Flora Nwapa has challenged those younger women (Catherine Acholonu from Nigeria, specifically) who criticize older writers' limitations to pick up their pens and create what they want to see themselves.

One important new development perhaps is that some women writers in

Africa have attempted to establish publishing enterprises. Flora Nwapa and Buchi Emecheta have both established presses (Tana and Ogwugwu Afor, respectively). But problems of distribution and foreign exchange hamper their full development as flourishing businesses. One hopes that this trend will allow other women writers to have a better chance to become published by presses that understand their experiences and the context of their writing.

REGIONAL, NATIONAL, AND ETHNIC INFLUENCES

Varying circumstances within different regions of Africa dispose women to differing priorities in their writing. Southern African women have struggled most urgently against racial oppression—not only Black writers such as Amelia House, Miriam Tlali, Fatima Dike, and Lauretta Ngcobo, but also white writers such as Nadine Gordimer and the white contributors to *Lip: From Southern African Women*.[8] Black women in South Africa must fight for the freedom to live and develop so that their literary creativity can flourish (see Davies, "Finding Some Space"). Fatima Dike, the South African dramatist, illustrates the possibility of turning the trauma of living through violence and racism into fierce, committed theater. Lauretta Ngcobo confesses that her novel *Cross of Gold* (1981) turns away from its initial focus on a woman and becomes a man's story, because she finds it difficult to focus only on women's issues and to develop sustained and strong women characters. Bessie Head, on the other hand, is equally concerned with race and gender in *A Question of Power* (1947). For some women in South Africa, where oppression is multiple, writing becomes an act of courage in adverse circumstances. Gcina Mhlope, an actress, poet, and short story writer, lives in a women's hostel in Johannesburg, where she cannot write late in the night because the hostel rises early, at 4 A.M. During weekends, when other women are out seeing boyfriends, she writes. Her attitude toward the deprivations, loneliness, and tension of living in such a situation is "You just have to cope" (8).

Similarly, women elsewhere in Africa find common ground in shared regional, linguistic, or religious experiences. In West Africa, for example, a central concern of women writers is the relation of tradition to Western cultural influences (Christianity, capitalism, urbanization). Women writers from Islamic cultures often question the role and place of women there, and to do so they must also recognize that to attack the culture on behalf of women may be seen as a threat to the entire social fabric. Their interest must therefore often balance the need for reform in relation to women with a need to protect their world against dissolution in the face of pressures from the West or from modernization. Alifa Rifaat's *Distant View of a Minaret* (1983) is powerful precisely because it gives us this balancing, a vision of a dissident womanhood within Islam that nevertheless intends to remain within that culture. Similarly, Zaynab Alkali's *The Stillborn* (1984; see Acholonu 1986) is a Nigerian woman's portrait of Muslim society from the perspective of a woman seeking personal development. Senegalese and Ivorian writers such as Bâ, Sow Fall, Diallo, and Adiaffi have expressed overwhelming concern with male prerogatives and the excesses of polygamy within the socially conscious literary and film tradition headed by Ousmane Sembène.

Certain national, ethnic, regional, and historical influences encourage women to write, while others do not. Today, Igbo women writers such as Nwapa, Udensi, Ulasi, Emecheta, Okoye, Onwueme, and Acholonu form a significant group, as do male Igbo writers (and there is a predominance of fiction writers in both groups). *Nigerian Female Writers: A Critical Perspective*, edited by Henrietta Otukunefor and Obiageli Nwodo (1989), testifies to Nigeria's current predominance. At an earlier period, most well-known women writers seem to have come from Ghana or Sierra Leone. Igbo culture may have particular elements within it, such as a tradition of storytelling and a respect for language skills, that predispose it to the development of literary arts, but then so do other ethnic groups. Nowhere is there a correlation between population size and the number of writers. For instance, the population of the Muslim north of Nigeria, for reasons that are primarily cultural, has produced the fewest writers. Precolonial Nigeria's strong oral literary traditions, which accorded respect to wordplay and to the verbal artist, has led to a flourishing written literary culture in modern times. Writing is more likely to be a chosen profession in cultures where it is respected and where creativity in writing is seen as an important extension of oral art. Many of the Arabic cultures, for example, have ancient traditions of poetry and prose fiction, but the woman's voice is often not heard.

Finally, a woman's perception of her culture can be markedly different from a male vision of it. In 1966 both Flora Nwapa's *Efuru* and Elechi Amadi's *The Concubine* were published. Whereas the former presents a water maid as a model for a woman trying to find a place for herself within traditional society as a single woman without children, the latter presents a water spirit incarnated as woman who, as the possession of a vengeful Sea King who destroys her happiness, becomes a destructive agent in the lives of men who love her without realizing what she truly is (Banyiwa-Horne 1986).

African Women's Prose

Storytelling is in many African societies a woman's genre, often used to instill morality in the young and for a variety of other aesthetic and functional reasons. Beginning writers, drawing on a tradition of women narrating, can therefore cross over from oral to written literature fairly easily. Flora Nwapa says the story of *Efuru* came to her while she was driving to her brother's house and that she wrote the novel within weeks.[9]

But the transition is not always easy. For one thing, writing in European languages can create difficulties in expression for writers whose mother tongues are African languages. Moreover, criticism of novels and stories still tends to be drawn from criteria that are conceptually European in origin as well as male-orientated. Critics must be careful not to imprison experimental new forms in old critical compartments out of sheer ignorance.

AUTOBIOGRAPHY

Women who want to be writers tend to undergo a period of self-examination, and autobiography thus becomes an important form for them. African women write autobiography in different tones, from the distanced, socio-cultural (Joyce Sikakane's *A Window on Soweto* [1977] and Noni Jabavu's *The Ochre People*) to the cautiously personal (Nafissatou Diallo's *A Dakar Childhood* [1975]) and the frankly personal, thinly disguised as fiction (Buchi Emecheta's *Second Class Citizen* [1975] and *In the Ditch* [1972]) (see Davies, "Private Selves"). Autobiography is of course a structured mode of writing, and related to fiction in the sense that it constructs the self as part of an integrated discourse. But it is not the same as autobiographical fiction, the difference being a question of the degree to which a piece of writing consciously embraces conventions of fiction as opposed to those of autobiography. The narrative voice may or may not admit to the material's auto-biographical nature. Bessie Head's novel *A Question of Power* (1977) is an example of the latter. It includes several important details that appear in her "Biographical Notes: A Search for Historical Continuity" (1982).

Although autobiography deals with personal experience, and although African women are clearly drawn to attempt autobiography, self-revelation may offend the strong sense of decorum and propriety with respect to the family that suffuses African life. Miriam Tlali's clearly autobiographical novel *Muriel at Metropolitan* (1975), for example, focuses on the world of work, on race issues in South Africa, and not on personal intimate revelation. (It was also heavily censored in South Africa, with several chapters deleted). In this hesitancy about baring the self, which is clearly present in many auto-biographical works, Buchi Emecheta is a notable exception, though she creates some distance from her personal experience in her first two novels by using a third-person narrative voice and by creating a separate persona, Adah, as the central character. Both works have been highly attacked for their frank criticism of Igbo customs relating to women. Chikewenye Ogun-yemi has said of Emecheta's *Second Class Citizen* that it is "aesthetically unsatisfying to a reader who comes from a culture where it is unethical to reveal the unpleasant details of a martial breakdown" (9).

But Ama Ata Aidoo has spoken about the emotional cost of trying to be honest:

> Most certainly my trials as a woman writer are heavier and more painful than any I have to go through as a university teacher. . . . You feel awful for seeing the situation the way you do, and terrible when you try to speak about it. . . . Yet you have to speak out, since your pain is also real, and in fact the wound bleeds more profusely when you are upset by people you care for, those you respect. (Aidoo 1984, 262)

Such conflicts are bound to arise when a writer's perception of "herstory" comes into opposition with protective nationalism or racial pride. Emecheta speaks of this problem:

> There are many who think I exaggerated in *Second Class Citizen*, that I distorted reality. But the cruelty with which I was treated by both my husband and by English society is truthfully rendered in the book. *Reality appears unbelievable the moment other people see it on paper.* My husband wasn't really a bad guy, but he wasn't able to accept an independent woman. My writing began to develop only after I had left him. As I wrote in my book, he actually destroyed my first efforts to put my experiences on paper, my first attempt to stake out my terrain. ("It's Me" 4, our italics)

It is no doubt the permanence of "putting it on paper," as well as the understandable protectiveness of a people toward a culture that has been distorted by Europeans, that causes African women writers to shy away from explicit and intimate details of personal oppression. But for Emecheta, as for many other writers who use personal experience in their creative work, it is the pain involved in telling the story, in reexperiencing it, that prompts the writing. The act of writing becomes a cathartic response, allowing what happened to be understood, to make sense. Emecheta needs to tell her readers what it is like to grow up female in a society that favors boys, and also of the struggle to make her personal choices, or of the husband who failed her: all of this serves to prepare us for the account of her eventual triumph over adversity. In American society, the confessional aspect of this kind of writing has been much more acceptable. Interestingly, Emecheta's equal openness about race and class oppression in English society has provoked little comment in England.

In this light, it is understandable why Noni Jabavu's *Drawn in Color* and *The Ochre People* are more travelogue than autobiography. On only a few occasions—in *Drawn in Color,* for instance, only when the writer leaves the family and is journeying on her own—is the inner self revealed in such experiences as her confrontation with a Boer immigration officer. Most of the revelations of private life are not of the author, however, but of a sister who is experiencing a bad marriage in Uganda. Much like Emecheta, who has been accused of betraying Africa by writing the kind of criticisms of African society that ignorant and racist Europeans want to read, Jabavu devotes large chunks of her narrative to commentary on what she sees as the unsavory lifestyles of the Ugandans, focusing on the issue of male privilege and concomitant loss of female self-esteem. Through all of this, Jabavu's personal life is never revealed. *The Ochre People* is another excursion into the culture and history of three geographical regions of South Africa—Middledrift, Confluence Farm, and Johannesburg—seen through the eyes of Jabavu's family. Her discussion of Aunt Daisy, "Big Mother," is the only telling of a woman's story, although there are brief vignettes on other women. The work juxtaposes family history and cultural history with the nascent system of apartheid.

For those who find personal detail irrelevant or even embarrassing or dangerous, individual stories are less important than the story of the group. An alternative approach is offered by Ellen Kuzwayo's *Call Me Woman* (1985), which provides an important model of group and personal life co-constructed; i.e., she tells her own story, but toward the end of it she includes references to other women's lives, seeming to emphasize the representative nature of her individual experience. Women enjoy telling their life stories, and several oral autobiographical narratives have been subsequently transcribed into print; among them are Iris Andreski's *Old Wives Tales: Life Stories of African Women* (1970), June Goodwin's *Cry Amandla: South African Women and the Question of Power* (1984), and "Going Up the Mountain" by Motlalepula Chabaku in *Sisterhood Is Global* (1984). The "life story" genre may become an important aspect of an African woman's aesthetic in circumstances where defending a culture is not an issue.

Between Emecheta's confessional style and Jabavu's sociocultural style is the sort of narrative found in Nafissatou Diallo's *A Dakar Childhood*, which centers on a Muslim family. The story is about the love between the small girl and her father and grandmother, and even where conflict arises (as when the father and grandmother confront each other over the head of the girl about her education), it is expressed as nothing more serious than the natural ups and downs of a happy and united family. Perhaps, as Diallo says within the fiction itself, the most important aspect of the story is the lifting of the Muslim "taboos of silence" about familial emotions—a brave thing to attempt.

A similar undertaking is Charity Waciuma's *Daughter of Mumbi* (1969), in which a surface text on Gikuyu culture and traditions clearly submerges a more personal text on the exploitation of women. Another is *Le baobab fou* (1982; The crazy baobab) by Ken Bugul (a pen name for Marietou Mbaye, a Senegalese sociologist). Bugul's novel—a kind of "fictional biography" that some critics say is autobiographical—deals with the story of a child who, alienated at home because of the circumstances of her birth and subsequent abandonment, becomes even more alienated through French colonial education. She travels to Europe and through a series of sexual and other misadventures, including a devastating abortion and drug addiction, loses touch with reality and identifies with the only thing that gave her stability at home, the baobab tree. Sekai Nzenza's *Zimbabwean Woman: My Own Story* (1988), by contrast, offers a specific grounding in a cultural context of women as bearers of tradition. Tainted by negative colonial values, though, she learns to hate herself and her blackness. Nevertheless, through the telling of her life she reconstructs herself with dignity.

A great deal of life writing is taking place, from the many collections of life stories to the controversial *Poppie Nongena: One Woman's Struggle against Apartheid* (1990). The life story, lived or completely fictional, is an important strand of African women's writing, crossing the generic boundaries of the novel and autobiography. Autobiographical narratives are cumulatively exposing their readers to the politics of African women's lives. Their importance lies not only in the vital information they provide but also in the formal shapes and thematic concerns they have contributed to African women's writing. Those themes include the construction of gender roles, marriage, family, tradition, the education of a girl to be a woman, and social power relations.

GENRE-CROSSING NARRATIVES AND THE NOVEL

In a sense, the epistolary novel, an eighteenth-century genre, is the most convenient form for sharing a personal story. This form has been popularized in the United States by Alice Walker's *The Color Purple* (1982). Senegalese writer Mariama Bâ's novel *Une si longue lettre* (1980; *So Long a Letter*, 1981) is in the form of an extended letter, written by Ramatoulaye to her friend Aissatou. Letter writing functions as a catharsis for Ramatoulaye, who can reveal all the hurt and joy she experienced throughout the various phases of her growing from girlhood to womanhood, and the many steps along the way that both she and Aissatou took together as girls and women. Because one expects personal documents such as letters to friends to be kept in strict confidence, the reader has a sense of eavesdropping on the narrator. The same device allows the narrator to bare herself completely, in the guise of sharing her secrets only with the one designated for hearing them. The letter novel, with its air of confidentiality, then becomes a truly intimate medium for the woman who wants to tell the story of her inner life.[10] The epistolary novel of women confiding in each other, like the novel in the form of diary entries, can thus be a more personal medium than autobiography, which assumes a public audience, and may therefore be particularly suited to the African woman writer who wants to adjust to revelation through the written word.

For some African women writers, the epistolary novel and other confessional genres, surprisingly, have antecedents from within Islamic culture, despite Muslim restrictions on public speech for women. Mbye Cham locates Mariama Bâ's approach within the Islamic custom of *mirasse*, which allows an Islamic widow to divest herself publicly of the gains and losses of the marriage.

The letter, the diary, and the life story—all shades of the same confessional mode—connect in Lauretta Ngcobo's *Cross of Gold*. In the first section of the novel, the central character, Sindiswe, tells her son:

> *I cannot now tell you the long story,* but I have some of my life stored away for you in my case. It is a strange story, my child. But from here, when all is over, you will go to Sharpeville, Number 20, Tema Street, where you will find a good friend of mine. . . . *She knows the whole story.* (9; our italics)

At the friend's house the son is given Sindiswe's diary, which contains her story and which charts her awakening into the consciousness of her part in the freeing of her people.

Ama Ata Aidoo, in *Our Sister Killjoy* (1977), experiments with a number of forms: poetry, prose, brief journalistic entries, anecdotes, and the letter. The final section of the book, "A Love Letter," is written to a male friend. It is not a love letter in traditional terms but rather an excursion into a number of issues—African and European slavery, African women's traditional assertiveness, the reality of loneliness in Western culture, motherhood, exile, male-female relationships—many of which she treats thematically in the rest of the novel. Of relevance to our discussion is Sissie's use of the letter, which she writes on her airplane flight home, as a purgation. Her decision not to mail the letter coincides with her looking out the window and realizing that she is in Africa. Realizing that she has been writing the letter throughout the flight and that it is "deservedly long," "too long," she questions sending it. More importantly, "*Once written it was written.* She had taken some of the pain away and she was glad. There was no need to mail it" (133; our italics).[11] The writing of the letter becomes a ritual of release, self-sufficient, coming out of the need to communicate.

Writing a novel is a difficult and painstaking undertaking; its sheer length requires not only skill but also time and space. Yet African women writers, despite their frustrations in achieving their work, have become increasingly proficient in full-length fiction. Many African women write about social and political issues, and about women's domestic and personal lives. Being a woman often involves being both emotional and analytical, physical and intellectual, and this duality comes across in the way African women write about the experience. Bessie Head's novel *A Question of Power* is a brilliant exposition of a disturbed consciousness and of a society in deep trouble. Many readers find it difficult, but its complexity comes not only from intellectuality but also from the intense emotional process that complicates the narrative form and meaning.[12] Flora Nwapa's *Efuru* tells the central character's story through details of her personal relations, motherhood, bereavements, business ventures—in short, from a whole life, private and public. In *So Long a Letter*, feelings shape the texture and form of the letter writing: "My heart rejoices each time a woman emerges from the shadows. I know the field of our gains is unstable, the retention of conquests difficult" (56).

Ramatoulaye's conflicts are characteristic of the conflicts expressed in plot and characters in many novels by African women, and they may be summed up as "a woman is often divided against herself: she loves to serve her family and society but often finds that her service denies her basic humanity as much as it supports and develops it." The hero (or anti-hero) in, for example, *A Question of Power*, or *So Long a Letter*, or Nwapa's novel *One Is Enough* (1981) is not sure of her choices, or of her self, but painfully aware of her restrictions and contradictions. Her uncertainty often comes across in the writing. In *One Is Enough* Amaka, the heroine, pours out questions: Is childlessness really the end of the world? Is she useless to society if she is not a mother? Is she useless to the world if she is unmarried? Is she going to cope if she leaves her husband? The novel shows Amaka making choices that negate these questions.

Plenty of novels, however, address the woman's condition in a reactionary manner. One of them, *Behind the Clouds* (1980) by Ifeoma Okoye, is an unevenly written saga of a wife who cannot have a child and whose husband has one with someone else. The jealousy described between the women is doubtless a reflection of actual commonplace behavior, but the novelist seems depressingly unaware of better possibilities.

By contrast, in searching for new forms, writers like Head and Bâ are also redefining women's experience, perceiving it from an assertive point of view that promises the chance of improvement in women themselves and in their condition, through change and through resistance to exploitation. Just as we have come to expect the bulk of African literature in modern forms to be anticolonial, radical, and desirous of better social conditions, so we have come to see the best of women's writing as expecting different and more developed relations among women themselves and between women and the rest of society, as well as heralding a more confident sense of self to come from self-examination. For some writers, such as Aminata Sow Fall of Senegal (*Le revenant* [1976; The ghost], *La grève des battu* [1979; *The Beggars' Strike*, 1981], and *L'áppel des arène* [1982; The call of the arena]), social detail is a mainspring of narrative style, for her interest is in the socioeconomic relations at the basis of social order. In illustrating her fictional thesis, she shows both men and women as victims of social collapse and economic privation.

African women writers' development from novel to novel is sometimes impressive, as in the case of Buchi Emecheta's steady growth from autobiographical works to novels proper (*Double Yoke* [1982]) to science fiction and allegory (*The Rape of Shavi* [1983]). *The Family* (1989) moves beyond Emecheta's usual focus on African communities to examine the life of a young woman from Jamaica who makes her home in London. Also, writers of short stories often attempt novels and vice versa. For example, the short story writer Grace Ogot wrote the novel *The Promised Land* (1966), the novelist Flora Nwapa has written short stories, and Bessie Head has written both novels and stories. As with other types of writing, each woman tries to turn the novel into something reflective of her focus on her traditional society or modern condition, and she develops whichever aspects of the genre are most appropriate for her vision of woman. Adaora Lily Ulasi, for example, has concentrated on detective novels such as *Many Thing Begin for Change* (1971). Many African women novelists deliberately keep their focus on personal, emotional, and domestic elements in the lives of women, letting the ideas come through indirect means and not theorizing about women's roles except emotively and generally. It is early yet to draw conclusions about what is happening with the novel as African women develop it as their own, but clearly it is changing as they use it to tell their own stories.

New writers continue to appear. Farida Karodia's *Daughters of Twilight* (1986) deals with a girl growing up in South Africa in the 1950s, the child of an Indian father and a "coloured" mother. Karodia now lives in Canada, where she is a full-time writer. Many people are also excited about Tsitsi Dangarembga's first novel, *Nervous Conditions* (1988), which won the African nomination for the Commonwealth Prize for Fiction. It is a well-crafted novel, told through the eyes of a young girl, Tambudzai, who witnesses as she struggles to go to school the intersection of colonial dominance and entrenched African patriarchal power. Jean-Paul Sartre's quote, "The status of 'native' is a nervous condition," in his introduction to Frantz Fanon's *The Wretched of the Earth* (1966) serves as her epigraph. Her pluralizing of the "condition" directs attention to the "gendered-female native" and the many conditions she confronts in society. A cousin, Nyasha, who is central to the narrative, suffers a nervous breakdown as she holds consciously the problems of oppression. And the entire family and community seem gripped by all these "nervous conditions." It is a worthy accomplishment for a first novel, one that holds the reader's attention from its controversial first line: "I was not sorry when my brother died."

Yet with all the new work being produced, much work by African women writers remains outside the pale of critical examination. Rebeka Njau's *Ripples in the Pool* (1975) deserves much more attention than it has received so far. Also, the work of Miriam Were gets only passing mention in larger studies. And writers such as Werewere Liking, whose works include *La puissance de Um* (1979; Um's power) and *Elle sera de jaspe et de corail* (1983; She will be of jasper and coral), which she calls a *chant-roman*, continue to fall through the cracks in literary scholarship, with some discussion in conferences but few published studies. Werewere Liking is offering some important genre-crossing work and is mounting radical critiques of the social construction of gender.

THE SHORT STORY

Short stories are produced both as collections by writers established in other genres and as separate pieces in journals and magazines. The better-known collections include Grace Ogot's *Land without Thunder* (1968), which came out two years after her novel *The Promised Land;* Ama Ata Aidoo's *No Sweetness Here* (1970); Flora Nwapa's *This Is Lagos and Other Stories* (1971) and *Wives at War* (1980); and Bessie Head's *The Collector of Treasures* (1977). Other writers with individual stories in magazines and journals include Amelia House, Miriam Tlali, Charity Waciuma, Miriam Were, Elvania Zirimu, Martha Mvungi, Mabel Segun, Efua Sutherland, and Catherine Acholonu. Anthologies help to make these pieces less fugitive; an excellent illustration is the fate of Efua Sutherland's anthologized story "New Life at Kyerefaso," which has now become quite well known. Similarly, Frances Ademola's *Reflections* (1962) helped popularize Mabel Segun's works. Charlotte Bruner's anthology *Unwinding Threads* (1983) includes a number of otherwise unavailable stories by several writers and is balanced regionally as well as chronologically. Bruner has Mabel Dove Danquah's "Anticipation," and Adelaide Casely-Hayford's "Mista Courifer" from the early period, as well as pieces by Efua Sutherland, Ama Ata Aidoo, Mariama Bâ, Flora Nwapa, Buchi Emecheta, Martha Mvungi, Charity Waciuma, Grace Ogot, Miriam Tlali, Amelia House, Alifa Rifaat, Fadma Amrouche, and others. But a large anthology devoted to short stories by African women is needed.

A number of South African women have published short stories. Zoe Wicomb's collection of semiautobiographical short stories (which some read as a novel) called *You Can't Get Lost in Cape Town* (1987) deals with life in a South African township, migration to England, and separation and alienation. Gcina Mhlope has written a few autobiographical sketches; "The Toilet" and "It's Quiet Now" were published in *Sometimes When It Rains: Writing by South African Women* and reprinted in *Somehow Tenderness Survives* (1988). Miriam Tlali, one of the most important of the preceding generation of South African women writers, has published *Mhloti* (1984; Teardrops), a collection of travelogues, short stories, interviews, and what she calls "new journalism." Most of these pieces first appeared in *Staffrider*, which was important in providing the avenue for a number of writers to publish their work. A second collection of short stories and articles, *Soweto Stories* (1989), will be published in South Africa as *Mehlala Khatamping (Footsteps in the Quag)*. Cheryl Clayton's *Women and Writing in South Africa: A Critical Anthology* (1989) testifies to the burgeoning of creative work in South Africa and provides a fairly extensive bibliography.

The form of the short story is related to the tradition of the personal anecdote as well as to the traditional folk tale or narrative. Yinka Shoga suggests that the reason African women writers use this form successfully is because of its concentrated nature. Perhaps this quality and its compactness explain its popularity among African women writers. Those writers marry two traditional elements in their stories: female conversational forms and such traditional African story forms as the cautionary tale, the dilemma tale, and the moral fable. But they use these elements often to examine the meaning of highly complex modern life. Ama Ata Aidoo's "In the Cutting of a Drink" (1970) is a moving tale of a brother who is sent to find his sister in the city and discovers that she is a prostitute: it expresses a concern for the plight of the woman in the city coupled with an original perspective on male-female (sister-brother) relations. Aidoo's "Certain Winds from the South" (1970) has her characteristic use of dialogue, a natural quick interchange that creates a sense of character and place, and that derives from her ear for women's talk. She often uses repetition, patterns of formal greeting, and conversational interjections and expressions. Her stories are the more economical for her sensitive use of dialogue to explore the center of relations between people. Similarly, Efua Sutherland uses traditional women's culture to good effect in her stories. Her "New Life at Kyerefaso" opens "Shall we say / Shall we put it this way," and goes on in a traditional manner with the story. It is not surprising that both Aidoo and Sutherland are dramatists, because the skills they display in their stories are also a dramatist's stock in trade. Sutherland's "New Life in Kyerefaso" has a rhythm that recalls alternating stabs and longer rhythms of the drum. Sometimes song is used in Sutherland's story, to amplify the plot and strengthen the theme.

By contrast, Mabel Dove Danquah's "Anticipation" and Adelaide Casely-Hayford's "Mista Courifer" are more of the written mode, with long passages expressed from the viewpoint of a third-person, omniscient narrator. Similarly, Grace Ogot's stories in *Land without Thunder* are told in an authoritative single narrative voice, often woven around a traditional story: "For many years Mboga had beseeched Ramogi, the ancestor of the Luo people to intercede on his behalf for his son." Her stories do not have the performance orientation of the work of Sutherland and Aidoo.

Thematically, a number of writers who are less innovative in the use of traditional forms demonstrate a clear consciousness of women's problems and their resourcefulness and strength. Flora Nwapa's stories are concerned with the problems of women in difficult circumstances in the city or in wartime. In "Daddy, Don't Strike the Match," the apparently bold and protective father kills himself in his laboratory by carelessness, whereas the mother takes the care of the children, thus ensuring their survival. She is the one who maintains the security of the family in difficult and changing circumstances, whereas he is modernistic and irresponsible. In "The Chief's Daughter," an attempt to follow an old Igbo tradition by which a father could keep a daughter with him, single, and adopt her children as his own is foiled by the daughter's desire to marry, and by her elopement. Her education overseas is blamed for her rebellion.

Bessie Head's stories, in *The Collector of Treasures,* show a thematic development from traditional to modern situations and from mythic to realistic treatments. The prose in her stories, as in her novels, is subtle and sometimes difficult. Her feminism is quite clear, though. In "Hunting" the men insist on sex without responsibility and the women are left with the consequences. Tholo, who lacks the surface showiness of some men, treats his woman well, but he is unusual. "Snapshots of a Wedding" shows a young woman modifying her personality to become a respectful wife who respects her people. The title story is set in a prison where a number of women are confined for killing their husbands. Two of them had castrated their husbands. In Kebonye's case, castration was in retaliation for her husband's sexual ill treatment of her and his habit of getting young girls pregnant. The setting of the story is crucial to understanding it: the women are in a cell and share stories as they eat together and offer each other support. Theirs is a female society and a culture subversive toward the male oppressors.

Miriam Tlali's story "Point of No Return" (Bruner 129–41; see also Davies, "Finding Some Space"), deals with a South African man and woman grappling with the conflict caused by his twin responsibilities, his political commitment to ending apartheid and his commitment to his family, and shows the woman reluctantly realizing that she does not have the luxury of being an attached, dependent wife, but must develop qualities of resource-fulness in herself. The story has a tighter construction than her first novel, *Muriel at Metropolitan,* which is interesting in its use of incident but loosely constructed and sometimes flat. In fact, all of the *Soweto Stories* are carefully crafted pieces dealing with South African folk struggling as they cope with difficult life experiences under apartheid. Amelia House's "Conspiracy" (Bruner 142–55) deals with a clandestine interracial relationship between a Black woman and a white man and with the larger notion of whether love is possible in such a situation. Its resolution demonstrates how apartheid causes fear and betrayal to permeate even intimate lives of both Black and white South Africans. A first sexual encounter is suddenly the center of a public situation, a police raid: "Their world caving in around them. Two very tiny people viewed by giants in boots. Lights. Policemen everywhere like cockroaches. Even more lights. More cockroaches" (155).

Just as the politics of race looms large in the works of South African women writers, so does the politics of gender in the works of women writers throughout Africa. African women are reading and writing off African patriarchy in different ways. Miriam Tlali, for instance, actively organizes women for writing in South Africa. And Catherine Acholonu, in Nigeria, published "Mother Was a Great Man" (1989), which raises interesting questions of the social construction of gender identity in an African context.

Drama

The full extent of women's participation in the immense variety of African traditional theatricality has not yet been documented. Because modern the-atrical ventures make demands on time in the evenings, when family respon-sibilities are most pressing, it is difficult for many women to participate in them. Also, acting is considered to be an immoral profession in many African societies, as elsewhere. Playwriting can be done at home, at least partly, but the dramatist needs involvement in a theater company in order to learn her craft.

Female modern dramatists are fairly rare in Africa, even in places where a strong male tradition of playwriting might have encouraged women to try as well. Yoruba drama is almost entirely a male affair (e.g., Soyinka, Ogun-yemi, Osofisan, Sowande). Although Zulu Sofola lives and works in the west of Nigeria because she is married to a Yoruba man, she is not Yoruba, but comes from Bendel, a culture close to Igbo. The dramatists Uwa Udensi and Catherine Acholonu are both Igbo. A younger playwright, Tess Onwueme, also from Bendel State in Nigeria, has written over twelve plays. She won the Association of Nigerian Author's Drama Prize in 1985 for *The Desert Encroaches*. Tess Onwueme's and Fatima Dike's works were shown at the First International Women Playwrights' Conference in Buffalo, New York, in 1989. Ghana has produced Efua Sutherland, Ama Ata Aidoo, and Patience Addo, whose *Company Pot* appeared in Gwyneth Henderson and Cosmo Pieterse's *Nine African Plays for Radio* (1973). Sutherland was a moving force in the establishment of the modern Ghanaian dramatic tradition at the Ghana Drama Studio and the Institute of African Studies at the University of Ghana at Legon. Her involvement in that development gave her a central role as director and the opportunity to participate in production. For younger women like Ama Ata Aidoo and Patience Addo, she was a groundbreaker, someone who showed that women could be primary creative sources in the theater.

In East Africa, Rebeka Njau, of Kenya, was writing in the 1960s (*The Scar* [1963]), and later on Micere Mugo, also of Kenya, worked with Ngũgĩ wa Thiong'o on *The Trial of Dedan Kimathi* (1976). Elvania Zimiru, of Uganda, wrote her *Family Spear* in 1974. Penina Muhando Mlama, of Tanzania, has written a number of plays in Swahili: *Hatia* (1972; Crime), *Tambueni haki zetu* (1972; Recognize Our Rights), and *Nguzo mama* (1982; A Pillar of a Mother). Her study *Culture and Development: The Popular Theatre Approach in Africa* (1991 [see Savory 1993]) uses her own experience in performance with the community to identify the developments in popular theater in Africa.

It is much easier for women to participate in theater if other women have preceded them. The establishment of major theater schools in African universities has been important here; both Efua Sutherland and Zulu Sofola have worked in association with academic institutions. Sutherland, however, has always had a firmly established contact with the world outside the university, through her work in children's drama, theater in Twi, and production tours of Ghana, as well as through her theater work in the city of Accra.

We could speculate that Sutherland and Aidoo emerged in Ghana partly because Akan culture allows for directorial and active women and thus permits the development of a woman's confidence to cope with theatrical work. But it would remain a shaky speculation, because we really do not know much about why fiction seems to outweigh drama (and even poetry) in women's writing in Africa. Perhaps the storytelling tradition is a powerful influence toward fiction. But sometimes telling a story becomes itself the structure of a play, as in the case of Efua Sutherland's *The Marriage of Anansewa* (1977). In other works, tradition itself is challenged, as in Bertha Msora's domestic drama *I Will Wait* (1984), which won a first prize in

Zimbabwe Publishing House's Playwriting Competition, and which portrays a woman who tries to challenge traditional attitudes to marriage by choosing her own man. Msora comes from a theatrical family and started acting when she was five years old. She has appeared in Ama Ata Aidoo's play *The Dilemma of a Ghost* (1965). But her desire to write more plays has to coexist with a busy life, for Msora is a married woman with three children and works as a market research executive with an advertising company. Professional modern drama is an exception rather than a rule in modern Africa, and outside university drama companies there is a need to combine jobs and theatrical commitment, which itself can limit opportunities to be productive.

As with other genres, we find that anthologies of African drama tend to be male-dominated. A dramatist such as Zulu Sofola, who has written many plays, has only a few in print, and some of those are now hard to find. But this body of drama is important in the establishing of women's perspectives on experience, and moreover, in the provision of good, central roles for actresses, permitting them to develop their skills and escape stereotypes. Efua Sutherland's *Edufa* has a range of significant roles for women, as do Aidoo's *Dilemma of a Ghost* and Sofola's *The Sweet Trap* (1977 [see Savory Fido 1987]). Each of these plays deals with cross-cultural, gender-specific conflicts in a different way. Sutherland deals with a husband's betrayal of his wife in *Edufa*, using many elements of ritual and symbolism but telling the story in the context of the man's modern capitalistic abandonment of his moral commitment to his wife, and of her firm stance with the other women for the morality of the past, a stance supported by Edufa's father. Aidoo presents a confrontation between the African family, the African-American wife, and their American-educated son, in which it is the women who finally resolve the tensions and not the "ghost" of a husband. The remarkable use of language registers in this play conveys the spectrum of usage from traditional, indigenous language to modern American English. Nonverbal symbolic languages are also important in the play. Sofola's domestic drama *The Sweet Trap* uses Western conventions to underline the alienation of the intellectual and professional African middle class from tradition and show how this alienation is at the root of tensions between men and women. Sofola sees tradition as a better place for women than modern middle-class life.

Women dramatists are concerned not only with the politics or the implications of women's experiences and roles but also with wider political issues. Micere Mugo's work with Ngũgĩ wa Thiong'o, *The Trial of Dedan Kimathi*, a socialist treatment of the Mau Mau/settler conflict in Kenya, includes an awareness of women's roles in that revolutionary context. The settler associates "my wife, my daughter, my property" together, but African men and women are shown as comrades and equals in their vision. Additionally, Ngũgĩ and Mugo demonstrate a symbolic unity of the sexes in creative work within the socialist framework. Uwa Udensi has written on the Biafran War (*Monkey on a Tree* [1975]). Elvania Zimiru, who tragically died in a car accident in 1979, was an actress, dramatist, and director. She often wrote on themes of general interest, like generational conflict. For a South African writer like Fatima Dike (*The Sacrifice of Kreli* [1977], *The First South African* [1979], *The Glass House* [1980]), playwriting is an emotional response to the dehumanization of her people (she was specifically affected by the rape and death of a seven-year-old girl whose body was found stuffed into a garbage can behind a row of shops where Dike worked). Her language is Xhosa, but she can reach more people by using English, and her treatment of interracial conflict and the violence of present-day South Africa is intended to reach the whole country. Gcina Mhlope was an actress with the Market Theatre in Johannesburg. Her work has been staged in the United States and Europe. *Born in the RSA*, staged at Lincoln Center in New York City, won an Obie Award. In 1988 her play *Have You Seen Zandile?* had its American premiere in Chicago.

Forms differ not only from dramatist to dramatist but from play to play within the work of one writer. Zulu Sofola, for example, uses the domestic drama and the symbolic, poetic play (*Reveries in the Moonlight* [1977] and *Omu Ako of Isele-Oligbo* [n.d.; both unpublished]), and has included some Igbo and Edo in her most recent English-language work. Sutherland seems to have found Euripedes' *Alcestis* a good inspiration for beginning *Edufa*, and she turned to a Ghanaian form and content entirely for her *Marriage of Anansewa*. This experimentation with form is characteristic of modern African drama in English by men as well as women, as in the increasing use in more recent plays of small elements of African-language writing. Sutherland and Aidoo use women's talk in their drama as they do in their stories, and they portray women performing rituals that sustain a traditional identity in a community. Werewere Liking's *Orphée d'Afric: Theatre-rituel* (1981; African Orpheus: Ritual theater) uses traditional Cameroonian rituals in a contemporary, creative manner. Tradition is often seen as a positive aspect of African life by women dramatists, and thus they frequently portray women in their plays as good guardians of it. Nevertheless, traditional female figures can also be perceived negatively. Catherine Acholonu's *The Trial of the Beautiful Ones*,[13] for instance, portrays a sea goddess, Owu, as a dangerous spirit who is defeated by the good male Christian figure of Michael.

Community and popular theater has developed in South Africa, where a group of Xhosa-speaking women have produced plays such as *Imfuduso,* a political play of resistance to apartheid. According to Beverly Couse, the play demonstrates that "the art of black South African women cannot be interpreted by the guidelines of white, western feminism, which still basically looks for the self-actualization of the individual, or for the enhancement of a unique art form" (12).

Poetry

A limitation in our assessment of the poetic achievement of African women is the difficulty of procuring volumes of poetry by individual poets published in Africa. Berrian lists a considerable number of volumes by individual poets, such as Grace Akello, Micere Mugo, and Clementine Madiya Faik-Nzuju,[14] but these volumes tend to be published by small publishing houses based in Africa and to have a limited and fairly localized distribution. Of these, Mugo's *Daughter of My People Sing* (1976) is perhaps best known. A number of poets, such as Amelia Blossom House (*Our Sun Will Rise* [1989]), write steadily and are well recognized. Omolara Ogundipe-Leslie has a volume, *Sew the Old Days and Other Poems* (see Ogundipe-Leslie, "Not Spinning"), and a number of her poems have appeared in a variety of journals.

Many of these poets are accomplished in other genres as well, but Noemia de Souza is known as a poet only. Beier and Moore list her as the "first African woman to achieve a genuine reputation as a poet" (253), whereas her entry in Herdeck (109) remarks that she wrote no poetry in the "relatively calm and happy period" of her marriage to a Portuguese man, during which period she lived in Lisbon. It is rare to find such linking of personal life and creative achievement in the discussions of male African writers. We will not investigate here the ring of the term "genuine reputation as a poet."

Noemia de Souza has a strong consciousness about women. In "Appeal," in *Poems of Black Africa* (1975), she asks, "Who has strangled the tired voice / of my forest sister?" The same poem describes a woman as "leashed with children." This awareness is clear in the work of many other women poets from Africa. Francesca Yetunde Pereira, of Nigeria, is most polemical in her "Two Strange Worlds," in *Poems from Black Africa* (1963). She writes:

> Woman
> What fools we are
> Invading unprotected
> The world of men so alien
> And ever manifesting
> Weakness in tenderness.

Efua Sutherland's lovely poem "The Redeemed," in *Messages* (1971), is written from a Christian standpoint, portraying the serpent's vision of an African Eve. The serpent intends to suck "sweet life out of eggs," but she defeats him:

> Her dark lips smiled.
> Her dark eyes beamed delight,
> The copper neck swerved back with its load
> And down the slope of the market road,
> She strode.

Grace Birabawa Isharaza's "The Smiling Orphan," in *Summer Fires* (1983), tells of an aunt's death and how the funeral was filled with people who had ignored the woman while she was alive. Only her daughter was with her when she was dying (her son was on "Official Duty").

Personal experience is strong in some poems, but confessional poetry is rare, perhaps because of attitudes toward disclosure in the poets' cultures. Mabel Segun has a wry poem about self-knowledge, "The Pigeon-Hole," in *Aftermath* (1977). She writes, "If only I knew for certain / What my delinquent self would do." Abena P. A. Busia has written of her father's death:

> Time finds us still your children
> and we make fellowship
> with fractured pieces of life passed
> like the fragments, of the wafer.
>
> (*Summer Fires*)

Her first volume, *Testimonies of Exile and Other Poems* was published in 1990. The "i" in Catherine Obianuju's Achonolu's "The Spring's Last Drop" (1982) is both personal and general in this maternal poem about sustenance in the midst of dwindling resources:

> i obianuju
> i shall provide my children
> with plenty
> i shall multiply this drop
> they will never taste
> of the sea.

Achonolu writes prolifically in both English and Igbo, with several volumes published in Nigeria.

Sometimes a poem expresses a political vision that is wide in scope, as in Ama Ata Aidoo's "Cornfields in Accra," in *Aftermath,* or Omolara Ogundipe-Leslie's "Song of the African Middle Class" in the *Penguin Book of Modern African Poetry.*

Much Negritude poetry idealized women and romanticized motherhood, making them synonymous with tradition, with Africa. For this reason, according to Andrea Benton Rushing, there are few negative images of women in African poetry, and those are limited to women who have rejected traditional women's roles. Women poets clearly have a different perspective, a more complex and realistic one, on themselves, and one hopes that perspective will begin to emerge as women write more and more in poetic form. From the beginning, African women have subverted conventions in their poems. Francesca Pereira, in her "Mother Dark," in *Poems from Black Africa,* offers a powerful mother image, "she was dark, very dark / and her voice shook the world," and then an image of the mother crying "loud in pain," because "her children now / Oppress her children." "Mother Africa" has been courageously fighting for her children's freedom, but now she is not heard because the oppression comes from within the family. A number of newer voices emerge all the time. Irene Assiba d'Almeida published five poems in "Black Women's Writing: Crossing the Boundaries," a special issue of *Matatu* (1989).

Jean Benjamin and the Bellville UWCO branch's "The Curse of Adam and Eve" is a performance poem that links the oppression of women at home and at work in South Africa, using both English and Afrikaans:

> I'm up at four
> In the morning
> Do the ironing
> The cleaning
> Dress the kids
> Get them to school
> Run to work
> Get there on time
> To stand in the production line.
>
> *Ek het is baas baas baas*
> *Sy naam is Klaas Klaas Klaas*
> *En hy vat hie*
> *Dan vat hy da*
> *Hy vat ans dew me kaar*
> *Push up production!*
> *Push up production!*
> *Haai girls laat ons line*
> *Fok die corruption!*
>
> [I've got a boss boss boss
> His name is Klaas Klaas Klaas
> He touch me here
> He touch me there
> He touch me everywhere
> "Push up production!"
> "Push up production!"
> "Hey girls, let's go"
> Fuck this corruption!]¹⁵

According to Benjamin, the words of this song are a rewriting of some popular lyrics that she realized were destructive when she heard one of her young daughters singing the popular version, which makes light of the abuse of women and even poses women as delighting in their acceptance of abuse.

Amelia House is clear in her articulation of resistance in the South African struggle. In the final poems of *Our Sun Rises* she links South Africa to a delivering woman whose labor must be induced:

> You amble on
> We can no longer
> Wait for nature's course
> We must deliver
> You
> With
> Force
>
> (63)

The link is made as well to her own daughter's birth and to all South African children, as her dedication indicates. It ends with "We Still Dance" (71), which is both an echo of an earlier poem, "I Will Still Sing" (21), and a forecast of victory and celebration.

The Writers' Themes

African women's writing consistently portrays women in various struggles for self-definition. A character's ability to define herself is shaped both by her understanding of the boundaries by which society circumscribes her and by her ability to transcend those boundaries and attain self-actualization while remaining nonetheless within her society. This struggle generates conflict, which is universally a source of creative power. In the writing of African women, certain themes present this process, and they may be summarized as follows: (1) the contradictions of motherhood; (2) the struggle for economic independence and success; (3) the precariousness of marital relationships; (4) tradition and modernity in relation to the role of women; (5) the politics of colonialism and neocolonialism and their effects on society in general and women in particular; and (6) the nature of power relationships in society.

Although certain texts, such as Buchi Emecheta's *The Joys of Motherhood* (1979), deal substantially with overturning myths about mothering, the subject comes up again and again as part of a play's or novel's theme (e.g., in Bâ's *Une si longue lettre,* in Sutherland's *Edufa,* and in Ngcobo's *Cross of Gold*). Sutherland's *Foriwa* (1967) presents an important mother-daughter relationship. In many works the struggle for economic success is central, as in Nwapa's *Efuru, Idu,* and *One Is Enough* and Njau's *Ripples in the Pool* (1978). Both *Ripples in the Pool* and *The Joys of Motherhood* treat the idea that women can become economically self-sufficient through prostitution.

These themes are frequently combined with differing emphases according to the writer's intention. Marriage and sexual relationships are often intertwined with the subject of motherhood; a notable exception is Nwapa's *Idu,* which deals with a husband-wife relationship that does not require the addition of children (although society would insist on the contrary). For Senegalese writers, Islamic polygamy in which a wife can be abandoned, is an important theme. In Sow Fall's *La grève des battù* (1979; *The Beggars' Strike,* 1981) a man is callous to his extremely supportive wife and takes another, younger wife who is less respectful of him; the same theme is also an important aspect of Bâ's *Une si longue lettre*. Many works show evidence that a new kind of woman is being envisaged by the writers, one who will challenge the societal order (as in Nwapa's *One Is Enough*).

The conflict between tradition and modernity is a theme that has concerned many African writers, both men and women, since joining these two worlds is a principal challenge of contemporary African experience. Women writers are concerned particularly with the woman's role in this process. For Ramatoulaye in *Une si longue lettre*, tradition is oppressive, something that can hurt as well as console. In Sutherland's *Edufa*, Ampoma's integrity is linked strongly to her loyalty to the spirit of tradition. In Bessie Head's *A Question of Power*, a woman confronting social rejection achieves inner peace by turning to nature, to growing plants and food and tending to children; in this way ancient traditions heal modern crises. Noni Jabavu in *The Ochre People* shows how a family blends the modern and traditional to avoid conflict between the two worlds.

Tradition often means woman as mother, grandmother, guardian of old ways, and teacher of those ways to the young. But assuming these roles is difficult when women see opportunities in societies moving toward modern technological development. The Hausa oral poet Binta Katsina therefore sings, "Women of Nigeria you could do every kind of work," and goes on to list being a minister, doing clerical work, driving cars, and flying planes, among others (Mack). Yet in many works, women writers indicate that the old authority figures, both men and women, still contribute a powerful sense of identity to the individual and relate her to her culture. That contribution may be destructive or constructive. In *A Question of Power*, both male authority figures, Sello and Dan, are damaging to Elizabeth in different ways. In Dangarembga's *Nervous Conditions*, the patriarchy refers to male and female elders who together maintain power relations in the clan. In the autobiographical writings of Diallo and Jabavu, patriarchal fathers are admired. It depends on the writer and her culture how these things are interpreted. Emecheta presents a negative image of maternal power through Ma Palagda in *The Slave Girl* (1977). Zulu Sofola has her central character Clara kneel to her husband in deference to a male authority figure, Dr. Jinadu, at the close of her play *The Sweet Trap* (1977).[16] Nwapa tends to show authority figures as being good or bad depending on how they wield authority. Overall, then, the variety of approaches to the meaning and value of tradition represents the present confusion of directions for many individuals caught in a situation of rapid change.

Women writers also add another dimension to the portrayal of political reality in Africa. In many works (Emecheta's *The Joys of Motherhood* or Bessie Head's *Maru*, for example), the condition of the woman is placed within a context of politics in the whole society. Perspectives are different. Sow Fall is much less sympathetic to the neocolonial politician Mour Ndiaye in *La grève des battù*, who lugs beef in the heat of the day to beggars who have been driven into a camp by his own directive, than is Head to Maru, a male leader with difficulties.

Domestic content in women's writing, however radical it may be about male-female relations, is less politically disturbing to society than the direct political statement of a Sada'aw in *Woman at Point Zero* (1975). Boitumelo, in an interview titled "Women Writers Speak," first published in *Staffrider*, quotes the young South African writer Manoko Mchwe on what constitutes women's literature:

> I believe a woman, as mother in her society, as the first teacher of her children and also as an ordinary member of society, is in a very good position to communicate with people she writes for. The usage of simple domestic language can be very effective as it will be easily understood, *but I must stress that a woman is not confined to write about domestic life*. I only gave that as an example. (76; our italics)

Feminism and African Women Writers

> "The female writer should be committed in three ways: as a writer, as a woman and as a third world person; and her womanhood is implicated in all three."—Omolara Ogundipe-Leslie, "The Female Writer"

The question of political and social responsibility and the writer is addressed to the African woman writer by the Ogundipe-Leslie formulation above. Ogundipe-Leslie is concerned that "many African female writers like to declare that they're not feminists, as if it were a crime to be a feminist" (11). This she attributes to successful intimidation of African women, which has resulted in women being apologetic for asserting women's rights. This became the central question in a trialogue between Micere Mugo, Ama Ata Aidoo, and Buchi Emecheta at the 1988 African Literature Association Annual Conference held at the University of Pittsburgh. It became clear in the ensuing discussion that all three writers were in support of the necessary links between gender, location, and writing because they were aware of the dangers of prescriptiveness. Further, all three writers felt that while they identified themselves with feminist politics, it had to be redefined within African contexts.

Not every woman who makes a statement through writing is necessarily a feminist. There is a tendency to ascribe feminism to a woman writer simply because she shows women grappling with society's definitions of women. A number of African women writers dislike the label feminist, but not its politics. Nwapa, for example, says in an interview with Alison Perry in 1984, "Just because I write about women people accuse me of being feminist." But she accepts Alice Walker's term *womanist* because it conveys a commitment to the "survival and wholeness of the entire people, male and female." Aidoo also says, "I shall not protest if you call me a feminist. But I am not a feminist because I write about women" ("Unwelcome Pals" 40). Similarly, Emecheta has expressed difficulties with the application of the term. According to Emecheta, "I will not be called a feminist *here*, because it is European. It is as simple as that. I just resent that. Otherwise, if you look at everything I do, it is what the feminists do, too; but it is just that it comes from Europe, or European women, and I don't like being defined by them" (Grandquist and Stotesbury 19).

Some theorists have sought to bring together the meaning of *feminist* that many African women adopt and use it within African contexts. Filomina Steady talks of an "African feminism" that conveys the strength of pre-colonial African women, their autonomy and respect for motherhood and woman's contribution to society. Ama Ata Aidoo in *Our Sister Killjoy* (1978) has her character Sissie say, "But wasn't her position among our people a little more complicated than that of the dolls the colonizers brought along with them who fainted at the sight of their own bleeding fingers?" (117). Ogundipe-Leslie sees activism for women as part of an attack on social exploitation in general: "Women's liberation is but an aspect of the need to liberate the total society from dehumanization. It is the social system which must change. But men do become enemies when they seek to retard or even block these necessary historical exchanges when for selfish power-interests, they claim as their excuse culture and heritage" ("Not Spinning" 503).

Disregarding terms, women writers largely share a determination to achieve a freedom for men and women within an overall humane and just society. Perhaps Ogundipe-Leslie's assertion that the female writer should be committed in three ways, "as a writer, as a woman and as a third world person" is an ideal close to the position of many women writers, although they may not choose to be called feminists. A special issue of *Current Writing: Text and Reception in Southern Africa*, "Feminism(s) and Writing in English in South Africa" (1990), contains several interesting essays on feminist theory and the role of feminism in South African liberation. The role and history of feminist politics or activism on women's rights in Africa is a discourse which African women are studying and clarifying for themselves.

Criticism and African Women's Writing

The critical reception given African writers has been slow and often inadequate, tending to focus on a few writers. White women critics have hardly recognized African women's writing. Some Black male critics have been involved in this field from the beginning, either usefully (Lloyd Brown) or superficially (Taiwo, Little). Major volumes of criticism on African women writers by single authors tend to be by men, while women critics tend to produce collaborative efforts. *Ngambika: Women and African Literature* (1986) is a collection coedited by Carole Boyce Davies and Anne Adams Graves.

Rhonda Cobham-Sander and Chikwenye Ogunyemi have coedited a special issue of *Research in African Literatures* (1988) on African women writers. Anne Adams is editing *70 African and Caribbean Women Writers: A Bio-Bibliographic Study* for Greenwood Press. Perhaps what this means is that male critics have been able to find the time needed to finish long and sustained work, whereas women need to write and edit collaboratively or communally to produce long pieces of criticism. Certainly even professional women have domestic responsibilities that interfere with their time for work, whereas men frequently can devote themselves to work without interruption. But a number of single-authored volumes by women are in progress. Much of the work has appeared as single essays, articles in journals and magazines, or chapters in books. Susheila Nasta edited *Motherlands* (1991), a collection of critical essays including pieces on Nwapa, Emecheta Bâ, Sa'adawi, Aidoo, Njau, Head, Macgoye, and by Aloena Busia, Judie Newman, Pro, Euke Bochmer, C. L. Innes, and Jane Bryce-Okunlola.

At any rate, interest in African women writers is rising. A number of special issues of academic journals have been devoted to the topic (*Research in African Literatures, African Literature Today, World Literature Written in English*). *Sage: A Scholarly Journal of Black Women*, which continues to publish work on Black women internationally, often includes work by and about African women. Others, such as *Callaloo*, have issues looking at Black women writers cross-culturally. Some professional associations, such as the African Literature Association's Women's Caucus, have developed a core of interested critics who discuss women's writing at the annual conferences, and a great deal of research is being done at African universities on women in general. Out of this kind of activity, sustained criticism is developing.[17]

But establishing the field is not without controversy and some clear resistance from male critics. Debate is healthy, but too often criticism speaks without understanding or sympathy—and this is not always a male shortcoming, by any means. Nadine Gordimer said that Flora Nwapa could not handle theme, and that the portrait of the main character in *Efuru* is obscured by "rambling details of daily life, mildly interesting but largely irrelevant" (20) and has responded similarly to Ellen Kuzwayo's *Call Me Woman* (1973). We should not desire total agreement about this body of literature, but we should tackle critical prejudice for what it is, the product of misunderstanding and sometimes of fear of change.[18] For whatever else this new literature represents, it certainly represents a stride into the future, determinedly carrying whatever is of use and value from the past. These women writers struggle to express their reality with honesty, with complexity, and with concern for their societies. We honor that effort.

Notes

1. Critics and editors define this group differently. Brenda Berrian's *Bibliography* includes European women married to African men, yet excludes Nadine Gordimer.

Chinua Achebe and Lyn Innes include Gordimer and Alifa Rifaat, from Egypt, in their *African Short Stories*. In forming any set of criteria, it is necessary to avoid simplistic categories. Although Gordimer is an African of European settler ancestry, her work has contributed greatly to our understanding of the African experience. Nevertheless, we have chosen not to discuss her work here, opting instead to concentrate on lesser-known writers. Similarly, we exclude Rifaat because, as an Arabic woman writing in North Africa, she already has a place within the African canon, and because the focus of this book is on sub-Saharan Africa.

2. Much of the information in this paragraph came from personal conversations, interviews, personal knowledge, or written reviews, and we have respected the privacy of sources.

3. For some writers, children's literature provides a way of bringing traditional women's uses of words and the modern writer's role together. Barbara Kimenye, of Kenya, is one of these writers.

4. A special issue of *Research in African Literatures* (forthcoming) edited by Omolara Ogundipe-Leslie and Carole Boyce Davies focuses specifically on African women oral artists.

5. *West African Review* published a number of extracts from Casely-Hayford's *Memoirs* (see Berrian 1). It is hard to see why in their introduction Dathorne and Feuser call her style "toffy-tainted," a description that seems needlessly insulting to a woman who was born into a certain elite, colonially educated place, where she could not help a certain linguistic stiffness, and at least did her best to fight for the preservation of creative aspects of her traditional culture, as well as for progressive ideas like the education of girls.

6. Berrian lists Kakaza, *Intyatyambo yomzi* (1913; The flower in the home) and *u Tandiwe wakwa Gcaleka* (1914; Tandiwe, a damsel of Gaikaland); Swaartbooi, *u Mandisa* (1933; Bringer of joy) and Dube, *Wozanazo izindaba zika Phoshozwayo* (1935; Tell us the stories of Phoshozwayo). Swaartboi was born in 1907, the daughter of a headmaster of a Methodist school; she became a teacher herself. Violet Dube was the pen name of Natale Nxumalo (née Nxaba), who was married to the Zulu writer and teacher James Alfred Walter Nxumalo.

7. Hughes includes Marina Gashe (according to Berrian, a pen name for Rebeka Njau), Aquah Laluah, and Francesca Pereira. Laluah (the pen name of Gladys Casely-Hayford, Adelaide's daughter) published two poems in the *Philadelphia Tribune*, 14 October 1937, and a small volume of partly Krio poetry, *Take 'um so* (1948).

8. Brown, Hofmeyr, and Rosenberg, voicing their regret that fewer Black women's voices are represented in *Lip* than they had hoped, note that white women "have had disproportionate recognition in the arts of our countries, because of their privilege and the oppression of others" (2). Not only such well-known white Southern African women writers as Olive Schreiner and Nadine Gordimer but also minor writers such as the novelist Yvonne Burgess (*A Life to Live*, 1973; *The Strike*, 1975) have much better access to publication than Black women in their societies.

9. Informal discussion, 1985 African Literature Association conference, Northwestern University, Evanston, Ill.

10. Beverly Mack's study of Hausa women's oral literature shows that "women find ways to work within the religious and literary parameters of their culture to speak their minds on political and social issues that affect them" ("Waya Daka" 28).

11. This is the same "letter to self/letter to God" motif Alice Walker employs in

The Color Purple. The letter becomes a prayer, in the mode in which Black women use prayer and testimonial to dramatize and release pain and suffering.

12. Oladele Taiwo, at the beginning of his *Female Novelists*, places female writers in Africa in relation to intellectual women writers of Europe by assuming that women's activism must come from outside Africa by some influence, in direct opposition to his position on the subject of European influences on male novelists in his earlier *Culture and the Nigerian Novel*.

13. Unpublished; produced by the Imo State Council for Arts and Culture, 7 and 26 February 1985.

14. See Berrian 49–76. Akello published a volume of poems, *My Barren Song* (1979). Faik-Nzuji has published several volumes in Kinshasa, e.g., *Murmures, Poemes* (1968).

15. Lyrics supplied by the author in Oxford, England, August 1989.

16. This incident caused controversy at Ibadan University, where it was performed for the Nigerian Association of University Women on International Women's Day, 1975. Sofola argues that modern women lose twice over, because they do not understand the advantages in traditional culture, where men and women respect each other and maintain a balance of power, and because modern relations between men and women are inadequate and produce bad behavior on both sides. Education misleads women, she argues, placing the blame on feminist influence from the West.

17. Also, such new anthologies as Charlotte Bruner's *African Women's Writing* (1993) bring more writers to critical attention. Unfortunately, as we go to press, we cannot extend this discussion to include new voices and newly discovered voices, such as Zaynab Alkalis, Orlanda Amarilis, Aminita Maïga Ka, Awuor Ayoda, Violet Das Lannoy, Daisy Kabagarama, Lina Magalia, Ananda Deri, Jean Marquand, Sheila Fugard, Gisèle Halimi, Leila Sebbar, Andrée Chedid, nor the new issues in this field that their work raises.

18. For instance, Wole Soyinka's failure to realize the significance of women poets in his *Poems of Black Africa* (1975) indicates that a major African writer had not developed a consciousness about a new literary tradition, at a time when he was breaking new ground creatively and intellectually in other areas.

Bibliography

Achebe, Chinua, and Lyn Innes, eds. *African Short Stories*. London: Heinemann, 1985.

Acholonu, Catherine Obianuju. "Mother Was a Great Man." In *Black Women's Writing: Crossing the Boundaries*, edited by Carole Boyce Davies, 43–51. Special issue of *Matutu* (Frankfurt), 6, no. 3 (1989).

———. "The Spring's Last Drop." *Afa* 1 (November 1982): 8–9.

———. "The Woman Comes of Age in the Nigerian Novel: A Study of Zaynab Alkali's *The Stillborn*." Paper presented at the annual conference of the African Literature Association, Michigan State University, East Lansing, 1986.

Ademola, Frances, ed. *Reflections: Nigerian Prose and Verse*. Lagos: African Universities Press, 1962.

———. "Ghana: To Be a Woman." In *Sisterhood Is Global: The International Women's Movement Anthology*, compiled and edited by Robin Morgan, 258–65. New York: Doubleday, 1984.

Aidoo, Ama Ata. "Unwelcome Pals and Decorative Slaves: The Woman Writer, the Woman As a Writer in Modern Africa." *Afa* 1 (November 1982): 34–43.

Akello, Grace. *My Barren Song*. Arusha, Tanzania: East Africa Publications, 1979.

Alkali, Zaynab. *The Stillborn*. London: Longman, 1984.

Awoonor, Kofi, and G. Adali-Morty. *Messages: Poems from Ghana*. London: Heinemann, 1971.

Balisidya, Ndayano May L. [Matteru]. "The Construction of Sex and Gender Roles in Penina Muhando's Work." *Sage* 1 (Summer 1988): 15–20.

———. "Language Planning and Oral Creativity." Ph.D. diss., University of Wisconsin, 1988.

Banham, Martin. *Early Nigerian Student Verse*. Ibadan, Nigeria: Ibadan University Press, 1959.

Bankier, Joana, and Deidre Lashgari, eds. *Women Poets of the World*. New York: Macmillan, 1983.

Banyiwa-Horne, Mary Naana. "African Womanhood: The Contrasting Perspective of Flora Nwapa's *Efuru* and Elechi Amadi's *The Concubine*." In *Ngambika: Studies of Women and African Literature*, edited by Carole Boyce Davies and Ann Adams Graves, 119–30. Trenton, N.J.: Africa World Press, 1986.

Barber, Karin. *I Could Speak until Tomorrow: Oriki, Women, and the Past in a Yoruba Town*. Washington, D.C.: Smithsonian Institution Press, 1991.

Barber, Karin, and P. F. de Morales Farias, eds. *Discourse and Its Disguises: The Interpretation of African Oral Texts*. Birmingham Center of West African Studies Series, no. 1. Birmingham, England: 1989.

Beier, Ulli, and Gerald Moore, eds. *Modern Poetry from Africa*. Harmondsworth: Penguin Books, 1963. Revised as *The Penguin Book of Modern African Poetry*. 1984.

Berrian, Brenda. *Bibliography of African Women Writers and Journalists*. Washington, D.C.: Three Continents Press, 1985.

Boitumelo. "Women Writers Speak." *Staffrider Magazine* 2, no. 4 (November/December, 1979). Reprinted as Appendix A in Amelia House, *Black South African Women Writers in English: A Preliminary Checklist*, 19–21. Evanston, Ill.: Northwestern University Program on Women, 1980.

Brown, Lloyd. *Women Writers in Black Africa*. Westport, Conn.: Greenwood Press, 1981.

Brown, Susan, Isabel Hofmeyr, and Susan Rosenberg, eds. *Lip: From Southern African Women*. Johannesburg: Ravan Press, 1983.

Bruner, Charlotte, ed. *African Women's Writing*. Oxford: Heinemann, 1993.

———. "A Decade for Women Writers." In *African Literature Studies: The Present State/L'état present*, edited by Stephen Arnold, 217–27. Washington, D.C.: Three Continents Press, 1985.

———. *Unwinding Threads: Writing by Women in Africa*. London: Heinemann, 1984.

Calder, Angus, Jack Mapanje, and Cosmo Pieterse, eds. *Summer Fires: New Poetry of Africa*. London: Heinemann, 1983.

Cham, Mbye. "The Female Condition in Africa: A Literary Exploration by Mariama Bâ." *Current Bibliography on African Affairs* 17, no. 1 (1984–85): 29–52.

Couse, Beverly. "Let Us Build Each Other Up." *Southern Africa Report* (February 1986): 11–12.

Darah, G. G. "The Creative Process as Social Praxis: The Case of Urhobo Dance

Songs." Paper presented at the Conference on African Oral Poetry, University of Ibadan, Nigeria, 1977.

Dathorne, O. R. *African Literature in the Twentieth Century.* London: Heinemann, 1976.

Dathorne, O. R., and W. Feuser, eds. *Africa in Prose.* Harmondsworth: Penguin Books, 1969.

Davies, Carole Boyce. "Finding Some Space: Black South African Women Writers." *Current Bibliography of African Affairs* 19, no. 1 (1986–87): 31–45.

———. "Private Selves and Public Spaces: Autobiography and the African Woman Writer." *CLA Journal* 34, no. 3 (1991): 267–89. Reprinted in *Crossing Boundaries in African Literatures* (African Literature Association annual, 1986), edited by Kenneth Harrow, Jonathan Ngaté, and Clarisse Zimra, 109–27. Washington, D.C.: Three Continents Press, 1991.

Dike, Fatima. *The First South African.* Johannesburg: Ravan Press, 1979.

———. *The Glass House.* Unpublished play.

———. *The Sacrifice of Kreli.* Johannesburg: Theatre One, A. D. Donker, 1977.

Emecheta, Buchi. "It's Me Who's Changed." Interview. *Connexions* 4 (Spring 1982): 4–5.

———. *Second-Class Citizen.* New York: George Braziller, 1975.

Etherton, Michael. *The Development of Africa Drama.* New York: Africana, 1982.

Faik-Nzuju, Clementine Madiya. *Murmures, Poemes.* Kinshasa: Editions Lettres Congolaises, Office National de la Recherche et du Developpement, 1968.

Fido, Savory Elaine. "A Question of Realities: Zulu Sofola's *The Sweet Trap.*" *Ariel* 18, no. 4 (October 1987): 53–66.

———. "Motherlands: Self and Separation in the Work of Buchi Emecheta, Bessie Head and Jean Rhys." In *Motherlands: Black Women's Writing from Africa, the Caribbean, and South Asia,* ed. Susheila Nastra. (London: Women's Press, 1991), 330–49.

Finnegan, Ruth. *Oral Literature in Africa.* Oxford: Oxford University Press, 1970.

Gordimer, Nadine. *The Black Interpreters: Notes on African Writing.* Johannesburg: SPRO-CAS/RAVAN, 1973.

Graham-White, Anthony. *The Drama of Black Africa.* New York: S. French, 1974.

Grandquist, Raoul, and John Stotesbury. *African Voices: Interviews with Thirteen African Writers.* Sydney: Dangaroo Press, 1989.

Gray, Stephen. "An Interview with Fatima Dike." Appendix B in *Black South African Women Writers in English: A Preliminary Checklist,* compiled by Amelia House, 22–32. Evanston, Ill.: Northwestern University Program on Women, 1980.

Hale, Thomas. *Scribe, Griot, and Novelist: Narrative Interpreters of the Songhay Empire.* Gainesville: University of Florida Center for African Studies, 1990.

Head, Bessie. "Notes from a Quiet Backwater I." In *A Woman Alone: Autobiographical Writings,* edited by Craig Mackenzie. London: Heinemann, 1990.

Henderson, Gwyneth, and Cosmo Pieterse, eds. *Nine African Plays for Radio.* London: Heinemann, 1973.

Herdeck, Donald E. *African Authors: A Companion to Black African Writing.* Vol. 1, *1300–1973.* Washington, D.C.: Black Orpheus Press, 1973.

House, Amelia. *Black South African Women Writers in English: A Preliminary Checklist.* Evanston, Ill.: Northwestern University Program on Women, 1980.

Hughes, Langston, ed. *An African Treasury.* New York: Pyramid, 1961.

————. *Poems from Black Africa*. Bloomington: Indiana University Press, 1963.

James, Adeola. *In Their Own Voices: African Women Writers Talk*. London: Currey, 1990.

Katsina, Binta. "Song for the Women of Nigeria." Appendix to Beverly B. Mack, "Waka Daya Ba Ta Kare Nika—One Song Will Not Finish the Grinding: Hausa Women's Oral Literature," in *Contemporary African Literature*, edited by Hal Wiley, Eileen Julien, and Russell J. Linneman, 15–46. Washington, D.C.: Three Continents Press, 1983.

Kuzwayo, Ellen. *Call Me Woman*. San Francisco: Spinster Ink, 1985.

Laluah, Aquah [Gladys Casely-Hayford]. *Take 'um so*. Freetown, Sierra Leone: New Era Press, 1948.

Liking, Werewere. *Elle sera de jaspe et de corail* [She will be of jasper and coral]. Paris: L'Harmattan, 1983.

————. *Orphée d'Afric: Theatre-rituel* [African Orpheus: Ritual theater]. Paris: L'Harmattan, 1981.

Little, Kenneth. *The Sociology of Urban Women's Image in African Literature*. Totowa, N.J.: Rowman and Littlefield, 1980.

Lyonga, Pauline Nalova. "Umahiri: A Feminist Approach to African Literature." Ph.D. diss., University of Michigan, 1985.

Mack, Beverly B. "Waka Daya Ba Ta Kare Nika—One Song Will Not Finish the Grinding: Hausa Women's Oral Literature." In *Contemporary African Literature*, edited by Hal Wiley, Eileen Julien, and Russell J. Linneman, 15–46. Washington, D.C.: Three Continents Press, 1983.

Mhlope, Gcina. "Block E, Room 24 Is Home of a Poetess." *New Nation* 27 (27 February–12 March 1986), 8.

Mlama, Penina Muhando. *Culture and Development: The Popular Theatre Approach in Africa*. Stockholm: Scandinavian Institute for African Studies, 1991.

Mugo, Micere. "Towards a Definition of African Orature Aesthetics." *Third World Book Review* 2, no. 3 (1987): 39–40.

Mvula, Enoch T. "Tumbuka Pounding Songs in the Management of Familial Conflicts." In *Crossrhythms*, edited by Daniel Avorghedor and Dkwesi Yankah, 93–113. Bloomington: Indiana University Folklore Publications, 1983. Edited by Susheila Nastra, *Motherlands: Black Women's Writing from Africa, the Caribbean, and South Asia*. (London: Women's Press, 1991).

Njau, Rebeka. *Ripples in the Pool*. London: Heinemann, 1978.

————. *The Scar. Transition* 3, no. 8 (1963): 23–28. Reprinted in *Eleven Short African Plays*, edited by Cosmo Pieterse. London: Heinemann, 1971.

Ogunbiyi, Yemi, ed. *Drama and Theatre in Nigeria*. Lagos: Nigeria Magazine, 1981.

————. "Not Spinning on the Axis of Maleness." In *Sisterhood Is Global*, edited by Robin Morgan, 498–504. New York: Doubleday, 1984.

Ogundipe-Leslie, Omolara. "The Female Writer and Her Commitment." *Guardian* (Lagos, 21 December 1983). Reprint in *Women in African Literature Today*, edited by Eldred Durosimi Jones, 5–13. London: Joseph Currey; Trenton, N.J.: Africa World Press, 1987.

Ogunyemi, Chikwenye. "Buchi Emecheta: The Shaping of a Self." *Komparatistiche* 8 (1983): 65–78.

Otukunefor, Henrietta, and Obiagele Nwodo, eds. *Nigerian Female Writers: A Critical Perspective*. Lagos: Malthouse, 1989.

Perry, Alison. "Meeting Flora Nwapa." *West Africa* 3487 (18 June 1984): 1262.

Reed, Clive, and John Wake. *A Book of African Verse*. London: Heinemann, 1964.

Rochman, Hazel. *Somehow Tenderness Survives: Stories of Southern Africa*. New York: Harper & Row, 1988.

Rushing, Andrea Benton. "Images of Black Women in Modern African Poetry: An Overview." In *Sturdy Black Bridges*, edited by Parker Bell and Guy Sheftall, 18–24. New York: Anchor Books, 1979.

Russell, Joan. "Women's Narration: Performance and the Marking of Verbal Aspect." In *Swahili: Language and Society*, edited by Joan Maw and David Parkin, 89–106. Vienna, Austria: Afropub, 1985.

Savory, Elaine (formerly Savory Fido), Review of Penina Mukando Relama, *Culture and Development: The Popular Theatre Approach in African Research in African Literatures* 24, no. 1 (Spring 1993).

Scheub, Harold. *African Oral Narratives, Proverbs, Riddles, Poetry, and Song*. Boston: G. K. Hall, 1977.

Shoga, Yinka. "Women Writers and Africa Literature." *Afriscope* (October 1973): 44–45.

Showalter, Elaine. "Feminist Criticism in the Wilderness." In *Writing and Sexual Difference*, edited by Elizabeth Abel, 23–35. Chicago: University of Chicago Press, 1982.

Sow Fall, Aminata. *L'áppel des arènes* [The call of the arena]. Dakar: Nouvelles Editions Africaines, 1982.

———. *La grève des battù*. Dakar: Les Nouvelles Editions Africaines, 1979. *The Beggars' Strike*. Translated by Dorothy Blair. London: Longman, 1981.

———. *Le revenant* [The ghost]. Dakar: Nouvelles Editions Africaines, 1976.

Soyinka, Wole. *Poems of Black Africa*. London: Secker & Warburg, 1975.

Taiwo, Oladele. *Culture and the Nigerian Novel*. London: Macmillan, 1976.

———. *Female Novelists in Black Africa*. London: Macmillan, 1984.

Tlali, Miriam. *Muriel at Metropolitan*. Johannesburg: Ravan Press, 1975; London: Longman, 1988; Washington, D.C.: Three Continents, 1979.

12 The Question of Language

in African Literatures

OYEKAN OWOMOYELA

Personne n'entend plus un peuple qui perd ses mots.
[Nobody listens to a people that has lost its voice.]
—François Mitterand

The phrase "Russian literature" customarily implies the Russian language; the phrase "Russian literature in Russian" is therefore tautological. Put differently, if a literature is Russian it is so by virtue of its creation out of the Russian culture and is necessarily in the Russian language. The same logic applies to English literature, French literature, Chinese literature, and so forth, and by extension to European literatures and Asian literatures, for example. In other words, one cannot separate a literature from the culture and the language that define it; mainly for that reason, works translated from one language to another lose some essential qualities that cannot cross linguistic and cultural barriers.

In this regard the widely recognized and acknowledged literatures of Africa are unique among the literatures of the world. Whereas elsewhere language in literature attracts attention and debate only in terms of the artistic effectiveness of its use, in Africa the major point of contention is in what language or languages the literatures may legitimately be expressed. To be sure, in the context of Spanish literature the preference for Castilian over Aragonese might occasion debate, and in English literature pundits might argue about the literary properties and legitimacy of Cockney or the Scottish brogue in comparison with the Queen's English, but in each case the choice would be between or among indigenous languages, one having achieved ascendancy over the other(s). In Africa the question is whether what the world regards as the literary expression of the African imagination should be in African or foreign tongues.

Houston Baker poses the crucial question in his "English as a World Language for Literature: A Session for the 1979 English Institute." Given that language is inseparable from thought, he asks, "How then, does Tewa or

347

Yoruba or Sotho thought achieve literary form in English? How, given the inseparability of thought and language, and the diversity of the world's language communities, should one approach the notion that English has global status as a literary language? What presuppositions are embodied in this view, and what are the implications?" (ix). More recently, and in a similar vein, a Yoruba scholar discussing the anomaly of practicing what passes as African philosophy in non-African languages cites Ludwig Wittgenstein's assertion that "the limit of our language is the limit of our world" (Makinde 17).

Modern African literatures are a product of the encounter between African and European cultures. Their development has been significantly influenced by the nature of that encounter, and later by colonial expediency and the exigencies of decolonization. An understanding of the linguistic anomaly that is a feature of those literatures thus necessitates an archeological probing of those events.

Archeology

The story effectively begins in the Victorian era, when European attitudes toward Africans were dominated by a strong belief in their inferiority to Europeans and some suspicion about their humanity. Africans were supposed to suffer from a mental "deficit," as Victorian natural scientists put it, that rendered them incapable of the sort of enterprises, intellectual or cultural, that other humans could accomplish. Their languages were held to reflect that deficit. Referring specifically to the Africans transplanted as slaves to the Caribbean, Edward Braithwaite notes that their native languages had to be "submerged" because the European slavers regarded them as those of beings who were "inferiors—nonhuman, in fact" (18).

In that prevailing atmosphere, when the question of African education arose it inevitably generated some controversy. Those who believed in the deficit argued that forcing too much education into the deficient African brains might have pathologically debilitating consequences. Others were not so much interested in Africans' mental health as in the possibility that education might adversely affect their perception of their proper place in relation to Europeans in the order of things. T. J. Jones, of the Phelps-Stokes studies, and, unfortunately, Booker T. Washington exemplify the conviction that Africans (and African Americans) should be offered only the sort of education that would ensure their usefulness to the dominant white society and would not give them any ridiculous idea of equality to whites. The proper education would teach only enough English to make them functionally useful; otherwise instruction would concentrate on menial and industrial subjects.[1]

Humanitarians and Christian missionaries unimpressed by the notion of an African "deficit," and wishing to disprove the racists' contention that the

African could not be civilized, set out to establish schools on the continent that would be isolated "islands of civilization," hermetically sealed off from surrounding Africa. They would be laboratories from which would issue finished, educated specimens, proof of African educability. These specimens would, of course, have shed all vestiges of Africa, including language, and would speak in the "tongue of 'civilization'" (Lyons 83). The missionaries "hoped that gradually they would expand their 'islands of civilization' until the last traditional African society would be not transformed but destroyed." The policy was no different from the one that underlay the establishment of residential schools for American Indians in the United States and Canada, as documented in such television programs as "White Man's Way" (the United States) and "Where the Spirit Lives" (Canada).

Whatever the missionaries' plans, practical considerations intervened to modify them, at least initially, and especially in "Anglophone" areas. They had to discharge their primary duty of spreading the gospel to people who had no knowledge of European languages and must therefore be reached, at least initially, in their indigenous languages. Moreover, the size of the task necessitated the employment of African helpers, who had to be literate in their own languages. The missionaries also faced the necessity of producing literature, preferably in applicable local languages, suitable for proselytization and, later, instruction. This was true even for Catholic missionaries, who did not bear the obligation the Reformation imposed on Protestants to make the Bible accessible to every believer (see Ologunde 279–80).

The onset of colonialism once again forced the missionaries' hand, as developments in the Yoruba area of Nigeria illustrate (see Ologunde 281–83). The missionaries still retained control of education during the infancy of the colonial era, with Yoruba as the medium of instruction. But the needs of the colonial administration soon assumed precedence over those of the missions. Rather than propagators of the gospel, the colonists needed messengers, clerks, civil servants, and court interpreters. The educational system responded to the development. The missionaries, always strapped for money for their projects, were induced with the grant of governmental subventions to embrace the change in orientation. But contrary to the popular notion that contemporary Africans surrendered to Europeans without a fight, in this instance nationalists protested the supplanting of their language by the European imposition (Ologunde 281–82).

A major difference in colonial ideology existed between Britain and France, the two most important colonial powers as far as the present discussion is concerned: while Britain favored "indirect rule," a system that was based on administration through the agency of indigenous rulers and that sought to preserve traditional institutions, France opted for assimilation, a system designed to transform her African subjects into Black French men and women. Christine Souriau has described the practical application of this policy of cultural domination, with regard to language, in the Maghreb, where Arabic was already established as a written, scholarly medium. The French policy discouraged instruction in Arabic, stopped financing local education, replaced Arabic-speaking personnel with French speakers practicing French ways (thus relegating the former to inferior status), and forbade French personnel to learn Arabic (320–21).

The task of linguistic assimilation was easier in sub-Saharan Africa, where no challenge existed to French like that which Arabic posed in the Maghreb. Indeed, even now the controversy about the choice between African and European languages is virtually confined to the Anglophone parts of the continent, because with regard to Francophone areas, Arabization has made it irrelevant in the Maghreb while sub-Saharan Africa has shown little evidence of discomfort with the primacy of French. In fact, while complaining about the encroachment of English on French around the world and chastising French diplomats for occasionally departing from French, François Mitterand singled out the leaders of Francophone Africa for their exemplary loyalty to the language. At the Brazzaville gathering of mayors from Francophone territories in 1987, Jacques Chirac in his capacity as mayor of Paris proposed as the group's motto, "Cooperation for development, friendship, *francophonie*" (see "Francophone Mayors Meet"). As S. K. Panter-Brick has shown (330, 341), *francophonie* as a concept developed in the early 1960s to enfold collectively all French-speaking peoples, but especially those who share a French identity—*la francité*. In practice the group has come to include only the peoples of France and Francophone Africa, not those of Belgium, Quebec, or even Francophone Antilles, even though these last are considered *départments* of France.

Regardless of the colonial power involved, colonial education throughout the African continent uniformly privileged European cultures and languages over African ones. Peter Lloyd writes of the schools:

> Some were government managed, others run by missionary bodies. In either case the schools were usually located in the capitals or principal towns; most were boarding schools. Those of the French colonial territories were overtly assimilationist—many indeed had the children both of African and settler European populations. In the British territories of East and Central Africa with settler populations segregated educational facilities existed. But although the principles of indirect rule and *association* (in contrast to *assimilation*) guided the colonial governments in their policies of developing indigenous political institutions, in the educational sphere their schools were run on the lines of the English boarding school. The content of the curricula was almost entirely European—the staff knowing little about Africa. These schools divorced the youth from his local community during the most formative years of his life. They thus produced men who were elitist in outlook. (20)

Dennis Brutus, the South African poet, testifies from his own experience that the African writer educated under the colonial system was exposed to the mainstream of the English literary tradition, which left a lasting impression on him or her. It is little wonder, then, that, as he also observes, "some African writers have been criticized for a too-slavish imitation of their English models" (7).[2] Edward Braithwaite's Caribbean experience parallels and corroborates Brutus's, for, as he remarks, the effect of English education was to make the Caribbean more familiar with Sherwood Forest and Robin Hood than with "Nanny of the Maroons, a name some of us didn't even know until a few years ago" (18).

A not so direct but equally eloquent testimony to the effects of colonial education comes from Africa's first winner of the Nobel Prize for literature, Wole Soyinka. *Aké*, his memories of a colonial childhood, pictures an idyll centered in the sequestered mission parsonage, in the care of "Wild Christian," his mother, and Essay, his schoolteacher father, whose passions were for scholarly disputations and cultivating roses; Sunday afternoons at the parsonage featured high tea ceremonies. The laureate recalls an occasion when a colorful police band parade lured him to wander far beyond Aké until he found himself at the end of the parade in the police compound. There an English officer gamely but unsuccessfully attempted to communicate with him in Yoruba. The befuddled young Soyinka asked another (Yoruba) officer standing by, in English, what the Englishman was saying. The Englishman was amazed at Soyinka's English, and a rapport immediately developed between them (46–47). Soyinka also recalls that contemplating the figures on the stained-glass windows of their church, who looked very much like *egúngún* (masqueraders), he wished that they would some day materialize, but only on condition that they spoke English, for only then could he converse with them (32–33).

When the colonial powers eventually came to see empires as misfortunes to be shed as speedily as possible (Austin 23), their desire was to leave affairs in the hands of Africans who could be relied upon to maintain a continuity with the policies of the colonial period. France's assimilationist policy was well designed to serve that purpose, but not so Britain's "indirect rule." That policy was therefore discarded in favor of the strategy devised by Andrew Cohen, the colonial officer most responsible for the dismantling of the British empire in Africa. The traditional rulers, bastions of "indirect rule," were useless in the new scheme of building modern states; the elite, who had been hitherto largely excluded from the legislative and representative councils, were now to be groomed as successors of the colonizers (see Robinson).

At Independence the westernized elite class comprised three elements: the politicians, who constituted the ruling class; the intellectuals; and the army, or "elite with guns" (Clayton 207). Among the three the degree of westernization was by no means uniform, and the division of functions not always stable. As in the case of Léopold Sédar Senghor, sometimes the first two classes or elements coincided or overlapped, and soon after Independence the military element would also often become the ruling element. Whatever the case, the writers constitute part of the intellectual branch of the elite segment, and their operative language is the one the colonizers left in their wake.

Postcolonial Linguistic Continuity

In order to explain the persistence of European languages in independent Africa one might simply argue that since other colonial legacies have persisted—some as important as the fragmentation of formerly cohesive ethnic groups into different colonial zones, and the agglomeration of hitherto disparate groups into single states—there is no good reason to expect that language would be an exception. There are, however, other reasons. As I noted earlier, modern African literature is a product of the assimilated elite. When they tried their hands at creative writing they had no other choice of language than that of their education. Also, given the stigma of inferiority that attached to the use of African languages in the colonial era, the educated African felt hardly any misgiving about preferring European substitutes. At this point one should stress that Soyinka's account of his early proficiency in English and corresponding inadequacy in Yoruba is to be understood as evidence of precociousness rather than a lament over some sort of cultural deprivation. He was, he was informing us, the proverbial *àsàmú*. According to a Yoruba proverb, *Omo tó máa jé àsàmú, kékeré ló ti nsenu sámú-sámú* (A child that will grow to unparalleled stature will show his or her genius from childhood.)

The enduring colonial imprint on the African intellectual is evident in J.-L. Miège's observation that the universities remain even after Independence "the best examples of the colonial past" (45). The differences among postcolonial Africans, he suggests, are not ethnic (they may be from the same ethnic group) but derive from their different colonial pasts, and are discernible in the different ways that they write, think, and live. Those differences between the Anglophone Yoruba of Nigeria and their Francophone relatives across the border in the Benin republic prove his point.

The consequence for African literatures is that they have come to mean writings in English, French, and Portuguese. Only as a conscious effort does one include, grudgingly, "African-language literatures," and then only because the customary assumption about what constitutes African literatures, and in particular what part language plays in the determination, has lately lost its early confidence.[3]

Proponents of the status quo have offered other reasons for retaining non-African languages for literary purposes. One such reason appears in Sartre's "Orphée noir," the preface to Senghor's 1948 *Anthologie de la nouvelle poésie nègre et malgache de langue française* (Anthology of the new negro and Malagasy poetry in the French language). Sartre pointed out that colonized peoples lacked a common language as a consequence of the manner in which the colonial powers constituted their colonies. In general, distinct peoples who had never had much to do with one another were consolidated willy-nilly into administrative units for colonial convenience. As a result, people who found themselves as subjects in the same colony, and eventually as citizens in the same postcolonial nation, often could communicate among themselves only in the language of their colonizer. Ezekiel Mphahlele therefore had a point when he said that ironically, "colonialism had not only delivered 'the writers' to themselves, but had delivered them to one another, had provided them, so to speak, with a common language and an African consciousness; for out of rejection had come affirmation" (2). For, he added, even where colonialism had receded on the continent, European languages still served as a unifying force (8).

Writers obviously have certain readers in mind when they settle on the language to employ, if indeed they have a choice. (The question does not arise for some writers, of course, who conceive their activity as part of an intra-cultural dialogue.) For Chinua Achebe, for example, the chosen audience is one involved in "international exchange" (*Morning* 82–83). Writing for that audience distinguished between "serious" and "nondescript" writers. The former are those like him who have something to say to the world, and who are consequently better off expressing themselves in European languages. The latter are those of a much more modest calling, who must accordingly be content with African languages. Lewis Nkosi's description of the delegates to the 1962 Kampala conference of Anglophone writers captures the affectation of self-importance that attends the consciousness of election to international responsibility evident in Achebe's statement: they were mostly young, sardonic writers, he wrote, whose mien suggested amazement "that fate had entrusted them with the task of interpreting a continent to the world" (Nkosi 1). Ngũgĩ wa Thiong'o has also testified that writers at that time understood their duty to be "to explain Africa to the world: Africa had a past and a culture of dignity and human complexity" (20). When later on, antipathies developed between writers and rulers, be they civilian or military, the writers found their most sympathetic champions among the audiences they had cultivated abroad, and, understandably, they continued to direct their messages and complaints to those audiences. Charles Larson has in fact contended that the sometimes impenetrable English Wole Soyinka affected in his writings was a deliberate stratagem to get his works past African censors to his foreign readers (24).

Yet another argument for not writing in African languages rests on a practical consideration such as the writer's need to reach enough readers to make writing worth his or her while financially. Thus Gerald Moore insists that a writer should express himself "in a language that gives him a hearing (and a living)," leaving the development of "vernaculars" to those who are content with a "vernacular audience" ("Polemics" 9). Similarly, the Senegalese novelist and filmmaker Ousmane Sembène commented at the 1963 Dakar conference of Francophone writers that writing, "which is now my job," is a social necessity, like the jobs of the mason, the carpenter, or the ironworker" (in Moore, *African Literature* 57). He went on to assure his audience that if he had taken the trouble he could have written his novel *Le docker noir* in Wolof, his native language. "But then," he asked, "who would have read it? How many people know how to read the language? . . . Even written in French, how many Africans have read *Le docker noir?* Eighty-five per cent of the people here are illiterate; the rest can read and write but they do not read African authors. That means that our public is in Europe" (58). Along the same lines, Chinua Achebe's brief article on African reading habits (in *Morning* 50–54) outlines the reasons why the African writer could not hope to make a living writing for Africans. African intellectuals, he reports, read (if they read anything at all) history, economics, mathematics, and the like, hardly ever fiction or poetry; they simply had not developed the leisure habit of reading such things, as their European counterparts had.

In addition to the better living that writing in European languages affords African writers, another determinate factor is the international acclaim that comes from direct access to the international custodians of literary taste, and the rewards such access entails. Not least among these is the frequent invitations favored writers receive to speak of their writing (and otherwise perform) before audiences around the world, but especially in Europe, the Americas, Australia, New Zealand, and formerly, even in the Soviet Union.[4] As important, and perhaps more important, are the many prizes available to writers who address themselves directly to the external world. The list of African writers in European languages who have won such honors is impressive, honors such as the Commonwealth Literature Prize, the Noma Award, the Guardian Fiction Prize, the Jock Campbell/New Statesman Prize, Prix Renaudot, Prix Saint-Beuve, Prix Charles Veillon, and, of course, the most coveted of them all, the Nobel Prize that Soyinka finally captured in 1986. Although some African writers have chosen to forgo the opportunity for such honors and have instead elected to stick with African languages, we cannot minimize the temptation that the allure of a possible Nobel Prize and the status of cosmopolitan celebrity represents for a young and aspiring artist.

In discussing the problem of language policy in contemporary Africa in general, one must be mindful of the implications of the reality that in African literary studies and in African studies as a whole, Africa itself is at the periphery, while the centers are located elsewhere—in Europe or America. As long as that condition persists it is logical to expect that the operative and favored languages will be those of the centers.

The benefits of producing "African" literatures in non-African languages do not accrue only in the direction of the African writers, for non-African literary scholars and critics have correctly noted that were Africans to write in African languages their works would be inaccessible to all but a handful of the non-Africans to whom they are available at the moment. Robert Plant Armstrong, for example, sees Amos Tutuola's preference for English despite his lack of facility in the language as a boon for his foreign readers. Because Tutuola's material is close to Yoruba folklore, Professor Armstrong writes, "he has doubly blessed the serious student who does not command enough of Yoruba to understand the traditional texts as they are traditionally communicated by writing in English" (151). Similarly, O. R. Dathorne defends the same writer's idiosyncratic English, describing it as "a sensible compromise, between raw pidgin (which would be unintelligible to European readers) and standard English" (72).

Dathorne apparently believed, as many other critics did, that Tutuola's "young English," as Dylan Thomas described it in his *Observer* review, was a deliberate put-on by the writer rather than the best English he was capable of, as was indeed the case. As late as 1987 the same misconception persisted on the part of some critics. As an example, Mark Axelrod faults Dan Kunene's handling of his characters' language in *From the Pit of Hell to the Spring of Life,* saying, "No attempt is made to alter the prose, as Amos Tutuola does . . . to make it sound less Anglicized and more African" (18).

From Expediency to Preference

The discussion so far indicates that expediency and certain exigencies determined the language of African literatures in the crucial formative stages. A logical inference would therefore be that with their passing, and the return of more auspicious circumstances, normality will ensure. On the contrary, however, the predominant sentiment is in favor of perpetuating the preemption of African languages by European ones. The proponents of that option have been eloquent and energetic in justifying it.

Frantz Fanon's famous observation that "to speak means . . . above all to assume a culture" (17–18) refers in general to colonized peoples' attitude toward the colonizers' languages, not specifically to their employment for creative literary expression, but the statement is particularly relevant to the literary enterprise. Christine Souriau elaborates on Fanon's statement, describing language as "a guide to social and political relationships within a community as also between different communities" (310). Its discussion, she goes on, is not always objective, because it is always colored by ideology. "But," she surmises, "perhaps it is unrealistic to seek objectivity in this area which touches directly on the problem of identity and its affirmation" (311). The enduring controversy on the subject bears her out on the issue of objectivity.

Jean Paul Sartre's celebrated "Orphée noir" represented Negritude as a rebuttal to colonialist slanders against the African experience. "When you removed the gag that was keeping these black mouths shut," he asked, "what were you hoping for? That they would sing your praise?" (5). He further contended that the African writer, even though he might write in a European language, was really not interested in any manner of communication with the white world, which he had pointedly obliterated from his consciousness the better to celebrate blackness. That contention prompted O. Mannoni's invocation of the Caliban-Prospero relationship, which has proved so useful to some advocates of African faithfulness to European languages. Mannoni countered Sartre with the view that the assimilated colonial was not indifferent to the colonizer; rather, in reaction to the trick the latter had played on him—lifting him out of his native milieu only to strand him in a limbo, short of complete acceptance—the colonial was embittered and full of hatred for the colonizer. The colonial's complaint, like Caliban's to Prospero, was that at first the colonizer seduced and taught him the colonizer's language, then abandoned him in inferiority (Mannoni 76–77).

I have already alluded to Achebe's variation on the argument, which seems to have lost little of its appeal with the receding of the colonial period. In a similar vein Kofi Awoonor invokes the Caliban-Prospero relationship and argues that just as Caliban turned Prospero's language into a weapon against him, so African writers have converted the appropriated European languages into "an internalized weapon of our self-assertion because what we are also doing in the same process is to liberate ourselves from the strangle hold of Western cultural structures" (149). Also along the same lines Ezekiel (Es'kia) Mphahlele, calling to mind the multiplicity of languages on the continent, sees English and French as affording Africans "the common language with which to present a nationalistic front against white oppressors" (8).

Soyinka in effect reiterates Awoonor's points in his Nobel Prize acceptance speech. In a ringing homage he describes his native Yoruba world as "that which I so wholeheartedly embrace, . . . a world that nourishes my being, one which is so self-sufficient, so replete in all aspects of its productivity, so confident in itself and in its destiny that it experiences no fear in reaching out to others and in responding to others." He adds that because that world forms "the prism of our world perception . . . our sight need not be and has never been turned permanently inwards. If it were, we could not so easily understand the enemy on our doorstep, nor understand how to obtain the means to disarm it." He goes on to say, "When we borrow an alien language to sculpt and paint in, we . . . begin by coopting the entire properties of that language as correspondencies to represent our matrix of thought and expression" (in Gates, "Rhetoric" 21). One can fairly comment that Soyinka doth protest too much, for the very reasons that necessitated his construing rejection of a language as a testimony to its self-sufficiency and a demonstration of affection for it.

Most revolutionary perhaps are those arguments that set out to relegate language to near or total irrelevance in the realm of literature. One example is the complex of opinions that have emerged in approbation of Amos Tutuola's writing in English. Their underlying thesis amounts to an assertion that an artist need not be a master of his or her medium. The dissertation by Chinweizu and his collaborators on this subject in *Towards the Decolonization of African Literature* is a notable example. They insist that literatures written in European languages by non-Europeans are distinct from European national literatures (9), a proposition that is unlikely to incite opposition. But in order to legitimize African writers' use (or misuse) of non-African languages they devise a revolutionary set of criteria for attributing literatures to cultures. Accordingly they argue that although language embodies and expresses cultural values "it is not a crucial generator of those values and cannot *alone* be relied upon to supply literary criteria" (12; their italics). To underscore the limited role they would assign to language in such matters they resort to a musical analogy: "Just because an African or an Afro-American plays a piano—a European invention—does not at all mean that the highlife or jazz he produces on it is European music, which therefore should be judged by the same standards as European music" (14). They thereupon propose a ranking of the criteria that should determine the categorization of literatures, according to which language places in the fourth and last slot, behind (1) primary audience, (2) the work's implicit cultural and national consciousness, and (3) the author's nationality by birth or naturalization (13).[5]

Mphahlele's objection to African languages arises from his conviction that they are simply inadequate, because they lack "a technical terminology and a vocabulary that meets the needs of systematic analytic contemporary thought" (8). Unfortunately, that patently untenable opinion is current among a distressing number of intellectuals in the African diaspora; Baker reports that a Yale University Professor from a formerly colonized portion of the world . . . claimed that he could not express his "most complex and striking notions" in any language other than English. "I suggested," says Baker, "that the Creole of his native island might be quite suitable for 'advanced thought' " (x).

Time after time some new argument surfaces to demonstrate, among other truths, that once one commits oneself to an option one's lucidity and objectivity regarding that option vis-à-vis alternatives become easy casualties. As an instance Olasope Oyelaran argues against replacing English with Yoruba in the relevant parts of Nigeria by suggesting that language and culture are not necessarily linked. He quotes Malcom Gutherie as authority to assert that English, unlike other languages, is culture-neutral (304), and that the Yoruba person who uses it presumably only avails himself or herself of a resource that belongs to all peoples of the world. Furthermore, he calls attention to the immense prestige it confers, adding:

> There is no doubt that social and parental attitudes towards the acquisition of English are exuberantly enthusiastic in Nigeria. . . . Even the Yoruba speaking Nigerians would sacrifice anything to acquire English, because it is the way to academic honors—the proverbial 'Golden Fleece' to all Nigerians. And academic honors are widely cherished as the *key* to material well-being. (309; Oyelaran's italics)

Another irresistible argument (in his view) for not disturbing the status quo is, ironically, that the Yoruba area is only part of a country that includes people who speak other languages; the promotion of Yoruba would, he thinks, be disruptive for the political arrangement (302). The same argument would of course apply to the other indigenous languages of the country. The irony of using the mosaic nature of postcolonial countries, which is blamed for necessitating the imposition of European languages in the first place, as a reason for not restoring African languages is inescapable.

In 1963 Obiajunwa Wali recommended that African writers follow the examples of Spenser, Shakespeare, Donne, and Milton, writers who opted for their national languages even though the fashion favored the more prestigious Latin (13–15). To continue writing in alien languages, he warned, would be to pursue "a dead end, which can only lead to sterility, uncreativity, and frustration." Moore, holding brief for the writers, rejected that course and offered his own vision of the future instead. "More likely than a simultaneous renaissance of hundreds of African vernaculars," he wrote, "is the gradual divergence and emergence of a distinctive African idiom in English, a process which has already taken place in America and the West Indies" ("Polemics" 9).

The arguments for retaining the hegemony of European languages in African letters are not uniformly spurious. Some have some cogency and deserve serious attention. One of these comes from Dennis Brutus. South Africans, he explains, are suspicious that attempts to turn them toward their own languages and cultures are simply another strategy to consolidate apartheid. He notes that a great deal of literature, both oral and written, is produced in South African languages such as Zulu, Xhosa, Sotho, and others. He continues:

> There is a very special bind here, though, that I ought to explain. Because the apartheid government—the minority white government—has tried to revive the old tribal structures and to force the Africans back into those structures in order to prevent them from participating in the present political process, the Africans tend to be suspicious even of their own languages and literary vehicles. They are fearful that these might be turned against them and used as one further pretext to force them back into a tribal mode within a broad policy of what are known as the Bantustans—a strategy that is aimed at forcing black Africans back into tribal structures. (11–12)

Coping Strategies

Having deprived themselves of the most obvious and customary index of the cultural grounding of their literary products, which would be the language of the particular culture, African writers in European languages have had to explore alternatives to suggest a cultural ambiance, in other words, to add a cultural flavoring. One of the best-known devices, exemplified in the early novels of Chinua Achebe, is the use of proverbs. Since traditional African discourse tends to rely to a considerable degree on proverbs, the writer creates frequent opportunities to insert them both in his authorial descriptions and in the dialogue of his characters. Another device is to suggest the lyricism and dignified profundity characteristic of traditional discourses by preferring words with Anglo-Saxon origins to those with Greek or Latin roots. While Achebe also adopted this device, the best examples occur in Ayi Kwei Armah's *The Healers* and *Two Thousand Seasons* (both 1979). The relative simplicity of Anglo-Saxon words, coupled with the relative brevity of sentences in the dialogue, justifies the description of the language in such works as simple, a description that has been mistaken by some critics for an imputation of artlessness. For example, Eustace Palmer objected to my pointing out this feature with regard to early Anglophone African writers. He took exception to what must have seemed to him a charge that the writers lacked complete mastery of their adopted language (113–14).

Other strategies include the literal translation of African idioms into English—either deliberately, as in the case of Nkem Nwankwo's *Danda* (1964), for example, or innocently, as in the early works of Amos Tutuola. The most famous use of this strategy is the bold experiment Gabriel Okara carried out in *The Voice* (1964), in which he combined Ijo syntax with English lexis. The freshness of the result is apparent in such passages as the following: "A stinking thing like a rotten corpse be, which had made us all, you and me, breathe freely no more for the many years past. Now we are free people be, free to breathe" (72). Where the writers wish to indicate some difference between an object they have in mind and the one commonly understood to be designated by the English word they have chosen, or where they have chosen to use the African word, they have usually resorted to what Niyi Osundare describes as "cushioning," brief (but sometimes extended) explanatory diversions, or the attachment of a comparable English term as an alternative. Again Achebe's earlier novels offer the best instances in such constructions as "*agadi-nwayi*, or old woman" (*Things Fall Apart* 9), "elders, or *ndichie*" (10), "hut, or *obi*" (11), "*chi* or personal god" (14), and so forth.

Generally speaking, with enough practice the writers develop the ability to integrate their chosen devices into their works seamlessly, such that they call little attention to themselves. Here again Achebe set the example, for his later works such as *A Man of the People* (1966) successfully and unobtrusively integrate his glosses with the contextual materials. These stratagems are not without pitfalls, for while certain readers and critics applaud the poetry of Armah's language in his historical novels, for example, others find his style somewhat too labored and affected. Moreover, however much the writers succeed in masking the dilemma that attends their choice of language, Osundare's observation that they are forced to spend an inordinate amount of time and energy on medium at the expense of content will remain valid. Instead of struggling with "lexical equivocations" (16) and "masochistic linguistic acrobatics" (21), he suggests, the writers would do better to write in their own languages.

Objections to the Deemphasis of Language

To reiterate the basic thesis of this discussion, the relegation of language to the margins in literature certainly defies logic and common usage, and has inevitably led those who attempt it into considerable difficulties. By its very nature literature is the manipulation of language, and the established practice is to base the determination of its cultural underpinning on the language of its expression. The nationality of the writer is not enough to assign his or her writing to a particular tradition. French literature is not simply the literature of French-speaking peoples, but literature written in French, and Arabic literature is similarly not simply the literature of Arabic-speaking peoples but literature written in Arabic. When one speaks of English, or French, or German literature one does not speak in political terms but rather in linguistic or cultural terms. The confusion would be eliminated if the lexical formulation were not the same for both. Consider, for example, Arab literature and Arabic literature. The former would be literature written by an Arab, whether it is in Arabic or not, and the latter would be literature written in Arabic, answering to whatever cultural values one associated with Arabic, whether the work was written by an Arab, an African, an Indian, or an Indonesian.

Significantly, in the discipline of literature one customarily refers to English literature rather than British literature, to emphasize the linguistic and the cultural rather than the political aspect. (On the other hand, one speaks of the British empire, rather than the English empire.) The point is that one may carry the passport of a nation (an African nation, for example) and yet write literature that would belong in a different tradition (say, Arabic or French).

Acceptance of the other criteria that some writers and scholars have offered instead of language poses its own problems. If one were to take the audience for which the work is written, one would have to conclude that those works the writers themselves concede were directed at Europeans to correct or debunk their slander against Africans must be regarded as European literature. Championship of European languages as the proper media for African writing has engendered, as one would expect, some confusion and inconsistency. Ngũgĩ lists Taban lo Liyong among the three lecturers whose activism resulted in the dethronement of English literature as the centerpiece of the literature department at Makerere University (94). Those lecturers believed that in an African institution African cultures (and African cultural products) should occupy that position, while those that belong to other parts of the world must position themselves around the periphery according to their relevance. Yet while fighting that entirely heroic battle on behalf of African cultural rehabilitation, lo Liyong also ridiculed Nigerian university graduates for finding fault with Tutuola's choice of English as his medium (160).

Similarly, in a BBC program in December 1986 Chinweizu responded to the award of the Nobel Prize to Soyinka by describing the laureate as a "euro-assimilationist type of writer as opposed to the frankly nationalist and Africanist kind of writer" (see "Soyinka on BBC"). He referred in particular to Soyinka's famous ridiculing of Negritude in its heyday, a ridiculing that, in Chinweizu's view, "marks the division . . . between the assimilationists who do not want to have much to do with African nationalism in cultural matters and the Négritude writers who made that part of their central theme" (20). He added:

> I thought that his works and the Nobel Prize deserve each other and for those of us who hold that the Nobel Prize is an undesirable prize in Africa and who also find most of Wole's works unreadable I thought from that position that his getting the Nobel would be a case of the undesirable honoring the unreadable. (21)

That indictment of Soyinka, a writer who prides himself on being an African nationalist, is undoubtedly harsh. Chinweizu's disapproval results from what he perceives as Soyinka's too intimate familiarity with Greco-European sensibilities and his incorporation of them in his works—and, of course, from what he regards as the opacity of Soyinka's English. Considered in light of the critic's rather visible and vocal campaign in favor of decolonizing African literature and the African mind, it is not surprising or unexpected. But while he objects that the difficulty of Soyinka's language, which makes him unreadable to university professors like himself, also renders him undesirable in Africa, he does not similarly object to the use of the English language itself, which makes African writers unreadable or unintelligible to most Africans. Thus, while dismissing Soyinka's Nobel Prize, earned for his English-language writings, he had no qualms about himself accepting the Association of Nigerian Authors Prize for his own English-language poetry in 1985.

Facing the Future

Several commentators have remarked on the brevity of the colonial period in Africa. John Hargreaves, one among them, observers, "In the long perspective of history, the period when Europeans exercised direct political control over West African peoples was brief: except in a few special areas closely involved in the conduct of oceanic trade, it nowhere exceeded the life-time of an old man" (73). In response to the question of whether these were "years of revolutionary importance," he cites J. F. Ajayi's representation of the colonial period as "just another episode . . . in the continuous flow of African history." Hargreaves continues:

> Africans who successfully practiced the "politics of survival" were able eventually to recover their sovereignty with their essential identities intact, having acquired new institutions, techniques and problems without suffering fundamental social or cultural upheaval. He could find unwanted support among those old imperialists who, shaking their heads over the latest news from Uganda or Angola, conclude that Africans are reverting to their unregenerate past; being colonized has done them no good at all. (73–74)

Osogbo, the town in which I grew up, was a colonial district headquarters—the seat of a district officer—and an important stop on the Lagos–Kano railway. It also had its European quarters and branches of assorted European commercial enterprises. Yet I knew people who lived their entire lives in the town without once coming in direct contact with a European, or ever once seeing a railway train. Such was the colonial experience for most Nigerians, not the sort that results in a sea change. It seems in retrospect hardly enough to obliterate permanently such an important cultural resource as language; but that prospect is a distinct possibility if the present attitude of writers and intellectuals toward African languages persists.

But there are reasons to believe that the trend is not irreversible. Ngũgĩ's announcement in 1986 that henceforth the vehicle for all his writing would be "Gĩkũyũ and Kiswahili all the way" (xiv) is a positive development. Before him Sembène had arrived at a similar decision, after an encounter with his people opened his eyes to the hiatus that separated him as a French speaker from them. When in 1979 he showed his French-language films to village audiences, for whom he professed to have made the films, they asked him why, if the films were for them, he had made them not in their language but in his own (Armes 83). "I had not at that moment realized how far I had alienated myself from my people," he commented. "I made a study of our films and then I realized that if I wanted to make films for my people, then it must be in their language." Since the choice of language implied the choice of audience, he vowed that he would thereafter direct himself to his own people and not to the world (Gabriel 38). If enough canonical literary figures followed suit they might persuade aspiring writers that they have a viable future as users of their own languages.

We may also take heart from the tendency of praise for African masters of European languages more and more to be alloyed. Thus, while he celebrates Soyinka's capture of the Nobel Prize, Henry Louis Gates also acknowledges that Africans' use of European languages signifies and repeats the economic dominance of Western Judeo-Christian, Greco-Roman cultures and their traditions over those of color ("Writing" 6).

Moreover, Africa can hardly remain immune from the nationalistic and linguistic revolutions that periodically erupt to reinstate submerged and subjugated national languages. Wali had such an eruption in mind when he urged African writers to take a leaf from the book of Spenser, Shakespeare, and Milton, and an example from the medieval revolt against the hegemonic languages of the period. He was on far surer grounds than Gerald Moore, who rebutted him with the experience of the West Indies, which he recommended for Africa also. Frederich Heer, describing in *The Medieval World* how subjugated peoples used their national languages as rallying points to assert their distinct identities, writes:

> Anguish, anger, sorrow, burning hatred and burning love presided over the birth of the national literatures of Europe. The growth of languages implies the growth of nations. The people came alive as their languages gathered strength in opposition to the Latin which was the trademark of Rome and of the universalizing culture of professors, clerks and officials. (360)

The medieval period in fact provides useful ammunition for those who would see national languages triumph over "universal" or "world" languages. Souriau notes several instances of resistance to linguistic domination through history, including the struggle in England between the eleventh and fourteenth centuries among the Britons, the Saxons, and the Normans, a struggle settled in favor of the English language in the area of London. The Latin Middle Ages, she observes, may be seen as evidence of cultural universalism, or as "organized domination by elites," but it also involved "the long neglect and underdevelopment of popular or national languages" (312). Braithwaite cites Dante Alighieri as the "forerunner . . . who, at the beginning of the fourteenth century, argued, in *De vulgari eloquentia* (1304), for the recognition of the (his own) Tuscan vernacular as the nation language to replace Latin as the most natural, complete, and accessible means of verbal expression" (22).

Our own times have their own instances of linguistic and cultural reassertion. In the months preceding the collapse of the Soviet Union in 1991 we watched Soviet Georgians revolt when authorities from the Kremlin attempted to relegate the Georgian language to parity with Russian within the Georgian republic. Latvians, Estonians, and Lithuanians similarly continued to demand that their languages be accorded priority in their republics over Russian, flatly rejecting the proposition that a universal Russian sway in the Soviet Union would cement "national" bonds or promote the "nation." The nations that matter most to these peoples are those defined by their languages and cultures, and these they were not about to surrender in preference for some meaningless geographical pastiche superimposed on them by a coercive will. Along the same lines, the French-speaking Canadian province of Quebec has rekindled the old smoldering fire of their campaign to make French the only legitimate language in the province, and thus to ensure that the French character of the province, at least of the majority of the population, is reflected in the language it uses, permits, or privileges. English, the dominant language of the Canadian nation as a whole, the provincial government would confine to shop signs well hidden within the stores. Without guarantees to that effect the Quebecois threaten to declare themselves a sovereign nation; so important are language and culture to them.

I have mentioned the allure of prestigious international prizes as one reason African writers steer away from their own languages and toward European ones. With the award of the Nobel Prize for literature for 1988 to Naguib Mahfouz, an Egyptian who writes in Arabic, that particular inducement for adopting "world languages" (meaning European languages)[6] has lost much of its force. Mahfouz caught the attention of the international community without compromising his tongue and culture; someday an African writer might afford enthusiasts for African languages an opportunity to celebrate by earning the prize with works in African languages.

The limitation that the multiplicity of African languages, or lack of a common African language, imposes on writing in African languages deserves a brief comment. The concept "African literature" is of a kind with, say, "Asian literature," or "European literature," in that all are geopolitical constructs that embrace a number of distinct elements, especially languages and nationalities. Africa encompasses a number of different nations (whether we mean true traditional nations or postcolonial pseudonations), just as do Asia and Europe. Therefore, just as "Asian literature" would be a convenient shorthand for a long list of literatures—Japanese, Korean, Chinese, Indian, and so forth—and just as "European literature" would similarly be a shorthand collectively for English, French, Dutch, German, Polish, and other literatures of the subcontinent, so "African literature" must be seen as a convenient shorthand for the many distinctive literatures of the African continent.

A critic may be justified in dismissing the tenor of the whole debate on the language of African literatures, as I have traced it in this discussion, as beside the point. The critic might argue that the debate does not take sufficient account of the fact that by derivation, in name and in practice, African literatures (*canonical* African literatures, that is) are imported Western forms, be they poetry, drama, fiction, autobiography, or the essay. That there are in certain cases more or less analogous indigenous forms is immaterial. Since African literatures are imitative, the critic might then argue, there is no reason why the imitativeness should exclude language, the medium of the art. After all, the argument would go, if there were a musical form called the "African symphony," one would not insist that its instruments and instrumentation be indigenous. That line of argument does, however, place the putative form at the margins of African life, where its threat to traditional institutions is limited. One cannot say the same of African literatures.

This discussion of the language of African literatures, whether canonical or hegemonic, has been more historicist than historical. One major reason is that the history of language in the discipline has been virtually a lack of history, a lack of movement, for little has changed since the pioneering producers of the literatures made their fateful and all but inevitable choice of their colonizers' languages for their writing. Wali's call for a return to African languages did occasion some debate, and the debate still continues. The optimism I expressed with regard to gestures on behalf of African languages (like Ngũgĩ's and Sembène's, referred to earlier, and Soyinka's recommendation of Swahili to all African writers at the time of the 1977 Second World Black and African Festival of Arts and Culture—Festac II) may prove unjustified, for they have been ineffectual. They have had little effect in redirecting aspiring African writers from European to African languages. Indeed, the African embarking on a literary career will be aware that no matter in what language Ngũgĩ writes, his work will be either simultaneously or immediately translated into "world languages," because his reputation has already been made, thanks to his English career. The new aspirant would understandably choose the same avenue and medium to establish himself or herself. And while Ngũgĩ has at least made the gesture of writing in Gĩkũyũ, Soyinka for his part has not followed his own recommendation and written in Swahili.

One could certainly write a rich history of the twists and turns in the debate on the proper language(s) for African literatures, but such an essay would be more appropriate in a history of African literary criticism. A historicist essay is proper in this context, especially because of the necessity of stressing the historicity of the displacement of African languages by European ones for the expression of what are nonetheless regarded as "African voices" (Rutherfoord 1970). Acceptance of the fact that historical developments, specifically those associated with the subjection and colonization of the continent by Europeans, gave rise to the anomaly would increase the likelihood of the acceptance of the corollary proposition that historical processes can correct it. In other words, when properly placed in the context of historical dialectics, the use of European languages by African writers loses the aura of necessity some Europhone writers and Europhile critics are wont to invest it with, and the various arguments that serve them as subterfuges also lose their force.

Notes

1. For a fuller discussion see chapter 5, "Prejudice and Policy, 1914–1960," in Charles H. Lyons's *To Wash an Aethiope White.*

2. In this regard see Chinweizu, Jemie, and Madubuike on the derivativeness of the poetry of Wole Soyinka and Christopher Okigbo, which they stigmatize as "The Hopkins Disease" (172ff).

3. As early as 1963 Donatus Nwoga voiced his objection to that assumption at the

Freetown seminar on "African Literature and the University Curriculum." "It has been suggested," he said, "that what we call African writing is really primarily English or French or Portuguese or Italian or Spanish literature, and only secondarily African. I would prefer to consider that what we call African literature is *primarily African* and *secondarily English or French etc.*" (Moore, *African Literatures* 84–85; Nwoga's italics).

4. It is something of an irony that Ngũgĩ's dissertation on why Africans should write in African languages took shape as a series of lectures he was invited to give at Auckland University in 1984. We may safely assume that he would not have received the invitation had he written in Gikuyu. He indirectly says as much when he writes (6) that he qualified to attend the 1962 conference of writers in Kampala, even though he was a student with only two stories in English to his name, while well-established writers in African languages were not invited. It is also interesting to note that the African Literature Association (USA) has honored Amos Tutuola by inviting him as an honored guest to one of its annual conferences, whereas (to my knowledge) it has not so honored established writers in African languages.

5. For an extended discussion of the debate on what standards African literatures should observe see Rand Bishop, *African Literature, African Critics: The Forming of Critical Standards, 1947–1966*, New York: Greenwood Press, 1988, especially chapter 2.

6. I am indebted here to Chinua Achebe's usage of the term in his discussion of the usefulness of English to the Third World writer (*Morning* 79).

Works Cited

Achebe, Chinua. *Morning Yet on Creation Day*. Garden City, N.Y.: Anchor Books, 1976.
———. *Things Fall Apart*. London: Heinemann, 1958.
Armes, Roy. *Third World Film Making and the West*. Berkeley and Los Angeles: University of California Press, 1987.
Armstrong, Robert Plant. *The Affecting Presence: An Essay in Humanistic Anthropology*. Urbana: University of Illinois Press, 1971.
Austin, D. G. "The Transfer of Power: Why and How." In *Decolonisation and After: The British and French Experience*, edited by Georges Fischer and W. H. Morris-Jones, 3–34. London: Frank Cass, 1980.
Awoonor, Kofi. "Tradition and Continuity in African Literature." In *In Person: Achebe, Awoonor, and Soyinka*, edited by Karen L. Morell, 133–63. Seattle: African Studies Program, University of Washington, 1975.
Axelrod, Mark. Review of *From the Pit of Hell to the Spring of Life* by Daniel Kunene. *Bloomsbury Review* 7 (1987): 18–19.
Baker, Houston A., Jr. "English as a World Language for Literature: A Session for the 1979 English Institute." In *English Literature: Opening Up the Canon*, edited by Leslie A. Fiedler and Houston A. Baker, Jr., ix–xiii. Baltimore: Johns Hopkins University Press, 1981.
Braithwaite, Edward Kamau. "English in the Caribbean." In *English Literature: Opening Up the Canon*, edited by Leslie A. Fiedler and Houston A. Baker, Jr., 15–53. Baltimore: Johns Hopkins University Press, 1981.

Brutus, Dennis. "English and the Dynamics of South African Creative Writing." In *English Literature: Opening Up the Canon*, edited by Leslie A. Fiedler and Houston A. Baker, Jr., 1–14. Baltimore: Johns Hopkins University Press, 1981.

Chinweizu, Onwuchekwa Jemie, and Ihechukwu Madubuike. *Toward the Decolonization of African Literature*. Vol. 1, *African Fiction and Poetry and Their Critics*. Washington, D.C.: Howard University Press, 1983.

Clayton, Anthony. "The Military Relations between Britain and Commonwealth Countries, with Particular Reference to the African Commonwealth Nations." In *Decolonisation and After: The British and French Experience*, edited by W. H. Morris-Jones and Georges Fischer, 193–223. London: Frank Cass, 1980.

Dathorne, O. R. "Amos Tutuola: The Nightmare of the Tribe." In *Introduction to Nigerian Literature*, edited by Bruce King, 64–76. New York: Africana, 1972.

Fanon, Frantz. *Black Skin, White Masks*. New York: Grove Press, 1968.

"Francophone Mayors Meet." *West Africa* 3653 (1987): 1607.

Gabriel, Teshome, H. *Third Cinema in the Third World*. Ann Arbor, Mich.: UMI Research Press, 1982.

Gates, Henry Louis, Jr. "On the Rhetoric of Racism in the Profession." *ALA Bulletin* 15, no. 1 (1989): 11–21.

———. "Writing, 'Race,' and the Difference It Makes." *Critical Inquiry* 12, no. 1 (1985): 2–20.

Hargreaves, John D. "Assumptions, Expectations and Plans: Approaches to Decolonisation in Sierra Leone." In *Decolonisation and After: The British and French Experience*, edited by W. H. Morris-Jones and Georges Fischer, 73–103. London: Frank Cass, 1980.

Heer, Frederich. *The Medieval World: Europe, 1100–1350*. Translated by Janet Sondheimer. New York: Mentor, 1961.

Irele, Abiola. *The African Experience in Literature and Ideology*. London: Heinemann, 1981.

Larson, Charles R. "Wole Soyinka: Nigeria's Leading Social Critic." *The New York Times Book Review*, 24 December 1972, pp. 6–7, 10.

Liyong, Taban lo. *The Last Word: Cultural Synthesism*. Nairobi: Modern African Library, 1969.

Lloyd, P. C. *The New Elites of Tropical Africa*. London: Oxford University Press, 1966.

Lyons, Charles H. *To Wash an Aethiope White: British Ideas about Black African Educability, 1530–1960*. New York: Teachers College Press, 1975.

Makinde, M. Akin. *African Philosophy, Culture, and Traditional Medicine*. Monographs in International Studies, edited by James L. Coban. Athens, Ohio: Ohio University Center for International Studies, 1988.

Mannoni. O. *Prospero and Caliban: The Psychology of Colonization*. New York: Praeger, 1956.

Miège, J.-L. "The Colonial Past in the Present." In *Decolonisation and After: The British and French Experience*, edited by W. H. Morris-Jones and Georges Fischer, 35–49. London: Frank Cass, 1980.

Mitterand, François. *Réflexions sur la politique extérieure de la France* [Reflections on France's foreign policy]. Paris: Fayad, 1986.

Moore, Gerald. "Polemics: The Dead End of African Literature." *Transition* 3, no. 11 (1963): 7–9.

———, ed. *African Literature and the Universities.* Ibadan, Nigeria: Ibadan University Press, 1965.

Mphahlele, Ezekiel. "Polemics: The Dead End of African Literature." *Transition* 3, no. 11 (1963): 7–9.

Ngũgĩ wa Thiong'o. *Decolonising the Mind: The Politics of Language in African Literature.* London: James Currey, 1986.

Nkosi, Lewis. "MAK/V(I)." In *Conference of Anglophone Writers*, edited by Ezekiel Mphahlele. Kampala: Makerere College, 1962.

Nwankwo, Nkem. *Danda.* London: Heinemann, 1964.

Okara, Gabriel. *The Voice.* London: Heinemann, 1964.

Ologunde, Agboola. "The Yoruba Language in Education." In *Yoruba Language and Literature*, edited by Adebisi Afolayan, 277–90. Ibadan, Nigeria: University of Ife Press, 1982.

Osundare, Niyi. "Caliban's Gamble: The Stylistic Repercussions of Writing African Literature in English." Paper presented at the 1982 Ibadan Annual Conference on African Literatures, University of Ibadan, Nigeria.

Oyelaran, Olasope. "Yoruba as a Medium of Instruction." In *Yoruba Language and Literature*, edited by Adebisi Afolayan, 300–312. Ibadan, Nigeria: University of Ife Press, 1982.

Palmer, Eustace. Review of *African Literatures: An Introduction*, by Oyekan Owomoyela. *Research in African Literatures* 12, no. 1 (Spring 1981): 110–15.

Panter-Brick, S. K. "La Francophonie with Special Reference to Educational Links and Language Problems." In *Decolonisation and After: The British and French Experience*, edited by W. H. Morris-Jones and Georges Fischer, 330–45. London: Frank Cass, 1980.

Robinson, Ronald. "Andrew Cohen and the Transfer of Power in Tropical Africa, 1940–1951." In *Decolonisation and After: The British and French Experience*, edited by W. H. Morris-Jones and Georges Fischer, 50–72. London: Frank Cass, 1980.

Rutherfoord, Peggy, ed. *African Voices: An Anthology of Native African Writing.* New York: Universal Library, 1970.

Sartre, Jean-Paul. "Black Orpheus." In *The Black American Writer*, vol. 2, *Poetry and Drama*, edited by W. E. Bigsby, 5–40. Baltimore: Penguin Books, 1969.

Souriau, Christine. "Arabisation and French Culture in the Maghreb." In *Decolonisation and After: The British and French Experience*, edited by W. H. Morris-Jones and Georges Fischer, 310–29. London: Frank Cass, 1980.

Soyinka, Wole. *Aké: The Years of Childhood.* London: Rex Collins, 1981.

"Soyinka on BBC." *ALA Bulletin* 13, no. 1 (Winter 1987): 18–23.

Thomas, Dylan. "Blythe Spirits." In *Critical Perspectives on Amos Tutuola*, edited by Bernth Lindfors, 7–8. Washington, D.C.: Three Continents Press, 1975.

"Tributes to Wole Soyinka." *ALA Bulletin* 13, no. 1 (1987): 18–26.

Wali, Obi. "The Dead End of African Literature?" *Transition* 3, no. 10 (1963): 13–15.

13 Publishing in Africa:

The Crisis and the Challenge

HANS M. ZELL

The indigenous book and publishing industries in most African countries are currently in a state of crisis after a decade of relative boom and rapid expansion. Much of Africa has become a bookless society. Because of foreign exchange constraints most libraries in Africa have been unable to purchase any new books for the past few years, much less maintain their journal subscriptions. Research and teaching, meanwhile, have been crippled.

The constantly deepening economic recession and chronic balance-of-payments problems in most African countries have taken a severe toll on publishing and book development in general, and on the output of new African writing in particular. Many publishing enterprises have become dormant; others have drastically cut back their operations, with far fewer new titles being published each year. The dearth of publishing outlets has meant that young writers and scholars are finding it difficult to place their work. Most literary magazines and scholarly periodicals have stopped publication or publish only sporadically, providing fewer and fewer publishing facilities and leading to a stifling of scholarship as well as creative writing.

Yet in the midst of the most adverse circumstances some remarkable books continue to come off African presses, and a new self-help marketing initiative by African publishers will henceforth greatly enhance the visibility of African publishing in Europe and North America.

Publishing in Crisis

The salient facts about Nigerian publishing are a vivid example of the handicaps under which publishers are laboring. In this previously oil-rich country, the introduction in 1986 of the second-tier foreign exchange market (an element in an overall structural adjustment program imposed by the International Monetary Fund) led to a dramatic devaluation of the naira.

Some sections of this paper first appeared in *Logos* 1, no. 2 (London, 1990).

369

From being on par with the dollar in the mid-1980s, by 1990 it required seven naira to purchase one dollar. Many of the materials for book production still need to be imported into Nigeria, including paper and printing equipment and supplies. But the loss of purchasing power of the naira has had a crushing effect on import prices, and publishers also face high customs tariffs. Nigerian publishers have thus ended up in a Catch 22 situation. They should be able to benefit from the much-restricted flow of imported books by filling the vacuum, yet they cannot do so because they face prohibitive import prices for the materials to publish locally. The demand is there, but it cannot be met, and this at a time when the need is probably greatest.

Elsewhere in Africa the situation varies from country to country, but few indigenous publishers have been able to meet the challenges of the book shortages caused by the economic crisis. Moreover, the majority of them are still at a disadvantage over the multinationals and are unable to compete with them on real terms. A viable indigenous publishing industry that can produce books on a scale that matches local needs is, sadly, still largely a dream in most parts of the continent.

It seems to be stating the obvious that African authors should have the realistic option of publishing within Africa, that the image of the cultural heritage of any country can best be projected by indigenous publishers, and that school textbooks should be available that emanate from and reflect the country in which they are used. Over the past two decades several international organizations, and many individuals, have suggested long-term measures that would favor the local production of books and aid the setting up of truly autonomous publishing enterprises—that is, enterprises that might be run without undue government interference or pressure and that could exist without massive subsidies. Numerous conferences and meetings in Africa on publishing and book development have been preceded by fine opening speeches by government ministers stressing the importance of books in national development and concluding with pious resolutions. And in the current discussions on the grave book famine in Africa it has been repeatedly and quite rightly stressed that book donations alone cannot and should not be seen as the long-term solution to the shortage of books in Africa, and that it is vital for indigenous publishers to be supported. Yet the indisputable fact remains that few African governments have taken positive and decisive action to support their indigenous book industries, certainly not in the private sector. Meanwhile, the book industries and library development continue to take a back seat in the pursuit of national development, despite pious conference resolutions to the contrary.

In the case of Nigeria again, and when there was a favorable environment in the early 1980s for the development of a strong autonomous publishing industry, the Nigerian government of the time provided neither encouragement to indigenous publishers, nor investment, nor concessions. The net result is that today there is a continuing reliance on the importation of finished books and the materials required for printing and paper manufacture.

Instances of rather more enlightened government attitudes may be found, in Zimbabwe, for example, and especially in Francophone West Africa, where the governments of Senegal, the Ivory Coast, and Togo jointly set up Les Nouvelles Editions Africaines, albeit with French publishing interests. Nouvelles Editions Africaines is now a major force in all areas of publishing, with a massive and impressive list, although it can be argued that their dominance and near monopoly has probably stifled the growth of small independent publishers.

MULTINATIONALS

The much-maligned multinationals, which so dominated the publishing scene in the 1960s and 1970s, are now largely out of favor with African governments, or certainly no longer play such a dominant role as they coexist, relatively peacefully, alongside indigenous publishers.

Over the years a great deal of stereotypical claptrap has been said and written about the multinationals, and while their sometimes exploitative role has been rightly exposed and criticized, some of the accusations—for example, that the multinationals are producing books that are not relevant to an African reader or an African environment—may have been true thirty years ago but are certainly no longer universally true today. There is plenty of evidence that many of the multinationals are now engaged in publishing African-oriented books and literature, conceived and published in Africa by Africans. In other cases, former branches of the multinationals have paved the way for new indigenous companies. For example, at Heinemann Kenya, while continuing some links with Heinemann's in the United Kingdom, the majority equity is now firmly in Kenyan hands, and the Heinemann Kenya list is probably one of the most innovative and enterprising in the whole of Africa. True, they too must first and foremost concentrate on the bread-and-butter lines and mainstream educational publishing, but the firm has also published a whole broadside of creative writing and popular fiction and has an extensive list of children's books and books in the African languages.

STATE PUBLISHING

The verdict on government involvement in publishing must be that by and large it hasn't worked. Parastatals, where they exist, are frequently hampered by bureaucracy, inefficiency, or lack of motivation on the part of their staff. Many state publishing enterprises were ill conceived, many of the projects supported by international lending agencies were simplistic in design, and much aid money in books or library development schemes was invested in an unplanned or uncoordinated way.

In some countries the government has decided that only books written by their own curriculum development advisors or curriculum institutes should be used as textbooks, the lack of competition leading sometimes to poor-quality material and depriving local publishers of a vital source of income.

In Kenya a completely new educational system and syllabus was introduced in the mid-1980s that brought with it the need for a vast number of new textbooks to replace existing ones. There were great expectations that this demand would benefit not only the transnationals but also the burgeoning indigenous publishers, who were keen to get a slice of the cake. The government subsequently decreed, however, that it would recommend only those books published by the state publishing corporations, such as the Jomo Kenyatta Foundation and the Kenya Literature Bureau, and only material written at its national curriculum development center. This decree set up the kind of incestuous arrangement—seen elsewhere in the past both in Africa and other developing countries—whereby books are written, vetted, approved, and published and distributed by the same state monopoly, leaving the market without competition and the private publishing sector out in the cold.

THE BOOK FAMINE

Collapsing economies and the chronic balance of payments problems in almost all countries of the continent have taken a heavy toll on educational budgets and, in turn, on libraries and the book industries. The picture of Africa at the beginning of the 1990s is largely that of a bookless society. Not only has there been a dramatic decline of funds available for book and journal purchases generally, but because of the foreign exchange constraints many university and public libraries in Africa have been unable to purchase any new books over the past four or five years, much less able to maintain their current periodicals collections. Most bookshops present a picture of empty shelves, schools are without books, research has been crippled, and teachers and scholars are divorced from the materials needed to pursue their studies, to maintain their understanding of developments taking place in their disciplines elsewhere in the world, and to keep their teaching or research up to date. African academics are more and more marginalized, unable to participate in contemporary academic debates or at conferences.

The scarcity of books has meant that neither the needs of educational institutions nor the general public can be met. The effects of the book famine also mean that devastating and quite possibly lasting damage is being inflicted across a whole generation of people going through primary, secondary, or university education in Africa today. A generation of students is now being taught by lecturers who are unable to gain access to current research and scholarship. The lack of books and teaching materials has led to students' having to rely on lecture notes provided by their teachers, and it hardly needs to be stated that such teaching methods cannot be conducive to enlightened learning and the acquisition of knowledge.

Meanwhile, in libraries the poor state of provision of books and journals has lead to a whole wave of vandalism, characterized by the mutilation of books and journals, or outright theft.

INDIGENOUS PUBLISHING

What is remarkable is that, despite the overall gloomy picture I have recounted in the previous pages, and despite the difficult economic conditions and lack of government encouragement, new indigenous imprints continue to mushroom all over Africa, and some privately owned firms have shown a great deal of imaginative entrepreneurial skill in the midst of adversity. This flowering is not quite the paradox it might seem. Established and new firms do flourish, but not always to their full potential, and not enough of them to meet the needs. There is, alas, also a high mortality rate among the new companies. Some of them have come to grief not only because of unfavorable economic conditions but because of sometimes inept financial management, poorly trained and motivated staff, inadequate day-to-day administration, or ineffective marketing and promotion, especially overseas.

New autonomous publishing firms invariably face the need to raise fairly substantial sums of high-risk and initially low-return investment capital, and most of them are badly undercapitalized. At the same time, I am always astounded by the constant woes and cries that new African or Third World publishers are grossly undercapitalized, as if this were something unique to struggling new publishers in the Third World, whereas in fact the new publisher starting off in Abingdon, Berkshire, or Tulsa, Oklahoma, faces precisely the same problems, admittedly in a somewhat different publishing environment.

There are particularly dynamic indigenous publishing companies in Zimbabwe, Kenya, Nigeria, and even in Ghana, which was especially hard hit by the economic recession. In Nigeria some indigenous imprints have had notable successes and have conducted aggressive local marketing campaigns for some of their output. Nigerian editions of books by prominent African writers such as Chinua Achebe or the Nobel laureate Wole Soyinka are now increasingly published locally at realistic, albeit still expensive, prices. Another positive development is the fact that Nigerian newspapers (Nigeria has a vigorous newspaper industry, with some thirty dailies in addition to dozens of weeklies) devote much more space nowadays to book reviews and articles on publishing and book development. There is also a vast crop of a whole new generation of writers looking for publishing outlets—many Nigerian writers now bitterly complain that local publishers have not risen to the occasion, or are extremely slack in submitting royalty statements, much less parting with hard cash!

Piracy, meantime, seems to be on the wane, although a number of Nigerian academics and writers have come out with some of the most extraordinary statements encouraging piracy. For example, Onwuchekwa Jemie, writing in the Nigerian *Guardian* (25 January 1987), a respected high-quality daily, lumped all publishers together as a class of "mostly liars and cheats," calling on book pirates to unite and make a major onslaught of illicitly reprinting everything they could lay their hands on. Happily, the call does not appear to have been taken up.

KEY ISSUES

The development of the book industries in Africa today has been affected, and will continue to be heavily affected, by infrastructural problems and the economic recession. Many social and cultural dimensions compound the problem: a multiplicity of languages, a still high level of illiteracy (over 50 percent of Africa's population is still illiterate), poor transport and communications, lack of training and expertise, and other obstacles have all played their part in hindering the development of the reading habit and the growth of a healthy book industry. For general publishing—or publishing in the African languages, or children's books—effective distribution is still the main headache, although some publishers have tried to come to grips with the problem and have explored novel and innovative ways of getting books to the marketplace and to the rural communities.

One of the most fundamental issues for publishers and writers alike is the matter of language. The question whether to write in an African language or in a European language has been vigorously argued, and debates about new norms, new ways for writers to reach the people, are recurring themes. An increasing number of African authors are trying to reach a national audience through an indigenous language, most prominent among them the Kenyan writer Ngũgĩ wa Thiong'o (who, paradoxically, is living in exile in London). Ngũgĩ has repeatedly stated that only through writing in an African language can an African sensibility truly develop, and that writing in an African language might compel African writers to become more relevant, more meaningful, and closer to the realities of African life. Dissenting voices have argued, however, that to write in any of the African languages would restrict their work to a small group of readers, and to select an international language provides them with a medium of communication that will allow their books to be published in many countries.

While this debate will no doubt continue, the language issue also greatly affects publishing developments: on the one hand, the vast number of languages creates special problems for African publishers, and on the other, African governments' decisions on language policy will significantly influence future publishing developments in Africa in general, and the success and viability of publishing in African languages in particular.

There have been repeated calls by African writers for African publishers— both the multinationals and the indigenous—to devote more time and spend more of their resources on publishing material in African languages for the general reader, and material intended for enjoyment rather than achievement reading. Some firms have bravely experimented in this area—some, for example, have published translations into African languages of works of fiction written in English by major African writers—but although there have been some modest successes, publishing in the African languages has often proved to be disappointing in commercial terms, certainly for titles for the general markets. New approaches will be needed, innovative experimentation in seeking out the audience, eliciting feedback and response, and ultimately meeting the challenge of a potentially vast local readership and bringing books into the economic reach of the rural poor. But no publisher in his right senses will want to dabble in such worthy causes unless either the books are subsidized or the publisher can also benefit from more mainstream publishing and the more lucrative educational book markets.

READERSHIP

Another key issue is that of readership and the reading habit. Attitudes toward books and reading in Africa have been governed by social circumstances and by cultural and economic factors. Economic factors are certainly a major issue: annual income per capita is still very low in most African countries, ranging from as little as $200 in the poorest nations to something in the region of $700–$800 in countries such as Nigeria and Zimbabwe. With such levels of income the problem is survival; there are precious few resources for buying books.

It has frequently been lamented in the past, by such prominent writers as Chinua Achebe, that Africans do not continue with reading once formal education or a university degree has been obtained. It is probably quite true that, in the past, reading was never a large part of the tradition of life in Africa, and more pleasure was derived from the oral tradition and the performing arts than from reading a book. But then the educational methods imposed on Africans by their erstwhile colonial masters hardly encouraged them to read for enjoyment. Reading was a serious business, not to be indulged in for pleasure. Reading was only for prescribed literature at school, an instrument with which to acquire academic knowledge and success and with which to pass examinations. Nonetheless, whereas much of the reading that takes place in Africa today may still be geared toward achievement reading, the remarkable success of a substantial number of general books in, for example, Nigeria, Kenya, and Zimbabwe has demonstrated that the readers are there. In Nigeria, for instance, Kole Omotoso's *Just before Dawn*, a lively blend of fact and fiction dramatizing the first one hundred years of Nigeria, has been a runaway best-seller and has sold in quantities well in excess of twenty thousand copies.

The emergence during the past decade of African-produced mass paperbacks of popular fiction has also created a new kind of readership. And while some controversy about the sometimes dubious quality of some of this popular literature continues, it has nonetheless created an appetite for reading among people who did not in the past want to read books for pleasure. It can also be argued that this popular fiction may sensitize the ordinary reader to progress ultimately to more serious works of creative writing.

In the meantime, it is clear that the whole question of the audience has to be more fully studied and investigated. More research has to be carried out to determine what people want to read—the preferred reading interests in different African countries—and how reading can contribute to the improvement and enrichment of the quality of life of the ordinary African reader. The question of the audience certainly presents a formidable challenge to African publishers.

AFRICAN BOOKS COLLECTIVE

The priorities of many publishers in Africa, of necessity, must still lie at home. But with the proliferation in particular of African scholarly and literary works, a great deal of African-published material is now much in demand by libraries, scholars, and other book buyers throughout the world. Unfortunately, overseas promotion by African publishers has been weak, the international markets have been barely touched, and export earnings have been negligible. Moreover, the acquisition of African publications by libraries in Europe and North America has been difficult. All this should now change, and another bright spot amid all the gloom is the early success— probably much to the surprise of several skeptics—of a new African self-help initiative, African Books Collective Ltd. From concepts and proposals first explored at a 1985 London meeting of a representative group of African publishers, this new operation has now started trading, following four years of preparatory work and fund-raising activities. The collective addresses both the needs of African publishers to more effectively promote and disseminate their output in the major English-language markets and the needs of libraries facing chronic problems in the acquisition of African-published material.

Nineteen African publishers have joined African Books Collective (ABC) as founding members and will produce joint lists and catalogues, with ABC providing centralized order fulfillment, billing, and shipping. The collective maintains small office premises in Park End Street in central Oxford and has on its premises a small showroom with a constantly changing display of titles distributed by the collective, in addition to sample copies of backlist titles not carried as part of the inventory but that may be obtained on special order. Warehouse premises are maintained separately in nearby Burford.

The unique nature of African Books Collective is that it is a nonprofit organization that aims only to cover its operational costs, although it naturally seeks to be profit-making on behalf of its constituent members by substantially increasing their export earnings. Overseas list prices are established in consultation with member publishers and on the basis of what the market will bear. African publishers fully benefit from the proceeds of the overseas markup, and their net sales earnings are substantially higher than what would be the case with conventional commercial distribution agreements.

Governed by a Council of Management consisting of elected representative publishers from East, West, and Central and Southern Africa, funding for the organization has come in part in the form of onetime membership fees paid by founding members and applied against capital and setting-up costs. However, in the light of ABC's nonprofit status and the preferential terms offered to publishers, who receive roughly 65 percent of net receipts, it was realized at an early stage that the initial volume of turnover and the proportion of the income retained by the collective would be insufficient to meet recurrent operational costs and that there would be considerable shortfalls of income over expenditures, at least in the first few years. The collective therefore sought seed money to meet the initial deficits and to separate finance capital and setting-up costs. The Ford Foundation, NORAD, and SIDA have provided financial support, and the Commonwealth Foundation provided partial funding for an inaugural meeting of the Council of Management. And while the money raised did not entirely meet the fund-raising targets, sufficient financial support was raised to enable the collective to set up an efficient operating base and to start trading.

African Books Collective's financial position is still rather precarious, and fund-raising activities continue to seek support for recurrent cost budgets. Setting up its own warehousing has not come cheap, but it will enable the collective to have full control of its distribution service and, even more vital, of its own credit and cash collection. About 400 titles were in distribution in 1990, for the most part recently published, with the expectation of adding some 150–200 new titles to the inventory each year. The emphasis is on scholarly and academic books, creative writing by African authors, and critical works on African literature, but certain general interest items and some children's books are also stocked.

The establishment of ABC has already generated a great deal of excitement among Africana librarians, and the collective is offering standing orders and "profile" plans to meet individual library requirements.

Literary Publishing in Africa South of the Sahara: A Brief Overview

Literary publishing in Africa does not have a long history: apart from some of the early Onitsha Market novels and a number of titles in African languages, literary book publishing activities, or literary imprints, did not begin to emerge on any scale until the early 1960s.

One of the earliest indigenous publishing ventures in Black Africa was the establishment of the Mbari Artists' and Writers' Club and Mbari Publications in Ibadan, Nigeria, in July 1961 by a group of writers, artists, and art lovers. Ulli Beier, a member of this group and arguably its prime inspirer, had earlier helped to launch the literary and cultural magazine *Black Orpheus*, together with the late Janheinz Jahn. The first issue of *Black Orpheus* was published in 1957, and between 1961 and 1965 Mbari released some thirty titles by a number of aspiring young African writers, both from Nigeria and other parts of Africa. They were little known at the time, but are now household names of modern African literature. Kofi Awoonor, Dennis Brutus, Es'kia Mphahlele, Christopher Okigbo, Wole Soyinka, and Tchicaya U Tam'si were among them. Almost all of their books published by Mbari— now long out of print and prized collectors' items—have since been reissued either individually or have been included in expanded collections of these authors. By the early 1970s, however, the operation became dormant and an initiative later by the University of Ife Press to revive its activities proved abortive.

On the other side of the continent, the bulk of literary publishing output came from the East African Publishing House, which, established in 1965, was instrumental in launching several series devoted to African creative writing, including the Modern African Library, with its best-selling *Song of Lawino* by Okot p'Bitek. Sadly, the East African Publishing House went into liquidation in 1988, but a number of the titles on its list have recently been reissued under the Heinemann Kenya imprint.

The early 1970s saw an explosion of mass paperback publishing of popular fiction, especially in Kenya, and where a number of publishers were suddenly discovering new markets. David Maillu's Comb Books were the pioneers in this area. The books were similar to the Nigerian Onitsha Market literature, but they were rather more sophisticated, more elitist, and better produced. Some of David Maillu's books came under fire, however, because of their sometimes cheap morality, and several were actually banned in Tanzania for a period. A whole broadside of popular paperbacks, most of them thrillers or romantic fiction, later on emerged in Nigeria as well.

In Francophone Africa publishing has mainly flourished with the help of either government or church support. Francophone book industries at first tended to lag behind their Anglophone counterparts. The situation was dramatically changed, however, with the founding in Dakar, in 1972, of Les Nouvelles Editions Africaines, as a joint undertaking of the governments of Senegal, the Ivory Coast, and Togo, along with French publishing interests. NEA has since progressed to a position where it is undoubtedly the leading publisher for the whole of French-speaking Africa. There is little competition, and the only two other sizeable publishing operations in French-speaking Africa are the Center d'Edition et de Diffusion Africaines (CEDA) in Abidjan and the church-sponsored Centre de Littérature Evangélique (CLE) in Yaoundé, Cameroon. As mentioned earlier, this lack of multiplicity of publishers has come in for some criticism, for providing African writers with limited outlets and putting them in a subservient position; the nature of the partnerships between Francophone African governments and French publishers has also come under some hard scrutiny. Nonetheless, the establishment of NEA must be considered one of the more enlightened publishing initiatives and it has helped to break the near-monopoly exercised by French publishers in the African markets in the past.

Literary publishing activities in Africa today are primarily concentrated in a few countries, which the following sections examine in turn.

WEST AFRICA

Nigeria, despite all the problems, maintains a lively publishing industry, and new imprints continue to emerge every year. Publishers with strong literary lists include Fourth Dimension Publishers; Heinemann Nigeria; Macmillan Nigeria; University Press, Ltd. (the former Oxford University Press Nigeria); and Spectrum Books of Ibadan, which has a reputation for the aggressive marketing of its products. Occasional works of literary criticism come from the university presses such as Ibadan University Press, Obafemi Awolowo University Press (formerly Ife University Press), and the University of Lagos Press. There are also several small imprints with high-quality literary lists, among them 'Biola Irele's New Horn Press, Ltd.; Chinweizu's Pero Press; Ken Saro-Wiwa's Saros International Publishers; Flora Nwapa's Tana Press; Dillibe Onyeama's Delta Publications; Agbo Areo's Paperback Publishers; Dafe Otobo's Malthouse Publishers; and Fountain Publications, the publishers of the Nigerian edition of Wole Soyinka's *Isara: A Voyage Round Essay.* And Update Communications in Lagos has recently published, on behalf of the Association of Nigerian Authors, several volumes of verse by young Nigerian poets.

As indicated earlier, however, indigenous publishers have had to take a lot of flak from Nigerian writers, who have accused them of being interested in publishing only for short-term gain and making a "fast buck," and of generally lacking vision. To some extent, perhaps, this is true; for one thing, good author relations do not seem to be high on the list of priorities of some publishers, and there also seem to have been some serious shortcomings in royalty accounting. For others, marketing and promotion beyond Nigeria appears to be nonexistent. It must also be said, however, that many writers—both established writers and aspiring ones—lack a real grasp of publishing realities, especially the realities of operating in a Nigerian situation. It takes a brave publisher to publish volumes of poetry or fiction by as yet little known writers: few retail outlets will be willing to stock them, and those that do may insist on sale-or-return terms and may return half the consignment in tatty condition a few months after they were supplied; or there may be serious collection problems. To sell books in neighboring countries, say, within the ECOWAS region—much less in other parts of Africa—is virtually impossible because of the currency problems.

In Ghana literary publishing has been severely curtailed in recent years because of the country's balance-of-payments problems, resulting in acute paper shortages and lack of spare parts to repair defective printing presses. The position is now beginning to improve again, and one imprint with an attractive and imaginative literary list is W. A. Dekutsey's Woeli Publishing Services, whose authors include Kofi Awoonor and Kofi Anyidoho.

FRANCOPHONE WEST AFRICA

Publishing in Francophone West Africa has already been mentioned briefly. Nouvelles Editions Africaines in Dakar, along with NEA operations in Abidjan and Lomé, heavily dominates the scene, with a massive literary list of over 250 titles of fiction, drama, and poetry, together with several collections and volumes of literary criticism. Many of the familiar and distinguished names from the literary as well as the academic world now appear on their list, and NEA has also published a wide range of writing by young and as yet little known authors. The late Mariama Bâ's remarkable first novel on the female condition in Africa, *Une si longue lettre,* was the first winner, in 1980, of the Noma Award for Publishing in Africa (the Japanese-sponsored five-thousand-dollar annual prize established to honor indigenously published African authors), and the novel subsequently appeared in sixteen different editions and translations. Five years later, NEA again won the (1985) Noma Award for a novel by the Cameroonian writer Bernard Nanga, *La trahison de Marianne,* which was awarded posthumously.

In the Côte d'Ivoire CEDA has an active literary list, and in Togo literary publishing is spearheaded by Yves-Emmanuel Dogbe's Editions Akpagnon, whose list includes fiction and poetry as well as several short story collections.

Publishing activities in the Cameroons have declined sharply in recent years. Notably, the well-known Editions CLE and small independent firms such as Buma Kor, Rene Philombe's Editions Semences Africaines, and Timothée Ndzaagap's Editions Populaire, in Bafoussam, seem to have been largely dormant for the past few years.

FRANCOPHONE AFRICA ELSEWHERE AND INDIAN OCEAN ISLANDS

In Francophone Central Africa there are sporadic outbursts of literary publishing activities, as well as a substantial amount of popular fiction publishing. Most of this comes from Zaire, where publishers in the forefront of literary publishing include Editions Lokole, Editions Impala, and Les Presses Africaines. The Presses Universitaires du Zaire publish a wide range of scholarly books, including several critical studies on African literature, and CEEBA in Bandundu produces several series of specialist volumes on African myths and folklore. In the neighboring Congo Popular Republic publishing is still in its infancy, but some volumes of poetry and drama have come from Leopold Pindy Mamonsono's Editions Heros dans l'Ombre, in Brazzaville.

Mamonsono was also the prime mover behind the establishment of the Association des Ecrivains d'Afrique Centrale, which organized an International Literary Symposium of African Writers against Apartheid in May 1987 in Brazzaville, and which established the Concours Littéraire International de Poesie contre l'Apartheid, with the first award going to Marouba Fall of Senegal.

Book production in the Indian Ocean island of Madagascar is primarily in the national language, Malagasy, and some of the major publishers include Editions Takariva, FOFIPA, and the Madagascar Print and Press Company. In Mauritius there is a dearth of publishing outlets for local writers, which has prompted many of them to publish their work in India. There is only one publishing house of any size, Editions de l'Océan Indien (jointly owned by the government of Mauritius with British and French publishing interests), which produces largely educational texts, although a small amount of creative writing, including several anthologies, has also appeared. Much of the local publishing is in Mauritian Creole by authors who double as their own publishers and distributors. On the island of Réunion, finally, is quite a flourishing literary publishing scene, and much of the initiative has come from the Association des Ecrivains Réunionais, which has published a sizeable number of books under the appropriately named imprint Editions Goute d'Eau dans l'Océan.

EAST AND CENTRAL AFRICA

In Kenya, which had the liveliest book industry in English-speaking Africa for many years, publishing activities, particularly in the literary arena, have dramatically declined over the past decade. Several publishers have gone bankrupt, notably the East African Publishing House, along with several small imprints. Publishers are given little encouragement to produce works of fiction or books aimed at the general markets, and they have to work in a generally hostile business environment. One notable exception is Heinemann Kenya under Henry Chakava, the publisher of Ngũgĩ wa Thiong'o and, as mentioned earlier, without doubt the most enterprising and most adventurous firm in the literary field, with an imaginative list of works of fiction, drama, and poetry, as well as creative writing in several African languages. The only other publisher with any significant literary output is Longman Kenya, which boasts a strong line of popular fiction, with Meja Mwangi as its star author. Occasional literary titles come from Foundation Books (in Swahili), the Kenya Literature Bureau, Oxford University Press Eastern Africa, Uzima Press, and Asenath Odaga's Lake Publishers, in Kisumu.

Literary publishing activities in Uganda are virtually nonexistent, although there is now evidence of one or two small new imprints emerging, for example, Crane Publishers in Kampala. In Tanzania the publishing industries face enormous obstacles, and the flow of new books from major publishers such as the Tanzania Publishing House has been dramatically cut back. Zambia, too, is another country where the development of an active indigenous book industry has been beset with many difficulties and, as elsewhere in Africa, has been tied up with the country's chronic balance-of-payments problems. Meanwhile, the state-sponsored Kenneth Kaunda Foundation (formerly the National Educational Company of Zambia) struggles on bravely and produces occasional literary items, as do one or two other publishers such as Multimedia Zambia and Dzuka Publishing.

In Malawi the main thrust of literary publishing has come from Popular Publications of Limbe, and their Malawian Writers Series has now grown to a respectable number of titles, consisting of short stories, folklore, drama, texts of oral narratives and poetry, and works of fiction in the country's main language, Chichewa.

SOUTHERN AFRICA

Probably the most exciting publishing developments in Africa at the present time are taking place in Zimbabwe, which has one of the continent's most dynamic publishing industries. Ironically, Zimbabwe is also the country that imposes and operates some of the most restrictive practices with regard to the free flow of books in Africa. On the one hand, Zimbabwe imposes a 20 percent duty on book imports (and slaps on a further 15 percent sales tax for good measure), and, on the other, makes the exporting of books as difficult and cumbersome as it possibly can. Local publishers first have to obtain an export license (or the Reserve Bank of Zimbabwe may insist on prepayment by the recipient for any books leaving the country, clearly an impractical requirement, especially where large consignments are involved), and all sorts of red tape and bureaucracy first have to be overcome before indigenous publishers are allowed to sell their books abroad, and actually earn their country some much-needed hard currency.

The major publishers of literature are College Press—with an impressive list of books in English by Zimbabwe's leading writers, and also publishing fiction and short story collections in Shona and Ndebele—the Zimbabwe Publishing House, Mambo Press, Longman Zimbabwe, and the Literature Bureau. Several recently established small imprints include the Anvil Press and Baobab Books. The tenth Noma Award for Publishing in Africa, awarded in 1989, went to the Zimbabwean writer Chenjerai Hove for his powerful novel *Bones*, published by Baobab Books in 1988, and which was also the recipient of the Zimbabwe Publishers Literary Award. *Nervous Conditions*, by Tsitsi Dangarembga, copublished by the Zimbabwe Publishing House and the Women's Press in the United Kingdom, won the Africa Region Commonwealth Prize for Literature for 1989.

In Lesotho and Swaziland local publishing is still largely underdeveloped, but a proliferation of government and scholarly publishing in Botswana has arisen to meet the needs of an expanding educational and scholarly market, and some of the multinationals, especially Macmillan, have set up sizeable operations in the country and are benefiting from one of the few booming economies in Africa today. But the size of the market is probably too small for any indigenous publishers to survive and prosper.

In Namibia local publishing has been virtually nonexistent apart from government and newspaper publishing and the output of a Native Language Bureau. In the wake of Namibian Independence in 1990, this situation will no doubt change, new indigenous imprints reflecting African aspirations will probably emerge soon, and already there is talk about the setting up of a Namibia Publishing House. The multinationals, too, will probably be clamoring for a slice of the new business that is going to be in the offing.

In Lusophone Mozambique and Angola publishing and the book trade is controlled by the government, through each nation's Instituto Nacional do Livro e do Disco. The INLD in Maputo has produced over two million books since its inception, and this number includes some splendid children's books as well as creative writing by Mozambican authors. In Angola the main initiative has come from the Angolan Writers Union, which has led to substantial print runs of the works by over seventy Angolan authors. In 1986 an INALD book from Angola, *Sobreviver em Tarrafal de Santiago* (Surviving in Tarrafal de Santiago),* Antonio Jacinto's lyric testimony to the human spirit triumphant over tyranny and injustice, won that year's Noma Award.

This overview of literary publishing in Africa will not attempt to report in depth about publishing in South Africa, which of course has a well-established book industry, and which has largely escaped the economic ravages elsewhere in Africa. Tribute must be paid, however, to a number of small independent companies who have actively encouraged Black expression in South Africa, and who have published a great deal of socially committed writing despite having to operate under a repressive regime that, until very recently at least, has faced them with threats of banning, harassment, or arrest. Ravan Press of Johannesburg is probably the best known among the small crop of publishers who have been in the forefront of oppositional publishing in South Africa over the past decade, courageously challenging apartheid ideology and actively promoting the struggle for a just, democratic and nonracial society. Ravan Press has a strong fiction list, several series of poetry and drama, as well as children's books. They have twice won the prestigious Noma Award—in 1988 for a history book aimed at a popular audience (by Luli Callinicos), and earlier, in 1984, for Njabulo Ndebele's short story collection *Fools and Other Stories*.

Three other imprints that must be mentioned are Adriaan Donker, David Philip, and Skotaville Publishers: Donker has a particularly strong poetry list; David Philip has an extensive list of fiction, drama, poetry and criticism;

---

*Tarrafal is the name of the concentration camp in colonial Cape Verde where the author was incarcerated for several years. *Ed.*

and Nadine Gordimer, the late Richard Rive, Miriam Tlali, Alan Paton, Jack Cope, Guy Butler, and Menan du Plessis are among David Philip authors. David Philip is also the publisher of the Africasouth Paperbacks series, reissues of works of Southern African literature that have been long out of print but that deservedly have now been rescued from neglect. The same series also includes original writing and books by a number of Black African authors whose work was previously banned in South Africa.

Skotaville Publishers is a wholly Black-owned publishing collective established in 1982 and named after Mweli Skota, secretary general of the ANC in the 1930s and a writer and editor as well as a politician. Skotaville was set up by the African Writers Association, and its two prime movers are Jaki Seroke and Mothobi Mutloatse, who work with a board of directors that includes Miriam Tlali, Sipho Sepamla, and Es'kia Mphahlele.

Among other alternative presses are a women's publishing cooperative named Seriti sa Sechaba Publishers, Buchu Books, and Jonathan Ball Publishers. Following the momentous events in South Africa early in 1990 and the signs that, at long last, there may now be some genuine reform in South Africa, there are exciting times ahead for all of South Africa's progressive publishers.

Literary Periodicals and Magazines

Literary journals in Africa, as elsewhere, tend to live a precarious existence. Many new journals are started in Africa each year; a few have been successful and prosper, but most others have sunk after the first issue or have become dormant after a year or two. Many have taken off with the best of intentions and fine first issues—and frequently with recklessly optimistic initial print runs—but have not survived beyond "volume I, number 1." High editorial standards, a sense of purpose and mission, and a clear focus are clearly all vital if a journal is to build for itself a reputation of excellence. But editorial vision is not enough, and one of the most persistent reasons for the high mortality rate among African literary journals—and indeed, literary magazines published elsewhere—is that in addition to usually feeble overseas promotion and marketing, the vital aspects of effective subscriptions management and fulfillment, and the business and administrative side, are usually neglected. Many journal publishers also seem not to realize just how difficult it is nowadays to start a new journal, how long it will take to attract, and thereafter retain, overseas library subscriptions, and that libraries in most parts of the world now face serious budgetary restraints and many must face canceling existing subscriptions, much less taking on new journals. Too many new journals are still started without editors or publishers first identifying their key market segments and determining just how large that market is, how that market can be reached and at what cost, how a new journal might be made attractive to that target market, and how long it might take (in most cases several years) to build up a solid subscriber base and to generate sufficient income to at least recover editorial, manufacturing, and marketing and promotion costs.

The late 1960s and early 1970s saw an abundance of African literary magazines, notably those published in East Africa. But all of them, *Busara*, *Dhana*, *Joliso*, *Umma*, and *Zuka*, have long since ceased publication. The most influential and most outspoken cultural and political magazine was *Transition*, once aptly described by Abiola Irele as a journal that was "not merely reporting about Africa or feeling its pulse, but charting the directions of its mind." *Transition* was published in Uganda between 1961 and 1975, edited by Rajat Neogy. It then moved to Ghana and was renamed *Ch'indaba* with its fiftieth issue, and Wole Soyinka became its new editor for a period until it ceased publication in 1976. Plans to recommence publication in London did not materialize. Happily, in 1991 *Transition* restarted publication from a U.S. base, with Henry Louis Gates and Kwame Appiah as editors, and Wole Soyinka as its editor-in-chief.

Another journal that continues to be sporadically revived is the famous *Black Orpheus*. Occasional issues have appeared in recent years under the imprint of the University of Lagos Press, and most recently under the editorship of Theo Vincent. The longest survivor, and arguably the most important and most successful literary magazine actually published in Africa, is *Okike* (Enugu, Nigeria) under the editorship of Chinua Achebe, although it, too, has suffered from frequent delays in publication. *Kiabara* (Port Harcourt, Nigeria) is another survivor published irregularly, but the attractively produced *New Culture* (Ibadan, Nigeria) unfortunately is one of the many literary magazines that had to suspend publication after only a year or two.

Francophone West Africa has two impressive journals in *Ethiopiques* (Dakar), published quarterly by the Fondation Léopold Sédar Senghor and edited by Moustapha Tambadou (a special issue, vol. 5, nos. 1–2 [1988], was devoted to "*les métiers du livre*"—the book trade), and the *Revue de littérature et d'esthétique négro-africaines* (Abidjan), edited by N'Guessan Djangone Bi and published by the Côte d'Ivoire branch of NEA. The well-known *Abbia* has been dormant for many years, but may well be resuscitated once more in the near future.

In Southern Africa literary and cultural journals of note are *Marang* (Gaborone), published, albeit irregularly, by the Department of English at the University of Botswana since 1980, and *Moto* (Harare), published by Mambo Press, a monthly digest of comments and events concerning Zimbabwe and the international scene, and including news and reviews of film, radio, and television programs as well as providing regular space for publication of creative writing by Zimbabweans.

In South Africa, the leading literary and cultural magazines are the large-format *ADA Magazine* (Howard Place); *The Classic* (Braamfontein), sponsored by the African Writers Association and published by Skotaville Publishers, which contains short stories, drama, poetry, critical writing, and graphics and photography; *Contrast* (Cape Town); *Critical Arts* (Durban); *Journal of Literary Studies* (Pretoria); UNISA *English Studies* (Pretoria); and the excellent critical forum *English in Africa* (Grahamstown), published twice yearly by the Institute for the Study of English in Africa at Rhodes University.

But perhaps the most interesting and most successful venture on the South African literary scene was the launching by Ravan Press, in 1978, of *Staffrider* (Braamfontein), which is still going strong and celebrated its tenth year of publication by issuing a special edition (vol. 7, nos. 3–4) bringing together some of the finest stories, poems, photographs, graphics, essays, and popular history published over the past decade. The magazine takes its name from the young men who ride "staff" on the crowded commuter trains from South Africa's Black townships, by climbing perilously on the roofs of the carriages or standing on the steps, entertaining or alarming their more sedentary fellow passengers. The name of the magazine therefore reflects the precarious lifestyle of young urban Blacks. *Staffrider* is under the control of an informal editorial collective, and whereas many well-known writers have appeared in its pages, it was principally conceived as an outlet for young and often inexperienced writers and to feature, in its arts sections, the work of community-based projects.

Among new literary and cultural journals that have commenced publication over the past several years are *Ngoma* (Lusaka, Zambia, 1986–), *Journal of the Humanities* (Zomba, Malawi, 1987–), *Uwa ndi Igbo/Journal of Igbo Life and Culture* (Nsukka, Nigeria, 1984–), *Ifè: Annals of the Institute of Cultural Studies* (Ile-Ife, Nigeria, 1987–), *Kriteria: A Nigerian Journal of Literary Research* (Onitsha, 1988–), *Mokwadi: Writers Workshop Journal* (Gaborone, Botswana, 1987–), *EJOLLS: Ekpoma Journal of Languages and Literary Studies* (Ekpoma, Nigeria, 1988–), and the *African Theatre Review* (Yaoundé, Cameroon, 1985–). Finally, the ANA *Review* (Lagos, 1985–), the annual journal of the Association of Nigerian Authors, is an absolutely goldmine of information for current literary activities in Nigeria. Unfortunately, the publication is "for private circulation only," restricted to members and the ANA seems to be determined that nobody outside Nigeria should hear about its activities!

Conclusion

Whereas the 1970s might have been described as a decade of boom and expansion, the 1980s can only be described as a decade of crisis for the African book industries. The chronic balance-of-payments problems in most African countries have had a crippling effect on publishing and book development. Government funds available for school textbooks, or library funds, have steadily and dramatically declined, with inevitable consequences for the book industries. And for lack of funds and hard currency, much of Africa is becoming a tragically bookless society.

Yet amid the most difficult circumstances, there is still evidence of a great deal of intellectual vigor and enterprise by African publishers. Moreover, despite the enormous problems and obstacles, there are important challenges to seize. New directions can open up if African publishers respond in the 1990s to the opportunity to develop, by publishing in African languages and promoting African-language literatures. New approaches will be needed: innovative experimentation in seeking out the audience, eliciting feedback and response, bringing books into the economic reach of the rural poor, and exploring new and more effective marketing and distribution channels. The challenge is there.

A positive development amid all the gloom is the establishment of African Books Collective. Essentially a marketing and distribution operation, it may represent a turning of the tide well beyond marketing. First, it will enhance the visibility of African book publishing output. Second, by collectively providing their own nonprofit organization, African publishers will improve their economic base, providing them with more hard currency sales earnings. Those earnings, in turn, will also stimulate increased publishing activities at home. Third, the existence of the collective will help African publishers to persuade top African writers and scholars to publish with them, rather than with overseas firms, and those publishers will be able to demonstrate to their authors that they can effectively project their work and standing in the international markets. These developments will help to promote the independence of African publishers and their authors on a basis of equality with their colleagues overseas.

Works Cited

Bâ, Mariama. *Une si longue lettre*. Dakar: Nouvelle Editions Africaines, 1979. *So Long a Letter*. Translated by Modupé Bodé-Thomas. London: Heinemann, 1981.

Dangaremba, Tsitsi. *Nervous Conditions*. London: Women's Press, 1988.

Ethiopiques. Special issue of *Les métiers du livre* 5, nos. 1–2 (1988). Dakar: Foundation Léopold Sédar Senghor.

Guardian (Lagos), 25 January 1987.

Hove, Chenjerai. *Bones*. Harare: Baobab Books, 1988.

Jacinto, António. *Sobreviver em Tarrafal de Santiago* [Surviving in Tarrafal de Santiago]. Luanda: Instituto Nacional do Livro e do Disco, 1985.

Nanga, Bernard. *La trahison de Marianne* [Marianne's treachery]. Dakar: Nouvelles Editions Africaines, 1984.

Ndebele, Njabulo. *Fools and Other Stories*. Johannesburg: Ravan Press, 1983.

Omotoso, Kole. *Just before Dawn*. Ibadan, Nigeria: Spectrum Books, 1988.

p'Bitek, Okot. *Song of Lawino*. Nairobi: East African Publishing House, 1966.

Soyinka, Wole. *Isara: A Voyage Round Essay*. Lagos: Fountain, 1989; New York: Random House, 1989.

The Contributors

J. Ndukaku Amankulor

J. Ndukaku Amankulor teaches at the University of Nigeria, Nsukka, where he heads the School of Dramatic Art. He has also taught at the University of California at Los Angeles, where he did his graduate studies in theater.

Robert Cancel

Robert Cancel teaches at the University of California, San Diego, in the Department of Literature. His research interest includes the fields of African oral traditions, literature, and film. His *Allegorical Speculation in Oral Society: The Tabwa Narrative Tradition* was published by the University of California Press in 1989.

Carole Boyce Davies

Carole Boyce Davies is an associate professor with joint appointments in English, Afro-American and African studies, and comparative literature at the State University of New York at Binghamton. Her research and teaching interests span African, Caribbean, and African-American literatures, with special focus on women writers and the relationship between oral and written literary traditions. She coedited, with Elaine Savory Fido, the volume of criticism *Out of the Kumba: Caribbean Women and Literature*, published by the African World Press in 1990.

Arlene A. Elder

Arlene Elder is a professor of English and comparative literature at the University of Cincinnati. She has published *The Hindered Hand: Cultural Implications of Early African-American Fiction* and essays on African-American, African, and Australian Aboriginal writing, and is working on a comparative study of African and African-American writers.

Elaine Savory Fido

Elaine Fido teaches at New York University. She has taught at universities in Ghana, Nigeria, and the Caribbean, and was involved in the development of the Women's Studies program at the University of the West Indies. Her interests include gender issues, women's writings, and theater in Africa and the Caribbean. She coedited, with Carole Boyce Davies, *Out of the Kumba: Women and Caribbean Literature*.

Russell G. Hamilton

Russell Hamilton is a professor of Brazilian and Lusophone African literatures and dean of the Graduate School at Vanderbilt University in Nashville, Tennessee. He is the author of *Voices from an Empire: A History of Afro-Portuguese Literature*, and *Literatura Africana, Literatura Necessaria*.

Thomas Knipp

Thomas Knipp teaches African literature and American literature at Saint Louis University. His publications on African poetry have appeared in wlwe, *Journal of Commonwealth Literature*, *The South Atlantic Review*, and elsewhere.

Edris Makward

Edris Makward is a professor of French and African literatures at the University of Wisconsin, Madison, where he has taught since 1967 and is currently the director of the African Studies Program. Before coming to Madison he was on the faculty of the University of Ibadan, Nigeria. He is the author of *African Literature* (Random House, 1972) and numerous other articles and essays on contemporary African and Caribbean literatures.

Oyekan Owomoyela

Oyekan Owomoyela is a professor of English at the University of Nebraska–Lincoln, where he teaches courses in African literatures, folklore, and film. His publications include *African Literatures: An Introduction* (Crossroads Press, 1973), *A Kì í: Yoruba Proscriptive and Prescriptive Proverbs* (University Press of America, 1988), *Visions and Revisions: Essays on African Literatures and Criticism* (Peter Lang, 1991), and several articles on African literatures, folklore, and philosophy.

Jonathan A. Peters

Jonathan Peters is a professor in African American studies at the University of Maryland, Baltimore County. He previously taught at the University of Alberta and the City University of New York's La Guardia Community College. He has traveled widely in Africa, Europe, and the United States. His previous publications include *A Dance of Masks: Senghor, Achebe, Soyinka* (Three Continents Press, 1978), and *Literature of Africa and the African Continuum* (Three Continents Press, 1989), which he coedited with Mildred Mortimer and Russell Linneman.

John F. Povey

John Povey was educated in the United Kingdom and in South Africa, and came to the United States to earn a doctorate at Michigan State University. In 1964 he was appointed to the African Studies Center at UCLA, where he introduced the first courses on African literature in English, a field in which he later published numerous articles and books.

Alain Ricard

Alain Ricard teaches at the Centre d'Etude d'Afrique Noire (Center of Black African Studies) at the University of Bordeaux. He has worked extensively with theaters in both Anglophone and Francophone West Africa. His books include *Théâtre et nationalisme: Wole Soyinka et Le Roi Jones* (1972; *Theatre and Nationalism*, 1983), published by Présence Africaine, and *Livre et communication au Nigéria* (Présence Africaine, 1975; Book and communication in Nigeria).

Servanne Woodward

Servanne Woodward is an associate professor at The Wichita State University, where she teaches French. She is a consulting reader for the *Continental Latin American and Francophone Women Writers* yearly Wichita Conference Papers. She recently published "La tête du serpent rusé: Grammaires et dictionaires bilingues en Afrique et aux Caribbes" in *Diogène* (1990).

Hans M. Zell

Hans Zell was the first editor-in-chief at Africana Publishing Corporation in New York before establishing his own publishing company in 1975. He has written and consulted extensively on publishing and book development in Africa. He is the author of *African Books in Print, The African Book World & Press*, and *Reader's Guide to African Literature*.

Index